FORMAL DESCRIPTION TECHNIQUES, IV

IFIP Transactions C: Communication Systems

International Federation for Information Processing

Technical Committee 6

C-2

FORMAL DESCRIPTION TECHNIQUES, IV

Proceedings of the IFIP TC6/WG6.1 Fourth International Conference on
Formal Description Techniques for Distributed Systems and
Communications Protocols, FORTE '91
Sydney, Australia, 19-22 November 1991

Edited by

K.R. PARKER
Telecom Research Laboratories
Clayton, Victoria, Australia

G.A. ROSE
Department of Computer Science
University of Queensland
Queensland, Australia

1992

NORTH-HOLLAND
AMSTERDAM • LONDON • NEW YORK • TOKYO

ELSEVIER SCIENCE PUBLISHERS B.V.
Sara Burgerhartstraat 25
P.O. Box 211, 1000 AE Amsterdam, The Netherlands

Distributors for the United States and Canada:
ELSEVIER SCIENCE PUBLISHING COMPANY INC.
655 Avenue of the Americas
New York, N.Y. 10010, U.S.A.

ISBN: 0 444 89402 0
ISSN: 0926-549X

© 1992 IFIP. All rights reserved.

No part of this publication may be reproduced, stored in a retrieval system or transmitted in any form or by any means, electronic, mechanical, photocopying, recording or otherwise, without the prior written permission of the publisher, Elsevier Science Publishers B.V., Copyright & Permissions Department, P.O. Box 521, 1000 AM, Amsterdam, The Netherlands.

Special regulations for readers in the U.S.A. - This publication has been registered with the Copyright Clearance Center Inc. (CCC), Salem, Massachusetts. Information can be obtained from the CCC about conditions under which photocopies of parts of this publication may be made in the U.S.A. All other copyright questions, including photocopying outside of the U.S.A., should be referred to the publisher, Elsevier Science Publishers B.V., unless otherwise specified.

No responsibility is assumed by the publisher or by IFIP for any injury and/or damage to persons or property as a matter of products liability, negligence or otherwise, or from any use or operation of any methods, products, instructions or ideas contained in the material herein.

pp. 51-60, 83-90, 149-164, 329-344: Copyright not transferred.

Printed in The Netherlands

Preface

Formal Description Techniques IV, or FORTE'91, is the fourth conference of the international FORTE series which was inaugurated by Prof. Ken Turner of Stirling University, Scotland. Previous FORTE conferences were held at Stirling (1988), Vancouver (1989) and Madrid (1990). FORTE'91 was held in Sydney, Australia, 19-22 November, 1991. FORTE is sponsored by IFIP TC 6 (Communications Systems) WG 6.1 (Architecture and Protocols for Computer Networks).

Formality is becoming accepted as essential in the development of complex systems such as multi-layer communications protocols and distributed systems. Formality is mandatory for mathematical verification, a procedure being imposed on safety-critical system development. Standards documents are also becoming increasingly formalised to capture notions precisely and unambiguously.

FORTE has focussed on the standardised languages SDL, Estelle and LOTOS but is open to other notations and techniques to encourage the continuous evolution of formal techniques. The FORTE'91 proceedings include 29 submitted papers, three invited papers, four industry reports and four tool reports organised in sections corresponding to the conference sessions.

The success of FORTE'91 was the result of the efforts of many people and the support of the sponsoring organisations. We thank Harry Rudin for his promotion of FORTE'91 within IFIP. Ken Turner was always available in providing FORTE background and procedures, and Son Vuong and Juan Quemada were generous in their advice and support during the long period of organisation of FORTE'91. We are grateful to the Program Committee and the other referees who collectively prepared over 200 reviews to provide the multiple basis for selection from over 70 submissions. We also thank all those who submitted papers for consideration, those who presented papers, our invited speakers and tutorial presenters for their excellent presentations, and the conference attendees, many of whom travelled long distances.

We are grateful to the Local Arrangements Committee comprising David Charrett(Chair), Carl Dobis, Elizabeth Price, Karen Rosenberg, Carol Seiffhart and Lou Sherwin. Carol and Lou in particular spent many hours making detailed arrangements and were constantly in attendance during the conference. Thanks also to Diana Dragisic and Wendy Johnston for their assistance over many months.

We thank Sun Microsystems (Aust) for the loan of equipment and Colin Fidge and Michael Homsey for their support to the tool demonstrators. We thank OTC for making their Conference Centre available, and the Centre's staff for excellent support services.

The financial support of the major sponsors OTC and Telecom Australia and of the co-sponsors Computer Sciences of Australia, Ericsson, and the Key Centre for Software Technology and the Software Verification Research Centre within the University of Queensland's Computer Science Department is gratefully acknowledged.

Ken Parker and Gordon Rose
FORTE'91 Co-chairmen

November 1991

Table of Contents

Preface	v
Table of Contents	vii
Committee Members	xi
Invited Speakers	xii
Sponsoring and Cooperating Organizations	xiii
List of Authors	xiv
List of Referees	xv

APPLICATIONS I

Using LOTOS in a Design Environment
M. Vigder and R.J.A. Buhr — 1

Using VDM to Specify OSI Managed Objects
L. Simon and L.S. Marshall — 17

INVITED PAPER

What is the Method in Formal Methods?
E. Brinksma — 33

PERFORMANCE AND RELIABILITY

Io: An Estelle Simulator for Performance Evaluation
E. Fernandez, D. Vazquez and J. Vinyes — 51

Modeling Timeouts and Unreliable Media with a Timed Probabilistic Calculus
H. Hansson — 67

INDUSTRY REPORTS

Formal Methods at AT&T – An Industrial Usage Report
J.A. Chaves — 83

The Adoption of Formal Methods within OTC
K. Rosenberg — 91

Linking Specifications with Implementations
M. Kooij   99

Experience of Using LOTOS Within the CIM-OSA Project
A. McClenaghan   109

APPLICATIONS II

An Exercise in Protocol Synthesis
P. van Eijk and J. Schot   117

Specification of a Distributed Coordination Function in LOTOS
I. Widya, F. Sadoun and G.-J. van der Heijden   133

XP, an Experiment in Modular Specification
G. Veltink   149

INVITED PAPER

Understanding Interfaces
S. Lam and A.U. Shankar   165

CHANGE MANAGEMENT

Modelling Dynamic Communication Structures in LOTOS
L. Fredlund and F. Orava   185

Dynamic Configuration in LOTOS
E. Najm and J.-B. Stefani   201

TIMED EXTENSIONS

An Upward Compatible Timed Extension to LOTOS
G. Leduc   217

Mapping Time-Extended LOTOS to Standard LOTOS
A. McClenaghan   233

LOTOS-like Process Algebras with Urgent or Timed Interactions
T. Bolognesi and F. Lucidi   249

TRANSFORMATIONS

Event Structures for Design and Transformation in LOTOS
R. Langerak   265

A Calculus to Define Correct Transformations of LOTOS Specifications T. Massart	281
Inverse Expansion S. Pavón, M. Hulström, J. Quemada, D. de Frutos and Y. Ortega	297

TOOLS AND ENVIRONMENT

A LOTOS Data Facility Compiler (DAFY) E. Lallemand and G. Leduc	313
The Superimposition of Estelle Programs: A Tool for the Specification and Implementation of Observation and Control Algorithms B. Caillaud	329
Design and Implementation of an Application Interface for LOTOS Processors K. Ohmaki, H. Tsuji, K. Yamanaka, Y. Sato, Y. Itabashi and T. Shimizu	345

VALIDATION

Formal Specification, Validation and Implementation of an Application Protocol with Estelle C.T. Nguyen, P. Hunel and M.C. Vialatte	361
Specification and Validation of a Simple Overtaking Protocol using LOTOS P. Ernberg, L. Fredlund and B. Jonsson	377
Protocol Trace Analysis Based on Formal Specifications M.C. Kim, S.T. Chanson and S.T. Vuong	393

LANGUAGE ISSUES

Inheritance in LOTOS S. Rudkin	409
Mixing LOTOS and SDL Specifications H. Saria, H. Nirschl and C. Binding	425
$\Lambda\beta$: A Virtual LOTOS Machine J.A. Mañas and J. Salvachúa	441

TOOLS REPORTS

FORSEE
J. Billington, G. Wheeler, B. Keck and K. Parker 457

Tools for Process Algebras
E. Madelaine and D. Vergamini 463

A Cross Compiling Experiment: A PC Implementation of a LOTOS Spec
J. Mañas, J. Salvachúa and T. de Miguel 467

The Lotosphere Integrated Tool Environment Lite
P. van Eijk 471

INVITED PAPER

Superposition Refinement of Parallel Algorithms
R.J.R. Back and K. Sere 475

VERIFICATION

Specification and Verification of a Sliding Window Protocol in LOTOS
E. Madelaine and D. Vergamini 495

Protocol Verification System for SDL Specifications Based on Acyclic Expansion Algorithm and Temporal Logic
H. Saito, T. Hasegawa and Y. Kakuda 511

PROCESS FOUNDATIONS

Process Algebra Traces Augmented with Causal Relationships
C.J. Fidge 527

Fairness in LOTOS
C. Wu and G. von Bochmann 543

A LOTOS Based Calculus with True Concurrency Semantics
J.-P. Courtiat and R.J. Coelho da Costa 559

Conference Chair

Ken Parker
Telecom Research Laboratories

Gordon Rose
Dept. of Computer Science, The University of Queensland

Program Committee

T. Bolognesi	CNUCE - Italy
E. Brinksma	U of Twente - The Netherlands
L. Cerchio	CSELT - Italy
A. Danthine	U of Liege - Belgium
M. Diaz	LAAS - France
R. Duke	U of Queensland - Australia
O. Faergemand	TFL - Denmark
F. Garijo	TIDSA - Spain
D. Hogrefe	U of Bern - Switzerland
J. Linn	NIST - USA
L. Logrippo	U of Ottawa - Canada
J. de Meer	GMD - Germany
T. Mizuno	Mitsubishi - Japan
E. Najm	INRIA - France
B. Pehrson	SICS - Sweden
J. Quemada	DIT-UPM - Spain
H. Rudin	IBM - Switzerland
R. Tenney	U of Massachusetts - USA
K. Turner	U of Stirling - Scotland
S. Vuong	U of British Columbia - Canada
A. Valmari	VTT - Finland
E. Wiedmer	ASCOM - Switzerland

Invited Speakers

Ralph-Johann Back	Abo Akademi University - Finland
Ed Brinksma	University of Twente - The Netherlands
Simon S. Lam	The University of Texas - USA

Sponsors and Cooperating Organizations

Major Sponsors

>IFIP TC6.1
>OTC Limited, Australia
>Telecom Australia

Co-sponsors

>Computer Sciences of Australia
>Ericsson Pty Ltd
>Key Centre for Software Technology, The University of Queensland
>Software Verification Research Centre, The University of Queensland

Cooperating Organizations

>IEEE (Victoria Branch), Australia
>SUN Microsystems, Australia

List of Authors

R. Back
J. Billington
C. Binding
G. Bochmann
T. Bolognesi
E. Brinksma
R. Buhr
B. Caillaud
S. Chanson
J. Chaves
R. Coelho da Costa
J. Courtiat
P. Ernberg
D. Fernandez
C. Fidge
L. Fredlund
S. Gomez
H. Hansson
T. Hasegawa
D. de Frutos
M. Hulstrom
P. Hunel
Y. Itabashi
B. Jonsson

Y. Kakuda
B. Keck
M. Kim
M. Kooij
E. Lallemand
S. Lam
R. Langerak
G. Leduc
F. Lucidi
E. Madelaine
J. Manas
L. Marshall
T. Massart
A. McClenaghan
T. Miguel
E. Najm
C. Nguyen
N. Nirschl
K. Ohmaki
K. Sere
Y. Ortega
K. Parker
K. Rosenberg
S. Rudkin

F. Sadoun
H. Saito
J. Salvachua
H. Saria
Y. Sato
J. Schot
T. Shimizu
L. Simon
J. Stefani
H. Tsuji
G. van der Heijden
P. van Eijk
E. Vazquez
G. Veltink
D. Vergamini
M. Vialatte
M. Vigder
J. Vinyes
J. Quemada
A. Udaya-Shankar
S. Vuong
G. Wheeler
I. Widya
C. Wu
K. Yamanaka

List of Referees

A. Azona	M. Hedlund	F. Orava
A. Bensink	D. Hogrefe	Y. Ortega-Mallen
C. Bernardeschi	V. Jones	K. Parker
T. Bolognesi	D. Karjoth	S Pavon
B. Botma	C. Kloos	J. Pettersson
E. Brinksma	M. Kristensen	A. Pras
S. Chanson	E. Lallemand	P. Quaglia
L. Cerchio	J. de Meer	J. Quemada
R. Clark	R. Langerak	K. Raymond
D. Cockburn	G. Leduc	G. Rose
F. Cornelius	J. Linn	B. Sarikaya
J.P. Courtiat	L. Logrippo	J. Schot
J. Curgus	D. Lopez	P. Sibille
M. Diaz	N. Lumello	P. Sjodin
P. Drabik	P. Maccario	A. Spichiger
E. Dubuis	J. Manas	W. Stoll
R. Duke	T. Massart	L. Tello
P. Ernberg	Maurizio	R. Tenney
D. Escrig	V. Mazzola	M. Tienari
O. Faergemand	T. Mizuno	K. Turner
A. Fantechi	C. Moiso	A. Valmari
L. Ferreira Pires	M. Naitalin	P. van Eijk
T. Garijo	E. Najm	G. Vazquez
S. Gianefranco	K. Nykland	F. Vernadat
J. Grabowski	A. Obaid	A. Vogel
J. Grobholz	A. Okkonen	S. Vuong
J. Gustafsson	A. Olsen	E. Wiedmer
A. Danthine	B. Pehrson	P. Wollper
G. von Bochmann	H. Rudin	

… … …
Using LOTOS in a Design Environment

Mark Vigder
vigder@sce.carleton.ca

R.J.A. Buhr
buhr@sce.carleton.ca

Dept. of Systems and Computer Engineering
Carleton University
Ottawa, Canada

Abstract

Implementation of reactive systems is recognized as a difficult problem in the field of computer system engineering. Much of this difficulty arises due to the interactions between many components executing concurrently and the distributed nature of many of the systems. This paper describes an approach which can be used for the design of such systems and how LOTOS was integrated into this approach. The design approach involves alternating between structural design and behavioural design with LOTOS being the language used for formally specifying behavioural design. Different styles of specification can be used for defining the behaviour of a set of interconnected components, and this paper introduces a new style, the slice style, which describes behaviour as interactions propagating through a set of components. A number of problems were encountered regarding the expressiveness of LOTOS; the problems encountered as well as the proposed solutions are presented.

1. Introduction

The work described in this paper is the result of an ongoing research project involved with the design of reactive systems. The design of such systems has proven to be a particularly difficult problem for computer system engineers for a number of reasons:
- Reactive systems usually require complex temporal behaviour.
- The system is often constructed from many concurrent components. The inherent concurrency of the system adds to the difficulty in correctly specifying behaviour.
- Reactive systems are often physically distributed over a number of processors. This requires a great deal of synchronization and communication between components to provide the required services.

This work was funded by the Telecommunication Research Institute of Ontario (TRIO).

One approach to reactive system design is to view the design process as involving both *structural design* and *behavioural design*[1, 2, 3] where structural design identifies the components from which a system is constructed and behavioural design identifies the behaviour which the system is required to exhibit.

1.1 Specifying Behaviour of Interconnected Components

This paper proposes a novel approach to specifying behaviour of interconnected components by using LOTOS[4] behaviour expressions to define behaviour along paths joining interconnected components (called *slices*). Before explaining this concept in more detail we first review some familiar LOTOS specification styles.

Behavioural specifications can be classified in one of two ways[5, 6]:

- A behaviour specification is *extensional* if it describes behaviour using only the interactions with which the system and its environment communicate. The specification does not use any knowledge of internal structure or internal interactions.
- A behaviour specification is *intensional* if it uses knowledge of internal structure and interactions in order to describe system behaviour.

An intensional specification of a system S requires that the designer first identify the set of components from which S is constructed and how these components are interconnected. Given that a system S is constructed from the component set $C=\{c_1, ... c_n\}$ the designer can specify how the components of C interact to provide the behaviour required of S. A number of different approaches can be taken by the designer when intensionally specifying the behaviour of S.

One possible approach to the problem is to use a *resource oriented style* of specification[5]. For each component $c \in C$ the designer can construct a behaviour specification B_c which represents the behaviour of component c. These individual component behaviour specifications can then be composed according to the interconnection of the components to give the overall behaviour of S. As an example of a resource style specification in LOTOS, assume that a system has been structurally decomposed as shown in figure 1. The system is constructed from components $S1$, $S2$ and $S3$; a,b,e represent interactions with the environment; c,d,f represent internal interactions between components with c,d being two way interactions and f being a three way interaction between $S1,S2$ and $S3$. Processes can now be defined which specify the behaviour of individual components, and these processes then composed to give the behaviour of the system as represented by the LOTOS behaviour expression of figure 3.

Slice Style of Specification

A resource oriented style of specification does not always reflect the approach taken by the designer when faced with the task of specifying the behaviour of interconnected components. Rather than looking at each component of C in isolation, often a designer will step through a scenario in which a triggering interaction at the edge of the system initiates a behaviour pattern where interactions propagate through different component of the system[7, 8]. Such behaviour patterns are not limited to individual components but involve many components of the system. What the designer is doing in these cases is identifying a set of components and interaction points which cooperate while executing a particular behaviour pattern, and then defining this behaviour pattern across these components. Such an approach is called a *slice style* of behaviour specification.

Given a design structure, the slice style requires the designer to first identify a slice of the design structure. A slice is a set of components and interaction points which trace a path through the design structure. Behaviour is then defined by showing sequences of interactions superimposed upon this slice. This generally involves the designer identifying some end-to-end behaviour which will be required of the system and showing how this end-to-end behaviour is provided by the components and interactions of the slice.

For example, given the structure of figure 1, a designer might identify one behaviour pattern where a triggering interaction at *a* initiates a behaviour requiring an interaction at *c* followed by one at *e* and then *f*. The slice associated with this pattern is illustrated in the leftmost diagram of figure 2. A process can then be defined which represents this behaviour pattern (process `slice_1` in figure 4). A similar behaviour pattern might be noted for the interaction points *b,d,e,f* (rightmost diagram of figure 2, process `slice_2` of 4). These behaviour patterns can then be combined to give the overall behaviour of the system as defined in figure 4

Comparing the specifications of figure 3 and 4 it can be seen that they specify equivalent behaviour but are organized very differently. In the first case using the resource style, the behaviour of each component is clearly identified as a process within the behaviour specification. In the second case using the slice style, each process does not specify the behaviour of a single component but rather specifies a behaviour pattern which slices across a number of components. Although both specifications are correct, one or the other may be useful for different purposes or at different stages of the design process. For example the slice style may be useful during the initial stages of the design development when the designer is investigating how the components of the system must be able to interact to provide the end-to-end behaviour. A resource style may be more applicable in later stages of design when the designer is refining the behaviour of individual components, or providing a specification from which a component can be implemented.

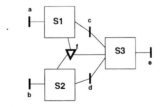

Figure 1 Design structure – an example.

2 LOTOS as a Design Representation Language

In attempting to use LOTOS as the language for specifying design behaviour within the design environment being developed, two problems were encountered. The first problem was

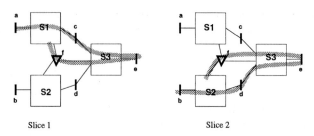

Figure 2 Slices of the design structure.

```
hide c,d,f in
  (S1[a,c,f] |[f]| S2[b,d,f]) |[c,d,f]| S3[c,d,e,f]
where
 process S1[a,c,f] : noexit := (*Behaviour of component S1*)
   P[a,c,f]
 endproc

 process S2[b,d,f] : noexit := (*Behaviour of component S2*)
   P[b,d,f]
 endproc

 process S3[c,d,e,f] : noexit := (*Behaviour of component S3*)
   P[c,e,f] |[e,f]| P[d,e,f]
 endproc

 process P[e1,e2,e3] : noexit :=
   e1; e2; e3; P[e1,e2,e3]
 endproc
```

Figure 3 Resource style behaviour specification.

```
hide c,d,f in
  cut_1[a,c,e,f] |[e,f]| cut_2[b,d,e,f]
where
 process slice_1[a,c,e,f] : noexit := (*Behaviour pattern of slice 1*)
   Q[a,c,e,f]
 endproc

 process slice_2[b,d,e,f] : noexit := (*Behaviour pattern of slice 2*)
   Q[b,d,e,f]
 endproc

 process Q[e1,e2,e3,e4] : noexit :=
   e1; e2; e3; e4; Q[e1,e2,e3,e4]
 endproc
```

Figure 4 Slice style behaviour specification.

trying to identify components involved in a particular interaction. Interactions are modeled as multiway synchronizations between components, with each interaction occurring at a named interaction point (see §3); each interaction between components is then represented as a LOTOS event. When defining behaviour of a system of interconnected components, it is important to define not only which interactions occur, but also which components were involved in the interaction. Knowing the name of the interaction point is not sufficient for determining the components involved. The problem is that since there is no explicit structural representation in LOTOS, it is not always clear from the LOTOS event which components were involved in the interaction[2]. If a resource style of specification is being used (e.g. figure 3) where the behaviour of each component is represented as a LOTOS process within the top level behaviour expression, it is possible to determine the components involved in the interaction by knowing the initial mapping between components and LOTOS processes and analyzing the behaviour expressions before and after the event occurred. Using a slice style of specification (e.g., figure 4), analysis of the behaviour expression cannot in general be used to determine the components of the interaction since the organization of the LOTOS behaviour expression does not mirror the design structure, i.e., processes of the behaviour expression describe behaviour patterns which may cut across many components. Therefore, when using the slice style there must be some way of explicitly encoding within the LOTOS event the identities of the components involved in the corresponding interaction.

The second problem with LOTOS which was encountered when using the resource style, was the inability to represent the behaviour of any arbitrary network of components where the method of component communication is synchronous rendezvous. The problem is illustrated in the structure of figure 5[3]. The system is constructed from three components A, B, and C, and three synchronous interaction points a,b,c. A and B synchronize on a and b and execute in parallel on c; A and C synchronize on a and c and execute in parallel on B; and B and C synchronize on b and c and execute in parallel on a. Using a resource style of specification a designer can construct processes P_A, P_B, P_C to represent the behaviour of the components A,B,C. However when the designer attempts to compose these processes to represent system behaviour, it cannot be done simply by combining these processes using the LOTOS operators. Since A and B synchronize on a and b, their combined behaviour is given by $P_{AB}=(P_A |[a,b]| P_B)$. When P_C is composed with P_{AB} to represent the system behaviour, neither the expression $(P_C |[a,b,c]| P_{AB})$ nor the expression $(P_C |[c]| P_{AB})$ correctly represent the intended behaviour; the former implies that a and b require three way synchronizations between A, B, and C; the later implies that C does not synchronize with A on a and with B on b.

Solutions to representing arbitrary component networks in LOTOS generally involve constraining in some way the system structures which can be represented (see for example [9]). This however was considered unacceptable in the design environment being developed as it unnecessarily constrained the design process. A solution to the problem can be realized if an explicit representation of the design structure exists as is presented in §3; a possible solution to representing arbitrary interconnections is presented in §4

3 A Formal Structural Representation

In order that a designer can proceed independently in the specification of structure and behaviour, it is necessary to have independent means of representing structure and behaviour. With LOTOS as the behaviour representation language, a structure representation must be developed. This section proposes a structural design representation which is compatible with

---

[2] Note that this problem does not exist in figure 1; because of the component interconnections, if the interconnection point is known the corresponding components can be determined. This is not true in general as described in §3

[3] Although figure 5 is an artificial example, it does illustrate a problem which was encountered while trying to specify real systems.

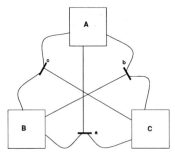

Figure 5

the LOTOS behavioural design representation. (For a more general discussion of some of the issues involved see [10, 11]). The proposed structural design allows a designer to identify the components of the system, and to interconnect the components.

A structural design specifies:

- The components from which the system is constructed.
- The interfaces to each of the components.
- The interconnections between the components.

Components communicate with each other by means of *interaction points* (IPs) (e.g., a,b,c,d,e,f in figure 1). An *interaction* is a unit of communication between components which occurs at an IP. Each interaction is modeled as a multiway synchronous rendezvous between two or more components. During the interaction components which are involved in the interaction can exchange data.

Each IP has a number of *sides*; the number of sides of the IP represents the number of components which will synchronize during the interaction. For example, an IP with three sides (e.g., IP f of figure 1) represents a synchronization between three components. In order for an interaction to occur at an IP there must be one component at each side of the IP willing to engage in the interaction. Thus one can view components as making offers at different IP sides. If there is at least one component offering at each side of an IP, then the IP is enabled and an interaction may occur. If more than one component is offering at an IP side, one of those components will be non-deterministically chosen to engage in the interaction; the remaining components will continue offering at the IP side.

For example in figure 1 the interaction point f identifies a three sided interaction. Since there is only one component attached to each side of f, any interaction which occurs at f must be a three way synchronization between components $S1,S2,S3$. During the interaction data can be exchanged between these components.

Formally an interaction point can be defined as follows.

Definition: interaction point (IP). An *interaction point (IP)* is a tuple $<e,e_{sides},e_{var}>$ where:

- e is a unique identifier.

- e_{sides} is a non-empty set of sides.
- e_{var} is a set of data variables.

The number of components which synchronize on the IP is given by $|e_{sides}|$ and is referred to as the *arity* of the IP. The data variables e_{var} represent the data which is transferred between components during the interaction.

From a structural point of view, a component is defined by identifying the IP sides to which it is connected. This leads to the following definition:

Definition: component. A *component* is a pair $<c,c_{sides}>$ where:
- c is a unique identifier.
- c_{sides} is a set of IP sides.

For a component $<c,c_{sides}>$, the set c_{sides} identifies the IP sides to which a component is connected. Once the IP sides are known, the complete interface to the component is defined and its interconnection to other components is specified. In particular, a component c_1 can communicate with a component c_2 only if they are connected to different sides of the same IP; the data variables of the IP identify data flows which the components must support during the interaction.

A design structure can now be defined as a set of interaction points and a set of components.

Definition: design structure. A *structural design* is a pair $<I,C>$ where:
- I is a set of interaction points
- C is a set of components

such that if $<e_1,s_1,v_1>,<e_2,s_2,v_2>\in I$ and $e_1 \neq e_2$ then $s_1 \cap s_2 = \emptyset$.

Given the above definitions, a formal representation of the structure of figure 1 can now be given. Assuming that the set of IP sides is $\{a1,a2,b1,b2,c1,c2,d1,d2,e1,e2,f1,f2,f3\}$, the structure $<I,C>$ is:

- $I = \{<a,\{a1,a2\},\{\}>, <b,\{b1,b2\},\{\}>, <c,\{c1,c2\},\{\}>, <d,\{d1,d2\},\{\}>, <e,\{e1,e2\},\{\}>,$
  $<f,\{f1,f2,f3\},\{\}>\}$
- $C = \{<S1,\{a2,c1,f1\}>, <S2,\{b2,d1,f2\}>, <S3,\{c2,d2,e1,f3\}>\}$

3.1 Integrating Structure and Behaviour

Once a design structure has been specified, a designer can proceed with defining the behaviour expected of the structure by means of interactions which occur at the interaction points.

Definition: Interaction. An *interaction* is a tuple $<i,C,g,V>$ where:
- $i=<e,e_{sides},e_{var}>$ is an interaction point.
- C is a set of components.
- $g : e_{sides} \rightarrow C$ is a function that maps the set e_{sides} onto C such that if $g(s)=<c,c_{sides}>$ then $s \in c_{sides}$.
- V is a set of data values which instantiate each variable of e_{var}.

For each interaction <i,C,g,V>, i represents the IP where the synchronization occurred, C is the set of components involved in the synchronization, g identifies which components were at which sides of the IP during the interaction, and V represents the data values passed between the components.

If behaviour is specified using LOTOS, then a way must be found to represent each possible interaction <i,C,g,V> as a LOTOS event. In LOTOS, each event consists of a gate name and a list of typed data values. Thus, a very straightforward representation of an interaction as a LOTOS event can be defined as follows:

- The interaction point identifier e is a gate name in the LOTOS behaviour expression.
- The event e has $|e_{sides}|+|e_{vars}|$ data values associated with it.
- The first $|e_{sides}|$ data values associated with gate e are the identifiers of the components which synchronize at IP e; the position of the identifier in the data value list can be used to associate a component with a particular side of the IP.
- The last $|e_{vars}|$ data variables associated with gate e correspond to the data values which are exchanged between components when they synchronize at IP e.

For the structure of figure 1 (in which no data is being passed between components) the interaction <c, {$S1,S3$}, {}> would be represented as the LOTOS event `c!S1!S3`.

4 Composing Component Behaviours

As described in §2, when using a resource style of specification there exist component interconnection topologies which cannot be represented in LOTOS as a simple composition of component behaviours (e.g., figure 5). However, if an explicit structural representation exists, it is possible to construct a behaviour expression from the component behaviours which does correctly represent the intended behaviour of the system. The problem can be stated as follows.

- Given
    - a design structure S=<I,C>.
    - for each $c \in C$ a LOTOS behavior expression B_c which represents the behaviour of component c.

- Construct a LOTOS behaviour expression B_S which represents the behaviour of S.

In order to construct B_S it is first necessary to define a LOTOS process `default[E](C:Component)` where `E` is a list of all the IP identifiers and `Component` is a data sort which includes all the component identifiers of the system. The behaviour of `default` can be described as follows:

- `default[E](c)` will continuously offer event e if and only if e represents an interaction in which component c is not involved.

Thus `default[E](c)` will engage in any event which represents an interaction in which component c is not involved and will refuse to engage in any event representing an interaction involving component c.

Given that $C=\{c1,c2,...cn\}$, the desired behaviour expression B_S can now be constructed as:

$B_S=$
$\quad(B_{c1}$ ||| `default[E](c1)`) ||
$\quad(B_{c2}$ ||| `default[E](c2)`) ||
$\quad$ ...
$\quad(B_{cn}$ ||| `default[E](cn)`)

To understand the behaviour of B_S, note that every line of the expression synchronizes on every event. If component `cj` is involved in the interaction represented by the event then the expression B_{cj} (or one derived from it) will synchronize with the event; else the expression `default[E](cj)` will synchronize.

Construction of the expression for B_S depends on the construction of the process `default[E](C:Component)`. Given a structural design $<I,C>$, the process `default` can be generated from the set of interaction points I. The method for doing this is as follows:

- For each $<e,e_{sides},e_{vars}>\in I$ define a process `default_e[e](C:Component)` as follows:

```
process default_e(C:Component) : noexit :=
  e ?c1 ?c2 ... ?cn ?d1 ?d2 ...?dm
    [(c1 ne C) and
     (c2 ne C) and
      ...
     (cn ne C)];
  default(C)
endproc
```
where $|e_{sides}|=n$ and $|e_{vars}|=m$.
- The process `default` can now be defined as follows:
```
process default[e1,...,ek](C:Component) : noexit :=
  default_e1[e1](C) |||
  default_e2[e2](C) |||
   ...
  default_ek[ek](C)
endproc
```
where e1...ek are the interaction point identifiers.

Using the above method, a behaviour expression representing the behaviour of the structure of figure 5 can be constructed as shown in figure 6.

5 Example — a Telephone System

One of the motivations for developing an explicit structural representation of a system which is independent of the behavioural representation is to allow the designer to use an

```
(PA ||| default[a,b,c](A)) ||
(PB ||| default[a,b,c](B)) ||
(PC ||| default[a,b,c](C))
where
  process default[a,b,c](X:Component) : noexit :=
    default_e[a](X) |||
    default_e[b](X) |||
    default_e[c](X)
  endproc
  process default_e[e](X:Component) : noexit :=
    e ?X1 ?X2 [(X1 ne X) and (X2 ne X)];
       default_e[e](X)
  endproc
  .
  .
  .
```

Figure 6

intensional approach to behaviour specification without being constrained to the resource style of specification. In particular, a designer may wish to use the slice style, identifying a particular set of interaction points and components and then showing how the required system services are provided by interactions propagating through these components. This section provides a small example of the slice specification style proposed within this paper. The example is a (overly simplified) telephone system in which only the connection establishment and termination is being modeled (i.e., the voice switching is ignored). (Similar examples using other specification approaches can be found in [12, 13]). The requirements can be specified as follows:

- There are a number of handsets which can be used for placing and receiving calls. Each handset has a unique identifier.
- At any time a user can request that a call be placed to another handset. The system will record that the call has been requested and service the request when possible.
- When the system establishes a connection, the users are notified of the connection.
- After a connection has been established the initiator of the connection can terminate the connection.
- A handset will never be engaged in more than one call at a time.

We start by specifying the system structure $<I,C>$. One possible structure is illustrated in figure 7, where each handset is represented by an identical component `tel(n)` and a central **switch** controls the connections between the handsets. An interaction point `tu` provides a means of communication between the user and the handset and an interaction point `ts` provides communication between the handsets and the central switch. Assuming for illustrative purposes three handsets, the structure is represented as:

- $I=\{<\texttt{tu},\{tu1,tu2\},\{X:tSig\}>, <\texttt{ts},\{ts1,ts2\},\{Y:sSig\}>\}$
- $C=\{<\texttt{switch},\{ts2\}>, <\texttt{tel(1)},\{tu2,ts1\}>, <\texttt{tel(2)},\{tu2,ts1\}>,$
       $<\texttt{tel(3)},\{tu2,ts1\}>\}$

The data types *tSig* and *sSig* contain the following values:

    tSig : *call(X)*   - -User requests connection to *X*.
             notify(X)   - -Notify user connection established with *X*.
             hangup   - -User terminates connection.

    sSig : *con_request(X)*   - -Connection requested to *X*.
             connect(X)   - -Connection established to *X*.
             disconnect   - -Current connection terminated.

We can now specify the sequence of interactions which is required to complete a call between two handsets. This requires defining behaviour across a slice involving two handsets and the central switch. This is a natural way of beginning the behavioural design process, where the designer identifies a service which must be provided by the system (setting up and terminating a call between two users) and then shows how the internal components of the system interact to provide this service. Generating complete and independent specifications of the individual components in a resource style is left to a later stage of the design process.

Completing a call requires interactions involving three components: the source handset, the destination handset, and the central switch. This process is defined as `call[tu,ts](src,dest)` in figure 8. Note that this process does not define the behaviour of an individual component, but rather includes within it the partial behaviour of three different components.

Multiple calls can be represented by executing the process `call[tu,ts](src,dest)` in parallel with different values for `src` and `dest`, as is done in the behaviour expression of figure 8. However, there is a requirement that one handset can be involved in at most one connection at a time. This requires an additional constraint to be added to the system. A design decision must now be made by the designer as to how this constraint will be included. There are two ways (at least) of satisfying this constraint: the individual handsets can enforce the constraint; or the `switch` can enforce the constraint. In this example the decision was made that the switch shall enforce the constraint, and this was done by representing the constraint as the process `maxOneCall[ts](X:setOfCalls)` where the data type `setOfCalls` is a set of pairs representing all the current connections between handsets.

The complete behaviour expression for a three handset system is given in figure 8.

Once the slice oriented specification has reached a sufficient level of completeness, the designer can use this specification in a number of ways during the development process. For example:

- *Conceptualizing the design problem.* By conceptualizing behaviour in terms of how sets of components interact a designer can see design issues which are not necessarily apparent by looking at each component in isolation. For example: Where are the performance bottlenecks? Is the decomposition of the system into components 'correct' or should a different decomposition be used? What is the best way of assigning functions to components.

- *Generating test sequences.* Since a slice style specification identifies behaviour patterns involving many components, it can form the basis for generating test sequences to be used during integration testing, where it is validated that the implemented components interact correctly with each other.
- *Refining the behaviour specification.* The slice style specification provides a starting point from which specifications for the individual components can be generated.

Research is continuing on providing theories, methods, and tools to assist in the above areas.

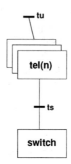

Figure 7 Structure of the telephone switching system.

6 Conclusions

The motivation for the work summarized in this paper was the desire to use LOTOS as a tool while developing designs for reactive systems. The design process presented here is one of alternating between structural specification of a system and behavioural specification of a system. Although LOTOS is a powerful behaviour description language, it lacks a means for representing structure explicitly. For this reason a formal representation of structural design was developed.

This formal representation resulted in two advantages being realized. First, LOTOS suffers from the weakness that when using the resource style it cannot represent any arbitrary network of components which communicate by synchronous rendezvous. However, by making use of the explicit structural representation of a system the intended behaviour of any network of components can be correctly represented.

The second advantage of having an explicit structural representation is that the two distinct elements of design (structure and behaviour) can be separately and formally represented, allowing more flexibility to the designer when specifying relationships between structure and behaviour. This flexibility facilitates the use of different specification styles, for example the slice style, where the designer is trying to understand and specify complex behavioural relationships which exist between sets of structural components.

```
hide ts in
 (* Three handsets -- calls can be going on concurrently*)
 (call[tu,ts](1 of telID,2 of telID)
 |||
 call[tu,ts](1 of telID,3 of telID)
 |||
 call[tu,ts](2 of telID,1 of telID)
 |||
 call[tu,ts](3 of telID,1 of telID)
 |||
 call[tu,ts](2 of telID,3 of telID)
 |||
 call[tu,ts](3 of telID,2 of telID))
 (*constrain any one handset to one call at a time*)
 |[ts]|
 maxOneCall[ts]({} of setOfCalls)

where

(*process call specifies the behaviour required of the source
  handset, the destination handset, and the switch, in order
  to complete a call*)
process call[tu,ts](src,dest : telID ) : noexit :=
  tu ?U:Component !tel(src) !call(dest);
   ts !tel(src) !switch !con_request(dest);
    ((ts !switch !tel(src) !connect(dest);
       tu !tel(src) ?U:Component !notify(dest);
         exit)
     |||
      (ts !switch !tel(dest) !connect(src);
       tu !tel(dest) ?U:Component !notify(src);
         exit)
    ) >>
      tu ?U:Component !tel(src) !hangup;
       ts !tel(src) !switch !disconnect;
        call[tu,ts](src,dest)
endproc

(*maxOneCall is a constraint of the switch which enforces one
  call per handset*)
process maxOneCall[ts](CallSet:setOfCalls) : noexit :=
  (choice Y:telID []
   ts ?X:Component !switch !con_request(Y);
    maxOneCall[ts](CallSet)
  )
```

Figure 8 Behaviour of the telephone switching system. (Continued . . .)

```
  []
    (choice T1:telID,T2:telID,X:telID,Y:telID []
    ts !switch !tel(X) !connect(Y)
        [(c(X,T1) NotIn CallSet) and
         (c(Y,T2) NotIn CallSet)];
      maxOneCall[ts](Insert(c(X,Y),CallSet))
    )
  []
    (choice X:telID,Y:telID []
    ts !tel(X) !switch !disconnect
        [c(X,Y) IsIn CallSet];
      maxOneCall[ts](Remove(c(X,Y), CallSet))
    )
endproc
```

Figure 8 Behaviour of the telephone switching system.

Bibliography

[1] R. Buhr, *Practical Visual Techniques in System Design: With Applications to Ada.* Englewood Cliffs, N.J.: Prentice Hall, 1990.
[2] R. Buhr, "Practical Visual Techniques for the Joint Refinement of Structure and Temporal Behaviour in Reactive System Design," in *Compeuro 90*, (Tel Aviv), 1990.
[3] D. Harel and A. Pnueli, "On the development of reactive systems," in *Logics and Models of Concurrent Systems* (K. Apt, ed.), NATO ASI Series F: Computer and System Sciences, Vol. 13, pp. 3–26, Berlin: Springer-Verlag, 1985.
[4] ISO/TC 97/SC 21, *Information processing systems - Open systems interconnection - LOTOS - A Formal Description Technique Based on the Temporal Ordering of Observational Behaviour*. International Organization for Standardization, 1987.
[5] C. Vissers, G. Scollo, and M. van Sinderen, "Architectural and Specification Style in Formal Descriptions of Distributed Systems," in *Proc. IFIP WG6.1, Protocol Specification, Testing, and Verification VIII*, pp. 189–204, North-Holland, 1988.
[6] C. Vissers, G. Scollo, M. van Sinderen, and E. Brinksma, "On the use of Specification Styles in the Design of Distributed Systems," Unpublished manuscript, 1990.
[7] M. Vigder, "Slicing a System: a Design Methodology with Examples in LOTOS," Tech. Report SCE-91-03, Dept. of Systems and Computer Engineering - Carleton University, Ottawa, 1991.
[8] R. Buhr, "Pictures that Play for Designing Concurrent Real Time Systems," Tech. Report SCE-91-08, Dept. of Systems and Computer Engineering - Carleton University, Ottawa, 1991.

[9] M. Haj-Hussein and L. Logrippo, "Specifying Distributed Algorithms in LOTOS," Technical Report TR-91-04, Computer Science Dept., University of Ottawa, Ottawa, 1991.

[10] R. Gotzhein, "The formal definition of the architectural concept 'interaction point'," in *Formal Description Techniques (FORTE 89)* (S. Vuong, ed.), North-Holland, 1989.

[11] P. King and G. Smith, "Formalisation of Behavioural and Structural Concepts for Communication Systems," in *Protocol Specification, Testing, and Verification* (L. Logrippo, R. Probert, and H. Ural, eds.), pp. 1–18, Amsterdam: North-Holland, 1990.

[12] M. Faci, L. Logrippo, and B. Stepien, "Formal Specifications of Telephone Systems in LOTOS," Technical Report TR-89-07, Computer Science Dept., University of Ottawa, Ottawa, February 1989.

[13] C. Morgan, "Telephone Network," in *Specification Case Studies* (I. Hayes, ed.), pp. 73–88, London: Prentice/Hall, 1987.

Using VDM to Specify OSI Managed Objects

Linda Simon and Lynn S. Marshall

Bell-Northern Research Ltd., P. O. Box 3511 Station C, Ottawa, Ontario,
Canada K1Y 4H7
ph: (613) 765-4932 / 765-4856, fax: (613) 765-4920 / 763-4222,
e-mail: ldsimon@bnr.ca / lynnmar@bnr.ca

Abstract

Protocol standards must be defined in a precise, unambiguous and concise manner as they serve as the basis for implementation and testing of compatible systems. It is this need which has resulted in the development within the International Organization for Standardization (ISO) of two formal description techniques (FDTs), viz. LOTOS and Estelle. These FDTs have been applied to the formal specification of a number of Open Systems Interconnection (OSI) communication protocol standards.

The formal specification of OSI network management protocols presents a number of interesting challenges as the structure and semantics of the information to be communicated across an interoperable interface is modelled as managed objects. The challenge arises in integrating existing formal techniques into the specific object-oriented framework developed by the ISO management standards.

The ISO management standards currently provide notational tools for describing the syntactical aspects of OSI managed objects. The choice of a particular specification language(s) for defining the behaviour of managed objects has been left open, although in practice only English has so far been used.

This paper examines the suitability of VDM as a candidate specification technique for use in formally specifying the behaviour of OSI managed objects. It builds on some earlier work reported elsewhere proposing a semi-formal technique for describing the behaviour of managed objects based on pre-conditions and post-conditions written in English.

To investigate the suitability of VDM to incorporate object-oriented concepts such as inheritance, we take as a case study a simplified Discriminator managed object class, described in English within the ISO management standards.

1 Introduction

1.1 Background

The International Organization for Standardization (ISO) is developing a set of standards for managing Open Systems Interconnection (OSI)-based networks. A fundamental aspect of ISO's technical approach to these standards is the adoption an object-oriented paradigm for the specification of management information to be communicated across an interface between two open systems. This approach has embraced a number of concepts and principles from general object-oriented design. However, it has not adopted all aspects of these concepts, and in some cases the terms and concepts have been modified. We therefore begin by reviewing the relevant concepts and definitions.

A managed object is an abstracted view or representation of a logical or physical resource to be managed across an interoperable interface. A resource can be anything that is subject to management, for example, a protocol state machine, a connection or a physical communications equipment such as a modem.

Each managed object is an instance of a managed object class that includes all managed objects that share the same definition. The definition of a managed object class consists of: the *attributes* visible at the managed object boundary, the *operations* that may be applied to the managed object, the *notifications* which are emitted by the managed object when some internal or external event occurs, and the *behaviour* exhibited by the managed object.

A managed object class (called a subclass) may be derived from an existing managed object class (called a superclass) by inheriting the characteristics of the superclass and defining additional/extended characteristics that apply to the new class. Only *strict inheritance* of characteristics is permitted; that is, deletion of any of the superclass characteristics is not allowed and the superclass characteristics can only be extended in a compatible manner.

1.2 Motivation

Since ISO protocol specifications represent the standards which are the basis for the implementation and testing of compatible OSI systems, it is essential that these specifications be unambiguous, complete and concise. Estelle and LOTOS are two Formal Description Techniques (FDTs) developed within ISO for the formal specification of ISO protocols. These FDTs have been applied in the development of formal descriptions of a number of OSI standards.

Within the OSI system managements standards, it is necessary to specify both:

1. the Common Management Information Protocol (CMIP) which has been specified by ISO as the general carriage protocol for communicating operations from managing systems to managed objects and for communicating notifications from managed objects to managing systems; and,

2. the structure and semantics of the information that is carried by CMIP—this is expressed as managed object class definitions.

Whereas Estelle and LOTOS may be applied to the formal specification of the carriage protocol (i.e. CMIP) [1], it is not apparent whether these FDTs are the most suitable languages for specifying the behaviour of OSI managed objects.

In order to use, for example, the LOTOS FDT there is a requirement to reconcile the OSI *management* concepts of managed object, notifications, operations, etc. with the LOTOS language concepts of process, event, etc. There are some difficulties in interpreting the concept of inheritance within the existing framework of LOTOS [2,3].

This paper examines the suitability of VDM as a candidate specification technique for use in formally specifying the behaviour of OSI managed objects. It is motivated, in part, by some earlier work reported in [4] which proposed defining managed object behaviour in terms of pre-conditions and post-conditions written in English. VDM is a formal method based on pre-conditions and post-conditions [5].

Another motivation, is that the VDM concepts of state and operations can be intuitively mapped onto the managed object concepts of attributes, and operations and notifications, respectively. Furthermore, work on interpreting the language Z (which is similar to VDM) in an object-oriented framework [6,3] suggest that object-oriented concepts including inheritance can be readily accommodated. Bear [7] has done some work on structuring VDM specifications, but he has not looked at inheritance.

To investigate the suitability of VDM as a candidate specification technique we take as a case study the Discriminator managed object class, which is based on a simplified version of the OSI managed object class described in natural language in [8].

The remainder of this paper is organized as follows. Section 2 provides an informal description of the Discriminator managed object. In Section 3, we discuss our experiences in developing a VDM formal description of the Discriminator and a subclass of the Discriminator. Section 4 provides an overview of the VDM specification itself. Section 5 presents some conclusions based on our experiences to date.

2 An Informal Description of the Discriminator Managed Object

In order to control the systems being managed, a managing system must be aware of changes in the configuration of system components (e.g. how the components of a managed system are interconnected) and the status of system components (e.g. whether components of a managed system are in-service, faulty, etc.). Notifications are used by managed objects (the representation of such system components) to report some information autonomously and hence, provide a mechanism for informing a managing system of such changes.

A managing system requires the ability to control which notifications it receives from which managed objects. It requires the ability to turn on and off the receipt of such notifications. It requires the ability to specify the destination (e.g. identities of other managing systems) to which particular notifications are to be sent. The purpose of the *Discriminator* managed object class is to satisfy such requirements.

Discriminator managed objects are described within the conceptual framework shown in Figure 1. When a notification is emitted by a managed object, it is conceptually processed by a local system function (called the event detection and processing function in Figure 1). This local function forms a *potential event report* which contains all of the information required to be forwarded externally to the managing system in a CMIP event report.

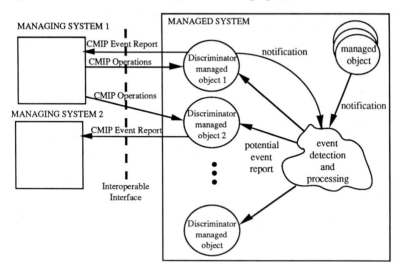

Figure 1: Discriminator Conceptual Model

Conceptually, this potential event report is distributed to all Discriminators that are contained within the local managed system. A Discriminator acts as a filter or sieve, selecting only those potential event reports that satisfy a given set of criteria specified by the *discriminator construct* attribute. For example, a Discriminator may select only potential event reports with event type = alarm from managed objects of class = *line card*.

If the discriminator construct evaluates to **true** for a potential event report and the Discriminator is in the *unlocked* administrative state and in the *enabled* operational state, then an event report will be directed to the managing system specified by the *destination* attribute.

With the exception of the operational state, all attributes of a Discriminator may be modified by a managing system by sending a *set* operation to that Discriminator. When the value of the administrative state is changed to *unlocked* (*locked*) the event forwarding activity is resumed (suspended). Event reports can be directed to a different managing system by changing the value of the destination attribute.

The values of all attributes of a Discriminator may be retrieved by sending a *get* operation to that Discriminator. The operational state attribute indicates whether the Discriminator is functional (state = *enabled*) or not functional (state = *disabled*).

A *create* operation may be sent by a managing system to request that a managed system create a Discriminator managed object, thereby requesting new or additional event forwarding controls be imposed. With the exception of the operational state, values to be assigned to the attributes when the object is created may be specified in the create operation request. If no values are supplied then default values are assumed.

A *delete* operation may be sent by a managing system to request the deletion of a Discriminator, thereby requesting that some event forwarding controls be terminated.

A Discriminator is itself a managed object and can therefore emit notifications. A Discriminator generates an *attribute change* notification whenever one of its attributes is changed. An *object creation* notification and an *object deletion* notification are emitted by a Discriminator when that Discriminator is created and deleted, respectively. These notifications are processed as potential event reports by all Discriminators, including the one which generated the notification.

Given the requirement for a Discriminator to process its own potential event reports, the following behavioural constraints are imposed on the Discriminator:

1. A Discriminator shall not be deleted until it has processed the *object deletion* potential event reporting resulting from the deletion request.
2. A Discriminator shall not enter the *locked* administrative state or change its destination until it has processed the *attribute change* potential event report resulting from its state change or destination attribute change, respectively.

3 Developing the VDM Specification

3.1 Issues Arising from the Informal Specification

Writing the formal description starting from an informal specification [8] turned out to be more difficult than originally expected. The concept of receiving potential event reports and passing on the appropriate ones seems quite simple. However, as explained in the previous section there are some special behavioural constraints. It required several iterations through reading the documentation, writing a formal description, and discussion, to reach an acceptable VDM specification of the simplified discriminator. Many concepts became clear as the work progressed and the specification took shape. However, while trying to formalize the specification, many questions arose which are not answered by the documentation. The fact that formalizing an informal description always requires many iterations and raises many interesting questions shows how valuable this exercise can be. For example, the ISO document [8] introduces an attribute, usage state, which reflects the ability of the Discriminator to accommodate more *users*. This attribute is never referred to by the operations defined for the class. Furthermore, the description of this attribute is ambiguous in the English language description; specifically, it is not clear whether the managed objects which generate the notifications are the users of the Discriminator. If this is the interpretation, then the Discriminator usage state could continuously cycle between idle (not processing information) and active (processing information to be forwarded). A change of usage state from active to idle causes the Discriminator to emit a notification which is then presented for discrimination, thus causing a change in usage state from idle to active (which in turn generates a notification to be presented for discrimination, etc.). Based on this analysis, a proposal to delete the usage state from the Discriminator object was submitted to the relevant standards committee [9].

The ISO Discriminator managed object class includes a scheduling capacity which allows a managing system to specify the intervals during which event reports will be selected for forwarding. In our simplified specification of the Discriminator the scheduler function was removed so this could be incorporated in a subclass and the concept of inheritance in VDM could be explored. It was later determined that this subclass was not an extension of the superclass (i.e. did not follow the rules of strict inheritance). This was not apparent from the informal documentation but was revealed in the formal description.

3.2 Incorporating VDM Within the Existing Syntactical Framework

A primary objective was to incorporate the VDM specification within the existing syntactical framework specified by the ISO Guidelines for the Definition of Managed Objects (GDMO) standard [10]. This standard defines notational tools, called templates, for documenting the attributes, operations, notifications and behaviour associated with managed objects of a specified class. A subset of the elements included in the managed object class template is shown in Figure 2. For complete details including a description of the syntactical conventions used in the template definition, the reader is referred to [10].

managed object class label MANAGED OBJECT CLASS
DERIVED FROM *list of superclasses this is derived from*
ATTRIBUTES
    list of attributes and their associated properties and syntax
ACTIONS
    list of operations and their associated parameters and syntax
NOTIFICATIONS
    list of notifications and their associated parameters and syntax
BEHAVIOUR
    behaviour description

Figure 2: Elements of the Managed Object Class Template

The language in which the behaviour description may be written has been left completely open by ISO, although in practice only natural language has so far been used. Here, we propose that VDM be used within the BEHAVIOUR element of the GDMO templates for formally describing the behaviour of the managed objects.

Abstract Syntax Notation One (ASN.1) [11] is used to specify the syntax of the data types associated with the attributes of a managed object and the parameters of the operations and notifications. An issue, therefore, concerns how to combine or integrate the behavioural component of VDM with ASN.1. The specifications presented in this paper are given entirely in VDM. The approach taken was to manually translate the ASN.1 specifications to VDM types. The automatic translation of ASN.1 to VDM or the provision of referencing/using the ASN.1 data descriptions within a VDM behavioural specification are potential areas of future investigation.

The DERIVED FROM element in the template is presumed to automatically import all characteristics from the superclass definition(s). A particular managed object class template, therefore, only specifies the *delta* or extended characteristics introduced by the subclass and does not repeat the superclass characteristics. GDMO specifies a set of rules for combining the characteristics specified in the superclass(es) template with the extended characteristics to derive the complete class definition. Our objective is to specify only the extended behaviour in the class template and to enhance GDMO to specify the rules for combining this VDM specification with the VDM specifications documented in the superclass(es) template. In the following subsection we identify the nature of these rules for providing extensible behavioural specifications.

3.3 The VDM Style Appropriate for Inheritance

One of the key features of the ISO Standards for OSI Managed Objects is the notion of inheritance. While VDM is not an object-oriented formal method, it is possible to adopt a VDM style appropriate for Managed Objects.

VDM provides the notion of *satisfiability* [5]. It provides a framework for showing that a concrete formal description is a valid implementation of (i.e. *satisfies*) a more abstract description. The *implementation* (concrete description) must meet the *specification* (abstract description) but may be defined on a larger domain and may be more determined (i.e. less non-deterministic). Thus for each operation the concrete pre-condition may be weaker and the post-condition may be stronger. This is exactly the concept necessary for strict inheritance in managed object terminology. A subclass must exhibit all the behaviour of the superclass, but may introduce additional (consistent) behaviour.

Thus a subclass specification of a managed object is derived from a superclass description by weakening the pre-condition and strengthening the post-condition of the applicable operations.

When expressing a subclass specification, only the additional information need be given. This will avoid repetition, aid in understandability, and tie in with the current GDMO Template format. Thus a subclass is assumed to inherit the operations exactly as stated in the superclass unless an extension is given. If an extension is given, the new pre-condition is "or"ed (∨) with the superclass pre-condition, and the new post-condition is "and"ed (∧) with the superclass post-condition. This will guarantee that the inheritance rules are met.

Taking the original discriminator specification and attempting to derive a subclass for it, again required several iterations. To extend the behaviour of an operation by only weakening the pre-condition and strengthening the post-condition requires that the superclass operation be in an appropriate form. While this research has not yet disclosed exactly what this appropriate form might be, some conclusions can be drawn.

The split between the pre- and the post-condition is very important. Generally it seems to be best to put as much information in the pre-condition as possible. This seems to make extension go more smoothly. If the operation has a pre-condition of **true** (e.g. returns a flag indicating whether or not the operation was successful), it may be necessary to introduce a new operation which does have a pre-condition. The original operation may *quote* (VDM's equivalent to subroutine call) this new operation and the new operation will be extensible. It is also important that the post-condition be extensible. The **others** clause of the **case** construct and the **else** clause of the **if** construct should be avoided.

A further consideration is necessary when extending a managed object. The OSI management standard [12] allows subclasses to define new attributes as needed. This capability could be provided in VDM by leaving part of the top level state undefined and adding the necessary definitions in the subclasses. This is not very elegant and we have adopted the RAISE [13] approach[1], which allows extra fields to be added later with no mention of them in the original description.

In addition to adding new data types to a subclass, we may also add additional parameters to an operation. GDMO standards allow "holes" to be left in operation and notification signature definitions which can be filled in by the subclasses. An extendable definition is indicated in ASN.1 by providing a parameter of the "ANY DEFINED BY" type. To avoid the need for signature changes in the VDM specification it is best to structure the signature of such operations in such a way that the parameters are a set of parameter type and value pairs, instead of a list of parameter values whose type is determined by the signature. The function describing the valid types of the parameter set can be extended in the subclass definition.

4 Overview of the VDM Specification

The entire specification will not be presented here. The authors will be pleased to provide copies of the complete specifications upon request. Mario Wolczko's VDM LaTeX macros [14] and the SpecBox Tool [15] were used to prepare the VDM specifications.

---

[1] RAISE stands for Rigorous Approach to Industrial Software Engineering. The RAISE Specification Language (RSL) supports model-oriented, algebraic, explicit, axiomatic, applicative, imperative, and concurrent styles. The RAISE Method is based on the stepwise refinement paradigm.

4.1 Architecture

The original plan was to model a single Discriminator in isolation. However, since two of the operations to be modelled are *create* and *delete* (which have cross-object constraints), it was necessary to take a step back and view the system at a higher level. The specification is presented in two layers, or modules. The upper *Coordinator* layer takes care of the creations and deletions but leaves most of the functionality to the lower *Discriminator* layer which produces notifications, and returns and changes attribute values as necessary.

The Coordinator level receives a request from outside the system, performs various checks, and then invokes (or, in VDM terminology, *quotes*) the corresponding Discriminator level operation for the chosen Discriminator(s).

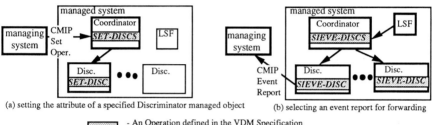

(a) setting the attribute of a specified Discriminator managed object   (b) selecting an event report for forwarding

▨ - An Operation defined in the VDM Specification
Disc. - Discriminator Layer VDM Specification
LSF - Local System Functions (e.g. event detection and processing function)

Figure 3: SET and SIEVE

Figure 3 shows the flow of control for two operations. In Figure 3(a) a *set* request is received from the managing system. The Coordinator passes this request on to the appropriate Discriminator. Figure 3(b) shows the Coordinator receiving a potential event report from the "event detection and processing function" within the local system. This is passed on to all Discriminators. Each Discriminator decides whether to forward the event report on to the managing system specified by its destination attribute.

4.2 Type and State Definitions

The state for the *Coordinator* level description is as follows:

compose *Discs* of
    dsinfo : *Dsinfo*
end

Dsinfo is further defined in a type definition:

Dsinfo = map *Discriminator-id* to *Disc*

Disc is the state for the *Discriminator* level:

compose $Disc$ of
    $info$: $Disc\text{-}info$
    $notif$: $[Not\text{-}msg]$
end

The discriminator information originally contains the five following fields. The keywords at least indicate that other fields may be added later. We could express this concept in standard VDM but this more elegant notation was inspired by RAISE (see section 3.3).

compose $Disc\text{-}info$ of at least
    $disc\text{-}id$: $Discriminator\text{-}id$
    $disc\text{-}const$: $Discriminator\text{-}construct$
    $dest\text{-}addr$: $Destination\text{-}address$
    $admin\text{-}state$: $Administrative\text{-}state$
    $op\text{-}state$: $Operational\text{-}state$
end

The subclass definition then provides the declaration:

extend $Other\text{-}info$ with
    $sched$: $Scheduler\text{-}info$
end

The subclass state contains everything in the superclass state and the scheduler field.

4.3 High Level Behaviour

The most complicated operation at the *Coordinator* level is the *CREATE-DISCS* operation. It has a variable number of parameters. Any parameter that is not supplied is assigned a default value.

CREATE-DISCS ($attrs$: $Attr\text{-}info$, $caller$: $Object\text{-}id$)
ext wr $dsinfo$: $Dsinfo$
pre dom $attrs \subseteq \{DISCIDTYPE, DISCCONSTTYPE, DESTADDRTYPE,$
    $ADMINSTATETYPE\} \wedge$
  ($DISCIDTYPE \in \text{dom } attrs \Rightarrow attrs(DISCIDTYPE) \notin \text{dom } dsinfo$)
post let $newdisc \in Disc\text{-}info$ in
  $newdisc.disc\text{-}id =$
    if $DISCIDTYPE \in \text{dom } attrs$ then $attrs(DISCIDTYPE)$ else $pickdefid()$

  $\wedge\ newdisc.disc\text{-}const =$
    if $DISCCONSTTYPE \in \text{dom } attrs$ then $attrs(DISCCONSTTYPE)$ else $EMPTY$

  $\wedge\ newdisc.dest\text{-}addr =$
    if $DESTADDRTYPE \in \text{dom } attrs$ then $attrs(DESTADDRTYPE)$ else $caller$

  $\wedge\ newdisc.admin\text{-}state =$
    if $ADMINSTATETYPE \in \text{dom } attrs$ then $attrs(ADMINSTATETYPE)$
    else $UNLOCKED$
  $\wedge\ newdisc.op\text{-}state = getopstate() \wedge$
  $\exists disc \in Disc \cdot post\text{-}\overleftarrow{CREATE\text{-}DISC}(mk\text{-}Disc(newdisc, \text{nil}), disc) \wedge$
  $dsinfo = \overleftarrow{dsinfo} \dagger \{newdisc.disc\text{-}id \mapsto disc\}$

The parameter *attrs* is a map from attribute name to attribute value. The pre-condition states what values may be present in this map and checks that the Discriminator id (if given) is unique. *CREATE-DISC* is quoted to trigger the object creation notification, and the new discriminator is added to the state. Use of the VDM *mk-* function is avoided since *newdisc* may have additional fields added by a subclass. Note that this operation does not return a boolean flag indicating success or failure. If that is included in this operation, it is not possible to extend the behaviour for the subclass definition. A *DO-CREATE* operation is added to deal with this. The user invokes *DO-CREATE* which quotes the pre-condition and, if necessary, the post-condition of *CREATE-DISCS* and returns a success flag.

When the scheduler is added for the subclass definition, *CREATE-DISCS* is extended as follows:

CREATE-DISCS
orpre dom $attrs \subseteq \{DISCIDTYPE, DISCCONSTTYPE, DESTADDRTYPE,$
   $ADMINSTATETYPE, SCHEDINFO\} \wedge$
   $(DISCIDTYPE \in$ dom $attrs \Rightarrow attrs(DISCIDTYPE) \notin$ dom $dsinfo)$
andpost $newdisc.sched =$
   if $SCHEDINFO \in$ dom $attrs$ then $attrs(SCHEDINFO)$ else $EMPTY$

Here the parameters and externals are omitted. They are assumed to be the same as in the superclass. The 'orpre'-condition given here is "or"ed with the superclass pre-condition, and this subclass 'andpost'-condition is "and"ed with the original post-condition to provide the complete subclass definition.

4.4 Discriminator Behaviour

The *Discriminator* module describes the behaviour at a per discriminator level.

The *SET-DISC* operation requests an attribute change. If the request is valid, it also triggers a notification. If the attribute value can be changed immediately, that will be done. In the case of a request to lock the discriminator or change the destination address, the change cannot be performed until the corresponding potential event report has been processed. The actual change to the attribute is performed by the *SIEVE-DISC* operation.

$SET\text{-}DISC$ $(a: Attr\text{-}pair)$ $success: Bool$
ext wr $info$: $Disc\text{-}info$
   wr $notif$: $[Not\text{-}msg]$
pre $notif =$ nil $\wedge$
   $a.attr \in \{DISCCONSTTYPE, DESTADDRTYPE, ADMINSTATETYPE\}$

post cases $a.attr$ of
$\quad DISCCONSTTYPE \rightarrow$ if $a.value \neq \overleftarrow{info.disc\text{-}const}$
$\qquad$ then $success \land info = \mu(\overleftarrow{info}, disc\text{-}const \mapsto a.value)$
$\qquad\quad \land\, notif = mk\text{-}Not\text{-}msg(ATTRIBUTECHANGE,$
$\qquad\qquad DISCCONSTTYPE, \overleftarrow{info.disc\text{-}const}, a.value)$
$\qquad$ else $\neg success \land info = \overleftarrow{info} \land notif = \overleftarrow{notif}$
$\quad DESTADDRTYPE \rightarrow$ if $a.value \neq \overleftarrow{info.dest\text{-}addr}$
$\qquad$ then $success \land info = \overleftarrow{info}$
$\qquad\quad \land\, notif = mk\text{-}Not\text{-}msg(ATTRIBUTECHANGE,$
$\qquad\qquad DESTADDRTYPE, \overleftarrow{info.dest\text{-}addr}, a.value)$
$\qquad$ else $\neg success \land info = \overleftarrow{info} \land notif = \overleftarrow{notif}$
$\quad ADMINSTATETYPE \rightarrow$ if $a.value \neq \overleftarrow{info.admin\text{-}state}$
$\qquad$ then $success \land$ if $a.value = LOCKED$ then $info = \overleftarrow{info}$
$\qquad\qquad\qquad$ else $info = \mu(\overleftarrow{info}, admin\text{-}state \mapsto a.value)$
$\qquad\quad \land\, notif = mk\text{-}Not\text{-}msg(ATTRIBUTECHANGE,$
$\qquad\qquad ADMINSTATETYPE, \overleftarrow{info.admin\text{-}state}, a.value)$
$\qquad$ else $\neg success \land info = \overleftarrow{info} \land notif = \overleftarrow{notif}$
end

This is one operation that was restructured to make the extension work smoothly. The original pre-condition was much shorter and the post-condition had an "others" clause and the operation returned a flag indicating success or failure.

This operation can be extended in the scheduler subclass as follows:

SET-DISC
orpre $notif =$ nil $\land\, a.attr = SCHEDINFO$
andpost $a.attr = SCHEDINFO \Rightarrow$
$\qquad$ if $a.value \neq \overleftarrow{info.sched}$
$\qquad$ then $success \land info = \overleftarrow{info}\,\land$
$\qquad\quad notif = mk\text{-}Not\text{-}msg(ATTRIBUTECHANGE, SCHEDINFO,$
$\qquad\qquad \overleftarrow{info.sched}, a.value)$
$\qquad$ else $\neg success \land info = \overleftarrow{info} \land notif = \overleftarrow{notif}$

The *SIEVE-DISC* operation is used to sieve a potential event report. An event report will then be forwarded if the appropriate conditions are met. If the potential event report is a change destination or lock yourself message, then the corresponding attribute is updated (since that was delayed until this point).

$SIEVE\text{-}DISC\ (per\text{:}\ Pot\text{-}event\text{-}report)\ er\text{:}\ [Event\text{-}report]$
ext wr $info\ :\ Disc\text{-}info$

post if $shouldpasson(per, \overleftarrow{info})$
   then $er = mk\text{-}Event\text{-}report(per, \overleftarrow{info}.dest\text{-}addr)$
   else $er = $ nil
$\wedge$ if $per.id = \overleftarrow{info}.disc\text{-}id \wedge per.notmsg.notif\text{-}type = ATTRIBUTECHANGE \wedge$
   $per.notmsg.attr = DESTADDRTYPE$
      then $info = \mu(\overleftarrow{info}, dest\text{-}addr \mapsto per.notmsg.new\text{-}attr)$
   else if $per.id = \overleftarrow{info}.disc\text{-}id \wedge per.notmsg = mk\text{-}Not\text{-}msg($
      $ATTRIBUTECHANGE, ADMINSTATETYPE, UNLOCKED,$
      $LOCKED)$
         then $info = \mu(\overleftarrow{info}, admin\text{-}state \mapsto LOCKED)$
   else $info = \overleftarrow{info}$

Problems are encountered when this operation is extended to describe the scheduler subclass. The scheduler can affect whether or not the event report should be passed on. There could be event reports that would be passed by the superclass that will now be rejected due to the value of the scheduler. This means that the behaviour has changed in a way that cannot be modelled simply by anding an additional clause to the post-condition. A new operation (which uses $SIEVE\text{-}DISC$) is needed to deal with this:

$SCHED\text{-}SIEVE\text{-}DISC$ $(per: Pot\text{-}event\text{-}report)$ $er: [Event\text{-}report]$
ext wr $info$: $Disc\text{-}info$
post $\exists ner \in [Event\text{-}report] \cdot \exists info' \in Disc\text{-}info \cdot$
   $post\text{-}SIEVE\text{-}DISC(per, mk\text{-}Disc(\overleftarrow{info}, \text{nil}), mk\text{-}Disc(info', \text{nil}), ner) \wedge$
   $er = $ if $ner = $ nil $\vee \neg scheduleron(\overleftarrow{info}.sched)$
      then nil
      else ner
$\wedge$ if $per.id = \overleftarrow{info}.disc\text{-}id \wedge per.notmsg.notif\text{-}type = ATTRIBUTECHANGE \wedge$
   $per.notmsg.attr = SCHEDINFO$
      then $info = \mu(\overleftarrow{info}, sched \mapsto per.notmsg.new\text{-}attr)$
   else $info = info'$

Thus the discriminator with a scheduler is not a strict subclass of the discriminator superclass.

5 Conclusions

Our work differs from [7,6] primarily in its intent. Our main focus has not been on extending, unconstrained, an existing specification language (i.e. VDM) to accommodate object-oriented concepts. Our objective has been to use an existing formal language within a *given* object-oriented syntactical framework provided by the ISO management standards.

Based on the work presented in this paper, we conclude that VDM, with its first-order logic and pre- and post-conditions, is well-suited for specifying the behaviour of managed objects. VDM specifications can be easily accommodated within the existing ISO management syntactical framework. Areas of future study identified in this paper include:

1. a formal treatment of the relationship between ASN.1 and VDM, and
2. the development of general guidelines for structuring pre- and post-conditions to facilitate extensibility.

Our experiences show that it is difficult to determine from an English language description of the behaviour of a given managed object, that this behaviour is compatible with the behaviour of another managed object class. The example subclass of the Discriminator we selected as the basis for analysis did not follow the ISO management rules for strict inheritance. This was not initially apparent from the informal description but was revealed in the process of developing the formal description.

It is essential that the ISO management rules for strict inheritance be followed in order to achieve interoperability between managing and managed systems. Specifically, it is a requirement for a managing system to be able to interoperate with a managed system which supports an extended class definition (i.e. a subclass definition), where the managing system knows only about the superclass definition. Formal methods, such as VDM, provide a critical tool for ensuring that managed object behaviour specifications are developed which are extensible and hence, facilitate interoperability.

Furthermore, our experiences show that by producing a formal description from an existing informal one, often reveals a number of ambiguities in the latter. As a result of our work, proposed changes to clarify ambiguities in the informal Discriminator specification have been submitted to the appropriate ISO standards committee.

In addition to facilitating the development of unambiguous, complete and correct specifications, a further benefit of using formal methods is that they provide the basis for formal and automated verification. Although outside the scope of this paper, given the formal specification it is possible to prove a number of properties of the Discriminator managed object.

References

[1] ISO. *Formal Specification of the CMIP Protocol Machine.* (ISO/IEC JTC1/SC21 WG4 N-1057), National Body Contribution from Australia, March 1990.

[2] Cusack, E., Rudkin, S. and Smith, C. *An Object Oriented Interpretation of LOTOS.* Proceedings of the Second International Conference on Formal Description Techniques (FORTE '89), 5–8 December 1989, Vancouver, B.C., pp. 265–284.

[3] ISO. *Working Document—Architectural Semantics, Specification Techniques and Formalisms.* (ISO/IEC JTC1/SC21 N-4887), 1990.

[4] OSI/Network Management Forum. *J-Team Technical Report on Modelling Principles for Managed Objects.* Issue 1, Draft 8, December 17, 1990.

[5] Jones, C. B. *Systematic Software Development Using VDM*. Prentice-Hall International, Second Edition, 1990.

[6] Duke, R., Rose., G. and Lee, A. *Object-Oriented Protocol Specification*. Proceedings of the Tenth International IFIP WG 6.1 Symposium on Protocol Specification, Testing and Verification, 12–15 June 1990, Ottawa, Ont., pp. 323–339.

[7] Bear, S. *Structuring for the VDM Specification Language*, in Proceedings VDM'88: VDM—The Way Ahead. Eds. R. Bloomfield, L. Marshall, R. Jones. Lecture Notes in Computer Science 328, September 1988, pp. 2–25.

[8] ISO. DIS Text of ISO/IEC 10164-5, *Information Technology—Open Systems Interconnection — Systems Management—Part 5: Event Report Management Function*. (ISO/IEC JTC1/SC21 N-4860), Output of the editing meeting held in Kyoto, Japan, May 1990.

[9] ISO. *Table of Replies for DIS 10164-5, Information Technology—Open Systems Interconnection—Systems Management—Part 5: Event Report Management Function*, Canadian Comments on DIS 10164-5, (ISO/IEC JTC1/SC21 N-5885), March 1991.

[10] ISO. DIS Text of ISO/IEC 10165-4, *Structure of Management Information Part 4—Guidelines for the Definition of Managed Objects*. (ISO/IEC JTC1/SC21 N-4852), Output of the May 1990, Editing Meeting held in Kyoto.

[11] ISO. Final Text of IS 8824, *Information Technology—Open Systems Interconnection—Specification of Abstract Syntax Notation One (ASN.1)*. (ISO/IEC JTC1/SC21 N-4720), April 1990.

[12] ISO. DIS Text of ISO/IEC 10165-1, *Structure of Management Information Part 1—Management Information Model*. (ISO/IEC JTC1/SC21 N-5252), Output of the editing meeting held in Paris, January 1990.

[13] Eriksen, Kirsten E., and Prehn, Søren. *RAISE Overview*. Computer Resources International A/S, 1991.

[14] Wolczko, Mario. *Typesetting VDM with LaTeX*. Department of Computer Science, University of Manchester, March 1988.

[15] Adelard. *SpecBox User Manual*. Coborn House Business Centre, London, UK, 1991.

What is the Method in Formal Methods? *

Ed Brinksma
Tele-Informatics and Open Systems Group,
University of Twente
P.O. Box 217, 7500 AE Enschede, The Netherlands
brinksma@cs.utwente.nl

Abstract

Many of the formal methods that abound in computer science are in fact just formal languages or calculi. They can be used to describe and analyse models of information systems of different complexities and application domains. Only to a much lesser extent are we also provided with methods that tell exactly how these models may be used to obtain working products. In this paper we attempt to analyse the difficulties of obtaining such methods by taking a look at the tension between the two fundamental approaches that underly the engineering of information systems: the *formal* approach, i.e. the internally consistent description of virtual objects, based on the principle of analysis by logical deduction, and the *scientific* approach, i.e. the externally consistent description of physical objects, based on the principle of validation (or refutation) by experimentation. One of our conclusions is that there is a need to be able to combine formal validation of designs, i.e. by mathematical means, with experimental validation of designs, i.e. by testing, within a single methodological framework. Some first ideas of what such a framework could look like are given.

1 Introduction

In many places it is argued that the use of formal methods is imperative to improve the quality of design of information systems.[1] This is a very defendable position, as many of the problems that occur when designing information systems can be traced back to ambiguities and incompleteness of problem statements and their solutions, and inconsistencies between specifications of different levels of abstraction along the design trajectory. Surely the availability of formalized notations with a precisely defined meaning provides an excellent basis for guarding precision and avoiding ambiguity, as well as a mathematical framework for comparison and correctness.

It is not by accident that especially in the area of open protocol systems the use of formal methods is receiving so much attention, as this area is characterized both by systems of great complexity, and a need to unambiguously describe their working to a widely dispersed group of users and manufacturers. This has led to the development, application, and even standardization of formal languages in this area, initially mainly for the purpose of specification, but more and more also for analytical purposes, and the support of the design process itself. Over the

---
*This work has been supported in part by the CEC research programmes ESPRIT (LOTOSPHERE, ref: 2303) and RACE (SPECS, ref:1046).
[1]We will use the term *information systems* generically to indicate all products of computer science engineering.

past few years much of this work has been reported at the FORTE conference series (with special emphasis on the standard techniques LOTOS [BoBr 87, ISO 8807], Estelle [ISO 9074], SDL [CCITT Z100]), and other conferences in the area such as the PSTV Symposia. It has also been one of the topics of some large (European) research projects, such as for example ESPRIT/SEDOS, ESPRIT/PANGLOSS, ESPRIT/LOTOSPHERE and RACE/SPECS.

The issue that we want to take up in this paper is more general: *What should be the role of formalisms in the design of information systems?* Formal methods as discussed above generally are not *design* methods, but merely formal notations and calculi that can be used to describe and analyse models of information systems of different complexities and application domains. Only to a much lesser extent are we provided also with methods that tell how exactly these models may be used to obtain working products. In this paper we attempt to analyse the difficulties of obtaining such methods. In doing so we take a look at the tension between the two fundamental approaches that underly the engineering of information systems: the *formal* approach, i.e. the internally consistent description of virtual objects, based on the principle of analysis by formal deduction, and the *scientific* approach, i.e. the externally consistent description of physical objects, based on the principle of validation (or refutation) by experimentation. Confronting these two approaches we will suggest a synthesis that we hope could form a proper basis to define the role and limits of formalisms in the design of information systems.

The rest of the paper consists of the following sections:

2 Design methods

3 Formalism and the design of information systems

4 A formal framework for validation

5 Conclusions

2 Design methods

It is not our intention to treat one or more design methods in detail here. Instead we wish to look at the problems of design or engineering from a general, qualitative point of view, because it appears that interesting observations can be made already at that abstract level.

The scientific method

It is illuminating to base our study of design methods on a comparison with a closely related model describing the *scientific* method. This method is described in terms of a general (although not undisputed) abstract model that explains the basic procedures for developing theories about phenomena in the physical world, and is one of the traditional topics of the philosophy of science. The basic model of the *empirical cycle*, as depicted in figure 1, to which we restrict ourselves here, has been developed on the basis of the ideas of the Viennese logical-positivist school (the *Wiener Kreis*) in the twenties of this century. It is important to observe that this model does not pretend to describe adequately the actual dynamics of scientific discovery, but is to be used to give an idealized account of it in the form of *a posteriori* rationalizations. This distinction is often indicated as that between the *context of discovery* versus the *context of justification* account of the development of science. Here, we will not concern ourselves with the refinement, variation, reinterpretation, and rejection of the empiral cycle as an appropriate model by later philosophical

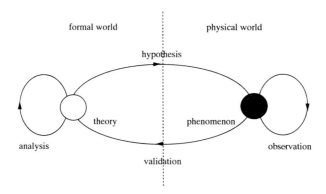

Figure 1: *the empirical cycle*

schools, as this rather crude approximation suffices for our immediate purposes. The interested reader is referred to the extensive literature on this topic, e.g. [Pop 59, Kuh 62, Lak 78, Fey 75].

Essentially, the empirical cycle describes the interaction between the growth of formal theories and the observation of physical phenomena that they intend to describe. The main features of the model are part and parcel of the education of every scientist, and include:

theory formation A formal account of the phenomena under consideration is constructed in terms of a logico-mathematical theory. This theory must be both *formally consistent*, i.e. be free of contradiction, and *physically sound*, i.e. describe the known facts adequately.

hypothesis deduction By *analysing* the formal model hypotheses about the phenomena in question are deduced. The physical interpretation of these hypotheses must have *observable* consequences.

experimentation By observing the phenomena under conditions determined by an *experiment* observation *data* are collected. The nature of the experiment is determined by the observations that relate to the formulated hypothesis.

validation The formal theory is *validated* on the basis of the new facts represented by the new observations. In the presence of the new facts it may be necessary to modify it to (re)establish its physical soundness.

For a more complete account of the standard model of the empirical cycle we refer to the literature of the philosophy of science, a good exposition can be found in [Nag 61].

The design method

It is remarkable that where the philosophy of science is an established discipline with a considerable tradition, there exists no clear counterpart with a similar recognition and tradition that could be called the 'philosophy of design'. Within all traditional engineering disciplines there does exist an abundance of publications on design and construction within the specific limits of their application areas (e.g. industrial design, civil engineering), in which they are studied

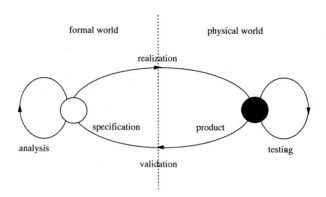

Figure 2: *the design cycle*

in connection to very pragmatic issues, such as the economic need and marketability of products, their production process, etc. Fewer publications deal with design *in abstracto*, see e.g. [Sim 81, JoT 63, Arc 65], of which especially [Sim 81] provides a very readable treatise on the ingredients of what he terms the '*sciences of the artificial*'. Almost all publications are concerned mostly with design in what could be called the *context of construction*, and much less with design in the *context of justification*. It is our feeling that the latter is of great importance when analysing the role of formal methods in the design process. We wil resist the temptation to find the reasons for this situation, but put forward a modification of the empirical cycle that can serve as a starting point for our analysis in figure 2. This model must be appreciated as just as crude an approximation to actual design as the empirical cycle is to actual scientific discovery.

The overriding difference with the empirical cycle is that in the design cycle the *specification* must be interpreted *prescriptively* in contrast with the *descriptive* nature of the formal theory in the empirical cycle. An important implication of this difference is that when the validation shows the model and the product to be incompatible, it is, in principle, the *product* that must be modified, not the model. We summarize the main ingredients of the design cycle:

specification Formally, design starts with the construction of a formal model, or *specification* of the product under construction. This specification can be subjected to mathematical analysis to show that the design satisfies desirable properties.

realization On the basis of the specification a *product* is constructed that is intended to *conform* to the specification. The realization is often, but not necessarily, guided by structural correspondance between the formal model and the lay-out of the product.

testing The product is *tested* for *conformance* to its specification by observing its properties and/or behaviour. This is done by carrying out tests that extract observable facts from the product.

validation The product is *validated* on the basis of the interpretation of the test results when compared to the formal specification. As result of the testing it may be necessary to modify the product or the realization procedure leading up to it.

The empirical cycle and the design cycle are, of course, not independent. In order to be able to specify formally an in principle realizable product, one must have the disposal of a well-corroborated scientific theory that can be used to describe the nature of the desired product. In this sense, science formally precedes engineering. In practice, however, engineering can precede science, as is illustrated by all products of engineering that predate modern science. In such cases the realization of products is based on informal and/or incomplete models, and in some sense the empirical and design cycles then merge: the validation process may then give rise to modifications of both model and product, and the development of a product adopts to some extent the character of a scientific experiment. We will come back to this interdependency and its effect on the design of information systems.

Refining the design method

A principal problem with the design cycle is that the realization of a product is not a formally deducible consequence of its model. This is different from the scientific method where the hypotheses can, in principle, be deduced from the formal theory. This lack of formal control gives rise to the adoption of an *iterative* design strategy, in which the design cycle is gone through several times.[2] The formal specification that contains sufficient structural detail to guide the realization process is not obtained at once, but via a number of approximations, i.e. the specification itself is subjected to a design procedure. The procedure is started with a first specification leading to a prototype product. This prototype is evaluated and leads to an adapted specification with which a new design cycle is started. This process is continued until a sufficiently detailed, final specification is obtained on the basis of which the product can be realized. The iterative design procedure is depicted in figure 3. Iterated design thus provides a way to move from abstract to more concrete specifications, i.e. formal models that contain more implementation related information.

It is important to observe that in iterated design not every design cycle needs to include a *physical* (prototype) product. As it is the objective of each (but the last) design cycle to obtain a modified formal specification, one may wish to make such modified specifications themselves the product of the design cycle. In such cases the whole cycle is embedded in the formal world, for which it would be appropriate to speak of *formal design*, sometimes also referred to as *mathematical* or *logical engineering*. In this context one also speaks of the *refinement* of specifications, whereas the term *realization* is reserved for the transformation into physical products. Both refinement and realization are sometimes referred to as *implementation*.[3] The identification of the (formal) product of a previous cycle with the specification of the next leads to the in software engineering well-known *cascading model*, as depicted in figure 4. Such formal design methods are of great importance for the design of information systems, but also a source of confusion, as we shall see.

Dynamic aspects of design

It should be pointed out that the role of formal methods in design can be understood only partly from the above representations of the design method in the context of justification. Where it is clear from these pictures that formal methods are needed to provide notations and calculi

---

[2]In the scientific method a similar iterative strategy is needed to resolve the dual problem: the impossibility to deduce formally a theory from observations. It should also be noted that the formal deducibility of hypotheses does not resolve the real problem in the scientific method; their selection and formulation form an important topic in the philosophy of science.

[3]The use of this terminology is confusing and inconsistent among authors; our account may not satisfy all.

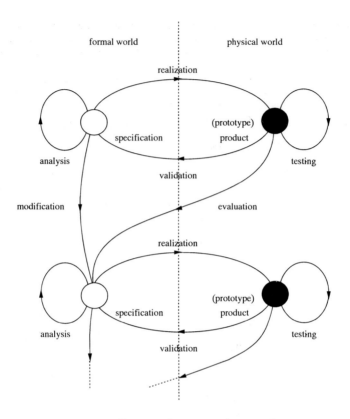

Figure 3: *the iterative design cycle*

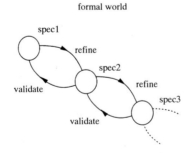

Figure 4: *the cascading model*

to support the activities of specification, refinement, and validation, they do not bring out the crucial need for formal support of the more dynamic aspects of the design process, viz. the generation and selection of alternative specification modifications. These are, together with the activities just mentioned, among the main topics in the curriculum for the theory of design suggested by Simon [Sim 81]:

- algorithms for choosing *optimal* design alternatives
- algorithms and heuristics for choosing *satisfactory* design alternatives
- heuristic search for design alternatives
- allocation of resources for search

3 Formalism and the design of information systems

Having looked at some general aspects of design methods, it is now time to investigate them in the more particular light of the engineering of information systems. As before, it is not our aim to suggest any concrete design method, but instead to try and analyse the situation and make a number of qualitative observations.

For a start we introduce two extreme positions or 'schools' with respect to the design of information systems. Although the individual computer scientist generally will not fall precisely within either of the categories, it is nevertheless our impression that they represent the two main methodological streams of computer science engineering.

Mathematical reductionism This school of thought sees computer science essentially as a branch of mathematics. The position finds its justification in the observation that a main category of products of computer science, viz. *software*, can be seen as *formal* objects. This would allow such products to be developed completely on the basis of formal design. In particular, it would allow the testing and validation of such products by mathematical means instead of experimentation.

Experimentalism Here, a more phenomenological view is taken of the products of computer science engineering. Initially, information systems are constructed on an experimental basis, and adapted on the basis of increasing knowledge and experience. The methodological basis is best described as a mixture of the scientific method and the design method: the validation feedback can give rise to modifications of both model and product.

Both positions are open to more or less serious criticism. Against mathematical reductionism two main counterarguments can be distinguished:

- *Misconception of product*: the formal interpretation of products ignores the fact that design must lead to *working* products. The formal correctness of a design does not guarantee the failure-free functioning of the product when embedded in its operational environment. In the case of software: the program may be correct but the compilation unreliable (as for example in silicon-compilers for VLSI-programming). Many information systems, moreover, cannot be seen as being exclusively composed out of software building blocks. The current trend to merge information processing with communication functions leads to increasingly heterogeneous systems in which the specifications of communication-oriented components are models of, in principle, physical phenomena. The methodological point that can be made here is that the validation of the ultimate product, is always the validation of a product in the physical world, which, by definition, cannot be subjected to formal proof.

- *Combinatorial explosion*: formal proofs of correctness are, it is true, a possibility in principle, but not in practice for realistic systems, as the combinatorial dimensions of such formal argumentation are unmanageable. This is a well-known argument, but it should be noted that it strikes against the *orientation* of current theories of (program) correctness, and is not aimed so much against the principle of validation with formal means. In many applications if would be satisfactory, for example, to show that failures occur with a certain small maximal frequency, and a complete proof correctness is not required. It might be possible to develop formal theories that could be used to prove such more tolerant forms of correctness more efficiently than their stricter versions. This remark can be compared to the emphasis in [Sim 81] on methods to find *satisfactory* solutions, instead of the more costly search for *optimal* solutions. To some extent the current semantic theories account for correctness on a *micro*-level, whereas a *macro*-level theory of correctness is needed. To compare: the theory of elementary particles is not used to explain how a radio works, although this could be done in principle (or so the physicists would have us believe) at the cost of a combinatorial explosion.

Combining both points it can be remarked that the mathematical approach seems to deal inadequately with the phenomenon of design errors. The ideological point of the mathematician is that '*errors shall not occur*', whereas that of the engineer could be described as '*errors will occur*'. The latter calls for an attitude that all methods of error detection, mathematical and otherwise, should be used together in good measure with the estimated cost of the occurrence of the error at hand. It also seems to require a different sort of underlying logic, in which local inconsistencies do not expand into global inconsistencies, as is the case in classical logic. We do not agree with those that argue that it is the discrete mathematical nature of the semantic models of computational behaviour that necessitate an 'all or nothing' theory of correctness, because it would not allow for a more continuous or approximative form of reasoning. Clearly, it is the choice of a two-valued logic of correctness that disallows such reasoning. The successful use of probabilistic models in the performance analysis of discrete systems, are a convincing case in point.

Our elaborate criticism of the mathematical reductionist position are not to be taken as an indication that we do not support tha large scale application of formal methods to the design of information systems. On the contrary, it must be interpreted as an indication of the interesting and subtle limitations of such applications, and an effort to determine where and how they can be applied best.

Seen in this light, it is a foreboding sign that we are much shorter in our criticism of the experimentalist approach to design. In our opinion it can never serve as a solid basis for the justification of designs because it tends to *corrupt* the design procedure. This corruption is due to the unclear interpretation of the feedback provided by validation: should the specification or the product be adapted? This flexibility of the approach undermines the systematic treatment of design obligations, and can easily lead to incompletely specified products with unknown behaviour, i.e. the typical 'nobody asked for it and nobody knows how it works' case. Ultimately this degenerates into design by uncontrolled trial and error, in which the specification is not used as a vehicle for analysis and all product modifications are carried out on a heuristic, or even arbitrary basis. Such procedures can lead to rather inefficient forms of design, that produce low quality design against relatively high costs, as for realistic information systems the modification of concrete products is usually much more costly than modifications at the (formal) specification level. These are precisely the ingredients of what has become known as the *software crisis*, but what in our view would be more accurately described as the *information system design crisis*. It were these problems that gave momentum to the development of the mathematical reductionist school.

The observant reader may wonder how then one may come to grips with systems for which there is not sufficient theoretical knowledge to get started with the iterative (formal) design strategy. The answer, without a moral undertone, is that one cannot *design* such systems.[4] To obtain the required knowledge of such systems, or parts of them, they can be studied using the *scientific method*, i.e. to develop theories on the basis of experimentation. Note that then, since one is then no longer in the business of design, this activity is methodologically pure again: the feedback from validation will unambiguously lead to the modification of the theory.

Once sufficient theoretical understanding has been gained the design activity can start. But if both of the mentioned methodological schools fail, although not in the same measure, what kind of design methodology do we need? We do not pretend to be able to provide any sort of complete answer to this question, but a number of methodological features can be established on the basis of the above discussion:

1. in order to maintain methodological *integrity* it should be based on the *standard design method*,

2. in order to deal succesfully with the *complexity* of the realization of information systems is should employ an *iterative design strategy*,

3. in order to improve the *quality* and the *efficiency* of dealing with complex designs it should include *formal design methods*, but

4. in order to ensure the ultimate correctness of *operational* products it should also include *conformance testing methods*, and

5. in order to allow the efficient development of *satisfactory* products it should include a *theory of approximate correctness*.

All together, it is an imposing list, and it may take a considerable time yet to produce the ingredients required. Also, we emphasize again that our remarks concerning the application of the design method and the scientific method should be understood in *context of justification* argumentation, implying that one must be able to disentangle the actual activities *a posteriori* into methodologically sound phases of development.

In section 4 we suggest basic elements of a single formal (sic!) (meta-)framework that integrates validation by formal and experimental means. At the same time it offers a basis for an approximative theory of correctness. Before presenting these ideas, however, we wish to digress shortly on the role of the computer science community in the development of sound design methods for information systems.

---

[4]This can be seen as an applied case of Wittgenstein's famous dictum "*Wovon man nicht sprechen kann, darüber muß man schweigen*", to be adapted in our case to "*What cannot be spoken about, cannot be designed*".

Digression: the CS community

One of the important tasks of the computer science community is the *production* and *evaluation* of methods, formalisms, and tools that support the design of information systems. It is our impression that the former element of this task, the production, is being paid much more attention to than the latter, evaluation. Almost any publication medium in the field may be consulted to find proposals for new methods, new languages, new logics, new architectures, new tools, etc. Real evaluations of such contributions are much harder to come by, if by this we mean a carefully developed demonstration of the success or failure of something or other on the basis of serious applications to design problems. This seems to be especially the case for the area of formal methods, where 'a hundred schools of thought do *not* contend', and consequently not too many flowers blossom.[5] No real scientific confrontation of ideas seems to take place, and competing work is ignored rather than opposed. A number of possible reasons can be suggested for this lack of scientific attitude:

- the absence of a firmly entrenched research tradition in computer science because of its relatively short existence, and because of that

- the adoption of research criteria from adjacent fields of science, notably mathematics, for which not applicability, but novelty and consistency are the main criteria for success, and therefore

- the relative scarcity of publications that deal with the evaluation of existing methods, systems, etc., and

- the great economic interest of computer science and its applications, which causes an influx of considerable means and stimulates growth rather than competition.

We strongly advocate that the scientific confrontation of ideas in computer science take place on a much larger scale than is currently the case. Competition, discussion, and evaluation should, in principle, lead to greater scientific progress and a greater relevance of the results of our work. It would also create a clearer picture for the potential users of our work, i.e. the industry, of which many are quick to point out that they are too slow in the uptake of our new ideas and products. It seems not unlikely that one of the factors that contributes to this situation is the embarrassment of choice between options, and the lack of real indications of their usefulness. To the resolution of the latter problem the industrial community can contribute much themselves by initiating and carrying out representative evaluation projects.

4 A formal framework for validation

In this section we give an outline of an approach to validation that encompasses correctness considerations both by formal means, i.e. mathematical proofs, and by experimental means, i.e. testing. This allows for a flexible strategy with respect to validation along the design trajectory, and merges the design of formal and physical products. Our overview is based on the more elaborate publications [Bri 88, Bri et al. 90, Bri 91]. The approach is based on the study of semantic equivalences and pre-orders of process behaviour that are based on formalized notions of observation, and has been strongly inspired by the theoretical work on testing equivalences started by De Nicola and Hennessy [DeHe 84, DeN 87].

---

[5]For those not versed in Chinese history the original reads *"Let a hundred flowers blossom, let a hundred schools of thought contend"*.

Implementation relations

We assume that we have at our disposal a formal theory of behaviour and a language in which we can denote behaviours as language expressions that are interpreted in the theory. We will use $B, B_1, B_2, \ldots$ to denote such *behaviour expressions*, and more in particular $S, S_1, S_2, \ldots$ to denote *specifications*, and $I, I_1, I_2, \ldots$ to denote *implementations*. The reader is reminded that the latter two are relative concepts in formal design, and what is an implementation at one stage can serve as a specification at the next.

In the context of the design process it is natural to postulate the existence of a relation R over behaviours, the *implementation relation*, such that S_1 R S_2 if and only if S_1 is a correct implementation of S_2. Thus each specification S determines the set of its implementations $Impl_R(S)$ defined by

$$Impl_R(S) =_{df} \{I \mid I \text{ R } S\} \qquad (1)$$

This formalized notion of correct design immediately implies a useful equivalence relation between specifications, viz.

$$S_1 \approx_R S_2 \quad \textit{iff} \quad \{I \mid I \text{ R } S_1\} = \{I \mid I \text{ R } S_2\} \qquad (2)$$

This definition tells us that two specifications are equivalent iff they determine the same set of implementations, which seems to be the desirable notion of equivalence in the context of design. If the relation R is a *pre-order*, i.e. reflexive and transitive, we write $\leq_R$ instead of just R. In that case a more intimate connection exists between $\approx_R$ and $\leq_R$, viz.

$$S_1 \approx_R S_2 \quad \textit{iff} \quad S_1 \leq_R S_2 \text{ \& } S_2 \leq_R S_1 \qquad (3)$$

Unless stated explicitly otherwise, we will assume our implementation relations R to be pre-orders $\leq_R$. An interesting account of how to deal with non-transitive implementation relations is given in [Led 90].

Observation frameworks

The main idea behind the unified treatment of different forms of validation is the formalization of the concept of *observation*. The definition of this concept should be such that it can be used as the formalization of physical observation in actual testing, as well as account for more idealized forms of observation that correspond to acts of verification. This spectrum can be brought in relation with the notions of *black box* versus *white box* testing, where no versus all structural detail of the implementation under validation are observable, respectively. Formal validation can be thought of as idealized testing in the presence of all structural information of the implementation, e.g. all states and all transitions are known. It is the compromise between these two extremes, also referred to as *grey box* testing, that could be an interesting basis for the study of approximative correctness for formal designs.

Definition 1 (Observation frameworks)
Let *Specs* be a universe of specifications. An *observation framework* OF over *Specs* is a triple $\langle \Sigma, \Omega, \Delta \rangle$ with

- Σ a set of *observations*

- Ω a set of *observers*

- $\Delta : \Omega \times \textit{Specs} \to \Sigma$ an *observation extraction* (function); for $O \in \Omega$ fixed we write $\Delta_O(S)$ instead of $\Delta(O, S)$.

□

Some remarks are in place to clarify this definition.

1. Σ is the universe of possible observations that can be made of a process in a given framework. Its elements may be structured objects of arbitray complexity built up out of more elementary *partial* observations. In most concrete cases the elements of Σ are *sets* of partial observations, such as *success, failure, deadlock, terminal state*, etc.

2. Ω represents the set of agents that carry out the observations. An important class of observation frames, the *reflexive* observation frames, are obtained by putting Ω=*Specs*. In the case of white box testing this is usually not sufficiently strong, however, and more potent observers are needed.

3. Δ is the function that produces for each process-observer pair the observation that is made. Together with Σ, it is obviously this extraction function that determines the strength of the method. In more experimental situations this function could, for example, be implemented by executing all runs of the combined process-observer system. In the case of a formal verification procedure S could be a logical formula, $O \in \Omega$ an assignment of values to variables, and $\Delta_O(S)$ the truth-value of S in the context of O.

We refer the reader to [Bri 91] for elaborations and examples of this formalized notion of observation. We now proceed to establish the connection between implementation relations and observations.

Operationalization of correctness

By operationalization of correctness we understand the explanation of what constitutes a correct implementation in the context of a given observation framework. This implies that for each notion of correct design in the form of an implementation relation, we can choose between the validation methods that correspond to those observation frameworks for which an operationalization can be obtained.

Definition 2 (Operationalization)
Let $\textit{OF}=\langle \Sigma, \Omega, \Delta \rangle$ be an observation framework over *Specs*, and let $\leq_R$ be an implementation relation over *Specs*. A relation $\textit{Obs}_R \subseteq \Omega \times \Sigma \times \Sigma$ is an *observation relation* for $\leq_R$ if

$$S_1 \leq_R S_2 \quad \textit{iff} \quad \forall O \in \Omega \ \textit{Obs}_R(O, \Delta(O, S_1), \Delta(O, S_2)) \tag{4}$$

The right-hand side part of (4) is referred to as the (*OF*-)*operationalization* of $\leq_R$.

□

Stated in words, an operationalization is a relation between observers and pairs of observations such that S_1 is a correct implementation of S_2 if and only if for all observers $\textit{Obs}_R$ holds for the observer and its applications to S_1 and S_2. In the traditional literature on testing equivalences [DeHe 84, Abr 87] equation (4) is exploited from 'right-to-left', i.e. new semantic pre-orders are generated by considering certain observation frameworks. We are also strongly motivated in the 'left-to-right' interpretation, i.e. given a notion of correctness to determine (different) ways to validate it. Note that if one can find observation frameworks that adequately model the relevant aspects of the testing of physical behaviour, (4) can be used as a basis for a theory of *conformance testing*. This direction of work is further elaborated in [Bri 88, Bri 91, Lan 90].

In the light of actual design procedures we can adapt equation (4) to bring out more clearly the usual situation in which a given specification S determines the correctness of an implementation I. If a formal specification S is given we can compute the $\Delta(O, S)$ 'in advance' to determine a family of predicates $\{Pass_O \mid O \in \Omega\}$, or *verdicts*:

$$Pass_O(V) =_{df} Obs_R(O, V, \Delta(O, S)) \qquad (5)$$

With this definition we can rewrite (4) into

$$I \leq_R S \quad \textit{iff} \quad \forall O \in \Omega \; Pass_O(\Delta(O, I)) \qquad (6)$$

This last formulation is especially attractive in the case of experimental validation, where $\Delta(O, S)$ is computed in advance on the basis of the formal specification S, and $\Delta(O, I)$ is determined by actual testing.

We can now formulate what we mean by a (formal or experimental) test, and other related concepts.

Definition 3 (Test)
Let $OF = \langle \Sigma, \Omega, \Delta \rangle$ be an observation framework over *Specs*.

1. A *test* T in OF is a pair $\langle O_T, P_T \rangle \in \Omega \times 2^\Sigma$, where O_T is the *observer* of T, and P_T is the *verdict* of T. An implementation I **passes** T iff $P_T(\Delta(O_T, I))$.

2. A *test suite* U in OF is a set of tests in OF. An implementation I **passes** U iff $\forall T \in U \; I$ **passes** T.

3. The *test* or *validation purpose* of a test (suite) T is the predicate $\Phi_T \subseteq Specs$ defined by $\Phi_T(I)$ iff I **passes** T.

□

Summarizing, if we take $\leq_R$ an implementation relation over *Specs*, $\{Pass_O \mid O \in \Omega\}$ the family of verdicts defined by (5), and define the test suite $U = \{\langle O, Pass_O \rangle \mid O \in \Omega\}$, then the test purpose $\Phi_U(I)$ is equivalent with $I \leq_R S$. In [Bri 91] methods are studied to obtain minimal subsets of U that have equivalent test purposes, which is, of course, the central question in *test generation*.

Note that the above presentation of testing in the context of test purposes includes validation by *model checking* (see e.g. [Emer 90]), as a special case. Model checking can be seen as testing for a priori given test purposes in a white box observation framework (the reachable states of an implementation must be observable).

Stratification of correctness

With respect to validation a 'divide and concur' strategy can be followed. A useful idea is to stratify the implementation relation R in the form of a *descending chain* of relations, e.g.

$$R_0 \supseteq R_1 \ldots \supseteq R_n = R \qquad (7)$$

The basic idea is to adopt an *incremental validation* scheme, starting with the validation of $I\ R_0\ S$, and then proceed with showing that $I\ R_{i+1}\ S$ under the hypothesis that $I\ R_i\ S$ has been validated. It is based on the assumption that it would be easier to validate less restrictive implementation relations first.

A strategy that has proved useful is to find Q_i that allow interesting validation techniques, and 'interpolate' between R_i and R_{i+1}, i.e.

$$R_{i+1} = R_i \cap Q_i \tag{8}$$

An example of this can be found in [Bri 88, Bri et al. 90], where the pre-orders $\leq_{trace}$ (*trace inclusion*) and $\leq_{fail}$ (*failure pre-order*) are considered. The intended implementation relation is $\leq_{fail}$, and $\leq_{trace} \supseteq \leq_{fail}$. It turns out that an interesting validation theory, that of *canonical testers*, can be developed for the relation **conf** with $\leq_{trace}\ \cap\ \mathbf{conf}\ =\ \leq_{fail}$. This enables the incremental validation of $\leq_{fail}$, by first validating $\leq_{trace}$, for which good formal verification methods exist, and then validating **conf**, for which interesting experimental validation methods exist.

In general stratification fits well with the formal design strategy, which itself follows a stratified approach that is determined by the consecutive iterations. It allows the designer to determine an optimal validation strategy for each design step, where a flexible choice between formal and experimental means is possible. This enables the transfer of information between these two modes of validation, i.e. to test a property experimentally relative to another property that has been established formally, or vice versa.

Approximation of correctness

When validation is based on a stratification of the implementation relation, it is attractive to establish a measure for the extent to which the correctness criterion that is implied by the ultimate implementation relation is approximated at each stage of the stratified validation. Such measures could form the basis for a decision on whether to stop or continue the validation by comparing the costs with the returns.

The descending chain of implementation relations in (7) corresponds to a chain of inverse implications between corresponding validation purposes, viz.

$$\Phi_0 \Leftarrow \Phi_1 \ldots \Leftarrow \Phi_n = \Phi \tag{9}$$

where $\Phi_i(I)$ is equivalent with $I\ R_i\ S$ for all $0 \leq i \leq n$ and S a given specification.

As validation purposes form a collection of (monadic) predicates over *Specs* they can be seen as the elements of a *Boolean algebra*. We can use this well-known model as a basis for the formalization of our correctness measures.

Definition 4 (Valuations)
Let $\mathcal{B}$ be a Boolean algebra of validation purposes. A *valuation* is a function $v : \mathcal{B} \to \mathcal{R}_{\geq 0}$ such that

$$\forall \Phi_1, \Phi_2\ \text{if}\ \Phi_1 \Leftarrow \Phi_2\ \text{then}\ v(\Phi_1) \leq v(\Phi_2) \tag{10}$$

□

Valuations provide measures of how 'interesting' properties are, where stronger properties must be more interesting than weaker ones. The real question is, of course, how to obtain such measures. In principle this cannot be determined by any formal method, because it is related to an appreciation of the environment in which the ultimate product is embedded. The occurrence of the same error may be rated entirely differently according to this embedding, e.g. as part of a device for playing computer games versus application in a nuclear plant. This means that such valuations must be regarded as system parameters whose actual values are provided externally. They could be part of the specification of a system, in which case they can be taken into account formally in the design process. The estimation of such parameters could intially be done on a heuristic basis, and subsequently be improved by using adaptive strategies, i.e. establishing new estimates by correcting the previous ones on the basis of their result. A more complete treatment of valuations and related concepts, especially in relation to the problem of *test selection*, can be found in [Bri et al. 91]. Here several methods for generating valuations are compared and evaluated, and an elaborate example is given of a valuation based on a probabilistic model for the occurrence of errors. It should be noted that the method behind this example is not generally applicable, as in many cases non-frequently occurring errors may be crucial for the application of a system. This is one of the reasons for not choosing stochastic theories as a basis for the approximation of correctness.

Valuations are not the most appropriate measure because they evaluate in terms of absolute values. Generally, of course, one is interested in the extent to which a given property or validation purpose has been approximated. Such measures can be obtained by applying a simple normalization procedure.

Definition 5 (Coverage)
Let $\mathcal{B}$ be a Boolean algebra of validation purposes, $\Phi \in \mathcal{B}$, and $v : \mathcal{B} \to \mathcal{R}_{\geq 0}$ a valuation. The *coverage* of Φ by Φ_a, $\text{cov}_\Phi(\Phi_a)$, is defined for all $\Phi_a \Leftarrow \Phi$ with $v(\Phi) \neq 0$ by

$$\text{cov}_\Phi(\Phi_a) =_{df} \frac{v(\Phi_a)}{v(\Phi)} \tag{11}$$

□

Finally, we need a measure of *cost* to compare with coverage. Only if these two elements are present we can rationalize validation strategies, e.g. on the basis of decision theory. As costs are typically tied to operational procedures, and not to properties, they must be assigned to tests. The only reasonable boundary condition on cost functions seems to be that if we validate more, it costs more. This leads us to the last definition.

Definition 6 (Cost assignment)
Let $\mathcal{K}$ be a collection of test suites over an observation framework OF. A *cost assignment* is a function $v : \mathcal{K} \to \mathcal{R}_{\geq 0}$ such that

$$\forall U_1, U_2 \in \mathcal{K} \text{ if } U_1 \subseteq U_2 \text{ then } c(U_1) \leq c(U_2) \tag{12}$$

□

Again, cost assignments are parameters whose values must be provided externally. In principle, the suggestions that were made for the determination of valuations would seem to apply here as well.

5 Conclusions

In this paper we have looked at the design of information systems in order to determine better the role that formal methods do and can play in this respect. Our analysis has been based on a study of *design* methods in the *context of justification*, i.e. the way in which the design process can be rationalized *a posteriori* to show the quality of the resulting product. As not much work exists in this area, a simple, abstract model of design has been proposed that contrasts the activity of design or engineering with the activity of scientific discovery. The latter has a standard, although not undisputed, model of justification known as the *empirical cycle*.

Based on the proposed model of the *design cycle* we have shown that design in general gives rise to iterative procedures to overcome the problem that product realizations do not logically follow from their specifications. We have indicated how intermediate prototype products may have the character of a formal object, which gives rise to formal design procedures and validation by mathematical means.

We have indicated the importance of formal design procedures in particular for the design of information systems, based on the formal character of software products, which are an important ingredient of such systems. It has been pointed out, however, that formal correctness cannot imply operational correctness, thus establishing the need for the *conformance testing* of products. Based on these observations we have analysed two main streams in the design of information systems, viz. *mathematical reductionism* and *experimentalism*. We have put forward that the school of mathematical reductionism fails to establish design methods that deal with the operational correctness of products, although they do certainly improve the quality of the design. We have also concluded that it currently only offers methods for the verification of absolute correctness, and does not provide in the need for approximative methods that are more in line with engineering needs. These are not aimed at the elimination of all errors, but at the elimination of all important errors. With respect to the experimentalist school we have argued that it can not serve as a basis for the justification of design because of the ambiguous interpretation of negative validation reslults, which easily leads to corruption of the design discipline.

On the basis of the analysis of the design of information systems and the criticism of the identified 'schools of design', the following list of features for a design method for information systems has been suggested.

1. in order to maintain methodological *integrity* it should be based on the *standard design method*,

2. in order to deal succesfully with the *complexity* of the realization of information systems is should employ an *iterative design strategy*,

3. in order to improve the *quality* and *efficiency* of dealing with complex designs it should include *formal design methods*, but

4. in order to ensure the ultimate correctness of *operational* products it should also include *conformance testing methods*, and

5. in order to allow the efficient development of *satisfactory* products it should include a *theory of approximate correctness*.

At the end of section 3 we have commented upon what we perceive as a lack of confrontation between the different schools of thought in computer science, in particular those concerned with formal methods. Whereas the concern for the mathematical consistency of formal methods is guarded by the adoption of a mathematically oriented research tradition, their evaluation with respect to their usefulness in the design of realistic information systems is (still) largely lacking. The coexistence of many formalisms without convincing indications of their applicability is confusing to their potential users. Here, also industrial cooperation is required to define and carry out representative application projects.

In section 4 we have presented some ideas on the validation of design that integrate formal reasoning with experimentation based validation. The notion of correct design is captured by so-called *implementation relations*, that associate with each specification the class of all its allowed implementations. These relations are then *operationalized* using an idealized notion of *observation*, defined in terms of *observation frameworks*. In this way different validation methods can be applied by operationalizing the same implementation relation in different observation frameworks.

We have indicated how such ideas can be further refined by *stratifying* the implementation relations, which leads to an *incremental validation* procedure, where each next step is based on the assumption that the validation of the preceeding step has been successful. By applying different validation methods for different steps this can be used to reduce proof obligations by testing, and test purposes by proving properties. We have concluded by suggesting a method to develop a theory for *approximative correctness*. This method involves the definition of *valuations*, which indicate the relative importance of individual correctness properties. Together with *cost assignments* for the validation methods used for these properties one can, in principle, optimize relative correctness against its cost. It has been pointed out that valuation functions and cost assignments are design parameters that cannot be obtained by formal means, but must be provided externally.

References

[Abr 87]   S. Abramsky, Observation Equivalence as a Testing Equivalence, TCS, Volume 53, 1987, Pages 225–241.

[Arc 65]   L.B. Archer, A systematic method for designers, (Council of Industrial Design, London, 1965).

[BoBr 87]   T. Bolognesi, E. Brinksma, Introduction to the ISO Specification Language LOTOS, Computer Networks and ISDN Systems 14 (1987), 25–59.

[Bri 88]   E. Brinksma, A Theory for the Derivation of Tests, in: Protocol Specification, Testing and Verification VIII, (North Holland, 1988). also: memorandum INF-88-19, University of Twente, Enschede, NL (1988).

[Bri 91]   E. Brinksma, A formal approach to testing distributed systems, memorandum INF-91-74, University of Twente, Enschede, NL (1991).

[Bri et al. 90] E. Brinksma, R. Alderden, R. Langerak, J. v.d. Lagemaat, J. Tretmans, A Formal Approach to Conformance Testing, in: J. de Meer (ed.), Proc. 2nd International Workshop on Protocol Test Systems, (North Holland, 1990), 349–363.

[Bri et al. 91] E. Brinksma, J. Tretmans, L. Verhaard, A Framework for Test Selection, to appear in: B. Pehrson, B. Jonsson, J. Parrow, editors, Protocol Specification, Testing, and Verification, XI, (North-Holand, 1991).

[CCITT Z100] CCITT, Specification and Description Language (SDL), Z.100, Geneva (March, 1988).

[DeHe 84]   R. De Nicola, M. Hennessy, Testing Equivalences for Processes, Theoretical Computer Science 34, (1984), 83– 133.

[DeN 87]   R. De Nicola, Extensional Equivalences for Transition Systems, Acta Informatica 24 (1987), 211–237.

[Emer 90]   E.A. Emerson, Temporal and modal logic, in: J. van Leeuwen (ed.), Handbook of Theoretical Computer Science, Volume B, Formal Methods and Semantics, pages 995–1072, (Elsevier/MIT Press, 1990).

[Fey 75]   P. Feyerabend, Against method : outline of an anarchistic theory of knowledge, (NLB, 1975).

[ISO 8807] ISO, Information Processing Systems, Open Systems Interconnection, LOTOS — A Formal Description Technique Based on the Temporal Ordering of Observational Behaviour, IS 8807 (1989).

[ISO 9074] ISO, Information Processing Systems, Open Systems Interconnection, Estelle — A Formal Description Technique based on a Extended State Transition Model, IS 9074 (1989).

[ISO 9646] ISO, Information Processing Systems, Open Systems Interconnection, OSI Conformance Testing Methodology and Framework, DIS 9646 (1989).

[ISO N6201] ISO, Information Retrieval, Transfer and Management for OSI, Working Draft on Formal Methods in Conformance Testing, Project 1.21.54, ISO/IEC JTC1/SC21 N6201.

[JoT 63]   J.C. Jones, D.G. Thornley, Proceedings conference on design methods, (Pergamon Press, 1963).

[Kuh 62]   T.S. Kuhn, The Structure of Scientific Revolutions, (University of Chicago Press, 1962).

[Lak 78]   I. Lakatos, Philosophical Papers, (Cambridge University Press, 1978).

[Lan 90]   R. Langerak, A Testing Theory for LOTOS using Deadlock Detection, in: E. Brinksma, G. Scollo, C.A. Vissers, editors, Protocol Specification, Testing, and Verification, IX, pages 87–98, (North-Holland, 1990).

[Led 90]   G. Leduc, On the Role of Implementation Relations in the Design of Distributed Systems using LOTOS, Dissertation, University of Liège, Belgium (1990).

[Nag 61]   E. Nagel, The Structure of Science : problems in the logic of scientific explanation, (Harcourt, Brace & World, 1961).

[Pop 59]   K.R. Popper, The Logic of Scientific Discovery, (Hutchinson, 1959).

[Sim 81]   H.A. Simon, Sciences of the Artificial, (MIT Press, 1981).

Io: An Estelle Simulator for Performance Evaluation

D. Fernández   E. Vázquez   J. Vinyes

Departamento de Ingeniería de Sistemas Telemáticos
Universidad Politécnica de Madrid – Spain

Address: ETS de Ingenieros de Telecomunicación
Ciudad Universitaria s/n E-28040 Madrid SPAIN

Email: dfernandez@dit.upm.es

April 20, 1991

Abstract

This paper describes a performance simulation tool based on Estelle. Estelle is a Formal Description Technique designed to specify the behavior of concurrent systems, in particular communication protocols. It is based on a state machine model extended with Pascal-like data structures and statements. Currently, Estelle is an International Standard of the International Standards Organization (ISO), and several development tools such as syntax-directed editors, compilers, and debuggers are available in the research community. The main objective of the tool described here is to integrate the evaluation of performance with other aspects of protocol development (validation, rapid-prototyping, etc) using common protocol models and tools for all of them.

The paper deals with practical aspects of simulation with Estelle, such as the use of the language to write simulation models, the tool features and its current status. A theoretical discussion about the applicability of formal description techniques to performance simulation, although important, is considered outside the scope of this paper.

1 Introduction

Formal Description Techniques (FDTs) are languages designed to define the structure and behavior of concurrent systems such as communication networks and protocols in a formal way. A system description written with one of these FDTs, usually called a specification, can be interpreted unambiguously and processed with automatic tools for different purposes, for example to verify logic properties, to refine the system design step by step and eventually obtain a prototype or implementation in a high-level programming language, and to generate test cases.

In general, the specifications written with the existing FDTs focus on functional aspects of the described systems, with little or no reference to time properties, so they are not suited to be used for performance evaluation purposes. However, several recent studies have considered the application of FDTs, possibly extended with time, for defining performance simulation models [1], [2], [3], [4], [11]. The rationale of this approach is to integrate the evaluation of performance with other phases of software development, using a single model of the system (or similar models at different levels of detail) in all of them, instead of a simulation model completely separated from the rest. This approach may significantly reduce the effort required to build and validate simulation models, taking advantage of existing specifications and tools based on FDTs.

The paper is organized as follows. Section 2 discusses in some detail the Estelle characteristics relevant to simulation. Section 3 describes the general structure and user interface of the simulation tool, and, finally, section 4 summarizes the work done up to now and the planned activities.

2 Simulation in Estelle

Estelle is one of the FDTs that has been more extensively used in the research community and it is currently an ISO International Standard [8]. Other standard FDTs are Lotos, defined also by ISO, and SDL, defined by CCITT.

Estelle [10] is based on the familiar concept of finite state machines or automata. In Estelle, a system is described as a hierarchically structured set of automata (called modules) which exchange messages through unlimited FIFO queues (called channels). The number of module instances and their interconnection pattern can change dynamically as the system evolves. Modules may have attributes that determine what module instances run in parallel and what instances run in interleaving. In addition to message passing, modules can communicate through restricted sharing of variables.

When a new module instance is created, it first executes an initialization section. Then, its subsequent behavior is defined by a set of state variables and a set of transitions. These transitions define the module response to different events and may be of one of two types: input or spontaneous. Input transitions fire in response to the reception of messages from other automata. Spontaneous transitions fire in response to internal conditions, for example when a state variable reaches a certain threshold, either as soon as the condition becomes true or when it has been continuously true during a given delay period. The set of conditions that must be satisfied to fire a given transition is called its predicate. Transitions may be qualified with a priority level. When a transition is actually fired, a set of associated actions is executed atomically, for example sending output messages, assigning new values to state variable, creating new module instances, etc. A module that has no transitions is called inactive.

The definition of state variables, transition predicates and actions is based on the Pascal programming language. Therefore, most Pascal features, such as simple data types, arrays, records, predefined operators, repetitive and conditional statements, functions and procedures, etc. are also available in Estelle.

As mentioned above, each active module has an attribute that determines its grade of parallelism with the rest of modules in the hierarchy of automata. In every specification there is always one or more special modules called *systems*, which are characterized by the fact that they and their subordinates behave independently of other systems. Systems can interchange messages through channels, but there is no synchronization among their behaviors. A system cannot be nested within an active module. Therefore, once initialized, it exists for the life-time of the specification. The behavior of a system depends on its attribute and the attribute of its children. They may run in parallel or in interleaving, but always synchronized.

The Estelle semantics [8] defines precise rules for interpreting an Estelle specification and determining which transitions can be fired in a given state, depending on module attributes, transition predicates, priorities, and delays. In the initial state, each system and the modules under it are evaluated in order to select a set of firable transitions (at most one per module). Once selected, all the transitions inside the set are executed, moving the system to a new state, in which it is evaluated again, giving a new set of firable transitions, and so on. The process of evaluating a system and its modules for choosing a set of executable transitions is called *system evaluation*.

In general, Estelle provides a simple and flexible way of defining the structure and behavior of communication systems. However, in order to obtain models suited for performance simulation [7] [9], three main language aspects must be improved, namely

- Quantitative description of time
- Probabilistic characterization of nondeterministic behaviors
- Definition of simulation parameters and measurements

These three aspects are briefly discussed below.

2.1 Time

The only Estelle construction related to time is the delay associated with spontaneous transitions. The delay construction means that the firing of a transition is delayed until some time in the future, provided that the transition predicate remains true during the delay period. (If the predicate becomes false as a result of state changes caused by intermediate transition firings, the delayed transition is canceled.) The specification of retransmission timers is a typical application of this construction in the protocol area: for example, a given data unit must be retransmitted provided that a valid acknowledgement has not been received during a certain time period.

However, Estelle does not make any assumption about temporal aspects such as the time consumed by each transition execution or by the evaluation of transition predicates. Estelle [8] simply states that:

- "time progresses as the computation does", so delayed transitions that are not canceled will eventually fire, and that
- "this progression is uniform with respect to the delay values of all the transitions involved", so transitions with short delays will fire before others with longer delays, but the exact firing times are not defined.

Knowing that a transition will eventually fire, or that it cannot fire in a given state, may be enough to verify that a protocol is logically correct, but usually it is not enough for performance evaluation purposes, where time information is of primary importance. To solve this problem, in the simulation tool described in this paper the user can specify two types of time parameters: transition execution times and system evaluation times.

The first parameter type models the time needed to carry out the actions associated with each transition. For example, protocol entities usually create new processes in response to connection requests coming from other entities. This is normally modeled in Estelle by a transition that fires when the request arrives and creates a new module instance that will serve the connection. In this case, the execution time associated to that transition may be used to model the time needed in a particular executing environment to create a new process, associate it with a network connection, etc.

The second parameter type, system evaluation times, models the time required to evaluate which transitions are firable in a given state to execute and choose the ones that will be actually executed. These parameters may be used to model the time needed in real protocol implementations to evaluate their state or the conditions required for system evolution, for example analyzing the headers of incoming data units, checking internal lists, etc.

In summary, the above time parameters represent the actual processing times associated to the actions performed by the simulated system and provide the basis for maintaining the simulated time clock characteristic of performance simulators. Now delay periods can be checked against this clock to determine the exact instants when delayed transitions may be executed.

2.2 Nondeterminism

An important property of Estelle specifications is that the order of transition firings may be partially undefined. For example, if in a certain system state several transitions can be fired in the same module, the Estelle semantics states that only one of them can be selected for execution. The user may force a particular selection by giving different priorities to these transitions or may leave the decision unspecified.

For performance simulation purposes, it is desirable to be able to characterize probabilistically these nondeterministic situations by assigning different selection probabilities to each of the involved transitions. For example, an unreliable communication channel may be modeled with two transitions that may fire in response to input messages: one that delivers the message to the receiver, and another that discards it. In this case, the selection probability assigned to the second transition would represent the message loss probability of the simulated channel.

These nondeterministic situations are resolved by our simulation tool in a simple way. Each transition may have a weight (real number), which is proportional to the probability of being chosen in a nondeterministic situation. This probability is calculated by dividing the corresponding weight by the sum of the weights of all the transitions involved in the choice. Each time a nondeterministic situation appears, the probabilities of all the transitions involved in it are calculated from their weights, and one of them is randomly chosen according to their relative probabilities.

In a similar way, in performance simulation it may be necessary to define delay intervals in terms of some suitable probability distribution. This can be used, for example, to represent variable propagation delays, message interarrival times, etc. The same consideration applies to the transition execution and system evaluation times added to the basic Estelle model. In this case, the time probability distributions would represent protocol operations that require a variable amount of time, for example the access to some data storage device.

At present, our tool allows to define variable delays, transition execution and system evaluation times using random distributions chosen by the user. The most common distributions (uniform, exponential, normal, etc.) are directly available and new distributions can be easily added.

Every time a transition starts executing or a system begins a evaluation period, a new value is generated according to the distribution selected by the user and associated to a timer. The expiration of this timer will signal the end of the execution or evaluation activity.

2.3 Definition of Measurements and Parameters

In principle, this problem can be solved directly in Estelle, since it includes all Pascal features related to operations with integer and real numbers. With this approach, the collection of measurements and the computation of mean values, confidence intervals, etc. would be programmed in Pascal and included in the actions associated to the appropriate transitions. In particular, the control of simulation experiments in terms of transient periods, duration of simulation runs, control of confidence intervals, etc. can be easily done with spontaneous transitions that fire when the desired conditions are met.

This approach may be convenient in simple cases, but the tool described in this article provides an alternative way of defining simulation experiments and measures that does not require any modification or addition to the Estelle specification (at least for the most common statistical computations). In this case, the definition is made through commands provided by the tool user interface (see subsection 3.2). Then, during the simulation the *required computations are done automatically by the tool, not by the specification*. This separation between measurement computations and behavior description is also found in modern simulation languages [12]. As an additional advantage, the measurement definition can be changed interactively without recompiling the specification.

Similar considerations apply to the selection of simulation parameters. They can be defined as normal Pascal constants or functions, at the cost of recompiling the specification every time a parameter value is changed. Alternatively, the Estelle mechanisms for leaving constant values or function bodies undefined [8] may be exploited in order to define simulation parameters. In this case, the parameter values can be supplied through the simulator interface or, in the case of functions, imported from library modules.

3 The Simulation Tool

At present our Estelle simulation tool, called **Io**, includes most of the functionalities outlined above. This section presents the main facilities provided by the tool and the next one summarizes the status of the current version.

It must be stressed that all the considerations about performance simulation with Estelle presented in section 2 are simply particular interpretations of Estelle specifications that are perfectly valid according to the standard Estelle semantics. They do not imply any change of or extension to the language. This is also true at the syntactic level: the information that specifies particular execution times, selection probabilities for nondeterministic situations present in the specification, etc is added in separate parameter files or through simulator commands, without changing the Estelle source file at all. (As an alternative this information may be given by using qualified comments, i.e. comments beginning with $, inside the Estelle specification file.)

Although performance evaluation was the main purpose of the tool, taking into account the advantages of integrating different aspects of protocol development as much as possible, Io was designed to be used for three purposes:

1. **Performance simulation.** This is the case discussed above. The specification is executed under control of the simulated clock according to the execution times and probability parameters defined by the user, in order to get estimations of characteristic system parameters, such as throughput, delay, etc.

2. **Logic simulation.** In this case, the specification is executed interactively through the simulator interface. The user can fire transitions one at a time or continuously until a certain condition is met (see "go on" menu below). The transition selection probabilities are ignored. Every time a nondeterministic situation is reached, the simulator asks the user to resolve it by means of a menu.

   In addition to selecting transitions, the user can inspect different system aspects such as module hierarchy, module states, firing conditions, message queues, etc (see figures in the appendix). This mode is useful for studying the specification behavior in detail, and also for testing and debugging measurement variable definitions before running long simulations.

3. **Prototype generation.** In this case, the specification is executed autonomously, that is, without including the simulator user interface. The simulated time clock that controls the delays in simulation mode is replaced by a real time clock provided by the host system, for example through an interruption vector. The interface between the system specified and the execution environment in which it will run has to be supplied by the user in one of the two ways explained in subsection 3.3.

3.1 Tool Structure and Functions

The process followed to simulate or get a prototype from a Estelle specification is depicted in figure 1. Io has two main parts: the Estelle to Modula-2 Translator (EMT) and the Simulator Kernel (SK). The former is written in C and the latter in Modula-2, and at present both run in PC compatible systems.

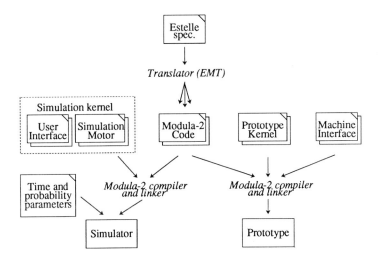

Figure 1: Simulator and prototype generation process

3.1.1 Estelle to Modula-2 Translator

The Estelle specifications processed by the tool are translated to the Modula-2 programming language [13] by means of EMT. In general, EMT generates one Modula-2 library module for every Estelle module type defined in the specification, plus a set of auxiliary library modules which contain information about channels and interactions.

For performance or logic simulation, the generated modules are compiled and linked with SK in order to obtain an executable program. The additional files that define the transition evaluation and execution times are plain text files that consist of character strings and numerical values. These files may be written by the user with any text editor or they may be generated directly by the translator if the necessary information is given in the specification using qualified comments.

3.1.2 Simulation Kernel

SK has two main parts: the simulation motor and the user interface. The *simulation motor* implements the simulation algorithm defined in [5], which is derived directly from the Estelle semantics. Essentially, it consists of an infinite loop that evaluates the specification state, determines which events may take place, chooses the one that will occur first, updates the simulated clock to the time of occurrence of that event and, finally, executes the chosen event, updating the measurement variables. Two event types are possible: transition execution and system evaluation. The first one is caused by the expiration of the execution timer of a transition that was chosen for execution in a previous system evaluation. The second is caused by the expiration of the evaluation timer of a system that previously ended the execution of all the transitions previously selected and began its evaluation.

If a nondeterministic choice arises during a system evaluation (i.e. several transitions ready to fire in the same module) the user may resolve it interactively by means of a menu, or may let the kernel do it by using the weights assigned to each transition.

The *user interface* has been implemented using windows, menus, and on-line help trying to provide a user friendly simulation environment. Commands can be introduced by clicking on menus with a mouse or through keyboard shortcuts. Simulation results are presented in separated windows (currently in text form only).

The available simulation commands are grouped in the following menus:

Modules. This menu includes commands to display information about the specification being simulated. For example, the user can see the hierarchy of modules that make up the specification, the state of each system (executing or evaluating), module internal states, transition states (executing, enabled, delayed, etc), messages waiting in queues, and some predefined statistics such as the number and rate of transition executions. See figures 5, 6, 7, 8, 10 and 11 in the appendix.

Go on. This menu offers several transition execution modes, namely step by step, until a given number of transitions has been fired, for a certain amount of (simulated) time, simulate indefinitely, or until a certain event occurs, for example the firing of a particular transition or the evaluation of a system. The simulation can always be stopped with a special combination of keys, even if the end condition has not been reached. See figure 2.

Configuration. This menu serves to select general configuration options, for example interactive or automatic mode, and to customize the format of the simulator output, ranging from a detailed history of all events (mainly transition executions, system eval-

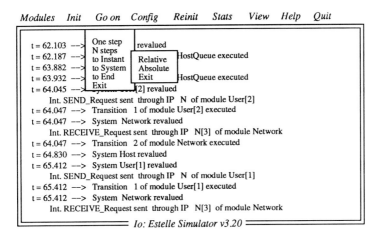

Figure 2: Simulation trace example

uations and messages passed) to a few user defined messages that flag important events. Configurations and simulator outputs can be saved in files for future use.

Statistics. This menu allows to define and display the measures that will be computed during the simulation. In order to define measures independently of the specification, Io implements three objects: *events*, *signals*, and *accumulators*, which are explained in the next subsection.

Other menus: Init, to initialize the specification; ReInit, to re-initialize the specification, resetting all user-defined statistics; View, to edit text files; Help, to get on-line help; and Quit.

3.2 Performance Measures

Events are actions performed by the simulated specification. Up to now, the following events have been identified: transition executions, system evaluations and interactions through message queues. All but the last are in fact refined in two distinct events, because they are not instantaneous, for example, beginning of a transition execution and end of execution. We plan to add new events in the future, such us the creation or release of a module.

The user can instruct the simulator to send a predefined *signal* to a certain *accumulator* every time a monitored event happens. The accumulator is the element that performs the required calculations and provides the desired results.

Currently, there are three accumulator types implemented in the simulator, namely "Time Recorders", "Average Timers" and "Counters".

A "Time Recorder" is simply a chronometer that recognizes two signals, on and off, which mark a number of time intervals. After any simulation period, the chronometer provides the total accumulated time and the ratio between this time and the simulation period duration.

The "Average Timer" can receive two signals, begin and end, used also to mark time intervals. After any simulation period, the average timer provides the mean interval duration of the intervals between begin and end signals.

Finally, the "Counter" receives up and down signals and provides the current count value (number of ups minus number of downs) and the average value over the simulated period. Other accumulator types and signals can be easily implemented.

The statistics menu includes commands to create accumulators of any the three predefined types and to associate their signals to particular events in the system. By identifying significant events in the specification and combining signals and accumulators in an appropriate way, the user can easily compute common metrics such as transmission delay, throughput, protocol efficiency, processor load, memory utilization, etc. Measurement definitions can be saved in files for future use.

Measurement example

Let us consider a specification of a simple communication network with a host and two remote users connected, where the CPU host is modeled by an Estelle module with two states, IDLE and WORKING, and three transitions: initialization (T1), accept job and change the state to WORKING (T2), and finish job and change the state to IDLE (T3). See figure 9.

In this system, the CPU load can be estimated by defining a chronometer accumulator that receives "on" signals when T2 is executed and "off" signals when T3 is executed. Figure 3 shows the relationship between CPU transitions and accumulator signals. After simulating the system for the desired period of time, the value of the accumulator gives the CPU load, absolute or relative to the total simulation time.

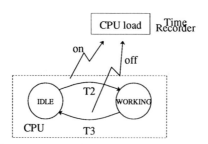

Figure 3: Example of accumulator usage (CPU load measurement)

In the above specification, the users are instances of an Estelle module with two states: READY and WAITING, and two transitions: T1, a transition that, after waiting for a random delay, sends a job to the host and changes the state to WAITING, and T2, an input transition fired by the arrival of the job response from the host, which changes the state back to READY. In this case, the average response time of the system composed by the network and the host can be estimated by creating an average timer accumulator that receives "begin" signals from T1 and "end" signals from T2. The relevant user transitions and the associated signals are shown in figure 4.

Finally, figure 12 shows sample values of the CPU load, the response time and other user-defined statistics included in the example, for example the number of jobs waiting to be served, etc. (Predefined or built-in statistics have been shown in figures 10 and 11.)

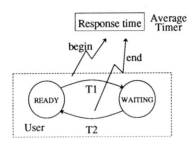

Figure 4: Example of accumulator usage (system average response time)

3.3 Prototype Generation

For prototype generation, a modified version of SK, called Prototype Kernel (PK), is used. PK is basically a simplification of SK that includes only a simplified simulator motor, excluding everything related with measurement variables or simulation control. The simulation clock used by SK, is replaced by a real clock provided by the execution environment in which the prototype will run. PK ignores the time parameters defined for performance evaluation purposes. Events take place as soon as possible.

Machine Interface. The user has to provide the interface between the prototype and the underlying machine. This can be done in two ways:

- Modifying the Modula-2 code generated by the tool, or
- Using Estelle mechanisms for leaving specification parts undefined (PRIMITIVE, EXTERNAL, etc).

The Modula-2 code generated by EMT is very clear and it is easy to add new code inside the actions of a transition or in the initialization part of a module. Besides, the syntax of Modula-2 and Estelle (Pascal) is very similar, so it is easy to identify the correspondence between the Modula-2 code and Estelle.

In any case, the first method requires some knowledge about internal aspects of the tool and, moreover, the changes made to the code will be overridden if the specification is translated again. For these reasons, the second method is generally recommended. In this case, the machine interface is defined using PRIMITIVE procedures and functions and undefined types and constants in the Estelle specification. The tool will create a new Modula-2 library module containing all these undefined parts, which must be filled by the user. In this way the hand-written code is confined to a separate module and will not be overridden by subsequent translations of the specification.

Hook Procedures. The user has also the possibility of inserting pieces of code inside de initialization part and the main loop of the simulation motor using a predefined library module. These pieces of code will be executed, respectively, when the prototype is initialized and each time an event takes place, and can be used to perform general actions that were not foreseen in the PK design.

Run-Time Debugging. For debugging purposes, a prototype and its machine interface may be linked with a "real-time" SK version instead of PK. In this way, the prototype runs autonomously but the user can stop its execution at any time by typing a special key combination. At this point, the screen contents is saved and the normal SK user interface is displayed, so the user can examine the execution state (module states, queue contents, etc), by using the simulation menus and commands described in 3.1.2. When the user selects any option from the "Go On" menu, the original screen is restored and the prototype execution is resumed.

4 Current Status and Future Work

The current version of Io is written in Modula-2 and runs on personal computers. Before the Estelle to Modula-2 translator was finished, the simulation kernel and the user interface were tested with several example specifications of moderate size, from a few hundred lines to a maximum of 1,200 lines, translated by hand. Some of these test specifications were simulated, for example a set of terminals that send jobs to a remote host through a communication network; others were implemented as autonomous programs, for example the call processing software of a simplified private telephone exchange.

At present, a first version of the translator is already available and we plan to simulate bigger specifications, in order to test the tool and the advantages of our simulation approach in real-life applications.

Additionally, we are working in the following areas:

- Definition of simulation experiments and parameters in a more powerful and flexible way. We are designing a new interface that will allow the user to run several simulations in batch and process the results later, giving for example medium values or confidence intervals. The new version will also include new types of accumulators whose value will be a function (average, maximum, sum, etc.) of other accumulators.

- A new tool version for UNIX workstations using the X-Window system.

References

[1] M. Ajmone, G. Balbo, G. Bruno, F. Neri. TOPNET: A Tool for the Visual Simulation of Communication Networks. IEEE J. Selected Areas in Communication, Vol. 8, Num. 9, December 1990.

[2] G. Albertengo, S. Forno, A. Fumagalli. TOP/PDT: A Toolkit for the Development of Communication Protocols. IEEE J. Selected Areas in Communication, Vol. 8, Num. 9, December 1990.

[3] F. Bause, P. Buchholz. Protocol Analysis Using a Timed Version of SDL. 3rd International Conference on FDTs, Forte 90, Madrid, November 1990.

[4] G. Bochmann, J. Vaucher. Adding Performance Aspects to Specification Languages. 8th IFIP WG 6.1 Conference on Protocol Specification, Testing and Verification. North-Holland, 1988.

[5] P. Dembinski, S. Budkowski. Simulating Estelle Specifications with Time Parameters. 7th IFIP WG 6.1 Conference on Protocol Specification, Testing and Verification. North-Holland, 1987.

[6] M. Diaz, et al (ed). The Formal Description Technique Estelle. North-Holland, 1989.

[7] D.G. Golden. Software Engineering considerations for the design of simulation languages. Simulation, Vol. 45, Num. 4, October 1985.

[8] ISO IS 9074. Estelle - A Formal Description Technique Based on an Extended State Transition Model. 1989.

[9] A.M. Law, W.D. Kelton. Simulation Modeling and Analysis. McGraw-Hill, 1982.

[10] R. J. Linn Jr. The features and facilities of Estelle. Open Systems Data Transfer. December 1988.

[11] C. Miguel. Tecnicas de descripcion formal aplicadas a la evaluacion de prestaciones de sistemas de telecomunicacion. Ph. D. Thesis, ETSI Telecomunicacion, Universidad Politecnica de Madrid, Spain. 1991.

[12] Simscript II.5 Programming Language. CACI, Los Angeles, 1986.

[13] N. Wirth. Programming in Modula-2. Springer-Verlag, 3rd corrected edition, 1985.

Appendix

This appendix collects the figures mentioned in the specification example described in section 3.2.

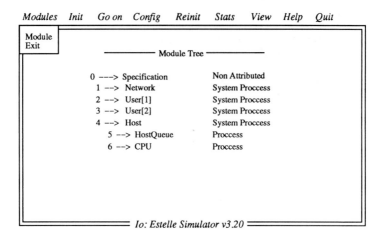

Figure 5: Module hierarchy example

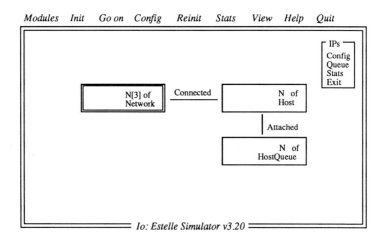

Figure 6: Channel configuration example

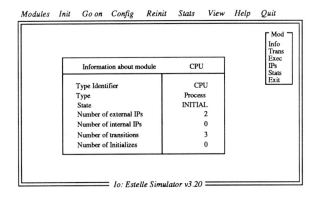

Figure 7: Module information example

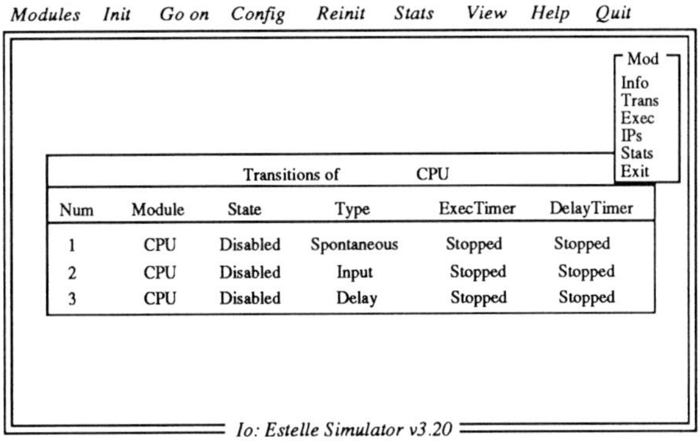

Figure 8: Transition information example

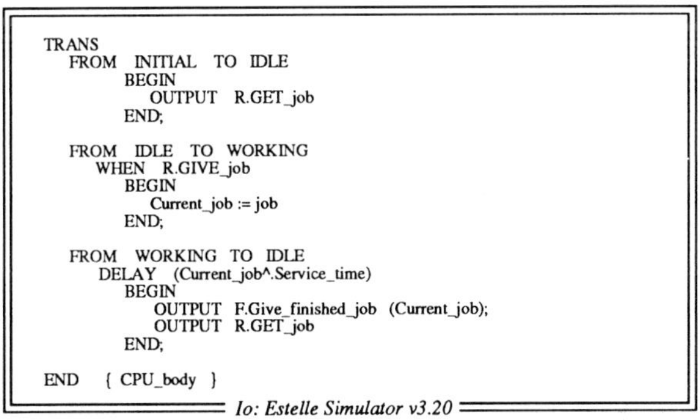

```
TRANS
    FROM INITIAL TO IDLE
        BEGIN
            OUTPUT R.GET_job
        END;

    FROM IDLE TO WORKING
        WHEN R.GIVE_job
        BEGIN
            Current_job := job
        END;

    FROM WORKING TO IDLE
        DELAY (Current_job^.Service_time)
        BEGIN
            OUTPUT F.Give_finished_job (Current_job);
            OUTPUT R.GET_job
        END;
END   { CPU_body }
```

Figure 9: CPU module transitions ("view" menu)

```
Modules  Init  Go on  Config  Reinit  Stats  View  Help  Quit
                                                              ┌ IPs ┐
                                                              Config
                                                              Queue
              ──────── IP Queue Statistics ────────           Stats
                                                              Exit
                  IP name  =      R
                  Module   =      CPU

                  Max Length        =  1.000
                  Mean Length       =  0.095
                  Max Time In Queue =  2.158
                  Mean Time In Queue=  1.569
                  Arrivals Rate     =  0.061
                  Total Elements    =  4.000




              ═══════ Io: Estelle Simulator v3.20 ═══════
```

Figure 10: Message queue built-in statistics

```
Modules  Init  Go on  Config  Reinit  Stats  View  Help  Quit

   SimTime = 100.342   Last reset = 0.000   ElapsedTime = 100.342


                                                              ┌ Mod ┐
                                                              Info
              ──────── Transition statistics ────────         Trans
          Trans #       Num executions        Exec rate      Exec
                                                              IPs
             1                1                 0.010        Stats
             2                6                 0.060        Exit
             3                6                 0.060

                          Total = 13            0.130



              ═══════ Io: Estelle Simulator v3.20 ═══════
```

Figure 11: Transition built-in statistics

```
Modules  Init  Go on  Config  Reinit  Stats  View  Help  Quit

   SimTime = 100.342   Last reset = 0.000   ElapsedTime = 100.342

                                                         ┌ Stats ┐
                                                         Reset
              ──────── Statistics created ────────       New statistic
          #    Name         Type            Values       Kill statistic
                                                         Kill All stats
          1  cpu_load     TimeRecorder    31.609 (=31.50%) Show signalers
          2  response_time AverageTimer   45.882           Load Estcript
          3  mean_service AverageTimer     5.268           Write Estcript
          4  t_bet_jobs   AverageTimer     3.324           Exit
          5  jons_in_queue Counter        20.000 mean= 8.996



              ═══════ Io: Estelle Simulator v3.20 ═══════
```

Figure 12: User-defined statistics

FORMAL DESCRIPTION TECHNIQUES, IV
K.R. Parker and G.A. Rose
Elsevier Science Publishers B.V. (North-Holland)
© 1992 IFIP. All rights reserved.

Modeling Timeouts and Unreliable Media with a Timed Probabilistic Calculus [*]

Hans Hansson

Swedish Institute of Computer Science [†]
and
Department of Computer Systems, Uppsala University

Abstract

We use an extension of Milner's Calculus of Communicating Systems (CCS) with discrete time and probabilities to model quantitative aspects of timeouts and unreliable media. As an illustration we provide a specification of the alternating-bit protocol.

1 Introduction

In a traditional process algebra, such as CCS [Mil89], timeouts are usually modeled with an internal non-deterministic choice between the possibility that the timeout will expire and the possibility that it will not. No information is provided on how frequent timeouts are or when the timeout will expire. Similarly, an unreliable medium is typically modeled as a non-deterministic choice between loosing the message or delivering it. No information is included on the transition delay or on how frequent losses are. Such specifications are likely to be underspecific in that they will specify behaviours that surely will not be included in the final implementation, e.g., the specification allows the timeout to expire "immediately" after it has been set, whereas in any implementation there will always be some delay (the timeout period) before the timeout expires. One way to overcome these limitations is to extend existing formalism with quantitative aspects dealing with time and probabilities.

Quantitative time is motivated by the need to model that certain time bounds are always met. Such real-time properties, often referred to as *hard deadlines*, are important in most applications. By explicitly modeling the passage of time it is possible to specify and verify not only *safety-properties* (nothing undesirable will happen) and *liveness-properties*

---

[*]This work was partially supported by the Swedish Board for Technical Development (ESPRIT/BRA project 3096 SPEC) and the Swedish Telecommunication Administration (project PROCOM).
[†]Address: SICS, Box 1263, S-164 28 Kista, SWEDEN, E-mail: hansh@sics.se

(something desirable will happen), but also real-time properties (something desirable will happen within an explicitly specified time period).

There are several motives for introducing probabilities, the most important being that

- reliability requires probabilities to be accurately modeled. For instance, much of the current work on protocol design is driven by the need to overcome unreliable communication media. However, in most existing formal methods the unreliability can only be specified as a possibility of failure, since the probability of failure across the medium cannot be quantified.
- some distributed algorithms actually rely on randomization.
- probabilities can be used to model *fairness*, e.g., a fair choice between two alternatives can be interpreted as: "there is a non-zero probability for each alternative".

Simultaneously introducing time and probabilities will, in addition to the real-time and reliability properties above, also allow *performance properties* to be specified and verified. Performance properties can either be related to the overall *average performance* of a system or to *soft deadlines*, such as "after a request for a service, there is at least a 98 percent probability that the service will be carried out within 2 seconds". Soft deadlines are of interest in systems in which a bound of the response time is important, but the failure to meet the response time does not result in a disaster, loss of lives, etc. Examples of systems for which soft deadlines are relevant are telephone switching networks and computer networks.

In this paper we will show that extending a formalism with time and probabilities will allow quantitative aspects of timeouts and unreliable media to be modeled. Our formalism, the Timed Probabilistic Calculus of Communicating Systems (TPCCS) is based on Milner's *Calculus of Communicating Systems* (CCS) [Mil89]. TPCCS has previously been presented in [HJ90] and [Han91].

In Section 2 we give an intuitive introduction to TPCCS and motivate it in light of the problems studied in this paper. In Section 3 we present the syntax and semantics of TPCCS. In Section 4 we apply the formalism to the alternating bit protocol to show how timeouts and unreliable media can be specified. Section 5 discusses verification. Finally, in Section 6 we conclude and present some related work.

2 Background and Motivation

Process algebras are structured description languages for concurrent systems. A number of process algebras have been proposed in the literature. Examples are Milner's Calculus of Communicating Systems (CCS) [Mil89], Hoare's Communicating Sequential Processes (CSP) [Hoa85] and Bergstra and Klop's Algebra of Communicating Processes (ACP) [BK84]. They all have some common features, e.g., they have operators corresponding to sequential composition, non-deterministic choice, and parallel composition of components. A number of semantic theories have been developed for these algebras by considering different types of equivalences (bisimulation equivalence, testing equivalence, failure equivalence, etc.).

CCS is a calculus for describing systems of processes that execute asynchronously and communicate by synchronizing over communication *actions*. A process is described in terms of its capability to communicate with other processes. The operational model of a process is defined as a *transition system*. A transition system consists of a set of *states* and *transitions* between the states, i.e., each transition has unique source and sink states. The transitions are *labeled* with actions, i.e., an action is associated to each transition.

Parallelism is modeled by the combined behaviour of two (or more) transition systems. In the combination, synchronization is modeled by joining transitions labeled with *complementary actions*. The parallel execution of two transitions that do not synchronize are in the combination modeled by arbitrary *interleaving* of the transitions. As an example of a CCS specification consider the system of two processes in Figure 1. The figure presents two transition diagrams (representing transition systems), where • denotes a state and an arrow denotes a transition labeled with the associated action (e.g. a). The leftmost transition diagram presents the transition system defined by the CCS process (agent in CCS terminology) $P = a.NIL + b.NIL$, where a and b are action names, NIL denotes deadlock (i.e., no action is possible), "." is the prefixing operator (e.g. $a.P$ denotes a process that initially can perform an a action and thereafter behave as P), and $+$ is the choice operator (i.e. $Q + R$ denotes a process that can behave as Q or as R). Consequently, the process P can initially either perform an a action or a b action after which it will deadlock. The rightmost transition diagram in Figure 1 gives the transition system for the CCS process $Q = \bar{a}.NIL + \bar{b}.NIL$, where a bar over an action denotes a complement action (e.g. $\bar{a}$ is the complement action of a).

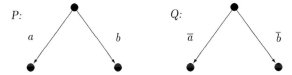

Figure 1: The simple CCS processes $P = a.NIL + b.NIL$ and $Q = \bar{a}.NIL + \bar{b}.NIL$

As stated above, when composing two processes in parallel they can synchronize on complementary actions. In CCS, the synchronization is considered to be internal to the two processes, and the special action τ is used to indicate this, i.e., in the combined transition system the synchronization is manifested by a transition labeled with a τ-action. The τ-action may not participate in any further synchronization. As an example, consider the combined transition diagram for the parallel composition of the processes P and Q in Figure 2. The processes P can when combined with Q either synchronize with Q by performing any of the communication events a or b jointly with Q (manifested by transitions

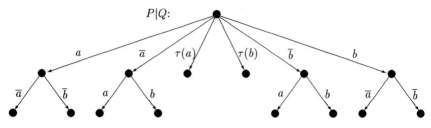

Figure 2: The behaviour of the composition $P|Q$

labeled with $\tau(a)$[1] and $\tau(b)$). Alternatively, P can independently of Q perform action a or action b. Similarly, Q can independently of P perform action $\bar{a}$ or action $\bar{b}$. Note that the communication in CCS is binary, in the sense that exactly two processes participate in each communication.

Figure 2 is also an illustration of the effects of interleaving, i.e., the parallel execution of the transitions in P and Q are modeled as the possibility of executing them in any order, but not simultaneously.

In CCS, choices between different alternatives (e.g., between the alternatives in Figure 2) are non-deterministic, i.e., we do not have any *a priori* information about which alternative that actually will occur.

Timeouts and Unreliable Media in CCS

As an illustration of how a timeout can be specified in CCS we give in Figure 3 (left)[2] a specification of a simple Sender process in a link-layer protocol. After the Sender

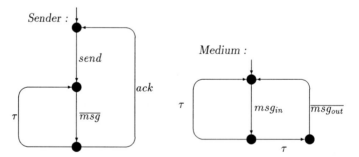

Figure 3: The CCS processes $Sender = send.S$, where $S = \overline{msg}.(ack.Sender + \tau.S)$ (left) and $Medium = msg_{in}.(\tau.Medium + \tau.\overline{msg_{out}}.Medium)$ (right)

has received a message to send from its user (action $send$), it will attempt to send the message (action $\overline{msg}$) after which the Sender process can do one of two things: either

---
[1] For clarity we will use the notation $\tau(a)$ to indicate that the τ originates from an a communication.
[2] Here and in the following we will use an extra arrow head to indicate the initial state.

an acknowledgement (action *ack*) will be received after which the Sender can continue sending new messages, or a timeout will expire (indicated with a τ-action) and the current message will be retransmitted. Note that the timeout might expire "immediately" after the message has been sent.

An unreliable medium can in CCS be specified in a similar way, as illustrated in Figure 3 (right). After the message has been received (action msg_{in}) the Medium makes an internal non-deterministic choice between loosing the message (no action) and delivering the message (action msg_{out}). Note that no information is provided on how frequent losses are.

2.1 Probabilistic Extensions

We introduce probabilities in CCS by a *probabilistic choice operator*. This operator defines a probability distribution over a set of possible behaviours, i.e., while the +-operator in CCS only indicates that both operands are possible, our new operator additionally gives quantitative (probabilistic) information on the outcome of the choice. Also, the probabilistic choice is independent from the environment, in that the probability distribution is not dependent on synchronizations with the environment. Intuitively, we view the distribution as an uncertainty of the internal state of a process. The probabilistic choice allows the designer to abstract away from the details of how choices are made, but still provide (quantitative) information on the outcome of the choice.

For each state in our model, either a probabilistic or a non-deterministic choice is made. For technical reasons we will use strict alternation between probabilistic and non-deterministic choices. We name our model the *alternating model*. As an example of an alternating process consider the vending machine described by the transition diagram in Figure 4 (left), where • denotes a non-deterministic state, i.e., a state where a non-deterministic choice is made, and ○ denotes a probabilistic state, i.e., a state where a probabilistic choice is made. Transitions originating from non-deterministic states are labeled with actions and they will be referred to as *non-deterministic transitions*. Transitions originating from probabilistic states are labeled with probabilities and they will be referred to as *probabilistic transitions*.

Intuitively, the vending machine in Figure 4 (left) accepts a *coin* and then, with probability 0.9 offers *tea* and *coffee* (giving the user a possibility to choose), and with probability 0.1 the machine will keep the coin without offering anything.

Probabilities and Unreliable Media

The probabilistic extensions of CCS can be used to specify quantitative aspects of unreliable media. As an example, consider the medium in Figure 4 (right) which, for each received message (action msg_{in}), with probability 0.1 will lose the message (no action) and with probability 0.9 deliver it (action $\overline{msg_{out}}$).

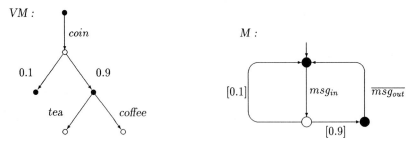

Figure 4: The unreliable vending machine $VM = coin.([0.1]NIL \oplus [0.9](tea.NIL + coffee.NIL)$ (left) and the unreliable medium $M = msg_{in}.([0.1]M \oplus [0.9]\overline{msg_{out}}.M)$ (right)

2.2 Timing Extensions

In our timing extension of CCS we will use *discrete time*. In such a model the advance of time can be viewed as a sequence of ticks, each tick corresponding to advancing the time (the global clock) one time unit. We assume that actions are instantaneous, i.e., no time is associated to the "execution" of actions. Time passes "between" actions, either when a delay is explicitly specified or when waiting to perform a communication action. When processes are composed in parallel, time will always pass simultaneously in all processes, i.e., "ticking" is a synchronous event that requires the participation of all processes. Furthermore, a process can never let time pass (tick) when an internal action (a τ-action) is enabled and when no internal action is possible the process can always let time pass. As a consequence, we characterize the timing model by: *arbitrary waiting* and *minimal delay*. That is, there is no *a priori* upper bound on the time (number of ticks) a process can wait for an external communication (arbitrary waiting), but at the same time, once an internal action is possible the process must not wait further (minimal delay). Minimal delay is essential since it guarantees progress by ensuring that two processes will communicate as soon as they are ready to do so. As an example of arbitrary waiting consider the process whose behaviour is described by the transition diagram in Figure 5 (left). This process can perform an arbitrary number of ticks. Note that we use the special

Figure 5: Arbitrary waiting illustrated by the process $a.NIL$ (left) and Minimal delay illustrated by the process $\tau.NIL$ (right)

"action" χ to indicate the passage of time. Minimal delay is illustrated by the process in Figure 5 (right). This process cannot perform any ticks (χ-actions), before performing the internal action (τ). In the sequel, we will in the transition diagrams use ⊙ to denote a non-deterministic state with a self-loop labeled with χ, i.e., a state in which the process can *idle*.

We introduce time in TPCCS through a special *timeout* operator ($\triangleright$), similar to the delay operator in ATP [NRSV90]. The timeout operator, not the special action χ, is used for explicit specification of delays. In fact, the action χ is – for technical reasons – only used to define the semantics of TPCCS, and is not allowed in the syntax. Intuitively, $G_1 \triangleright_i G_2$ denotes a process that after i time units becomes G_2, unless G_1 performs an action prior to that. If G_1 can perform an action (within i time units) and become G_1' then $G_1 \triangleright_i G_2$ can perform the same action and become G_1', otherwise $G_1 \triangleright_i G_2$ will become G_2 after i time units.

Timing and Timeouts

As an example of a timeout, consider the simple timeout handler in Figure 6 (left). The timeout handler is ready to perform a timeout after two time units (ticks) unless it has been aborted before the second tick. Another example is the vending machine in Figure 6

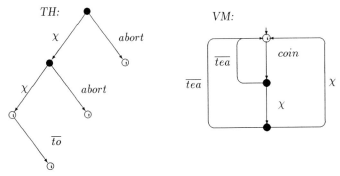

Figure 6: The behaviour of the simple timeout handler $TH = abort.NIL \triangleright_2 \overline{to}.NIL$ (left), and the Vending Machine: $VM = coin.(\overline{tea}.VM \triangleright_2 VM)$ (right).

(right). Intuitively, the vending machine accepts a *coin* and then offers *tea* to its user for two time units. If the user does not demand *tea* during this time period the vending machine will return to its initial state (waiting for another coin to be inserted).

3 Timed Probabilistic CCS

In this section we present a subset of our calculus, *Timed Probabilistic Calculus of Communication Systems* (TPCCS). The operators not presented here are *recursion* (**fix**) and *relabeling* ([ ]). A complete definition of TPCCS is given in [Han91].

3.1 Syntax

Let Λ be a set of symbols denoting actions ($\chi, \tau(a) \notin \Lambda$, for any a). For every $a \in \Lambda$ there is a complementary action $\bar{a}$. The set of complementary actions form the set $\bar{\Lambda}$. Also, we will use the convention $\bar{\bar{a}} = a$. Let $Act = \Lambda \cup \bar{\Lambda}$, ranged over by a, b etc. Let Tau be a set of non-communicating actions, defined as $Tau = \bigcup_{a \in Act} \tau(a)$, where $\tau(a) = \tau(\bar{a})$. Intuitively, $\tau(a)$ denotes that the origin of the non-communicating action is a synchronization between the actions a and $\bar{a}$, i.e., in contrast with CCS, internal synchronizations (communications) will be "observable". Note however that, as for the τ in CCS, $\tau(a)$ cannot participate in any further synchronizations. We will use τ to range over Tau. We will use the convention: $\overline{\tau(a)} = \tau(a)$. Let χ denote a special tick-action indicating the passage of time, and let $Act_T\chi = Act \cup Tau \cup \{\chi\}$, ranged over by α, β etc.

Let $[0,1]$ be the set of probabilities, ranged over by q, r, s etc.

In the syntax we define two types of expressions. Let E_N be the set of *non-deterministic expressions*, ranged over by N, N_1 etc., and let E_P be the set of *probabilistic expressions*, ranged over by P, Q, P_1 etc. The syntax is given by:

$$P \quad ::= \quad \sum_{i \in I} [q_i] N_i \quad \Big| \quad P \backslash a \quad \Big| \quad P | P$$

$$N \quad ::= \quad \sum_{i \in I} \alpha_i.P_i \quad \Big| \quad N \triangleright P \quad \Big| \quad N \backslash a \quad \Big| \quad N | N$$

The $\sum$-operator will be referred to as *probabilistic choice*. We require that the sum of probabilities in a probabilistic choice should add up to 1, i.e., in the expression $\sum_{i \in I}[q_i]N_i$ we must have $\sum_{i \in I} q_i = 1$. The \-operator will be referred to as *restriction*, and the |-operator will be referred to as parallel composition. The additional non-deterministic operators will be referred to as: *non-deterministic choice* ($\sum$) and *timeout* ($\triangleright$).

Intuitively, the probabilistic choice ($\sum$) defines a probability distribution over a set of non-deterministic processes, i.e., $\sum_{i \in I}[q_i]N_i$ will with probability q_i behave as N_i.

The non-deterministic choice ($\sum$) defines a set of alternative interactions, i.e., $N = \sum_{i \in I} \alpha_i.P_i$ can perform any α_i and then behave as the subsequent P_i. In addition, due to the arbitrary waiting and minimal delay requirements, N can only perform the action χ if none of the α_is is a non-communicating action ($\in Tau$). The result of performing the χ-action will be the probabilistic process $\sum[1]N$, which with probability 1 will behave as N.

Intuitively, timeout ($\triangleright$) defines what will happen when time passes, e.g., $N \triangleright P$ will when time passes become P, unless N performs an action prior to that.

Intuitively, restriction $G\backslash a$ denotes a process that behaves as G with the difference that $G\backslash a$ cannot perform any a or $\bar{a}$ action. In the example we will use restriction with respect to sets of actions, with the obvious meaning, e.g. $G\backslash\{a,b\}$ denotes $G\backslash a\backslash b$.

Intuitively, parallel composition $G_1|G_2$ denotes the concurrent behaviour of G_1 and G_2, where G_1 and G_2 can communicate on common actions. As a consequence of the arbitrary waiting and minimal delay requirements, $G_1|G_2$ can perform a χ-transition only if both G_1 and G_2 can perform χ-transitions, and if there is no possibility of communication between G_1 and G_2.

3.2 Semantics

Let $\rightarrow\ \subseteq E_N \times Act\tau\chi \times E_P$ be the non-deterministic transition relation; a triple in $\rightarrow$ is written $N \xrightarrow{\beta} P$. Let $N \not\xrightarrow{\beta}$ denote that there are no transitions labeled with β from N and let $N \xrightarrow{\beta}$ denote that there is some transition labeled with β from N. Let $\mapsto\ \subseteq E_P \times [0,1] \times E_N$, be the probabilistic transition relation; a triple in $\mapsto$ is written $P \xmapsto{q} N$.

The operational semantics for TPCCS is given in Table 1.

Note that, due to the alternation between probabilistic and non-deterministic expressions, an extra "[1]" is needed in the rules **par1** and **par2**. In order for $\mapsto$ to define probability distribution functions, we let (in the rule **p-choice**) choices with syntactically equal non-deterministic expressions define one probabilistic transition. The probabilistic choices made by processes executing in parallel are independent, hence, the rule **p-par** defines the combination of two independent probability distribution functions. Intuitively, **choice-idle** states that if no τ-transition is possible non-deterministic choices can let time pass (tick) without changing. The **par-tick** rule states that both processes in a parallel composition must tick in order for the parallel composition to tick, i.e., ticking is a synchronous action. Also, due to the minimal delay requirement a parallel composition can not tick if a communication between the composed processes is possible. The rule **to-tick** states that the timeout occurs when the process ticks, and **to-act** states that if the first process in a timeout performs an action then the timeout capability will be lost. It is evident, from the definitions of $\rightarrow$ and $\mapsto$, that TPCCS has a clear separation of actions and probabilities.

We also use the conventions:

$$NIL \text{ means } \sum_{i\in\emptyset}\alpha_i.P_i \qquad \alpha_1.P_1 \text{ means } \sum_{i\in\{1\}}\alpha_i.P_i$$

$$\sum_{i\in I}\alpha_i.P_i + \sum_{j\in J}\alpha_j.P_j \text{ means } \sum_{k\in I\cup J}\alpha_k.P_k \qquad (I\cap J = \emptyset)$$

$$[p_1]N_1 \oplus [p_2]N_2 \text{ means } \sum_{k\in\{1,2\}}[q_k]N_k$$

choice :	$\dfrac{\overline{}}{\sum_{i\in I}\alpha_i.P_i \xrightarrow{\alpha_j} P_j} j \in I$	**p-choice :**	$\dfrac{\overline{}}{\sum_{i\in I}[q_i]N_i \xmapsto{p} N_i} \; p = \sum_{\substack{N_j \equiv N_i \\ j\in I}} q_j$
restrict :	$\dfrac{N \xrightarrow{\beta} P}{N\backslash a \xrightarrow{\beta} P\backslash a} \beta, \overline{\beta} \neq a$	**p-rest:**	$\dfrac{P \xmapsto{q} N}{P\backslash a \xmapsto{q} N\backslash a}$
com-par :	$\dfrac{N_1 \xrightarrow{a} P_1 \, , \; N_2 \xrightarrow{\overline{a}} P_2}{N_1|N_2 \xrightarrow{\tau(a)} P_1|P_2}$	**p-par :**	$\dfrac{P_1 \xmapsto{q} N_1, \quad P_2 \xmapsto{s} N_2}{P_1|P_2 \xmapsto{q*s} N_1|N_2}$
par1 :	$\dfrac{N_1 \xrightarrow{\alpha} P}{N_1|N_2 \xrightarrow{\alpha} P|[1]N_2}$		
par2 :	$\dfrac{N_2 \xrightarrow{\alpha} P}{N_1|N_2 \xrightarrow{\alpha} [1]N_1|P}$		
choice-idle :	$\dfrac{\sum_{i\in I}\alpha_i.P_i \not\xrightarrow{}}{\sum_{i\in I}\alpha_i.P_i \xrightarrow{\chi} [1]\sum_{i\in I}\alpha_i.P_i}$		
par-tick:	$\dfrac{N_1 \xrightarrow{\chi} P_1 \, , \; N_2 \xrightarrow{\chi} P_2 \, , \; \forall a \in Act.(\; N_1 \xrightarrow{a} \text{ implies } N_2 \not\xrightarrow{\overline{a}})}{N_1|N_2 \xrightarrow{\chi} P_1|P_2}$		
to-tick :	$\dfrac{N \xrightarrow{\chi}}{N \triangleright P \xrightarrow{\chi} P}$		
to-act:	$\dfrac{N \xrightarrow{\alpha} P_1}{N \triangleright P \xrightarrow{\alpha} P_1} \; \alpha \neq \chi$		

Table 1: Operational semantics for TPCCS. Non-deterministic rules (left) and probabilistic rules (right).

We can now define the generalized timeout operator used in the introduction:

$$N \vartriangleright_n P \equiv N \vartriangleright [1](N \vartriangleright_{n-1} P) \quad (n > 1)$$
$$N \vartriangleright_1 P \equiv N \vartriangleright P$$

3.3 Results — TPCCS

In [Han91] we extend the strong bisimulation equivalence of CCS [Mil89] to TPCCS and present a corresponding sound and complete axiomatization. In particular, we define an expansion theorem which can be used to transform a parallel expression (containing |-operators) to a sequential expression (not containing any |-operator). We also present a method for extending TPCCS with additional operators, and we define operators for delays, interrupts, timeouts, and scheduling. Furthermore, we prove that the probabilistic labeled transition systems defined by the operational semantics are: (1) finite state, (2) without sink state (every state has at least one successor), (3) deterministic w.r.t. χ-transitions (every state has at most one outgoing χ-transition), (4) obeying the minimal delay requirement, i.e., every non-deterministic state has either at least one outgoing χ-transition or one outgoing transition labeled with an action in Tau, but not both, (5) alternating, i.e., any sequence of transitions in strictly alternates between probabilistic and non-deterministic transitions, (6) probabilistically well-defined, i.e., the sum of probabilities labeling outgoing transitions from probabilistic states is 1. In addition, we prove that any transition system satisfying these properties is equivalent to some TPCCS process.

4 The Alternating Bit Protocol

To illustrate how TPCCS can be used to model timeouts and unreliable media we present a specification of the Alternating Bit Protocol (ABP) [BSW69]. ABP is a simple communication protocol that provides error free communication over a medium which may lose messages. Our description of ABP consists of four entities: a sender, two media (one in each direction), and a receiver. The structure of the communication system, as well as the communication primitives are shown in Figure 7.

Figure 7: The structure of the communication system

In the protocol, a retransmission mechanism is used to overcome the unreliability of the medium. Retransmissions are initiated by a timeout. Timeouts will occur in the sender when the delay between issuing a message to the medium and receiving an acknowledgement is too long. This occurs either if the transmission delays in the medium or receiver are too long, or if a message or an acknowledgement is lost.

In our model we will assume that 10% of the messages are lost in the media (MEDIUM and Ack-MEDIUM in Figure 7). Also, to model transmission delays, we assume a one time unit delay in the media. We specify the components as follows:

The sender:
$$S \equiv send.S_1$$
$$S_1 \equiv \overline{in_0}.(acks_0.S_2 \triangleright_3 S_1)$$
$$S_2 \equiv send.S_3$$
$$S_3 \equiv \overline{in_1}.(acks_1.S \triangleright_3 S_3)$$

The sender accepts a *send* primitive from a user and then attempts to transmit it (by issuing an *in* primitive) over the faulty medium until an acknowledgement (*ack*) is received. Note that there is a retransmission timer which will time out three time units after an *in* action has been issued, unless an acknowledgement is received. Also, a one bit sequence number is associated to messages and acknowledgements to prevent duplicates from being offered to the user on the receiving side and to prevent late acknowledgements from being confused with an acknowledgement of the currently outstanding message.

The media:
$$M \equiv in_0.M_1 + in_1.M_2$$
$$M_1 \equiv [0.1]\,(NIL \triangleright M) \oplus [0.9]\,(NIL \triangleright M_3)$$
$$M_2 \equiv [0.1]\,(NIL \triangleright M) \oplus [0.9]\,(NIL \triangleright M_4)$$
$$M_3 \equiv \overline{out_0}.M \triangleright M$$
$$M_4 \equiv \overline{out_1}.M \triangleright M$$

$$Mack \equiv ackr_0.Mack_1 + ackr_1.Mack_2$$
$$Mack_1 \equiv [0.1]\,(NIL \triangleright Mack) \oplus [0.9]\,(NIL \triangleright Mack_3)$$
$$Mack_2 \equiv [0.1]\,(NIL \triangleright Mack) \oplus [0.9]\,(NIL \triangleright Mack_4)$$
$$Mack_3 \equiv \overline{acks_0}.Mack \triangleright Mack$$
$$Mack_4 \equiv \overline{acks_1}.Mack \triangleright Mack$$

The media model faulty communication channels where messages (data or acknowledgements) might be lost. We regard corrupted messages as lost, i.e., we assume that there is some mechanism, e.g. a checksum, used to detect and discard corrupted messages. The media accept an input (an *in/ackr* action) which is lost with probability 0.1 and with probability 0.9 offered, after a one time unit transmission delay, to the receiver/sender for one time unit (as an *out/acks* action). If the receiver/sender is not prepared to accept the action during this time the possibility to receive it will be lost. This is intended to model a medium where the transmitted signal is active only during a short time (one time unit in our case).

The receiver:
$$R \equiv out_0.\overline{rec}.\overline{ackr_0}.R_1 + out_1.\overline{ackr_1}.R$$
$$R_1 \equiv out_1.\overline{rec}.\overline{ackr_1}.R + out_0.\overline{ackr_0}.R_1$$

The receiver waits for a message with the appropriate sequence number (0 or 1). When such a message arrives it offers the message to its user (as a $\overline{rec}$ action) until the user accepts it, thereafter an acknowledgement is sent to the sender. Note that, duplicates are acknowledged but not offered to the user.

The transition diagrams corresponding to S, M, $Mack$, and R are shown in Figure 8. Remember that ⊙ denotes a state in which the process can *idle*.

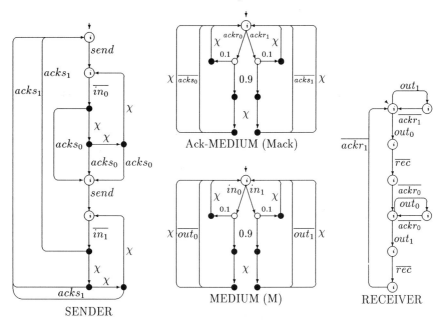

Figure 8: The behavior of S, M, $Mack$, and R

We can now define the communication system depicted in Figure 7 by composing the sender, the media, and the receiver as follows:

$$CS \equiv (S|M|Mack|R) \setminus \{in_0, in_1, out_0, out_1, acks_0, acks_1, ackr_0, ackr_1\}$$

By using the expansion theorem in [Han91] we can transform CS to a sequential expression from which it is straightforward to draw a transition diagram. It turns out that this transition diagram has 142 states. To allow evaluation of the performance of the modeled system we place it in an environment with the following user which is always prepared to engage in *send* and *rec* actions:

$$U \equiv \overline{send}.U + rec.U$$

We can then define the system obtained when composing CS and U:

$$Sys \equiv (CS|U) \setminus \{send, rec\}$$

Intuitively, Sys is a closed system consisting of a user (U) which is continuously using an alternating bit protocol (processes S and R contained in CS) to transfer messages over an unreliable medium (M and $Mack$ also contained in CS). In Figure 9 we give the corresponding transition diagram.

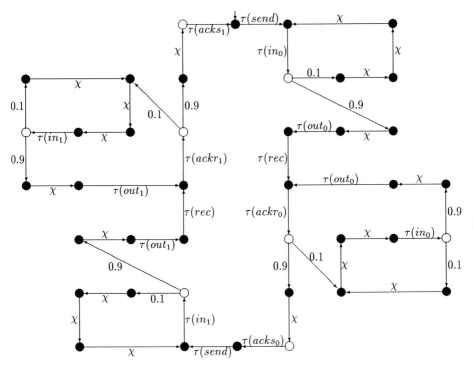

Figure 9: The behavior obtained when composing sender, media, and receiver of the ABP with an environment that is always prepared to engage in communications

5 Verification

In [Han91] we extend the branching time temporal logic CTL [CES83] with quantitative time and probabilities[3]. In the extended logic, TPCTL, it is possible to formulate invariance properties (properties that are always true), eventualities (properties that eventually will become true), precedence properties (properties of type: one event must occur before another), real-time properties (e.g. properties that will become true within some specified time), reliability properties (e.g. properties that are true with a specified probability),

---

[3]TPCTL is similar to our previous logic PCTL [HJ89], the main difference being that TPCTL is interpreted over alternating models whereas PCTL is interpreted over discrete time Markov chains.

and performance properties (e.g. properties that with a specified probability become true within some specified time).

For verification we have defined an algorithm which can be used to establish if a TPCCS specification satisfies a TPCTL formula (model checking). Also, we have developed a tool implementing the model checking algorithm as well as an algorithm for deciding the bisimulation equivalence mentioned in Section 3.3.

The following are two examples of TPCTL properties that we have verified to hold for the alternating bit protocol specification given in Section 4:

$$send \; \mathcal{A} \; \overline{rec} \qquad (1)$$

$$\tau(send) \underset{\geq 0.9999}{\overset{\leq 10}{\leadsto}} \tau(rec) \qquad (2)$$

Intuitively, Property 1 states that the system (Process CS) behaves as a one element buffer, i.e., initially $send$ precedes $\overline{rec}$ and there is a strict alternation between $send$ and $\overline{rec}$ actions. Intuitively, Property 2 states that for the closed system (Process Sys) there is at least a probability 0.9999 that a $\tau(rec)$-action will occur within 10 time units after the occurrence of a $\tau(send)$-action. Property 1 is an example of a precedence property, whereas Property 2 is a performance property.

6 Conclusions

We have illustrated how quantitative aspects of timeouts and unreliable media can be modeled in TPCCS, a calculus extending Milner's CCS with discrete time and probabilities. In the TPCCS timing model, time passes either when a delay is explicitly specified or when no action is possible. That is, there is no *a priori* upper bound on the time a process can wait for external communications, but on the other hand, once an action is possible the process is not allowed to wait any longer (minimal delay). Probabilities are introduced as uncertainties of the internal state of processes, in the sense that we define action independent probability distributions over sets of possible future states of processes. This is achieved by defining two transition relations: one for probabilities and one for actions. Our timing model is inspired by the timing models in ATP [NRSV90] and timed CCS [Wan91]. Our probabilistic extension of CCS is inspired by work of Larsen and Skou [LS89], as well as van Glabbeek, Smolka, Steffen and Tofts [vGSST90]. TPCCS is, as far as we know, the first example of a process algebra in which time and probabilities are combined.

Separating probabilities from actions, as we have done in TPCCS, is a general idea which allows probabilities to be introduced independently of the original calculus. It seems for this reason possible to in a similar way extend other calculi, such as for instance the control part of LOTOS [EVD89], with probabilities.

In the specification of the alternating bit protocol we show that – using TPCCS – we can model quantitative aspects of timeouts and unreliable media. This allows modeling at a less abstract level compared to previous specifications of the same protocol (e.g. [Mil89]). Other specification formalisms which include notions of time and probabilities are the timed and stochastic extensions of Petri nets [HV87, ABC86]. The advantage of using process algebra compared to Petri nets is mainly the modular specification style inherent in the algebras.

References

[ABC86]   M. Ajmone Marsan, G. Balbo, and G. Conte. *Performance Models of Multiprocessor Systems.* MIT Press, 1986.

[BK84]   J.A. Bergsta and J.W. Klop. Process algebra for synchronous communication. *Information and Control*, 60:109–137, 1984.

[BSW69]   K. Bartlett, R. Scantlebury, and P. Wilkinson. A note on reliable full-duplex transmissions over half duplex lines. *Communications of the ACM*, 2(5):260–261, 1969.

[CES83]   E.M. Clarke, E.A. Emerson, and A.P. Sistla. Automatic verification of finite-state concurrent systems using temporal logic specifications: A practical approach. In *Proc. 10th ACM Symp. on Principles of Programming Languages*, pages 117–126, 1983.

[EVD89]   P. Eijk, C. Vissers, and M. Diaz, editors. *The Formal Description Technique LOTOS.* North-Holland, 1989.

[Han91]   H. Hansson. *Time and Probabilities in Formal Design of Distributed Systems.* PhD thesis, Department of Computer Systems, Uppsala University, 1991. Available as report DoCS 91/27, Department of Computer Systems, Uppsala University, Sweden, and as report 05 in SICS dissertation series, SICS, Kista, Sweden.

[HJ89]   H. Hansson and B. Jonsson. A framework for reasoning about time and reliability. In *Proc. 10th IEEE Real -Time Systems Symp.*, S:a Monica, Ca., 1989. IEEE Computer Society Press.

[HJ90]   H. Hansson and B. Jonsson. A calculus for communicating systems with time and probabilities. In *Proc. 11th IEEE Real -Time Systems Symp.*, Orlando, Fl., december 1990. IEEE Computer Society Press.

[Hoa85]   C.A.R. Hoare. *Communicating Sequential Processes.* Prentice-Hall, 1985.

[HV87]   M.A. Holliday and M.K. Vernon. A generalized timed Petri net model for performance analysis. *IEEE Trans. Software Eng.*, SE-13(12), 1987.

[LS89]   K.G. Larsen and A. Skou. Bisimulation through probabilistic testing. In *Proc. 16th ACM Symp. on Principles of Programming Languages*, 1989.

[Mil89]   R. Milner. *Communication and Concurrency.* Prentice-Hall, 1989.

[NRSV90] X. Nicollin, J.-L. Richier, J. Sifakis, and J. Voiron. ATP: an algebra for timed processes. In *Proc. IFIP TC2 Working Conference on Programming Concepts and Methods*, Sea of Gallilee, Israel, April 1990.

[vGSST90] R. van Glabbeek, S. A. Smolka, B. Steffen, and C. Tofts. Reactive, generative, and stratified models of probabilistic processes. In *Proc. 5th IEEE Int. Symp. on Logic in Computer Science*, 1990.

[Wan91]   Y. Wang. CCS + Time = an interleaving model for real time systems. In *Proc. 18th Int. Coll. on Automata Languages and Programming (ICALP)*, volume 510 of *Lecture Notes in Computer Science*, pages 217–228. Springer Verlag, 1991.

Formal Methods at AT&T - An Industrial Usage Report

John A. Chaves

AT&T Bell Laboratories
Naperville, Illinois 60566

ABSTRACT

We will describe the experience we have at AT&T with the integration of formal validation tools into the design process of code for our 5ESS® telephone switch. A tool called *sdlvalid*, for the formal validation of specifications written in the CCITT language SDL, has been in routine usage in one development area since 1989. Use of validation within the constraints of the existing development methodology has met with some success, but the need to develop an integrated approach to large scale development and validation has been identified. The NewCoRe[1] project is developing an approach for the systematic application of formal methods for design and verification specifically for use in the context of large scale software development. We seek to integrate a controlled refinement approach with automated support for partial and full validation, and test generation.

1. INTRODUCTION

1.1 Background

AT&T designs and manufactures telephone switching systems for the U.S. and international markets. One of these systems, the 5ESS® switch, is a complex, distributed architecture machine. The software for the 5ESS switch, covering administrative, switching, and signaling functionality, contains over three million lines of source code. Many different signaling systems are supported by the 5ESS switch. The latest of these is the CCITT Signaling System 7 (SS7). SS7 is a layered architecture protocol, much like the OSI model, though with fewer layers. At the application level of SS7 there are a number of User Part protocols. Two examples are the Telephone User Part (TUP), and the ISDN User Part (ISUP)[1].

Developing the software for a SS7 User Part is a complex undertaking. It may take 10, 20, or more developers and support staff up to one or two years to produce a working implementation. That implementation may contain 20k or more lines of C source code. It is not unusual to have to produce many different versions of the same User Part to satisfy a number of different markets. Different countries can interpret the CCITT specification differently and also frequently extend the protocol to meet their own specialized needs.

---

1. The name *NewCoRe* is derived from the goal of the project: to explore New development methods based on Controlled Refinement techniques.

The nature of the User Part protocols makes them difficult to develop by techniques that rely on hierarchical decomposition of functionality. Each protocol consists of a base specification covering the basic call processing requirements, and a large number of features that interact with the base and with each other. There is no natural hierarchy of functionality that can be exploited in the design of the software. If a software organization is chosen to optimize one aspect of the functionality or feature, it will be at the expense of other aspects of the functionality. As a result, specifications of the protocol tend to be relatively flat (i.e. not have a deeply hierarchical structure).

Contributing to the complexity of development are other issues ranging from vague customer specifications to the logistics of developing for a large existing system. Some of the challenges offered are:

- Ten or more developers must simultaneously contribute to the specification
- Requirements are subject to change at any time through release of the code
- Numerous system architectural and interface constraints must be considered
- The final product contains 20K or more weakly hierarchical source lines of code

To deal with these adverse conditions, conservative design methodologies have been used. Reliance has been on people using informal methods, and not on machine labor for the development of systems. Reliability of the systems was ensured mainly by extensive use of design reviews and system testing.

1.2 Formalization of Development Process

Prior to 1989, the SS7 User Parts and similar protocols were developed using specification techniques of informal text, pseudocode, and informal SDL[2]. The standard design methodology, then and now, is the waterfall model consisting of separate stages for requirements, high and low level design, coding, and testing. The same specification techniques are applied from requirements through low level design. Defects in requirements or design specifications are identified by a manual review process. A variety of review types are used including document reviews, scenario walkthroughs, and audits of related documents. Those defects that are not detected early are found, and fixed at a greater expense, at a later stage of development. Many defects are uncovered and fixed during the manual coding and testing stages.

At that time, the trend had been to rely more on SDL specification and less on text specification. While use of the SDL was still informal, it resulted in more structure and less ambiguity than a text specification. AT&T has an extensive in-house SDL tool set that has helped encourage the use of SDL. Included are tools for simulating SDL behavior, editing both text and graphic SDL, conversion between text and graphic SDL, syntax checking, printing and summarizing an SDL specification. None of these tools require that the SDL be a formally rigorous specification. It is sufficient for the SDL to be syntactically correct. Even the simulator has a mechanism whereby ambiguous statements are referred to the user for interpretation.

The first use of formalized SDL came as the result of the availability of the validation tool *sdlvalid*[3]. *Sdlvalid* is based on Holzmann's *supertrace* algorithm[4] and provides the most extensive validation capability available today. Without a tool that can check the syntactic and semantic correctness of a formal SDL specification, internal consistency and conformance to requirements can only be checked by manual review. The specification then has a tendency to drift towards the informal. Only through frequent and consistent application of a verification tool can a large scale specification be kept formal.

1.3 Early Validation Results

A development of the TUP protocol targeting a number of different international markets began in 1988. Formalized SDL was chosen as the specification language supported by use of *sdlvalid* as the validation tool. No other changes were made to the development methodology. The traditional requirements, high level design, low level design, code and test intervals were used. Validation was applied in part to the requirements and the high level design. It was discontinued for the low level design and coding intervals. The strategy was successful, but limitations were apparent.

A large number of protocol errors were identified early and corrected. There is evidence that merely the anticipation of validation caused a more rigorous specification technique and prevented some errors from ever finding their way into the specification. The developers felt that the process of writing the formalized specification raised more unsolved issues and identified more errors than use of the validation tool did, though the actual numbers were not documented. The type of errors found during formalization were generally simpler than those found later by the validator.

The application of *sdlvalid* identified over one hundred defects. The deviant behaviors flagged by the validator manifested themselves as unspecified message receptions, system deadlocks, and violations of various user specified assertions. Many different types of specification errors led to the conditions identified by the validator. Some of these errors would have been found during the standard review process, though many would have survived until the coding or testing intervals, or possibly been discovered after installation at a customer site. All discovered errors were corrected during the requirements or high level design intervals.

1.4 Methodology Limitations

Some fundamental limitations of applying validation within the traditional design methodology prevented our taking full advantage of the technology. One difficulty is the lack of a formal linkage between each of the development intervals. The benefits of a validation completed on one interval are diminished when the next interval is started anew, using the previous interval only as an informal reference point. Unless the validated specification can be carried forward from one development interval to the next and directly integrated into the final code product, the results are significantly weakened.

Another difficulty is the mechanism for running validations on a monolithically growing specification while multiple developers need access to it. At any point in time, some portions of the specification are under development. In order to run an effective validation, all portions of the specification must be periodically frozen - in coherent form and at the same level of abstraction. Then, after the validation is run and errors are corrected, development can continue. This takes an exceptional amount of planning to accomplish and puts a significant burden on the development process. To alleviate these difficulties, both methodology changes and new tools are required.

1.5 Improving the Process

The next protocol to be developed was ISUP, starting in 1990. Evaluation of the TUP project results led to the decision to continue using the same methodology for ISUP. The development would use formalized SDL and *sdlvalid* validation while fitting it into the traditional development methodology.

A parallel project was also launched to develop a new methodology and extended tool set to be used for large scale formal protocol development. Instead of studying the problem in the abstract, the NewCoRe project is to build a working version of the ISUP protocol in the course of developing the supporting tools and methodology. It is structured as a collaborative effort between the Bell Laboratories research area and the 5ESS switch development area.

2. THE NewCoRe PROJECT

2.1 Requirements

It is not hard to imagine an idealized protocol development process: the protocol is specified formally at several levels of abstraction, it is validated at each level, code is automatically generated from the final specification level, and tests are automatically generated from one of the more abstract levels. Compared to the traditional development process, where the first point of formalization is the code itself, significant gains in quality and productivity can be expected. However, such a process is difficult to implement even under highly controlled conditions. Large scale development brings its own set of challenges to the process. Our task is to produce such a process explicitly to support large scale development.

Technology transfer issues play a major role in shaping our approach. A new development methodology may be resisted for reasons such as lack of understanding, lack of agreement to support the new process, and the conservative tendency to cling to familiar ways. Our experience is that one of the bigger issues is that of training and support for the entire group of developers. Documentation and other educational materials tend to be sparse for a new or still evolving tool set, yet this is when they are needed most. We can ease many of these concerns by carefully building an evolutionary path from the old methodology to the new. The tools that are developed to make this happen must satisfy three strict, though self-imposed, requirements:

1. The tools can be applied effectively to large-scale projects.
2. Usage of the tools must require minimal training.
3. The tools must fit smoothly into the existing (SDL based) design environment at AT&T.

In addition to the needs imposed by software development, maintenance must be considered. The software lifecycle for 5ESS switch protocols can run into the decades and involve hundreds of developers over that time. Homogeneity of the software structure of the various subsystems within the switch contribute to the ease of maintenance. Often, when a piece of software is developed with a specialized technology, it must also be maintained using that same technology. This is especially the case when automated techniques are applied in the generation of the design or code. Care must be taken when introducing new technology to ensure that any gains made during development are not lost through poor support of the maintenance cycle.

2.2 Approach

The development steps from requirements through code generation involve writing abstract, and initially ambiguous, descriptions of the desired system behavior and then replacing the descriptions with increasingly more detailed ones. Each development step is an opportunity for validation to ensure that desirable new behavior has been added to the system, and that none of the old behavior has been broken. We seek to streamline this process by integrating the refinement and validation steps.

The paradigm for the development process is that of the UNIX® tool 'make'. Design units are composed independently and dependency information is maintained. The composite system specification is built automatically from the individual design units. While the composite system specification is used for validation, presentation, and other purposes, it is never modified. All changes are applied through the individual design units. As a design unit evolves, previous and more abstract specifications of it are still maintained. When a prior design step must be revisited due to changing requirements or an evolving design, it and all subsequent design steps already completed are rebuilt and validated automatically.

The organization of the system is carefully designed to maintain the independence of the design elements and to simplify their dependencies. A developer's task in this process is to produce a series of design units, in increasing levels of detail, that implement the requirements. We have found that such a structuring produces designs in which the original requirements can be readily mapped to the final code instead of losing their mapping in a large composite specification.

2.3 Specification Organization

The primary unit of organization for the specification, as used in customer requirements and in developer designs, is the 'feature'. Traditionally, User Part protocols are outlined first in terms of a minimal call processing capability, and then supplemented with many features. Some of these features are readily recognized as visible customer services such as call waiting. Most, however, deal with specialized internal requirements of the protocol or the system and its hardware. These features are the main unit of organization for requirements, the higher levels of design, and for testing. It is important to consider the contribution each feature makes to the overall behavior of the system, and the interactions between different features.

Typically, features do not fit cleanly into the overall system SDL specification. Each feature will usually affect multiple SDL states, multiple inputs, and have complex interactions with existing code. Traditionally, features are spliced into the base SDL until the specification is complete. The SDL is, for the most part, not hierarchically organized into procedures but left flat. Any deep hierarchical organization, while perhaps optimized for one feature, would be to the detriment of other features added later.

Our approach requires the reorganization of the SDL specification, and of the features, into specification 'chunks'. Instead of adding behavior to the base SDL by merging new SDL into the old, the new SDL retains its form as a unit of behavior. Each chunk communicates to other chunks only through a well defined interface of communication variables and not through shared code. For example, consider the following simplified SDL code fragment:

```
              DECISION 'cot_required';
              (FALSE):
                      ...more SDL...
                      DECISION 'digits_expected';
                      (FALSE):
                              OUTPUT ROUTE_REQUEST TO SYSTEM;
                      ENDDECISION;
              ENDDECISION;
```

This shows a typical nested decision, built from unrelated features, to implement part of the protocol control. It is not unusual to find deeply nested decisions integrating the combined requirements of many different features. Such an approach scatters the impact of a feature throughout the specification in a way that makes it difficult to understand and manipulate. The same SDL fragment separated into chunks might look like:

```
base:         TASK 'hold_route = FALSE';

chunk1:       DECISION 'cot_required';
              (FALSE):
                      ...more SDL...
              (TRUE):
                      TASK 'hold_route = TRUE';
              ENDDECISION;

chunk2:       DECISION 'digits_expected';
              (TRUE):
                      TASK 'hold_route = TRUE';
              ENDDECISION;

base:         DECISION 'hold_route';
              (FALSE):
                      OUTPUT ROUTE_REQUEST TO SYSTEM;
              ENDDECISION;
```

The introduction of a boolean variable `hold_route` allows the developers to separate the effects of the different features on system behavior. In this example, the behavior supplied by either feature (noted by `chunk1` and `chunk2`) may be omitted, included, or elaborated without disturbing the rest of the specification. New features may also be added cleanly within the `base` framework.

Each chunk has a well defined interface to its environment. This includes message data, system data, system interfaces, and inter-chunk communications. Each feature, being composed of a set of chunks, also has a well defined interface to its environment. This interface can be derived from the composite interfaces of the individual chunks. A feature can now be treated as a distinct and manipulatable unit of system behavior. This characteristic provides the basis for abstracting the effects of feature behavior on the system. We can understand how a feature interacts with the system and other features without being concerned with the logic for its decisions. The first specification for a feature can abstract away all internal behavior and show only the range of its external interactions. Subsequent versions of the specification can show increasing levels of detail in internal decision making.

2.4 Controlled Refinement

The full system specification is composed of SDL supporting basic call processing and the collection of features required for the application being developed. The first level of specification of the system will abstract the behavior of the features, and possibly omit entirely some of the features. As development proceeds, more of the feature behavior is added, and missing features are introduced. Structural changes may be necessary for the base SDL and for the features to support unanticipated feature interactions as the system evolves.

Some steps of the development process can be illustrated as follows:

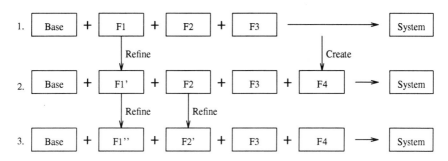

In the first step of this example, the base architecture is created along with abstract versions of three of the features. The system specification is built from these and some aspects of the functionality are validated. In the second step, a fourth feature is created and one of the previous features is refined. Once again, the new composite system is built and validated. In subsequent steps, features continue to be refined and validated until all requirements detail has been specified.

Developers have complete discretion to decide the order of development. As the system is constructed, dependency information is maintained to allow automatic reconstruction of the earlier stages. Validation is integrated into the process such that if any prior design step must be revisited, the entire set of subsequent builds and validations is automatically repeated.

2.5 Validation

Validation is used on the first level specification and throughout the rest of the development. The number of full system validations performed is minimized by use of partial validations and conformance proofs. The validation done on the earliest specifications are against general behavioral criteria that should not be violated as the abstract features are replaced by real ones. When possible, features can be validated for correct functionality independently - without the base system. Then, when an independently validated feature is used to replace its abstraction, a conformance proof is used to show that the real feature cannot have behavior worse than its abstraction. That is, all assertions made about the behavior of the abstraction are shown to remain true. When this is the case, it is not necessary to re-validate the entire system.

At the end of this process, the resulting system has been covered by the validator from the most abstract level of specification to the final, most detailed version. This final version is suitable for automatic generation of C code. Thus, all of the protocol behavioral specification is produced under the cover of validation. Some additional code must be manually written to support the protocol code. Typically, this code deals with system interface details and other machine specific tasks and little is to be gained by including it in the validation process.

2.6 Automated Test Generation

The formal specification of requirements and high level design provides an opportunity for automatic generation of tests for the system. Ideally, the validated development process should produce correct code. However, testing will be required to validate the process. We will automatically build tests loosely corresponding to unit testing from the more detailed SDL specifications, and overall system testing from the more abstract SDL. New test generation techniques developed specifically for SDL specifications will be applied[5].

3. CONCLUSION

We have described some of AT&Ts experiences with the adoption of formal techniques in one area of protocol development for the 5ESS switch. We have also described the NewCoRe project, which is advancing the state of the practice in 5ESS switch development with respect to formal protocol development techniques. The challenges facing the NewCoRe project range from research issues to development and technology transfer issues. Failure to address any one of these areas adequately will delay the further introduction of formal techniques to the development environment.

If the NewCoRe project succeeds, the set of validation tools will be extended with others that can support stepwise refinement proof techniques. The test generation and other tools will be integrated into a coherent tool set and will be documented with a supporting methodology.

REFERENCES

1. CCITT, *Specifications of Signalling System No. 7*, Recommendations Q.721-Q.766, CCITT IXth Plenary Assembly, Nov. 1988, ISBN 92-61-03521-3.

2. Saracco, Roberto and Smith, J.R.W. and Reed, Rick, *Telecommunications Systems Engineering using SDL*, Elsevier Science Publishers, Amsterdam, The Netherlands, 1989, ISBN 0-444-88084-4.

3. Holzmann, Gerard J. and Patti, Joanna, *Validating SDL Specifications: an Experiment*, Proc. 9th IFIP WG6.1 Int. Workshop on Protocol Specification, Testing, and Verification, North-Holland Publ., Amsterdam, 1989.

4. Holzmann, Gerard J., *Design and Validation of Computer Protocols*, Prentice Hall, Englewood Cliffs, NJ, 1991, ISBN 0-13-539925-4.

5. Yannakakis, Mihalis and Lee, David, *Testing Finite State Machines*, Proceedings of the 23rd annual ACM Symposium on Theory of Computing, New Orleans, May 1991, pp. 476-485.

# The Adoption of Formal Methods Within OTC

Karen Rosenberg

Network Software Systems R&D
OTC Limited, Australia

Abstract

This paper examines the incorporation of formal description techniques (FDTs) into the software development practices of OTC. The role of academia in this process is also discussed. Experiences within OTC have identified several problems and possibilities of FDTs. One of the aims of this paper is to provide other organisations with the benefits of OTC's experience. To achieve this, elements of a possible strategy for the successful transfer of FDT technology, including a training strategy are also described.

1 Introduction

Since 1986, OTC has undertaken investigations into formal description techniques (FDTs) in order to determine their applicability to practical telecommunications problems. This investigation has been accomplished through collaboration between OTC Research and Development (R&D) and the Key Centre for Software Technology at the University of Queensland (UQ). This investigation of FDTs has spawned several trials in the use of FDTs within OTC projects, as well as bringing to light various insights, problems and possibilities of FDTs.

This paper complements [3] in which UQ's perspective of the collaboration is discussed. The intention in this paper is to present OTC's experiences with using FDTs, including bridging the gap between academic research and industrial application.

Probably the largest use of formal techniques in industry was that of IBM Hursley in their development of CICS. A technical report written by Collins et al.[2] describes the results of this application of FDTs and includes some quantitative comparisons with conventional techniques. Rather than present quantitative comparisons, this paper discusses some of the issues involved with introducing formal techniques into industry, especially into medium size organisations. Issues discussed include technology transfer, training and support tools.

Section 2 of the paper gives a short background to software engineering within OTC in order to place the rest of the paper in context. Section 3 outlines the projects within OTC in which FDTs have been applied as part of the collaboration. Section 4 then discusses the extent to which OTC's adoption of FDTs has succeeded. Finally, Sections 5 and 6 present some insights into the use of FDTs, and identify problems found and possible future directions.

2 Background

Until recently, operational areas within OTC developed their own, free-standing, PC-based systems to meet their own particular needs. These small systems were developed in isolation without an overall OTC-wide framework. It has since been recognised that these developments, which initially met particular needs, should be integrated into OTC-wide systems. In recognition of this need, network management and operational support systems are now under internal development within OTC.

With the development of these integrated large systems, the need for a corporate-wide software development framework has become more apparent. Although software development lifecycle guidelines are being used by information systems areas, the operational areas within OTC are not yet using a common software development framework. These guidelines are currently under development.

Part of the charter of OTC R&D is to develop new techniques that can improve telecommunications services through better systems. This includes support for external R&D where appropriate. In 1986, OTC R&D initiated collaboration with the Key Centre for Software Technology at UQ in order to explore the application of formal techniques to the development of telecommunications systems.

3 Bridging the Gap between Academia and Industry

3.1 A First Development Project

A primary goal of any collaboration between industry and academia is to achieve a transfer of technology from academic research to industrial application. In an endeavour to close the loop between the methods being developed as part of UQ's research and the software development techniques of OTC, the formal specification technique, Z[4, 7], was used on an OTC R&D internal project. This project started in 1988 and aimed to develop a fault-tolerant communications processor (FTCP) as part of an intelligent network platform. This particular project was chosen to have formal methods applied to it as it was a medium-large scale project that R&D needed to develop, rather than just another FDT case study. Technical details of this project are discussed in [3].

This project provided an opportunity for significant progress of the collaboration. It formed the most cooperative task of the collaboration, with UQ acting as a *consultant* in the area of formal methods. A certain amount of technology transfer was achieved from UQ to OTC R&D which then allowed for OTC to be more involved in later tasks of the collaboration. Both parties also received much needed feedback on the collaboration's research to-date and had an opportunity to apply formal methods to a medium-scale project.

This project had a profound effect on the collaboration. The FTCP specification, written in Z, grew to be quite large (37 separate schemas[3, Section 3]). Both UQ and OTC agreed that Z did not scale well to specifications of this size. This was due to the fact that specifications written in Z are mainly flat, with Z not containing sufficient structuring techniques. Experience within OTC suggested that adding object-oriented extensions to Z might produce a more practical and scalable formal description technique. It seemed that the object-oriented features of encapsulation and inheritance would enable highly modular specifications to be written. Through encapsulation, the state of an object and operations on the object state are grouped together. Inheritance allows new objects to take on the properties of existing objects, thereby allowing for re-use of previous specifications and the production of smaller specifications.

Another reason for this suggestion was that an object oriented specification technique, together with OTC R&D's existing object oriented software development practices would provide less of a paradigm shift than previously existed between Z and OTC R&D's software development practices. The same paradigm, object orientation, could be used in all phases of software development. The concept of viewing a specification in terms of objects also promised to provide a very close match to the real-world situation being modelled.

3.2 Telecommunications Case Studies

The FTCP project was the catalyst for developing the object-oriented specification technique, Object-Z. During the development of Object-Z, UQ needed and OTC wanted to provide feedback on many aspects such as style and syntax. Simultaneously, R&D was interested in the issues involved in broadband signalling. Thus, a project was started to investigate broadband signalling systems using object-oriented specification techniques.

One of the "features" of this project was that the functionality requirements of broadband signalling systems were either non-existent or unclear. A main aim of the project was to more clearly define broadband signalling systems. Thus, much of the time spent on the project was spent testing concepts. It was found that Object-Z could be used at a high-level to test these different concepts and was useful in proving/disproving them.

The specifications written as part of this project were also used as case studies to test different versions and styles of Object-Z. This provided much needed feedback on the developing technique. This was especially useful in testing different styles of specifying aggregations and of structuring large specifications.

3.3 Discussions Based on Formal Specifications

Most formal description techniques are based on discrete mathematics. Thus, many people say that one must be familiar with the underlying theory in order to be able to use these techniques. During the above projects, however, the specification writers were able to use Z and Object-Z specifications in discussions with others who had little if any formal background. As mentioned in Section 3.1, staff within R&D were familiar with object-orientation. Therefore, in the case of Object-Z, they were familiar with the object model on which Object-Z is based.

Generally, problems occurring in the specifications were of two types, viz. Object-Z problems and modelling/concept problems. Problems with Object-Z were referred back to UQ whereas problems with the system being modelled were discussed with people within R&D. Where necessary, the formal notation of Object-Z was verbally rephrased into informal English in order to get down to the underlying problems. Invariably, the concept was able to be discussed and the problem solved with very little Object-Z explanation.

4 Achievements and Failures in Adopting Formal Techniques

In hindsight, OTC's original expectations were quite naïve. It took longer than expected for OTC to reap the benefits of the collaboration. Clearly, much research was and still is needed to develop a formal description technique suitable for use in the development of OTC's telecommunications systems.

Throughout the life of the OTC/UQ collaboration, there has been a strong intellectual research commitment on the part of OTC R&D to the collaboration. Recently, other groups within OTC have become much more involved in the internal development of medium-to-large scale development projects and thus have begun to show interest in the application of formal techniques to these projects. However, OTC has still not closed the gap between pure research into FDTs and their use by development teams within OTC.

If the aim of the OTC/UQ collaboration was to achieve a technology transfer from university to industry, then it has not really achieved this at a significant level. Currently, development teams within OTC are not using FDTs and there is no commitment to do so in the near future. One of the reasons that OTC R&D has been unsuccessful in achieving this technology transfer is that, as yet, OTC R&D has not had the right kind of project to trial formal techniques. Software development projects within OTC R&D tend to be either "small" prototype systems, or commercialisation projects with strict deadlines. To trial formal techniques on a project requires a medium to large project, together with the additional resources (time and people) to initially trial the new technique, e.g. to initially educate the people on the project in the new technique.

Although the collaboration has not *yet* achieved significant technology transfer, it has achieved several minor goals. Throughout OTC, there has been an increase in the knowledge of and interest in formal description techniques. Another aim common to most industry/academia collaborations is to increase academia's knowledge of industry applications. This aim has been achieved as staff and students at UQ now have much more telecommunications experience than before the collaboration.

5 Perceived Problems and Future Directions

5.1 The Need For Support Tools

As mentioned in [3, Section 6], FDTs cannot be seriously used in industry until support tools are available. Various types of support tools are necessary, including the ability to:

- edit and create formal specifications
- check the syntax of specifications
- check the semantics of specifications

The future OTC/UQ collaboration will concentrate on the development of the above support tools for Object-Z.

Many semantic aspects of a specification could be checked, e.g. type checking, access violations and polymorphism checking (for object-oriented specification techniques). Other minor tools would be useful when developing specifications, e.g. analysis of communication between objects in an object-oriented FDT.

Not much has been said in this paper about formal refinement of specifications to implementations. Although such a tool would be ideal, the theory is a long way off from becoming an industrial reality. An intermediate solution would be to have guidelines as to the manual conversion of specifications to implementations.

Another useful tool would be a specification/implementation library of verified functions/objects, i.e. critical functions/objects could be refined into formally verified, i.e. correct, implementations. The verified implementations could then be re-used in several projects without the developer having to re-implement the same specifications. One problem with such a scheme, however, is that a specification does not address issues such as efficiency and portability that a corresponding implementation would need to address. In this case, the library of specified implementations would act as a library of *default* implementations. Such a library would be very useful for prototyping specifications.

5.2 A Strategy For Technology Transfer

Experience within OTC suggests that formal methods will be most useful when used in development projects, much more so than in research projects. As mentioned in Section 2, one role of R&D is to develop new techniques that can improve services through better systems. However, in general, the "real" projects are in development sections, rather than in R&D. New techniques, such as formal methods, need to be tried out on these "real" projects.

Perhaps it is the role of R&D to investigate new techniques, gain the commitment of development sections to try them out and then consult with the development teams on the application of the new techniques to their development projects. Through such consultations, R&D can provide the extra resources required in order to try out new techniques.

The task of gaining the commitment of development sections to try out new techniques presents a problem. Without understanding a new technique and the possible benefits it offers, it is difficult for a development manager to give his/her commitment to the use of the technique. This issue will be discussed further in Section 5.3 on Training.

5.3 A Training Strategy

The adoption of formal methods, or any new technique, into an organisation requires the following different types of training:

- management education in order to gain the commitment of management to the new technique, e.g. a seminar focussed on FDTs in general.

- technical training on the use of a particular technique, e.g. an Object-Z workshop.

- training on how to incorporate the new technique into existing techniques, e.g. when and where to use FDTs in software development.

The issue of management education is a difficult one. In general, management do not want to be concerned with the technical details of a new technique. On the other hand, if management do not understand a new technique, how can they then be committed to its use or, for example, sign off a specification if they don't understand what it means? As suggested by [5], training courses in the use of FDTs need to be attended by *both* management and the people who will be applying the technique.

Technical training in the use of FDTs should be of one, two or even three weeks duration. Also, such in-depth training should only occur if the attendees will then go back to the organisation and apply FDTs to a project. The benefit from such in-depth training will be lost if the techniques are not used soon after the course. For example, one such course discussed in [5], consisted of two-weeks training and a one-week workshop that began to apply FDTs to the project on which the organisation wanted to use formal methods. This presents the same management problem as above. How can a manager commit a whole section to an extensive training course without understanding the technique himself/herself? For this to be possible, the manager needs to be convinced of the potential for benefits.

Another issue brought to light in [5] is that of critical mass. If an organisation wants to use formal methods, there should be a section within the organisation that is well-versed in the technique. OTC has definitely not achieved "critical mass" in formal methods. Although there are quite a few people within OTC who know about formal methods, they are in very different sections of the organisation. There is no single section within OTC that could begin a project with formal methods without training quite a few people first.

5.4 The Role of FDTs in Software Development

Although a lot of work has been done in developing formal description techniques, not much work seems to have been done to investigate where, when and how these techniques should be used in the development of software systems. As mentioned in Section 5.3, training in these areas needs to provided as part of the adoption of FDTs into an organisation's existing development practices.

FDTs have traditionally been used in the specification of complex sections of applications such as protocol specification. However, it is hoped that FDTs will have a much wider application base than these. Within OTC R&D, Object-Z has been used on several different types of systems and stages of the software development lifecycle.

5.4.1 Incorporating FDTs into Mainstream Software Development

Over the last couple of years, a small group within OTC R&D has been looking at software engineering techniques, with an emphasis on the object-oriented paradigm. This object-oriented emphasis was due to OTC's relatively long involvement in the development of C++ and the perceived advantages that the object-oriented paradigm gives to the partitioning of large systems (see Section 3.1).

Many software engineering techniques have been investigated including several object-oriented analysis/design methodologies. Examples include ER modelling, dataflow diagrams, Coad and

Yourdon's OOA[1], Rumbaugh's OMT[6], etc. Although the authors of these methodologies often refer to them as "formal", they are not rigorous in the same way that formal description techniques are. The rigorous nature of FDTs promises to enhance general software development, especially in the areas of software quality and assurance. Some indications of this are described in [2].

A disadvantage of formal techniques such as Object-Z is that it can be very difficult to view the whole system, as can be done with the use of a diagramming technique. Both non-object-oriented techniques such as Yourdon's SA[8] and SD[9], and object-oriented techniques, such as Coad and Yourdon's OOA, allow complete systems to be viewed as the relationships/interactions between entities/objects.

Thus, the combination of a formal method together with a graphical software development methodology should prove a powerful combination, providing a rigorous, yet useful software development technique.

An FDT, such as Object-Z, may also be useful as a backbone, or framework, joining various techniques used in object-oriented development. In most object oriented methodologies, some sort of textual *class specification* is used, with detail being added as the development proceeds. The use of Object-Z for these class specifications would provide an unambiguous specification which should reveal anomalies much earlier in the lifecycle. This use of a formal method as a backbone to a software development methodology applies equally well to non-object-oriented development.

This section has only given a cursory overview of the ways in which FDTs can be used in software development. Further detail, however, lies outside the scope of this paper.

6 Conclusions

Although the OTC/UQ collaboration on formal techniques has not achieved a significant transfer of FDT technology from UQ to OTC's *mainstream* development groups, people within OTC are now much more aware of FDTs, especially within R&D. The collaboration with UQ has enabled OTC to investigate FDTs and UQ to be exposed to telecommunications problems.

This paper has outlined several problems and future possibilities of FDTs that have become apparent during OTC's investigations. In particular, the following areas of required research have been identified:

- support tools
- the role FDTs can play in mainstream software development

One of the main aims of this paper is to give the benefit of OTC's experience in the adoption of formal methods to other organisations embarking on the same path. In order to do this, elements of a strategy for the transfer of FDT technology have been outlined. Most importantly, management needs to be involved in training in order to have the commitment to fully adopt FDTs. Research groups within organisations also have a role to play in such technology transfer, especially in providing the extra resources required on development projects to trial new techniques.

Acknowledgments

The author would especially like to thank Roger Duke (UQ), Graham Dumpleton and David Charrett (OTC) for their invaluable comments during the preparation of this paper. The author would also like to thank Gordon Rose, Paul King and Graeme Smith for the very interesting discussions we have had throughout the collaboration.

The permission of the Managing Director of OTC to publish this work is gratefully acknowledged. The views and opinions expressed in this work are those of the author and do not necessarily imply OTC policy or future service offerings.

References

[1] P. Coad and E. Yourdon. *Object-Oriented Analysis*. Prentice-Hall, 2nd edition, 1991.

[2] B. Collins, J. Nicholls, and I. Holm Sørensen. Introducing formal methods: the CICS experience with Z. Technical Report TR12.260, IBM United Kingdom Laboratories Ltd., Hursley Park, December 1987.

[3] R. Duke, G. Rose, and G. Smith. Transferring formal techniques to industry: A case study. In J. Quemada, J. Mañas, and E. Vazquez, editors, *Formal Description Techniques III*, pages 279–286. North-Holland, 1990.

[4] I. Hayes, editor. *Specification Case Studies*. International Series in Computer Science. Prentice-Hall, 1987.

[5] C. Jones. Formal methods and their role in industry. *ASWEC'91*, July 1991. Tutorial.

[6] J. Rumbaugh, M. Blaha, W. Premerlani, F. Eddy, and W. Lorenson. *Object-Oriented Modeling and Design*. Prentice-Hall, 1991.

[7] J.M. Spivey. *The Z Notation: A Reference Manual*. International Series in Computer Science. Prentice-Hall, 1989.

[8] Edward Yourdon. *Modern Structured Analysis*. Yourdon Press/Prentice Hall, 1989.

[9] Edward Yourdon and Larry Constantine. *Structured Design*. Prentice Hall, 1979.

Linking Specifications with Implementations*

Martin Kooij [a]

[a] PTT Research, P.O. Box 421, 2260 AK Leidschendam, The Netherlands

Abstract

This paper describes the development in the RACE Project SPECS, on the way to link formal specifications of communications systems to their actual implementation by means of introducing an intermediate layer.

1. INTRODUCTION

In this paper it is described how an intermediate layer between an algebraic specification and an implementation can help in bridging the world of specifications and implementation, reconciling the different "modes" of understanding of implementors and specifiers. The main issues that played a role in designing this intermediate layer are presented. We hope that these issues clear some common misunderstandings. Why do we think this presentation is useful for a forum like FORTE? In the world of formal methods it is always a problem how to relate formal specifications with implementations. On the one hand this problem is of a technical nature (on which subject we digress in section 3.) on the other hand it is just a matter of education. People working in implementations have a different background from those working in formal specifications. By defining an "execution model" as an intermediate layer we hope to bridge the gap.

Firstly, however, we will present an overview of the project to set the stage and present a context in which this intermediate layer has to function.

2. OVERVIEW OF THE SPECS PROJECT

The SPECS Project aims at integrating diverse specification languages, supplying methods and a framework on which analysis tools are implemented to analyse complex communication systems. SPECS is meant to support the whole trajectory from specification to implementation.

It is worthwhile to highlight the technical approach that was chosen to accomplish this. A common semantical layer was designed, called the CRL (Common Representation Language)[1].

---

*This work was partly supported by and carried out in the context of the RACE Project 1046, SPECS, Specification and Programming Environment for Communication Software.

This layer had to be powerful enough to capture the semantics of several (existing and new) specification languages. Tools are to be build on this common semantic layer, thus enabling tools to be reused if new specification languages are to be added in the architecture, and to express the behaviour of complex systems that are designed partly in one language, partly in another. The SPECS project makes an implementation of this architecture for the two language LOTOS[2] and SDL[3].

The CRL that is designed to serve as this common layer is an algebraic specification formalism based on ACP[4], and is thus similar to LOTOS. The layer is extended with a logical formalism to define data types. This logical formalism is an extension of conditional algebraic equational formalism as found in e.g. LOTOS and SDL. This formalism is sufficiently powerful to express a wide range of specifications of communication systems.

During the progress of the project it became increasingly clear that meeting the goal of supporting the whole trajectory from specification to implementation was more difficult than was initially thought. One of the causes was the difficulty of bridging the gap between the concepts of an algebraic specification formalism like ACP or LOTOS (and much less so SDL) and the concepts that play a role in the implementation phase. In order to better support implementation it was decided to design an intermediate layer between specification of the *tower languages*, the user languages, and implementation. This layer could serve as a vehicle for expressing the issues in the implementation phase of software development. This layer was placed alongside the algebraically oriented CRL, that serves its purpose as the main vehicle for analysis of specifications.

Following SPECS usage we will from now on consider the CRL layer to consist of two languages: the I-CRL, for Implementation oriented CRL, and the A-CRL for Analysis oriented CRL.

In this paper we will discuss the rationale for the implementation oriented intermediate layer I-CRL and its design principles in the next two sections. A short overview of the structure of I-CRL and some conclusions are presented after that.

3. RATIONALE FOR THE INTERMEDIATE LAYER

Firstly we will digress by discussing the concept of a wide spectrum language, and how it could ideally support the implementation phase, secondly we indicate how the I-CRL layer differs from a wide spectrum approach and why this approch was chosen.

To support the whole spectrum from specification to implementation one would like to have *one* language supporting the whole trajectory: a wide spectrum language. A wide spectrum language is able to express

- *specifications:* what the externally observable behaviour of the system is.

- *building blocks:* the primitives that are available in the platform on which implementation will be done.

- *implementations:* realisations of the specifications in terms of the building blocks, showing how the building blocks are used to realise the specification.

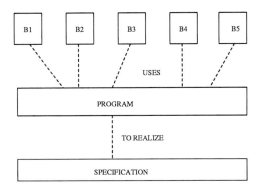

Figure 1: A program uses building blocks to realize a specification

- *stepwise development:* the combined use of implementations and specifications at the same time.

In figure 1 it is pictured how a program is effectively a specification of how building blocks available from some underlying system (be it hardware, be it software), are assembled to realize the behaviour of some specification. These two functions of a program we will return to later in section 4.2..

Another feature of wide spectrum languages, set up in the way described above, is the ability to *stack* designs: the building blocks itself could be regarded as specifications to be implemented by means of other building blocks. This enables to reason about how, e.g, a specification is implemented by a Pascal program, and how the Pascal programming language is implemented by an assembly language program, and how assembly language is implemented by VLSI hardware.

For sequential programming a rather successful design of a truly wide spectrum language is COLD-K[5], or to a lesser extent VDM[6]. For an interesting approach on the use of a wide spectrum language in the implementation phase see the thesis by Loe Feijs[7].

Such a wide spectrum language, however, is not readily available for distributed programming. One the one hand most concurrent specification languages do not really succeed having an effective means to describe within the language the various objects that play a role as building blocks in the implementation layer. Often (and rightly so) these language minimise on the number of concepts used (e.g, only synchronous or only asynchronous communication). On the other hand most implementation languages carry too much detail to support an effective specification semantics.

As sketched above, a wide spectrum language for concurrency is not available, for use in SPECS, given the current state of technology. The research needed for designing it would exceed the resources available in SPECS, an we had to resort to another way. This resulted in the concept of an I-CRL alongside the A-CRL to express the "building blocks" and the "implementation", these concepts being outside the realm of A-CRL. The configuration of A-CRL and I-CRL in the architecture of SPECS is shown in figure 2. We cut down to less ambitious goals, but

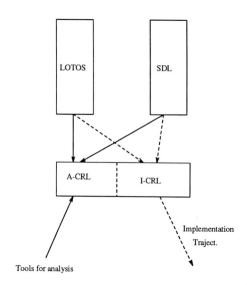

Figure 2: Architecture of SPECS, with I-CRL layer

useful in the context. Instead of building a general wide spectrum language, we were able to focus on building a layer that on the one hand is able to "talk about" some predefined, well known and proven concepts that play a role in the implementation of distributed programs, and on the other hand has a clear relation with the algebraic semantics of A-CRL. Thus it could serve a a bridge between some fixed specification level (algebraic concurrent specifications) and a fixed implementation level (distributed programming). One thus loses two important aspects of wide spectrum languages: the ability to *define* building blocks for implementations and thus the ability to *stack* designs and the possibility to mix, in one language, specifications and implementations. However, one wins a certain simplicity.

4. THE DESIGN CRITERIA OF THE INTERMEDIATE LAYER

The purposes of I-CRL are many-fold and are enumerated below. I-CRL should be designed in such a way that it has the possibility:

1. to serve as an common implementation platform from which it is possible to derive product quality code for telecom applications (see also item number 5);

2. to serve as a platform where many of the design decisions can be be made concerning the implementation structure of the resulting program;

3. to serve as the target for which translators from LOTOS and SDL that focus on the production of code can be designed;

4. to have a semantics that is easy relatable to the specification in A-CRL;

5. to enable to define modules that are separately compilable on current van Neumann, fixed bit length, machines, operating in a modern networked environment.

Each of these goals for I-CRL warrants some elaboration on what it means for the design of the language.

4.1. Quality code

To be able to achieve quality code from an I-CRL program it means that the building blocks that are described in I-CRL are a close match to existing building blocks. Ideally one would like to have a language where all kinds of building blocks could be described. If there is a fixed set of building blocks available one would want rather a union of the building blocks of the possible underlying systems than an intersection. This allows the designers to actually *use* and *select* the features of the underlying implementation platform. This process is often called *targetting*.

On the other hand one wants to avoid a plethora of options and features that make the semantics untractable. In this paper it is tried to find a balance for I-CRL between these two by abstracting from the facilities found in the underlying operating systems in such a way that features are clearly recognizable by people working in implementation, but abstract enough to avoid semantic complications. Moreover some building blocks found in operating systems that do not directly relate to telecom applications, like password and file access handling are not described in I-CRL. Also many features of programming languages like register variables, variable aliasing and parameter passing mechanism are not included. These decisions removes a lot of options and keeps the semantics tractable.

4.2. Implementation Structure

The I-CRL has two kinds of semantics, firstly the *intensional* semantics in terms of possible program transitions, that can be used to compare a program in I-CRL with a specification. This allows us to reason on the fact whether a program realizes the behaviour stated in a specification. Secondly a program written in I-CRL has an *extensional* semantics; from the syntax of the program the structure of the implementation can be seen. To state this in another way: from the program itself it can be seen *how* the available building blocks are used to achieve the desired behaviour.

One can compare this to a Pascal program implementing a sorting algorithm. On the one hand it has an *intensional* semantics (e.g., a denotational semantics) that defines the behaviour of the program: it sorts an array. One the other hand it has an *extensional* semantics that defines how variables and control flow are used to to achieve the sorting. One could easily imagine two Pascal program having the same intensional semantics but a completely different extensional semantics. The idea is that I-CRL can be seen as having this structure also: an *intensional* semantics that describes its behaviour (in terms of A-CRL or transition systems), and an *extensional* semantics that describes how the operating system is used to achieve the behaviour. The extensional semantics is not formally defined.

During the translation from specification language to I-CRL a lot of pre-defined (for prototyping), or user directed (for optimisation), choices can be made concerning the design decisions to be taken. The more abstract the specification language is the more decisions have to be made. Of course one can additionally chose to modify an I-CRL program in such a way that the intensional semantics stay the same, but its extensional semantics is changed, e.g., by allocating a process to another host.

4.3. Target for the translators from LOTOS and SDL

Effectively these translators define a semantics in the execution domain for LOTOS and SDL specifications. It should be so that design decisions about the allocation of processes and the architectural structure are made in this phase. SPECS is currently also investigating the possibility to translate TTCN (a notation for executable tests) to I-CRL. Currently, within SPECS an intermediate layer based on communicating state machines is defined[8], with the intention that results on these translations can be reused in the I-CRL discussed in this paper.

4.4. Relation with A-CRL

The relation with A-CRL should be found in comparing the intensional semantics of the behaviour of an I-CRL program with the specification of a behaviour in A-CRL. When this connection is established trust can be placed in the correct execution. It should also be possible to study the correctness of the triangle:

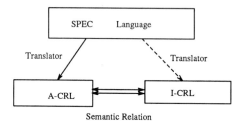

That such translations can be designed is shown in the thesis by Zuidweg[9]. This part is also published as [10].

4.5. Separate Compilability

In I-CRL there should be a concept of "a separately compilable module". The problem with such a concept is that it is strongly related with the underlying architecture and operating system. If the operating environment is very powerful, then certain constructs that are separately compilable in that powerful setting will not be in a more primitive operating environment. If we have an environment that has all process algebra operators as primitives, then every process[1] is trivially

---
[1] in the process algebra sense.

compilable. In a production quality environment it is, we think, unrealistic to assume the full set of process operators to be available as building blocks. Moreover we can assume that we will not be able to define an open, distributed, operating system that is capable of exchanging abstract data. Rather we define a separately compilable module as

> A *separately compilable module* is an I-CRL program that makes use of designated building blocks only, and where the binary bit patterns of the communications are known. The building blocks that can be used are those of current van Neumann machines operating in a modern, networked, environment.

In I-CRL we have a facility to delineate such a designated building block.

5. THE STRUCTURE OF I-CRL

To give some structure to the wealth of facilities that I-CRL needs to provide, we separate the facilities in several topics. Moreover, to keep the connection within the SPECS environment more simple we will have a separation of data and control, as is the case in the user specification languages and A-CRL. Furthermore we separate between local-area issues and wide-area issues. Local-area issues are issues that play a role on the same machine, or perhaps on a LAN with very high speed links, wide-area issues are issues about communication between machines connected by (slower) network lines. Of course wide-area is a superset of local-area. Wide-area issues also apply to single machines: it should be possible to communicate with a local machine as if it was on a network connection. Shared memory, however, is only available in the local-area setting.

1. *local-area control:* The control flow mechanisms

2. *local-area communications:* possible communication mechanisms in local-areas (synchronous).

3. *wide-area control:* control flow mechanisms that are possible over a wide-area network.

4. *wide-area communications:* communication mechanism on wide-areas (asynchronous).

5. *data definitions:* Implementation algorithms to implement data types and functions.

6. *data abstractions:* Relating abstract data specifications with implementations.

7. *data transport:* coding from data values to bitstreams.

We will work out each of these issues in sections. In this paper none of the issues is shown in any detail. It is, however, very interesting to study the details used in the I-CRL definition. The definition will be published in a public SPECS report end of this year[11].

5.1. Local control

Local control is done by the definition of finite state machines with variables. The state machines can either do "commands": for communication or control, or propose "actions" (possibly parameterised with data) to the outside world. Every state machine is accompanied with a number of "handlers": state machines that tell what to do in exceptional cases. Possible command include commands to wait some time, for the implementation of timers. State machines can have three kinds of variables. These are the local variables that are initialised by other machines at startup time: *the parameter variables*, local variables and variables shared with other state machines implementing *shared memory*. The reason to choose these kind of state machines is twofold, on the one hand the semantics of state machines are close to the transition system semantics of algebraic specification languages, on the other hand current results on the translations to communicating state machines of [8] can be reused within the project.

5.2. Local communication

Local communication is concerned with *shared actions* and *shared variables*. It describes how so called "filters" can combine proposed actions of state machines, thus giving the possibility of synchronously cooperating state machines. These filter combine, or rename, or just pass proposed actions to other filters, up to the level of a special filter: the native operating system, that can be a simulation environment that prints the string `ring-the-bell` on the receipt of a action called `ring-the-bell` or a real environment that actually rings a bell upon receipt of the action.

5.3. Wide area control

This addresses the stopping and starting of other state machines (process creation) and the calling of other state machines (remote procedure calls). These activities are inspired by the RPC mechanism in TCP/IP and ROSE class 1 and 5 of OSI[12]. Note that according to our definition of the applicability of wide area issues to local area issues this includes the creation of processes on the same machine.

5.4. Wide area communication

This is always the most problematic issue: asynchronous communication. The exact semantics vary from language to language and from operating environment to operating environment. As we are not the first in trying to structure existing connection possibilities, we did some research into documentation of existing operating environments.

In UNIX[2] the concept of STREAMS (see for example [13]) is a reasonable abstraction of asynchronous communication where various protocols stacks can be inserted to accommodate a wide range of behaviours. Thus it can be used as a framework for asynchronous communication in I-CRL. We see as advantages that is is reasonable abstract, implementable, and readily available in most UNIX operating system environments. SDL Channels, various communication channels, and TCP/IP like communication all can be fitted into a STREAMS framework.

---

[2] Unix is a trademark of AT&T.

The idea is that a stream is a buffered connection to some device (call it contact point) on the machine you are working on. A user process can insert modules to filter the stream both upwards and downwards, thus providing a protocol stack. There is a concept of urgent data that goes into the front of the buffer.

The way the contact point (on the "end" of the stream) behaves depends on the actual device: an RS232 port, a terminal, a file system, an ethernet connection, or, if the operating system has inserted a few default filters, an IP or an OSI network connection. It seems useful to define a minimal but useful set of contact point behaviours for I-CRL (e.g, a Transport Layer OSI Network Connection[14] and an SDL channel). Effectively this mechanism gives us a reasonable set of contact points on which we can developed some theory on the behaviour, on the other hand we are free to define more, or variations, if needed.

5.5. Data definitions

In this section it is possible to use algorithms (say a normal programming language) to implement the data part. One uses a standard set of available data types (integers, characters) and data type combinators (arrays, lists, records).

5.6. Data abstractions

Not all programs need a section on data abstractions. However, if an I-CRL program is to be compared with a specification one need to establish a relation between the concrete data types in I-CRL and the (abstract) data types in the specification. It is shown in this section how the algorithms are used to implement corresponding the operations on the abstract data types, e.g., linking a tree representation of a set to the abstract definition of a set. In this examples it should be indicated which concrete operations on the tree correspond with what abstract operations on the set.

In a proof connecting the I-CRL program with the A-CRL specification, one will have to proof that the implementation of the data type indeed implements all properties that are stated in the data type specification.

5.7. Data transfers

In this section coding rules how to translate data values into bit patterns are described. For this the standard ASN.1[15] is used and the companion standard for the basic encoding rules[16]. These standards tell how to define types and values, and their coding into bits patterns. These rules are only needed when you want to have a separately compilable module. In that case the information which bit patterns the implementation must generate must be known, because these can not change after compilation. This holds for all communication outside a compilable module. Within a module the compiler may decide on the internal structure of the data.

6. CONCLUSION

A need for a wide spectrum language for concurrency is shown. A less ambitious, but more practical solution, of an intermediate layer language between specification and implementation is discussed. This layer is, better than specification languages, able to express concepts needed to reflect design decisions in the life cycle of software when going from specification to implementation. Targetting, the selection of available options, is possible in the language.

This discussion concentrates on the design criteria, the functionality and the structure of the layer, and not on the technical details. In related work, however, it is shown that this approach works, and a layer with the desired properties can be build.

Of course, whether a layer designed according to the design requirements stated, will in practice serve its intended function remains to be seen. Early results within SPECS show encouraging results, but are not definitive.

I want to thank Michel Dauphin for fruitful discussions on the design of I-CRL and the referees for their comments on an earlier version of this paper.

References

[1] SPECS-SEMANTICS. Definition of CRL/MR version 2.1. RACE Report 46/SPE/WP5/DS/A/017/b1, SPECS Consortium, 1990.
[2] LOTOS — a formal description technique based on the temporal ordering of observational behaviour. ISO/TC97/SC21 21 N, July 1987. Draft International Standard 8807.
[3] Specification and description language SDL. CCITT, ITU Z.100, 1988.
[4] J. C. M. Baeten and W. P. Weijland. *Process Algebra*, volume 18 of *Cambridge Tracts in Theoretical Computer Science*. Cambridge University Press, 1990.
[5] L. M. G. Feijs, H.B.M. Jonkers, C. P. J. Koymans, and G. R. Renardel de Lavalette. Formal definition of the design language COLD-K. Report METEOR/t7/PRLE/7, METEOR, 1987.
[6] C.B. Jones. *Systematic Software Development Using VDM*. Prentice-Hall, second edition, 1990.
[7] L.M.G. Feijs. A formalisation of design methods. Ph.d.thesis, Philips, 1990. Eindhoven.
[8] G. Karjoth. XFSM: A formal model of communicating state machines for implementation specifications. Technical Report RZ 2209, IBM Research Division, 9/12/1991.
[9] J. Zuidweg. Concurrent system verification with process algebra. Ph.d.thesis, PTT Research, 1990. Leidschendam.
[10] L.G. Bouma and J. Zuidweg. Structured design of a translation from LOTOS to MR. *Formal Aspects of Computing*, January 1991.
[11] SPECS-SEMANTICS. Definition of CRL/MR version 3. RACE Report 46/SPE/WP5/DS/A/010/b1, SPECS Consortium, December 1991. To be published.
[12] Remote Operations – Part1: Model notation and service definition. ISO/JTC1, 1987. Draft International Standard 9072-1, CCITT X.219.
[13] *SunOS 4.1: STREAMS Programming*. from SunOS 4.1 manual set.
[14] Transport service definition. ISO/JTC1, 1986. International Standard 8072, CCITT X.214.
[15] Specification of Abstract Syntax Notation One (ASN.1). ISO/JTC1, 1987. International Standard 8824, CCITT X.208.
[16] Specification of Basic Encoding Rules for ASN.1. ISO/JTC1, 1987. International Standard 8825, CCITT X.209.

Experience of Using LOTOS Within the CIM-OSA Project[1,2]

Ashley Mc Clenaghan

Department of Computing Science and Mathematics
University Of Stirling, STIRLING FK9 4LA, Scotland

Abstract

The **Computer Integrated Manufacturing – Open Systems Architecture** (CIM-OSA) project [1, 2, 3] has recently started to use the FDT LOTOS [4] in the development and formal representation of its **Integrating Infrastructure** (IIS) reference architecture. This paper briefly introduces CIM-OSA, presents an overview of the LOTOS application strategy, and reviews the results so far (which have been very positive).

1 Introduction to CIM-OSA

When the need to develop an Open Systems Architecture for Computer Integrated Manufacturing (CIM) was recognised, the Commission of the European Communities launched Project 688 CIM-OSA within its Esprit[3] framework in 1986[4].

CIM-OSA's primary objectives include: producing CIM system models and guidelines; bottom-up integration across CIM systems; and influencing standards. At the heart of these objectives lies the development of a **CIM Reference Architecture**. This defines generic structures (framework guidelines) which can be used to create a completely structured description of an enterprise as a system. The CIM-OSA Reference Architecture is a complex knowledge base consisting of many orthogonal concepts, modelling strategies and guidelines at several different levels of abstraction and genericism.

CIM-OSA proposes three steps towards an integrated enterprise: physical system integration, application integration, and finally business integration. Integration at the level

---

[1]The author would like to acknowledge the financial support of the Esprit CIM-OSA Consortium (AMICE), Department of Computing Science (University of Stirling), Hewlett-Packard Laboratories (Bristol), and the Department of Education for Northern Ireland (DENI).
[2]The opinions expressed in this paper are the author's, and are not necessarily those of CIM-OSA.
[3]European Strategic Programme for Research and Development in Information Technology.
[4]establishing the CIM-OSA Consortium AMICE, consisting of 21 companies form 7 European countries.

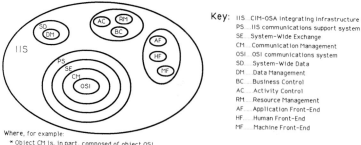

Figure 1: The Architecture of the IIS

of business functions can only be reached if a sufficient level of integration between applications and physical systems is realised. Towards this goal CIM-OSA has identified what it considers as a set of services *common* to most CIM systems. This composite set of services is known as the **Integrating Infrastructure** (IIS).

The IIS provides an *information technology platform* on top of which any "particular" CIM-OSA system can be built. This information technology platform encompasses a set of services which are common to the needs of most CIM systems. In some sense, the IIS resembles a "CIM-OSA operating system".

2 The Benefits of FDTs for CIM-OSA

At present the CIM-OSA **Formal Reference Base** (FRB) provides *informal* (English language text with supporting diagrams) descriptions of the IIS. Certain aspects of the descriptions are incomplete (at a specification-level), with architectural, functional and informational elements missing. Ambiguity is another problem found in the FRB descriptions – this is mainly a result of ambiguity in natural language prose. Also, inconsistencies occur in the descriptions of IIS subsystems and their inter-communication.[5]

Once the FRB was established, the need to introduce some kind of formalism to all areas of the project (Reference Architecture and IIS) became obvious, and LOTOS was chosen to this end (to formalize IIS descriptions). The development of LOTOS descriptions of IIS elements has helped identify the above mentioned problems of incompleteness and inconsistency. The creation of LOTOS descriptions has forced decision making processes which solve ambiguities and other problems. This development process has made designers conscious of issues such as: level of abstraction; the identification of architectural, functional and informational elements which are important at the specification-level; and what constitutes a good specification-level design and why. Moreover, since the IIS is part of a "reference architecture" it is even more desirable that its description have all the properties of formal representation.

---

[5]We would like to emphasize that such problems are by no means unique to the CIM-OSA project but are characteristics of informal descriptions in general.

LOTOS support tools (SEDOS, Esprit and Spider, Hewlett-Packard) are being used to verify the correctness of LOTOS IIS descriptions, and will be used in testing the correctness of implementation-level models against LOTOS specification-level descriptions.

Further reasons to use formal languages are well documented in the LOTOS literature.

3 Our Strategy for the Application of LOTOS

In the previous section we addressed the reasons for using LOTOS. Given our choice to use LOTOS, we then had to decide what aspects of the IIS we should formalize. Using the FRB as a guideline, we identified that LOTOS descriptions should capture the following important aspects of the IIS:

1. The compositional structure of the IIS (in terms of elements, and elements composed of elements, etc.).

2. Interfaces between IIS elements (which elements interface with which elements, etc.).

3. The extent to which the reference architecture constrains the behaviour and information content of interactions between IIS elements.

The IIS is a fairly typical distributed computing system, consisting of a number of interacting composite components which form a complex web of interaction and dependency. Therefore, unlike OSI, the IIS cannot completely be described in terms of neat symmetric strata.

With this in mind, we chose to view the IIS from an object-based perspective (see figure 1). IIS *objects*[6]/components are described in terms of behaviour and information exchange at their interfaces. Such an *interface description* describes an IIS object's rôle as a *server* (similar to the OSI "service definition" idea) but, in addition, the interface description may also describe the object's rôle as a *client*.

Addressing the description of IIS compositional structure (*compositional description*), we identified two important forms: *composite objects* and *interacting objects*. Composite objects can be expressed in terms of their composing objects, in conjunction with some additional constraints; and the architectural relationship between interacting objects can be reflected in the parallel composition of their interface descriptions.

The remaining sections of this paper provide an indication of our general approach to the development of IIS LOTOS descriptions.

4 Interface Descriptions

In general, interfaces are the boundaries between architectural elements which have been identified as being of some significance for specification or design purposes. We consider

---
[6]Autonomous entities; encapsulating a number of properties, behaviour and data; with well defined interfaces to their environments.

each architectural element in the system as an object. An *interface description* of an object describes how the environment can interact[7] with that object.

In LOTOS we can model an interface as a gate[8] at which a number of constraints act to impose allowable/*signature* behaviour and information content on all events occurring at that interface. A LOTOS event then denotes an interaction of some nature (e.g. communication of a message) between the object and its environment.

4.1 Generic Interface Example

Now consider a fictitious component X, which has all the important generic characteristics of an IIS component. We can represent X's interface, in LOTOS, by a gate **x** (say), but now consider how we can make this X interface description more concrete (detailed), in terms of the behaviour and information content of events occurring at this interface.

The following list summarizes the important generic interface characteristics of IIS objects.[9]

1. Usually interactions (occurring at an interface) take the form of *Request-Confirm* pairs, an asynchronous communication model in which information (the Request) is conveyed from the "service-user" to the "service-provider" and subsequently, information (the complementary Confirm) is conveyed in the opposite direction.

    In general, though, the communication model is more complex than this. Normally an object not only assumes the rôle of service-provider (*server*) but also of service-user (*client*). Thus the object (acting a server rôle) may receive an incoming Request and may (acting a client rôle) solicit the services of other objects, before returning a complementary Confirm to the service-user which initiated the original Request.

2. An object (service-provider) can support a number of concurrent Request-Confirm interactions.

3. Often the previous history of interactions at the object-interface affects the information content and behaviour of all subsequent interactions at that interface.

4.1.1 Representing Information Exchange

Addressing the first point in section 4.1, we can model Request-Confirm interactions as suitably structured LOTOS events occurring at a gate representing the object-interface. So in our X-Interface example this this would suggest pairs of LOTOS events (with corresponding ACT ONE data types) with coarsely the following structure:

```
x!X_DataUnit(Request,userID,         x!X_DataUnit(Confirm,userID
         interactionID,data1)                interactionID,data2)
```

---

[7] Remember that interaction is a two-way process.
[8] LOTOS gates identify interaction points.
[9] Readers are referred to the FRB items (e.g. [9]) for more detailed descriptions of IIS components, and to [5] for an example of a more complete LOTOS specification of one such component: the **System-Wide Exchange (SE)**.

4.1.2 Supporting Concurrent Interactions

Given our decision to represent Request-Confirm interactions as LOTOS events we must now consider how to capture X's multiple concurrent interaction model in LOTOS (point 2 in section 4.1). Consider the following LOTOS fragment:

```
process INVOCATION_CONSTRAINTS [x] : noexit :=
    ONE_INVOCATION [x] ||| INVOCATION_CONSTRAINTS [x]
where
  process ONE_INVOCATION [x] : noexit :=
    x ? xdu1: X_DataUnitSort [xdu1 is Request];
    x ? xdu2: X_DataUnitSort [(xdu2 is Confirm) and (ExtractUserID(xdu1) eq
                              ExtractUserID(xdu2)) and (ExtractInteractID(xdu1)
                              eq ExtractInteractID(xdu2))];
    stop
  endproc (* ONE_INVOCATION *)
endproc (* INVOCATION_CONSTRAINTS *)
```

The process INVOCATION_CONSTRAINTS realizes object X's constraints on multiple concurrent Request-Confirm invocations. Each instantiation of the ONE_INVOCATION process models one Request-Confirm pair instance: one Request event and then a complementary Confirm event.

4.1.3 Applying Orthogonal Constraints

Point 3 in section 4.1 indicates that the previous history of event occurrences at an interface often affects the subsequent history of event occurrences at the same interface. The realization of this usually means allowing all event occurrences to affect some *state information* (which captures all important aspects of the previous history) and, reciprocally, having all event occurrences constrained (in some way) by this state information. The important point to comprehend about this scheme is that these *history constraints* need to be applied orthogonally to the constraints on invocations (as expressed in INVOCATION_CONSTRAINTS). To understand why, we need to remember that Request-Confirm pair invocations can occur concurrently, and that this is modelled in LOTOS through the parallel interleaving of events which represent these Request-Confirm pair invocations. With this in mind we should realize that complementary Request-Confirm event pairs do not necessarily occur consecutively but may be separated by event occurrences corresponding to other Request-Confirm invocations.

Hence for history constraints to affect every single event occurrence, and to be affected by every single event occurrence, they need to be applied in conjunction with INVOCATION_CONSTRAINTS. Such a conjunction is reflected, in context, in the LOTOS text below, showing that the X-Interface-Description defines object X in terms of observable behaviour at its interface (represented by the LOTOS gate x).

```
specification X-Interface-Description [x] :noexit :=
   (* Appropriate data type definitions *)
behaviour   (* ...As a conjunction of constraints *)
```

```
INVOCATION_CONSTRAINTS [x] || STATE_CONSTRAINTS [x] (state_info)
endspec (* X-Interface-Description *)
```

4.1.4 Partitioned Interfaces

Often an object assumes the rôles of both *client* (invoking services encapsulated by other objects) and *server* (providing services to other objects). All interactions of an object, both as client and server, between it and its environment occur at the object's interface. Until now we have represented this interface by a single LOTOS gate, but it is often convenient to partition the complete interface of an object into a number of more *limited* interfaces (also representing these by LOTOS gates). This allow us to explicitly partition server rôle interaction concerns from client rôle interaction concerns, and to explicitly reflect compositional architecture in terms of interactions with other objects.

For example, if we parameterise process `ONE_INVOCATION` by separate gates to explicitly separate client/server interaction concerns, then the process body might be re-written as (expressed in pseudo-LOTOS):

```
(  x-server          ? Request1; (* Receive (acting as a server) a request.  *)
   x-as-client-of-y  ! Request2; (* Solicit object Y to help in computation. *)
   x-as-client-of-y  ? Confirm2; (* Receive a result back from object Y.     *)
   x-server          ! Confirm1  (* Send (acting as a server) the completed  *)
)                                (* result back to the Request1 originator.  *)
[] (* OR *)
   (* ...Similarly for other possible communication combinations... *)
```

5 Compositional Descriptions

We are now in a position to describe the observable properties of any IIS object in LOTOS — in other words we have the know-how necessary for formalizing all the FRB-IIS-component interface descriptions. What we have not yet addressed is the description of the compositional structure of the IIS, i.e. expressing object composition in terms of other objects, and allowable object interaction.

The question of composition leads us to look at two separate scenarios: Firstly, **composite objects** where one object is, in part, composed of (or contains) what can be recognized as another object, distinct in its own right. Secondly, **interacting objects** where a collection of objects interact with one another, forming a complex lattice of dependency.

The first case is really a more specific example of the second, since one composite object can be viewed as two interacting objects, one of which (the *contained* object in the original view) can only directly interact with the other object (the residuum when the contained object is removed from the composite object in the original view). It is arguable that the first scenario still deserves recognition as a distinct case because, in many instances, it is a sufficient and powerful way of conceptualizing systems, e.g. in layered communication systems such as OSI, and indeed the stratified communication support system (PS in figure 1) in the IIS itself.

The above two scenarios are identified because each of them nicely fit parts of the IIS architecture. Looking back to figure 1 we can see that the IIS communications support system is realized by the composite object PS, containing composite object SE, which in turn contains the composite object CM, and so on. Similarly we can describe SD in terms of composite objects.

If we consider object CM (in figure 1) to be described by the LOTOS interface description:

```
specification CM-Interface-Description [cm] : noexit ....
```

then we can describe the composite object SE (figure 1) as:

```
specification SE-Interface-and-Compositional-Description [se] : noexit
   (* Appropriate data type definitions for the SE object *)
behaviour
   hide cm in        CM-Interface-Description[cm]
              |[cm]| Additional-Constraints-for-SE-Interface-Description[se, cm]
endspec (* SE-Interface-and-Compositional-Description *)
```

The two important points to note about the above description are that: only the SE interface is observable to the environment (the interface to CM is *hidden*); and although not observable to the environment, the coarse compositional structure of SE is described as a conjunction of the characteristics of the contained CM object with some additional constraints, which (approximately speaking) represent the functionality of the residual entity when object CM is removed from the composite object SE (study figure 1). In other words, these additional constraints model how occurrences at the SE interface are related to occurrences at the (hidden) CM interface.

Turning our attention to the IIS **Business Service Complex** (BS) (objects BC, AC and RM in figure 1): Our model of interacting objects seems most suitable for its description since BC, AC and RM do not interact with one another in a linear-chain fashion but in fact incur a cyclic dependency (BS, unlike PS, is not a layered complex.) The architecture of interacting objects may be captured in LOTOS by combining the involved objects' descriptions in an appropriate parallel composition.

Taking a wide perspective we conclude that the whole IIS can be described in terms of interacting (composite) objects.

6 Conclusions

Even in the short time that LOTOS has been employed in the CIM-OSA project, it has had a considerable impact, and has gained project-wide acceptance as an integral part of the development of the IIS reference architecture. Our initial use of LOTOS has shown that the so called "Formal Reference Base" IIS descriptions are neither as rigorous nor as complete as required. The application of LOTOS has lead not only design corrections, but also to the development of better designs.[10] Development of LOTOS descriptions has

---

[10]See [5] for specific examples.

also helped the overall coherence between the project workpackages (responsible for the development of each of the IIS services). Before the use of LOTOS their descriptions were not entirely compatible — a fact not immediately evident from examining the informal FRB descriptions.

In this paper we have shown the suitability of LOTOS for capturing both the component interface characteristics, and the compositional structure of CIM-OSA's IIS.

Acknowledgements

I would like to especially thank Prof. Kenneth Turner (Uni. of Stirling), Patrick Viollet and Daniel Boisson (Hewlett-Packard, Lyon), Stewart Black (Hewlett-Packard, Bristol), and Pierre De Swert (Cap Gemini Sesa, Brussels) for their help involving CIM-OSA.

References

[1] Dirk Beekman. CIM-OSA: computer integrated manufacturing — open systems architecture. *Int.J. Computer Integrated Manufacturing. Vol.2, No.2*, pp94–105, 1989.

[2] Esprit Consortium AMICE. *Architecture Description — CIM-OSA AD 1.1*. Technical Report R0391/1, 1990.

[3] Esprit Consortium AMICE. *Management Overview — CIM-OSA AD 1.1*. Technical Report R0391/0, 1990.

[4] ISO. *Information Processing Systems – Open Systems Interconnection – LOTOS – A Formal Description Technique Based on the Temporal Ordering of Observational Behaviour*. Technical Report ISO 8807, 1989.

[5] Ashley Mc Clenaghan. *On the Specification of the CIM-OSA System Wide Exchange*. Technical Report, CIM-OSA. (Department of Computing Science and Mathematics, University of Stirling, Scotland), 1990.

[6] Kenneth J. Turner. A LOTOS-based development strategy. In *[10]*, pages 157–174, November 1989.

[7] Marten van Sinderen. Generic service and protocol structures. In *ESPRIT Conference '90, Brussels*, Uni. of Twente, Dept. Informatics, Netherlands., 1990.

[8] Chris A. Vissers, Giuseppe Scollo, Marten van Sinderen, and Ed Brinksma. *On the Use of Specification Styles in the Design of Distributed Systems*. University ot Twente, Fac. Informatics, 7500 AE Enschede, NL.

[9] WP-J. *FRB Series on "System Wide Exchange (SE)"*. Technical Report CIM-OSA C5-12xx Series, Esprit Consortium AMICE (CIM-OSA), 1989.

[10] *FORTE'90, Third International Conference on: Formal Description Techniques*, Madrid, November 1990.

An Exercise in Protocol Synthesis

Peter van Eijk and Jeroen Schot
pve@cs.utwente.nl
schot@cs.utwente.nl
University of Twente, Fac. Informatics
P.O. Box 217
7500 AE Enschede, NL

Abstract

It has been claimed earlier that a protocol should be designed on the basis of a service definition. In this paper we work through an example in which this is done entirely in LOTOS and entirely with correctness preserving transformations. It is thus an example of applying formal methods in a design *process*, and not just in a design representation. We believe that the techniques introduced in this paper constitutes a novel contribution to the craft of protocol design.

1 Introduction

The goal of this paper is to show an example of a systematic derivation of a protocol from a service, in LOTOS. One approach to the design of correct protocols is to prove the equivalence of the protocol to the service it provides, after the protocol is designed. In contrast, in the approach illustrated here a protocol is actually *derived* or *synthesized* from a service in a systematic way. Correctness of the protocol is an inherent property of such a design process, hence we use the term *correctness preserving transformation* to refer to such design steps.

In the more general framework of systematic development of (distributed) systems, the stepwise refinement approach is a widely recognized strategy for the synthesis of high quality systems out of (standard) components. The approach limits the complexity of the design process by dividing it into a number of manageable steps [PV90]. The transformation that is presented in this paper can thus be seen as a type of design step that is frequently taken in the aforementioned design approach.

When a number of transformation steps are taken in succession, it is important to preserve the specification structure and properties as much as possible, and this is what our approach attempts to do. In the algorithms of [KvBK89] and [Lan90], this principle is violated by the requirement to transcribe the input specification to action prefix normal form expressions. In a design process one wants to postpone such a transformation to the latest possible stage, because it removes structure. In practical distributed system design, it is likely that after a protocol has been defined, it will be further structured into lower level components until a mapping onto implementation elements (i.e. hardware/software components) is easily performed. For these steps, the method presented here can be applied as well.

The method that we present here takes a service and transforms this into a protocol based on an implicit underlying service. Our method is based on the algorithms described in [Lan90]. The direct application of the original algorithms can result in unnecessary PDU exchanges, as we will explain in Section 6. We will show that our approach avoids these.

Other promising work in this area can be found in [vSF91], where the transformation suggested by Parrow[Par89] is extended with heuristic protocol derivation constructs, and can be applied for the simultaneous derivation of both sender and receiver components. In this approach, input from the human designer in terms of decisions and suggestions is required, in order to cover a large area of protocol functions. This work can be seen as complementary to ours, and integration is worked on by the authors.

Our derivation approach consists of a novel combination of transformation steps, most of which are based on existing theory. Additional theory is provided to fill up the remaining gaps. These transformation steps are partly automated by software tools. For the purpose of illustration and evaluation of the approach, we apply the derivation on a simple service specification, yielding a formally correct protocol. We also address the relation between our design steps and the overall design methodology.

The paper assumes knowledge of LOTOS [vEVD89, ISO88] and related design methods. In Section 2 we present the specification of the service that our design starts from. In Section 3 we discuss the relevant theory for our development, followed by a discussion of the tools used in Section 4. The actual derivation is presented in Section 5, which constitutes the bulk of this paper. In Section 6 we discuss the approach and future directions it may take. The conclusion constitutes Section 7.

2 The Service Specification

The service that we base our development on is simple, but fairly complete. It is a single data connection, between users A and B. Setting up the connection is asymmetric: gate a represents the calling side. Data transfer is bidirectional, but limited to one outstanding message per direction. After the connection has been released, which can only be caused by the service users, the specification is exited. The connection release is unconfirmed.

For the purpose of deriving the bare bones of the protocol, we left out a number of data parameters: connection endpoint identification (for N users and multiple connections per service access point), quality of service negotiation (therefore, a user confirmed connection setup is not required), SDU parameters of the data primitives (the actual contents of the data transferred is irrelevant), and disconnect reason (which normally indicates whether the user or the provider released the connection). We also limited our example to one connection.

The style of the LOTOS specification is constraint-oriented, with a distinction between local and remote constraints, along the lines of [vS90].

- In the local constraints, the ordering of service primitives at the calling and called side is defined. They have been structured according to the phases of a connection: connection-establishment >> data-phase [> disconnect (at the calling side, the connect phase has to be split up in two steps).

- The remote constraints of the service specification are structured into a number of independent constraints using the ||| operator, which expresses the independency between its operands. Each of the remote constraints defines a relation between an event occurring at one of the sides, and a subsequent event at the opposite side.

The functionality of the specification is exit, expressing successful termination. This termination happens when calling, called and remote synchronize on exit. calling and called can do this after a disconnect service primitive. The process remote can then do nothing, so it is disabled by the exit. By structuring the service specification in this way, we can discern between successful termination and possible deadlocks. A protocol derived from this service will then automatically have the property of synchronized termination, i.e. it will not be the case that one entity terminates while the other waits forever. In the protocol there will thus be PDU exchanges that guarantee the synchronized termination. Exhaustive analysis of the specification using a simulator shows that all sequences of events end in an exit, and none in a deadlock.

```
specification simple[a, b] : exit

type sp is
sorts
  sp
opns
  conreq, conind, conconf, datreq, datind, disreq, disind : -> sp
endtype (* sp *)

behaviour
 connection [a, b]
where
  process connection[a, b] : exit:=
   (calling [a] ||| called [b]) |[a, b]| remote [a, b]
  endproc (* connection *)
```

```
process calling[a] : exit:=
  a!conreq; (a!conconf; datal [a] [> disconl [a])
endproc (* calling *)

process called[b] : exit:=
  b!conind; (datal [b] [> disconl [b])
endproc (* called *)

process remote[a, b] : exit:=
  (connect[a, b]    ||| datar [a, b] ||| datar [b, a] |||
     disconr [a, b]    ||| disconr [b, a])      [> exit
endproc (* remote *)

process connect[a,b] : noexit:=
  a!conreq; b!conind; a!conconf; stop
endproc (* connect *)

process disconl[a] : exit:=
  a!disind; exit  [] a!disreq; exit
endproc (* disconl *)

process disconr[a, b] : noexit:=
  a!disreq; b!disind; stop
endproc (* disconr *)

process datal[a] : noexit:=
  datreqs [a] ||| datinds [a]
endproc (* datal *)

process datreqs [a] : noexit:=
  a!datreq; datreqs[a]
endproc (* datreqs *)

process datinds [a] : noexit:=
  a!datind; datinds[a]
endproc (* datinds *)

process datar[a, b] : noexit:=
  a!datreq; b!datind; datar [a, b]
endproc (* datar *)
endspec (* simple *)
```

3 The Theory

We prove the equivalence of the service and the protocol by transforming the service to a protocol using correctness preserving transformations. The theory underlying our proof is not very complicated, and consists mainly of congruence laws and theorems. Each congruence law can be used as a transformation in two directions, in the same way as a pair of converse rewrite rules. A proof of equivalence is then conducted by rewriting one side of the equivalence through a sequence of rule applications, leading to the other side of the equivalence.

The first set of laws to consider come from the LOTOS standard[ISO88]. In particular we use most of the congruence laws in B2.2.f, e.g.

```
hide s1 in p1[s1] ||| hide s2 in p2[s2]
                        ==
hide s1, s2 in (p1[s1] ||| p2[s2])
```

We call the transformations that correspond to these laws *hide pushers*. Another law is B2.2.h (instantiation), which allows the substitution of a process instantiation by its body and vice-versa, although we call these *unfolding* and *folding* respectively.

Useful for the analysis of possible behaviour are *expansion theorems*, which derive from a behaviour expression its action prefix normal form. By repeated expansion, a behaviour can be transformed into a form that consists of only action prefixes, choices, and process instantiations. This is called a fully expanded behaviour. Note that this transformation destroys all structure of a specification.

Besides the equivalences and congruences in the LOTOS standard, we have used a few others in our proof. The minor ones are explained in the text. The more fundamental ones follow here.

The transformation that is perhaps the most central to our derivation is *decomposition of functionality* [Lan90], also known as bipartition or splitting of functionality. This transformation splits a process into two processes, communicating over a gate, in such a way that the processes only have this communication gate in common. This transformation is only defined on fully expanded behaviours. As discussed elsewhere, this is a disadvantage if one attempts to apply this transformation in a naive way. However, in our derivation we circumvent this disadvantage.

Another important group of congruences is formed by the *regrouping of parallel processes transformations* (RPPT for short)[Bol90]. These can be thought of as generalized associativity and commutativity laws. An example is the following.

```
(c[a] ||| c[b]) |[a,b]| (r[a,s] |[s]| r[b,s])
                        ==
(c[a] |[a]| r[a,s]) |[s]| (c[b] |[b]| r[b,s])
```

The RPPT preserve strong bisimulation congruence. The decomposition of functionality preserves weak bisimulation equivalence. In [vS89, VSvSB90] similar equivalences are proposed and applied.

4 The Tools

A number of tools can or have been used in conducting the proof described in this paper. An overview of the current state of the art in tools is in [vE91]. The current situation is that not every transformation or equivalence proof is fully automated, or for full LOTOS. It is probably unavoidable that in research of this nature the development of tools, theory and their applications progresses hand in hand. Below we mention the available relevant tools, categorised according to the portion of theory they implement. Most tools support theory from more than one category though.

Tools embodying the congruence laws in the LOTOS standard are in two categories: manual single step transformation, such as [vE89, vE90, L+90], and automatic equivalence checkers, such as AUTO[MV90].

Examples of more expansion oriented tools are Smile [vEE91], ISLA [LOBF88] and LOLA [QPF89]. These are typically used to analyse a behaviour in a step by step operational way. Smile was used in this experiment.

Of the last two functions from the previous section (splitting and regrouping) prototype implementations have been made in the ESPRIT Lotosphere project (2304), based on the structure editors discussed in [vE89]. The functions are applied by selecting, in the editor, an expression, supplying the additional information in a form, and executing a command. These prototypes have been used. As a result of this experiment, these tools are now being improved.

5 The Derivation

In essence the transformation starts with a splitting of each remote constraint separately. After a sequence of relabellings and hide pushings, the inner parallel expressions are regrouped, leading to the desired end structure of a process for each side.

5.1 Splitting the Remote Constraints

The process `remote` consists of 5 remote constraints. Each of these constraints is split separately. An example of the splitting of such a component is:

```
process datar[a, b] : noexit:=
   a!datreq; b!datind; datar[a, b]
endproc (* datar *)
```

which becomes according to [Lan90]:

```
process datar[a, b] : noexit:=
  hide synca, syncb in
     datara[a, synca, syncb] |[synca, syncb]| datarb[b, synca, syncb]
endproc (* datar *)
```

```
process datara[a, synca, syncb] : noexit:=
  a!datreq; synca; syncb; datara[a, synca, syncb]
endproc (* datara *)

process datarb[b, synca, syncb] : noexit:=
  synca; b!datind; syncb; datarb[b, synca, syncb]
endproc (* datarb *)
```

The transformation introduces two synchronisation messages, one for the data transfer (synca), and one for the flow control (syncb) [1]. After applying this transformation to each remote constraint, and pushing up the hide constructs, the process remote changes to the following.

```
process remote[a, b] : exit:=
  hide  s1, s2, s3, s4, s5, s6, s7, s8 in
   ( ( (connecta[a, s1, s2] |[s1, s2]| connectb[b, s1, s2]) |||
       (datara[a, s3, s4] |[s3, s4]| datarb[b, s3, s4]) |||
       (datara[b, s5, s6] |[s5, s6]| datarb[a, s5, s6]) |||
       (discona[a, s7] |[s7]| disconb[b, s7]) |||
       (discona[b, s8] |[s8]| disconb[a, s8])
     ) [> exit
   )
endproc (* remote *)
```

Pushing up the hide yet further now yields:

```
process connection[a, b] : exit:=
  hide  s1, s2, s3, s4, s5, s6, s7, s8 in
    (calling[a] ||| called[b])|[a, b]|
         remote[a, s1, s2, s3, s4, s5, s6, s7, s8, b]
endproc (* connection *)

process remote[a, s1, s2, s3, s4, s5, s6, s7, s8, b] : exit:=
   ( (connecta[a, s1, s2] |[s1, s2]| connectb[b, s1, s2]) |||
     (datara[a, s3, s4] |[s3, s4]| datarb[b, s3, s4]) |||
     (datara[b, s5, s6] |[s5, s6]| datarb[a, s5, s6]) |||
     (discona[a, s7] |[s7]| disconb[b, s7]) |||
     (discona[b, s8] |[s8]| disconb[a, s8])
   ) [> exit
endproc (* remote *)
```

---

[1] It is possible to define a protocol in which these two functions are performed by a single message (synca), but it implements a two slot buffer service instead of a one slot buffer service.

5.2 Regrouping the Remote Constraints

The body of the process remote now has to be regrouped according to a RPPT. After that and the folding of its two components into remotea and remoteb it becomes:

```
process remote[a, s1, s2, s3, s4, s5, s6, s7, s8, b] : exit:=
  (remotea[a, s1, s2, s3, s4, s5, s6, s7, s8]
        |[s1, s2, s3, s4, s5, s6, s7, s8]|
   remoteb[ s1, s2, s3, s4, s5, s6, s7, s8, b])[> exit
endproc (* remote *)

process remotea[a, s1, s2, s3, s4, s5, s6, s7, s8] : noexit:=
  connecta[a, s1, s2] ||| datara[a, s3, s4] |||
  datarb[a, s5, s6]      ||| discona[a, s7]      ||| disconb[a, s8]
endproc (* remotea *)

process remoteb[ s1, s2, s3, s4, s5, s6, s7, s8, b] : noexit:=
  connectb[b, s1, s2] ||| datarb[b, s3, s4] |||
  datara[b, s5, s6]      ||| disconb[b, s7]      ||| discona[b, s8]
endproc (* remoteb *)
```

The next step is rather small, the [> exit in remote still works globally, and should be distributed. This is possible because the congruence

```
(A |[..]| B) [>exit   ==  (A [>exit |[..]| B [>exit)
```

holds if A and B have functionality noexit. The result is then:

```
process remote[a, s1, s2, s3, s4, s5, s6, s7, s8, b] : exit:=
  remotea[a, s1, s2, s3, s4, s5, s6, s7, s8] [> exit
      |[s1, s2, s3, s4, s5, s6, s7, s8]|
  remoteb[s1, s2, s3, s4, s5, s6, s7, s8, b][> exit
endproc (* remote *)
```

After this, remote can be unfolded in the top level behaviour.

5.3 Regrouping on the Top Level

On the top level we have now a composition of 4 processes:

```
process connection[a, b] : exit:=
    hide  s1, s2, s3, s4, s5, s6, s7, s8 in
              (calling[a] ||| called[b])
                    |[a, b]|
```

```
( (remotea[a, s1, s2, s3, s4, s5, s6, s7, s8] [> exit )
       |[s1, s2, s3, s4, s5, s6, s7, s8]|
   (remoteb[s1, s2, s3, s4, s5, s6, s7, s8, b] [> exit ) )
endproc (* connection *)
```

which can be regrouped into:

```
process connection[a, b] : exit:=
  hide  s1, s2, s3, s4, s5, s6, s7, s8 in
  (calling[a] |[a]| (remotea[a, s1, s2, s3, s4, s5, s6, s7, s8] [> exit ))
            |[s1, s2, s3, s4, s5, s6, s7, s8]|
  (called[b]  |[b]| (remoteb[s1, s2, s3, s4, s5, s6, s7, s8, b] [> exit ))
endproc (* connection *)
```

So that the final specification becomes:

```
specification simple[a, b] : exit

type sp is
sorts sp
opns conreq, conind, conconf, datreq, datind, disreq, disind : -> sp
endtype (* sp *)

behaviour
connection [a, b]
where
  process connection[a, b] : exit:=
    hide  s1, s2, s3, s4, s5, s6, s7, s8 in
    (calling[a] |[a]| (remotea[a, s1, s2, s3, s4, s5, s6, s7, s8] [> exit ))
    |[s1, s2, s3, s4, s5, s6, s7, s8]|
    called[b] |[b]| (remoteb[s1, s2, s3, s4, s5, s6, s7, s8, b] [> exit )
  endproc (* connection *)

  process calling[a] : exit:=
    a!conreq; (a!conconf; datal [a] [> discon1 [a])
  endproc (* calling *)

  process called[b] : exit:=
    b!conind; (datal [b] [> discon1 [b])
  endproc (* called *)

  process remotea[a, s1, s2, s3, s4, s5, s6, s7, s8] : noexit:=
    connecta[a, s1, s2] ||| datara[a, s3, s4] |||
    datarb[a, s5, s6]   ||| discona[a, s7]    ||| disconb [a, s8]
  endproc (* remotea *)
```

```
process remoteb[s1, s2, s3, s4, s5, s6, s7, s8, b] : noexit:=
  connectb[b, s1, s2] ||| datarb[b, s3, s4] |||
  datara[b, s5, s6]       ||| disconb[b, s7]      ||| discona[b, s8]
endproc (* remoteb *)

process connecta[a, synca, syncb] : noexit:=
  a!conreq; synca; syncb; a!conconf; synca; stop
endproc (* connecta *)

process connectb[b, synca, syncb] : noexit:=
  synca; b!conind; syncb; synca; stop
endproc (* connectb *)

process disconl[a] : exit:=
  a!disind; exit  [] a!disreq; exit
endproc (* disconl *)

process discona[a, synca] : noexit:=
  a!disreq; synca; stop
endproc (* discona *)

process disconb[b, synca] : noexit:=
  synca; b!disind; stop
endproc (* disconb *)

process datal[a] : noexit:=
  datreqs [a] ||| datinds [a]
endproc (* datal *)

process datreqs [a] : noexit:=
  a!datreq; datreqs[a]
endproc (* datreqs *)

process datinds [a] : noexit:=
  a!datind; datinds[a]
endproc (* datinds *)

process datara[a, synca, syncb] : noexit:=
  a!datreq; synca; syncb; datara[a, synca, syncb]
endproc (* datara *)

process datarb[b, synca, syncb] : noexit:=
  synca; b!datind; syncb; datarb[b, synca, syncb]
endproc (* datarb *)
endspec (* simple *)
```

This specification then constitutes a (synchronous) protocol implementing our service. These are equivalent by construction. Their equivalence has also been proved through the use of AUTO[MV90].

5.4 Mapping to PDUs

The synthesis of the 'protocol' implied the introduction of several gates, through which the entities communicate. Each gate represents one distinct message. This could obviously be transformed into one gate with several messages. These messages can then be seen as corresponding to PDUs. The following table gives the mapping of these to their more traditional names.

gate	PDU	direction
s1	ConReq	a→b
s2	ConConf	b→a
s3	Data	a→b
s4	Ack	a→b
s5	Data	b→a
s6	Ack	b→a
s7	Dis	a→b
s8	Dis	b→a

5.5 What is the Protocol Entity?

The top level structure of the final specification consists of two behaviour expressions that have synchronous communication over the 's' gates and do not communicate over both a and b. These expressions, one of which is

```
(calling [a] |[a]|
    (remotea [a, s1, s2, s3, s4, s5, s6, s7, s8] [> exit ))
```

can be used as the protocol entities. Although correct, the result is not optimal in some sense. This is because they allow more behaviour than is possible in synchronisation with their peer entity. For example, an unfolding of the simulation tree of the expression above shows that, in its initial state, it will allow the events s5 and s8 to happen, which the other side will never do. The reduction we seek may serve two purposes: to serve as the basis for the derivation of tests of isolated protocol entities, and to reduce the size of a state machine implementation.

An approach to restrict the behaviour is to take the constraints posed by the other side into consideration. The idea is that the calling side should only do whatever the called side allows it to do (and vice versa). From the theoretical side one would like to use a notion of 'equivalence in context' to reduce the protocol entity. From an architectural viewpoint one would like to derive explicitly the local constraints that apply on the synchronisation messages.

In any case, these protocol entities are written in a constraint-oriented style, and further transformational design is desirable. Possibilities for this include other applications of the splitting transformation, e.g. to divide the protocol entity in a sender and a receiver component, and transformations to a state machine.

6   Discussion and Future Directions

An alternative to our approach is to expand the original service into an extended state machine, and apply the splitting transformation directly on that. This leads to a significantly larger number of message exchanges ('PDUs'). For example, in a certain state of the data phase of the service, a data request service primitive is possible on both sides. Schematically this looks like

   a; stop ||| b; stop

which expands to

   a; b; stop [] b; a; stop

and contains a choice between events on distributed gates. The splitting transformation then introduces polling exchanges to resolve this distributed choice. The distributed choice, however, is an artifact of the expansion, which is based on interleaving semantics. In our approach we do not expand, and the distributed choice does not appear. As another way of escaping the artifacts of interleaving semantics, event structure based approaches [Lan91] seem promising.

In our example the set of PDUs is *not* a design decision, they fall out rather naturally given the remote constraints. It is interesting to note that this set contains more or less the same number of PDUs as a manual design for this service.

Our protocol synthesis has identified PDUs and their relation with the primitives of the service implemented. The PDUs are exchanged using synchronous communication. The extension of this method to the use of an asynchronous error free underlying service can be easily performed using algorithm 4 of [Lan90]. Lack of tools for this transformation has prevented us from doing this experiment. It appears possible to extend the algorithms to support unreliable underlying services.

In our example we have abstracted from the exchange of data values. There does not appear to be a fundamental theoretical problem in doing our derivation on a service with data exchange. The equivalences used are either applicable to full LOTOS or can be extended to full LOTOS. However, the development of this theory and the supporting tools still needs to be done. Also feasible appears to be the adaptation of transformations in order to handle services with an arbitrary number of access points and connection endpoints. These are usually distinguished by parameters on a single gate, rather than by different gates.

7 Conclusion

In this paper we have presented a new transformation method for the derivation, or synthesis, of a correct protocol from a service specification. The essence of this method is to exploit the structure of the service specification by splitting each remote constraint separately, and then regroup processes. As a result our method leads to fewer PDU types than direct application of a splitting transformation, and it preserves most of the structure of the service specification. Therefore it can be applied in earlier steps of a design process. We have indicated to which extent existing tool functions and theory can be employed and what improvements are possible.

Acknowledgements

The equivalence proof using AUTO was conducted by Eric Madelaine and Jean-Bernard Saint of INRIA Sophia-Antipolis. The tool functions for the splitting and regrouping transformations were implemented by Elisabetta Zuppa and Cinzia Bernardeschi of CNUCE. Useful comments on drafts of this paper were given by Henk Eertink, Rom Langerak, Pippo Scollo, and Marten van Sinderen.

References

[Bol90] T. Bolognesi. A graphical composition theorem for networks of LOTOS processes. In *Proceedings of ICDCS-10, Tenth International Conference on Distributed Computing Systems*. IEEE Computer Society Press, 1990.

[ISO88] ISO. IS 8807 information processing systems - Open Systems Interconnection - the definition of the specification language LOTOS, 1988.

[KvBK89] F. Khendek, G. von Bochmann, and C. Kant. New results on deriving protocl specifications from service specifications. In *Proceedings SIGCOMM 89 Communication Architectures and Protocols*, volume 19, pages 136–145, 1989.

[L+90] G. León et al. ASDE: Design of a transformational environment for LOTOS. In S. T. Vuong, editor, *Formal Description Techniques, II - Proceedings of the FORTE 89 Conference*, pages 501–515, Amsterdam, 1990. North-Holland.

[Lan90] R. Langerak. Decomposition of functionality: a correctness-preserving LOTOS transformation. In L. Logrippo, R. L. Probert, and H. Ural, editors, *Proceedings of the tenth international conference on protocol specification, testing and verification*, pages 229–243, Amsterdam, 1990. North-Holland.

[Lan91] R. Langerak. Event structures for design and transformation in LOTOS. Technical Report INF-91-45 TIOS 91-14, University of Twente, Enschede Netherlands, 1991. accepted for FORTE 91.

[LOBF88] L. Logrippo, A. Obaid, J. P. Briand, and M. C. Fehri. An interpreter for LOTOS, a specification language for distributed systems. *Software - Practice and Experience*, 18(4):365–385, April 1988.

[MV90] E. Madelaine and D. Vergamini. AUTO: A verification tool for distributed systems using reduction of finite automata networks. In S. T. Vuong, editor, *Formal Description Techniques, II - Proceedings of the FORTE 89 Conference*, pages 61–66, Amsterdam, 1990. North-Holland.

[Par89] Joachim Parrow. Submodule construction as equation solving in CCS. *Theoretical Computer Science*, 68:175–202, 1989.

[PV90] L. F. Pires and C. A. Vissers. Overview of the LotosPhere design methodology. In Commission of the E.C. DG XIII, editor, *ESPRIT Conference 1990*, pages 371–387, Dordrecht, 1990. Kluwer Academic Publishers.

[QPF89] J. Quemada, S. Pavon, and A. Fernandez. Transforming LOTOS specifications with LOLA - the parameterised expansion. In K. J. Turner, editor, *Formal Description Techniques - Proceedings of the FORTE 88 Conference*, pages 45–54, Amsterdam, 1989. North-Holland.

[vE89] Peter van Eijk. LOTOS tools based on the cornell synthesizer generator. In H. Brinksma, G. Scollo, and C. A. Vissers, editors, *Proceedings of the ninth international symposium on protocol specification, testing and verification*, Amsterdam, 1989. North-Holland.

[vE90] Peter van Eijk. Tools for LOTOS specification style transformation. In S. T. Vuong, editor, *Formal Description Techniques, II - Proceedings of the FORTE 89 Conference*, pages 43–52, Amsterdam, 1990. North-Holland.

[vE91] Peter van Eijk. Tools for LOTOS, a Lotosphere overview. Technical Report INF-91-25, TIOS-91-7, University of Twente, Enschede Netherlands, 1991. Submitted to Computer Networks and ISDN Systems.

[vEE91] Peter van Eijk and Henk Eertink. Design of the LotosPhere symbolic LOTOS simulator. In J. Quemada, J. Mañas, and E. Vazquez, editors, *Formal Description Techniques, III - Proceedings of the FORTE 90 Conference*, Amsterdam, 1991. North-Holland.

[vEVD89] P.H.J. van Eijk, C. A. Vissers, and M. Diaz, editors. *The Formal Description Technique LOTOS - results of the ESPRIT/SEDOS project*. North-Holland, Amsterdam, 1989.

[vS89] M. van Sinderen. A verification exercise related to specification styles in LOTOS. Technical Report INF-89-18, University of Twente, Enschede Netherlands, 1989.

[vS90]   M. van Sinderen. Generic service and protocol structures. Technical Report INF-90-61, University of Twente, Enschede Netherlands, 1990. Submitted to Computer Networks and ISDN Systems.

[vSF91] M. van Sinderen and Luís Ferreira Pires. FDT-based protocol design. In *Computer Networks 1991*, Wrocław, Poland, 1991.

[VSvSB90] C. A. Vissers, G. Scollo, M. van Sinderen, and H. Brinksma. Specification styles in distributed systems design and verification. Technical Report INF-90-05, University of Twente, Enschede Netherlands, 1990. to appear in Theoret. Comput. Sci. special issue dedicated to Tapsoft 89.

Specification of a Distributed Coordination Function in LOTOS

Ing Widya[a], Franck Sadoun[b] and Gert-Jan van der Heijden[c]

[a]Tele-Informatics Group, University of Twente, PO Box 217, 7500 AE Enschede, The Netherlands

[b]SYSECA Logiciel, 315 St. Cloud Cedex, France

[c]Océ Nederland B.V., P.O.Box 101, 5900 MA Venlo, The Netherlands

Abstract

This paper presents the application of a design method on the specification of a realistic OSI protocol in LOTOS, and reports on some experiences acquired during this specification. The protocol selected is a subset of ISO Transaction Processing protocol. This paper emphasizes on the specification rationale of the protocol and in particular that of the Multiple Association Coordination Function. This function is suitable for a design exercise due to its responsibility to coordinate distributedly the interworking of the encapsulating protocol entity with the other entities which are involved in a transaction. The design process described in this paper starts with a non-formalized protocol description and yields a formalized specification which incorporates some implementation aspects. This will enable further elaboration of the specification towards an implementation. The work presented here is accomplished within a project that aimed at the development of a LOTOS based design method which satisfy industrial needs. In this perspective, this work may be regarded as an industrial assessment of that part of the design method which concerns with the formal specification of a non-formalized description.

1 Introduction

ESPRIT II project 2304 (LotoSphere) [1] is a project that develops an integrated design method for distributed systems, and in particular for communication protocols. The method is based on the formal description technique LOTOS [2] and must satisfy industrial needs, such as design guidance, correctness preserving transformation techniques and tools, predefined constructs and structures, and the availability of well documented and easy to use tools. Some tasks within the project have to assess the industrial applicability of the design method, i.e. the language, tools and theories, see e.g. [3]. One of the tasks specifies and implements some OSI application layer protocols in accordance with the method. This task has decided to specify in LOTOS and implement in ISO Design

Environment (ISODE) [4] the Commitment Concurrency and Recovery (CCR) [5], the Association Control Service Element (ACSE) [6], and Transaction Processing (TP) [7] protocols. Due to the complexity of TP the specification-implementation trajectory of TP will only yield an implementation oriented specification in LOTOS, i.e. a LOTOS specification which in a design sense is close to an implementation. This paper deals with TP specification.

The interoperability aspect of a distributed transaction system, e.g. a travel agency reservation system, is typically complex. This is due to distributed coordination problems which arise when transactions execute in a concurrent and failure sensitive environment. Although ISO [8, 9] has restricted its transaction model to self-contained transactions with its (remotely) distributed participants being associated in tree structured relationships, the protocol remains being complex. The TP protocol layer must manage the multiparty relationship, coordinate the interworking between the distributed entities, and map the multiparty relationship onto several bipartite relations. This mapping is implied by the bipartite, i.e. end-to-end, relationships of entities in the underlying service provider. These functionalities are provided locally by an OSI Application Layer protocol component, the so-called Multiple Association Coordination Function (MACF) [10]. Specification of the TP protocol, and particularly the TP-MACF, is a suitable design example to assess the design method because of the distributed nature of TP, which usually involves several interworking participants.

This paper presents the specification of TP protocol in LOTOS, particularly the MACF component, and emphasizes on the specification rationale. It also reports on some of the experiences gained during the specification. This paper is not concerned with the design of a TP service or the design of a TP protocol. It is only concerned with the specification of a subset of ISO - Transaction Processing protocol. The ISO protocol version used for deriving the LOTOS specification is the (first) Draft International Standard (DIS) [7]. Though ISO-TP is still under development and has thus not yet reached its stable International Standard status, this DIS version has reached a form which is acceptable to start the design exercise with.

In the next section, some relevant characteristics of transaction processing are described. Section 3 gives a brief overview of the design method. Section 4 outlines the applied design approach and section 5 discusses the particular design objectives and the functionalities selected to be specified. In section 6 the protocol architecture is discussed. In the section thereafter some relevant LOTOS structures of TP-MACF are described. These structures reflect the design decisions and illustrate the possibility to map directly informal requirements onto (formal) LOTOS-constructs, as is advocated in the design method.

2 Transaction Processing

This section introduces application transactions and the ISO Transaction Processing in brief. It is not meant as a complete introduction to Transaction Processing, it merely describes matters which are relevant for the specification being elaborated in the next sections.

A *transaction* may be defined as a set of interrelated, distributed, and on-line operations that fulfils certain properties, see e.g. [11]. The main characterizing property is the all or nothing effect of the distributed operations of a transaction, called *atomicity*. Other properties are for example the consistency of the operations and the non-interfering property of concurrent transactions, i.e. the isolation of partial results.

Application transactions are for instance travel agent transactions, banking transactions, and transactions in design systems. The following example of a travel agent transaction shows the distributed nature of a transaction.

A client of a travel agency may wish to book a holiday. This client requires a return flight from A to C, which includes an intercontinental flight from A to B and a domestic flight from B to C. It is not necessary, however, to fly with the same company for both flights. The client needs further a car and hotel accommodation. These booking operations typically require an on-line multiparty communication between the travel agency, the hotel-, car lease-, and plane reservation systems. If one of the operations involved can not be satisfied, the client may wish to cancel all reservations (Atomicity). It is furthermore unacceptable for the travel agent to make a mistake, i.e. to work inconsistently, or that another transaction interferes by reserving the same seat.

ISO-TP concerns with the *interoperability* of distributed processing of application transactions. It provides the users communication and coordination facilities which can be used to enforce the required transaction properties. Coordinating services for concurrency, e.g. commitment and rollback service elements, play a major role in TP.

As shown in the previous example, the distributed operations of a transaction are usually clustered. In practice, each cluster forms a particular usage (i.e. an *invocation*) of an application subsystem. These subsystems may be distributed over several system sites. In ISO-TP, clusters are interrelated in a *tree structure*. Thus, a tree models the multiparty relationship between the local activities of the TP service users involved in a transaction. The user who initiates the transaction is called the *root*. During processing of a transaction a user may expand the transaction tree dynamically by establishing new transaction branches. This user becomes the superior and the remote users become subordinates. Users who do not have subordinates are *leafs*. The other users, who have a superior and at least one subordinate, are called the *intermediates*.

ISO-TP makes also use of the concept: dialogues. A *dialogue* expresses the relationship between two TP service users in the same way as an application association expresses the relationship between two application protocol entities. A dialogue is supported by an application association. This association is hidden from TP service users. Similar to transaction branches, dialogues can only be structured as trees.

In general, a transaction tree and a dialogue tree do not coincide. A transaction tree may be viewed as the support for the interworking of the distributed activity between users who are related in a dialogue tree. A dialogue tree may support several disjoint transaction trees at a time. Moreover, dialogues and dialogue-trees may persist after the termination of the supported transactions. This allows sequences of transactions being executed over the same dialogue trees.

To support the transaction processing model described above, ISO-TP provides the following services:

- dialogue and transaction control facilities.
- error and calamity reporting and handling facilities.
- facilities to invoke other OSI application services.
- facilities to synchronize application activities.

TP functionalities are classified in the following functional units (FUs):
Kernel, Commit, Handshake, Shared Control, Polarized Control, and Unchained FU.
The Kernel FU is mandatory. It contains service elements related to dialogue control, data transfer, and error reporting. The Commit FU contains facilities for the interchange of concurrency control primitives. If this functional unit is not selected, TP loses its characterizing feature. In this case, the users by themselves have to take care for commitment, rollback and recovery. Handshake FU is optional. It allows pairs of users to synchronize their processing activities. Shared and Polarized Control FUs are mutual exclusive. If Shared Control is selected, both users have control over the dialogue and both may issue request primitives, which are subjected to the normal constraints. In case of Polarized Control being selected, only one user has full control over the dialogue at a time. If Unchained FU is *not* selected, a transaction starts automatically when a dialogue is established and a new transaction starts immediately after termination of the previous transaction. If this functional unit is selected, a TP service user may exclude (or include) subordinate users from (or in) a transaction.

It was mentioned earlier that TP protocol layer has the responsibility to map the tree structured users relationship onto a set of bipartite associations. Therefore, it must posses the coordinating function MACF. In addition, the protocol includes the following functions:

- application association and dialogue management and control,
- dialogue and transaction recovery, and
- optionally, some auxiliary functions for efficiency purposes.

3 The applied design method

The applied design method [12] is basically a top-down method. In this method, a design process typically consists of several design steps. Each step refines the design created during a previous step by taking appropriate design decisions which are in accordance with an overall design objective. The method guides the designers in making the appropriate decisions by means of some design quality criteria, e.g. propriety, parsimony, orthogonality and open-endedness criteria [13, 14]. The practical necessity of these intermediate steps is usually imposed by the complexity of the design. The method also supports an iterative design approach. This gives the designers the opportunity to iterate, i.e. improve or adapt, their design decisions by evaluating the achieved properties and the quality of their designs.

The design method distinguishes three consecutive phases in a design trajectory, i.e. the architectural, the implementation and the realization phases.

In the *architectural phase*, the requirements on properties of the system to be designed are captured. These requirements comprises user requirements. They may further be enriched or be constrained by other types of requirements, for instance some project constraints. The composition of all proper requirements yields an architectural specification, also called an architecture. This specification shows *what* the system is able to do for the users and expresses the constraints on properties of the system. Ideally, designers should not be burdened by realizability aspects in the architectural phase, especially when designing complex systems. In practice, however, knowledge about realization oriented predefined constructs and structures helps designers in minimizing the number of the design iterations. In the *realization* phase, the intermediate design will be mapped onto physical resources and so the realization will emerge. The *implementation phase* is needed to bridge the gap between the architectural and the realization phase.

Unfortunately, boundaries between these design phases are usually vague. It is often not clear when an architectural phase ends and the implementation phase begins.

The applied design method supports further a *cyclic* design approach, meaning that a design may be processed through several design cycles. Designers may start with a small subset of the ultimately required functionality of the system to be designed. In this way, designers are able to acquire the necessary experiences and insights on the design as well as on the design method and tools. After completing or during a particular cycle the designers may concurrently start another cycle by incorporating more functionality into the design. A necessary condition for the success of this approach is to keep the designs pertaining to a particular cycle open-ended, i.e. obeying the open-ended principle during designs of each cycle. This approach enables gradual growth of the system complexity, gives a better control on the design process, and yields high quality designs, especially in the case of large complex systems.

4 Technical Approach

In the beginning of the project, it was planned to take an existing TP protocol specification in LOTOS as a starting point of the specification-implementation trajectory. However, after an assessment of that specification it was decided to start the design process with a fresh design cycle. This was due to the fact that the existing LOTOS specification was based on an earlier version of the ISO protocol standard, i.e. the *second Draft Proposal* standard [15]. In the view of the design method, the existing specification contains some architectural deficiency. For example, the lack of an interface to the application service elements ACSE and CCR. This will confuse the evaluation or validation of specification refinements with respect to the non-formalized protocol procedures described in the TP standard. It will also prevent a modular design approach, where specifications of components will be aggregated into a more complex one. The architecture of the protocol described in the (first) DIS version [7, 8, 9] is on the other hand a considerable improvement of the previous one. This protocol version is therefore more suitable to use.

In accordance with the design method, the first design cycle specifies a subset of ISO TP functionality. This subset includes some essential characteristics of a transaction processing system. The details will be discussed in the next section. The selected subset fulfils the project constraint which requires a sufficiently complex system to get a genuine design exercise. But, to meet the project limitation on resources, the complexity of the design must be manageable. A system constraint which enables a modular design approach, where groups of designers may work independently on the components of TP, is the definition of an explicit interface to ACSE and CCR protocols. These constraints form an input to the requirement capturing phase of the chosen design trajectory.

Moreover, the specification elaborated here applies the concepts and structures of the ISO Application Layer Structure [10]. Its architectural structure resembles the structure of the non-formalized protocol description in the standard. This approach yields a LOTOS specification which architecture is well founded and which is easier to produce.

The specification presented in this paper is expressed in the so-called *resource-constraint oriented* style [16]. This style reflects functional resources at the top level and expresses mechanisms (or constraints on properties) at the detailed level of the hierarchical specification. This style perfectly suits the design approach which starts with a non-formalized protocol description, that expresses the protocol components and their interactions. In this style, some implementation issues may be incorporated. The specification presented here should be viewed as an intermediated product of the implementation phase, thus a product beyond the architectural phase.

5 Selection of the functionalities and possible design cycles

The first design cycle yields a simplified transaction processing protocol which only supports serial and concurrent but non-interfering transactions in an error free environment. Efficiency aspects in TP protocol are omitted in this cycle. Only some of the characterizing elements of transaction processing are incorporated in the specification.

The selected functional units are the Kernel, Shared Control and the Commit FUs. Not selected are the Handshake and Unchained Transaction FUs. Not all service elements and options of the selected functional units are specified. The rollback and recovery facilities are excluded for simplicity of the first design cycle. Consequently, the error- and calamity reporting services are excluded, because collisions of the corresponding service primitives may initiate rollback services. Reusability of dialogues and application associations are not incorporated either. Dialogues must therefore be released by the TP service user at termination of each transaction. The protocol machine will then release the corresponding application association. As a result of the previous choices, transaction and dialogue trees coincide. This simplifies the specification. Other protocol efficiency aspects such as the concatenations of PDUs are omitted in the design.

A possible extension of functionality in a next design cycle is the inclusion of facilities to support concurrent transactions in an error-free communication system. Recovery or rollback facilities may then be included in the specification. Reusability of dialogues and application associations could also be considered in the next design cycle.

6 TP Protocol Architecture

In this section, it will be shown that by applying some generic architectural structures the skeleton architecture of the protocol, i.e. the top level description of the architectural specification, can be derived without the need to know the details of the non-formalized specification. During construction of this skeleton architecture, some design quality criteria, e.g. open-endedness, orthogonality and parsimony, have to be taken into account. A further elaboration of the chosen structures yields a well structured protocol specification.

It was mentioned earlier that the specification described in this paper conforms with the ISO Application Layer Structure. The protocol layer is decomposed further into a TP specific and a Common Application (CA) layer, see also [18]. The latter is defined on top of the presentation service and contains the ACSE and CCR protocols. Its service provider supports therefore end-to-end relationships over OSI with concurrency control facilities. Due to this decomposition, the TP specific protocol layer is "thinner" and thus more easy to specify. The decomposed structure has better testing facilities and suits a modular design approach because the ACSE and CCR services have been made more explicit. The architectural details of the CA service and protocol could be found in [18] and will not be described here.

A disadvantage of the decomposition described previously is the division of certain protocol components, i.e. the single association objects, in a part which resides in a CA entity and the rest in the associated TP specific entity. Protocol efficiency aspects like the concatenations of TP-APDUs are also hard to specify in LOTOS when using this layered architecture. However, if these aspects are required, it is always possible to merge a CA entity into the TP entity, while retaining their main structures, in a new design cycle.

For the sake of convenience the TP specific protocol layer and entities are called the TP protocol layer and entities, respectively, in the sequel.

6.1 Gates and event structures of the protocol entity

For some reasons, probably the property of TP service primitives which can be classified into primitives that deals with single dialogues or transaction branches (e.g. data transfer primitives) and primitives that deal with multiple dialogues or transaction branches (e.g. commitment primitives), the existing protocol specification in LOTOS mentioned in section 4, uses two external gates at the TP service boundary. The architecture described here uses *one* gate at this boundary. The reason for this is that TP service users should not be burdened by details concerning gates selection, the protocol machine must resolve these issues.

Events at the service gate, called the `tp` gate, have the following structure.

```
tp   tpsap   tpcei   branchid   TP-service-primitive
```

The variable `tpsap`, which stands for Transaction Processing Service Access Point, associates to one Application Entity in the restricted model described here. The variable `tpcei` is used for the identification of one Application Entity Invocation, i.e. a particular usage of the entity. The `branchid` variable has been introduced to distinguish between the transaction branches (i.e. dialogues in this model).

An analysis on the interactions between (the components of) the TP and the corresponding CA entity, and the LOTOS feature which requires interoperating processes to synchronize on events, yields the definition of a pair of gates at the CA service. These gates are called `ca` and `p`. The primitives of ACSE and CCR synchronize at gate `ca` and primitives of the presentation service which are used by TP entities synchronize at `p`. The fact that ACSE and CCR primitives are disjoint allows a shared use of gate `ca`. Events at gate `ca` have the following structure:

```
ca   casap   cacei   CA-service-primitive
```

The `casap` variable identifies the CA Service Access Point. The CA Connection Endpoint Identifier `cacei` associates to a CA association. The event-structure at the presentation-level is similar to the previous structure, thus having the following structure.

```
p   psap   pcei   P-service-primitive
```

6.2 The general part of the TP protocol behaviour

The following specification of TP protocol layer comprises commonly used LOTOS structures, see e.g. [17, 18]. In the specification, some implementation issues are incorporated, e.g. the number of available entity invocations. For simplicity of the following specification, a TP entity and the corresponding CA entities have the same address values. Otherwise, a table containing tuples of TP and CA addresses must be maintained. For clarity, only relevant parts of specifications are depicted in the following.

```
process TP_protocol[tp](ads:SetOfAdr): noexit :=
hide ca,p in
  (TP_P_layer[tp,ca,p](ads) |[ca,p]| CA_Service[ca,p](ads))
where

process TP_P_layer[tp,ca,p](ads:SetOfAdr): noexit :=
  choice ad:Adr [] [ad IsIn ads] -> ( TP_P_Entity[tp,ca,p](ad)
                                      |||
                                      TP_P_layer[tp,ca,p](Remove(ad,ads))
                                    )
endproc (* TP_P_layer *)
```

```
process TP_P_Entity[tp,ca,p](ad:Adr): noexit :=
let freeinvocs:SetOfInvocs = Makeset(...identifications...) in
TP_PE_invocations[tp,ca,p](ad,freeinvocs)
where
process TP_PE_invocations [tp,ca,p](ad:Adr,freeinvocs:SetOfInvocs):
                                                          noexit :=
    choice invoc:InvocId [] [(invoc IsIn freeinvocs)] -> i;
       ( TP_PE_invocation [tp,ca,p] (ad,invoc)
         |||
         TP_PE_invocations [tp,ca,p] (ad,Remove(invoc,freeinvocs))
       )
endproc

process TP_PE_invocation[tp,ca,p](ad: Adr,invoc:InvocId):noexit :=
let freebranches:SetOfBr = Makeset( ...identifications...) in
    TP_Node [tp,ca,p] (ad,invoc,freebranches)
    >>
    TP_PE_invocation [tp,ca,p] (ad,invoc)
endproc

endproc
```

A TP_Node is a TP protocol entity invocation and is either a root or a leaf (/intermediate) node. It contains a set of Single Association Objects (TP_SAOs) and a coordinating component MACF (i.e. the process MACFRoot or MACFLeafOrIntermediate). A single association object represents the local part of a transaction branch, including the local parts of the supporting dialogues and application association. A TP_SAO contains a TP application service element (TP-ASE), a user definable service element (U-ASE), and possibly some other application service elements. The ACSE and CCR service elements, which usually belong to a single association object, are defined in the CA layer. The interactions between MACF and TP_SAOs take place at the gates nn and uu. These gates are hidden from the environment because the interactions are internal to the protocol machine. The nn gate is used for interactions concerning TP-ASE related primitives. The uu gate is used for interactions concerning U-ASE primitives. The definition of two separate gates, instead of one, fulfils the open-ended principle. In this way, the "user" definable events of U-ASE are not constrained by TP-ASE events.

```
process TP_Node [tp,ca,p](ad:Adr,invoc:InvocId,freebranches:SetOfBr):
                                                          exit :=
       TP_RootNode[tp,ca,p](ad,invoc,freebranches)
       []
       TP_LeafOrIntermediateNode[tp,ca,p](ad,invoc,freebranches)
endproc
```

```
process TP_RootNode [tp,ca,p](ad:Adr,invoc:InvocId,freebranches:SetOfBr):
                                                                    exit :=
    hide nn,uu in
      ( MACFRoot [tp,ca,nn,uu] (ad,invoc,freebranches)
        |[nn,uu]|
        TP_SAOs [nn,ca,p,uu] (ad,invoc,Root,freebranches) )
endproc

process TP_LeafOrIntermediateNode [tp,ca,p](ad:Adr,invoc:InvocId,
                                        freebranches:SetOfBr):exit :=
    hide nn,uu in
      ( MACFLeafOrIntermediate [tp,ca,nn,uu] (ad,invoc,freebranches)
        |[nn,uu]|
        TP_SAOs [nn,ca,p,uu] (ad,invoc,Intermediate,freebranches) )
endproc

process TP_SAOs[nn,ca,p,uu](ad:Adr,invoc:InvocId,role:NodeRole,
                            freebranches:SetOfBr):exit:=
    choice br_id: BrId [] [br_id IsIn freebranches]   ->
      ( TP_SAO[nn,ca,p,uu] (ad,invoc,br_id,role)
        |||
        TP_SAOs[nn,ca,p,uu] (ad,invoc,role,Remove(br_id,freebranches)) )
endproc
```

Some protocol specifications, especially the ones which are directly transformed from service specifications, contain processes which synchronize at the external gates to constraint the events of the environment, see e.g. [18]. These processes are not defined here because the specification is derived from the non-formalized ISO description, which should incorporate these constraints in the protocol procedures. However, if the non-formalized description is incomplete, i.e. the protocol standard does not fully comply the service standard, the missing constraints on the ordering of the environment primitives must be derived from the service definition.

7 TP - MACF structures

TP-MACF is the component of the TP protocol machine which coordinates the multiparty interworking with remote protocol machines over OSI. Its functionality includes:

- establishment, management, release of application associations
- distribution of users service primitives to the appropriate TP-ASE, U-ASE, or CA service invocation of a particular dialogue or transaction branch, and the collection of the received primitives for the user.
- distributed coordination of certain transaction activities over OSI multiple application associations on users demand.

It was mentioned earlier that a TP protocol entity invocation is either a root node or a leaf (/intermediate) node and never both. A leaf node is potentially an intermediate node. The first event received by a protocol entity invocation determines the role of the node. The node is a root if this event is a request to initiate a dialogue, i.e. a TP-BEGIN-DIALOGUE request. Otherwise, it is a leaf or an intermediate node.

Service elements which affect multiple relations, i.e. branches to all direct subordinates of the particular node, are specified in the process **ManageBranches**. This process represents the behaviour of a superior of these transaction branches. In case of a leaf or an intermediate node, it also represents the behaviour of a subordinate of a branch. In a tree structured relationship a leaf or an intermediate node has one and only one superior. On the other hand, the service elements which affect individual transaction branches or dialogues are specified in the process **M_Branches** and, in case of a leaf or an intermediate node, the process **M_SubBranch**. The process mentioned first concerns with the superior behaviour. The second one concerns with the direct subordinate behaviour. In a leaf or an intermediate node these processes are interleaved. The global coordination is performed by **ManageBranches** and the user. The occurrence of events of the process **ManageBranches** is constrainted by the state of the process **M_Branches** or **M_SubBranch**. This yields full synchronization at gates **tp** and **ca**. The decomposition reflects the properties of transaction processing captured earlier and yields a well structured MACF architecture, where concerns are well separated. The specifications of the coordination functions are then the following.

```
process MACFRoot[tp,ca,nn,uu](ad:Adr,invoc:InvocId,freebranches:SetOfBr):
                                                              exit :=
     ManageBranches[tp,ca](..,Root,freebranches,{} of SetOfBr)
     |[tp,ca]|
     M_Branches[tp,nn,ca,uu](..,atomicactionid(..,..),..)
endproc

process MACFLeafOrIntermediate[tp,ca,nn,uu](ad:Adr,invoc:InvocId,
                                      freebranches:SetOfBr):exit:=
     (* some events ordering concerning the set up of the association
        and the dialogue from the superior are defined here *)
     ;
     ( ManageBranches[tp,ca]( .... )
       |[tp,ca]|
       (M_Branches[tp,nn,ca,uu](...) ||| M_SubBranch[tp,nn,ca,uu](...)) )
endproc
```

In section 2, it was observed that the number of used transaction branches grows dynamically during processing of a transaction. A commit (or rollback in the general case) request stops this grow, and only then the protocol machine is informed on the actual number of direct subordinates. Thus, the process **ManageBranches** comprises a growing (of transaction branches) phase and a commit phase successively. In the growing phase, this process counts and administrates the transaction branches. In the commit phase, it solves the two phase commitment procedures of each transaction branch and coordinates the multiple commitment. The specification of the commitment procedure is a straightforward translation of the multiple associations commitment procedure described in the ISO protocol standard and will not be presented here. The process `GrowingPhase` is recursive in the sense that it calls `ManageBranches`. A request to prepare a commitment enables the process `CommitPhase` when some preconditions, e.g. the acceptances or submissions of CCR-Begin service primitives, are fulfilled. This state machine structure enables parameter values to be passed from the growing to the commit phase. Thus,

```
process ManageBranches[tp,ca] (..,role:NodeRole,freebranches:SetOfBr,
                               usedbranches:SetOfBr)             :exit:=
   GrowingPhase[tp,ca](..,role,freebranches,usedbranches,..)
   []
   [(* preconditions *)] -> CommitPhases[tp,ca](..,role,usedbranches,..)
endproc
```

The process `M_Branches` consists of several interleaved processes `M_Branch` which represent the superior side behaviour of individual branches. These processes are identified by `br_id` and are invoked one by one when receiving a request until the commitment phase.

```
process M_Branches[tp,nn,ca,uu](ad:Adr,invoc:InvocId,rootinfo:AtActId,..)
                                                                 :exit:=
   tp!ad!invoc?br_id:BrId?tpsp:TPSPSort[IsTP_BEGIN_DIALOGUEreq(tpsp)];
   (* note: value br_id is determined by ManageBranches *)
   ( M_Branch[tp,nn,ca,uu](ad,invoc,br_id,GetRecepientTPSUTitle(tpsp),
                           GetSelectedFUs(tpsp),rootinfo)
   |||
     M_Branches[tp,nn,ca,uu](ad,invoc,rootinfo,..)
   )
   []                                       (* growing phase termination *)
   tp!ad!invoc?br_id:BrId?tpsp:TPSPSort[(IsTP_COMMITreq(tpsp) and ..) or
                                        IsTP_CONTINUE_COMMITreq(tpsp)];
   M_B_AbsorbPrimitives[tp](ad,invoc)
endproc (* M_Branches *)
```

M_Branch comprises the following phases:

association establishment superior side >> dialogue establishment >>
data transfer >> dialogue release and association release

Note that the dialogue and application association release phase are defined within an application entity invocation, which terminates after the end of each transaction. This is a consequence of the selected functionality and the chosen constraints. A (late) dialogue rejection indication may disrupt the normal behaviour of M_Branch.

To enable interleaved interactions on different branches, M_Branch must accept service primitives for the particular branch immediately, without waiting for the establishment of the application association or dialogue. This is due to the unconfirmed TP-BEGIN-DIALOGUE service element and the LOTOS synchronization property. The process M_B_TpspQueue and a queue are defined in M_Branch to accept and store these primitives. After dialogue establishment, M_B_EmptyQueue will pass these primitives for further processing, and meanwhile it may accept other primitives submitted by the local TP user. This process exits when the queue is empty. A simplified version of the process M_Branch is shown below.

```
process M_Branch[tp,nn,ca,uu](ad:Adr,invoc:InvocId,br_id:BrId,
                              rtt:Adr,sfu:Selected_Functional_Units,
                              rootinfo:AtActId): exit:=
  ( M_B_AssociationEstablishmentSuperior[nn](br_id,rtt)
    |||    (* allows interleaving at gate "tp" *)
    M_B_TpspQueue[tp](ad,invoc,br_id,empty_queue)
  ) >> accept tpspqueue:TpspQueue,ca_result:AssociateResult,... in
      ( [(ca_result eq accepted) and ... ] ->
            nn!br_id!NN_BEGIN_DIALOGUEreq(ad,rtt,sfu,DummyDCI);
            ca!ad!MkCEI(invoc,br_id)!CBEGINreq(atActIdMas(rootinfo),
                              atActIdSuf(rootinfo),br_id,nulldata);
            (( M_B_EmptyQueue[tp,nn,uu](ad,invoc,br_id,tpspqueue,..)
               |||
               M_B_ReceiveRemotePrimitives[tp,nn,ca,uu](ad,invoc,br_id,..)
            ) >> accept dialoguestate:DialState,... in
                ( [dialoguestate eq accepted] ->
                        M_B_Data[tp,uu](ad,invoc,br_id,..)
                  []
                  [dialoguestate eq rejected] -> exit(..,true of Bool,..)
                  []
                  [dialoguestate eq unknown]  ->
                        ( M_B_Data[tp,uu](ad,invoc,br_id,..)
                          [> M_B_DialogueReject[tp,nn](ad,invoc,br_id) )
                )
                >> accept ...,dialoguerejected,dialogueend:Bool in
                ( [not(dialoguerejected)] -> (* normal dialogue end *)
                        M_B_End[tp,nn,ca](ad,invoc,br_id,..)
                  []
                  [dialoguerejected] ->
                        M_B_ReleaseAssociation[ca](ad,invoc,br_id)
                )
            )
      []
      [(* appl. association rejected *)] ->
                        (* indicate properly to the user *)
      )
endproc
```

Process M_B_Data represents the data transfer phase. It contains two interleaved processes, one sends data to the remote entity, the other receives data from the remote entity. The first process exits on receiving a user request to end the dialogue. Control is then passed to M_B_End which terminates the branch behaviour by releasing the dialogue and application association.

```
process M_B_Data[tp,uu](ad:Adr,invoc:InvocId,br_id:BrId,..):
                                        exit(..,Bool,Bool):=
    M_B_PassDown[tp,uu](ad,invoc,br_id)
    |||
    M_B_PassUp[tp,uu](ad,invoc,br_id,..)
endproc

process M_B_PassDown[tp,uu](ad:Adr,invoc:InvocId,br_id:BrId):
                                        exit(..,Bool,Bool):=
    tp!ad!invoc!br_id?tpsp:TPSPSort[IsTP_DATAreq(tpsp)];
    uu!br_id!U_DATAreq(UserData(tpsp));
    M_B_PassDown[tp,uu](ad,invoc,br_id)
    []
    tp!ad!invoc!br_id?tpsp:TPSPSort[IsTP_DEFERRED_END_DIALOGUEreq(tpsp)];
    exit(..,any Bool,true of Bool)
endproc
```

The process M_SubBranch, which represents the subordinate behaviour of a transaction branch, is complementary to M_Branch and will therefore not be described here.

8 Status of the work

The specification has successfully passed tests with respect to syntax and static semantic checks according to the requirements in clause 3 of ISO/DIS 8807. Simulations on the complete specification are finished successfully. The tools used for the previously mentioned checks, tests and simulations are SCLOTOS, LISA, TOPO and SMILE [19, 20, 21].

This work has been undertaken within the LotoSphere (ESPRIT II 2304) project and has consumed around 2 manyears in total. British Telecommunication was involved in the preparation phase. The geographically distributed location of the designers and the limited time reserved for this work hampered the progress of this specification.

9 Acknowledgement

This work has been supported by the CEC under the ESPRIT II program in project 2304.

10 Conclusions

This paper presents parts of a specification of a TP protocol, and in particular the distributed coordination function MACF, in LOTOS. The complete specification has successfully passed syntax, static semantic checks and is successfully simulated. The protocol is specified in the resource oriented style because this style fits the chosen design trajectory which starts with the non-formalized ISO protocol description, which reflects the protocol resources and which includes the protocol procedures. This specification is a precursor of an implementation oriented specification since it incorporates some implementation aspects. A next design step is for instance the transformation of the specification into a state (machine) oriented specification.

The specification has been undertaken to assess a design method on its industrial applicability. For this reason a subset of the ISO TP functionality is selected. This yields a genuine, i.e. non-trivial, design exercise which complexity is manageable. The specification of the chosen subset of TP protocol in LOTOS was not easy. This is due to the distributed and complex nature of TP and the designers initial lack of experience in LOTOS. A cyclic and iterative design approach is essential in such design circumstance. Though functionality has been reduced, some design iterations were needed before a well structured specification is achieved. This is partly caused by the remote distances between the cooperating designers.

Some of the constraints on primitives ordering incorporated in the presented specification, have been taken from the ISO service definition and not from the protocol standard. Knowledge of transaction processing and a good understanding of TP model and service help designers in recognizing orthogonal (i.e. independent) components in the protocol and enables the preservation of the open-ended property in the specifications. The latter is possible because placeholders for additional functionalities are then more easy to identify. Background in transaction processing applications is also useful, especially for interpretating complicated and sometimes vaguely described protocol procedures. The recognition of the orthogonal components mentioned previously and the use of design quality criteria yields a well structured architecture, which refines the architecture reflected in the protocol standard. The use of the generic application layer constructs and structures improves the architecture in clarity and structure. The basically top-down design method assists designers in preserving the captured user requirements during the elaboration of the details of the specification. The use of design tools helps designers further in validating the produced specifications and hence it reduces design time.

The produced specification reflects the design decisions and illustrates the possibility to map informal requirements onto LOTOS structures. Thus, the design method has shown its merits in this design exercise.

References

[1] C.A.Vissers, J.v.d. Lagemaat "Report on LotoSphere" Proc.ESPRIT Technical Week, Brussels, Nov. 1989

[2] ISO, "LOTOS - a Formal Description Technique Based on the Temporal Ordering of Observational Behaviour", ISO/IS 8807, 1988.
[3] J. Navarro and P. San Martin, "Experience in the Development of an ISDN Layer 3 Service in LOTOS", Proc. of FORTE'90, J. Quemada et.al. (eds), Madrid, Nov. 1990, page 403 - 413
[4] M.T. Rose, "The ISO Development Environment: User's Manual", ISODE 6.0, Performance Systems Int. Inc., Jan. 1990.
[5] ISO, "Protocol Specification for the Commitment, Concurrency and Recovery Service Element" ISO/IS 9805.3,
[6] ISO, "Protocol Specification for the Association Control Service Element", ISO/IS 8650, 1988.
[7] ISO/DIS 10026-3 Information Processing Systems - Open Systems Interconnection - Distributed Transaction Processing - Part 3: Protocol Specification, 1990.
[8] ISO/DIS 10026-1 Information Processing Systems - Open Systems Interconnection - Distributed Transaction Processing - Part 1: Model, 1990.
[9] ISO/DIS 10026-2 Information Processing Systems - Open Systems Interconnection - Distributed Transaction Processing - Part 2: Service Definition, 1990.
[10] ISO, "Application Layer Structure", ISO/IS 9545, 1989.
[11] A.M. Fletcher, "An Overview of the OSI Transaction Processing Standard", Proc. Int. Open Systems '89, Online Publ., 1989, page 153 - 162.
[12] L.F. Pires and C.A. Vissers, "Overview of the LotoSphere Design Methodology", ESPRIT Conf. 1990, Brussels Nov. 12 - 15, 1990.
[13] G. Scollo, C.A. Vissers and A. Di Stefano, "LOTOS in Practice", in *Information Processing 86*, H.J. Kugler (editor), IFIP 1986, Elsevier Science Publ. BV., page 869 - 875.
[14] P. San Martin (editor), "Task 1.1 Deliverable", ESPRIT II 2304 Internal Deliverable Lo/WP1/T1.1/N0015, 1990.
[15] ISO/DP 10026-3 Information Processing Systems - Open Systems Interconnection - Distributed Transaction Processing - Part 3: Protocol Specification.
[16] C.A. Vissers, G. Scollo and M. van Sinderen, "Architecture and Specification Style in Formal Descriptions of Distributed Systems", Proc. IFIP WG6.1, PSTV VIII, North Holland, 1989, page 189 - 204.
[17] ISO/PDTR 10167 Information Processing Systems - Open Systems Interconnection - Proposed Draft Technical Report on Guidelines for the Application of Estelle, LOTOS and SDL
[18] M. van Sinderen and I. Widya, "On the Design and Formal Specification of a Transaction Processing Protocol", Proc. of FORTE'90, J. Quemada et.al. (eds), Madrid, Nov. 1990, page 515 - 532.
[19] J. Manas, T. de Miguel, T. Robles, and J. Salvachua, "Automatic Compilation versus Hand Coded Implementation of LOTOS Data Types", in Proc. of Forte'89.
[20] H. Eertink and D. Wolz, "Symbolic Execution of LOTOS Specification", Technical Report University of Twente, Memoranda Informatica 91-47, TIOS 91/016, May 1991.
[21] M. Caneve and E. Salvatori (eds), "Lite User Manual", ESPRIT II 2304 internal report Lo/WP2/N0034, April, 1991.

XP, an experiment in modular specification

Gert Veltink

Programming Research Group, University of Amsterdam, Kruislaan 403, 1098 SJ Amsterdam, The Netherlands. e-mail: veltink@fwi.uva.nl

Abstract
Previous experiences in the design of the formal description technique PSF have shown that it is hard to come up with just the right language constructs. The main problems we have encountered have to do with modularization concepts. Therefore we want to carry out an experiment in which we take a step back and try to find the basic elements for a specification language based on process algebras and abstract data types. After separating these basic elements we extend the language with one possible view of modularization. To stress the fact that this is an experiment we will call the resulting language XP (eXPeriment). A list of design goals is given and the language constructs introduced are tested against these goals.

1. Introduction & Motivation

Previous experience in the design of the formal description technique PSF [MV89a,MV90], has shown that it is easier to make mistakes in the design of a language then to find the correct concepts at once. Part of the problems with PSF come from the fact that it uses ASF [BHK89] for the specification of its data types and modularization concepts. Experiences and not in the least complaints of PSF users, as well as people implementing the computer tools for the PSF toolkit, have instigated this experiment in language design. In this experiment we first try to find the basic entities that make up a formal description technique based on process algebras and abstract data types, and then add one possible way of modularization. The resulting language is called XP for eXPeriment.

Related work and languages that have influenced the design of XP are in alphabetical order: C [KR78], COLD [FJKR87], Eiffel [Mey88], LOTOS [ISO89], μ-CRL [GP91], Occam [INM88], Perspect [Wie88] and PSF [MV90]. The design goals for XP have been:

- 1. incorporate a notion of modularization to support programming-in-the-large;
- 2. try to minimize dependencies among modules and try to minimize their interfaces;
- 3. keep the language as small as possible in order to be able to learn the language by heart without too much effort;
- 4. try to aim at maximal orthogonality among the different language constructs;
- 5. try to make the language look like an ordinary programming language in order to try to open the field of formal description techniques to a wider audience, but still keep in mind that we want to be able to supply a formal semantics for the language;
- 6. try to make the meaning of a specification clearer by grouping together things that belong together, and aim at a maximal understanding of a module without having to look across the module boundaries;
- 7. do not be afraid to let the language design be influenced by the implementation;

Note: This work was partially supported by ESPRIT Project no. 3006, CONCUR.

We are fully aware of the fact that we have set ourselves a very ambitious goal, and are not afraid to admit that we will surely fail in meeting all the design goals given above. However we think or rather hope that we can learn as much from this experiment and the errors we make, as we have learned from the design of PSF.

We will now shortly make some remarks referring to the design goals in random order. It is our firm belief that writing specifications in languages like LOTOS and PSF is just another form of programming. All problems encountered in the design of a program in a conventional programming language come up in the construction of specifications, even 'evil' things like *debugging* and *hacking*. This justifies the use of the word *programming-in-the-large* in 1 and also relates to goals 5 and 7.

A lot of languages are too large or too complicated to be understood fully: PSF, COLD, Ada [Bar82,ANSI83]. A return to the *small and simple* can be seen nowadays in hardware: RISC-architectures, as well as software: design of Occam (it even takes its name from this principle), Eiffel and μ-CRL. This relates to goals 2, 3 and 4.

We think more effort should be put into research into the psychological processes involved in using programming languages and we would encourage a better feedback of such results to the designers of computer languages. This relates to goal 6.

The outline of this article is as follows. In section 2 we introduce the objects, the mathematical entities that are subject to importing and exporting and the language constructs closely related to these objects. Section 3 deals with the actual importing, exporting and hiding of objects. In section 4 we deal with aspects of normalization of XP. The communication between processes is explained in section 5. In section 6 we shortly state what the semantics of XP looks like. A description of the implementation of the XP prototype is given in section 7, and section 8 contains an example of a specification in XP and finally section 9 contains a comparison with Extended LOTOS [Bri88,Bri90].

2. OBJECTS

As stated in the introduction, XP has been developed to study modularization concepts, so it deals with imports and exports. The first natural question then seems to be: "What do we want to import or export?" The answer in XP is: *objects*! We consider four classes of such objects in XP, things that can be more or less 'touched' in the mathematical world, two data and two process object classes. In the next sections we will introduce these objects and will discuss their properties and the relationships between them.

2.1. Data Objects

Just like the facilities for specifying abstract data types in PSF and LOTOS, XP offers constructs to specify data by means of (conditional) equational specifications. The semantical interpretation of the equations in XP is the initial algebra semantics [EM85,GM85]. In the implementation a set of equations is considered a term rewriting system in which the left-hand side rewrites into the right-hand side of an equation. We demand that the resulting term rewriting system is *semi-complete*. The first data object in XP is a sort. In the next example we will give an example of the *definition* of the sort Boolean:

```
sort Boolean {};
```

The introduction of an object starts with a *keyword*, `sort` in this case. Keywords referring to objects will consist of four characters. The *object keyword* is followed by a *declaration* of the object stating the object's name and possible type. An object name can be any string of minimal length one, consisting of lower-case and upper-case characters, digits and underscores ('_') in any order. A *declaration* can be turned into a *definition* by supplying the object's attributes between '{' and '}'. Because a sort has no further attributes, there is nothing written between the brackets in the *definition* in the example above. Finally, the definition is closed by a semicolon. The semi-colon in XP is always used as a logical end-of-line. Like in traditional programming languages, this feature greatly facilitates the process of synchronizing for the parser during error recovery. The other data object is the function. The keyword for a function is: func. An example of the definition of the boolean function not:

```
func not(Boolean): Boolean {
      not(true())  = false();
      not(false()) = true();
   };
```

The declaration of the function contains its *input type* between parentheses followed by a colon, and the *output type*. In XP a colon always indicates that the following entity will be a *type*. In case of a more complex input type the sorts are separated by commas. We currently restrict ourselves to simple output types, so we do not allow tupled output. In XP we adhere to a strict *declare before use* strategy. This implies in the example that the sort Boolean and functions true() and false() already had to be declared.

In XP we want to be able to disambiguate the class to which an object belongs syntactically. This explains why all functions, even constants, must be followed by a pair of parentheses. The main reason for this is to avoid name clashes with variables that are introduced in the next example. This approach has great advantages not only for the tools manipulating specifications, but also for humans.

Unlike in other specification languages, it is obligatory in XP to specify, along with the definition of the function, all rewrite rules that directly apply to the function being defined. This means that all equations used in a definition, have the function being defined as outer function symbol. Moreover we require that all objects that are used in a definition already have been declared. We argue that this requirement will lead to clearer specifications, because it forces grouping things that belong together and thus increases legibility and comprehension. Variables can be used in the definition of equations as shown in the following example:

```
func and(Boolean,Boolean): Boolean {
    for x: Boolean;
       and(true(),x)  = x;
       and(false(),x) = false();
   };
```

Variables are introduced by the for keyword and are strongly typed. They must be declared before the equations and their scope is limited to the equations of the function being defined. Variables occurring at the right-hand side of an equation must also occur at the left-hand side. It is possible in XP to use conditional axioms. The next fragment will give an example of the use of conditional equations:

```
eq( f(a,b),g(c,d) ) = true()  <=
    eq(a,c) = true(),
    eq(b,d) = true();
```

2.2. Process Objects

Next, we will introduce two objects to specify process behaviour: *atoms* and *processes*. The keywords in the XP syntax are atom and proc. The process part of XP will, like PSF, be based on ACP [BW90]. For more specific information on ACP we refer to [BW90]. An atom or atomic action is an indivisible element of the process theory on which XP is based. Processes are constructed from atomic actions by combining them by means of operators. We will come back to these aspects when we describe the process operators. Firstly we will focus on the definition of atoms.

To avoid name clashes with the objects introduced so far all atomic actions are followed by a pair of angular brackets '<' and '>'. An example of a definition of an atom:

```
atom receive_data<Data> {};
```

As can be seen in this example, atomic actions can be parameterized by data types. The next example shows the specification of a process object. It has also been taken from the sender of an alternating bit protocol.

```
proc RM[Boolean] {
    for b:Boolean
      RM[b] =
      alt {
      for d:Data;
        seq {
          receive_data<d>;
          SF[b,d];
        }
      }
    };
```

It is clear from this example that process identifiers are followed by a pair of rectangular brackets: '[' and ']' to distinguish them from the other objects. There are three basic operators to combine process expressions. These are the: sequential composition (`seq`), alternative composition (`alt`) and the parallel composition (`par`). There are three simple process expressions: the `skip` expression, an atomic action and a 'process invocation' (`SF[b,d]` in the example). The `skip` represents the internal action like the `skip` in PSF or the `i` in LOTOS. There is one type of complex process expression which is formed by an operator and a list of process expressions, see `seq { ... }` in this example. The intuitive semantics of the three operators is the following:

- `seq`, sequential composition.
  seq { x_1; x_2; ...; x_n; } is the process that first executes x_1, after termination of x_1 continues with x_2 and so on until it reaches x_n on which termination, the complete expression terminates.
- `alt`, alternative composition.
  alt { x_1; x_2; ...; x_n; } is the process that first makes a non-deterministic choice from its summands x_1 up to x_n, and then proceeds with the execution of the chosen summand.
- `par`, parallel composition.
  par { x_1; x_2; ...; x_n; } is the process that represents the simultaneous execution of all processes x_1 up to x_n,

The three operators can be of any arity (≥ 1) and the `par` and `alt` can be parameterized (generalized) by variables. Allowing this construct means that we have to able to enumerate all elements of the data set. Better orthogonality would have been achieved if we would allow `seq` also to be parameterized. However, this would imply that we also have to define an ordering of the data elements. The definition of the `alt` construct in the example is an instance of a generalized alternative composition. The generalized commands are formed by inserting the `for` keyword and a list of variables after the operator.

One of the main problems for implementations of specification languages is the fact that the variables introduced here, can be typed with an infinite sort. A possible solution is to put a restriction on these variables. A simple restriction is to allow only variables that are typed with a sort that is defined as an enumeration of constants. In [Wie88] part of this problem is tackled by forcing data type specifications to be *persistent*. More research has to be carried out to be able to loosen restrictions on data types and still be able to check the finiteness of a data type and to generate all its elements.

The decision to choose prefix notation for the process operators and strong suggestion of indentation, has been influenced by Occam [INM88]. However, we do not want to force any indentation like Occam does. In PSF these process operators are all binary and are denoted using an infix notation. Grouping of sub-expressions and disambiguation of the parse tree in PSF is performed by inserting parentheses. We have experienced that already relatively small process expressions can become hard to read and understand when the process structure has a high branching degree (extensive use of alternative and parallel composition) and when larger variable names are used. In understanding such expressions one has to find matching parentheses all the time. We believe that using the syntax proposed for XP we can more or less overcome this traditional problem due to the use of different brackets, prefix notation and clearer standard indentation.

There is one last construct to be dealt with in this section on processes: the guard. Each process expression can be preceded by a guard. A guarded expression has the following form:

[s = t] -> <process expression>

The guard is an equation between two data terms and the semantics is equal to the semantics of the *guarded command* from [BBMV91]. If the guard is true the expression is equal to the expression without the guard. If the guard is false the expression evaluates to a *deadlock* [BW90]. Deadlock can not be expressed in the XP syntax, but is part of the semantical domain of the processes. In an actual implementation this means that we first normalize the two terms in the data model. If after normalization they are syntactically equal, the guard is *true* and *false* otherwise. To allow the user more flexibility the guard can be negated. The '=' can be replaced by '!=' to express the fact that the guard is *true* when the two terms are not equal and *false* otherwise. The demand for semi-complete term rewriting systems is needed to be able to introduce negation. By using guards we can express general *if-then-else* and *case/switch* constructs.

3. MODULES AND VISIBILITY OF OBJECTS

One of the topics of this paper, as stated earlier, is modular specification. We think of a specification as a collection of modules that together define a meaning. This implies that we have to provide means to let the different modules cooperate. Suppose module *A* wants to use an object *f* defined in module *B*. This cooperation can only occur if both modules explicitly state that they agree with such interaction. In this case it means that module *B* has to make object *f* visible to module *A*, and module *A* has to specify that it wants to use object *f* from module *B*.

A module in XP consists of a series of declarations and definitions of objects grouped between the keywords: `module` and `end`. A module can contain definitions of objects of all four classes. These definitions can occur in any order within a module, as long as the *declare before use* rule is respected. This approach differs from PSF where data and process modules are strictly separated and where objects have to be introduced in a fixed order.

One of the design goals of XP is to minimize the dependencies and interfaces between modules, in order to achieve a better comprehension of a (part of a) specification at modular level. This means that we do not want to inspect a whole series of other modules if we want to understand the module at hand.

It is our opinion that in the example above there is only one natural dependency, namely *A* depends on *B*, because *A* uses an object defined in *B*. In XP module *B* would make its object *f* visible to the *world* by exporting it. Module *A* imports *f* and states that it imports the *f* from *B*. If we would have demanded from *B* to give a list of modules that might use *f*, we would have introduced another dependency.

There are numerous languages that treat import by importing a complete module. This means that if module A imports module B all objects that are exported from B become visible in A. Apart from needlessly polluting the name space of A, such a treatment can lead to unexpected name clashes. Consider the following example. Module A defines objects a and u, and module B defines objects b and u. A third module, say C, wants to use object a from A and b from B so it imports A and C. Module C now can use objects a and b but due to the import it also has caused a name clash between the two different objects u. The problem here is that one is unaware of this name clash because the attention is focussed on a and b. The situation is even worse in ASF and consequently PSF where every object that once has been exported, is automatically added to the export section of the importing module. We consider these import mechanisms as undesirable, because the interfaces between the modules become too large and indistinct.

To tackle this problem of import, in XP, each object that is used in a module and is not defined there should be declared. The declaration of an object also involves stating its full type. In combination with the *declare before use* strategy this guarantees that a compiler will be able to disambiguate every occurrence of an object and is able to do complete type checking, on the modular level. These strategies therefore support *separate compilation* of modules and guarantee that all errors that occur when combining modules are errors in the interface definitions. This way of checking on separate levels, first within a module and then between modules, gives more information about the nature of mistakes in the specification. In the next program fragment we will give examples of *imports*:

```
sort Boolean              { <- Booleans };
func false() : Boolean    { <- Booleans.f };
```

Import of an object is indicated by the backwards arrow: '<-'. It is possible to rename an object on import as shown in the `func` section. The function locally known as *false* is in fact function *f* from module *Booleans*. Because we are now able to change the names of objects we should discuss overloading and name clashes. We will treat these topics in the next section.

In the previous example we have shown how objects can be imported. Now we will focus on how objects can be made visible to the outside world. There are several options to choose from when deciding how visibility is controlled. One possibility is to group all items that should be exported in one special section, as is done in PSF. A disadvantage of this approach is that we have experienced in actually writing specifications, this leads to a lot of *copy-paste* actions in the editor to shift lines from and to the export section.

A similar problem occurs in the definition of Ada packages which are made up of a separate specification and implementation part. In this situation inconsistencies between the two parts are introduced very easily, because all objects that are exported must be specified twice. We prefer the approach chosen in Eiffel to overcome this problem. Here the specification part of a class is generated from the implementation part using the *short* tool [Mey88].

By dismissing the approaches used in PSF and Ada, we are forced to explicitly define the visibility of each object by attaching a *visibility tag* to each definition and declaration of an object. Therefore we introduce two operators controlling the visibility of objects. The first operator is the *export* operator: '->', which is the counterpart of the *import* operator. The second one is the *hiding* operator, written as: '-|'.

Now we are able to define the visibility of each object by attaching either the *export* or the *hiding* operator to it. Attaching a tag to every definition and declaration can become a cumbersome job and so we want to consider a rule for default visibility. In doing this we are left with two options. We can either take as default that all objects are defined locally and that we have to export them explicitly or we can take exporting as default and consequently have to *hide* all objects that should not be visible to the outside world.

It is hard to choose just one of both approaches because we have found by inspecting medium-sized specifications in PSF [JM89,Mul89,MM90] that there is an asymmetry towards visibility control between data and process objects. We have experienced that in specifications almost all data objects are exported and that almost all process objects, except the top process and atoms intended for external communication, are hidden. Therefore in XP, export is default for data objects and hiding is default for process objects. Its usage is shown in the following:

```
func true() : Boolean  { <- Booleans } -|;
atom receive_data : <Data> {} ->;
```

There are two semantical constraints we impose on a module M in which a sort S is introduced.
- the initial algebra of sort S must be described completely within M.
- all functions necessary to construct normal forms of S, are exported from M.

4. OVERLOADING & ORIGINS

In the context of a modular specification with modules importing one and another it is easy to get in trouble with the names given to the objects involved. In XP we have tried to minimize the possibilities of name clashes between objects. In the section on objects we have shown that different types of brackets are used to disambiguate the different objects at a syntactical level. The only remaining possibility for a name clash which can not be solved, could be between a variable and a sort. In the current design of the syntax there is no place where a clash could occur between these two. (The situation could however change when we would add more sophisticated features like parameterization and inheritance to the language.) This naming convention is of great importance for the compiler as well as humans. We have experienced that in PSF a number of different highly undesirable ambiguities can occur which, apart from leading to unclearer specifications, took a lot of effort to be solved in the implementation. We will recall the main problems here shortly. For a more thorough description see [Vel90].

- variables can clash with constant functions in data terms: `and(true,x)`
- atoms can clash with processes in process definitions: `X = a.Z.X`
- sets can clash with sorts in, for example, set definitions: `H = K/{ item }`

All above-mentioned problems have been solved in XP by the cooperation between the strict naming convention for objects and the *declare before use* strategy. As a result overloading of names between different objects is always allowed. Overloading of names of objects from the same object class is allowed only if the objects have different input types (recall that the full type of an object is always known). This implies that overloading of sorts as well as overloading of constant objects (non-parameterized objects) within the same object class is prohibited. Another source of ambiguity can come from the use of variables. In XP there are several types of variables:

- variables used in the specification of rewrite rules
- variables used in the definition of generalized process operators
- variables used in the definition of the communication function
- variables representing parameters of processes

It is required in XP that it must be possible to disambiguate all different variables on the basis of their names only. This implies that within the scope of any variable it is impossible to find an occurrence of another variable with the same name. This approach is different from PSF where it is possible to temporarily override a variable by declaring another variable with the same name in an inner block.

Just like in ACP and LOTOS we want to assign semantics to a normalized or flattened specification in XP. (We would prefer to be able to assign modular semantics to a modular specification language, but we believe that this is more difficult.) As a result of this it is possible that hidden objects can clash in the normalization process, that is, they can not be disambiguated by their names only. Clashes between visible objects can be taken care of by careful renaming, but it would be illogical to demand that renamings for hidden objects are to be given. In ASF, and subsequently PSF, this problem is solved by introducing the *origin rule*. In XP we will introduce a similar *origin rule*, which is simpler than the one from ASF.

A specification S in XP consists of a series of modules M_1 to M_n, all with different names. In S each object is fully disambiguated by a pair of names. The first item of this pair is the name of the module in which the object has been defined, the module of *origin*. The second item is the object's original name in the module of origin. In the sequel this pair of names will be called the *origin name*. The origin name will be used during the normalization procedure. The origin rule now reads:

if in one module there are two objects:
- with the same name
- from the same object class
- with the same input type

then their origin names must be equal.

Violations of the origin rule must be detected and reported during the normalization phase. The treatment of the origin names in combination with renamings in XP has as a consequence that one object can have different names. This is different from ASF (PSF) where it is possible to rename a function on import and then extend its properties by adding equations that only hold for the new renamed version of the function. Such features should not be incorporated in simple renamings on import, but should be studied thoroughly in the setting of *inheritance*, *generics* and *polymorphism* as known from the field of object oriented languages.

5. COMMUNICATION

So far we still not have described interaction between processes. XP processes can communicate by sharing occurrences of atomic actions. Which atomic actions are shared is given by an explicitly defined communication function. The communication function γ is a commutative binary function, that has two arguments, the two components of a communication, and yields the result atom ($\gamma(a,b) = c$). This approach differs from CSP: $\gamma(a,a) = a$ [Hoa85] (on which LOTOS is more or less based) and CCS: $\gamma(a,\bar{a}) = \tau$ [Mil80]. Defining a communication function in ACP does not force this communication to happen in the expansion of a process. To understand this we have to look at the expansion theorem:

a.X ∥ b.Y = a.X ⫼ b.Y + b.Y ⫼ a.X + (a|b).(X ∥ Y)

The ⫼ (left merge) is a ∥ (merge) with the restriction that the first action has to be performed by its left operand. Due to the interleaving semantics the merge of the two processes P ∥ Q can proceed as one of three alternatives. Either the first atomic action to be performed comes from P, from Q, or the two initial atomic actions on either side communicate ('|'-operator). To exclude the first two possibilities we can put the complete process into the scope of the so-called encapsulation operator (∂_H), that renames elements from the set of atomic actions H into *deadlock*. In an alternative composition, *deadlock* is never chosen whenever there is an open alternative. Intuitively this means that when there is the possibility to proceed, a process will not deadlock. The derivation of $\partial_{\{a,b\}}$(a.X ∥ b.Y) is now given as:

$\partial_{\{a,b\}}$(a.X ∥ b.Y)
= $\partial_{\{a,b\}}$(a.X ⫼ b.Y + b.Y ⫼ a.X + (a|b).(X ∥ Y))
= $\delta.\partial_{\{a,b\}}$(X ⫼ b.Y) + $\delta.\partial_{\{a,b\}}$(Y ⫼ a.X) + $c.\partial_{\{a,b\}}$(X ∥ Y)
= $c.\partial_{\{a,b\}}$(X ∥ Y)

From practical experience with PSF case studies [JM89,Mul89,MM90] we have learned that in a specification the encapsulation operator is normally used only once per module, namely to encapsulate the top process. (In verifications however the encapsulation operator is 'pushed' into the process expressions as deeply as possible using the so-called conditional axioms [BBK87] to reduce the state space complexity of a process expression. See [MV91] for an example of the use of conditional axioms in verifications.) Using this knowledge we have tried to get rid of the *encaps* operator in the process *specification* and have decided to let it coincide with the module boundaries. This means that every process that is exported from a module is put into the scope of an encapsulation operator implicitly.

Unlike ACP or PSF, in XP the atomic actions, per module, are divided into three categories: *inert atoms*: actions that do not engage in any communication, *communicating atoms*: actions that form the 'components' of a communication, *result atoms*: actions that are the result of a communication

Next we put some restrictions on the communication schemes that can be defined. Like PSF we demand that a *result atom* is not able to take part in a communication as a *communicating atom*, this is called *firm handshaking* in PSF. As opposed to PSF where the communication function is a global property of the specification, in XP each module defines its own communication function. This means that an exported *result atom* can be a *communicating atom* at a higher level, that is the module into which it is imported. Due to this layered design in XP we do not need the alternative of the *consistency of communications* restriction from PSF.

A second restriction on the XP communication scheme is that we want communication to take place at the level at which it has been defined. Therefore we do not allow *communicating atoms* to be exported from a module (although their result can). Using the two abovementioned restrictions, we can now define the encapsulation set for a module implicitly to be exactly the set of all communicating atoms from that module.

There is another renaming operator in ACP and PSF similar to the encapsulation operator; the abstraction operator (τ_I). This operator acts as a kind of filter and renames all atomic actions from a set I into the internal action; τ in ACP and `skip` in PSF. In XP we also want to let this operator coincide with the modular constructions. From the PSF case studies we have observed that the 'favourite' application of the abstraction operator is as in the following example:

$$\tau_I \circ \partial_H(X)$$

This strongly suggests that we should treat the abstraction operator in a way similar to the encapsulation operator. The abstraction set of a module is implicitly defined as the union of all *inert atoms* and *result atoms* that are *not* exported from that module. Although we have been discussing communication between atoms we have not yet given the XP syntax. In XP the definition of a possible communication is an attribute of the *result atom*.

```
atom c<> {
       c<> = a<> | b<>;
     };
```

Because of the commutativity of γ, the definition in the example defines both $\gamma(a,b) = c$ and $\gamma(b,a) = c$. The definition of a communication between parameterized atoms involves the introduction of variables:

```
atom funny<Boolean,Boolean> {
     for x:Boolean; y: Boolean; z:Nat; w:Char;
       funny<x,y> = f<x,z> | g<z,y,w>;
     };
```

One could argue that the restrictions put on the communication function in XP affect the idea of the communication function from ACP. We agree with this but claim that in most applications we have seen so far the restrictions are no real limitations. One problem that we see however, is the modelling of broadcasting in which one process sends an action that can be received by a possibly infinite number of listening processes.

6. SEMANTICS

The semantics of XP is defined in a way similar to the semantics of PSF. As already mentioned in the section on overloading and origins, the semantics of XP can only be assigned to a flattened or normalized version of the specification. We will not give the flattening process here in detail, but the main idea is that all modules from a specification are merged into one module, while for all objects the names are replaced by their *origin names*.

As the semantics for the data types we use the initial algebra semantics as defined in, for example, [EM85,GM85]. We also assign an initial algebra to atomic actions parameterized with *closed* data terms and define an equivalence relation in the following way:

$a<v_1, v_2, ..., v_n> = b<u_1, u_2, ..., u_m>$ whenever:
 the origin name of a is equal to the origin name of b
 $\forall i, 1 \leq i \leq n: v_i = u_i$ in the initial algebra of the sort of v_i and u_i.

The processes are given an *operational semantics* defined with the aid of action relations [Plo82]. We will give part of the table listing the action relations for XP just to get an idea of this approach. For a complete table of action relations we refer to the action relations for PSF defined in [MV90], because the semantical basis of XP and PSF is closely related.

Table 1
Action rules

atom	$a \xrightarrow{a} \sqrt{}$			
seq 1	$\dfrac{x \xrightarrow{a} x'}{seq\{x; L\} \xrightarrow{a} seq\{x'; L\}}$	seq 2	$\dfrac{x \xrightarrow{a} \sqrt{}}{seq\{x; L\} \xrightarrow{a} seq\{L\}}$	
alt 1	$\dfrac{x \xrightarrow{a} x'}{alt\{L; x; M\} \xrightarrow{a} x'}$	alt 2	$\dfrac{x \xrightarrow{a} \sqrt{}}{alt\{L; x; M\} \xrightarrow{a} \sqrt{}}$	
par 1	$\dfrac{x \xrightarrow{a} x'}{par\{L; x; M\} \xrightarrow{a} par\{L; x'; M\}}$	par 2	$\dfrac{x \xrightarrow{a} \sqrt{}}{par\{L; x; M\} \xrightarrow{a} par\{L; M\}}$	
par 3	$\dfrac{x \xrightarrow{a} x'; y \xrightarrow{b} y'; \gamma(a,b) = c}{par\{L; x; M; y; N\} \xrightarrow{a} par\{L; x'; M; y'; N\}}$			
par 4	$\dfrac{x \xrightarrow{a} x'; y \xrightarrow{b} \sqrt{}; \gamma(a,b) = c}{par\{L; x; M; y; N\} \xrightarrow{a} par\{L; x'; M; N\}}$	...		

For each element [a] of the initial algebra of atomic actions we define a binary relation $\xrightarrow{[a]}$ and a unary relation $\xrightarrow{[a]} \sqrt{}$ on closed process expressions. If a is an atomic action, and [a] its equivalence class (so [a] ∈ IA), we write $\xrightarrow{a}$ instead of $\xrightarrow{[a]}$.

$x \xrightarrow{a} y$ means that the process expression represented by x can evolve into y, by executing the atomic action [a].

$x \xrightarrow{a} \sqrt{}$ means that the process expression represented by x can terminate successfully after having executed the atomic action [a]. The special symbol $\sqrt{}$ can be looked upon as a symbol indicating successful termination of a process.

The relations $\xrightarrow{a}$ are generated by the rules in table 1, that is, $x \xrightarrow{a} y$ only holds if this can be derived using these rules. In the following table we will use some symbols that have a special meaning. These symbols are: a,b,c: atomic actions or skip, x,y: process expressions, L,M,N: possibly empty lists of process expressions.

7. IMPLEMENTATION

A syntax checker for XP has been implemented using the standard compiler construction tools Lex [LS79] and Yacc [Joh79]. Due to the careful design of the PSF toolkit [Vel91] we have been able to reuse large parts of the toolkit in implementing XP. In the following section we will give a short description of the PSF toolkit and its usage in the implementation of XP.

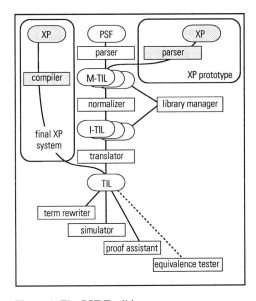

Figure 1. The PSF Toolkit

7.1. The PSF Toolkit

At the centre of the toolkit, see figure 1, is the Tool Interface Language (TIL) [MV89b] through which all tools can communicate. From the picture we see that the PSF specification at the top is translated into TIL using two intermediate languages called M-TIL and I-TIL. In the course of this translation the library manager is used which supports and controls separate compilation of PSF modules.

Each PSF module is translated into exactly one M-TIL module. M-TIL is similar to TIL, but it still contains information about the modular structure of the specification. Because TIL supports no modular structure at all, a PSF specification has to be flattened. This is done in the normalization phase in which the I-TIL language is used. The complete description of the translation from PSF to TIL, including the definitions of the M-TIL and I-TIL languages, can be found in [Vel90].

At the bottom of the picture we see the different tools. At present a simulator, a term rewriter and a proof assistant have been implemented. The simulator and proof assistant are fully interactive programs that are implemented using the X-Windows system. We are currently working on interfacing the toolkit with Aldébaran [Fer91], an existing tool for equivalence testing using bisimulation decision techniques. The XP trajectory is added to this picture using grey items.

The best way to make the toolkit available for XP would be to write a type checker and normalizer that produce TIL. However, we are currently working on a program that translates XP into M-TIL to be able to produce a prototype quickly. In implementing XP following this approach, we can also reuse the PSF type checker and normalizer. However, there is one main drawback. Due to design goals of XP, *declare before use* and *full typing*, the type checker and normalizer for XP can be constructed more efficiently and can have better performance than the PSF equivalents. So by choosing for the implementation of XP through a rapid prototype, we lose efficiency.

8. EXAMPLES

In this section we will give the specification of two of the modules from an alternating bit protocol as an example.

```
module Booleans

  sort
    Boolean {};

  func
    true(): Boolean {};
    false(): Boolean {};

    not(Boolean): Boolean
    {
      not(true()) = false();
      not(false()) = true();
    };

    and(Boolean,Boolean): Boolean
    {
    for x: Boolean;
      and(true(),x) = x;
      and(false(),x) = false();
    };

    or(Boolean,Boolean): Boolean
    {
    for x: Boolean;
      or(true(),x) = true();
```

```
      or(false(),x) = x;
    };
end

module Sender
  sort
    Boolean     { <- Booleans };
    Data        { <- Data };
    Frame       { <- Frames };
    Ack         { <- Acknowledgements };

  func
    false() : Boolean              { <- Booleans };
    true()  : Boolean              { <- Booleans };
    not(Boolean) : Boolean         { <- Booleans };
    frame(Boolean,Data) : Frame    { <- Frames };
    error() : Ack                  { <- Acknowledgements };
    ack(Boolean) : Ack             { <- Acknowledgements };

  atom
    receive_data<Data> {} ->;
    send_frame<Frame> {} ->;
    receive_ack<Ack> {} ->;

  proc
    RM[Boolean];
    S[]
    {
    S[] =
      RM[false()];
    };

    SF[Boolean,Data];
    RM[Boolean]
    {
    for b:Boolean;
    RM[b] =
      alt {
      for d:Data;
        seq {
          receive_data<d>;
          SF[b,d];
        }
      }
    };

    RA[Boolean,Data];
    SF[Boolean,Data]
    {
    for b:Boolean; d:Data;
    SF[b,d] =
      seq {
        send_frame<frame(b,d)>;
        RA[b,d];
      }
    };
```

```
RA[Boolean,Data]
{
for b:Boolean; d:Data;
RA[b,d] =
  alt {
    seq {
      alt {
        receive_ack<error()>;
        receive_ack<ack(not(b))>;
      }
      SF[b,d];
    }
    seq {
      receive_ack<ack(b)>;
      RM[not(b)];
    }
  }
};
```

end

9. COMPARISON WITH EXTENDED LOTOS

In this section we will shortly discuss a comparison between XP and the proposal for modularization techniques in Extended LOTOS as put forward in [Bri88,Bri90].

We think that the main difference between XP and Extended LOTOS is the fact that the latter is really an extension of LOTOS. This implies that LOTOS constructs are kept in the design. As an example we give the *where* construct in process definitions in LOTOS. We think this feature can be dropped in a setting that supports modules for process specification. XP has been redesigned from scratch. Due to this fact the syntax of XP is more orthogonal.

Extended LOTOS allows parameterization of data types, but not of processes, where XP does not support any notion of parameterization. In our approach we would aim at introducing parameterization concepts for both data and process specification in a unified framework.

A final remark is that XP focuses on the objects that constitute a module, whereas Extended LOTOS treats modules as the entity of modularization operations. An example for this is the renaming of objects in a module which is done by defining a function for this module that maps identifiers onto identifiers. In a setting in which some form of overloading is present, we think this is not sufficient, and suggest that identifiers should be extended with their types.

10. CONCLUSIONS

In this paper we have introduced a new specification language called XP. We have tried to focus on the issues involved in modularization, and tested the language constructs that we have introduced, against the design goals expressed in the introduction. In some cases the choices to be made were simple, in other cases we had to deal with conflicting interests.

We think we have succeeded in trying to exploit the syntax of XP to do as much disambiguation as possible. The fact that the language and its syntax checker were developed at the same time, together with previous experience gained from the design of PSF, has contributed greatly to this achievement.

We claim that XP is easier to explain to a novice and its language constructs are easier to remember for a user of the language than PSF, while retaining comparable expressiveness. Because of this fact, the implementation of the XP compiler will also be much simpler than its PSF counterpart.

We have shown that one of the design goals of the PSF toolkit, ease of reuse of large parts of it, has been met by creating the translation from XP to M-TIL.

Future developments on extending the XP language can involve a lot of different approaches. We could try to add more expressiveness to the data objects. Two relatively simple extensions come to the mind. Allow functions to have tupled outputs as a result. This would lead to the parallel of *records* or *structs* in conventional programming languages. In this case tuples should also be valid parameters to functions and processes and we must consider special functionality to update information stored in a tuple without having to unpack, modify and pack the tuple completely. The other is an extension to the syntax of the functions. Experiments in the COLD project [FJKR87] have shown that people are more productive in writing specifications when the syntax of a formal description technique is capable of mimicking the concepts from their province as closely as possible. This would suggest that allowing the user to specify the syntax of the functions using an arbitrary context free grammar, as done in the ASF+SDF project [Kli91], instead of plain prefix notation would increase productivity.

A much harder problem to tackle will be the investigation of how concepts like: *generics*, *inheritance* and *polymorphism* can be added to the language. We think it can be expected that adding such features to the current design of XP can cause conflicts. It is our opinion that this is almost impossible to avoid, because the factors involved are very complex, and that there is no problem in redesigning the language when new features dictate this. This project therefore can also be seen as an experiment in layered design of formal description techniques.

Acknowledgements

The author would like to express his thanks to Hans Mulder for his valuable comments on the problems he has experienced in using the PSF language and his willingness to discuss earlier drafts of XP. Several suggestions including the dot notation for renaming on import and the syntax for hiding are in fact due to him. Moreover thanks are due to Jan Bergstra, Sjouke Mauw, Chris Verhoef and the anonymous referees for their comments on earlier drafts of this paper.

11. REFERENCES

[ANSI83] American National Standards Institute, Inc., *The Programming Language Ada™ Reference Manual*, ANSI/MIL-STD-1815A-1983, LNCS 155, Springer Verlag, 1983.

[Bar82] J.G.P. Barnes, *Programming in Ada*, Addison-Wesley, 1982.

[BBK87] J.C.M. Baeten, J.A. Bergstra & J.W. Klop, *Conditional axioms and a/b-calculus in process algebra*, in: Proceedings IFIP Conference on Formal Description of Programming Concepts III, Ebberup, (M. Wirsing, ed.) pp. 77-103, North-Holland, 1987.

[BBMV91] J.C.M. Baeten, J.A. Bergstra, S. Mauw & G.J. Veltink, *A process specification formalism based on static COLD*, in: *Algebraic Methods II: Theory, Tools and Applications*, J.A. Bergstra & L.M.G. Feijs (eds.), LNCS 490, pp. 303-335, Springer Verlag, 1991.

[BHK89] J.A. Bergstra, J. Heering & P. Klint, *The algebraic specification formalism ASF*, in: *Algebraic specification*, J.A. Bergstra, J. Heering & P. Klint (eds.), pp. 1-66, ACM Press Frontier Series, Addison-Wesley 1989.

[Bri88] E. Brinksma, *On the design of Extended LOTOS*, doctoral dissertation, University of Twente, 1988.

[Bri90] E. Brinksma, *Specification modulis in LOTOS*, in: *Formal Description Techniques, II*, S.T. Vuong (ed.), pp. 101-115, North-Holland, 1990.

[BW90] J.C.M. Baeten & W.P. Weijland, *Process Algebra*, Cambridge Tracts in Theoretical Computer Science 18, Cambridge University Press, 1990.

[EM85] H. Ehrig & B. Mahr, *Fundamentals of Algebraic Specifications, Vol. I, Equations and Initial Semantics*, Springer-Verlag, 1985.
[Fer91] J.C. Fernandez, *Aldébaran, A tool set for deciding bisimulation equivalences*, in: Proceedings CONCUR '91, Amsterdam, (J.C.M. Beaten & J.A. Bergstra, eds.), 1991. (to appear in LNCS series).
[FJKR87] L.M.G. Feijs, H.B.M. Jonkers, C.P.J. Koymans & G.R. Renardel de Lavalette, *Formal Definition of the Design Language COLD-K*, METEOR/t7/PRLE/7, 1987.
[GM85] J.A. Goguen & J. Meseguer, *Initiality, induction and computability*, in: Algebraic Methods in Semantics (M. Nivat & J.C. Reynolds eds.), pp. 460-541, Cambridge University Press, 1985.
[GP91] J.F. Groote & A. Ponse, *The Syntax and Semantics of μCRL*, to appear as a Technical Report in the CS series. Centre for Mathematics and Computer Science, Amsterdam, 1991.
[Hoa85] C.A.R. Hoare, Communicating Sequential Processes, Prentice-Hall, 1985.
[INM88] INMOS Limited, *occam® 2 Reference Manual*, Prentice Hall, 1988.
[ISO89] International Organization for Standardization, *IS 8807, Information processing systems - Open systems interconnection - LOTOS - A Formal Description Technique Based on the Temporal Ordering of Observational Behaviour*, ISO 1989.
[JM89] H. Jacobsson & S. Mauw, *A Token ring network in PSFd*, Report P8914, Programming Research Group, University of Amsterdam, 1989.
[Joh79] S.C. Johnson, *YACC: yet another compiler-compiler*, in: UNIX Programmer's Manual, Volume 2B, pp. 3-37, Bell Laboratories, 1979.
[Kli91] P. Klint, *A meta-environment for generating programming environments*, in: Algebraic Methods II: Theory, Tools and Applications, J.A. Bergstra & L.M.G. Feijs (eds.), LNCS 490, pp. 105-124, Springer Verlag, 1991.
[KR78] B.W. Kernighan & D.M. Ritchie, *The C programming language*, Prentice-Hall, 1978.
[LS79] M.E. Lesk & E. Schmidt, *LEX - A lexical analyzer generator*, in: UNIX Programmer's Manual, Volume 2B, pp. 39-51, Bell Laboratories, 1979.
[Mey88] B. Meyer, *Object-Oriented Software Construction*, Prentice Hall, 1988.
[Mil80] R. Milner, *A calculus of communicating systems*, Springer LNCS 92, 1980.
[MM90] S. Mauw & Gy. Max, *A formal specification of the Ethernet protocol*, Report P9007, Programming Research Group, University of Amsterdam, 1990.
[Mul89] J.C. Mulder, *The inevitable coffee machine*, Report P8915, Programming Research Group, University of Amsterdam, 1989.
[MV89a] S. Mauw & G.J. Veltink, *An introduction to PSF_d*, in: Proc. International Joint Conference on Theory and Practice of Software Development, TAPSOFT '89, (J. Díaz, F. Orejas, eds.) LNCS 352, pp. 272-285, Springer Verlag, 1989.
[MV89b] S. Mauw & G.J. Veltink, *A Tool Interface Language for PSF*, Report P8912, Programming Research Group, University of Amsterdam, 1989.
[MV90] S. Mauw & G.J. Veltink, *A process specification formalism*, Fundamenta Informaticae XIII (1990), pp. 85-139, IOS Press, 1990.
[MV91] S. Mauw & G.J. Veltink, *A proof assistant for PSF*, to appear in: Proceedings of the Workshop on Computer-Aided Verification, Aalborg 1991.
[Plo82] G.D. Plotkin, *An operational semantics for CSP*, in: Proc. Conf. Formal Description of Programming Concepts II, Garmisch 1982 (E. Bjørner, ed.), pp. 199-225, North-Holland, 1982.
[Vel90] G.J. Veltink, *From PSF to TIL*, Report P9009, Programming Research Group, University of Amsterdam, 1990.
[Vel91] G.J. Veltink, *The PSF Toolkit*, Report P9107, Programming Research Group, University of Amsterdam, 1991.
[Wie88] F. Wiedijk, *Voorlopig rapport over de specificatie-taal Perspect*, Report P8811, Programming Research Group, University of Amsterdam, 1988. (*in Dutch*)

Understanding Interfaces*

Simon S. Lam
Department of Computer Sciences
The University of Texas at Austin
Austin, Texas 78712

A. Udaya Shankar
Department of Computer Science and
Institute for Advanced Computer Studies
University of Maryland
College Park, Maryland 20742

Abstract

The concept of layering has been applied to the design and implementation of computer network protocols, operating systems, and other large complex systems. However, to reap the benefits of a layered architecture—i.e., to be able to design, implement, and modify each module in a layered system individually—a composition theorem such as one we formulated and proved recently is necessary. To arrive at the theorem, we explore the semantics of interfaces. In particular, we investigate how modules should be designed to satisfy interfaces as a service provider and as a service consumer. The requirements are then presented formally, as well as our composition theorem for a general model of layered systems.

1. Introduction

Consider the design of a system to provide services through a user interface U. Instead of designing a monolithic system to provide these services, the system design may be decomposed into components that are implemented separately. For example, Figure 1 shows a system design with two modules, M and N, interacting across interface L, and with users of the system interacting with M across interface U. The intention of the design is that N provides the services of interface L (formally, N *offers* L), and M provides the services of U while utilizing the services of L (formally, M *using* L *offers* U).

The design in Figure 1 can be used only if the following claim can be established: M while interacting with N does indeed provide the services of U to users of the system. The above claim can be established in general by proving the following composition theorem: If M using L offers U, and N offers L, then the composite system consisting of M interacting with N offers U. To prove the theorem, we need to understand how to specify interfaces,

---
* The work of Simon S. Lam was supported by National Science Foundation grant no. NCR-9004464. The work of A. Udaya Shankar was supported by National Science Foundation grant no. NCR-8904590.

and how modules should be designed to satisfy interfaces as a service provider and as a service consumer. Specifically, we need formal definitions for *interface*, *M offers I*, and *M using L offers U*, where M denotes a module and I, U, L denote interfaces.

We emphasize that these formal definitions are needed not only for the composition theorem but also for practical applications, i.e., for the designer of a module to check that the module does satisfy each one of its interfaces. With the composition theorem, we are assured that each module in Figure 1 can be designed, implemented, and modified *individually*. The internals of M can change so long as M satisfies L as a service consumer and satisfies U as a service provider. Similarly, the internals of N can change so long as N satisfies L as a service provider. This we consider to be the *key benefit of decomposition*.

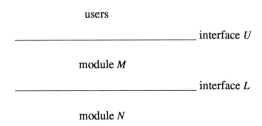

Figure 1. A system of two interacting modules.

Figure 1 is a simple illustration of the concept of layering (described by Dijkstra more than two decades ago [4]). Layering has been applied to the design and implementation of computer network protocols, operating systems, and other large complex systems. It is surprising that a composition theorem applicable to layered systems has not been formulated and proved. (In fact, to our knowledge, it has not even been formally stated by designers of layered systems.) Without formal semantics for the notions of *interface, using an interface*, and *offering an interface*, and a composition theorem based upon the semantics, we cannot get the key benefit of decomposing a system into modules or layers—because there are no applicable guidelines for designing each module to satisfy its interfaces.

The main result of this paper is a composition theorem for a general model of layered systems. Specifically, a layered system is organized as a stack of layers, with a finite number of modules in each layer. Each module offers a set of interfaces. Each module may use a set of interfaces offered by other modules, each of which resides in a lower layer of the stack. More precisely, a system can be represented by a directed acyclic graph where each node is a module, and each arc, say an arc from node M to node N, represents an interface whose service provider is N and whose service consumer is M. (Conversely, any directed acyclic graph represents a layered system in our model.)

For computer networks, we note that each module in our model represents a protocol (e.g., data link, transport, routing) rather than a protocol entity (i.e., a process). When there are several modules in a layer (e.g., the transport layer), they represent different protocols (e.g., TCP, TP4 and UDP).

The balance of this paper is organized as follows. In Section 2, we explore informally the semantics of interfaces, subsequently arriving at the concept of a "two-sided" interface. The requirements for a module to satisfy such an interface as a service consumer and for a module to satisfy it as a service provider are discussed. In Section 3 we present formal definitions. Our composition theorem is presented in Section 4. The concept of module implementation and theorems relevant to this concept are presented in Section 5.

2. Exploring Interface Semantics

A physical interface is where a module and its environment interact. For different kinds of physical interfaces, such interactions take on a variety of physical forms. For a vending machine, an interaction may be the insertion of a coin. For a workstation, an interaction may be the striking of a key on a keyboard. For a communication protocol, an interaction may be the passing of a set of parameter values. For a hardware circuit, an interaction may be the changing of voltages on certain pins.

Semantically, we model interface interactions between a module and its environment as discrete event occurrences. An interface event occurs only when both the module and environment are simultaneously executing the event (*simultaneous participation*). Such an occurrence is observable from either side of the interface. Thus an interface may be specified by a set of sequences of interface events; each such sequence defines an allowed sequence of interactions between the module and its environment. This semantic view of an interface is akin to the *specification* of a process in CCS [15], CSP [5] and Lotos [2], or the specification of an I/O automaton [14].

Let S denote the specification of a module M. Most definitions of M satisfies S in the literature have this informal meaning [5,6,13,14]: If every possible observation of M is described by S, then M satisfies S. (Specific definitions differ in many ways: (1) in whether interface events or states are observable, (2) in whether observations are finite or infinite sequences, (3) in the formalism for specifying these sequences, and (4) in the conditions under which interface events can occur.)

A straightforward way to define interface semantics is to use the following paradigm: every module is viewed by an observer situated in its environment. From the viewpoint of the observer, the module is completely enclosed by a physical interface that is semantically specified by S, a set of sequences of interface events. Informally, the module satisfies its interface if and only if every possible observation of the module is described by S.

In what follows, we first illustrate this paradigm with an example. We then discuss why it is inadequate for achieving our *goal* stated in Section 1—namely, to find conditions sufficient for designing, implementing, and modifying each module in a layered system individually; in particular, each module can be designed and implemented by a different person or team. Clearly, these conditions should be as weak as possible for them to be useful in practice.

Observer as paradigm

Consider the design of a vending machine that is made up of two modules, a control module and a storage module. (See Figure 2.) The control module has the following specification (in CSP notation [5]):

$$CONT = (coin \to request \to response \to choc \to CONT)$$

The intent of the designer can be stated as follows. A customer comes up to the vending machine and inserts a coin. Having accepted the coin, the control module sends a request to the storage module. Having got the request, the storage module responds by releasing a chocolate to the control module, which then dispenses the chocolate to the outside of the vending machine. The storage module has the following specification:

$$STOR = (request \to response \to STOR)$$

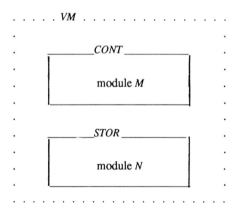

Figure 2. External views as specifications.

Let *VM* denote the parallel composition of *CONT* and *STOR* with interactions between the two modules hidden.

$$VM = (CONT \mid\mid STOR) \setminus \{request, response\}$$
$$= (coin \to choc \to VM)$$

VM represents the allowed interaction sequences between the vending machine and its environment. Note that these allowed interaction sequences (as well as those between the control and storage modules) are not explicitly specified. Instead, they are derived from $CONT$ and $STOR$. (This approach of system design is characterized as *compositional* or *bottom-up*.)

Suppose we have shown that VM satisfies the intended property for a vending machine. Let M denote a module that implements $CONT$, and N a module that implements $STOR$. (See Figure 2.) We can then use *observational equivalence*, defined by Milner [15], to be the *satisfies* relation between a module and its specification to arrive at a composition theorem—namely, if M is observationally equivalent to $CONT$, and N is observationally equivalent to $STOR$, then we claim that the composite system consisting of M interacting with N is observationally equivalent to VM.

Actually, various weaker notions of equivalence can be used instead of observational equivalence. In fact, to have a useful composition theorem, the *satisfies* relation between a module P and its specification S should be much weaker. Specifically, consider an implementation relation from [2,3], stated informally as follows:

P is an implementation of S iff

(**I1**) P can only execute events that S can execute, and

(**I2**) P can only refuse events that S can refuse.

For the vending machine example, we claim that if M is an implementation of $CONT$ and N is an implementation of $STOR$, then the composite system consisting of M interacting with N is an implementation of VM. However, for reasons given below, the requirements **I1** and **I2** are still too strong for achieving our goal.

Events controlled by environment

Consider module M in Figure 2, which implements $CONT$. Module M participates in the execution of four events, *coin*, *choc*, *request*, and *response*. In applying the implementation relation (or observational equivalence) to M and $CONT$, all four events are treated in the same way. However, there is clearly an intuitive distinction between the events $\{choc, request\}$, for which module M has control of, and the events $\{coin, response\}$, for which module M does not have control of.

Consider an occurrence of the event *coin*, requiring insertion of a coin by a customer in the environment of the vending machine, and participation by module M to accept the coin. Note that the *initiative* to insert a coin can only be taken by a customer in the environment; hence, the environment has control of the *coin* event.

In addition to initiative, control of an event also includes a notion of *responsibility*, e.g., the coin inserted by the customer is not a "bad" coin. The specification *CONT* above is unsatisfactory because it requires module *M* to have perfect discrimination of good and bad coins—a highly unreasonable premise—in the sense that in order for a module and *CONT* to satisfy the implementation relation, the module must accept only good coins and refuse all bad ones.

A more reasonable specification for the module is that it accepts only objects of a certain size, shape and weight. For such a module, a bad coin can be one of these cases:

- It is an object larger than the specified size of the coin slot. When a customer tries to insert the object, it is blocked (refused).
- It is an object that meets the size specification but not the shape or weight specification. When a customer inserts the object, it is accepted. Having accepted the object (e.g., a piece of scrap metal), module *M* breaks down or malfunctions in an arbitrary manner. (Can we blame the module or the designer of the module?)
- It is an object that meets the specification of size, shape and weight (e.g., a counterfeit coin). When a customer inserts it, it is accepted and module *M* dispenses a chocolate.

In each of the three cases, we believe that the behavior of module *M* is satisfactory and the module should not be considered as failing its specification. However, such would be the conclusion if the implementation relation were the criterion for *M* to satisfy *CONT*; hence it is too strong.

The reader, one who is familiar with CSP (or Lotos), might disagree with this conclusion. Clearly, we can replace the event *coin* by three events, *big.object*, *bad.object*, and *good.object*, with *good.object* representing both genuine and counterfeit coins. We can then rewrite the specification *CONT* as described above for the three cases. In fact, we can and should rewrite *CONT* to describe what module *M* must do for every possible sequence of objects that a customer may try to insert.

Indeed, CSP (or Lotos) is sufficiently expressive for specifying how a module responds to all kinds of inputs from its environment. The moral of the story here, however, is not about expressiveness, but something else, namely: In designing a module, we have *information* that certain events are controlled by the environment of the module. Such information is not utilized in the definition of the implementation relation. Consequently, unless the module's specification (i.e., *CONT* in the example) is designed to explicitly make use of this information and, moreover, all possible input sequences from the environment are accounted for in the specification, the implementation relation is too strong.

Similarly, consider the event *response* that is under the control of module *N* but not under the control of module *M*. If module *M* fails to dispense a chocolate because module *N* does not respond to a request from *M*, or the response of module *N* is bad, then module *M* should not be considered as failing its specification.

In Section 3 below, when we define an interface, each event is identified to be under the control of the service provider or consumer of the interface. Intuitively, we employ the following approach: for every event under the control of the consumer, it is the responsibility of the consumer, rather than the provider, to ensure that the event is not a bad input. In our definitions of *M offers I* and *M using L offers U*, we make use of information that certain events are controlled by the environment of *M* to arrive at "safety constraints" that are similar to, but weaker than, **I1** and **I2**. With our definitions, there is no need to *explicitly* account for all possible input sequences when specifying the interfaces of a module.

Designing module vs. testing black box

In *testing* an existing module—specifically, one whose internal states are either unobservable or too complicated to comprehend—the tester is the outside observer and the module is regarded as a black box. In designing a module to satisfy its interfaces, however, there is no need to consider the module as a black box. In fact, we do not, for the following reason.

Consider a vending machine and a tester. The tester can initiate interaction with the vending machine by inserting a coin or some object. However, it cannot initiate interaction with the vending machine in the *choc* event. Having inserted a coin, the tester can only wait to interact in the *choc* event. Suppose an indefinite duration of time has elapsed and there is no sign of chocolate. The tester cannot conclude that the vending machine has refused the *choc* event (because real time is not part of the interface semantics).

In designing a module, there is no need to view it as a black box. In our approach, the designer of a module is the one who demonstrates that the module satisfies its interface as a service provider, and the designer knows the module's internal behaviors. (See "progress constraints" in definitions of *M offers I* and *M using L offers U* in Section 3.)

Decompositional vs. compositional approach

In general, let S denote a system specification, and $\{S_i\}$ specifications of individual modules in the system. In a compositional approach, $\{S_i\}$ are specified first and S is derived from them. If S does not have the intended system property, the module specifications $\{S_i\}$ are redesigned. On the other hand, in a decompositional or top-down approach, the system specification S is first given and module specifications $\{S_i\}$ are derived from S.

When there are constraints on how a system should be decomposed into processes, as in the design of many distributed algorithms—e.g., one process in each node of a network performing a parallel computation—a compositional approach is appropriate. On the other hand, to design a system beginning with no constraint other than S, a decompositional approach provides the maximum freedom of choice on how to decompose the system.

Decomposing a system specification S into a set $\{S_i\}$ of module specifications is a difficult task in general. For a layered system, however, the task is facilitated by the hierarchical provider-consumer relationships between pairs of modules in the system. In this case, S corresponds to the "topmost" interface offered to the users of the system. Other interfaces in the system can be derived from S by a topdown approach as follows. Consider any interface U in the system. To design a module that offers the services of U, we may assume that certain services are offered by other modules through a set of interfaces $\{L_j\}$. In this manner, interfaces offered by other modules in lower layers of the system are specified.

Contract as paradigm

Our interface semantics differs in several ways from those based upon the paradigm of an external observer [2,5,14,15]. First, each module in a system is specified by a set of interfaces rather than a single external view (e.g., module M specified by interfaces U and L in Figure 1). We think of an interface to be like a legal contract between two modules in the system (e.g., interface L in Figure 1), or between a module and the environment of the system (e.g., interface U in Figure 1).

Each interface has a service provider on one side and a service consumer on the other. The allowed interaction sequences between the service provider and consumer are specified *explicitly*. Specifically, let I denote an interface between M and N. (See Figure 3.) In our design approach, I is first specified to be a set of allowed interaction sequences between M and N. Specifications of M and N are to be derived from I.

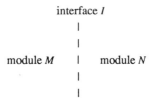

Figure 3. Interface I constraining behaviors of both M and N.

Note that the *same* set of interaction sequences constrains the behaviors of both M and N. This is like a legal contract between two parties: the same document contains the entire bilateral agreement, and is interpreted by each party to determine its privileges and obligations. For example, consider a loan agreement between a debtor and a creditor. The identity of either the debtor or the creditor may change (e.g., a house is sold and its mortgage assumed by the buyer). The loan agreement remains in force so long as it has been honored by its debtor and creditor, whose actual identities over time might have changed.

We refer to interface *I* illustrated in Figure 3 as a *two-sided interface* because, like a bilateral agreement, *I* encodes all information that the designers of M and N need to know and the same *I* is to be satisfied by both M and N—albeit the obligations of service provider and service consumer are not exactly the same.

Each event in interface *I* is explicitly defined to be under the control of M or N. This additional semantic information gives rise to definitions—of what it means for a service provider and a service consumer to satisfy an interface—that are adequate for our goal, i.e., design, implement and modify modules individually. (See Section 3 for details.)

The notion of control is not new (e.g., see [13]). In the theory of I/O automata [14], the events of an I/O automaton are partitioned into events under its control and events controlled by the automaton's environment. Each I/O automaton, however, is required to be input-enabled, i.e., every input event, controlled by its environment, must be enabled to occur in every state of the automaton. With this requirement, the class of interfaces that can be specified using I/O automata is restricted. For example, a module with a finite input buffer such that inputs causing overflow are refused cannot be specified. A consequence of the restriction is that it is not always possible to use an I/O automaton to encode all the semantic information that a designer wants to include in a specification, e.g., the input buffer size. Such information has to be supplied separately by other means. (The theory of I/O automata differs from ours in other ways also. For example, the specification of an I/O automaton is defined to be its external view as seen by an outside observer; specifically, the *satisfies* relation is the usual one, i.e., an automaton M satisfies its specification S if every possible observation of M is described by S.)

Obligations of service provider and consumer

Consider Figure 3. Since interface events are partitioned into events under the control of M and events under the control of N, in general interface *I* can be satisfied only if M and N cooperate with each other in some manner. In order to design each module individually, terms of the required cooperation must be completely encoded in *I*.

For illustration, we consider some special cases, i.e., the terms of cooperation are in the form of a set of guarantees a module must ensure given that the other module satisfies a set of assumptions, where assumptions and guarantees are assertions of safety or progress. (For this section, assumptions and guarantees are stated informally and only very simple ones are illustrated. See Part II of our report [11] for a general and more rigorous presentation of safety and progress assertions in our method.)

A safety assertion is a statement that something bad never occurs. An example of some safety assumptions and guarantees for M and N is shown below.

(S1) M never executes e_1 $\Rightarrow$ N never executes e_2

(S2) N never executes e_2 $\Rightarrow$ M never executes e_1

(The consequent of **S1** is a guarantee of N given an assumption about M, which is the antecedent of **S1**. Similarly, the consequent of **S2** is a guarantee of M given an assumption about N, which is the antecedent of **S2**.)

A progress assertion is a statement that something good eventually occurs. An example of some progress assumptions and guarantees for M and N is shown below.

(**P1**) M eventually executes e_3 $\Rightarrow$ N eventually executes e_4

(**P2**) N eventually executes e_4 $\Rightarrow$ M eventually executes e_3

Suppose M and N are designed individually and it has been proved that N satisfies **S1** and **P1** and M satisfies **S2** and **P2**. To infer that the composite system of M and N satisfies the guarantees—more generally, to prove a composition theorem—we must take care that circular reasoning is not used. The possibility of circular reasoning in composing processes has been addressed by other researchers. For processes that communicate by CSP primitives, Misra and Chandy gave a proof rule for assumptions and guarantees that are restricted to safety properties [16]. Using different models, Pnueli [17] presented a proof rule and Abadi and Lamport [1] presented a composition principle that are more general in that the class of assertions includes progress properties (albeit the class is still restricted).

In summary, we know the following: Safety assumptions and guarantees can be composed without circular reasoning. (For **S1** and **S2**, this is intuitively evident.) But with progress assumptions and guarantees, such as **P1** and **P2**, circular reasoning is involved.

In formulating our composition theorem below, circular reasoning is avoided in a straightforward manner. Specifically, each interface in our model is between a service provider and consumer. Therefore, we need only assert that the provider eventually performs a service given that the consumer eventually does something good. (E.g., for a vending machine, if eventually a customer inserts a coin, then the vending machine eventually dispenses a chocolate.) Thus, if N is the service provider and M the service consumer of interface I in Figure 3, only **P1** is meaningful (but not **P2**). Since our composition theorem applies to layered systems that are modeled by a set of modules organized as the nodes of a directed acyclic graph, circular reasoning is avoided.

Our *implements* **relation**

In the next section, we formally define M *offers* I and M *using* L *offer* U, where M denotes a module and I, U and L interfaces. These definitions embody our semantics for a module satisfying an interface as a service provider and as a service consumer. Each module in a system can be designed separately given all of the interfaces offered and used by the module, However, having derived a module, say M_1, that satisfies all of the given interfaces, it is useful to have an *implements* relation to facilitate additional refinements of M_1 in the manner described below.

Suppose M_1 has been designed such that M_1 offers I and M_1 using L offers U for arbitrary interfaces I, U and L. Suppose M_2 is derived from M_1 by a series of refinements. The *implements* relation should be defined such that it is as weak as possible and allows the following to be inferred: If M_2 implements M_1, then M_2 offers I and M_2 using L offers U.

Consider Figure 3. Having derived modules M_1 and N_1 that cooperate to satisfy I, our *implements* relation is then used in the same way as the implementation relation [2,3] described above. It is however a weaker relation because interface events are under the control of either the service provider or consumer. Its definition, given in Section 5 below, is similar to that of M *offers* I.

3. Definitions

We first define some notation for sequences. A *sequence over E*, where E is a set, means a (finite or infinite) sequence $(e_0, e_1, \cdots)$, where $e_i \in E$ for all i. A *sequence over alternating E and F*, where E and F are sets, means a sequence $(e_0, f_0, e_1, f_1, \cdots)$, where $e_i \in E$ and $f_i \in F$ for all i.

Definition. An interface I is defined by:
- *Events*(I), a set of events that is the union of two disjoint sets,

    Inputs(I), a set of input events, and

    Outputs(I), a set of output events.
- *AllowedEventSeqs*(I), a set of sequences over *Events*(I), each of which is referred to as an allowed event sequence of I.

By definition, output events of I are under the control of the service provider of I, and input events of I are under the control of the service consumer (user) of I. For interface I, define

$$SafeEventSeqs(I) = \{w : w \text{ is a finite prefix of an allowed event sequence of } I\}$$

which includes the empty sequence.

Definition. A state transition system A is defined by:
- *States*(A), a set of states.
- *Initial*(A), a subset of *States*(A), referred to as initial states.
- *Events*(A), a set of events.
- *Transitions*$_A(e)$, a subset of *States*$(A) \times$ *States*(A), for every $e \in$ *Events*(A). Each element of *Transitions*$_A(e)$ is an ordered pair of states referred to as a transition of e.

A *behavior* of A is a sequence $\sigma=(s_0, e_0, s_1, e_1, \cdots)$ over alternating *States*(A) and *Events*(A) such that $s_0 \in Initial(A)$ and (s_i, s_{i+1}) is a transition of e_i for all i. A finite sequence σ over alternating *States*(A) and *Events*(A) may end in a state or an event. A finite behavior, on the other hand, ends in a state by definition. The set of behaviors of A is denoted by *Behaviors*(A). The set of finite behaviors of A is denoted by *FiniteBehaviors*(A).

For $e \in Events(A)$, let $enabled_A(e) \equiv \{s : \text{for some state } t, (s, t) \in Transitions_A(e)\}$. An event e is said to be enabled in a state s of A iff $s \in enabled_A(e)$. An event e is said to be disabled in a state s of A iff $s \notin enabled_A(e)$.

Notation. Let σ be a sequence over a set F. For any set E, $image(\sigma, E)$ is the sequence over E obtained from σ by deleting all elements that are not in E.

Definition. A module M is defined by:

- *Events*(M), a set of events that is the union of three disjoint sets:

    Inputs(M), a set of input events,

    Outputs(M), a set of output events, and

    Internals(M), a set of internal events.

- *sts*(M), a state transition system with *Events*$(sts(M))$=*Events*(M).

- *Fairness requirements of* M, a finite collection of subsets of *Outputs*$(M) \cup Internals(M)$. Each subset is referred to as a fairness requirement of M.

By definition, a module has control of its internal and output events, but its input events are under the control of its environment.

Convention. For readability, the notation $sts(M)$ is abbreviated to M wherever such abbreviation causes no ambiguity, e.g., $States(sts(M))$ is abbreviated to $States(M)$, $enabled_{sts(M)}(e)$ is abbreviated to $enabled_M(e)$, etc.

Let F be a fairness requirement of module M. F is said to be enabled in a state s of M iff, for some $e \in F$, e is enabled in s. F is said to be disabled in state s iff F is not enabled in s. In a behavior $\sigma=(s_0, e_0, s_1, e_1, \cdots, s_j, e_j, \cdots)$, we say that F occurs in state s_j iff $e_j \in F$. An infinite behavior σ of M satisfies F iff F occurs infinitely often or is disabled infinitely often in states of σ.

For module M, a behavior σ is an *allowed behavior* iff for every fairness requirement F of M: σ is finite and F is not enabled in its last state, or σ is infinite and satisfies F. Let *AllowedBehaviors*(M) denote the set of allowed behaviors of M.

We are now in a position to formalize the notion of *a module offers an interface*. Consider an interface I. Let σ be a sequence over a set of states and events.

Definition. σ is allowed wrt I iff $image(\sigma, Events(I)) \in AllowedEventSeqs(I)$.

Definition. σ is safe wrt I iff one of the following holds:
- σ is finite and $image(\sigma, Events(I)) \in SafeEventSeqs(I)$.
- σ is infinite and every finite prefix of σ is safe wrt I.

In what follows, we use $last(\sigma)$ to denote the last state in a finite behavior σ, and @ to denote concatenation of two sequences. (For sequences consisting of a single element, say e, the sequence notation $<e>$ is abbreviated to e for simplicity.)

Definition. Given a module M and an interface I, M *offers* I iff the following conditions hold:

- Naming constraints:
  $Inputs(M) = Inputs(I)$ and $Outputs(M) = Outputs(I)$.
- Safety constraints:
  For all $\sigma \in FiniteBehaviors(M)$, if σ is safe wrt I, then
  $\forall e \in Outputs(M): last(\sigma) \in enabled_M(e) \Rightarrow \sigma@e$ is safe wrt I, and
  $\forall e \in Inputs(M): \sigma@e$ is safe wrt $I \Rightarrow last(\sigma) \in enabled_M(e)$.
- Progress constraints:
  For all $\sigma \in AllowedBehaviors(M)$, if σ is safe wrt I, then σ is allowed wrt I.

Note that module M is required to satisfy interface I only if its environment satisfies the safety requirements of I. Specifically, for any finite behavior that is not safe wrt I, the two Safety constraints are satisfied trivially; for any allowed behavior of M that is not safe wrt I, the Progress constraint is satisfied trivially. That is, as soon as the environment of M violates some safety requirement of I, module M can behave arbitrarily and still satisfy the definition of M *offers* I.

The two Safety constraints can be stated informally as follows: First, whenever an output event of M is enabled to occur, the event's occurrence would be safe, i.e., if the event occurs next, the resulting sequence of interface event occurrences is a prefix of an allowed event sequence of I. Second, whenever an input event of M (controlled by its environment) can occur safely, M does not block the event's occurrence.

For an input event of M whose occurrence would be unsafe, module M has a choice: it may block the event's occurrence or let it occur.

A module M with upper interface U and lower interface L is illustrated in Figure 1. The environment of M consists of the user of U and the module that offers L. In what follows, we use "σ is safe wrt U and L" to mean "σ is safe wrt U and σ is safe wrt L."

Definition. Given module M and interfaces U and L, M *using* L *offers* U iff the following conditions hold:

- Naming constraints:
  $Events(U) \cap Events(L) = \emptyset$,
  $Inputs(M) = Inputs(U) \cup Outputs(L)$, and
  $Outputs(M) = Outputs(U) \cup Inputs(L)$.
- Safety constraints:
  For all $\sigma \in FiniteBehaviors(M)$, if σ is safe wrt U and L, then
  $\forall e \in Outputs(M): last(\sigma) \in enabled_M(e) \Rightarrow \sigma@e$ is safe wrt U and L, and
  $\forall e \in Inputs(M): \sigma@e$ is safe wrt U and $L \Rightarrow last(\sigma) \in enabled_M(e)$.
- Progress constraints:
  For all $\sigma \in AllowedBehaviors(M)$, if σ is safe wrt U and L, then
  σ is allowed wrt $L \Rightarrow \sigma$ is allowed wrt U.

The definition of M *using* L *offers* U is similar to the definition of M *offers* I in most respects. The main difference between the two definitions is in the Progress constraints. For module M using interface L, it is required to satisfy the progress requirements of interface U only if the module that offers L satisfies the progress requirements of L.

Note that M *using* L *offers* U reduces to M *offers* U when L is a *null* interface—i.e., $Events(L)$ is empty, and $AllowedEventSeqs(L)$ has the null sequence $<>$ as its only element.

4. Composition Theorem

We first define how modules are composed.

Definition. A set of modules $\{M_j: j \in J\}$ is compatible iff $\forall j, k \in J, j \neq k$:

$Internals(M_j) \cap Events(M_k) = \emptyset$, and $Outputs(M_j) \cap Outputs(M_k) = \emptyset$.

Convention. For any set of modules with distinct names, $\{M_j: j \in J\}$, it is assumed that $Internals(M_j) \cap Events(M_k) = \emptyset$, for all $j, k \in J, j \neq k$.

The above convention can be ensured by, for instance, including the name of each module as part of the name of each of its internal events. Thus to check that a set of modules $\{M_j: j \in J\}$ is compatible, it suffices to check that their output event sets are pairwise disjoint.

Notation. For a set of modules $\{M_j: j \in J\}$, each state of their composition is a tuple $s = (t_j: j \in J)$, where $t_j \in States(M_j)$. We use $image(s, M_j)$ to denote t_j.

(Note that the ordering of module states in the tuple is arbitrary. In fact, the state of the composite system can be represented by an unordered tuple provided that, for all $i, j \in J$, $States(M_i) \cap States(M_j) = \emptyset$. This requirement can be ensured by including the name of each module as part of its state.)

Definition. Given a compatible set of modules $\{M_j: j \in J\}$, their composition is a module M defined as follows:

- *Events* (M) defined by:

  $Internals(M) = [\bigcup_{j \in J} Internals(M_j)] \cup [(\bigcup_{j \in J} Outputs(M_j)) \cap (\bigcup_{j \in J} Inputs(M_j))]$

  $Outputs(M) = [\bigcup_{j \in J} Outputs(M_j)] - [\bigcup_{j \in J} Inputs(M_j)]$

  $Inputs(M) = [\bigcup_{j \in J} Inputs(M_j)] - [\bigcup_{j \in J} Outputs(M_j)]$

- *sts* (M) defined by:

  $States(M) = \prod_{j \in J} States(M_j)$

  $Initial(M) = \prod_{j \in J} Initial(M_j)$

  $Transitions_M(e)$, for all $e \in Events(M)$, defined by: $(s, t) \in Transitions_M(e)$ iff, $\forall j \in J$,

  if $e \in Events(M_j)$ then $(image(s, M_j), image(t, M_j)) \in Transitions_{M_j}(e)$, and

  if $e \notin Events(M_j)$ then $image(s, M_j) = image(t, M_j)$.

- *Fairness requirements of* $M = [\bigcup_{j \in J} Fairness\ requirements\ of M_j]$.

Definition. A set of interfaces $\{I_j: j \in J\}$ is *disjoint* iff $\forall j, k \in J$, $j \neq k$,

$Events(I_j) \cap Events(I_k) = \emptyset$.

Theorem 1. Let modules, M and N, and disjoint interfaces, U and L, satisfy the following:

- M using L offers U
- N offers L

Then, M and N are compatible and their composition offers U.

Since the composition of any two compatible modules is also a module, Theorem 1 is easily extended to the following theorem for an arbitrary number of modules organized in a linear hierarchy.

Theorem 2. Let $M_1, I_1, M_2, I_2, \cdots, M_n, I_n$ be a finite sequence over alternating modules and interfaces, such that the following hold:

- $I_1, I_2, \cdots,$ and I_n are disjoint interfaces.
- M_1 offers I_1.
- For $j=2, \cdots, n$, M_j using I_{j-1} offers I_j.

Then, modules $\{M_1, \cdots, M_n\}$ are compatible and their composition offers I_n.

Theorem 2 can be used for the design and specification of layered systems by considering each system layer as a module in our theory. For some complex systems, however, it is desirable to consider each system layer as a set of modules. For example, the transport layer of a computer network may consist of a set of different transport protocols (TCP, TP4, UDP, etc.).

We next formulate and prove a composition theorem for a general model of layered systems.

Definition. The composition of a set of disjoint interfaces, $\{I_j : j \in J\}$, is an interface I defined by:

- *Events* (I) that is the union of

$$Inputs(I) = \bigcup_{j \in J} Inputs(I_j), \text{ and}$$

$$Outputs(I) = \bigcup_{j \in J} Outputs(I_j)$$

- *AllowedEventSeqs* $(I) = \{w : w$ is a sequence over *Events* (I) such that
$$\forall j \in J : image(w, Events(I_j)) \in AllowedEventSeqs(I_j)\}$$

Definition. Given a set $\{U_1, U_2, \cdots, U_n, L_1, L_2, \cdots, L_m\}$ of disjoint interfaces, M using $L_1, L_2, \cdots, L_m$ offers $U_1, U_2, \cdots, U_n$ iff M using the composition of $\{L_1, L_2, \cdots, L_m\}$ offers the composition of $\{U_1, U_2, \cdots, U_n\}$. Also M offers $U_1, U_2, \cdots, U_n$ iff M offers the composition of $\{U_1, U_2, \cdots, U_n\}$.

Before considering a layered architecture in general, we first prove the following *basic composition theorem*:

Theorem 3. Let modules, M and N, and disjoint interfaces $\{U, L, V\}$, satisfy the following:

- M using L offers U
- N offers L, V

Then, M and N are compatible and their composition offers U, V.

Note that Theorem 3 subsumes Theorem 1. Specifically, it reduces to Theorem 1 when V is a null interface. A proof of Theorem 3 is presented in [10]; it is quite long, requiring seven lemmas.

Definition. A layered system with layers 1 through J is defined by

- *Modules*, a set of modules with distinct names partitioned into sets $Modules(j)$, $j=1, \cdots, J$, one for each layer.
- *Interfaces*, a set of disjoint interfaces partitioned into sets $Interfaces(j)$, $j=1, \cdots, J$, one for each layer.
- for each module $M \in Modules$, $U(M)$, a set of interfaces to be offered by M, and $L(M)$, a set of interfaces to be used by M.

such that the following Naming constraints are satisfied:

(1) for all $j=1, \cdots, J$:

$$Interfaces(j) = \bigcup_{M \in Modules(j)} U(M)$$

(2) for every $M \in Modules$:

  (a) $M \in Modules(j) \wedge j > 1 \Rightarrow L(M) \subseteq \bigcup_{k<j} Interfaces(k)$

  (b) $Inputs(M) = [\bigcup_{I \in U(M)} Inputs(I)] \cup [\bigcup_{I \in L(M)} Outputs(I)]$

  (c) $Outputs(M) = [\bigcup_{I \in U(M)} Outputs(I)] \cup [\bigcup_{I \in L(M)} Inputs(I)]$

(3) for every pair of distinct modules M and N:

  $U(M) \cap U(N) = \emptyset$
  $L(M) \cap L(N) = \emptyset$

The above Naming constraints ensure that *Modules* is a compatible set of modules.

In our model of layered systems, a module in layer j can use an interface offered by any module in a lower layer, provided that no other module is using the same interface. (This provision is simply a naming constraint. In fact, a module can offer services to multiple users concurrently. But by tagging interface event names with user names, the interface offered to each user is distinct.) A layered system corresponds to a directed graph whose nodes are modules and whose arcs are defined as follows: for modules M and N in *Modules*, there is an arc from M to N iff for some interface I in *Interfaces*, N offers I and M uses I. It is not hard to see that every layered system in our model can be represented by a directed acyclic graph. Furthermore, every directed acyclic graph represents a layered system allowed by our model.

Let *Services*(*j*) denote the services available to the user(s) of layer *j*. Formally,

$$Services(1) = Interfaces(1)$$

and for *j* >1

$$Services(j) = [Interfaces(j)] \cup [Services(j-1) - \bigcup_{M \in Modules(j)} L(M)]$$

Theorem 4. For a layered system, if the following hold:

- $\forall M \in Modules(1)$: M offers $U(M)$
- for $j=2, \cdots, J$, $\forall M \in Modules(j)$: M using $L(M)$ offers $U(M)$

Then, $\bigcup_{k \in \{1, \cdots, J\}} Modules(k)$ is a set of compatible modules and their composition offers *Services*(*J*).

5. Implementation Theorems

To define our *implements* relation between two modules, we extend the definitions of "safe wrt" and "allowed wrt" as follows. Let M and N denote modules, and let σ be a sequence over a set of states and events.

Definition. σ is safe wrt N iff for some $w \in Behaviors(N)$,

$$image(w, Inputs(N) \cup Outputs(N)) = image(\sigma, Inputs(N) \cup Outputs(N)).$$

Definition. σ is allowed wrt N iff for some $w \in AllowedBehaviors(N)$,

$$image(w, Inputs(N) \cup Outputs(N)) = image(\sigma, Inputs(N) \cup Outputs(N)).$$

Definition. Given modules M and N, M *implements* N iff the following conditions hold:

- Naming constraints:
    Inputs(*M*)=*Inputs*(*N*) and *Outputs*(*M*)=*Outputs*(*N*).
- Safety constraints:
    For all $\sigma \in FiniteBehaviors(M)$, if σ is safe wrt N, then

    $\forall e \in Outputs(M)$: $last(\sigma) \in enabled_M(e) \Rightarrow \sigma@e$ is safe wrt N, and

    $\forall e \in Inputs(M)$: $\sigma@e$ is safe wrt $N \Rightarrow last(\sigma) \in enabled_M(e)$.
- Progress constraints:
    For all $\sigma \in AllowedBehaviors(M)$, if σ is safe wrt N, then σ is allowed wrt N.

Suppose a module has been designed and shown to satisfy a set of interfaces. Subsequently, we may want to refine it to derive new modules. The following theorems are useful for justifying such refinement steps.

Theorem 5. Let M and N be modules and I an interface. If M implements N and N offers I, then M offers I.

Theorem 6. Let M and N be modules, and U and L be interfaces. If M implements N and N using L offers U, then M using L offers U.

Theorem 7. Let M_1, M_2 and M_3 be modules. If M_3 implements M_2 and M_2 implements M_1, then M_3 implements M_1.

6. Concluding Remarks

Proofs of the theorems and lemmas in this paper are presented in [10]. For interfaces and modules specified in the relational notation [8], we have developed a proof method based upon the theory in this paper [11]. A small example illustrating application of our method to the specification of a connection management protocol can be found in [9]. Nontrivial applications of our method to the specification and verification of protocols for concurrency control and secure access control can be found in [7] and [12] respectively.

Acknowledgement

We thank Michael Merritt of Bell Laboratories for his constructive criticisms of our proof method in [7], which motivated us to develop the theory presented in this paper.

References

[1] M. Abadi and L. Lamport, "Composing Specifications," in *Stepwise Refinement of Distributed Systems*, J. W. de Bakker, W.-P. de Roever and G. Rozenberg (Eds.), LNCS 430, Springer-Verlag, 1990.

[2] T. Bolognesi and E. Brinksma, "Introduction to the ISO Specification Language LOTOS," *Computer Networks and ISDN Systems*, Vol. 14, 1987.

[3] S. D. Brookes, C. A. R. Hoare, and A. D. Roscoe, "A Theory of Communicating Sequential Processes," *JACM*, Vol. 31, No. 3, 1984.

[4] E. W. Dijkstra, "Hierarchical Ordering of Sequential Processes," *Acta Informatica*, Vol. 1, 1971.

[5] C. A. R. Hoare, *Communicating Sequential Processes*, Prentice-Hall, Englewood Cliffs, N.J., 1985.

[6] S. S. Lam and A. U. Shankar, "Protocol Verification via Projections," *IEEE Transactions on Software Engineering*, Vol. SE-10, No. 10, July 1984.

[7] S. S. Lam and A. U. Shankar, "Specifying Modules to Satisfy Interfaces: A State Transition System Approach," Technical Report TR-88-30, Department of Computer Sciences, University of Texas at Austin, August 1988; revised, January 1991, to appear in *Distributed Computing*.

[8] S. S. Lam and A. U. Shankar, "A Relational Notation for State Transition Systems," *IEEE Transactions on Software Engineering*, Vol. 16, No. 7, July 1990; an abbreviated version entitled "Refinement and Projection of Relational Specifications" in *Stepwise Refinement of Distributed Systems*, J. W. de Bakker, W.-P. de Roever and G. Rozenberg (Eds.), LNCS 430, Springer-Verlag, 1990.

[9] S. S. Lam and A. U. Shankar, "A Composition Theorem for Layered Systems," *Proceedings 11th Int. Symp. on Protocol Specification, Testing and Verification*, Stockholm, June 1991.

[10] S. S. Lam and A. U. Shankar, "A Theory of Interfaces and Modules I—Composition Theorem," Technical Report, Department of Computer Sciences, University of Texas at Austin, in preparation.

[11] S. S. Lam and A. U. Shankar, "A Theory of Interfaces and Modules II—Proof Method," Technical Report, Department of Computer Sciences, University of Texas at Austin, in preparation.

[12] S. S. Lam, A. U. Shankar and T. Y. C. Woo, "Applying a Theory of Modules and Interfaces to Security Verification," *Proceedings Symposium on Research in Security and Privacy*, IEEE Computer Society, May 1991.

[13] L. Lamport, "A Simple Approach to Specifying Concurrent Systems," *Comm. ACM*, Vol. 32, No. 1, January 1989.

[14] N. Lynch and M. Tuttle, "Hierarchical Correctness Proofs for Distributed Algorithms," *Proceedings of the ACM Symposium on Principles of Distributed Computing*, Vancouver, B.C., August 1987.

[15] R. Milner, *A Calculus of Communicating Systems*, LNCS 92, Springer-Verlag, Berlin, 1980.

[16] J. Misra and K. M. Chandy, "Proofs of Networks of Processes," *IEEE Transactions on Software Engineering*, Vol. SE-7, No. 4, July 1981.

[17] A. Pnueli, "In Transition from Global to Modular Temporal Reasoning About Programs," NATO ASI Series, Vol. F13, *Logics and Models of Concurrent Systems*, K. R. Apt (ed.), Springer-Verlag, Berlin, 1984.

Modelling Dynamic Communication Structures in LOTOS*

Lars-åke Fredlund and Fredrik Orava[†]
Swedish Institute of Computer Science
Box 1263, S-164 28 Kista, Sweden

Abstract

We study how to formally specify dynamically changing communication structures in the specification language LOTOS. We present a method for modelling dynamic communication structures by encoding link names as data values together with a sufficient condition on the communication structure guaranteeing that the modelling is possible. As an example we formally specify the handover procedure in the GSM protocols. Using automated tools we prove the specification equivalent with a more abstract description of the system.

1 Introduction

Most work in the literature on formal protocol specification and verification [PSTV, FORTE] address the functional behaviour of protocols, while little attention has been paid to other aspects of protocols, e.g. the mobility of nodes in mobile telephone networks. Although work has been published on specification of mobile networks [CV89, DRL90], these papers do not concentrate on the mobile aspects. Exceptions are [OP90, OP91, EFJ91]. In [OP90, OP91] mobility of nodes in a mobile telephone network is directly expressed and verified in the rigorous mathematical framework of the π-calculus [MPW89a, MPW89b], a process calculus where mobility is one of the basic concepts. In [EFJ91] a system with dynamic communication structure is specified and verified in LOTOS [vEVD89] by modelling the communication media as LOTOS processes. The purpose of this paper is to demonstrate how mobility of nodes can be modelled directly in the standardized specification language LOTOS.

As an example of a system with a dynamic communication structure we will specify and verify a part of a protocol intended to be used in the Public Land Mobile Network (PLMN) proposed by the European Telecommunication Standards Institute (ETSI).

---

*This work was partially supported by the Swedish Board for Technical Development (ESPRIT/BRA project 3006, CONCUR) and the Swedish Telecommunication Administration (project PROCOM).
[†]Authors' email: fred@sics.se; fredrik@sics.se

In Section 2 we discuss how to model a dynamically changing communication structure in LOTOS and characterize the class of communication systems we consider in this paper. In Section 3 we give an overview of the structure of the Public Land Mobile Network and explain informally the handover procedure. The formal specification of the handover procedure in LOTOS is contained in Section 4. We prove the protocol equivalent with a more abstract description of the system. The specification of the protocol is generalized and the result is discussed. Finally in Section 5 some concluding remarks are drawn.

2 Dynamic Communication Structures

Consider a model of synchronously communicating processes where *processes* are interconnected and can communicate via named *links*. If each communication via a specific link involves exactly two processes, then the communication via the link is *binary* and the link is a binary link. By the *communication interface* of a process we understand the set of names of links the process may use to communicate with its environment. Consider the scenario depicted in Figure 1(left). Let the communication interface of P, Q and R be $\{a,b\}$, $\{a,c\}$ and $\{b\}$ respectively. The processes P and Q can communicate through the link a and the processes P and R can communicate through the link b but R and Q cannot communicate because they do not share any link. Note that the communication interface of Q includes the link name c although Q is not connected to any other process via a link with this name. Assume now that this communication structure is changed so that Q and R can communicate directly. One way to model this change is as a transmission to R of a link that Q can use for communication, say c. The situation is now as in Figure 1(middle), Q and R can communicate through the link c. In this section we discuss how to model this kind of dynamically changing communication structure in LOTOS.

2.1 Problem Description

The scenario described above requires at least two features of the specification language at hand: the ability to dynamically change the communication interface of a process by adding and removing links, and the ability to communicate links between processes. The

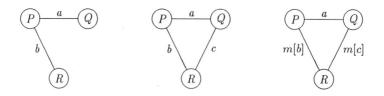

Figure 1: Left: Three processes before reconfiguration. Middle: Three processes after reconfiguration. Right: Modeling link passing.

LOTOS specification language lack both these capabilities. In LOTOS the processes have a static communication interface and communication between processes is accomplished by synchronizing on common gates. When specifying a process in LOTOS the specifier has to decide from the very beginning which gates the process may use for communication. Once this is decided the interface cannot be changed, i.e. the process cannot communicate via any other gate. Furthermore, in LOTOS it is not possible to communicate gate names between processes, it is only possible to transmit values of (user specified) datatypes.

However, we can model passing of links in the following manner. We consider links, e.g. b in the example above, to be pairs consisting of a *medium* and a *channel*. Two processes communicate by naming both medium and channel, e.g. $medium_i[channel_j]$. We model transmission of links by passing channel names (e.g. $channel_j$) between processes. Consider again the example in Figure 1 (right). In this example m is a medium containing two channels, b and c. Communication is accomplished by naming both the medium and the channel. Initially, P communicates with R via $m[b]$. The transmission of the link c to R is modelled by P transmitting, via $m[b]$, the channel name c to R. The processes Q and R can now communicate through $m[c]$.

These considerations suggest the following method for specification of dynamically changing communication structures in LOTOS. Assume two sets of processes, S_1 and S_2, where (some of) the processes in S_1 communicate with (some of) the processes in S_2 via a set of links, L. Some of the members of L may be transmitted in communications via other links in L. We model the set of links, L, by one gate m (common to all processes in S_1 and S_2) and a set of channel identifiers, C, one for each link in L. A communication via a link $l_i \in L$ is specified as a synchronization on the common gate m together with the channel identifier c_i, corresponding to the link l_i, as in: m !c_i. According to the semantics of the parallel composition operator in LOTOS, only processes which specify the same channel identifier can synchronize. The transmission of the channel c in the example in Figure 1 would be specified as m !b !c and the reception as m !b ?l:ChannelId. The receiver, R, subsequently uses the received value, stored in the variable l, as a channel identifier to communicate with the process Q, as in m !l. Note that we do not require gate names to be transmitted, nor do we change the communication interface of the processes.

Unfortunately, not all process configurations can be handled in this way. The success of the method depends crucially on the semantics of the parallel composition operator and the actual communication structure. A parallel composition in LOTOS (or CSP [Hoa85]), P |[A]| Q, requires participation of both P and Q in a synchronization on a gate in the set of gates A. This is in contrast to e.g. CCS [Mil89] where a parallel composition $P | Q$ may offer a synchronization on a port common to P and Q if one of the components offer a synchronization. If, in the example in Figure 1, P and Q also would communicate via m, then the three processes P, Q and R would have to agree on every communication on m, in particular all three processes would have to agree on the transmission of the channel name c to the process R. This would violate our intuition that a link is transmitted from one process to another.

2.2 Characterization

In this subsection we characterize the class of process configurations where we can model a dynamically changing communication structure as outlined in the previous subsection. The idea is to divide the set of process into groups such that a link name is only passed between a pair of groups. If more than two processes are going to use the same link name then we must make sure that we can arrange the processes such that communication over links with the common name always occur between two groups.

We first investigate which process configurations we can model in LOTOS. We then describe how we model dynamic communication structures within this class.

Definition 1 A *communication graph* C is a triple $\langle V, N, E \rangle$ where:

- V is non-empty set of *nodes*.
- N is a set of *link names*.
- E is a set of *edges*, $E \subseteq 2^V \times N$.

□

We will interpret V as a set of processes and E as communication capabilities, or links, between the processes. Note that an edge in a communication a graph can connect more than two processes and thus represent a multi-way communication. If all edges in the graph connect exactly two processes then the graph is binary.

Definition 2 A communication graph $\langle V, N, E \rangle$ is *binary* if $E \subseteq V \times V \times N$. □

Example 1 In Figure 2 we give examples of different communication graphs. In the leftmost communication graph process P can communicate with process R via a link named a and process Q can communicate with process R via a link named a, but P and Q cannot communicate. In the middle graph all three processes can communicate with each other. Finally, in the rightmost graph all three processes can participate in a three-way communication.

In LOTOS (and CSP) it is possible to model processes with general communication graphs. In CCS all processes have a binary communication graph. Networks of synchronously communicating processes has been studied in detail by Milner ([Mil79]) and Parrow ([Par90a, Par90b]). We are in this paper interested in binary communication and will from now on only consider binary communication graphs.

Definition 3 Let C be a communication graph $\langle V, N, E \rangle$. We define $V(C)$ (the nodes of C), $N(C)$ (the link names of C) and $E(C)$ (the edges of C) as:

- $V(\langle V, N, E \rangle) = V$

- $N(\langle V, N, E \rangle) = N$
- $E(\langle V, N, E \rangle) = E$

□

Definition 4 Let C be a binary communication graph. The *sort* of a node $v \in V(C)$ is defined by: $sort_C(v) = \{l \mid \exists v' \in V(C) \wedge (v, v', l) \in E(C)\}$. □

We will now give sufficient conditions on communication graphs guaranteeing that it is possible to model the corresponding communication structure in LOTOS. The idea is to consider *binary aggregations* of the communication graph, i.e. groupings of the nodes of the communication graph connected by sets of link names. A communication graph can be implemented in LOTOS (or CSP) if there exists a binary aggregation representing the same communication capabilities as the communication graph.

Definition 5 A *binary aggregation* B of the binary communication graph $C = \langle V, N, E \rangle$ is a triple $\langle X_1, X_2, L \rangle$ such that

either X_1 is a singleton set $\{v\}$, $v \in V(C)$ and $X_2 = \emptyset$ and $L = \emptyset$

or

1. X_1 and X_2 are binary aggregations of C
2. $L \subseteq N(C)$ such that $L \cap (\mathcal{L}(X_1) \cup \mathcal{L}(X_2)) = \emptyset$, where

$$\mathcal{L}(\langle Y_1, Y_2, L \rangle) = \begin{cases} \emptyset & \text{if } Y_1 = \{v\} \text{ and } Y_2 = L = \emptyset \\ \mathcal{L}(Y_1) \cup \mathcal{L}(Y_2) \cup L & \text{otherwise} \end{cases}$$

□

Note that the nodes of a binary aggregation are binary aggregations themselves. The condition on the sets of links in the second clause above guarantees that no link name connecting two groups occur inside the groups. This will guarantee that all communication between the processes in the binary aggregation is binary.

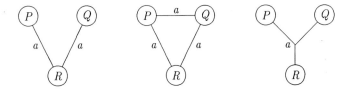

Figure 2: Examples of different communication graphs.

Definition 6 Let B be a binary aggregation $\langle X_1, X_2, L \rangle$ of the binary communication graph C. The *occurrence* of $v (\in V(C))$ in B, denoted $\mathcal{O}_v(B)$, is defined by:

$$\mathcal{O}_v(\langle X_1, X_2, L \rangle) = \begin{cases} 1 & \text{if } X_1 = \{v\} \text{ and } X_2 = L = \emptyset \\ 0 & \text{if } X_1 = \{u\} \text{ and } X_2 = L = \emptyset \text{ and } u \neq v \\ \mathcal{O}_v(X_1) + \mathcal{O}_v(X_2) & \text{otherwise} \end{cases}$$

□

Definition 7 Let $B = \langle X_1, X_2, L \rangle$ be a binary aggregation of C. Let $l \in N(C)$ and $v, u \in V(C)$. We say that l *connects* v *and* u *in* B if

either $\mathcal{O}_v(X_1) > 0$ and $\mathcal{O}_u(X_2) > 0$ and $l \in L$, or vice versa

or l connects v and u in X_1

or l connects v and u in X_2

□

Definition 8 Let C be a binary communication graph. The binary aggregation B of C is *faithful* to C if the following three conditions are satisfied:

1. if $v \in V(C)$ then $\mathcal{O}_v(B) = 1$.

2. for all $(v, u, l) \in E(C)$ it is the case that l connects v and u in B.

3. if l connects v and u in B and $l \in sort_C(v) \cap sort_C(u)$ then $(v, u, l) \in E(C)$.

□

Informally, if a binary aggregation B is faithful to a binary communication graph C, then B represents the same communication capabilities as C. Let p be a LOTOS process. By *gates*(p) we denote the set of gates on which p can synchronize. Let C be a binary communication graph with n nodes, $\{v_1, \ldots, v_n\}$, and let $\{p_1, \ldots, p_n\}$ be LOTOS processes such that $sort_C(v_i) = gates(p_i)$. We say that the binary communication graph C can be modelled in LOTOS if there exists a LOTOS expression P, only containing the parallel composition operator and $p_1, \ldots, p_n$, such that p_i can synchronize with p_j on gate l if and only if $(v_i, v_j, l) \in E(C)$. In [FO] we prove that a binary communication graph C can be modelled in LOTOS if there exists a faithful binary aggregation B of C. Intuitively, a binary aggregation $\langle X_1, X_2, L \rangle$ of a communication graph can be viewed as an abstract LOTOS process, X1|[L]|X2, with the sets of link names, L, corresponding to the set of gates in the parallel composition operator.

The result extends to dynamically changing process configurations if we take all links in consideration, i.e. also links a process may receive in future communications. Thus, if the system under specification has a binary communication graph with a faithful binary aggregation when we also take future links in consideration, then we can model the dynamic aspects of the system as described in the Section 2.1. The modelling can be performed in the following way. For each subset L of link names in the binary aggregation, use L as the name of the medium and the link names in L as channel names.

Example 2 In Figure 3 we give examples of binary communication graphs (denoted $C_1, \ldots, C_4$ from left to right). In Figure 4 we give example of binary aggregations (denoted $B_1, \ldots, B_4$ from left to right) of $C_1, \ldots, C_4$. Only B_4 is faithful to C_4. The binary aggregation B_1 does not satisfy requirement 2 of Definition 8 relative to C_1. The binary aggregations B_2 and B_3 do not satisfy requirement 3 in Definition 8 relative C_2 and C_3 respectively. This is because a connects Q and R in B_2 and $a \in sort_{C_2}(Q) \cap sort_{C_2}(R)$ but $(Q, R, a) \notin E(C_2)$. The same holds for C_3 and B_3.

Note that, with our modelling, the scope of a link name is static. The scope of a link name, l, is the set of processes which are members of the binary aggregations which are connected by an edge labelled with a set L containing l. Once the system is modelled as described above we have also decided which link names a process may use for communication in the future. The process may not know about all of these link names at all times, some of them may become known to the process as result of a communication. However, a link cannot move outside of its static scope. This is in contrast to the π-calculus where a link name may move freely between processes and where the scope of a link name changes as the system executes.

We end this section by pointing out that even if there is no binary aggregation faithful to the communication graph under consideration it may still be possible to model dynamically changing communication capabilities by, for example, modelling the media explicitly as processes. This is done in e.g. [EFJ91].

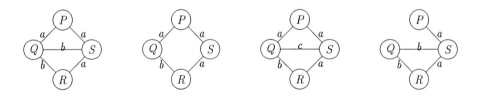

Figure 3: Examples of different communication structures as communication graphs.

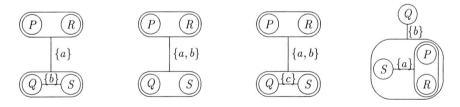

Figure 4: Examples of aggregated communication graphs

3 The Handover Procedure in GSM

In this section we will give an overview of the operation of the handover procedure intended to be used in the GSM Public Land Mobile Network (PLMN). The presentation in this section is based on earlier work by one of the authors [OP90, OP91].

The PLMN is a cellular system consisting of Mobile Stations, Base Stations, Mobile Switching Centers, and Location Registers. A *Mobile Station* (MS) is a unit mounted in e.g. a car providing service to an end user. A *Base Station* (BS) manages the interface between the Mobile Stations and a stationary network. Each Base Station controls radio communication within a designated geographical area, called a *cell*. All communication with Mobile Stations in a cell is routed through the Base Station responsible for the cell. A *Mobile Switching Center* (MSC) manages a set of Base Stations. Communication between two Mobile Switching Centers, and between an MSC and an external network, uses an existing stationary network. Communication between an MSC and a BS may also employ this network. The *Location Registers* record the status of the PLMN. Each Mobile Station is associated with a *Home Location Register* to which all incoming calls to the station are routed. This register contains information about where to find the associated Mobile Station.

3.1 The Handover Procedure

The purpose of the handover procedure is to change the communication partner of the Mobile Station from the Base Station in the current cell (in the following called the *old* Base Station) to a new Base Station (called the *new* Base Station) in another cell. This procedure is needed to ensure that a Mobile Station moving across a cell boundary is constantly in contact with the MSC (via a Base Station). Without such a handover communication with the Mobile Station could be disrupted because of the restricted range of the radio equipment.

The network (MSC) initiates the handover by transmitting a *handover command* message to the Mobile Station via the old Base Station. The handover command message contains parameters enabling the Mobile Station to locate the radio links of the new Base Station. When transmitting this message the network (MSC) suspends transmission of all messages except for messages related to the handover procedure. Upon receipt of a handover command message the Mobile Station disconnects the old radio links and initiates the establishment of low layer connections on the new radio links. In order to establish these connections the Mobile Station sends *handover access* messages to the new Base Station. The purpose of the access messages is to synchronize the Mobile Station with the new Base Station. When the low layer connections are successfully established, the Mobile Station sends a *handover complete* message to the network via the new Base Station. When the handover complete message has been received the network resumes normal operations and releases the old radio links; these are now free and can be allocated to another Mobile Station.

There are a number of ways in which the handover procedure may fail, we mention here only a few. If the Mobile Station is unable to establish the low layer connections on the new radio links it will try to reestablish the connections on the old links. If this succeeds the Mobile Station sends a *handover failure* message to the network via the old Base Station, and resumes operation on the old links as if no handover attempt had been made. If the Mobile Station does not succeed in reestablishing the connections on the old links the Mobile Station is isolated and recovery procedures are invoked. The network may also time out before it receives a response (handover complete or handover failure) to a handover message. The old links are then released and all connections with the Mobile Station are cleared.

An abstract view of the handover procedure is that the Mobile Station receives, via the link to the old Base Station, a new link to the new Base Station. In the next Section we will model this abstract view of the handover procedure in LOTOS using the method of Section 2.

4 Handover in LOTOS

4.1 Formal Definition of the Handover Procedure

In this section we specify the handover procedure in LOTOS. We consider a simple scenario with one Mobile Switching Center (MSC), a single Mobile Station (MS), and two Base Stations (BS_1 and BS_2) with one radio channel each (see Figure 5(left)). Section 4.2 discusses a generalized formal definition.

The MSC is connected to the Base Stations via two links, b_1 to BS_1 and b_2 to BS_2. A Base Station consists of a number of Controllers (short for Radio Channel Controllers) each one controlling one radio channel. Radio channels are used for communication between Mobile Stations and Controllers. In our specification we assume that all names of radio channels are unique.

In Figure 5(middle) we show the binary communication graph of the system, and in Figure 5(right) we show a faithful binary aggregation of the communication graph, thus

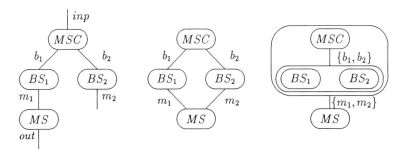

Figure 5: Left: The initial configuration of links in the scenario. Middle: All future communications in the scenario. Right: A binary aggregated communication graph constructed from the Middle figure.

proving that the communication structure of the system can be modelled in LOTOS using the method of Section 2.1.

In the LOTOS specification we introduce the gate ether for communication via links m_1 and m_2, and a gate f for communication via the links b_1 and b_2. The data type RaCh is defined to range over the radio channels m1 and m2, and BaseNo ranges over the Base Station links b1 and b2. We identify a Radio Channel Controller by its Base Station link (bi) and radio channel (mj). A value of type Address is composed of a BaseNo value and a RaCh value, and can be constructed using the mk_address constructor. To access the subparts of an address, the operations b_no(Address) and ra_no(Address) are available.

A Mobile Station is identified by a logical channel number which is enumerated by the LOTOS data type Channel_no. Input on the gate inp, of type Data_sort, is qualified with a logical channel number so that the system can forward the message to the correct Mobile Station.

The Mobile Switching Center

The MSC is the coordinator of the system. It directs input to Mobile Stations and initiates handovers. The MSC is composed of three different types of processes: for each Mobile Station there is a CC process which coordinates the communication between the MSC and the Mobile Station (via a Controller), and a HC_LCC process which initiate handovers. For each radio channel not in use there is a HC_AC process storing the address of the radio channel.

These processes coordinate their activities by participating in three-way synchronisations over a gate l internal to the MSC. Each synchronization involves a HC_LCC process which initiates a handover to another Base Station, a HC_AC process which offers a free radio channel, and a CC process which executes the handover in communication with the Radio Channel Controllers (and indirectly the Mobile Station). As a result of the handover, a second three-way synchronization on the l gate occurs where a free radio channel is returned to the HC_AC process. Figure 6 contains formal definitions of the different types of processes.

The CC process receives input to the Mobile Station on the inp gate, and sends the data to the appropriate Radio Channel Controller (as indicated by the a parameter) via the f gate. Alternatively, a handover starts when the address of a new radio channel is received on the l gate. The CC process then transmits a ho_cmd command with the new address as a parameter to the old Radio Channel Controller. CC may then receive a ho_com message from the (formerly) passive Controller indicating a successful handover. CC then sends a ch_rel command to the (formerly) active Controller to request its now unused radio channel. Alternatively, CC receives a ho_fail command indicating that the handover failed.

A Base Station

In our specification, the Base Stations BS_1 and BS_2 are defined as a composition of Radio Channel Controller processes (see Figure 7). The behaviour of an active Controller

```
process CC[inp, l, f](c: Channel_no, a: Address): noexit :=
    inp !c ?v: Data_sort;
    f !b_no(a) !ra_no(a) !data !v;
    CC[inp, l, f](c, a)
[]
    l !c ?a_new: Address;
    f !b_no(a) !ra_no(a) !ho_cmd !ra_no(a_new);
    (   f !b_no(a_new) !ra_no(a_new) !ho_com;
        f !b_no(a) !ra_no(a) !ch_rel;
        f !b_no(a) !ra_no(a) ?m_old: RaCh;
        l !c !a;
        CC[inp, l, f](c, a_new)
        []
        f !b_no(a) !ra_no(a) !ho_fail;
        l !c !a_new;
        CC[inp, l, f](c, a)
    )
endproc (* CC *)

process HC_LCC[l](c: Channel_no, a: Address): noexit :=
    l !c ?a_new: Address [b_no(a_new) nequal b_no(a)];
    l !c ?b: Address;
    (   [b equal a_new] -> HC_LCC[l](c, a)
        []
        [b nequal a_new] -> HC_LCC[l](c, a_new)
    )
endproc (* HC_LCC *)

process HC_AC[l](a: Address): noexit :=
    l ?c: Channel_no !a; l !c ?b: Address; HC_AC[l](b)
endproc (* HC_AC *)
```

Figure 6: Formal definitions of CC, HC_LCC and HC_AC processes

is given by the process RCa, and a passive Controller is described by the process RCp.

An active Controller awaits messages from the MSC on the f gate which are forwarded to the Mobile Station on the ether gate. If a ho_cmd message is received, the Controller waits for one of two things to happen. Either the MSC requests the now unused channel, i.e. the handover succeeded and the Controller is no longer connected to the Mobile Station. The Controller then returns its channel to the MSC and becomes passive. If instead the handover fails a ho_fail messages is received from the MSC. The Controller then continues in active mode as before.

A passive Controller awaits a ho_acc message from a Mobile Station on the ether gate, qualified by the radio channel m. When so activated, the Controller sends a ho_com message to inform the MSC of a successful handover, and continues in active mode.

```
process RCa[f, ether](b: Base_no, m: RaCh): noexit :=
    f !b !m !data ?v: Data_sort;
    ether !m !data !v;
    RCa[f, ether](b, m)
[]
    f !b !m !ho_cmd ?m_new: RaCh;
    ether !m !ho_cmd !m_new;
    RCwait[f, ether](b, m)
where

    process RCwait[f, ether](b: Base_no, m: RaCh): noexit :=
        f !b !m !ch_rel; f !b !m !m; RCp[f, ether](b, m)
    []
        ether !m !ho_fail;
        f !b !m !ho_fail;
        RCa[f, ether](b, m)
    endproc (* RCwait *)
endproc (* RCa *)

process RCp[f, ether](b: Base_no, m: RaCh): noexit :=
    ether !m !ho_acc; f !b !m !ho_com; RCa[f, ether](b, m)
endproc (* RCp *)
```

Figure 7: Formal definitions of a Radio Channel Controller

A Mobile Station

A Mobile Station accepts data messages from a Controller via a radio channel (ether !m); these messages are forwarded on the out gate. If instead a ho_cmd message (containing a new radio channel) is received, the Mobile Station tries to establish contact with the new Controller by sending a ho_acc message on the new radio channel. If this fails, a ho_fail message is sent on the old radio channel, and the Mobile Station continues to use this radio channel. The formal definition of a Mobile Station is shown in Figure 8.

4.2 Generalized Protocol Specification

In the formal definition of the handover procedure we have already catered for alternative scenarios. The number of Mobile Stations in a scenario can be varied simply by instantiating a different number of MS processes. The number of Base Stations and radio channels can be adjusted by instantiating a different number of RCa or RCp processes, and the MSC can be adapted similarly. The complete specification of the handover procedure, and its service specification, can be found in [FO].

4.3 A Service Specification of the Handover Procedure

The observable behaviour of the protocol, as perceived on the external gates inp and out should resemble a buffer which accepts data items on the inp gate and transmits them

```
process MS[ether, out](m: RaCh): noexit :=
    ether !m !data ?v: Data_sort; out !v; MS[ether, out](m)
[]
    ether !m !ho_cmd ?m_new: RaCh;
    MStry[ether, out](m, m_new)
where
    process MStry[ether, out](m: RaCh, m_new: RaCh): noexit :=
        ether !m_new !ho_acc; MS[ether, out](m_new)
    []
        ether !m !ho_fail; MS[ether, out](m)
    endproc (* MStry *)
endproc (* MS *)
```

Figure 8: Formal definition of a Mobile Station

on the out gate. The buffer has three places since the MSC, BS and MS processes can hold one data item each. The effect of a handover is to empty all buffers by delivering their contents on the out gate before new data can be accepted on the inp gate. Thus, even though a handover is not directly observable, its effects will be.

In a scenario with two Mobile Stations and three Base Stations with a single Radio Channel Controller each, only one handover at a time is possible (since there is only one free radio channel). This leads us to design a service specification with buffers competing for critical resources, i.e. free radio channels. For example, the service specification of the above scenario contains three processes: two buffer process (representing the Mobile Stations), and a critical resource modelled as a semaphore (representing the free radio channel).

In Figure 9 we show the definition of the semaphore and the process SS1 which specifies the buffer in a state where it stores one data item. Note that in correspondence with our specification of the handover procedure, a handover can only take place between radio channels in different Base Stations. The outcome of a handover is represented as a nondeterministic choice in Sem between returning the new or the old Base Station identifier.

The process SS1 can either receive a new data item (v) and become the process SS2 (a buffer holding two items), or output one data item (v1) and become SS0 (an empty buffer), or a handover starts (wait). Before the handover ends (signal), the buffer is emptied.

4.4 Verification

One of the chief motivations for our work on modelling mobile systems in LOTOS was to enable reasoning about mobile systems using the validation tools that are available for LOTOS. In this section we report on a verification of the handover protocol. We show that the handover procedure as formulated in LOTOS is observation equivalent [Mil89]

```
process Sem[wait, signal](b: Base_no, semNo: Nat): noexit :=
    wait !semNo ?b_old: Base_no [b_old nequal b];
    (     signal !semNo !b_old; Sem[wait, signal](b, semNo)
      []
          signal !semNo !b; Sem[wait, signal](b_old, semNo)
    )
endproc (* Sem *)

process SS1[inp, out, wait, signal]
            (c: Channel_no, b: Base_no, v1: Data_sort): noexit :=
    inp !c ?v: Data_sort;
    SS2[inp, out, wait, signal](c, b, v1, v)
[]
    out !v1; SS0[inp, out, wait, signal](c, b)
[]
    wait ?semNo: Nat !b;
    out !v1;
    signal !semNo ?b_new: Base_no;
    SS0[inp, out, wait, signal](c, b_new)
endproc (* SS1 *)
```

Figure 9: Formal definitions of two parts of the service specification: a semaphore, and the process SS1

to a service specification.

The verification proceeded as follows: first we translated the handover procedure and service specifications in LOTOS to labelled transition systems using the CÆSAR tool[GS90]. Then each labelled transition system was reduced with respect to strong bisimulation equivalence using the Aldébaran tool[Fer89]. These reduced transition systems were then compared with respect to observation equivalence (using Aldébaran).

The scenario with one Mobile Station and two Base Stations with one radio channel each has a reduced state space of 87 states. The reduced state space of the scenario consisting of two Mobile Stations and three Base Stations with a single radio channel each, is approximately 7 000 states, well within the limits of verifiablity. For both these scenarios we defined the range of messages to be three: i.e. the system can receive three different messages (of type Data_sort) on the inp gate. For verifying so called data-independent protocols, a range of three different messages has been shown to be sufficient [Wol86].

We also experimented with a scenario of two Base Stations with two radio channels each, and two Mobile Stations. In this scenario, two handovers can take place simultaneously. Using a computer with 32Mb of memory approximately 600 000 states could be generated, unfortunately not enough to represent the whole state space and thus the automatic verification failed. Of course, the specification could still be simulated, and we conducted several experiments using the Hippo tool [Tre89].

5 Conclusions

We have studied how to specify dynamically changing communication structures in the specification language LOTOS. Our result is a method to model communications of links by encoding link names as LOTOS data values together with a sufficient condition on the communication structure of a system guaranteeing that the modelling is possible.

We have formally specified the GSM handover procedure in the standardized specification language LOTOS. Using automated tools we have been able to prove the specification equivalent with a more abstract description of the system. The description of the handover procedure in this paper extends the description in [OP90] by allowing more than one radio channels in each Base Station and several Mobile Stations and has inspired the description in [OP91].

Acknowledgment

We are grateful to Joachim Parrow whose comments on the manuscript helped us improve this work substantially. We also wish to thank the anonymous referees for many helpful comments.

References

[CV89] R.C. Cam and S.T. Vuong. A formal specification, in LOTOS, of a simplified cellular mobile communication system. In *Proc. 2nd International Conference on Formal Description Techniques*, 1989.

[DRL90] R. Duke, G. Rose, and A. Lee. Object-oriented protocol specification. In *Proc. Protocol Specification, Testing, and Verification X*, 1990.

[EFJ91] P. Ernberg, L. Fredlund, and B. Jonsson. Specification and validation of a simple overtaking protocol using LOTOS. In *Proc. 4th International Conference on Formal Description Techniques*, 1991.

[Fer89] J-C. Fernandez. Aldébaran: A tool for verification of communicating processes. Technical Report RTC 14, IMAG, Grenoble, 1989.

[FO]   L. Fredlund and F. Orava. Modeling dynamic communication structures in LOTOS. Technical report, Swedish Institute of Computer Science. In preparation.

[FORTE] Proceedings of the international conferences on Formal Description Techniques, 1988-1990. North-Holland.

[GS90] H. Garavel and J. Sifakis. Compilation and verification of LOTOS specifications. In *Proc. Protocol Specification, Testing, and Verification X*, 1990.

[Hoa85]   C.A.R. Hoare. *Communicating Sequential Processes.* Prentice-Hall, 1985.

[Mil79]   R. Milner. Flowgraphs and flow algebras. *J. ACM*, 26(4):794–818, 1979.

[Mil89]   R. Milner. *Communication and Concurrency.* Prentice Hall, 1989.

[MPW89a]   R. Milner, J. Parrow, and D. Walker. A calculus of mobile processes, part I. Technical Report ECS-LFCS-89-85, Department of Computer Science, University of Edinburgh, 1989. Accepted for publication in *Information and Computation*.

[MPW89b]   R. Milner, J. Parrow, and D. Walker. A calculus of mobile processes, part II. Technical Report ECS-LFCS-89-86, Department of Computer Science, University of Edinburgh, 1989. Accepted for publication in *Information and Computation*.

[OP90]   F. Orava and J. Parrow. Algebraic description of mobile networks: an example. In *Proc. Protocol Specification, Testing, and Verification X*, 1990.

[OP91]   F. Orava and J. Parrow. An algebraic verification of a mobile network. Technical Report SICS R91:002, Swedish Institute of Computer Science, 1991. Accepted for publication in *Formal Aspects of Computing*.

[Par90a]   J. Parrow. The expressive power of parallelism. *Future Generation Computer Systems*, 6:271–285, 1990. Also in *Proc. Parle'89 Vol II*:pages 389-405, LNCS 366.

[Par90b]   J. Parrow. Structural and behavioural equivalences of networks. In *Proceedings of the 17th International Colloquium on Automata, Languages and Programming, LNCS 443*, pages 540–552, 1990. Accepted for publication in *Information and Computation*.

[PSTV]   Proceedings of the IFIP WG6.1 international symposia on Protocol Specification, Testing, and Verification, 1981-1991. North-Holland.

[Tre89]   J. Tretmans. HIPPO: A LOTOS simulator. In P.H.J. van Eijk, C.A. Vissers, and M. Diaz, editors, *The Formal Description Technique LOTOS*, pages 391–396. North-Holland, 1989.

[vEVD89]   P.H.J. van Eijk, C.A. Vissers, and M. Diaz, editors. *The Formal Description Technique LOTOS*. North-Holland, 1989.

[Wol86]   P. Wolper. Specifying interesting properties of programs in propositional temporal logic. In *Proc. 13th ACM Symp. on Principles of Programming Languages*, pages 184–193, 1986.

Dynamic Configuration in LOTOS

Elie NAJM

Institut National de Recherche en Informatique et Automatique (INRIA)
Domaine de Voluceau – Rocquencourt
BP 105 – 78153 Le Chesnay Cedex – FRANCE
E-mail : najm@inria.inria.fr

Jean-Bernard STEFANI

Centre National d'Etudes des Télécommunications (CNET)
38-40 rue du Général Leclerc
92131 Issy-les-Moulineaux – FRANCE
E-mail : jbs@tchang.cnet-pab.fr

Abstract

Distributed Systems offer new challenges and and new opportunities for the application of Formal Description Techniques (FDTs). Dynamic Reconfigurtion of Systems (either predicted or spontaneous) is one of the major issues to be addressed. The process part of LOTOS is based on a CCS-like process calculus, and, as such, lacks the basic dynamic reconfiguration capabilities. Such capabilities are naturally mirrored in Object Based languages and in Milner's & al π-calculus. In the paper, we demonstrate that when one considers Full LOTOS, i.e., LOTOS including Act One and Value-Passing, these capabilities can be modelled. OL1 is a simple language designed to exhibit the essential dynamic characteristics of object-based languages. A semantics preserving translation of OL1 into LOTOS is given. A major "byproduct" of this translation is the definition of a new specification style for LOTOS: the *object-based* style.

1 Introduction

1.1 Dynamic reconfiguration

Distributed systems should potentially offer a flexible environment for modification and extension. Components should be included and removed to attend changes in the enviromnement or the user's requirements. Another point is that faults are expected to occur in any system, mainly in physical systems. It is important, then, that distributed systems can tolerate some faults in order to offer acceptable service. If distributed systems are to be practical they must accomodate such changes.

In general, these evolutionary changes cannot be predicted at the time the system is designed. Also, in a large number of cases, it is not possible either for economic or safety reasons to stop a whole computer system in order to change part of it. Therefore, distributed systems should support dynamic reconfiguration, which is the property (ability) to modify and extend a system while it is running.

As an example, consider a system which comprises a faulty element. We may want to remove the faulty element and replace it with a new correct one. We must then refer to a given element and be able to manipulate the whole configuration.

Even this simple and usual kind of reconfiguration problem is difficult to specify directly using existing standardized formal description techniques (FDTs). Dynamic reconfiguration, in this sense, is one of the challenges for the application of FDTs in the general area of Open Distributed Processing [25].

1.2 Dynamic reconfiguration and objects

In the ODP framework, which draws heavily on recent distributed system research, the basic notion is that of object. As defined in [15] an object is a model of a self-contained part of a system, which encapsulates data and behaviour, and can interact with other parts of the system. A configuration is thus seen as a collection of objects. Objects in a configuration can interact among themselves and with the environmement of the configuration.

This notion of configuration is a very general one: it allows for objects in a configuration to be created, destroyed, or to change their potential interaction partners. For the time being, we know of no adequate formal model of such a notion that could capture all the required dynamicity in the idea of configuration. There are, however, both specification and programming languages which do exhibit some form of dynamic reconfiguration.

First, we have concurrent object-based languages (see e.g. [29]). In these languages, configurations indeed take the form of collections of interacting objects. Dynamic reconfiguration is achieved through the change in objects interaction patterns : communication is pairwise, based on objects identity and dynamic reconfiguration is made possible through the passing of object identifiers as interaction parameters.

A second type of language which exhibits some form of dynamic reconfiguration is given by Milner's π-calculus, or calculus of mobile processes [20, 21]. The π-calculus extends CCS by allowing the passing of gate names as interaction parameters.

The forms of dynamic reconfiguration present in these languages are very close to one another. They are powerful but remain relatively limited. For instance, they do not allow higher order features which can be found in e.g. CHOCS [26]. Nevertheless, in absence of a formal definition of configuration, and of a full-blown theory of dynamic reconfiguration, it would be interesting to investigate further these forms of dynamic reconfiguration.

1.3 Object-basis and LOTOS

One of the basic question to consider is whether dynamicity can be captured using existing standardized FDTs. In particular, it is important to consider whether they can be expressed in LOTOS.

The process part of LOTOS (basic LOTOS) is based on a CCS-like process calculus, and, as such, lacks the basic dynamic reconfiguration capabilities of object-based languages and of the π-calculus. The integration of ACT ONE in full LOTOS, however, gives the language considerable expressive power. It would then be interesting to see whether one can capture, in full LOTOS, the kind of dynamicity exhibited in object-based languages and in the π-calculus.

In this paper, we show how one can indeed capture in full LOTOS object-based dynamic reconfiguration features. This is done by considering a simple object-based language with a formally defined semantics, OL1, and translating it into LOTOS. The choice of OL1 was motivated by the fact that it exhibits, in a simple form, the allegedly essential characteristics of object-based concurrency :

- an explicit notion of object identity,
- explicit object creation,
- explicit pairwise communication between named objects,
- implicit parallelism between objects.

Also, OL1 has a formal semantics based on standard Structured Operational Semantics rules. This makes our proof of equivalence easier. OL1 is defined in [23]. The remainder of the paper is organized as follows: in section 2 we briefly introduce OL1, its syntax and semantics, in section 3 we show how to translate OL1 in LOTOS, in section 4 we prove the translation correct with respect to the original OL1 semantics and in the conclusion, we comment on the translation we have obtained, and perhaps on its limitations.

2 An Object-Based Language: OL1

OL1 was defined [23] to capture, in a process calculus setting, elementary features of object-based concurrency: object-identity with explicit object creation, and communication between named, concurrent objects. For simplicity, communication in OL1 is based on atomic rendez-vous.

2.1 Syntax

Names

OL1 is based on a set NN of *names* (also called *object-ids*) with $u, v, w, \ldots$ as typical elements. NN is endowed with a *naming* function, $\nu : NN \times 2^{NN} \to NN$, satisfying:

$$\forall u, u' \in NN, \forall \theta, \theta' \in 2^{NN} : (u \neq u') \lor (\theta \neq \theta') \Rightarrow \nu(u, \theta) \neq \nu(u', \theta').$$

Function ν is used to uniquely name new objects: $\nu(u,\theta)$ is the name generated for a new object created by u in the context where θ is the set of names already generated by u.

Objects

An object of OL1 is a couple $(u : B)$ where u is the name of the object and B its *behaviour-expression*. The name of an object carries with it the set of names this object has already generated. When this set is relevant, it is noted as a superscript to the name, e.g. $(u^\theta : B)$. A collection of interacting objects is represented in OL1 by an *object-expression*:

$$(u_1 : B_1) \mid \cdots \mid (u_n : B_n)$$

where $\mid$ is the (proven to be commutative and associative) *parallel* operator.

Behaviour-expressions

Behaviour-expressions are elements of a CCS-like calculus. Assuming the following sets:

- the set NN as defined above,

- a set VV of *name-variables* or simply *variables* (elements of which will be denoted $x, x', y, y', ...$). NN and VV are disjoint,

- the set NV of *name-expressions* which is defined as $NV=NN \cup VV$ (elements of NV will be denoted $z, z', z1, ...$),

- a set GG of *gates* or *operations* (elements of which will be denoted $g, h, g', h', ...$),

- a set AA of agents (elements of which will be denoted $A, A', A1, ...$),

the set $\mathcal{B}(OL1)$ of *behaviour-expressions* of OL1, is defined by the following grammar where B is the generic element:

B ::=	stop	*Inaction*
$\mid$	$a; B$	*Action-prefix*
$\mid$	$B + B$	*Choice*
$\mid$	$[z = z']B$	*Guard* : B is enabled iff the names z and z' are equal
$\mid$	$[z \neq z']B$	*Guard* : B is enabled iff the names z and z' are different
$\mid$	$<?x> B$	*Name generation*: a new name is generated and stored in x
$\mid$	$A(z1, ..., zn)<z>$	*Agent instantiation*

For each agent, we assume a defining equation in the form: $A(x1, ..., xn) <x> = B$, where $FV(B) \subseteq \{x, x1, ..., xn\}$, ($FV(B)$ is the set of free-variables of B).

Actions

The originality of the OL1 calculus, compared to CCS, lies mainly in its actions: OL1 actions are invocations of other objects and may involve object creations. Actions are defined by the following grammar:

a	::=	e	Simple action
	|	$a\ c$	Action with object creation
e	::=	i	Internal action
	|	$U \cdot g\ p$	Invocation action:
			- U is the invoked object
			- g is the invoked gate
			- p is the invocation parameter
U	::=	z	z is the name of the invoked object
			(the invoked object is known)
	|	$\star x$	invocation of any object
			(the name of the responding object is stored in x)
p	::=	$!z$	the name z is offered
	|	$?x$	a name is accepted and stored in x
c	::=	new $A(z1,...,zn) <z>$	An new Object is created:
			- z is its name,
			- $A(z1,...,zn) <z>$ is its behaviour.

(In object-oriented terminology: new $A(z1,...,zn) <z>$ creates an instance of the class defined by the Agent-definition: $A(x1,...,xn) <x> = B$.)

Binding and Bound occurences

- $x1,...,xn$ and x are binding in: $A(x1,...,xn) <x> = B$,
- x, x', and y are binding in: $\star x \cdot g\ p\ ; B$, $<?x'> B$ and $U \cdot g\ ?y\ ; B$,
- all other types of occurences are non-binding occurences,
- e new $A(...) <x>$ occurences of x can be bound only by $<?x>$ occurences.

Shorthand notation

In OL1, in order to ensure the proper unique assignment of names to objects, the only allowed name generation construts (i.e., constructs of the form $<?x>$) are those resulting from the following shorthand notation where name generation and name assignment are combined:

$<?x1> \cdots <?xn>\ \ e\ \ \ \text{new } A1(...) <x1> \cdots \text{new } An(...) <xn>\ \ ;\ \ B$
is shortened to: $e\ \ \ \text{new } A(...) \ll x1\gg \cdots \text{new } An(...) \ll xn\gg\ \ ;\ \ B$

Example

A factory is an object that processes a create operation. On invocation of this operation, a factory object returns the name of a newly created object of class A to the invoker. The definition of class factory in OL1 is given by the following equation:

$$\text{Factory} = *x \cdot \text{create }?x'\ \text{new}A(x') \ll y\gg;\quad x \cdot \text{return }!y;\ \text{Factory}.$$

Here, each Factory object (i.e. instance of class Factory) is equipped with two operations: *create* and *return*. On invocation of the *create* operation, a new A object is created. The name of the invoker (a priori unknown to the factory object) is stored in x. The *return* invocation is then invoked on x to pass the name of the newly created A object.

2.2 Semantics

The semantics of OL1 is given in the form of Structured Operational Semantics rules. The semantical domain we consider is a set of labelled transition systems denoted $\mathcal{LTS}(OL1)$, which is defined by its set of labels and set of states:

- the labels of $\mathcal{LTS}(OL1)$ are elements of the set $\mathcal{ACT}(OL1)$ which is given by:

$$\mathcal{ACT}(OL1) = \{\ \text{i}\ \} \cup \{\ (u:v\ g\ w)\ |\ g \in G,\ \text{and}\ u,v,w \in NN\ \}$$

Intuitively, the labels of $\mathcal{LTS}(OL1)$ are actions which involve object u as a server, gate g as an operation, object v as a client, and w as an input/output value.

- the states of $\mathcal{LTS}(OL1)$ are elements of the set $\mathcal{S}(OL1)$ which is defined by the following grammar (where S is the generic element):

$$S ::= (u^\theta : B)\quad |\quad S\ \text{``}|\text{''}\ S$$

Note that the superscript θ will be often ommitted, for example when its value is not relevant.

The meaning of an expression B of $\mathcal{B}(OL1)$ is obtained by borrowing a name u from NN: the semantics of B is the labelled transition system rooted at $(u : B)$. In this paper, we consider only the labelled transition systems obtained with the SOS rules given below. However, it is worth mentionning that in the semantics of B, the name u which is used can be abstracted through the definition of "matching" bisimulations [23].

The derivation system of $\mathcal{LTS}(OL1)$ is given by a set of SOS rules. We define first the following:

- $req : \mathcal{ACT}(OL1) \setminus \{ i \} \rightarrow NN$ is the function defined by $req(u : v\ g\ w) = v$. Intuitively, given a label $(u : v\ g\ w)$, req returns the client object name.
- for S in $\mathcal{S}(OL1)$, $obj(S)$ denotes the set $\{\ u\ |\ \exists B$ such that $(u : B)$ occurs in $S\}$. Intuitively, $obj(S)$ denotes the set of object names which appear in S.
- a function, $dom : \{\ *x, ?x, !u, u\ \} \rightarrow 2^{NN}$, is defined thus:

$$dom(?x) = dom(*x) = NN \text{ and } dom(!u) = dom(u) = \{\ u\ \}.$$

- $L[d1/f1, ..., dn/fn]$ denotes the expression obtained from the syntactical element L by replacing in L the free occurrences of fi by di. We will further consider $u/*x$ and $u/?x$ to mean the substitution u/x and we consider u/u to stand for the identity substitution.

We are now ready to give the semantical rules for OL1. In these rules, a transition will be denoted $S \xrightarrow{\alpha} S'$ where α is an element of $\mathcal{ACT}(OL1)$.

Internal action

This rule gives the behaviour of an object which must first perform a silent action:

$$(\text{Act0}) \quad \frac{}{(u : i\ ;\ B) \xrightarrow{i} (u : B)}$$

Simple invocation

This rule gives the behaviour of an object which performs first a simple invocation. The invoked object, V, can be explicitely designated (e.g. $V = v$) or unknown (e.g. $V = *x$). The invocation parameter, p, can be either a name offer (e.g. $p = !w$) or the acceptance of a name (e.g. $p = ?y$).

$$(\text{Act1}) \quad \frac{v \in dom(V) - \{\ u\ \} \text{ and } w \in dom(p)}{(u : V \cdot g\ p\ ;\ B) \xrightarrow{(u : v\ g\ w)} (u : B[\sigma])} \quad \text{where } \sigma = v/V, w/p$$

Creating a new name

This rule creates a new unique name using the function ν:

$$(\text{Nam}) \quad \frac{(u^{\theta'} : B[u'/x]) \xrightarrow{\alpha} S}{(u^{\theta} :<?x> B) \xrightarrow{\alpha} S} \quad \text{where } u' = \nu(u, \theta) \text{ and } \theta' = \theta \cup \{u'\}$$

Creating a new object

Given a new name v, this rule creates a new object with name v by placing it in parallel with the rest of existing objects:

(Act 2) $$\frac{(u:a;B) \xrightarrow{\alpha} (u:B[\sigma]) \mid S}{(u:a \text{ new } A(...)<v>;B) \xrightarrow{\alpha} (u:B[\sigma]) \mid (v^\emptyset : A(...) <v> [\sigma]) \mid S}$$

Choice

(Cho1) $$\frac{(u:B1) \xrightarrow{\alpha} S}{(u:B1+B2) \xrightarrow{\alpha} S}$$ (Cho2) $$\frac{(u:B2) \xrightarrow{\alpha} S}{(u:B1+B2) \xrightarrow{\alpha} S}$$

Guards

(Test1) $$\frac{(u:B) \xrightarrow{\alpha} S \text{ and } z=z'}{(u:[z=z']B) \xrightarrow{\alpha} S}$$ (Test2) $$\frac{(u:B) \xrightarrow{\alpha} S \text{ and } z \neq z'}{(u:[z \neq z']B) \xrightarrow{\alpha} S}$$

Recursion

(Rec) $$\frac{(u:B[vj/xj,v/x]) \xrightarrow{\alpha} S}{(u:A(v1,...,vn)<v>) \xrightarrow{\alpha} S} \quad \text{where } A(x1,...,xn) <x>= B$$

Immersion left and immersion right

These rules indicate how two object configurations can be merged, provided there is no invocation from an object in one of the configurations to the second one:

(Par1) $$\frac{S1 \xrightarrow{\alpha} S1', \ (obj(S1) \cap obj(S2) = \emptyset), \ ((\alpha = i) \text{ or } (req(\alpha) \notin obj(S2)))}{S1 \mid S2 \xrightarrow{\alpha} S1' \mid S2}$$

(Par2) $$\frac{S2 \xrightarrow{\alpha} S2', \ (obj(S1) \cap obj(S2) = \emptyset), \ ((\alpha = i) \text{ or } (req(\alpha) \notin obj(S1)))}{S1 \mid S2 \xrightarrow{\alpha} S1 \mid S2'}$$

Rendez-vous

This rule indicates when and how communication can take place between two object configurations. Communication is enabled when two objects, one in each configuration, are invoking one another. Thus, the two objects can communicate in one atomic and synchronous step.

(Par3) $$\frac{S1 \xrightarrow{(u:v\ g\ w)} S1', \ S2 \xrightarrow{(v:u\ g\ w)} S2', \ (obj(S1) \cap obj(S2) = \emptyset)}{S1 \mid S2 \xrightarrow{i} S1' \mid S2'}$$

Example

A factory object and its client: we consider the Factory class as defined at the end of section 2.1. We consider a Factory object u, with one of its client, v. The initial configuration has only u and v to start with. It can be denoted thus:

$$(u^\theta : \text{ Factory}) \mid (v : \quad u \cdot \text{ create }!u' \: ; \quad u \cdot \text{ return }?t \: ; \: B)$$

From this initial configuration, using the rules above, we obtain the following transitions (where $w = \nu(u, \theta)$ and $\theta' = \theta \cup \{w\}$):

$$(u^\theta : \text{ Factory}) \mid (v : \quad u \cdot \text{ create }!u' \: ; \quad u \cdot \text{ return }?t \: ; \: B)$$
$$\downarrow i$$
$$(u^{\theta'} : \quad v \cdot \text{ return }!w; \text{ Factory}) \mid (v : \quad u \cdot \text{ return }?t \: ; \quad B) \mid (w^\emptyset : A(u') <w>)$$
$$\downarrow i$$
$$(u^{\theta'} : \text{ Factory}) \mid (v : B[w/t]) \mid (w^\emptyset : A(u') <w>)$$

v has communicated with u, by invoking operation create. On invocation, w is created, and its name is passed in a second invocation, on operation return, to v.

3 Translation of OL1 into LOTOS

The translation of OL1 into LOTOS induces within LOTOS a real specification style, one might call the object-based style (in constrast with the object oriented style which is concerned with the inheritance). In the sequel, we introduce the translation of the different OL1 concepts. Equivalent concepts will emerge within LOTOS: "object", "object-expression", "object-name", "name-generation", "object-creation" "object-invocation", etc... Our starting point is an OL1 object-expression:

$$(u_1^{\theta_1} : B_1) \cdots (u_n^{\theta_n} : B_n)$$

3.1 Names

We need first to define the sets NN and 2^{NN} and the naming function ν in the Act One setting. The data type definitions of sorts NN and SNN (the Act One name for 2^{NN}) and of their operations are given in the appendix. In order to make our specification self-contained, we have defined a concrete construction for NN: the set NN is generated starting from an enumerated set of *root-names*. However, only the abstract properties of operation ν (no equations are associated to ν) are relevant to our translation.

3.2 Objects

The natural way of putting "objects" together in LOTOS is in expressions of the form:

$$OB_1 \,|[G_1]|\, \cdots \,|[G_{n-1}]|\, OB_n$$

It is worth noting that these expressions are static, i.e., the fact that two objects OB_i and OB_j of the configuration can or cannot interact will not change over time. On the other hand, we would like to model the potentiality that any couple of objects are able to get into interaction on any gate and at any moment after the initial state. This can only be achieved by making any two objects of the initial configuration share and synchronise on all gates. Thus, the only possible form of expression where we may succeed in modelling the dynamic movement of partnership is the one where all $|[G_i]|$ are equal to $||$:

$$OB_1 \,||\, \cdots \,||\, OB_n$$

Moreover, due to the nature of the $||$ operator which synchronises all actions, and taking into account that OL1 actions involve at most 2 objects, each LOTOS "object" should be able to produce, at any state, "idle" actions. The aim of "idle" actions is to let global actions of the configuration happen even when not all objects are partners in these actions. Thus the above expression can be refined to become:

$$(\; BH_1 \;|||\; Idle_1 \;) \,||\, \cdots \,||\, (\; BH_n \;|||\; Idle_n \;)$$

Considering that the "idle" actions of each object should occur on <u>all possible gates</u>, and considering also that LOTOS processes can be parametrized with only finite sets of gates, the gates to gates mapping is only possible if OL1 is defined over a finite set of gates. Let G be such a finite set, the above expression can be refined to become:

$$(\; BH_1 \;|||\; Idle_1[G] \;) \,||\, \cdots \,||\, (\; BH_n \;|||\; Idle_n[G] \;)$$

Furthermore, in OL1, an object is a named behaviour-expression. This is mirrored in LOTOS by parametrizing the behaviour-expressions of the object, i.e., BH_i and $Idle_i$, by the name of this object – as it will be explained in the following subsection, this name is explicitely offered in each action of the object together with the name of the invoked partner.

Moreover, the non-idling part of the LOTOS object will be involved in the application of function ν when creating new objects. For this reason, it should be parametrized with the set of already generated names. Thus, the above LOTOS "object" expression is refined to become:

$$(\; BH_1(u_1, \theta_1) \;|||\; Idle[G](u_1) \;) \,||\, \cdots \,||\, (\; BH_n(u_n, \theta_n) \;|||\; Idle[G](u_n) \;)$$

3.3 Actions

When translating OL1 into LOTOS, we need also to deal with the mapping of semantical actions (i.e., labels of the transition systems) in order to discuss the semantics preservation of the translation.

In OL1, two actions are synchronisable iff they are symmetrical. For example, actions

$\alpha_1 = (u : v\ g\ w)$ and $\alpha_2 = (v : u\ g\ w)$ are synchronisable. In LOTOS, synchronisation takes place only when the actions are identical. Since we need to preserve the synchronisation of actions in our translation, two symmetrical actions should be mapped onto the same LOTOS action.

For this reason, we have defined the image of a couple of OL1 symmetrical actions, $(u : v\ g\ w)$ and $(v : u\ g\ w)$, to be the LOTOS action: $(g\ !pair(u, v)\ !w)$, where $pair(x, y)$ is the operation of pairing names. The data type describing pairs and their operations is given in the appendix.

3.4 The translation function

In the LOTOS behaviour-expressions and process definitions that are generated in our translation, we will use the parameters n:NN as and s:S_NN to stand for the object-name and the set of already generated names, respectively. We define first the *Idle* process:

$Idle[G](n:NN) := $ choice g in G [] $\quad g\ ?p : PAIR\ ?x : NN\quad [\text{not}(\text{is\_in}(n, p))]\ ;\ Idle[G](n)$

The OL1 to LOTOS translation function, $\mathcal{T}$, is structurally defined as follows:

Object-expressions

$\mathcal{T}(S_1\ |\ \cdots\ |\ S_n)\quad =\quad \mathcal{T}(S_1)\ ||\ \cdots\ ||\ \mathcal{T}(S_n)$
$\mathcal{T}((u^\theta : B))\quad =\quad (\text{ let n} : NN = u,\ \text{s} : S\_NN = \theta\ \text{in}\ \mathcal{T}(B)\ )\ |||\ Idle[G](u)$

Agent-defintions

$\mathcal{T}(\ A(x_1, ..., x_n) <x> = B\ )\quad =\quad P_A[G](n:NN, s:S\_NN, x_1, ..., x_n, x:NN) = \mathcal{T}(B)$
(to each OL1 agent-definition we associate a LOTOS process-definition)

Behaviour-expressions

$\mathcal{T}(\text{stop})\quad =\quad \text{stop}$
$\mathcal{T}(B_1 + B_2)\quad =\quad \mathcal{T}(B_1)[]\mathcal{T}(B_2)$
$\mathcal{T}([z = z']B)\quad =\quad [z\ \text{eq}\ z'] ->\ \mathcal{T}(B)$
$\mathcal{T}([z \neq z']B)\quad =\quad [z\ \text{ne}\ z'] ->\ \mathcal{T}(B)$
$\mathcal{T}(<?x> B)\quad =\quad \text{let}\ x = \nu(n, s)\ \text{in let s} = \text{insert}(x, s)\ \text{in}\ \mathcal{T}(B)$
$\mathcal{T}(A(z_1, ..., z_n) <z>)\quad =\quad P_A[G](n, s, z_1, ..., z_n, z)$
$\mathcal{T}(i\ ;B)\quad =\quad i\ ;\mathcal{T}(B)$
$\mathcal{T}(z \cdot g\ ?y; B)\quad =\quad g\ !pair(n, z)\ ?y : NN;\ \mathcal{T}(B)$
$\mathcal{T}(z \cdot g\ !z'; B)\quad =\quad g\ !pair(n, z)\ !z'\ ;\quad \mathcal{T}(B)$
$\mathcal{T}(*x \cdot g\ ?y; B)\quad =\quad g\ ?x : PAIR\ ?y : NN\ [\text{is\_in}(n, x)]\ ;\ \text{let}\ x : NN = \text{other}(n, x)\ \text{in}\ \mathcal{T}(B)$
$\mathcal{T}(*x \cdot g\ !z'; B)\quad =\quad g\ ?x : PAIR\ !z'\quad [\text{is\_in}(n, x)]\ ;\ \text{let}\ x : NN = \text{other}(n, x)\ \text{in}\ \mathcal{T}(B)$

$$\mathcal{T}(a\ \text{new}A(z_1,...,z_n)\mathord{<}z\mathord{>}; B) = \mathcal{T}(a; B)\ [\ C||\mathcal{T}(B)\ /\ \mathcal{T}(B)\ ]$$
$$\text{where } C = \mathcal{T}(\ (z^{\{\}} : A(z_1,...,z_n)\mathord{<}z\mathord{>})\ )$$

4 Semantics Preservation

The transition system of an object expression, say S, and the one associated to its LOTOS image $\mathcal{T}(S)$, are "almost" strongly equivalent. Some definitions and notations are needed in order to clarify and proof this claim:

- let S be an OL1 object-expression: $[\![S]\!]_1$ denotes the labelled transition system associated to S using the OL1 derivation rules given in section 2.2,

- let L be a LOTOS behaviour-expression: $[\![L]\!]_2$ denotes the labelled transition system associated to L using the standard LOTOS semantics,

- by construction, the set $[\![\mathcal{T}(\text{OL1})]\!]_2$, which is a "LOTOS" labelled transition systems, is such that the labels are in the form: $g\ !\text{pair}(u,v)\ !w$, and the states are in the form: $(\ BH_1\ |||\ Idle[G](u_1)\ )\ ||\ \cdots\ ||\ (\ BH_n\ |||\ Idle[G](u_n)\ )$

  Over the states of $[\![\mathcal{T}(\text{OL1})]\!]_2$ we define function obj as follows:
  if $s = (BH_1|||Idle[G](u_1)\ )||\cdots||(BH_n|||Idle[G](u_n)\ )$, then $obj(s) =_{def} \{u_1,...,u_n\}$

- on the set $[\![\mathcal{T}(\text{OL1})]\!]_2$, we define $\#$: a relabelling/restriction operation. for $lts \in [\![\mathcal{T}(\text{OL1})]\!]_2$, $\#(lts)$ is the smallest transition system satisfying:

  - if $(s \xrightarrow{i} s') \in lts$ then $(s \xrightarrow{i} s') \in \#(lts)$,
  - if $(s \xrightarrow{g\ !\text{pair}(u,v)\ !w} s') \in lts$ and $\{u,v\} \subseteq obj(s)$ then $(s \xrightarrow{i} s') \in \#(lts)$,
  - if $(s \xrightarrow{g\ !\text{pair}(u,v)\ !w} s') \in lts$ and $u \in obj(s)$ and $v \notin obj(s)$ then $(s \xrightarrow{(u\,:\,v\ g\ w)} s') \in \#(lts)$,
  - if $(s \xrightarrow{g\ !\text{pair}(u,v)\ !w} s') \in lts$ and $v \in obj(s)$ and $u \notin obj(s)$ then $(s \xrightarrow{(v\,:\,u\ g\ w)} s') \in \#(lts)$.

($\#$ replaces LOTOS actions by equivalent OL1 actions and discards idle actions where no objects of the LOTOS "object" expression are involved.)

4.1 Property of $\mathcal{T}$

Now we can give a precise meaning to our claim: the translation $\mathcal{T}$ preserves strong equivalence modulo the restriction/relabelling: $\#$. This claim is formalised and proved as follows:

Proposition: $\forall S \in \text{OL1}$: $[\![S]\!]_1 \sim \#([\![\mathcal{T}(S)]\!]_2)$

Proof: For the sake of brevity, the full proof is not included in the paper. The proof is based on the construction of a bisimulation relation, R, between the states of $[\![S]\!]_1$ and those of $[\![\mathcal{T}(S)]\!]_2$. The relation R is constructed as follows:

S R L iff $\exists L'$ such that $L' = \mathcal{T}(S)$ and $L' \equiv L$; where $\equiv$ is the equivalence relation on LOTOS behaviour-expressions which is induced by the two rewrite rules:
other$(x, \text{pair}(x, y)) \rightarrow y$,   and
let $x : sort = E$ in $L \rightarrow L[E/x]$

5 Conclusion

We have presented a translation of OL1, a process calculus representative of concurrent object based languages, into LOTOS. By this translation we have demonstrated the ability of LOTOS to capture the dynamic features supported by object-oriented languages in general. Our translation may have shown some limitation. For instance, we had to consider OL1 as defined over a finite set of gates. We could however have mapped OL1 gates on an ACT One sort and thus, relax this limitation. It is worth noting that a sort *gates* would also allow them to move between processes. An interesting investigation in that direction might be the simulation of the π-calculus within LOTOS.

The intoduction of motion in processes has, in general, a drawback: systems become more difficult to analyse. An exception [7] is worth mentionning. In [7], LOTOS is extended and enhanced dynamic capabilities are introduced in the language. For instance, in this "extended" LOTOS, a parallel operator can be a process which may dynamically *rearrange* the communication structure of its arguments. Although this extension does not provide the expressive power to deal with process creation and with configurations of arbitrary numbers of processes, it has the advantage of bringing dynamicity without loosing the analytic properties of static structures.

Our translation has induced an "object-based" style in LOTOS. In this style, processes share a broadcasting medium which they use to listen (with idle actions) and to invoke their partners by naming them. The main criticism to this style is, may be, the use of the maximal synchronistion operator and of the Idle loop process which look unnatural when compared to OL1 and other object-based languages. Another point is that we had to use, for the definition of this style, a second level of semantics: a relabelling/restriction of the (LOTOS) labelled transition systems is necessary in order to interpret (LOTOS) behaviour-expressions as configurations of objects.

Acknowledgments: The authors would like to thank Paulo Cunha for his valuable remarks and comments. The work carried out in this paper has been, in part, supported by the Esprit2/ISAX project.

References

[1] P. America, J.W. de Bakker : "Designing equivalent semantic models for process creation" - Theoretical Computer Science 60, 1988.

[2] ESPRIT Project n 2267 (Integrated Systems Architecture) - Advanced Network Systems Architecture Reference Manual - Architecture Project Management Cambridge, UK- March 1989.

[3] H.E. Bal, J.G. Steiner, A.S. Tanenbaum : "Programming Languages for Distributed Computing Systems" - ACM Computing Surveys, Vol.21, N!3, September 1989.

[4] A. Black, N. Hutchinson, E. Jul, H. Levy, L. Carter : "Distribution and abstract types in Emerald" - IEEE Transactions on Software Engineering, SE 13 (1), January 1987.

[5] T. Bolognesi, E. Brinksma, "Introduction to the ISO Specification Language LOTOS", Computer Networks and ISDN Systems 14 (1987), pp25-29.

[6] G. Boudol : "Notes on Algebraic Calculi of Processes" - Advanced NATO School Series on Logics and Models for Verification and Specification of Concurrent Systems, Springer-Verlag 1985.

[7] H. Brinksma: "On the design of Extended LOTOS" – PhD thesis, University of Twente, The Netherlands, November 1988.

[8] E. Cusack, S. Rudkin, C. Smith : "An Object-Oriented Interpretation of LOTOS" - in Proceedings FORTE 1989 - Vancouver, December 1989.

[9] E. Cusack, M. Lai :"Object-oriented Specification in LOTOS and Z or, My Cat Really Is Object-Oriented !" - Proceedings Workshop on the Foundations of Object-Oriented Languages, Noordwijkerhout, The Netherlands - 1990.

[10] P. Dasgupta, R. Leblanc, W. Appelbe : "The Clouds distributed operating systems : functional description, implementation details and related work" - 8th International Conference on Distributed Computer Systems, San Jose, CA, USA. June 1988.

[11] H. Ehrig, B. Mahr: "Fundamental of Algebraic Specification 1" - EATC" Monographs on Theoretical Computer Science - Spinger-Verlag 1985.

[12] U. Engberg, M. Nielsen : "A Calculus of Communicating Systems with Label Passing" - Report DAIMI PB 208 - Aarhus Denmark - May 1986.

[13] J. Fiadeiro, T. Maibaum : "Describing, Structuring and Implementing Objects" - Proceedings Workshop on the Foundations of Object-Oriented Languages, Noordwijkerhout, The Netherlands - May 1990.

[14] International Standard 8807 - "LOTOS : A Formal Description Technique Based on the Temporal Ordering of Observational Behavior" - 1988

[15] document SC21 N4887: "Working document - Specification Techniques and Formalisms for ODP - Part 2 Descriptive Model" - ISO/IEC JTC1, June 1990.

[16] B. Liskov, R. Scheifler : "Guardians and actions : linguistic support for robust distributed programs" - ACM Transactions on Programming Languages and Systems. Vol 5 n 3, July 1988.

[17] T. Mayr : "Specifications of object-oriented systems in LOTOS" - In proceedings FORTE 1988.

[18] B. Meyer : "Object-oriented Software Construction" - Prentice-Hall 1988.

[19] R. Milner : "Communication and Concurrency" - Prentice-Hall 1989.

[20] R. Milner, J. Parrow, D. Walker : "A Calculus of Mobile Processes - Part I" - LFCS Report 89-85. University of Edinburgh June 1989.

[21] R. Milner, J. Parrow, D. Walker : "A Calculus of Mobile Processes - Part II" - LFCS Report 89-86. University of Edinburgh June 1989.

[22] R. Milner : "Functions as Processes" - INRIA Research Report n 1124, February 1990 - INRIA, Rocquencourt, France.

[23] E. Najm, J.B. Stefani: "Object Based Concurrency: A Process Calculus Analysis" in the 4th International Joint Conference on the Theory and Practice of Software Development TAPSOFT 91 – Brighton, UK (1991).

[24] R.K. Raj, E. Tempero, H.M. Levy, N.C. Hutchinson, P. Black: "The Emerald Approach to Programming" - Technical report 88-11-01 University of Washington, WA, USA - November 1988.

[25] J.B. Stefani: "Open Distributed Processing: The Next Target for the Application Of Formal Description Techniques" in the 3rd International Conference On Formal Description Techgniques FORTE 90 – Madrid, Spain (1990).

[26] B. Thomsen: "A Calculus of Higher Order Communicating Systems" in Proceedings of 16th Anual Symposium on Principles of Programming Languages, pp 143-154, 1989.

[27] C.A. Vissers: "FDTs for Open Distributed Systems, a Prospective View" in Proceedings 10th IFIP WG6.1 Workshop on Protocol Specification, Testing and Verification, Ottawa, Canada (1990).

[28] P. Wegner : "Dimensions of Object-Based Language Design" in Proceedings OOPSLA 1987.

[29] A. Yonezawa, M. Tokoro, eds : "Object-Oriented Concurrent Systems" - MIT Press 1987.

Appendix: Definition of Types

```
TYPE ROOT_NAMES
  sorts   RN

  opns   root     :              -> RN
         enum     :  RN          -> RN
ENDTYPE

TYPE NAMES is ROOT_NAMES, Boolean
  sorts   NN, S_NN

  opns   name              :                  RN              ->  NN
         {}                :                                  ->  S_NN
         insert            :                  NN, S_NN        ->  S_NN
         ν                 :                  NN, S_NN        ->  NN
         _eq_, _ne_        :                  NN, NN          ->  bool

  eqns   forall x, y : NN, s : S_NN
         ofsort NN
           x eq y                   =>   x = y;
         ofsort bool
           x = y                    =>   x eq y = true;
           x ne y                   =    not(x eq y)
         ofsort S_NN
           insert(x, insert(x, s))  =    insert(x, s);
           insert(x, insert(y, s))  =    insert(y, insert(x, s));
ENDTYPE

TYPE PAIRS is NAMES
  sorts   PAIR

  opns   pair     :        NN, NN      ->  PAIR
         is_in    :        NN, PAIR    ->  bool
         other    :        NN, PAIR    ->  NN

  eqns   forall           x, y :  NN
         ofsort           PAIR
           pair(x, y)         =    pair(y, x);
         ofsort           bool
           is_in(x, pair(x, y)) =  true;
         ofsort           NN
           is_in(x, pair(x, y)) =  true    =>  other(x, pair(x, y)) = y;
ENDTYPE
```

An upward compatible timed extension to LOTOS

Guy Leduc

Research Associate of the National Fund for Scientific Research (Belgium)
Université de Liège, Institut d'Electricité Montefiore, B 28, B-4000 Liège 1, Belgium
Tel: + 32 41 562698   Fax: + 32 41 562989
E-mail: u514401@bliulg11.bitnet or leduc@montefiore.ulg.ac.be

Abstract

We propose a timed extension of LOTOS, denoted TLOTOS, which is upward compatible with the standard LOTOS. It means first that a timed behaviour expression which does not use any language extension will have the same semantics as in standard LOTOS. In addition, we have pushed this upward compatibility one step beyond by requiring and obtaining that all the familiar equivalence laws of standard LOTOS be preserved, e.g. $B [] B \sim B, B [] stop \sim B$. This is needed in order to keep the intuition of a standard LOTOS user unchanged. TLOTOS has been mainly inspired by other approaches such as Moller & Tofts's TCCS (Temporal CCS), Hennessy & Regan's TPL (Temporal Process Language) and Nicollin & Sifakis's ATP (Algebra of Timed Processes). Our model is not strictly asynchronous (like standard LOTOS, CCS, CSP, ACP) nor strictly synchronous (like SCCS, CIRCAL, Meije). For compatibility and simplicity, we decided to keep the model asynchronous for a large part and, for dealing with time, to introduce a "synchronous part" by way of a new basic "synchronous" or timed action in the asynchronous semantic model. The design of our TLOTOS is presented together with other possible design alternatives which are all rejected according to our compatibility or expressive power requirements. The solution that we obtain is simple and satisfactory, and its operational semantics is presented in depth. Two examples are provided to illustrate the use of TLOTOS.

1. Introduction

In recent years, many quantitative timed extensions of well-known asynchronous process algebras have been proposed, as well as new timed process algebras. CSP [Hoa 85], CCS [Mil 89], ACP [BeK 85], LOTOS [ISO 8807] have been extended to Timed CSP [ReR 88, Ree 90], TCCS (Temporal CCS) [MoT 89], TIC [QAF 89], ACP_ρ [BaB 90], CELOTOS [HTZ 90], $ACP_{\tau\epsilon}^t$ [Gro 90], Timed-Interaction LOTOS [BLT 90, BoL 91], Timed CCS [Wan 90, Wan 91] and TPCCS [HaJ 90, Han 91]. New process algebras have been proposed which are intended to model time in a quantitative way: first, synchronous process algebras such as SCCS [Mil 83], Meije [AuB 85] or CIRCAL [Mil 85] and, in a second step, timed process algebras such as TPL (Temporal Process Language) [HeR 90], ATP (Algebra of Timed Processes) [NRS 90, NS 90, NSY 91], PADS (Process Algebra for Distributed Systems) [Azc 90]. An overview and synthesis on Timed Process Algebras may be found in [NS 91].

In this paper, we present a timed extension of LOTOS, denoted TLOTOS, with the objective of upward compatibility with standard LOTOS. This means that LOTOS will be a proper subset of TLOTOS (i.e. LOTOS specifications will be correct TLOTOS specifications, and their semantics will be unchanged). In addition, we have been able to preserve all the LOTOS strong and weak bisimulation laws in TLOTOS. This is fundamental in order to facilitate as much as possible its use by those who were trained on standard LOTOS. These are our requirements for claiming (true) upward compatibility. They will be further developed in section 2.

TLOTOS has been inspired by other approaches such as TPL [HeR 90], ATP [NS 90], $ACP_{\tau\epsilon}^t$ [Gro 90] and PADS [Azc 90]. Our model is between a strictly asynchronous algebra (like LOTOS, CCS, CSP, ACP) and a strictly synchronous one (like SCCS, CIRCAL, Meije). The idea has been suggested in the works previously mentioned here-above and may be informally presented as the addition of a "synchronous action" in an asynchronous algebra. The motivation is twofold. First, this way of doing is clearly in the line of an upward extension of LOTOS since the basic asynchronous model is our starting point. Second, this corresponds to the fact that distributed systems are mainly systems which behave most of the time asynchronously, but resynchronize themselves periodically. It is therefore unacceptable to burden a whole specification with timing considerations when only a small subset of it really depends on time. This is the main shortcoming of purely synchronous models.

The timed action that we will add in LOTOS may be defined with different properties in mind, which would lead to several possible extensions. The design of TLOTOS will thus be explained by presenting other possible design alternatives which will be all rejected according to our requirements of compatibility and expressing power. In this process, we do not claim of course to have explored all the possible timed extensions of LOTOS. However, we have tried to be as exhaustive as possible with respect to the possible extensions based on the fundamental concept of a distinct timed action.

The timed action is the basic element of the extended semantics. At the syntactic level, several additional constructs are needed to benefit totally from this new expressive facility. These constructs will be introduced and illustrated. Let us note that, at this level, other operators might have been used or could advantageously replace the chosen ones. We have simply selected an existing set of such timed operators (viz. those proposed in ATP) in order to avoid unneeded additional notations. However, this choice is not arbitrary: we think that the ATP timed operators are simple, easy to use and understand, and perfectly adequate to model many timed behaviours such as time-outs, watchdogs, ... TLOTOS is proposed with its operational semantics for the main operators.

In order to illustrate the use of TLOTOS, we will also present two small examples. The first one is the transmitter entity of the well-known alternating bit protocol. The second one is a unidirectional medium which introduces delays on the exchanged messages.

2. Upward compatibility with LOTOS

The main objective of this timed extension that we are looking for is its upward compatibility with current LOTOS [ISO 8807]. This means that, in TLOTOS, a behaviour expression which does not use any language extension should have the same semantics as in standard LOTOS. This allows the description in TLOTOS of untimed behaviours, exactly in the same way as in LOTOS. This requirement is necessary to achieve upward compatibility, but we would like to require more. We would like to use TLOTOS with the same intuition as LOTOS. This means that behaviour expressions which were (strongly, weakly, ...) bisimulation equivalent in LOTOS should remain equivalent in TLOTOS. In other words, we want to preserve all the familiar laws of LOTOS: e.g. $B \ [] \ B \sim B$, $B \ [] \ stop \sim B$, the commutativity and associativity of various operators such as choice or parallel composition with the same gate list. Whereas the first requirement only applies to the LOTOS subset of TLOTOS, this last requirement applies to the full TLOTOS.

The first requirement can be achieved as follows: first, we should preserve, in the operational semantics, all the axioms and inference rules of the LOTOS operators; second, if new axioms and inference rules are added for **standard LOTOS operators**, they should not allow new transitions when the **operands** are untimed processes. By contrast, the axioms and inference rules of the new timed operators remain unconstrained by this first requirement. Indeed, in this case, any behaviour expression in TLOTOS which does not use any new operator, will be an untimed behaviour expression, and will thus have exactly the same Labelled Transition System (LTS) as in LOTOS. A precise definition of a LTS will be given later on.

The second requirement, however, will add further constraints to the new axioms and rules of the standard operators.

Basic design choices of LOTOS also have to be preserved in order to achieve this upward compatibility. For instance, actions will remain atomic and instantaneous (i.e. with duration 0), and the semantics of parallelism will still be based on interleaving. We will see that this combination may lead to a satisfactory approximation of real parallelism. Intuitively, sequences of instantaneous actions may be considered to occur during the same unit time interval. If the set of possible interleaved sequences are all specified, this may be an adequate model of true parallelism. These sequences will be separated from subsequent actions (i.e. which should occur at a later time) by means of a special timed action, as presented later on in this paper.

3. Basic choices related to the timed extension

We decided to follow the approaches of TCCS, TPL and ATP to define TLOTOS, i.e. the definition of a model which is not strictly asynchronous (like LOTOS, CCS, CSP, ACP, ...) nor strictly synchronous (like SCCS, CIRCAL, Meije).We think that an appropriate model should be asynchronous for a large part, but should allow the expression of precise timing constraints. An asynchronous model as a starting point is thus justified for two reasons: first, an asynchronous model is in general simpler than a synchronous one; second, since we are looking for an upward compatible extension of the asynchronous model of LOTOS, we think that this approach is more natural and also simpler.

One problem remains however: the introduction of a "synchronous part" in the LOTOS asynchronous model. The basic idea has been presented in TPL, ATP, ACP_ϵ^t and PADS, and consists in introducing a new basic action in the semantic model. This action, which will be denoted χ (like in ATP) in the sequel, is called a timed action. Its occurrence models the passing of one unit of time. A process may thus either execute an observable action (i.e. a synchronization with its environment), or execute an asynchronous internal action (the well-known i), or execute a timed action χ modelling the passing of one unit of time.

This χ action is however a very low level construct which would, if introduced as such in the language, unnecessarily complicate TLOTOS, as well as its use for the description of time-dependent systems. Therefore, following ATP, we decided to make χ invisible at the syntactic level of the language. This is quite similar to the introduction, in the semantic model only, of the δ action, modelling a successful termination: no δ action ever appears in a LOTOS behaviour expression, it is hidden in a syntactic construct which is, in this case, the *exit* process.

We will follow the same approach, and define several new syntactic constructs whose semantics refer to the χ action. Some additional axioms and inference rules of standard LOTOS will also be defined and make use of this χ action.

We will adopt the same three basic timing constructs as in ATP. We only present two of them in section 3 for illustration, the third one will be justified later on in section 4.

Notations

L is the alphabet of observable actions.

$L^i = L \cup \{i\}$, $L^\delta = L \cup \{\delta\}$, $L^\chi = L \cup \{\chi\}$, $L^{i,\delta} = L \cup \{i,\delta\}$, $L^{i,\delta,\chi} = L \cup \{i,\delta,\chi\}$, ...

$P \ -a \rightarrow P'$ where $a \in L^{i,\delta,\chi}$, means that process P may engage in action a and, after doing so, behave like process P'.

$P \ -a \not\rightarrow$ where $a \in L^{i,\delta,\chi}$, means that $\neg (\exists P', \text{ such that } P \ -a \rightarrow P')$, i.e. P cannot accept (or must refuse) the action a.

The *start delay* operator (or time-out operator), $\lfloor\ \rfloor^d$

$\lfloor P \rfloor^d(Q)$ is a process which behaves like P provided P <u>starts</u> before d units of time, otherwise it behaves like Q. Note that d is required to be strictly greater than 0, and that, when d = 1, it may be omitted. Its operational semantics is defined by the following four inference rules [NS 90]:

(SD1)	$\dfrac{P \xrightarrow{a} P'}{\lfloor P \rfloor^d(Q) \xrightarrow{a} P'}$ $(a \in L^{i,\delta}, d \geq 1)$	(SD3)	$\dfrac{P \xrightarrow{\chi} P'}{\lfloor P \rfloor^{d+1}(Q) \xrightarrow{\chi} \lfloor P' \rfloor^d(Q)}$ $(d \geq 1)$
(SD2)	$\lfloor P \rfloor^1(Q) \xrightarrow{\chi} Q$	(SD4)	$\dfrac{P \xrightarrow{\chi}\!\!\!\!\!/\ \ \ \ \$}{\lfloor P \rfloor^{d+1}(Q) \xrightarrow{\chi} \lfloor P \rfloor^d(Q)}$ $(d \geq 1)$

The process $\lfloor P \rfloor^d(Q)$ would advantageously replace the following imprecise construction often used in standard LOTOS for modelling a time-out:
   $P\ []\ (Time\text{-}out\ (d) >> Q)$ where $Time\text{-}out\ (d:nat) := exit$
As an example, the figure 1 gives the LTS[§] associated with the process $\lfloor a;\ stop \rfloor^2(b;\ stop)$.

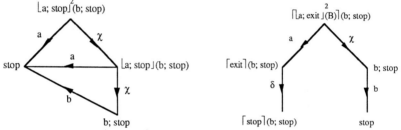

Figure 1: the LTS of $\lfloor a;\ stop \rfloor^2(b;\ stop)$ Figure 2: the LTS of $\lceil \lfloor a;\ exit \rfloor^2(B) \rceil(b;\ stop)$

When a well-defined semantics is given to *stop* in the next section, we will see that a simple delay of d units of time before the start of a process Q will be introduced as follows:
$$\lfloor stop \rfloor^d(Q)$$
The idea is that this process may only execute the trace χ^d and then behave like Q.

As mentioned in [NS 90], one might think (by looking at the union of their premises, and at their common inferred part) that the rules SD3 and SD4 could be replaced by a single simpler axiom such as $\lfloor P \rfloor^{d+1}(Q) \xrightarrow{\chi} \lfloor P \rfloor^d(Q)$. However, this is not intuitively satisfactory in the case of nested delays as explained on the following example from [NS 90]: in such a semantics, the process $\lfloor \lfloor a;\ P \rfloor^1(b;\ Q) \rfloor^2(R)$ would not have the ability to execute b; in fact, it would be equivalent to $\lfloor a;\ P \rfloor^2(R)$.

[$] This is called a negative premiss. This is the first time that we encounter one of them. This kind of transition system specification may create inconsistencies in general. In TLOTOS, these potential problems have been analysed in [Led 91].

[§] A precise definition of a LTS is given later on. Moreover, at this stage, without knowing the semantics of action-prefix and *stop* in TLOTOS, it may seem too early to give the LTS associated with this process. Therefore, this LTS should be considered only as a didactic aid to understand the operator. In fact, it will turn out to be the correct LTS according to semantics that we will define. This note is also valid for the subsequent examples.

The *execution delay* operator (or watchdog operator), $\lceil \ \rceil^d$

$\lceil P \rceil^d$ (Q) is a process which behaves like P before the dth unit of time, and like Q afterwards provided P has not terminated successfully before this d^{th} unit of time (i.e. executed a δ action). When d = 1, it may be omitted. Its operational semantics is defined by the following four inference rules:

(ED1)	$\dfrac{P -a \rightarrow P'}{\lceil P \rceil^d(Q) -a \rightarrow \lceil P' \rceil^d(Q)}$ ($a \in L^i, d \geq 1$)	(ED3)	$\dfrac{P -\chi \rightarrow P'}{\lceil P \rceil^1(Q) -\chi \rightarrow Q}$	
(ED2)	$\dfrac{P -\delta \rightarrow P'}{\lceil P \rceil^d(Q) -\delta \rightarrow P'}$ ($d \geq 1$)	(ED4)	$\dfrac{P -\chi \rightarrow P'}{\lceil P \rceil^{d+1}(Q) -\chi \rightarrow \lceil P' \rceil^d(Q)}$	($d \geq 1$)

The process $\lceil P \rceil^d$ (Q) would advantageously replace the following imprecise construction often used in standard LOTOS for modelling a watchdog:
   $P \mathrel{[>} (Time\text{-}out\,(d) \mathrel{>>} Q)$ where $Time\text{-}out\,(d{:}nat){:}exit := exit$

An example is presented in figure 2. In this case, it appears that B cannot be executed. The reason is that B cannot start before time 2 and, on the other hand, the watchdog is programmed to start at time 1. The LTS would have been the same for $\lceil La;\ exit \rceil^1(B) \rceil$ (b; stop) since the watchdog has the priority at time 1 according to the semantics.

ED1, ED3 and ED4 are given in [NS 90], whereas ED2 is different from its analogous rule where the consequent is instead $\lceil P \rceil^d(Q) -i \rightarrow P'$. This difference has the following interpretation: in ATP a δ action[1] is intended to cancel only one level of execution delay, whereas our semantics cancels all the levels of execution delay. Our choice is justified because it is very close to the semantics of the disabling operator where δ cancels all the levels of disabling. It is therefore interesting to keep this interpretation for cancellations of "pending watchdogs".

4. Modelling urgency on action occurrences

We think that a timed model cannot be useful if it does not allow the expression that a given synchronization must occur urgently, i.e. as soon as possible; which means, in our context, before the next χ action. This requirement is closely related to the ability to model timers: without urgent actions, there is no way to specify the necessity for an action to occur at (or before) a specific time instant, or to occur as soon as possible.

An interesting and easy way to provide this capability in our framework is achieved by keeping unchanged the axioms of the action-prefix operator and *exit* process, i.e.

$a; B -a \rightarrow B$ remains of course an axiom (remember that $a \neq \chi$),

but $a; B$ does not allow a χ action, i.e. a cannot be delayed: $a; B -\chi \not\rightarrow$

In particular, in $i; B$ the internal action i must occur before the next χ action.

Similarly, $exit -\delta \rightarrow stop$ remains valid,

but the successful termination cannot be delayed: $exit -\chi \not\rightarrow$

This is the approach chosen in TCCS [MoT 89], ATP [NS 90] and $ACP_{t\epsilon}^{\iota}$ [Gro 90] which contrasts with the one followed in Timed CSP [ReR 88, Ree 90], TPL [HeR 90] and TPCCS [Han 91] where only internal actions occur urgently (the so-called *maximal progress* property).

---

[1] δ is denoted ξ in ATP and has a different semantics with respect to the parallel composition, i.e. all parallel processes are not required to terminate simultaneously.

By specifying carefully when a χ action is enabled by way of the two timed operators presented above, this allows the specification of processes which behave asynchronously most of the time but resynchronize periodically on χ actions.

In order to allow a process to wait an arbitrary delay before starting its execution, we follow the same approach as in [NS 90] and provide a third timed operator.

The *unbounded start delay* operator, $\lfloor \, \rfloor^\omega$

$\lfloor P \rfloor^\omega$ is a process which behaves like process P except that it may wait an arbitrary long delay before starting. This operator disables the "as soon as possible" rule on the first possible actions of P. Its operational semantics is defined by the following three inference rules [NS 90]:

(USD1)	$\dfrac{P - a \rightarrow P'}{\lfloor P \rfloor^\omega - a \rightarrow P'}$ ($a \in L^{i,\delta}$)	(USD3)	$\dfrac{P - \chi \not\rightarrow}{\lfloor P \rfloor^\omega - \chi \rightarrow \lfloor P \rfloor^\omega}$
(USD2)	$\dfrac{P - \chi \rightarrow P'}{\lfloor P \rfloor^\omega - \chi \rightarrow \lfloor P' \rfloor^\omega}$		

Examples are presented in figures 3 and 4.

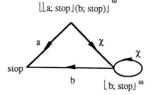

Figure 3: the LTS of $\lfloor a; stop \rfloor^\omega$ Figure 4: the LTS of $\lfloor \lfloor a; stop \rfloor (b; stop) \rfloor^\omega$

In conclusion, unless specifically disabled by an unbounded start delay operator, all actions (observable or not) are required to occur as soon as possible, i.e. before the next χ action. As previously explained, another fundamental exception is when these actions are in the scope of one of the other two timed operators (see rules SD2, SD3, SD4, ED3, ED4).

5. Possible semantics for the timed extension

In this section, we will try to survey all the possible ways to define the semantics of the TLOTOS basic operators, taking account of the requirements and basic choices of the previous sections.

A first basic decision is the semantics of process *stop*, i.e. does it allow a χ action or not?

The two approaches exist. In TPL [HeR 90], ATP [NS 90], PADS [Azc 90] and TPCCS [Han 91], the process which plays the role of *stop* allows a χ action, and *stop* satisfies the following axiom: $stop -\chi \rightarrow stop$. In TCCS [MoT 89] and ACP$_{t\varepsilon}^{!}$ [Gro 90] the opposite decision has been taken; in this case, *stop* not only refuses any action, but also stops the progression of time. Even if it may seem to be an undesirable effect at first glance, we may argue in favour of this second approach. First, when *stop* is used explicitly in a specification, it is intended to model that the process has reached a final state where nothing more will happen; therefore, the fact that time is also stopped does not matter any more, since time is no more needed. Second, if *stop* is not modelled explicitly, but results from a synchronization deadlock between processes, this is an error situation which is certainly not wanted; therefore, in this case too, the fact that time is stopped does not matter. An additional argument in favour of the second semantics is the upward compatibility with LOTOS: the LTS associated with *stop* remains the same, i.e. a unique node without transition. In the first semantics, the LTS associated with *stop* becomes a LTS with a unique node, but with a loop labelled by χ. Therefore, in order to preserve an upward compatibility with LOTOS in this case, we have to be sure that the semantics of any process equivalent to *stop* in standard LOTOS (e.g. *a; stop // b; stop*) is also this LTS with a χ loop. In other words, in order to remain consistent in this case, we must be sure that any process may never refuse the whole alphabet $L^{i,\delta,\chi}$ (since even *stop* cannot). In ATP, when a process may reach a state where it refuses $L^{i,\delta,\chi}$, this is a particular case of a so-called non well-timed process.

Let us summarize this by giving the two possible semantics for *stop*:
(A1) no axiom for *stop*, or
(A2) $stop -\chi \rightarrow stop$

The second basic LOTOS construct is the *choice* operator. We have to preserve the usual inference rules of choice, but some alternatives exist to define the semantics of this operator w.r.t. the χ action. For instance, if χ would be considered as an ordinary action, like in $ACP_{t\epsilon}^t$ [Gro 90], we would have the following inference rule (nondeterminism of choice w.r.t. time):

(B) $\dfrac{P -\chi \rightarrow P'}{P \;[]\; Q -\chi \rightarrow P'}$ and its symmetric

However, this rule contradicts our ASAP criterion: suppose that $Q -a \rightarrow Q'$ (with $a \in L^{i,\delta}$), then $P \;[]\; Q$ would allow χ, which is in contraction with the ASAP criterion stating that, in this case, a **must** occur before χ. The ASAP criterion appears as a way to restrict the occurrence of χ actions in a very simple way: give χ a lower priority than other actions in $L^{i,\delta}$ **in the scope of a choice operator**.

Note that the absence of such a rule allows anyway the modelling of a process which may (or may not) execute the action a of Q before the next χ action; it suffices to use the unit delay operator which has been specifically designed for that purpose: $\lfloor Q \rfloor (P')$ in this case.

Being aware of this difficulty, we come naturally to the question of replacing the classical choice rule by (an)other one(s). Several possibilities will be described and their consequences analysed, and finally our proposal will be derived.

Two basic questions that we have to consider when dealing with choice and time are the following:
- may time resolve a choice ?
- may time pass differently for both sides of a choice ?

The first question may also be expressed as: is the choice operator nondeterministic with respect to time ?

In addition to the classical choice rules, let us provide possible answers for the treatment of χ actions in terms of inference rules (the symmetric rules are implicit in the sequel).

(B1) $\dfrac{P -\chi \rightarrow P',\; Q -a \not\rightarrow\;\; \forall\; a \in L^{i,\delta}}{P \;[]\; Q -\chi \rightarrow P'}$
(B3) $\dfrac{P -\chi \rightarrow P',\; Q -\chi \rightarrow Q'}{P \;[]\; Q -\chi \rightarrow P' \;[]\; Q'}$

(B2) $\dfrac{P -\chi \rightarrow P',\; Q -a \not\rightarrow\;\; \forall\; a \in L^{i,\delta}}{P \;[]\; Q -\chi \rightarrow P' \;[]\; Q}$
(B4) $\dfrac{P -\chi \rightarrow P',\; Q -a \not\rightarrow\;\; \forall\; a \in L^{i,\delta,\chi}}{P \;[]\; Q -\chi \rightarrow P'}$

B1 expresses that time may resolve a choice, i.e. when no observable action can be executed in Q (however χ may be offered by Q), a χ action from P may be executed and thereby resolve the choice in favour of P.

B2 expresses that time may pass differently on both sides of a choice, i.e. when no observable action can be executed in Q (however χ may be offered by Q), a χ action from P may be executed without resolving the choice (i.e. Q remains enabled afterwards but time has not passed for Q).

B3 expresses that time may pass in both P and Q without resolving a choice. This rule is present in TPL and ATP.

B4 is only relevant when combined with *A1*, it expresses the same idea as *B1*. Moreover, *B4* is useless in the presence of *B1*, i.e. $B1 = B1 + B4$.

With respect to these axioms and rules, *stop* and *choice* in TPL and ATP are defined by A2 + B3 + the classical rules for choice.

Let us consider how these rules *B1,... B4* may be combined together with *A1* and *A2* while preserving well-known and desirable properties of LOTOS operators, such as the strong bisimulation equivalence between $B \, [] \, stop$ and B, or between $B \, [] \, B$ and B, or between $(A \, |[\gamma]| \, B) \, |[\gamma]| \, C$ and $A \, |[\gamma]| \, (B \, |[\gamma]| \, C)$, ...

Before going further in this discussion, we give the classical definitions of a LTS and the strong bisimulation equivalence. Note that in this last definition, the χ action is considered like any other action.

Definition (strong bisimulation)

Consider a $LTS = <S, L^{i,\delta,\chi}, T, s_0>$. A relation $\underline{R} \subseteq S \times S$ is a strong bisimulation iff :

$\forall <B_1, B_2> \in \underline{R}, \forall a \in L^{i,\delta,\chi}$, we have

(i) if $B_1 -a \rightarrow B_1'$,   then $\exists B_2'$ such that $B_2 -a \rightarrow B_2'$ and $<B_1', B_2'> \in \underline{R}$

(ii) if $B_2 -a \rightarrow B_2'$,   then $\exists B_1'$ such that $B_1 -a \rightarrow B_1'$ and $<B_1', B_2'> \in \underline{R}$

This is the classical definition of a strong bisimulation, where χ is considered as any other action.

Now we define the strong bisimulation equivalence between two LTS's.

Two LTS's $Sys_1 = <S_1, L^{i,\delta,\chi}, T_1, s_{0_1}>$ and $Sys_2 = <S_2, L^{i,\delta,\chi}, T_2, s_{0_2}>$ are strong bisimulation equivalent, denoted $Sys_1 \sim Sys_2$, iff

$\exists$ a strong bisimulation relation $\underline{R} \subseteq S_1 \times S_2$, such that $<s_{0_1}, s_{0_2}> \in \underline{R}$

The weak bisimulation would be defined similarly by replacing, in the definition of the strong bisimulation, the action $a \in L^{i,\delta,\chi}$ by the sequence $\sigma \in (L^{\delta,\chi})^*$. Note that the χ action is considered, like δ and unlike i, in the sequences.

Possible associations of axioms and rules

Since *A1* and *A2* are inconsistent, let us first examine the case where *A2* is selected.

A2 + B1 or A2 + B2

It is shown in [Led 91] that $B \, [] \, stop \sim B$ is not preserved. Take B := $\lfloor stop \rfloor$(b; Q).

In addition, for A2 + B2, it is also shown in [Led 91] that $B \, [] \, B \sim B$ is not preserved either. Take B := $\lfloor stop \rfloor^2$(b; Q).

A2 + B3

This combination is more subtle. It has been investigated in [Led 91] where it was shown that it makes it impossible to preserve the properties of the parallel composition, e.g. $a; stop \, |[a]| \, stop \sim stop$ together with the associativity of $|[\gamma]|$. This problem is not discussed in [NS 90] where the combination A2 + B3 was chosen for ATP, but let us note that this problem might have a different nature because their parallel composition is defined differently, i.e. like in ACP [BeK 84].

A2 + B4
This combination has no interesting expressive power since *B4* is only applicable when one of the alternatives cannot execute any action (even χ), whereas even *stop* may execute a χ action according to *A2*.

A1 + B2
It is shown in [Led 91] that $B \; [] \; B \sim B$ is not preserved. Take B := $\lfloor stop \rfloor$(b; Q).

A1 + B3 + ¬ B1 + ¬ B2 + ¬ B4
It is shown in [Led 91] that $B \; [] \; stop \sim B$ is not preserved. Take B := $\lfloor stop \rfloor$(b; Q).

Remaining possible combinations of inference rules
A1 + B1   or   A1 + B4   or   A1 + B1 + B3   or   A1 + B3 + B4
We can see that *A2* and *B2* are naturally rejected.

Among the four remaining possibilities, we have selected *A1 + B3 + B4* for the following reasons.

The second case *A1 + B4* is not expressive enough since it only allows the passing of time when one process in the alternative behaves like stop.

In addition, rule *B1*, when combined with *A1*, means that time may resolve a choice; which is not intuitively appealing, e.g. if $P -\chi \to P'$ and $Q -\chi \to Q'$, then $P \; [] \; Q$ may lead by χ either to P' or to Q'. The pair *A1 + B4* has not this drawback even if *B4* is very similar to *B1*. These considerations reject cases 1 and 3.

Therefore, it remains *A1 + B3 + B4*.

As a conclusion to this section, we may say that, on the basis of an ASAP principle (viz. χ has a lower priority than other actions **with respect to choice**) and the objective of an upward compatibility with standard LOTOS, we have been able to reject many inference systems for the choice operator. Theoretically, four of them remained. Finally, we have selected one of them on two bases: expressive power and intuitive understanding of time.

6. The proposed operational semantics of TLOTOS

Based on the preliminary study of section 5, our proposed TLOTOS is thus the following.

Stop
(S)   No axiom for stop, i.e. axiom *A1* above, or stated otherwise $stop \not\to^a \; \forall \; a \in L^{i,\delta,\chi}$

Action prefix

(AP) $a; P -a \to P$ $(a \in L^i)$

This semantics expresses the ASAP criterion, i.e. action a should occur before the next χ action since no χ action is enabled. As mentioned earlier, at the syntactic level, no χ action (as well as no δ action) may appear in an action-prefix construction. A χ action is transparently introduced however when one uses the timed operators presented in sections 3 and 4. This is similar to the introduction of a δ action by way of the *exit* construct.

Termination

(Ex) $exit -\delta \to stop$

This semantics also expresses the ASAP criterion, i.e. δ should occur before the next χ action since no χ action is enabled.

Idling

(Id) $idle -\chi \to idle$

This process, already introduced in PADS, plays the role of the *stop* process of ATP (where it is denoted δ). It may be considered as a shorthand notation for $\lfloor stop \rfloor^{\omega}$.

Choice

The choice operator has been discussed in length in section 5. The rules $B3$ and $B4$, as well as the classical choice rules are reproduced hereafter for completeness.

(Ch1)	$\dfrac{P \xrightarrow{a} P'}{P\ []\ Q \xrightarrow{a} P'}$	$(a \in L^{i,\delta})$	(Ch3)	$\dfrac{P \xrightarrow{\chi} P',\ Q \xrightarrow{a} \not\ \ \forall\ a \in L^{i,\delta,\chi}}{P\ []\ Q \xrightarrow{\chi} P'}$
(Ch2)	$\dfrac{P \xrightarrow{\chi} P',\ Q \xrightarrow{\chi} Q'}{P\ []\ Q \xrightarrow{\chi} P'\ []\ Q'}$			Plus the symmetric rules Ch1' and Ch3'

Parallel composition

The rules for parallel composition are the well-known rules, except that they have been extended to express transitions in the presence of χ actions. We have decided not to allow the introduction of a χ action in the list of gates of the parallel composition operator in order to keep χ actions hidden at the syntactic level (again this is also the case for δ). Formally, if γ is the list of gates of the parallel operator, we have the requirement that $\gamma \cap \{\delta, \chi\} = \emptyset$. However, we have to decide whether the parallel composition enforces or not an implicit synchronization on χ actions. This is again related to the ASAP criterion: if one of the processes running in parallel may execute alone a χ action, this makes it impossible to impose that some actions of the other process occur ASAP, i.e. before this χ action. A way to achieve this is to enforce an implicit synchronization on χ, as for δ actions. Furthermore, this synchronization means that time must pass at the same pace in both processes; which is intuitively appealing.

(PC1)	$\dfrac{P \xrightarrow{a} P'}{P|[\gamma]|Q \xrightarrow{a} P'|[\gamma]|Q}$	$(a \in L^i - \gamma)$	(PC2)	$\dfrac{P \xrightarrow{a} P',\ Q \xrightarrow{a} Q'}{P|[\gamma]|Q \xrightarrow{a} P'|[\gamma]|Q'}$	$(a \in \gamma \cup \{\delta, \chi\})$
Plus the symmetric rule PC1'					

Note that the parallel operator has the so-called "must-timing" semantics (in the sense of [QAF 89]). It can be argued that this semantics is counter-intuitive for the interleaving operator, and that a "may-timing" semantics (in the sense of [QuF 87]) is more intuitive. Let us first recall the usual argument against "must-timing" on the following example: consider the interleaving B ||| C, and suppose that B := b; B'. With a "must-timing" semantics, such as the TLOTOS semantics, if the environment does not offer b, then C will only be allowed to proceed until it comes to a state where a timed action is required to occur. Therefore, C is not independent from B because a deadlock of B may induce a deadlock of C at the next time instant. This is a priori counter-intuive because it violates the independence between B and C.

Let us try to explain why we are anyway in favour of a "must-timing" semantics. Let us first note that, even in standard LOTOS, processes B and C are not independent since they are required to synchronize on termination. In TLOTOS, this synchronization is stronger because it is extended to the point that B and C have to synchronize "periodically" on every timed action. Therefore, a special care is required in the design of B and C in order to avoid such unwanted propagation of local deadlocks from B (or C) to the whole combined process B ||| C. This is up to the designer to specify this or not. For instance, such deadlock of C by B is avoided if the designer accepts to specify the system as $\lfloor b; B' \rfloor$(idle) ||| C : if action b does not occur before the next timed action then B becomes idle, and does not block C. This way of doing offers the possibility to simulate a "may-timing" behaviour on top of the basic "must-timing" semantics. We think that the opposite is not feasible.

In conclusion, a "must-timing" semantics is necessary in TLOTOS to express urgency of actions in composed processes. Of course, requiring such strong requirements may have dangerous consequences such as time deadlocks when the environment is not ready to participate in these urgent actions. But this is the normal price to pay. The designer may always specify a "may-timing" behaviour if it is the intended behaviour. The only drawback is an additional complexity in the resulting behaviour expression.

Hiding

The rules for hiding are the classical LOTOS rules. Again we require that no χ action be allowed in the list of hidden gates (as for i and δ) for two reasons. First, χ does not appear at the syntactic level, and second it would be counter-intuitive to hide the passing of time. Formally, if γ is the list of hidden gates, we have the requirement that: $\gamma \cap \{i, \delta, \chi\} = \varnothing$.

(H1) $\dfrac{P -a\rightarrow P'}{\text{hide } \gamma \text{ in } P -a\rightarrow \text{hide } \gamma \text{ in } P'}$ $(a \in L^{i,\delta,\chi} - \gamma)$	(H2) $\dfrac{P -a\rightarrow P'}{\text{hide } \gamma \text{ in } P -i\rightarrow \text{hide } \gamma \text{ in } P'}$ $(a \in \gamma)$

Enabling

For the enabling operator, a χ action is considered as another non-δ action, and the classical rules remain unchanged.

(En1) $\dfrac{P -a\rightarrow P'}{P >> Q -a\rightarrow P' >> Q}$ $(a \in L^{i,\chi})$	(En2) $\dfrac{P -\delta\rightarrow P'}{P >> Q -i\rightarrow Q}$

Disabling

The three usual rules $Di1$, $Di2$ and $Di3$ hereafter are the classical inference rules for disabling. $Di4$ and $Di5$ have been added to provide χ transitions and follow the same spirit as the choice operator in order to preserve the expansion theorem of the disabling operator.

(Di1) $\dfrac{P -a\rightarrow P'}{P [> Q -a\rightarrow P' [> Q}$ $(a \in L^i)$	(Di4) $\dfrac{P -\chi\rightarrow P', Q -\chi\rightarrow Q'}{P [> Q -\chi\rightarrow P' [> Q'}$
(Di2) $\dfrac{P -\delta\rightarrow P'}{P [> Q -\delta\rightarrow P'}$	(Di5) $\dfrac{P -\chi\rightarrow P', Q -a\not\rightarrow \;\forall\; a \in L^{i,\delta,\chi}}{P [> Q -\chi\rightarrow P'}$
(Di3) $\dfrac{Q -a\rightarrow Q'}{P [> Q -a\rightarrow Q'}$ $(a \in L^{i,\delta})$	Plus the symmetric rule Di5'

Instantiation

(In) $\dfrac{P [g_1/h_1, \ldots g_n/h_n] -a\rightarrow P', \; Q [h_1, \ldots h_n] := P}{Q [g_1, \ldots g_n] -a\rightarrow P'}$ $(a \in L^{i,\delta,\chi})$

Timed operators

The timed operators have been defined in sections 3 and 4: *SD1, SD2, SD3, SD4, ED1, ED2, ED3, ED4, USD1, USD2* and *USD3*. It can be seen that:
- all the axioms and rules of LOTOS are preserved;
- when new axioms and rules are added, the operators are nevertheless defined such that no new transitions are created in the LTS **when the operands are untimed processes**.

These two criteria imply the upward compatibility: untimed TLOTOS processes have the same semantics as their corresponding (i.e. equal) standard LOTOS version.

In section 5, the semantics of *stop* and *choice* have been selected on an additional requirement: usual equivalence laws should be preserved in order to facilitate as much as possible the use of TLOTOS by those who were trained on standard LOTOS.

With these axioms and rules, it has been shown in [Led 91] that the usual strong bisimulation laws are preserved, e.g. P [] stop ~ P, P [] P ~ P, P |[γ]| (Q |[γ]| R) ~ (P |[γ]| Q) |[γ]| R, ...
Some interesting laws related to the three timed operators are also provided in [Led 91].

7. Examples

We just provide two small examples of the use of the start delay and the unbounded start delay operators on the transmitter of the alternating bit protocol, as well as on a possible medium.

We first present the usual standard LOTOS specification (figure 5) and then the specification in TLOTOS.

In this example, $nat0$ is a positive natural number, sdu is the service data unit that the protocol must transfer, pdu is an operation which builds a protocol data unit from a sdu and a bit, bit is a renaming of $bool$ with 0 for $false$, 1 for $true$ and $compl$ for not.

```
Process Transmitter [in,s,r] (time:nat0) :noexit := T [in,s,r] (0 ofsort bit,time)
  where process T [in,s,r] (b:bit,t:nat0) :noexit :=
    in?x:sdu; Send [s,r] (x,b,t) >> T [in,s,r] (compl(b),t)
  where process Send [s,r] (x:sdu,b:bit,t:nat0) :exit :=
    s!pdu(x,b);
    (r?ack:bit [ack=b]; exit
    [] r?ack:bit [ack ne b]; Send [s,r] (x,b,t)
    [] (Time-out (t) >> Send [s,r] (x,b,t)))
  where process Time-out (t:nat0) :exit := exit endproc
  endproc (* Send *)
  endproc (* T *)
endproc (* Transmitter *)
```

Figure 5: The transmitter in standard LOTOS

The difference between this specification and the next one (figure 6) is twofold.

```
Process Transmitter [in,s,r] (time:nat0) :noexit := T [in,s,r] (0 ofsort bit,time)
  where process T [in,s,r] (b:bit,t:nat0) :noexit :=
    ⌊in?x:sdu; Send [s,r] (x,b,t)⌋^ω >> T [in,s,r] (compl(b),t)
  where process Send [s,r] (x:sdu,b:bit,t:nat0) :exit :=
    s!pdu(x,b);
    ⌊r?ack:bit [ack=b]; exit [] r?ack:bit [ack ne b]; Send [s,r] (x,b,t)⌋^t
    (Send [s,r] (x,b,t))
  endproc (* Send *)
  endproc (* T *)
endproc (* Transmitter *)
```

Figure 6 : The transmitter in TLOTOS

First, in TLOTOS we have to disable at some places the ASAP criterion on the occurrence of actions, e.g. when the transmitter is waiting at in for a sdu to transfer. Without the introduction of an unbounded time delay, the action in would be required to occur before the next χ action. This is not reasonable because we do not know anything about the behaviour of the external user who can deliver its sdu's at any time. The unbounded delay operator allows the transmitter to idle until the matching at in between this user and the transmitter, which is the expected behaviour in this case.

Second, we have to quantify correctly the time-out mechanism by replacing the imprecise process *time-out* by an adequate start delay operator. The overall structure is preserved: the branch *time-out (t) >> send* is just (simplified and) placed as a second argument of the start delay operator, while the other alternatives are embedded in the first argument of this operator. The parameter t is then simply added to quantify the time-out delay.

It can be seen that the action at s is not embedded in an unbounded start delay operator. This is because we want to enforce that this sending occur immediately (i.e. before the next χ action) after the reception at *in* of a sdu. This should be used with care, because it may create unexpected time deadlock when the transmitter is synchronized with the medium. However, when designing a protocol, one knows exactly the underlying medium (or service), and we suppose here that this medium is always in a state where it may receive the pdu.

The ASAP principle is very useful to model that no time passes for instance between an r action and the subsequent *exit* or call to process *send*, as well as during the relay between *send* and T.

As another small example, we provide the specification of a unidirectional underlying medium (figure 7), which is always ready to receive, may loose pdu's and introduces a constant delay d.

Process Medium [in,out] (d:nat0) **:noexit** :=
$\lfloor$in?x:pdu; exit$\rfloor^\omega$ >>
    ($\lfloor$i; idle$\rfloor^d$ (out!x; idle)
    |||
    $\lfloor$stop$\rfloor$ (Medium [in,out] (d)))
endproc (* Medium *)

Figure 7: A medium in TLOTOS

In this specification, the medium cannot accept two successive *in* actions within the same unit of time (see last line of the specification). This choice is arbitrary, but illustrates a means to preserve the FIFO ordering of pdu's. Of course, as a consequence, this simple medium does not allow more than d pdu's in transit.

Again, the action *out* is required to occur immediately after the delay d, which may be problematic if the receiver is not ready to receive at any time. In this case, *out* should be embedded in an unbounded delay operator as usual.

Finally, let us note the use of process *idle*. It cannot be replaced by *stop* because this would create a time deadlock. This is due to the semantics of the parallel composition which requires that all processes in parallel execute their χ actions simultaneously in order to proceed.

8. Comparison with other works

In this section, we will briefly compare our proposal with previous works on timed extensions in several process algebras, including LOTOS. We will start with the approaches which are the closest to ours (ATP [NS 90], TPL [HeR 90b], ACP$_{t\epsilon}^t$ [Gro 90], TCCS [MoT 89], PADS [Azc 90], Timed CSP [ReR 88, Ree 90], Timed CCS [Wan 90, Wan 91] and TPCCS [Han 91]), and compare the differences between the basic choices in the semantics of the operators (see table below).

The LOTOS parallel composition operator is specific, and our work cannot be strictly compared with others. For instance, in TPL and TCCS, the parallel operators are binary. In ATP and ACP$_{t\epsilon}^t$ they are multiway but with a different semantics, viz. the ACP one.

Some other works are also worth mentioning here even if they are based on other principles: ACP$_\rho$ [BaB 89], TIC [QuF 87, QAF 89] and Timed-Interaction LOTOS [BLT 90]. All these models have chosen to work with timestamps associated to the actions, either directly in the language syntax or at the semantic level.

Our options	Choices similar to ours	Choices different from ours
Presence of a distinct timed action χ	σ in TPL, χ in ATP and TPCCS, t in ACP$_{t\varepsilon}^t$ and PADS	No equivalent in TCCS, Timed CCS and Timed CSP which are based on delays
Timed action not allowed in action-prefix	ATP, TPCCS	Allowed in TPL, ACP$_{t\varepsilon}^t$, PADS
Stop is a time deadlock	TCCS, ACP$_{t\varepsilon}^t$, PADS	in ATP, TPL, Timed CCS and TPCCS, *stop* (or *NIL*) is like our *idle*.
ASAP Action-prefix	ATP, TCCS, ACP$_{t\varepsilon}^t$, synchronous actions of PADS	Only internal actions in TPL, Timed CCS, Timed CSP and TPCCS occur ASAP
Choice is deterministic w.r.t. time	ATP, TPL, "+" in TCCS[1], Timed CSP, Timed CCS, PADS and TPCCS	Nondeterministic in ACP$_{t\varepsilon}^t$
Non-urgent actions via $\sqcup^\omega$	$\sqcup^\omega$ in ATP	δ in TCCS, "nolimit value" in PADS, implicit in TPL, Timed CCS, Timed CSP and TPCCS, no equivalent in ACP$_{t\varepsilon}^t$

9. Conclusion

We have presented TLOTOS which is an upward compatible extension of LOTOS. Its operational semantics has been given. The use of TLOTOS has been illustrated on two small examples which prove that TLOTOS is powerful and easy to use. LOTOS specifications may be easily adapted to TLOTOS when one wants to formalize some time-dependent parts which were specified in an imprecise way in LOTOS.

Finally, we would like to recall all the basic choices of TLOTOS:

- The existence of a distinct action χ to model the passing of one unit of time. Therefore, time is discrete and abstract.
- The ASAP principle on non-χ actions in an action-prefix construction, which means that these actions should occur before the next χ action.
- The determinism of the choice operator with respect to time, which means that χ actions cannot resolve a choice.
- The absence of χ actions at the syntactic level, i.e. as a first argument of an action-prefix or in the gate lists of the parallel composition or hiding operators.
- The introduction of timed behaviours by way of three timed operators instead of timestamps in actions.
- The synchronization on χ actions imposed by the parallel composition, in order to model that time progresses at the same pace in all the components of a system.
- The priority of the outermost χ action in nested delay operators.
- The disabling of all levels of execution delay operators by way of δ.
- The timelock behaviour of *stop*, and the introduction of a new *idle* process which allows time to pass.

One may argue that the modelling of time by a distinct action which is not always enabled is counter-intuitive, since this means that time may be stopped at some places when actions cannot proceed, e.g. $a; P$ may stop time if action a cannot be matched by the environment. This prob-

---

[1] In TCCS, $\oplus$ is closer to our $\sqcup$ operator

lem may yet be presented in another way. If a process proposes a long (possibly infinite) sequence of actions before offering a χ action by way of one of the timed operators, this can be considered as a non implementable system, because the execution of so many actions is impossible in one unit of time. In our model, where actions take no time, this is of course a non problem, but this approximation may be questionable. In conclusion, time is considered here as an abstract time (by contrast to physical time). It is a convenient assumption at a conceptual level, and timed actions should be considered here as an abstract time reference which is **not** strongly bound to a physical time by a kind of "periodic" sequence of clock ticks.

TLOTOS expresses naturally urgency on observable **actions**, but cannot express adequately urgency on observable **interactions**, i.e. that an action should occur as soon as all the partners involved in an interaction are ready to do so. This problem is presented in depth in [BLT 90] and considered as a basic expressive power limitation. Note that this is **not** a lack of (theoretical) expressive power, but a lack of flexibility. Theoretically, there is no difference between an observable action and an observable interaction in LOTOS. However expressing urgency on interactions is closely related to the ability of expressing urgency in a modular way, which is essential in practice. The more general approach we know of has been proposed in Timed-Interaction LOTOS [BLT 90] where an "asap" operator (and the more general "timer" operator) is defined which solves this problem and allows the expression of urgency on interactions. This lack of flexibility in TLOTOS to express urgency on interactions is probably its main shortcoming. A simple way to add this flexibility in TLOTOS would be to include this "asap" operator. However we are currently working on another kind of extension.

Section 7 illustrates how a standard LOTOS specification (containing imprecise and unquantified timed behaviours) may be rewritten in TLOTOS. It appears that in many places, the LOTOS "action-prefix" needs to be changed into a careful combination of TLOTOS (asap) "action-prefix" and the unbounded start delay operator. This is somehow unsatisfactory because we would like to keep the major part of a standard LOTOS specification unchanged. This problem is also under study in the above-mentioned extension of TLOTOS.

Finally, let us recall that, in [Led 91], we have proved that the operational semantics of TLOTOS is consistent, and that strong bisimulation is a congruence. Examples of equivalence laws associated with the three timed operators, and the details of the rejection of the combination A2 + B3 in section 5 are also included in this report.

Acknowledgements

I am grateful to the anonymous referees for their judicious comments.

References

[AuB 84]   D. Austry, G. Boudol, *Algèbre de Processus et Synchronisation,* Theoretical Computer Science 30 (1984) 91 - 131 (North-Holland, Amsterdam).

[Azc 90]   A. Azcorra-Saloña, *Formal Modeling of Synchronous Systems,* Ph. D. Thesis, ETSI Telecomunicación, Universidad Politécnica de Madrid, Spain, Nov. 1990.

[BaB 90]   J.C.M. Baeten, J.A. Bergstra, *Real time process algebra,* Rept. No. P8916b, University of Amsterdam, Amsterdam, March 1990.

[BLT 90]   T. Bolognesi, F. Lucidi, S. Trigila, *From Timed Petri Nets to Timed LOTOS,* in: L. Logrippo, R. Probert, H. Ural, eds., Protocol Specification, Testing and Verification X, (North-Holland, Amsterdam, 1990).

[BoL 91]   T. Bolognesi, F. Lucidi, *LOTOS-like process algebras with urgent or timed interactions,* in: K. Parker, G. Rose, eds., FORTE'91 (North-Holland, Amsterdam, 1992).

[Car 82]   L. Cardelli, *Real Time Agents,* in: M. Nielsen, E.M. Schmidt, eds., Automata, Languages and Programming (LNCS 140, Springer-Verlag, Berlin Heidelberg New York, 1982) 94-106.

[DaS 89]   J. Davies, S. Schneider, *An introduction to timed CSP,* Rept. No. PRG-75, Oxford University Computing Laboratory, Programming Research Group, Aug. 1989.

[Gro 90]   J. F. Groote, *Specification and Verification of Real Time Systems in ACP*, in: L. Logrippo, R. Probert, H. Ural, eds., Protocol Specification, Testing and Verification X, (North-Holland, Amsterdam, 1990).
[HaJ 90]   H. Hansson, B. Jonsson, *A calculus for communicating systems with time and probabilities*, in: 11th IEEE Real-Time Systems Symposium, Orlando, Florida, 1990, IEEE Computer Society Press
[Han 91]   H. Hansson, *Time and Probability in Formal Design of Distributed Systems*, Ph. D Thesis, DoCS 91/27, Uppsala University, Dept. of Computer Science, P.O. Box 520, S-75120 Uppsala, Sweden.
[HeR 90]   M. Hennessy, T. Regan, *A temporal process algebra*, in: J. Quemada, J. Mañas, E. Vazquez, eds., FORTE '90, Madrid, Spain, Nov. 90 (to be published by North-Holland, Amsterdam, 1991).
[HTZ 90]   W. van Hulzen, P. Tilanus, H. Zuidweg, *LOTOS Extended with Clocks*, in: S. T. Vuong, ed., FORTE '89 (North-Holland, Amsterdam, 1990).
[ISO 8807]   ISO/IEC-JTC1/SC21/WG1/FDT/C, *IPS - OSI - LOTOS, a Formal Description Technique Based on the Temporal Ordering of Observational Behaviour*, IS 8807, February 1989.
[Led 91]   G. Leduc, *On the design and properties of TLOTOS*, Rept. No. S.A.R.T. 91/04/13, Université de Liège, Dept. Systèmes et Automatique, B28, 4000 Liège, Belgium, May 1991.
[Mil 83]   A.J.R.G. Milner, *Calculi for Synchrony and Asynchrony*, Theoretical Computer Science, Vol. 25, No. 3, July 1983, 267-310 (North-Holland, Amsterdam).
[Mil 85]   G. Milne, *CIRCAL and the Representation of Communication, Concurrency and Time*, ACM Transactions on Programming Languages and Systems, Vol. 7, No. 2, April 1985, 270-298.
[MoT 89]   F.Moller, C. Tofts, *A temporal calculus of communicating systems*, Rept. No. ECS-LFCS-89-104, University of Edinburgh, Department of Computer Science, Edinburgh, Dec. 89.
[MRF 91]   J.M. Martin Espinosa, J. M. Robles Roman, L. Fuertes Prieto, *Concurrent Modelling in LOTOS as a solution to real time problems*, in: J. Quemada, J. Mañas, E. Vazquez, eds., FORTE '90, Madrid, Spain, Nov. 90 (to be published by North-Holland, Amsterdam, 1991).
[NRS 90]   X. Nicollin, J.-L. Richier, J. Sifakis, J. Voiron, *ATP : An algebra for timed processes*, in: M. Broy, C.B. Jones, eds., IFIP Working Conference on Programming Concepts and Methods, Sea of Gallilee, Israel (North-Holland, Amsterdam, 1990).
[NS 90]   X. Nicollin, J. Sifakis, *The Algebra of Timed Processes ATP: Theory and Application*, Rept. No. RT-C26, Projet Spectre, LGI-IMAG, Dec. 1990.
[NS 91]   X. Nicollin, J. Sifakis, *An Overview and Synthesis on Timed Process Algebras*, in: K.G. Larsen, ed., Computer-Aided Verification, III, Aalborg, Denmark, July 1991.
[NSY 91]   X. Nicollin, J. Sifakis, S. Yovine, *From ATP to Timed Graphs and Hybrid Systems*, in: REX Workshop "Real-Time: Theory and Practice", Mook, The Netherlands, June 1991.
[QAF 89]   J. Quemada, A. Azcorra, D. Frutos, *A timed calculus for LOTOS*, in: S. T. Vuong, ed., FORTE '89, Vancouver, Canada, Dec. 89 (North-Holland, Amsterdam, 1990).
[QuF 87]   J. Quemada, A. Fernandez, *Introduction of Quantitative Relative Time into LOTOS*, in: H. Rudin, C.H. West, eds., Protocol Specification, Testing and Verification, VII, (North-Holland, Amsterdam, 1987, ISBN 0-444-70293-8) 105-121.
[Ree 90]   G.M.Reed, *A Hierarchy of Domains for Real Time Distributed Computing*, in: M. Main, A. Melton, M. Mislove, D. Schmidt, eds., Mathematical Foundations of Programming Semantics (LNCS 442, Springer-Verlag, Berlin Heidelberg New York, 1990) 80-128.
[ReR 88]   G.M.Reed, A.W. Roscoe, *A Timed Model for Communicating Sequential Processes*, Theoretical Computer Science 58 (1988) 249 - 261 (North-Holland, Amsterdam).
[Tof 88]   C. Tofts, *Temporal Orderings for Concurrency*, Rept. No. ECS-LFCS-88-49, University of Edinburgh, Department of Computer Science, Edinburgh, April 88.
[Wan 90]   Y. Wang, *Real-Time Behaviour of Asynchronous Agents*, in: J.C.M. Baeten, J.W. Klop, eds., CONCUR '90, Theories of Concurrency: Unification and Extension, LNCS 458 (Springer - Verlag, Berlin Heidelberg New York, 1990, ISBN 3-540-53048-7) 502-520.
[Wan 91]   Y. Wang, *CCS + Time = an Interleaving Model for Real Time Systems*, in: ICALP'91, Madrid, Spain, July 1991.

Mapping Time-Extended LOTOS To Standard LOTOS[1]

Ashley Mc Clenaghan.

Department of Computing Science and Mathematics,
University Of Stirling, STIRLING FK9 4LA, Scotland.

Abstract

This paper explores the mapping between standard LOTOS and a *time-extended* derivative of LOTOS in which a notion of quantitative time is implicit and time constraints are easily expressed. This work is notable on two accounts. Firstly we propose a time-extended LOTOS which unifies and incorporates many features deemed desirable by separate authors in this field. Secondly, we investigate two semantics-preserving functions which map time-extended LOTOS to standard LOTOS. The intention is that *translated* time-extended LOTOS descriptions are then amenable to existing LOTOS tools and analysis techniques.

We relate ideas in this paper to existing work, and conclude with a list of issues requiring further investigation.

1 Introduction

In order to fully specify time-dependent systems we must use a description technique which fully supports this aspect of their behaviour, i.e. the expression of *quantitative timing concerns*. Cohen et al. [4] caution that to omit quantitative timing requirements may subtract an entire dimension from the description. Such omission may prove a useful abstraction but this does not necessarily *simplify* the description. Absence of timing information can lead to a large increase in the number of system states, which may in fact result in an erroneous description because of additional, unexpected behaviour. Cohen et al. sum this up by saying that: "the apparent distinction between the measures of time introduced for the mathematical concern of *correctness* and those introduced for the engineering concern of *performance* may be wholly illusory because what we originally perceived as a performance concern impacts on correctness". Further justifications of the need for description techniques which express quantitative timing concerns can be found in [4].

---

[1]The author would like to acknowledge the financial assistance of the Department of Computing Science (University of Stirling), Hewlett-Packard Laboratories (Bristol) and the Department of Education for Northern Ireland (DENI).

Process algebras have proved useful in capturing descriptions of complex, concurrent, communicating systems. LOTOS [7] is one such algebra. The formal basis of LOTOS provides it with the combined descriptive and analytic power necessary to tackle such complex systems. However LOTOS lacks the built-in facility to express quantitative time which explains our efforts to form a time-extended derivative of LOTOS for the description and analysis of time-dependent systems.

We begin by defining intuitively what we think is a desirable time-extended version of LOTOS. Then two possible strategies for mapping between this time-extended LOTOS and standard LOTOS are outlined — one using *time tick events* (t-events) and the other *time-stamped* events. Their points of interest, merits and drawbacks are considered. We conclude with a list of issues worthy of further investigation, and a summary of this paper.

2 Motivation and Requirements

The motivation for our work stems from the need to evolve an extended version of LOTOS in which the notion of *quantitative* time is implicit and in which timing constraints may be easily expressed. Standard LOTOS only allows us to describe the relative ordering in time of events. This may not be sufficient to fully describe systems with explicit timing constraints.

Any time-extended LOTOS should possess the following **two** important facilities:

1. The facility to specify that an event may occur only at constrained times (i.e. that time influences the occurrence of events).

2. The facility to measure durations between events (not necessarily consecutive).

A variety of solutions for extending LOTOS with time have already been proposed. These include: using *i-transitions* as timed events; Quemada *et al.* TIC calculus for LOTOS [10, 9]; W. van Hulzen *et al.* CELOTOS [12] which measures time intervals with clocks; denoting time using ADTs in standard LOTOS [3]; and a "real-time" simulator developed by C. J. Fidge [6].

Our attempt to unify many of the time-enhancements considered desirable by such authors has resulted in a time-extended version of LOTOS which we call T-LOTOS. Our other aim is to devise a function for mapping T-LOTOS descriptions to standard LOTOS descriptions.[2] We investigate two possible mapping algorithms but show that neither is complete. That is to say that it is not, in general, possible to map (unrestricted) T-LOTOS descriptions to equivalent finite LOTOS descriptions.

However, we conclude that complete mapping functions do exist for restricted subsets of T-LOTOS and observe that some such subsets may be useful.

---

[2] Such a mapping function can then be used to form the basis for a T-LOTOS to LOTOS translator tool which captures the semantics of T-LOTOS source descriptions in the structure of the derived LOTOS descriptions.

3 Representing Time

In LOTOS we conceive the behaviour of systems as sets of events constrained by sets of predicates. Conveniently, this underlying model also supports quantitative time extensions to LOTOS.

To enable the expression of quantitative timing concerns we want to be able to associate each event with a time (i.e. a measure of the interval between some fixed point in time and its occurrence). We can conceptualize the effect of time by predicates which impose time constraints on system events. Such a time predicate is responsible for two main tasks:

- To effect the propagation of time throughout the system. This has two consequences: events occur only at appropriate times; and the time (i.e. the duration from the start of the system) is known throughout the system during all time intervals.

- To effect the perpetual incrementation of the time by some measure of duration.

The realization of the above two tasks requires the representation of events located in time. This requirement can be satisfied in LOTOS by a number of approaches that include:

- The progression of time may be represented by the occurrence of specially designated events (*t-events*, see [1]). The the location in time of all other events can be established by considering their occurrence (ordering) relative to the t-events.

- All events could carry a *time-stamp* which denotes the location in time of their occurrence. Such a time-stamp may be part of the value structure of an event (i.e. an event parameter — an ACT ONE sort in an *experiment-offer* statement).

These two schemes form the bases for our two mapping algorithms. Their realizations, merits and drawbacks are discussed in the remaining sections.

4 Principles of T-LOTOS

This section very briefly and informally introduces T-LOTOS.

We extend the syntax of standard LOTOS *action-denotation* expressions (and **exit** events) to provide an optional *time-clause* delimited by braces, i.e. {...}. All time values referenced within time-clauses are absolute (i.e. measures of time relative to the start time of the specified system), and are denoted by natural numbers (i.e. the **NaturalNumber** type). *Sub-time-clauses* occur within time-clauses and are separated by commas. Sub-time-clauses can be used to constrain an event offer to ranges and sets of times, and allow the exact time of an event occurrence to be established by recording it in a variable. Examples of (sub-)time-clauses are:

a{2}	Event a is offered only at time 2.
b{Range(6,t1)}	Event b is offered only between time 6 and time t1 (de-referenced), inclusive.
c{Not(Range(1,4))}	Event c is not offered between time 1 and time 4, inclusive.
d{Range(5,9),@t2}	Event d is offered only between time 5 and time 9, inclusive, and if it does occur then its actual time of occurrence will be recorded in the variable t2, which can be made use of later in this behaviour expression.
e{Before(4)}	Event e is offered only before time 4.
f{4,After(4)}	Event f is offered only at time 4 and after.

Notice that the @ operator allows the exact time of an event occurrence to be established. For example: x{Range(2,5),@t1} constrains event x to occur between the times 2 and 5 (inclusive). Also, the actual time that event x does occur will be recorded in the variable t1, which can employed later in the rest of the behaviour expression. Hence the @ operator not only facilitates the *measurement* of durations between events (not necessarily consecutive), but also allows us to express time constraints *relative* to any system event.

Any event without an explicit associated time is simply constrained to occur between the immediately preceding and succeeding events. Thus: a{3};b;c{5} constrains b to occur within the absolute time range 3 to 5 (inclusive). From this last example it appears that two (or more) events can occur at the same moment in *time*, e.g. events a and b at absolute time 3. If so, this is contradictory to the use of the interleaving semantics of LOTOS. This apparent contradiction is resolved if we accept the following explanation. When two events x and y apparently occur at the same time but are actually composed as x;y, x occurs a negligible/unmeasurable duration before y, given the granularity at which we can measure time durations in this particular system.

All sorts and operations within time-clauses are of the type TimeType. The definitions for TimeType are presented to the T-LOTOS user as a predefined type definition. TimeType will contain the appropriate sort and operation definitions for time metrics, intervals, relations, etc.

5 Mapping Algorithm Using t-events

The first mapping algorithm is based on translating the *implicit*[3] quantitative time information contained in a T-LOTOS description to *explicit* time information in the form of special t-events[4] in the resulting LOTOS description. Each t-event represents the passing of one unit of time.[5] This is most similar to the proposal in [1] and similarities can also be found with work in [10, 9, 12].

---

[3] In the sense that the supporting quantitative time mechanism is hidden to the T-LOTOS user.

[4] In T-LOTOS t-events can be considered special in a similar way that δ events are in LOTOS.

[5] Of course the relationship between real-life units of time and the interval between t-event occurrences does not have to be one-to-one, or in any other way proportional, although in general we will choose that this be so.

The following subsections outline the translation to t-events, highlighting the main points of interest.

5.1 Action-Prefix Expressions

The following translation of an action-prefix expression conveys the essence of our t-event translation strategy. Consider translating the following behaviour expression[6]:

_TRANS_ACTION_PREFIX(b{Range(2,t1),@t2}; B[c,e])

Using our algorithm this is expanded to the following LOTOS text[7]:

```
EVENT1[b,c,e,t](thetime,t1)
...where   process EVENT1[b,c,e,t](thetime,t1:TimeSort) : noexit :=
              t?newthetime:TimeSort; EVENT1[b,c,e,t](newthetime,t1)
              [] [(2 le thetime) and (thetime le t1)]->
                  b; _TRANS_PROC_INST( B[c,e] )
           endproc
```

Notice that (in the expanded text) the choice between the t-event and the b event supports the requirement that time (in terms of t-events) should be able to proceed independently of any other concerns. The b event is constrained to be offered only at appropriate times, and the actual time of its occurrence (the value of newthetime) will be used in the subsequent steps of the translation (e.g. substituted for t2 where appropriate). The current time, thetime, is passed into process EVENT1 so that EVENT1 can decide whether or not it is an appropriate time to offer event b.

To impose a proper quantitative time ordering on these events a global time process must also be composed in a conjunction with the rest of the translated system description. This global time process continually offers to synchronize with **all** t-events in the system, negotiating a monotonically increasing[8] quantitative time for these events.

Internal (or i) events are treated similarly to other events in T-LOTOS — i.e. they can be given quantitative timing constraints. It should be noted that t-events are no substitute for i events — both are conceptually different. The former represents the passing of time, the latter represents some spontaneous transition within the system. What is more, the use of the i event to represent the passage of time has the disadvantage that time-related properties cannot be proved if the internal event is used for other purposes also (see [12]).

5.2 Choice Expressions

What should: (x{2}; P[x]) [] (y{1}; Q[y]) mean? Two possibilities for time-extended semantics are immediate or deferred choice. For *immediate choice* the above expression would be translated to:

---

[6]We use _TRANSxxx to denote a translation function.
[7]**Note:** We have rationalised the translated text and omitted some context information which must be maintained. Also notice how T-LOTOS expressions are translated into new (uniquely named) processes.
[8]When a t-event t!n occurs, all subsequent t-event occurrences will be of the form t!m, where $m > n$.

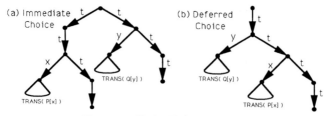

Figure 1: Choice Behaviour Trees

```
EVENT1[x,t](thetime) [] EVENT2[y,t](thetime)
```

(EVENT1 and EVENT2 are of the form shown in section 5.1 above.) Expanding this results in:

```
   (t;t;((x; _TRANS( P[x] ) ) [] (t; (* t offers ad infinitum*) )))
[] (t;((y; _TRANS( Q[y] ) )    [] (t; (* t offers ad infinitum*) )))
```

When this expression is evaluated, two t-events are offered[9] at the choice statement. When one of these occurs it immediately determines which of the events x or y can subsequently occur. One interpretation of these semantics is that since we often choose to have time-constrained events mark the finish of actions with durations, the description is saying that the actions corresponding to the events x and y mutually exclude one another. Immediately one of these actions starts to happen the other action (and hence the other representing event) cannot occur. (See behaviour tree (a) in figure 1.)

Translating the same time-extended choice statement as above, but using the *deferred choice* strategy will result in the expression expansion:

```
t;((y; _TRANS( Q[y] ) ) []
    (t;((x; _TRANS( P[x] ) ) [] (t; (* t offers ad infinitum *) ))))
```

This defers as late as possible, the decision as to whether or not an event such as x or y will occur. Events x and y still mutually exclude one another but, in this instance, if event y does not occur at time 1, event x may still occur at time 2. In the immediate choice translation, if event y was offered but did not occur at time 1, event x would never be offered. (Compare the behaviour trees in figure 1.)

Of these two time-extended semantic models for choice, deferred choice seems the closest to the standard LOTOS choice semantics, and also is the closest to the *intuitive* interpretation (by the author at least) of the time-extended syntax for choice expressions. Therefore we adopt the deferred choice model over the immediate choice model.

Translating time-extended deferred choice expressions is not as straightforward as it may initially seem. The algorithm must identify all action-denotations (and stop, exit expressions) which form direct alternatives to each other. Each set of such alternative action-denotations we call a 'choice set'. For example, the events x, y and z in the following T-LOTOS fragment form a choice set.

---

[9]The t-event may cause non-determinism if composed in parallel with itself, as any other event may. We might interpret a choice between t-events as a choice between different 'time streams'.

```
w; ((x{2}; Q) [] (y{4}; R) [] S[z])
...where    process S[z] : noexit := z{3}; P endproc
```

Translating the choice set:

```
_TRANS_CHOICE_SET( (x{2}; Q) [] (y{4}; R) [] S[z] )
```

gives us:

```
CHOICE_SET1[x,y,z,t](thetime)
...where    process CHOICE_SET1[x,y,z,t](thetime:TimeSort) : noexit :=
                t?newthetime:TimeSort; CHOICE_SET1[x,y,z,t](newthetime)
                [] _TRANS_CHOICE_ALT_ACTION_PREFIX( x{2}; Q )
                [] _TRANS_CHOICE_ALT_ACTION_PREFIX( y{4}; R )
                [] _TRANS_CHOICE_ALT_PROC_INST( S[z] )
            endproc
```

If an action-denotation element in a choice set is not referenced as a choice alternative, we translate this as shown in section 5.1. Where such an action-denotation is referenced as a choice alternative we translate it as shown below.

```
_TRANS_CHOICE_ALT_ACTION_PREFIX( y{4}; R )
```

expands to:

```
EVENT3[y,t](thetime)
...where    process EVENT3[y,t](thetime:TimeSort) : noexit :=
                [thetime eq 4]-> y; _TRANS_PROC_INST( R )
            endproc
```

Notice how CHOICE_SET1 implements deferred choice by always offering the t-event, and offering the other events when appropriate. Process EVENT3 significantly differs from the EVENT1 process (shown in section 5.1) in that it does not itself offer t-events as an alternative to its y event, but instead relies on the CHOICE_SET1 process for this t-event alternative. If EVENT3 were to offer an alternative t-event and this occurred, all the other alternative events in the CHOICE_SET1 expression would then be excluded from ever occurring. This would not reflect our intended semantics for the deferred time-extended choice expression.

5.3 Parallel Expressions

All parallel behaviour expressions which share a common time must synchronize on the t-events which represent the passage of time.[10] This implies that:

```
_TRANS_PARALLEL( choice-exp |[gate-id-list]| parallel-exp )
```

---

[10]T-LOTOS is based on a "synchronous model" of time.

will be translated to:

_TRANS_CHOICE(choice-exp) |[gate-id-list, t]| _TRANS_PARALLEL(parallel-exp)

The EVENTn processes, described in the previous subsections, ensure that all behaviour expressions in a parallel combination always offer to synchronize on t-events at least. Thus time can always progress throughout an expression consisting of sub-expressions combined in parallel even if one or more of these sub-expressions deadlocks (with respect to any events other than t-events). This is the avoidance of "synchronism deadlock" in [1].

5.3.1 Synchronous Exits

Translating T-LOTOS terminating (exiting) behaviour expressions combined by a parallel operator poses yet another problem. Thus far we have seen that in the LOTOS text (translated from T-LOTOS) we explicitly pass each behaviour expression the current time value (via the thetime parameter). To establish this current time we need to be able to determine the exiting time of the enabling behaviour expression. If the enabling expression is a set of synchronously exiting parallel behaviour expressions we must devise some means of negotiating the final synchronous exit time of the complete parallel expression.

To solve this problem (but see section 5.5) we replace all such synchronizing exits with special WAIT processes of the form:

```
process WAIT[t](thetime:TimeSort) :exit :=
     exit(thetime)
  [] t?newthetime:TimeSort;WAIT[t](newthetime)
endproc (* WAIT *)
```

The WAIT process offers to exit immediately with the time of the last event in the instantiating behaviour expression. However if exit synchronization at this time with the other parallel expressions is not possible, the WAIT process offers to synchronize on t-events to update its 'exit time' and recurses, continually trying to synchronize its exit with the other parallel expressions. Thus in this way, any one behaviour expression, in a set combined by a parallel operator, can wait until all other behaviour expressions in the set are ready to terminate with it.

In general the WAIT process must be tailored to the exact functionality of its context, i.e. the WAIT process must offer the same list of exit values.

5.4 Disable Expressions

Consider the translation of a T-LOTOS disable expression:

_TRANS_DISABLE(b{2}; B[b,c]) [> D[d])

This is translated to:

```
EVENT1[b,c,d,t](thetime)
...where  process EVENT1[b,c,d,t](thetime:TimeSort) : noexit :=
              t?newthetime:TimeSort; EVENT1[b,c,d,t](newthetime)
              [] [thetime eq 2]-> b; _TRANS_DISABLE( B[b,c] [> D[d] )
              [] _TRANS_DISABLING_PROC_INST( D[d] )
          endproc
```

Notice how _TRANS_DISABLE allows disabling at any instant, by offering the disabling expression as an alternative to all events.

_TRANS_DISABLING_PROC_INST translates all the possible events in the disabling expression much in the same way as _TRANS_CHOICE_ALT_ACTION_PREFIX (section 5.2) does, thus relegating the responsibility of updating time (via t-event synchronization) to the disablable expression.

5.5 Limitations of the t-event Based Approach

In the previous subsections we have not explicitly stated that the t-event based mapping can take any T-LOTOS description, statically analyse it and translate it into an equivalent finite LOTOS description. It cannot. Unfortunately it is not, in general, possible to translate T-LOTOS disable expressions which are embedded inside a recursive definition[11] to equivalent finite LOTOS. Two possible means of overcoming this difficulty are:

- Restrict the expressive power of T-LOTOS by either forbidding the expression of disable expressions inside recursion, or by altering the disable operator to force the T-LOTOS user to explicitly state at what times disabling may occur, e.g. [{time_constraint}>. (The times at which disabling may occur are immediately derivable from [{time_constraint}> . This is in contrast to the [> P[x] form of the disable operator, for which we would have to analyse P[x] to establish such times.)

- Integrate the translation algorithm into LOTOS simulation/expansion tools (such as SPIDER, HIPPO, LOLA [13, 14]). In effect this means that we rewrite the expansion theorems [7, section B.2.2] so that expansion of T-LOTOS expressions yields choice LOTOS (with data values) and the appropriate placing of t-events.

A lesser problem with this algorithm is that WAIT processes (section 5.3.1) cannot force a parallel set of behaviour expressions to exit at the *earliest* time possible.

6 Mapping Algorithm Using Time-Stamps

This mapping algorithm translates the *implicit*[12] quantitative time information in T-LOTOS descriptions to *explicit* time information (time-stamps) incorporated into the value structure of events. Thus T-LOTOS event offers such as:

---

[11]For example, expressions such as: P[x,y] ...where process P[x,y] : noexit := x2; P[x,y] [> D[y] endproc

[12]In the sense that the supporting quantitative time mechanism is hidden to the T-LOTOS user.

```
a ? x:X [x eq y] {Range(3,t1)};...
b ! z {Not(4),@t2};...
a;...
```

are mapped[13] to the LOTOS text:

```
a ? t:TimeSort ? x:X [x eq y, (t ge 3) and (t le t1)];...
b ? t2:TimeSort ! z [t2 ne 4];...
a;...
```

To impose a proper quantitative time ordering on these events, a global time process must also be composed in a conjunction with the rest of the translated system description. This global time process continually offers to synchronize on *all* events in the system, negotiating a monotonically increasing[14] quantitative time-stamp for these events.

However, LOTOS allows the dynamic declaration of new gates, which makes it impossible to pre-determine the set of all possible system events from simple static analysis of the T-LOTOS text. It is also generally impossible to 'dynamically evolve' such a global time process, i.e. to establish an initial global time process which synchronises on observable gates, and to then reconfigure this time process on-the-fly as each hide operator in the given T-LOTOS system is realized. This is because it proves impossible to manage the synchronization between an initial global time process and its newly evolved gates.

It is possible, through static analysis of any T-LOTOS description, to pre-determine a set of observable action-denotations (gate-identifiers together with experiment-offer structures) such that this set has the potential to synchronize with any observable events in the system. This set can then be used to construct a global time process in conjunction with the rest of the processes in the translated system. A global time process for the example above is:

```
process GLOBAL_TIME[a,b](thetime:TimeSort) : noexit :=
        a!thetime?v:X; GLOBAL_TIME[a,b](thetime) (*    Offer to synchronize with *)
     [] b!thetime?v:Z; GLOBAL_TIME[a,b](thetime) (*    the rest of the system    *)
     [] a; GLOBAL_TIME[a,b](thetime)             (*    at 'thetime'.             *)
     [] GLOBAL_TIME[a,b](thetime+1)              (* OR Offer to synchronize at   *)
endproc                                          (*    succeeding 'times'.       *)
```

For simulation an internal event would have to be introduced to guard the recursion, but the principle is that if an event happens at time 3 (say) then the next event may happen at time 5 (say) without the specification having to explicitly *move* in constant duration steps through the time series 3 to 5, in this case.

Of course this now means that we restrict quantitative time relations to be expressible *only* over observable events. This restricted form of T-LOTOS we term RT-LOTOS.

---

[13]Approximately.

[14]In the sense that when an event time-stamped t occurs, all subsequent event occurrences will be time-stamped $t + n$, where $n \geq 0$.

6.1 Justification for Investigation of RT-LOTOS

Our objective in developing RT-LOTOS is to extend the idea of a good **specification**[15] style (for LOTOS) to cover specifications in which quantitative time constraints are captured. Most authors advocate the constraint-oriented style for high-level specifications in view of its assertional characteristics. We argue that limiting the expression of quantitative time relations to *only* observable events is not only sufficient for the specification of time-dependent systems, but also provides a guideline for "good" specifications of such systems. It is on this basis that we feel justified in developing a restrictive time-extended version of LOTOS (RT-LOTOS).

6.2 Using RT-LOTOS

In this section we discuss examples of how RT-LOTOS can be used to specify certain aspects of quantitative time-dependent systems.

Consider writing a specification for a system which, after the user presses a button, will either two seconds later turn on a green light, or three seconds later turn on a red light. In RT-LOTOS we would write:

`press_button{@t1};(i;greenlight{t1+2};exit [] i;redlight{t1+3};exit)`

We might have considered writing:

`press_button{@t1};(i{t1+2};greenlight;exit [] i{t1+3};redlight;exit)`

but RT-LOTOS does not allow us to place quantitative time constraints on internal events. In the above example we can see that this is a welcome restriction, since the second solution (if it were legal in RT-LOTOS) would be more restrictive than the first in that it states at what time the system determines (invisibly) which one of the two possible behaviour paths to take after the `press_button` event. Moreover, this second specification does not actually fulfill the requirements since there are no constraints[16] to restrict the actual `greenlight` and `redlight` events to occur two and three seconds, respectively, after the `press_button` event. This example emphasizes the point that for specifications we are interested in stating only relations among observable events, and that this is also true for quantitative time relations.

A possible concern is the inability to express quantitative time constraints on `exit` events. The wish to have quantitatively timed `exit` events (in contrast to other ordinary internal events) would be to time the successful termination of behaviour expressions. If we consider specifying an untimed system whose successful termination should be established by the user (environment), we would write something like:

`...;theend;exit`

---

[15] Note that here we are assuming a clear distinction between (extensional) specifications and (intensional) "how-to" descriptions.

[16] Given that we only use the underlying time-stamp model to determine the quantitative time of event occurrences.

where theend is an observable event. The exit (or δ event which the exit produces) is merely an artifact of the LOTOS model and not an integral part of the specification itself. Therefore we establish the successful termination of this system by synchronizing on the theend event. Similarly we could establish the time of the successful termination of this system by synchronizing on a (quantitatively timed) RT-LOTOS event.

6.3 The Semantics of RT-LOTOS

The semantics of RT-LOTOS are not unlike those presented by Quemada et al. for TIC in [9]. The major difference is that we treat internal events as untimed whereas Quemada et al. allow timed internal events. In effect this means that the semantics of RT-LOTOS is a 'subset' of the semantics of TIC.

The main difference between RT-LOTOS and TIC can be seen in our slightly different definitions for (what TIC calls) "time choice" (an extension of action prefix). Borrowing the presentation style of TIC semantics, RT-LOTOS "time choice" semantics are:

$$aT; B - at \to B \quad iff \quad ((a \neq i) and (t \in T))$$
$$or((a = i) and (T = \emptyset) and (\mathcal{F}(s_0) = t))$$

where if $\mathcal{F}(s_0)$ is a function which returns the time at the initial state s_0 of the behaviour (given the labelled transition system $< S, AT, TR, s_0 >$ in [9]). Informally, this states that either an observable event a ($\neq i$) may occur at time t, where t is an element of the set T of times at which a may occur; or that an internal event a ($= i$) may occur at time t, where the set T is empty (i.e. no quantatitive time constraints on internal events) and t is the time in the state $aT; B$. We thus treat transitions involving internal events as transitions for which the time value between the two states does not alter.

6.4 Limitations of this Time-Stamp Based Algorithm

Given an RT-LOTOS specification, establishing whether action-denotations (apart from explicit i action-denotations) can never be *realized* as observable events is, in general, undecidable. This means that the translation algorithm produces a global time process which contains superfluous synchronization offers. Although not elegant, this does not affect the correctness of the resulting specification. A more worrying point about the algorithm's inability to distinguish such action-denotations is that it cannot detect if the RT-LOTOS specification contains hidden event offers with attached time-clauses. (In RT-LOTOS hidden events are not permitted time-clauses.)

7 Further Work

This section lists some of the issues arising from the investigation summarized in this paper.
In this document we have only explained the principle points of translating T-LOTOS/RT-LOTOS to standard LOTOS using simplified, stand-alone examples. We are developing

a *yacc* based translator program (using the time-stamp algorithm) to back up the ideas presented in this document, and to try out some case studies in the use of RT-LOTOS to consolidate this work.

We might consider inventing new useful operators for T-LOTOS. For example; with the present proposals we can express *truly* parallel actions (assuming that T-LOTOS events mark the end of actions which have duration). For example, in:

(a{3}; b{4}; c{7}; exit) ||| (e{2}; f{5}; g{6}; exit)

the complete behaviour expression can finish at time 7 even though the total duration of the actions associated with all the events is 13. Thus the operators |||, || and |[]| (denoting varying degrees of synchronization) can express true parallelism for actions.

For the description of some systems it may be useful to express interleaved concurrency for action sequences. For the last example this would imply that the complete behaviour expression would finish on time 13, no actions whatsoever would overlap in time, the relative ordering and duration time for all actions in any one of the sub-expressions (above) would remain constant, and that actions of the two sub-expressions would be interleaved in any order. We could have the T-LOTOS translator mechanically produce the (possibly complex) event permutations and combinations required to implement interleaved action concurrency. Fidge, in [6] describing his LOTOS real-time simulator, discusses the interleaved concurrency operators ///, // and /[]/ which are based on a similar notion.

Another possibility includes adding an *interrupt* operator '[<>' such that:

(a; b; exit) [<> I

would be equivalent to:

(I >> a; b; exit) [] (a; I >> b; exit) [] (a; b; I >> exit)

An interrupting expression (I in the above example) would interrupt the textually preceding expression at any instant (not violating any time constraints which may be imposed on the initial event of the interrupting expression). After the interrupting expression had exited, the interrupted expression would resume from the point of interruption.

Further work is required to see how best to integrate the concepts of global and local time within T-LOTOS. Global time is not a concept that is readily available in the implementation of distributed time-dependent systems. In an implementation the notion of global time might be supported through a simulated global clock which is maintained by synchronizing[17] all local (physical) clocks.

It may prove useful extend T-LOTOS to reflect the idea of local time. We could use the new syntactic construct {local} as part of a process instantiation statement[18] to indicate that time constraints within the process are with respect to its own local time. Local times may actually progress at different rates with respect to one another, or their progressions may be just multiples of some base rate.

---

[17]To within error tolerance limits (see [8]).

[18]It may be useful to further extend the syntax so that local time may start on any event and not just on process instantiation.

However, introducing the idea of local time into T-LOTOS may not be absolutely necessary. In [4], Cohen et al. merge Lamport's [8] concept of "logical time" together with Morgan's observations on implementing designs which assume global time. From this they conclude that if global time is used as a description or design device, the implementation may still be based on local clocks if it maintains the "logical clock" properties of the original description.

Another area for exploration is that of "divergence and realism", as discussed in [1]. This may not be a problem for an asynchronous model but in a synchronous model this may violate the "realism requirement" that an infinite number of events may not occur within a finite period of time. This implies that a T-LOTOS description may be wrong if the total time consumed (in the real system) by events occurring within a time interval becomes of the same order of magnitude as the time interval itself. Thus we must be careful if we either construct recursive loops containing events with no time constraints, or have unbounded creation of processes in parallel (see [9]). This issue relates to the notion of zero separation between events as an approximation of negligible duration, which is in itself controversial notion.

The concept of "must" and "may" timing has been discussed in [2]. In a synchronous calculus such as T-LOTOS based on the t-event mapping algorithm, implementing *must* timing may simply be a matter of *denying* the possibility of always choosing the t-event (i.e. letting time pass). Thus *forcing* (given the synchronous basis) any possible ordinary events (which can occur during that time interval) to occur *before* offering to let time progress. In this way we may be able to offer the user of T-LOTOS the facilities for expressing both *must* and *may* timing constraints in the same description. In the timestamp based RT-LOTOS (which is non-synchronous) the concept of "must" and "may" timing depends on the 'openness'[19] of the underlying semantic model. This topic requires further investigation.

We will investigate generic specification and modelling styles and constructs for the description of real-time systems. We will integrate the use of T-LOTOS into strategies for the development of real-time systems (mapping T-LOTOS descriptions to implementations).

We might consider associating time durations with LOTOS operations for the modelling of real systems, where the LOTOS description is a fairly direct representation of the system in question. For example, we could model interprocess communication delays in multiprocessor systems by imposing time durations for process synchronization. Similarly we could model system interrupts, context swaps, etc. by imposing time durations for process disabling and enabling operators. Work towards such aims has been discussed in [5, 6].

In this paper, the only tool proposed for the support of T-LOTOS/RT-LOTOS has been a translator. Other tools or tool enhancements might be considered to help support the use of T-LOTOS. Examples of these include enhancing current LOTOS simulators to produce symbolic traces which are annotated with timings. This should help in the analysis of systems which have real-time constraints. We could modify LOTOS simulators to have them automate (to some degree) the incrementation of time. Such modifications

---

[19]An 'open' model admits the occurrence of unspecified environment events, whereas a 'closed' model describes the whole universe. Thus in an open model, time may progress even if this is not explicitly denoted in the specification, but in the closed model all progression of time is denoted in the specification.

would help make the treatment of time seem more implicit when symbolically executing a translated T-LOTOS description.

8 Conclusion

The general objective of our work is to gain a better understanding of the philosophy, requirements, and practicalities of introducing time into LOTOS. Our more specific objective is to evolve an extended version of LOTOS (T-LOTOS) in which the notion of *quantitative* time is implicit and in which timing constraints may be easily expressed. We have explored two possible T-LOTOS to LOTOS mapping algorithms — one based on *t-events* and the other on *time-stamps*.

Neither algorithm has been found to be complete in the sense that neither is powerful enough to map complete T-LOTOS (as defined informally in section 4) descriptions to semantically equivalent finite LOTOS descriptions. We have suggested various means for overcoming this difficulty. For the t-event based algorithm we have suggested either restricting the use of the disable operator, or incorporating the algorithm in an *expansion tool* to map T-LOTOS to LOTOS on-the-fly.

For the time-stamp based algorithm we advocate restricting quantitative time relations to be expressible only over observable events. This stricter form of T-LOTOS we call RT-LOTOS. We argue that RT-LOTOS not only facilitates the expression of quantitative time relations, but also constrains the user to develop well formed constraint-oriented specifications of such systems.

It is arguable whether the t-event method is more constructive than than the time-stamp method. We think that both convey exactly the same amount of information, and that neither one restricts any refinement more or less than the other. ('Constructiveness' is a subjective measure anyway.)

What is important is to recognize the increased ease of expression which T-LOTOS affords in describing quantitative time-dependent systems, and the usefulness that an automatic translator for T-LOTOS would allow in exploitation of existing LOTOS tools and analysis techniques.

Basically we have been trying to develop a unified and pragmatic approach for adding quantitative time to LOTOS.

Acknowledgements

I would like to thank my supervisor Prof. Kenneth Turner, Dr. Robert Clark and Paul Gibson (a fellow Ph.D. student at Stirling) for their help and encouragement.

References

[1] Arturo Azcorra and Juan Quemada. *Proposal for the Introduction of Time in*

LOTOS. Technical Report Lo/WP3/T3.3/UPM/N0013/V01, LOTOSPHERE (ESPRIT), January 1990.

[2] T Bolognesi. Timed LOTOS: which way to go? In *British Telecom – British Computer Society/FACS Group Meeting on LOTOS – London*, September 1990.

[3] Dr. Robert G. Clark. *Using LOTOS in the Object-Based Development of Embedded Systems*. Technical Report, Department of Computing Science and Mathematics, University of Stirling, Scotland., 1990.

[4] B. Cohen, D.H. Pitt, and J.C.P. Woodcock. *The Importance of Time In The Specification of OSI Protocols: An Overview and Brief Survey of the Formalisms*. Technical Report ISSN 0262-5369, National Physical Laboratory, Teddington, Middlesex, TW11 0LW, U.K., November 1986.

[5] José Manuel Martin Espinosa, José Miguel Robles Roman, and Luis Fuertes Prieto. Concurrent modelling in LOTOS as a solution to real time problems. In *[14]*, 1990.

[6] C.J. Fidge. A LOTOS interpreter for simulating real-time behaviour. In *[14]*, 1990.

[7] ISO. *Information Processing Systems – Open Systems Interconnection – LOTOS – A Formal Description Technique Based on the Temporal Ordering of Observational Behaviour*. Technical Report ISO 8807, 1989.

[8] Leslie Lamport. Time, clocks, and the ordering of events in a distrubuted system. *Communications of the ACM*, 21(7):558–565, July 1978.

[9] J. Quemada, A. Azcorra, and D. Frutos. TIC: a timed calculus for LOTOS. In *[13]*, pages 195–209, 1990.

[10] Juan Quemada and Angel Fernandez. Introduction of quantitative relative time into LOTOS. In *The IFIP WG 6.1 Seventh International Conference on Protocol Specification, Testing, and Verification VII*, pages 105–121, North-Holland, 1987.

[11] Prof. Kenneth J. Turner. *The Formal Specification Language LOTOS: A Course For Users*. Department of Computing Science, University of Stirling, Stirling, August 1989.

[12] Wilfried H.P. van Hulzen, Paul A.J. Tilanus, and Han Zuidweg. LOTOS extended with clocks. In *[13]*, pages 179–193, 1990.

[13] *The IFIP TC/WG 6.1 Second International Conference on Formal Description Techniques for Distributed Systems and Communications Protocols, FORTE '89*, North-Holland, Vancouver, Canada, 1989.

[14] *FORTE'90, Third International Conference on: Formal Description Techniques*, Madrid, November 1990.

LOTOS-like process algebras with urgent or timed interactions[1]

T. Bolognesi [a] and F. Lucidi [b]

[a]CNUCE / C.N.R. Pisa - Italy (e-mail: bolog@fdt.cnuce.cnr.it)
[b]Fondazione U. Bordoni - Roma - Italy

Abstract A LOTOS-like timed process algebra is first introduced, which offers operators for specifying the urgency of a specified action, but also of an interaction involving two or more processes, and other fundamental time-related behaviours. The formal semantics of the language consists of two independent sets of inference rules which handle, respectively, the occurrence of actions and the passing of time. The language can specify in a natural way the "wait-until-timeout" scenario, and, due to its time related operators, it can simulate Turing machines. A refinement is then presented where one can specify time intervals for the occurrence of actions and interactions. The models appear as a most natural transposition in the realm of process algebras of the well known Time Petri Nets of Merlin and Farber and, as such, are proposed as a simple, sound and effective basis for timed extensions of the LOTOS standard.

1. Introduction

We present here two closely related process algebras meant to describe the time dependent behaviour of sets of interacting processes. Our initial objective was the enhancement of a small subset of LOTOS [2, 3] with facilities for expressing time-related features. One of the primary application areas of LOTOS is that of communication protocols; for a realistic specification of such systems it becomes crucial to be able to express time parameters such as message transmission delays or timeout periods (for an account on time in communication protocols, see [21]). Standard LOTOS cannot express time parameters and time dependent behaviours.

Our starting point has been Basic LOTOS, that is, LOTOS without data expressions and data exchange. More precisely, we have considered a small subset of Basic LOTOS, consisting of the *four* operators of:

- action prefix,
- choice,
- parallel composition with multi-way synchronization,
- process instantiation *without* gate relabelling

(that is, process instantiations are not allowed to associate new gate names to the names of their corresponding process definitions). We have excluded all the other operators of Basic

---

[1] Work partly supported by ESPRIT Project 2304 LotoSphere

LOTOS, such as hiding, enabling and disabling. The reason for such 'economy' is the following: our basic, untimed language, should include fundamental operators, but is not required to provide full (theoretic) expressivity, that is, it should not be able to simulate Turing Machines. It is a well known fact that the complete set of Basic LOTOS operators does provide such full expressivity; a similar result holds for the *seven* operators of CCS (inaction, action prefix, choice, parallel composition, restriction, recursion, relabelling). But then, we want to add time-related operators to our 'weak' sublanguage in such a way that its expressivity is indeed increased to the Turing level.

In fact, such an exercise was already done in the area of Petri Nets, and our work has been largely inspired by results in that area. Our initial requirement was to *imitate* as closely as possible the timed Petri Nets proposed by Merlin and Farber (called Time Petri Nets hereafter), since it appeared to us as a most simple and natural approach and, at the same time, it provably offers enhanced expressive capabilities with respect to (untimed) place-transition Petri Nets. Indeed [11] proves that Time Petri Nets can simulate Turing machines, while it is known that standard Petri Nets can't.

Our first proposal for a timed enhancement of LOTOS is presented in [6], where we argue that a *Timed-Interaction* approach is preferable to the *Time-Action* approach of [19] and [18], based on the observation that the former is analogous to the adequately expressive Time Petri Nets of Merlin and Farber, while the latter is the equivalent to another Timed Petri Net model [24] (in turn equivalent to a model proposed in [9]) whose expressive weakness is proved in [4]. The *syntax* of the Timed-Interaction LOTOS presented in [6] is essentially the same that we present at the end of the present paper. However, the formal semantics provided in [6], in SOS (Structured Operational Semantics) style, is quite complex and suffers from several weak points. It makes use of negative clauses in some of the premises, and it requires the application of two rewrite rules before applying inference rules of transition to some expressions. Even worse, we subsequently found [7] that such rewrite rules are not sufficient for properly handling all possible combinations of the *timer* and *parallel composition* operators.

A completely new formulation of the formal semantics of our timed enhancement of LOTOS is achieved here by considering the approach adopted for TCCS by Tofts and Moller [22], where the time and action dimensions are handled separately from one another. Such idea has proved to be extremely effective in achieving a simplified and, in our opinion, quite elegant formulation of the semantics of our timed algebras.

We present two closely related timed enhancements of LOTOS. The first one is called U-LOTOS (U for urgency); it is informally introduced in Section 2, where the analogy with Time Petri Nets is also illustrated, while its formal semantics is provided in Section 3. The main time-related feature of this language is represented by the *urgency* operator *'asap a'* , used to express the fact that a given action *or interaction a* is to be performed urgently, as soon as *all* the involved partners are ready for it. Ultimately, the effect of such operator is to prevent the passing of time as an alternative to the occurrence of an a-event. The expressive power of the language is discussed in Section 4.

The second proposed enhancement is called T-LOTOS (Timed-interaction LOTOS), and is presented in Section 5. The key time related feature is in this case the *'timer a(t1, t2)'* operator, used to express the fact that a given action *or interaction a* is to be performed within the indicated time window (t1, t2), where the implicit timer is started as soon as *all* the involved partners are ready for it. T-LOTOS is an enhancement of U-LOTOS itself, in the sense that the timer operator is a generalization of the urgency operator: *'asap a'* is equivalent to the special case *'Timer a(0, 0)'*. The formal semantics of T-LOTOS is obtained by appropriately enhancing, one by one, the components of the formal semantics of U-LOTOS. In the conclusive Section 6, we consider the relations of our timed models with existing timed algebras, and we mention some points for further study.

2. U-LOTOS: syntax and informal semantics

We assume that time be discrete, and we represent it by natural numbers. Process actions take no time, and this may be the case even for action sequences. For example, a trace of system behaviour can be denoted by 'S1==(2)==>S2--a-->S3==(3)==>S4--b-->S5--c-->S6--d-->..'. S1 to S6 are system states; after a delay of 2 time units, action a is instantaneously executed; then, after 3 time units, the action sequence $b.c.d$ is instantaneously executed, and so on.

The syntax of U-LOTOS is described by the following grammar, where B, $B1$ and $B2$ denote behaviour expressions, t is a time value (a natural number), P is a process identifier, a is an action identifier, G is a possibly empty set of gate identifiers:

B	::=	
|	a.B	(* action prefix *)
|	(t).B	(* time prefix *)
|	B1 + B2	(* choice *)
|	B1 |G| B2	(* parallel composit. over the gates of set G (synchronization gates) *)
|	asap G in B	(* urgency of actions (interactions) at the gates of set G (urgent gates) *)
|	P	(* process instantiation *)
|	**1**	(* time passing process (*derived* operator) *)
|	**0**	(* time deadlock process (*derived* operator) *)
|	B1 ||| B2	(* interleaving (shorthand for B1 |Ø| B2) *)

A process definition has the form: $P := Bp$, where P is a process-identifier and Bp is the defining behaviour expression of P. A *specification* in U-LOTOS has the form:

    B   [where   P1 := B1, ..., Pn := Bn]

where B is a behaviour expression, 'where' is a keyword introducing a list of process definitions, called the (process definition) *environment* of B, the Pi's are process identifiers, and the Bi's are behaviour expressions (the part in square brackets is optional). Indeed, we shall frequently omit to indicate the (non empty) environment of a behaviour expression, for notational conciseness.

Action prefix expression $a.B$ denotes a process that can perform an a-action at any time, and then transform into process B. Time prefix expression $(t).B$ denotes a process that transforms into process B after t time units. The choice expression $B1 + B2$ denotes a process for which time passes until one of the two alternative behaviours, $B1$ or $B2$, performs an action, thus eliminating the other. The parallel expression $B1 /[G]/ B2$ denotes a process where two components proceed in time independently from each other, except for actions at the synchronization gates in G, which are merged into a single action that must occur simultaneously in both of them.

The urgency expression *asap G in B* denotes a process that behaves like B, except that as soon as an action (at some gate) in the set G is ready for execution, it is immediately executed. If $P := B$ is a process definition, where P is a process identifier and B is a behaviour expression, then the process instantiation expression P denotes a process that behaves like B.
Symbol **1** denotes the (instantiation of) the time passing process, which is unable to perform any action and can only age. Process **1** is defined as follows: **1** := (1). **1**. Finally, we can also define a process **0**, called *time deadlock*, for which any action or time delay is impossible. This is achieved by imposing a synchronization over some action a between a process urgently needing to perform action a and another one unable to perform it at all: **0**:= (asap a in a. **1**) \|[a]\| **1**.

U-LOTOS exhibits several analogies with the Time Petri Nets of [12]. These are standard Petri Nets where transitions are labelled both by an action identifier and by a time interval (t1, t2), where t1, t2 ≥ 0. The idea is that, as soon as a (t1, t2)-labelled transition is *enabled* by the tokens, an implicit timer is started: the transition is actually *fireable* when t1 ≤ timer ≤ t2.

We are not interested here in providing a compositional mapping between Time Petri Nets and some timed version of LOTOS, and, indeed, the consideration of the existing gap between untimed Petri nets and process algebras does not encourage us to do so. What we want to import from Time Petri Nets to our timed algebras is the peculiar way in which time parameters are used in describing the behaviour of concurrent systems.

Different timing policies in Petri Nets and LOTOS-like process algebras are contrasted in Figure 2.1.

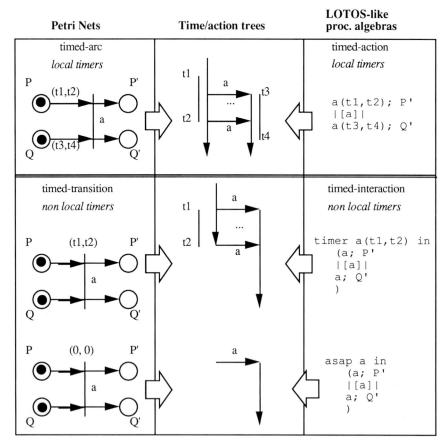

Figure 2.1 - Different timing policies in Petri Nets and LOTOS-like algebras

In the timed Petri Net model of [24] time labels are associated to the arcs connecting a place to a transition. [4] proves that such *timed-arc policy* fails to increase the expressivity of untimed Petri Nets. In the timed enhancements of LOTOS proposed in [19] and [18], time labels are associated to the action prefix construct, thus following what we may call a *timed-action policy*. An analogy can be established between the timed-arc and timed-action policies. In both cases the time interval has a completely *local* significance, that is, the implicit timer is started at the occurrence of a local event: in the Petri Net case, the event is that of a token entering a place; in the timed LOTOS case, it is the instantiation of a timed action prefix expression.

By contrast, the Time Petri Net model of [12] follows a *timed-transition policy*, as explained above, thus providing an increased expressivity w.r.t. the untimed model, as shown in [11]. Time intervals do not have local significance any more: the implicit timer is started as soon as *all* the enabling places are ready for the transition; correspondingly, in our timed algebras we want to be able to say that the timer is started as soon as *all the processes* involved in the synchronization are ready for it. The ability to detect the instant when all processes are ready is implicit in the *asap* operator of U-LOTOS, and we may say that U-LOTOS is indeed analogous to the subset of Time Petri Nets where synchronization transitions (those with more than one input arc) have a (0, 0) time label. The possibility to start a countdown at the moment when all processes become ready for synchronization shall be offered by the *timer* operator of T-LOTOS (see Section 5). It must be observed that both U-LOTOS and T-LOTOS include the time prefix construct $(t).B$, that models the idea of a strictly local timer.

As a simple example of application of U-LOTOS, and of the analogy between the ways in which time intervals are used in such process algebra and in Time Petri Nets, we specify a *symmetric timeout system* in U-LOTOS (Figure 2.2) and as a Time Petri Net (Figure 2.3). Observe that all the U-LOTOS operators are used in this example. Observe also that the urgency of actions *timeout1* and *timeout2* could have been as well expressed within the definitions of processes P and Q, while this is not possible for the synchronization action *a*.

S := asap [a, timeout1, timeout2] in (P |[a]| Q)

where
P := d1. (a.P + (t1).timeout1.**1**)
Q := d2. (a.Q + (t2).timeout2.**1**)

Figure 2.2 - U-LOTOS specification of a symmetric timeout system

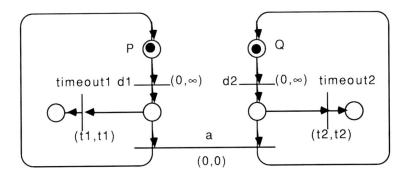

Figure 2.3 - Timed Petri Net for the symmetric timeout system of Figure 2.2

3. Formal semantics

The formal semantics of U-LOTOS is essentially given in the SOS (Structured Operational Semantics) style of [17], and consists of three elements:

- a set of inference rules for deriving action transitions;
- a set of inference rules for deriving aging (time passing) transitions;
- an auxiliary function which detects the immediate executability of an action.

The two sets of rules for action and aging transitions are provided in Table 3.1.

The inference rules for action transitions define the transition relation B1---a--->B2, where B1 and B2 are behaviour expressions and a is an action identifier. A consequence of separating action and aging rules is that when we write B1--a--> B2, we mean that B1 performs action a immediately. Another nice consequence of providing two separate sets of inference rules is that the action transition rules of U-LOTOS turn out to be *identical* to those of basic LOTOS [3] (note that in the latter the *asap* operator is not present, the choice operator '+' is denoted by the box symbol '[]', and in *action prefix* a semicolon is used in place of the dot).

In an *action prefix expression*, the action can occur immediately (rule a1). In a *choice expression* the possible immediate actions are those of its components (rules a2 and a3). With the *parallel operator*, the two parallel components can proceed independently from each other with actions that are not in the set of synchronization actions (gates) G, while they must proceed together on the actions in G (rules a5, a6, and rule a4).

Table 3.1 - U-LOTOS inference rules for action and aging transitions

Syntax		Action transitions		Aging transitions	
action prefix	a. B	a1)	a.B--a-->B	t1)	a.B==t==>a.B t>0
time prefix	(t). B t>0	-		t2) t3)	(t+t').B==t==>(t').B t, t'>0 (t).B==t==>B t>0
choice	B1 + B2	a2) a3)	B1--a-->B1' ――――――― B1+B2--a-->B1' symmetric of rule above	t4)	B1==t==>B1' and B2==t==>B2' ――――――――――― B1+B2==t==>B1'+B2' t>0
parallel	B1 |[G]| B2	a4) a5) a6)	B1--a-->B1' and B2--a-->B2' and a in G ―――――――――――― B1|G|B2--a-->B1'|G|B2' B1--a-->B1' and a not in G ――――――――― B1|G|B2--a-->B1'|G|B2 symmetric of rule above	t5)	B1==t==>B1' and B2==t==>B2' ―――――――――― B1|G|B2==t==>B1'|G|B2' t>0
urgency	asap G in B	a7)	B--a-->B' ――――――― asap G in B --a--> asap G in B'	t6)	B==t==>B' and $\forall a \in G$. not $\alpha_a(B)$ ――――――――――― asap G in B ==t==> asap G in B'
proc. inst.	P	a8)	B--a-->B' and P:=B is a proc.def. ―――――――――― P--a-->B'	t7)	B==t==>B' and P:=B is a proc.def. ―――――――――― P=t==>B'

The *urgency operator 'asap'* is a 'passthrough' operator with respect to actions: the actions of expression *asap G in B* are exactly those of expression *B* (rule a7). Note that the operator does *not* impose any priority of urgent actions over non urgent ones. For example, in the context of a 'wait-ack-until-timeout' scenario, if the ack-arrival and timeout events are possible at the same time, the choice is nondeterministic. The rule for *process instantiation* indicates that the actions of a process instantiation are those of the behaviour expression of its associated process definition (rule a8).

The inference rules for aging transitions define the transition relation B1===t===>B2, where *B1* and *B2* are behaviour expressions and *t* is a time value. Thus, these rules define whether and how a behaviour can be aged.

An *action prefix expression* can age unboundedly without transforming into a different expression (rule t1). The same holds for *choice* and *parallel expressions*, provided that the two arguments of the operator be able to do so (rules t4 and t5). Rules t2 and t3 indicate that the time interval of a *time prefix* need not be consumed in a single transition. It must be observed that the inverse behaviour (e.g. combining two sequential time intervals: if B==t'==>B', then (t).B==(t+t')===>B') is not admitted, since it would eliminate the effect of the urgency operator, as discussed below. The *urgency operator 'asap'* is meant to allow the passing of time only if no urgent action is immediately possible. That is, the operator imposes a priority of urgent actions over aging transitions. This is expressed by rule t6, which is the only rule that uses the function α_a defined below. The *asap operator* has a special dynamic nature, in the sense that, at the semantic level, it operates at the time when the first occurrence of action *a* becomes possible: its effect is the pruning of the time axis at that point in time. The reason for not admitting the inference rule for combining two sequential time transitions (as discussed above) is now clear: in behaviour

$$\text{asap a in} \quad ((t1). a. \mathbf{1} \ |[a]| \ (t2). a. \mathbf{1})$$

we would allow a '==t3==>' transition, with t3 > t1 and t3 > t2, thus ignoring the necessity of an a-transition at time max(t1, t2).

Rule t7 for process instantiation, combined with the similar rule a8, indicates that we can always replace a process identifier with the behaviour expression of its associated process definition. As an immediate consequence of the inference rules for aging transitions and of the definition of the time passing process '$\mathbf{1}$', we have that $\mathbf{1}==1==>\mathbf{1}$. Rule (t6) makes use of a function α_a, which is defined below.

Definition 3.1   (Function α_a)

Function α_a: Processes ---> {true, false}, parametric in action *a*, is a boolean function meant to indicate whether or not process B can immediately perform an a-action.

α_a (a.B)	=	true	
α_a(b.B)	=	false	if b ≠ a
α_a((t).B)	=	false	(t > 0)
α_a(B1 + B2)	=	α_a(B1) or α_a(B2)	
α_a(B1 |G| B2)	=	α_a(B1) and α_a(B2)	if a is in G
	=	α_a(B1) or α_a(B2)	if a is not in G
α_a(asap b in B)	=	α_a(B)	b = a is admitted
α_a(P)	=	α_a(B)	if P := B is a process definition.

Proposition 3.1 (consistency of relation '--a-->' and function α_a)
If "B where P1 := B1, ..., Pn := Bn" is a *guarded U-LOTOS specification*, then B--a-->B', for some B', iff $\alpha_a(B)$ = true.
Proof   See Appendix A, which also includes the definition of guarded specification.•

4. Expressivity

Two alternative points of view are possible for discussing the *expressivity* of many languages or formalisms. On one hand one may use informal but convincing arguments and examples (e.g. Figures 2.2 and 2.3) for showing that the language under consideration is indeed able to express a given set of desired concepts or constructs in a concise and intuitive way. As an alternative to such (psychology-oriented) approach, one may take the formal, well-established, language-theoretic approach, and show that the formalism under study is capable of expressing the widest possible class of formal languages, that is, it is capable of simulating Turing Machines. We can pose such problem with respect to U-LOTOS since, by abstracting away from the aging transitions in the time/action trees that the language ultimately expresses, we can indeed view the paths on such trees as words of a language (this point is further discussed in the conclusions).

We show here that U-LOTOS can simulate Turing Machines by proving that it can simulate two-counter machines, which, in turn, can simulate Turing Machines [13]. In deriving such result we shall take advantage of the analogy between our timed LOTOS and the Merlin-Farber's Time Petri Nets: two-counter machines can be simulated by such Petri Nets, as shown in [11], and, although no formal mapping between Time Petri Nets and U-LOTOS is available, the analogy between the two models has been helpful in deriving the construction introduced below from the one of [11].

An input-free two-counter machine is a 6-tuple

<States, S0, Sfin, I, C1, C2>

where:

States	is a finite set of states; we shall let P, Q and R range in this set;
S_0	is the initial state;
S_{fin}	is the final state;
I	is a finite set of instructions;
C1 and C2	are counters, each of which can store a nonnegative integer.

The counters are initially set to 0. The types of instructions and their meanings are listed in Table 4.1 below. P, Q , and R are states.

Table 4.1 - Types of instructions for two counter machines

Instruction		Meaning
(P, incr-i, Q)	i = 1, 2	in state P, increment Ci by one and go to state Q.
(P, decr-i, Q)	i = 1, 2	in state P, decrement Ci by one and go to state Q.
(P, test-i, Q, R)	i = 1, 2	in state P, test counter Ci: go to Q if Ci = 0, otherwise go to R.

The machine is deterministic, so that there is at most one instruction for each state P. Computations that attempt to decrement any empty counter are undefined. •

We do not provide here the U-LOTOS specification of a generic two-counter machine; it can be found in [8]. For giving an idea of the construction, we provide in the example below the U-LOTOS specification of just one small machine.

Example

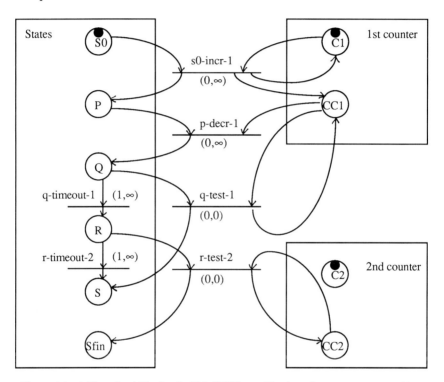

Figure 4.1 - A Time Petri Net for the U-LOTOS specification of a two-counter machine

The Time Petri Net of Figure 4.1 corresponds to the two-counter machine M = <States, S_0, S_{fin}, I, C1, C2> where:

States	= {S_0, P, Q, R, S, S_{fin}}
S_0	is the initial state;
S_{fin}	is the final state;
I	= {(S_0, incr-1, P), (P, decr-1, Q), (Q, test-1, R, S), (R, test-2, S, S_{fin})};
C1 and C2	are the two counters, initially set to 0.

The U-LOTOS specification of such machine is:

```
Two-counter-machine := asap [q-test-1, r-test-2] in ( S₀
                                                    |[ s₀-incr-1, p-decr-1, q-test-1, r-test-2 ]|
                                                    (C1 ||| C2)
                                                   )
where
S₀    :=   s₀-incr-1. P
P     :=   p-decr-1. Q
Q     :=   (1). q-timeout-1. R   +   q-test-1. S
R     :=   (1). r-timeout-2. S   +   r-test-2. S_fin
S_fin :=   1

C1    :=   s₀-incr-1. (C1 ||| CC1)
CC1   :=   q-test-1. CC1    +   p-decr-1.  1
C2    :=   1
CC2   :=   r-test-2. CC2
```

5. T-LOTOS

T-LOTOS is an extension of U-LOTOS: it offers a *timer operator* which is a generalization of (and replaces) the *urgency operator 'asap'* of the latter. U-LOTOS expression *'asap a in B'* is equivalent to the T-LOTOS expression *'timer a(0, 0) in B'*. T-LOTOS is inspired by the Time Petri Nets model [12], while we have already observed that U-LOTOS is analogous to the subset of Time Petri Nets where synchronization transitions (those with more than one input arc) have a (0, 0) time label. Although from a theoretic point of view U-LOTOS already provides maximum expressive power, we investigate also T-LOTOS because the direct availability of a timer operator for synchronizations offers further expressive flexibility to the specifier, and also because the step from the formal definition of U-LOTOS to that of T-LOTOS is relatively short.

We adopt here the same notational conventions applied for the U-LOTOS grammar. Furthermore, $\tau \geq 0$ shall be a time value indicating the age of an action, that is, the time during which it has been enabled.

```
B     ::=
      a. B                (* action prefix (as in U-LOTOS) *)
|     aᵗ. B               (* aged action prefix: an a-action of age τ is possible now, that is, an a-
                             action has been enabled during the last τ units of time.
                             This is an auxiliary operator not directly available to the user of the
                             language, but generated by the aging of an action prefix.
                             We have: a. B == a⁰. B *)
|     (t).B               (* time prefix (as in U-LOTOS) *)
|     B1 + B2             (* choice: as in U-LOTOS) *)
|     B1 |G| B2           (* parallel composition (as in U-LOTOS) *)
|     P                   (* process instantiation (as in U-LOTOS) *)
|     timer a(t1, t2) in B
                          (* timer: as soon as an a-action is enabled, it starts aging: a is fireable
                             within the associated time interval; indeed, it must be fired within that
                             interval, unless it is disabled by the firing of another action. *)
```

A *process definition* has the form: $P := B_P$, where P is a process-identifier and B_P is the defining behaviour expression of P. A specification in T-LOTOS has the same form of a U-

LOTOS specification: $B[\text{where } P1 := B1, ..., Pn := Bn]$. For simplicity, we have assumed that the timer operator can handle an action at a time (however, timers can be nested).

The semantics of T-LOTOS is obtained by piece-wise refinement of the U-LOTOS semantics. An important difference is that in the new model actions contain an indication of the action age, that is, the amount of time during which the action has been enabled. Thus an action transition has the form

$$B \; \text{--}a^\tau\text{-->} \; B',$$

which reads: B can (but does not have to) immediately perform an action a of age τ, thus transforming into B'. The two sets of rules for action and aging transitions are provided in Table 5.1.

Table 5.1 - T-LOTOS inference rules for action and aging transitions

Syntax	Action transitions	Aging transitions
aged act. prefix $a^\tau. B$ $\tau \geq 0$	a1) $\quad a^\tau.B\text{--}a^\tau\text{-->}B$	t1) $\quad a^\tau.B==t==>a^{\tau+t}.B \quad t>0$
time prefix $(t). B$ $t>0$	-	t2) $\quad (t+t').B==t==>(t').B \quad t, t'>0$ t3) $\quad (t).B==t==>B \quad t>0$
choice $B1 + B2$	a2) $\quad \dfrac{B1\text{--}a^\tau\text{-->}B1'}{B1+B2\text{--}a^\tau\text{-->}B1'}$ a3) symmetric of rule above	t4) $\dfrac{B1==t==>B1' \text{ and } B2==t==>B2'}{B1+B2==t==>B1'+B2'} \quad t>0$
parallel $B1 \;|[G]|\; B2$	a4) $\dfrac{B1\text{--}a^{\tau 1}\text{-->}B1',\; B2\text{--}a^{\tau 2}\text{-->}B2',\; a \text{ in } G}{B1|G|B2\text{--}a^{\min\{\tau 1,\tau 2\}}\text{-->}B1'|G|B2'}$ a5) $\dfrac{B1\text{--}a^\tau\text{-->}B1',\; a \text{ not in } G}{B1|G|B2\text{--}a^\tau\text{-->}B1'|G|B2}$ a6) symmetric of rule above	t5) $\dfrac{B1==t==>B1' \text{ and } B2==t==>B2'}{B1|G|B2==t==>B1'|G|B2'} \quad t>0$
timer timer $a(t1,t2)$ in B	a7) $\dfrac{B\text{--}a^\tau\text{-->}B'}{\text{timer } a(t1,t2)\text{in } B\text{--}a^\tau\text{-->}\text{timer } a(t1,t2)\text{in } B'}$ $t1 \leq \tau \leq t2$ a8) $\dfrac{B\text{--}b^\tau\text{-->}B'}{\text{timer } a(t1,t2)\text{in } B\text{--}b^\tau\text{-->}\text{timer } a(t1,t2)\text{in } B'}$ $b \neq a$	t6) $\dfrac{B==t==>B' \text{ and } \text{age}_a(B)+t \leq t2}{\text{timer } a(t1,t2)\text{in } B==t==>\text{timer } a(t1,t2)\text{in } B'}$ $t>0$
proc. inst. P	a9) $\dfrac{B\text{--}a^\tau\text{-->}B' \text{ and } P:=B \text{ is a proc.def.}}{P\text{--}a^\tau\text{-->}B'}$	t7) $\dfrac{B==t==>B' \text{ and } P:=B \text{ is a proc.def.}}{P=t==>B'}$

The rules for T-LOTOS are similar to those for U-LOTOS. The differences are as follows.

- Rule t1. After an aging transition of an aged action prefix, the updated age of the action is recorded in the transformed expression.

- Rule a4. The age of a synchronization action is the minimum of the synchronization actions of the two interacting processes, since synchronization was enabled by the most recently enabled component action.
- Rule a7. An action controlled by a timer can only occur if its age is within the timer interval. The remaining actions are handled by the new Rule a8.
- Rule t6. A timer expression cannot age to the extent of letting a timer dependent action (when present) grow older than the timer upper bound.

In complete analogy with the case of U-LOTOS, rule t6 makes use of a special function, which is now the function age_a, whose definition is given below, in denotational style. Intuitively, $age_a(B)$ yields the age of the oldest action a in expression B that could be performed immediately if there were no timer constraints. We are interested in the *oldest* action because we do not want action ages to surpass the upper time bounds imposed by the active timers. The conventional value $-\infty$ is used to indicate that an a-action is not available (enabled).

Definition 5.1 (Function age_a)

The function age_a: Processes $\longrightarrow \{-\infty\} \cup N$, parametric in action a, is the set of natural numbers (time values), is defined as follows:

$age_a(a^\tau; B) = \tau$; $\qquad age_a(B1+B2) = \max\{age_a(B1), age_a(B2)\}$;

$age_a(b^\tau; B) = -\infty, \quad a \neq b$; $\qquad age_a(B1|[a]|B2) = \min\{age_a(B1), age_a(B2)\}$;

$age_a((t).B) = -\infty, \quad (t > 0) \qquad age_a(B1|[b]|B2) = \max\{age_a(B1), age_a(B2)\}, \quad a \neq b$;

$age_a(P) = age_a(B) \ (P := B$ is a proc.def.$) \qquad age_a($timer $b<\tau 1, \tau 2>$ in $B) = age_a(B) \ (b = a$ admitted$)$•

The consistency of the definitions of function age_a with those of the relations '--a-->' and '==t==>' is captured by the following proposition, whose proof is omitted.

Proposition 5.1 (consistency of function age_a and relations '--a-->' and '==t==>')

(a) If $age_a(B) = -\infty$, then $\forall \tau \geq 0$. not B--a^τ-->.

(b) If B--a^τ-->, then $age_a(B) \geq \tau$.

(c) If B--a^τ--> and B==t==>B', then $age_a(B') = age_a(B) + t$.

6. Conclusions

U-LOTOS and T-LOTOS are the result of an effort to transpose in the realm of process algebras the main ideas and features of the Time Petri Net model of [12]. The syntax of a timed process algebra closely related to such timed nets was already presented in [6]; however, a completely satifactory definition of its formal semantics, as presented here, has been possible only by adopting the SOS style of semantic definition used by Tofts and Moller for their TCCS [22], where two horthogonal sets of rules are provided, respectively for action and aging transitions, and auxiliary functions are used, defined on the recursive structure of behaviour expressions.

We examine now some related work. The literature on timed process algebras is growing, thus we shall only consider those approaches that seem to be more closely related to U-LOTOS and T-LOTOS. Firstly we consider TCCS, Timed Calculus of Communicating Systems [22] and ATP, Algebra for Timed Processes [16] (an algebra closest to the latter is presented in [10]).

Some of the elements that U-LOTOS and T-LOTOS have in common with these two models are listed below.

1. At the semantic level, all these models distinguish between the time passing event and all the other observable actions, *which take no time to execute*. A nice consequence of this fact is that it becomes very easy to express action necessity: an action must be executed immediately when no alternative time passing transition is possible.

2. Inference rules are provided for explicitly expressing the fact that time events occur synchronously in all the parallel components of the system, so that time progress is the same in all such components.

3. All these algebras offer a choice operator that behaves similarly to parallel composition in the fact of merging the time events of its components into a unique (global) time event: the actual choice can only be made via an observable event. (However TCCS offers an additional, 'time-driven' *weak choice* operator, and a variant of ACP [10] has also a choice operator which is nondeterministic w.r.t. time.)

Some differences among these models are independent of their time related features, and are due to the facts that TCCS is a timed extension of CCS [14], ATP borrows some features of ACP [5], and our algebras are based on LOTOS. Thus the communication features of these timed algebras reflect those of their untimed counterparts; for example, TCCS only supports two-way synchronization, while multi-way synchronization is possible for ATP and for our LOTOS extensions, although in the latter the action set has less structure than in ATP.

The key time-related features of these models, and their differences, can be summarized as follows.

1. In TCCS and in ATP, an action prefix $a.B$ expresses the fact that a must occur immediately; however, by using a delay prefix operator $\delta.B$ (which is a primitive operator in TCCS, and a derived operator in ATP and in SCCS [15]), one can introduce an arbitrary delay before the (first) actions of B. In timed LOTOS we take a somewhat dual approach: the arbitrary delay of the action in an action prefix $a.B$ is built in the language (similarly to Milner's ASCCS [15]), while the urgency of the action (occurring now or in the future) can be expressed by applying the *asap a* (in U-LOTOS) or *timer a(0, 0)* (in T-LOTOS) operator. In our opinion the combination of a *delayed* action prefix with an *urgency* operator offers an advantage over the combination of an *urgent* action prefix with a *delay* operator: once the urgency operator is explicitly available, it can be applied not only locally, to an action prefix, but also at a more global level, to a synchronization event in a parallel composition. This usage is indeed the one that provides U-LOTOS with maximum expressivity, as it appears by considering the construction in Section 4.

2. Both Timed LOTOS and TCCS offer a primitive, explicit time delay prefix operator *(t).B*, which is also available in ATP as a derived operator, and reads: "wait for t time units and then behave like B". Such operator embodies, again, a concept of *local time*: one can think of the implicit timer as being started locally by the process whose specification contains the operator. Unlike TCCS and ATP, in our timed LOTOS time can be controlled *also* in a *distributed* way: when a timer operator is applied to a synchronization event of a parallel composition, the implicit timer is started as soon as *all* composed processes enable that event.

To our knowledge, no timed process algebras offer elementary constructs that reflect the idea of (implicit) non-local timers, where non-locality is understood as discussed above. In our opinion this fact is a major justification for the introduction of U- and T-LOTOS (the simplicity of their formal semantics being a second important motivation).

Timed extensions to LOTOS have been proposed in [19], and subsequently refined in [18]. A nice feature of these proposals is that they probably represent the most direct and minimum timed extension to the syntax of basic LOTOS: time intervals can only be associated to an action in the action-prefix context. The price for this is a reduced expressivity. The expressive weakness of the timed-action vs. timed interaction policy (timed-arc vs. timed-transition policy for Petri Nets) was already discussed in Section 2 and in [6]. For instance, in the specification of the symmetric timeout system of Figures 2.2 and 2.3, one cannot conceive the system as the parallel composition of two processes, but is forced to create a single global process where the interleaving of events d1 and d2 is made explicit.

Another timed extension of LOTOS is presented in [23]; more than a basic calculus, this Clock-Extended LOTOS has the flavour of an implementation-oriented enhancement of the language that offers constructs for explicitly starting, reading and resetting timers upon the occurrence of events. The formal semantics is correspondingly complex, but the comparison with timed process algebras is probably inappropriate. (An unpleasant feature of this language is that a time deadlock is never possible: thus, action necessity cannot be expressed). Some ideas on the explicit manipulation of timers in LOTOS are discussed also in [1].

Further investigations are under way in the following directions:

- Provide equivalence and congruence laws for the operators of U-LOTOS and T-LOTOS.

- Identify derived operators of U-LOTOS; to what extent the general timer operator of T-LOTOS can be simulated in U-LOTOS ?

- In proving the expressivity of U-LOTOS we have taken a language-theoretic approach which is unable to discriminate between deterministic and non-deterministic behaviours: we consider the traces of an action-tree but ignore the actual branching structure of it. It seems desirable to define and adopt finer methods for measuring the theoretic expressivity of process algebras such as U-LOTOS. Nevertheless, we insist that the language-theoretic approach, as we have applied, is a prerequisite for any further investigation. For example, it is quite clear (although no proof has been provided) that U-LOTOS without the time-related operators of time-prefix and urgency is *unable* to simulate Turing Machines: we have taken this fact as an indication that these two operators have been well chosen. It would be interesting to apply similar considerations and criteria to other timed process algebras.
- Compare U-LOTOS with the approach in [20]: the semantics of these two algebras are given in completely different styles, however the *hiding* operator of the latter seems to partly resemble the *asap* operator of the former.

Acknowledgement We would like to express our gratitude to Sebastiano Trigila for discussions on various aspects of the work presented here, and to an anonymous referee for having suggested the definition of the time deadlock process.

References

[1] E. Brinksma, "On the Design of Extended LOTOS", Ph.D. Thesis, University of Twente, 1988.

[2] E. Brinksma (ed.) - ISO - Information Processing Systems - Open Systems Interconnection - "LOTOS - A Formal Description Technique Based on the Temporal Ordering of Observational Behaviour", IS 8807, 1989.

[3] T. Bolognesi, E. Brinksma, "Introduction to the ISO Specification Language LOTOS", *Computer Networks and ISDN Systems*, Vol. 14, No 1, 1987.

[4] T. Bolognesi, P. Cremonese, "The Weakness of Some Timed Models for Concurrent Systems", Technical Report CNUCE C89-29, CNUCE - C.N.R., Pisa, October 1989.

[5] J. A. Bergstra, J. W. Klop, "Process Algebra for Synchronous Communication", *Information and Control*, 60 (1-3), 1984.

[6] T. Bolognesi, F. Lucidi, S. Trigila, "From Timed Petri Nets to Timed LOTOS", Proceedings of the Tenth International IFIP WG6.1 Symposium on Protocol Specification, Testing, and Verification, L. Logrippo, R. L. Probert, H. Ural editors, North-Holland 1990.

[7] T. Bolognesi, F. Lucidi, S. Trigila, "New Proposals for Timed-Interaction LOTOS", Technical Rep. 5-B-55-90, Fondazione U. Bordoni, Roma, Italy, 1990.

[8] T. Bolognesi, F. Lucidi, "Timed process algebras with urgent interactions and a unique powerful binary operator", to appear in Lecture Notes in Computer Science, Springer-Verlag, 1992.

[9] T. Bolognesi, H. Rudin, "On the Analysis of Time-Dependent Protocols by Network Flow Algorithms", Proceedings of the IFIP WG6.1 Fourth International Workshop on Protocol Specification, Testing, and Verification, Y. Yemini, R. Strom, S. Yemini editors, North-Holland 1985, pp.491-514.

[10] J. F. Groote, "Specification and Verification of Real Time Systems in ACP", Proceedings of the Tenth International IFIP WG6.1 Symposium on Protocol Specification, Testing, and Verification, L. Logrippo, R. L. Probert, H. Ural editors, North-Holland 1990.

[11] N. D. Jones, L. H. Landweber, Y. E. Lien, "Complexity of some problems in Petri Nets", Theoretical Computer Science 4, 1977, pp. 277-299.

[12] P. Merlin, D. J. Farber, "Recoverability of Communication Protocols - Implications of a Theoretical Study", IEEE Trans. Commun., Vol. COM-24, Sept. 1976, pp. 1036-1043.

[13] M. Minsky, "Recursive unsolvability of Post's problem", Ann. of Math. 74, 1961, pp. 437-454.

[14] R. Milner, A Calculus of Communicating Systems, Lecture Notes in Computer Science, Vol.92, Springer-Verlag, 1980.

[15] R. Milner, "Calculi for Synchrony and Asynchrony", Theor. Computer Science, 25, 1983.

[16] X. Nicollin, J.-L. Richier, J. Sifakis, J. Voiron, "ATP: An Algebra for Timed Processes" Project SPECTRE, Groupe Spécification et Analyse des Systemes, Laboratoire de Génie Informatique de Grenoble, Technical Report RT-C16, Jan. 1990.

[17] G. D. Plotkin, "A structural approach to operational semantics", Tech. Rep. DAIMI FN-19, Aarhus Univ., Computer Science Dept., Denmark, 1981.

[18] J. Quemada, A. Azcorra, D.Frutos "A Timed Calculus for LOTOS", Proceedings of FORTE '89 Second International Conference on Formal Description Techniques for Distributed Systems and Communications Protocols, Vancouver,Canada, December 1989.

[19] J. Quemada, A. Fernandez, "Introduction of Quantitative Relative Time into LOTOS", Proceedings of IFIP WG 6.1 Seventh International Conference on Protocol Specification, Testing, and Verification, H.Rudin, C. H. West Editors, North-Holland, 1987, pp. 105-121.

[20] G. M. Reed and A. W. Roscoe, "A Timed Model for Communicating Sequential Processes", Journal of Theoretical Computer Science, 56, pp. 249-261, 1988.

[21] H. Rudin, "Time in Formal Protocol Specifications", Proceedings of the GI/NTG Conference on Communication in Distrib. Systems, Karlsruhe, West Germany, March 11-15, 1985, Springer-Verlag Informatic Series N. 95, pp. 575-587.

[22] F. Moller, C. Tofts, "A Temporal Calculus of Communicating Systems", Proceed. of CONCUR'90, LNCS N. 458, North-Holland, 1990.

[23] W. H. P. van Hulzen, P. A. J. Tilanus, H. Zuidweg, "LOTOS Extended with Clocks", proceedings of FORTE '89, Second International Conference on Formal Description Techniques for Distributed Systems and Communication Protocols, S. T. Vuong editor, North-Holland 1990.

[24] B. Walter, "Timed Petri-Nets for Modelling and Analyzing Protocols with Real-Time Characteristics", Proceedings of 3rd IFIP Workshop on Protocol Specification, Testing, and Verification, (H.Rudin, C. H. West Editors), North-Holland, 1983, pp. 149-159.

Appendix A

Definition A.1   (guarded U-LOTOS expression)
A *guarded U-LOTOS expression* is any expression derived from the root symbol E of the grammar below, which is built on top of the grammar for U-LOTOS expressions whose root is B.

E   ::=   x.B | (t).B | E1+ E2 | E1 |[G]| E2 | asap G in E.

B   ::=   x.B | (t).B | B1+ B2 | B1 |[G]| B2 | asap G in B | P.   •

Proposition A.2   A guarded U-LOTOS expression is a U-LOTOS expression.
Proof   By structural induction on the set of guarded expressions, with a partial order '>' where 'x.B' and '(t).B' are the bottom elements (also elements of B, trivially), and E1+ E2 > E1, E1+ E2 > E2, E1 |[G]| E2 > E1, E1 |[G]| E2 > E2, asap G in E > E.   •

Clearly, a guarded expression has the property that any process identifier in it can only appear in the context of a prefix sub-expression (*a.B* or *(t).B*) of it.

Proposition A.3   If E is a guarded expression, then E--a--> iff $\alpha_a(E)$ = true.
Proof   By structural induction on the set of guarded expressions, with a partial order '>' where 'x.B' and '(t).B' are the bottom elements. We shall refer to the inference rules of Table 1.
Basis   If E = x.B, then: E--a--> iff x = a (by rule a1) iff $\alpha_a(x.B)$ = true (by definition of α_a). If E = (t).B, then E--a--> is false (since no action transition rules exist for time prefix) and $\alpha_a(x.B)$ = false (by definition of α_a), thus the double implication holds.   •
Step   If E = E1 + E2, then: E--a--> iff E1--a--> or E2--a--> (by rules a2 and a3), iff $\alpha_a(E1)$ = true or $\alpha_a(E2)$ = true (by the inductive hypothesis), iff $\alpha_a(E)$ = true (by definition of α_a).
Similarly, if E = E1 |G| E2, then E--a--> means that either rule a4 was applied, or rule a5 was applied (the case of rule a6 is symmetric). In the first case: E--a--> iff E1--a--> and E2--a-->, with a in G, iff $\alpha_a(E1)$ = true and $\alpha_a(E2)$ = true, iff $\alpha_a(E)$ = true. In the second case: E--a--> iff E1--a-->, with a not in G , iff $\alpha_a(E1)$ = true, iff $\alpha_a(E)$ = true. If E = asap G in E1, then: E--a--> iff E1--a-->, iff $\alpha_a(E1)$ = true, iff $\alpha_a(E)$ = true.   •

Definition A.4   (guarded U-LOTOS specification)
The U-LOTOS specification *'B where P1 := B1, ..., Pn := Bn'* is *guarded* if, by recursively substituting for a finite number of times the expressions Bi's for the process identifiers Pi's occurring in B and in the Bi's themselves, it is possible to obtain an *expanded* U-LOTOS specification *'E where P1 := E1, ..., Pn := En'*, where E and the Ei's are guarded expressions.

Clearly the two transition systems associated respectively with a U-LOTOS specification and with any of its expansions are strong-bisimulation equivalent, as implied by the substitution rules a8 and t6. Furthermore it is easy to realize that a guarded U-LOTOS specification can only transform, after an action or aging transition, into another guarded U-LOTOS specification.

Proposition 3.1 (consistency of relation '--a-->' and function α_a)
If *'B where P1 := B1, ..., Pn := Bn'* is a guarded U-LOTOS specification, then B--a-->B', for some B', iff $\alpha_a(B)$ = true.
Proof   Without loss of generality, we consider the expanded version E where P1 := E1, ..., Pn := En of the given, guarded specification, so that E and the Ei's are guarded expressions. The proof is done by structural induction on the set of guarded expressions, with a partial order '>' where the bottom elements are the process identifiers Pi's, and the partial order is defined by: x.B > B, (t).B > B, E1+E2 > E1, E1+E2 > E2, E1|[G]| E2 > E1, E1|[G]| E2 > E2, asap G in E > E. We shall refer to the inference rules of Table 3.1.
Basis   Let P be a process identifier. We have: P--a--> iff the specification contains some process definition P := Ep, where Ep is a guarded expression, and Ep--a--> (by rule a8), iff $\alpha_a(Ep)$ = true (by Proposition A.3), iff $\alpha_a(P)$ = true (by definition of α_a).   •
Step   The cases E = x.B and E = (t).B are handled as done in the 'basis' part of the proof of Proposition A.3. The remaining cases of the choice, parallel and urgency operators are handled as done in the 'step' part of that proof.   •

Event structures for design and transformation in LOTOS

Rom Langerak*
Department of Computer Science
University of Twente
PO Box 217 7500 AE Enschede The Netherlands
langerak@cs.utwente.nl

November 13, 1991

Abstract

An event structure semantics for LOTOS is introduced in an intuitive and graphical way. The usefulness of event structures for design and transformation is sketched in several examples: decomposition of functionality, design of a FIFO-buffer, and action refinement. In the appendix a comparison is made between several different event structure models.

1 Introduction

In this paper we explore the use of event structure semantics for the ISO-standard specification language LOTOS [BoBr87, LOT89]. LOTOS belongs to the family of process algebraic languages, together with e.g. CCS [Mi80], CSP [BHR84] and ACP [BeKl85]. The semantics of these languages is usually formulated in terms of labelled transition systems. A labelled transition system consists of states together with transitions between the states; the transitions are labelled by actions. In order to abstract away from irrelevant details, preorders and equivalences are defined over labelled transition systems.

This type of semantics is an example of so-called *interleaving* semantics: parallelism (or independence) is modelled by an interleaving of actions. This means that the typical equation a ||| b = a ; b [] b ; a holds. So the independence of a and b is interpreted in the following way: a and b can occur in any order, but not at the same time. In the past years interleaving semantics has been studied with rather satisfying results: apart from an operational semantics (Plotkin's SOS rules [Pl81]), several axiomatisations and

---
*This work was supported in part by the CEC under ESPRIT project 2304 LOTOSPHERE

observational characterisations have been found. Because of the simplicity of the underlying mathematics, interleaving semantics is widely used in formal methods for protocol specification, verification and testing.

Interleaving semantics is based on an abstraction with several characteristics:

- It considers the system as a whole, i.e. it looks only at the global state of a system, thereby disregarding its distributed nature.

- It is observational in nature; it considers what can globally be observed, not how the system is designed. Independence of actions is therefore not reflected in the semantics.

- It completely abstracts away from time aspects like the duration of an event.

At certain stages in designing a system these abstractions are perfectly natural. When a system is considered at a high level of abstraction, most notably during the initial phases of the design trajectory, interleaving semantics is quite appropriate. For instance, the way the parallel operator is used to capture requirements in the so-called constraint oriented approach [Br89] works nicely with interleaving semantics. Any non-interleaving semantics would cause unnecessary complications here. Interleaving semantics is also suited for deriving test suites for conformance testing, in the light of its observational character.

At later stages in the design trajectory, however, a specification serves not only as a reference for the observational behaviour of a system, but also as a prescription for the implementation of a system [Vi90]. The abstractions of interleaving semantics are then not so attractive anymore:

- The implementation of a distributed system will consist of several systems at different locations, each having its own local state. This is not reflected by the global state assumption of interleaving semantics.

- The intention of an implementor to have certain events executed independently may not be adequately captured in an observational framework. Sometimes these intentions will only affect performance characteristics and not observational functionality. The fact that independence is not reflected makes it hard to decide when events do not have to be implemented in mutual exclusion.

- At lower levels of abstraction one cannot disregard the duration of an event. This is especially a problem for action refinement.

Because of these points (and not just because interleaving semantics does not allow events to be observed simultaneously !) there is the need for a semantics suitable for lower levels of abstraction.

Many alternatives to interleaving semantics have been proposed, classified under the name of non-interleaving or "true concurrency" semantics. A prominent branch of non-interleaving semantics is formed by the family of *event structure* semantics. Event structures have as their basic objects labelled events which model the occurrence of actions.

There are several kinds of event structures with subtle differences [Wi89, BoCa89, Re90, La91, Re91], but all basically study relations of causality, conflict and independence between events.

Although event structures were first proposed more than ten years ago [Wi80], their role in studying formalized protocol design has been rather limited so far. There are several reasons for this. Event structures have been invented on the basis of mathematical intuitions rather than design considerations. The literature is therefore quite mathematical and in general not particularly easy to read. This might scare away more practically oriented researchers, especially since it takes some time to get used to the concepts and way of thinking of non-interleaving semantics.

We think this is a pity since there are intuitions behind event structures that are basically simple and pleasingly graphical in nature. The application of event structures to distributed system design might lead to a fresh and fruitful approach of several problems in this area.

Therefore in this paper we present a simplified version of event structures in an intuitive way, showing just pictures and avoiding mathematical formalism (section 2). We then use event structures in several examples which are non-trivial but still simple enough to be presentable : an example of decomposition of functionality (section 3), the specification of a FIFO-buffer (section 4), and an action refinement of the buffer (section 5). In the appendix we discuss some differences between the event structure proposals that exist in the literature.

So this paper aims at providing an intuitive understanding for studying event structures, and to give a motivation for using them in distributed system design.

2 Event structures

In this section we introduce the main concepts of event structures. There exist several brands of event structures with subtle differences between them, but in the following sections we will not deal with these differences. All the examples are chosen in such a way that they apply to all kinds of event structures in a similar way. The event structures presented here are in fact *bundle* event structures but this is only noticeable in just a very few cases. In the appendix the differences between several event structure proposals are explained.

Basic ingredients

Event structures consist of events and relations between events.

Events:
Events model the occurrence of actions, the fact that "something happens". The events are labelled: each event is labelled with an action. In this paper we represent events by dots; different events are represented by different dots. Different events may have the same label. We allow the internal action i as a label.

So a •   b •   • i   are examples of events.

In transition systems dots represent *states* whereas in event structures they represent *events*; it is important not to confuse them.

We will often denote an event by its action label if no ambiguities arise.

Causality or **precedence**:

This is a binary relation between events. We depict it as an arrow: a • ⟶ • b   This is read as "a precedes b" or "a causes b". It has the intended meaning that whenever a system run includes this occurrence of b, the event labelled with a has to have happened already. Accordingly,

a •
       ↘
         • c   means : for c to happen, both a and b should
b • ↗

have happened already.

Conflict:

This is a symmetric binary relation between events. We depict it as a dotted line:

a • ·········· • b

The intended meaning is that a and b will never both happen in a single system run. Conflict is closely connected with the idea of choice. In the above figure, the environment has to decide whether a or b happens.

Independence or **parallelism**:

This is a symmetric binary relation between events that is simply indicated by the absence of a precedence or conflict relation between the events.   a •   • b   means that a and b are independent. This means if both events are enabled, they can occur in any order or simultaneously, so they neither need to happen in parallel nor to occur one before the other.

Basic LOTOS examples

We will illustrate event structure semantics by giving small Basic LOTOS [1] examples in order to get more intuition for the intended meaning of event structures.

With each LOTOS expression we give an event structure representing its semantics. We remark that it is possible to obtain these event structures from the LOTOS expressions in a well-defined and compositional way.

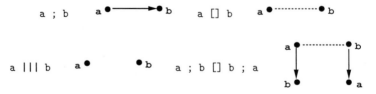

---

[1] We will often deviate a bit from the LOTOS syntax, e.g. by not writing down STOP processes

These last two examples show that parallelism differs from interleaving for event structures. Suppose the execution of an event takes some time. Then in the parallel expression b is always enabled, regardless of the execution of a. However, in the interleaving case it might be the case that in order to execute b, one has to wait until the execution of a is finished.

Note also that different occurrences of the same action in a LOTOS expression here lead to different events.

In the last event structure there are some implicit conflicts, e.g. between the two a-labelled events. These conflicts could be added without changing the interpretation of the event structure. In the next example there are two occurrences of b in the LOTOS expression. However, these two occurrences synchronize and therefore lead to only one event labelled b.

a ; b |[b]| (b [] c)

The next example shows how synchronization, as it were, "glues" event structures together on synchronizing events :

a ; b ; c |[b]| d ; b ; e

The next example shows a case of deadlock :

a ; b |[a,b]| b ; a

This event structure contains a circularity: for a to happen, b has to have happened first, but for b to happen, a has to have happened first. The result is deadlock, and the above event structure is equivalent to the empty event structure that has no events.

A last example:

a ; (b ; c ||| d ; e)

The reader is invited to write down the synchronisation tree for this example, in order to appreciate the conciseness of the event structure semantics !

Equivalences over event structures

Event structures provide a rather discriminating semantics. For example, the processes a = a• and a [] a = a•⋯⋯•a are distinguished. There may be good reasons to distinguish these processes. For instance, when one is interested in the robustness of processes one might argue that the second process is more robust than the first as it offers more capabilities for doing a.

For most applications, however, event structures are a bit too strong. In such cases the same approach as for labelled transition systems can be taken, namely the definition of equivalences over event structures [Gl90]. In this way the discriminating power of event structures can be tuned down to the desired level. It is even possible to define an equivalence such that the resulting semantics has the same discriminating power as an interleaving semantics. This is important as it ensures the "upward compatibility" of event structure semantics with interleaving semantics.

By defining a suitable equivalence it is possible to obtain a "weak" semantics that takes no notice of internal events at certain places. In the next sections we want to identify e.g. event structures like a•—i→•—→•b and a•—→•b. We do not formally define such an equivalence but rely on intuition in order to justify the removal or introduction of certain internal events in an event structure.

3 Decomposition of functionality

In this section we look at the problem of splitting a process into two synchronizing processes under the following conditions. Suppose we have partitioned the set of observable actions of a process into two sets. We look for two processes, synchronizing on a hidden gate, such that each process has as observable actions one of the sets of the partitioning. As an example, in the next picture we see a process B that is split into two processes B1 and B2 such that B1 has all a actions and B2 has all b actions, synchronizing over gate sync that is hidden to the environment:

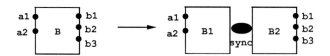

This decomposition transformation plays a role in the modularisation of a design and can be used as a first step in deriving a protocol from a service specification.

In [La90] a solution to this problem has been presented that is correct w.r.t. weak bisimulation equivalence, i.e. B is weak bisimulation equivalent to hide sync in B1 |[sync]| B2. Although weak bisimulation is in itself an attractive equivalence, in this situation the solution is intuitively not satisfactory. The reason for this is that the solution is based on the synchronisation tree of a process. Synchronisation trees form an interleaving model that ignores the independence of actions. Therefore independent actions still have to synchronize which produces an inefficient solution; still this is allowed by weak bisimulation as it is also incapable of representing independence explicitly.

As an example, let us take the process B = a1 ; (b1 ; b2 ||| b3 ; a2) and let us try to decompose it according to the above picture. The synchronisation tree is given in the next figure:

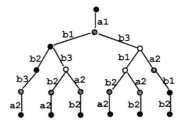

Two kinds of special states have been indicated:

- states marked °. These are states in which a choice between events from different processes has to be resolved by means of polling.

- states marked ⊗. These are states in which an action from one process is followed by an action from the other process so the processes have to synchronize.

In the synchronization tree there are three polling states and seven synchronization states leading to eight different synchronization messages. The resulting processes are rather complex; we do not show them.

We next show how to decompose the process B on the basis of its event structure model as given in the next figure:

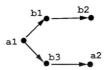

We are first going to perform the following transformation on this event structure. Whenever an event e from one process causally precedes events from the other process, we intersect between this event e and the other events a new event labelled sync!i for some value of i that has not been used before. This sync!i event precedes all events that e preceded and is preceded by e. This inserted event stands for a synchronisation between the processes; it will be hidden to the environment. This results in the next event structure:

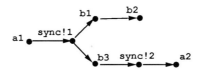

Next we project this event structure for B1 and B2 on the union of the respective action sets with the set of synchronization events. This leads to the following two event structures:

So the resulting decomposition is:

```
hide sync in (a1 ; sync!1 ; sync!2 ; a2)
             |[sync]|
             (sync!1 ; (b1 ; b2 ||| b3 ; sync!2)
```

which is much simpler than the solution based on the synchronisation tree: there are only two synchronizations and no polling.

Of course we still need to formally define this method of solution, and the sense in which it is correct, but we hope to have given some flavour of the usefulness of the event structure model for this decomposition problem.

4 Specification of a FIFO buffer

In this section we show how event structures can be used during the specification phase. As an example we take the specification of a FIFO buffer. To simplify we assume that only integers can be input and output.

It is rather easy to specify a FIFO buffer in LOTOS using an abstract datatype specification of a queue (in LOTOS abstract datatypes can be specified using the language ACT ONE). So a specification of a buffer might look like this:

```
Fifo(s:queue) = [s unequal empty] -> out!first(s) ; Fifo(rest(s))
                [] in?x:int ; Fifo(add(x,s))
```

We do not give the abstract datatype specification that belongs to this process but we are sure the reader can fill in these details. The complexity of this specification is largely "hidden" in the abstract datatype part. This is not always desirable; one might look for a specification that makes use only of the datatype int.

A more serious problem with this specification is that it prescribes a mutual exclusion between input and output: at any moment, one may either choose to input or to output. However, intuitively input and output should be to a certain extent independent. If several integers have been input, it should be possible to output them in parallel with inputting new integers! The mutual exclusion constraint is especially unnatural if one imagines input and output taking place at different locations. In order to solve this problem, let us look at an event structure for a FIFO buffer:

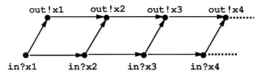

We have extended the event structure model a bit by allowing variables in the labels of the events; there are restrictions in doing this but they need not bother us here. The names of the variables serve only to indicate the binding relations and are themselves irrelevant. We invite the reader to convince himself that this event structure is indeed an adequate model of a FIFO buffer. Note e.g. that after in?x1, out!x1 and in?x2 can happen in parallel, i.e. independent of each other.

So the question is how to obtain a LOTOS specification that corresponds to this event structure? As a first step, we cover the event structures with "cells". Each cell communicates with the other cells over some gates that will be hidden. Each binding relation between two variables is local to a single cell:

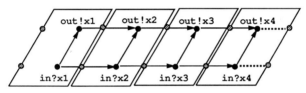

We give names to the newly introduced events that serve to synchronize the cells and obtain in this way the following event structure for a single cell:

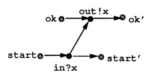

This cell functions as follows: first it is started by a previous cell by start. It can then input an integer. This integer can then be output after "receiving" an ok from the previous cell (indicating that that cell has output its integer). After inputting, the cell initiates the next cell by start'; it signals the fact that the integer has been output by ok'.

It is possible to give a LOTOS specification for this cell. We can however obtain a simpler LOTOS specification if we overspecify the cell a bit: we only let the ok take place after the integer has been input.

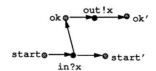

This overspecification does not really influence the correct functioning of the cells but just simplifies the specification somewhat. The LOTOS specification is now given by:

```
Cell = start ; in?x:int ; (start' ||| ok ; out!x ; ok')
```

We now have to connect the cells. It seems as if we would need an infinite number of different start and ok actions, but this can be avoided by using a simple renaming trick:

```
Cells = hide start',ok' in Cell
                          |[start',ok']|
                          Cells[start'/start,ok'/ok]
```

We only have to start the Cells process by giving it a start and an ok:

```
FIFO = hide start,ok in (start ||| ok)
                        |[start,ok]|
                        Cells
```

The event structure corresponding to this process FIFO is the following, where we have represented internal events by grey dots:

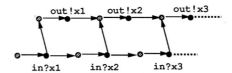

This event structure is equivalent to the event structure of a FIFO buffer modulo an equivalence that "forgets" the internal events.

We can compare this result with the following FIFO buffer specification, taken from [Le87]:

```
Cell'(x) = out!x ; in?y:int ; Cell'(y)
FIFO' = in?x:int ; hide mid in FIFO'[mid/out]
                               |[mid]|
                               Cell'[mid/in](x)
```

This specification uses a different kind of cell and only one synchronization gate. The corresponding event structure:

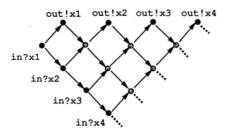

During the use of this buffer, the number of internal events between the input and output of an integer increases.

In [Br91] a method is described to derive a specification of a queue based on solving context equations. This method is based on interleaving semantics; still the result seems to have as it were by coincidence the desired independence between input and output. The relationship between the approaches needs further investigation.

5 Action refinement of a FIFO buffer

In this section we look at a brief example of action refinement. We refine the FIFO buffer of the previous section into a buffer where each message consists of two integers that are input one after the other. So in and out are to be replaced by in1 and in2 respectively out1 and out2.

This refinement step involves the following design decision: is it allowed to output the first part of a message *before* the second part has been input, yes or no ? For both answers to this question it is possible to find reasonable arguments. Let us first suppose the decision is *no*, i.e. the first part of a message can only be output after the second one has been input. In order to refine the buffer we refine the Cell process of the previous section. It is not hard to see that for this design decision the next event structure is reasonable:

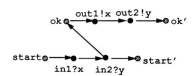

Note that out1 can only happen after in2 has happened. The LOTOS process that corresponds to this event structure:

```
Cell1 = start ; in1?x:int ; in2?x:int ; ( start'
                                          |||
                                          ok ; out1!x ; out2!x ; ok')
```

In this example, we see that we could have obtained Cell1 from Cell by simply syntactically substituting in1?x:int ; in2?y:int for in?x:int and out1!x ; out2!y for out!x. This is a mere coincidence, as the next refinement shows. Moreover, we would not have been sure which design decision we had taken by just performing this syntactic substitution.

This action refinement does not preserve the "global atomicity" of the input and output actions: the refined process has e.g. traces in1.in2.out1.in1... and in1.in2.in1.out1... which shows that at the global level input and output are not atomic anymore. In our opinion this shows that observations of the global state are not suitable when dealing with action refinement.

We now look at the other possible decision, namely: it is allowed to output the first part of a message before the second part has been input. Let us look at the following cell process:

```
Cell2 = start ; in1?x:int ; ( ok ; out1!x ; out2?z:int ; ok'
                              |[out2]|
                              in2?y:int ; (out2!y ||| start' ))
```

This process is not the result of a syntactic substitution of the original cell process. Is it acceptable as a refinement of the cell process, given this design decision ? This question is hard to answer on the basis of an interleaving semantics of the process. But consider the corresponding event structure:

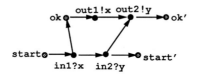

It is not hard to check on this event structure that it is a refinement of the original cell process. Note that `out1!x` can take place before `in2?y:int`.

The conclusion of this example is twofold. Firstly, it is not always possible to consider action refinement as a syntactic substitution. Secondly, event structures are a promising model to study action refinement as they are not based on global observations of the system. For a treatment of action refinement using event structures, although restricted to syntactic substitution, we refer to [GlGo90].

6 Conclusions

In an intuitive and preliminary way we have introduced an event structure model and illustrated it with LOTOS examples. We have shown how to use this model in several transformation and design problems. Event structures have originally been invented on the basis of mathematical considerations whose relation to practical problems was not always made clear. This does, however, not imply that event structures are just a toy for theoreticians. We hope to have demonstrated two things:

- the graphical and intuitive nature of event structure, which provides a way of thinking about concurrency that is different from the well-known interleaving semantics and provides new insight.

- the suitability of event structures for tackling several design and transformation problems.

Of course our presentation has simplified some issues a bit. We do not claim that one can completely skip the mathematics of the event structure models!

The treatment of the problems in sections 3, 4, and 5 has necessarily been brief. In the future we would like to study more complete approaches for solving these problems. Naturally tool support will be an essential factor in the success of these approaches. Currently at University of Twente a tool is being developed for the automatic generation and simulation of event structures from Basic LOTOS specifications.

Acknowledgements

I would like to thank Ed Brinksma, Arend Rensink, Jan Tretmans and especially Bart Botma for support, discussions and comments.

References

[BeKl85] J.A. Bergstra, J.W. Klop. *Algebra of communicating processes with abstraction.* TCS 37, pp.77-121, 1985

[BoBr87] T. Bolognesi, E. Brinksma. *Introduction to the ISO specification language LOTOS.* Comp. Networks and ISDN Systems, 14 (1987), pp. 25-59.

[BoCa89] G. Boudol, I. Castellani. *Permutations of transitions : an event structure semantics for CCS and SCCS.* LNCS 354, pp. 411-427, Springer-Verlag, 1989.

[BoCa90] G. Boudol, I. Castellani. *Three equivalent semantics for CCS.* LNCS 469, pp. 96-141. Springer-Verlag, 1990.

[BoCa91] G. Boudol, I.Castellani. *Flow Models of Distributed Computations: Event Structures and Nets.* to appear, Technical Report INRIA, Sophia Antipolis, 1991.

[Br89] E. Brinksma. *Constraint-Oriented Specification in a Constructive Formal Description Technique.* LNCS 430, pp. 130-152, Springer Verlag,1989.

[Br91] E. Brinksma. *From data structure to process structure.* proc. Third Workshop on Computer Aided Verification, Aalborg, July 1991.

[BHR84] S.D. Brookes, C.A.R. Hoare, A.W. Roscoe. *A theory of communicating sequential processes.* JACM 31 (1984), pp. 560-599.

[Gl90] R.J. van Glabbeek. *Comparative Concurrency Semantics and Refinement of Actions.* PhD. Thesis, Free University of Amsterdam, 1990.

[GlGo90] R. van Glabbeek, U. Goltz. *Refinement of actions in causality based models.* LNCS 430, pp. 267-300, Springer Verlag, 1990.

[La90] R. Langerak. *Decomposition of functionality : a correctness preserving LOTOS transformation.* Protocol Specification, Testing, and Verification X, pp. 229-242, North-Holland, 1990.

[La91]   R. Langerak. *Bundle event structures : a non-interleaving semantics for LOTOS*. Memoranda Informatica, University of Twente, June 1991.

[LoGo87] R. Loogen, U. Goltz. *A non-interleaving semantic model for nondeterministic concurrent processes*. Aachener Informatik -Berichte 87-15, RWTH Aachen, 1987.

[LOT89]   ISO, Information Processing Systems, Open Systems Interconnection. *LOTOS - A Formal Description Technique Based on the Temporal Ordering of Observational Behaviour*. IS8807, 1989.

[Le87]   G.J. Leduc. *The Intertwining of Data Types and Processes*. Protocol Specification, Testing, and Verification VII, pp. 123-136, North-Holland, 1987.

[Mi80]   R. Milner. *A Calculus of Communicating Systems*. LNCS 92, Springer-Verlag, 1980.

[Pl81]   G.D. Plotkin. *A structural approach to operational semantics*. Technical Report DAIMI FN-19, Comp. Sci. Dept., Aarhus University, 1981.

[Re90]   A. Rensink. *Selection Structures*. Memoranda Informatica 90-71, University of Twente, Nov. 1990.

[Re91]   A. Rensink. *Pattern Sets*. Memoranda Informatica 91-24, University of Twente, April 1991.

[Vi90]   C.A. Vissers. *FDTs for Open Distributed Systems, a Retrospective and a Prospective View*. Protocol Specification, Testing, and Verification X, pp. 341-362, North-Holland, 1990.

[Wi80]   G. Winskel. *Events in Computation*. PhD Thesis, CST-10-80, University of Edinburgh, 1980.

[Wi89]   G. Winskel. *An introduction to event structures*. LNCS 354, pp.364-397, Springer-Verlag, 1989.

Appendix: Different event structure models

In this appendix we discuss the main differences between several event structure models, namely prime event structures, flow event structures, bundle event structures and stable event structures. This list is not exhaustive; we do not treat e.g. the selection structures of [Re90] or the pattern sets of [Re91]. In [BoCa91] it has been pointed out that the different models do not have the same expressivity w.r.t. the set of system runs that can be expressed. If we denote "strictly more expressive" by $>$, then it turns out that stable e.s. $>$ flow e.s. $>$ bundle e.s. $>$ prime e.s.

Prime event structures
This is the best known event structure model [Wi80, Wi89, LoGo87]. It is characterized

by the fact that the causality relation is a partial order, and the conflict relation satifies the so-called *inheritance* property: if an event is in conflict with some event, then it is in conflict with all the causal successors of that event. E.g. if we see [diagram: a above, b→c] in an event structure, then we can conclude that also the conflict between a and c is present, so we will find [diagram: a, b→c with conflict] Because of the inheritance property, every event will be enabled in a unique way. Consider the following LOTOS expression with its associated prime event structure:

(∗)   (x ; a [] x ; b) |[x]| x ; c

Because c can be enabled by two different synchronizations on x, it is in prime event structures necessary to have two different events labelled c.

Prime event structures are conceptually simple and graphically attractive. However, the unique enabling property of events (as illustrated in the example above) can lead to an explosion of events in certain situations. In addition, the semantics of the parallel operator leads to very complicated constructions.

Flow event structures

In flow event structures [BoCa89, BoCa90, BoCa91] the causality relation is not necessarily a partial order nor does the inheritance property hold. This makes it possible to enable an event in different ways. For example, in the flow event structure  the event c can be enabled by either a or b. The price for this is a rather complicated enabling condition. Constructions in flow event structures are less complicated than in prime event structures, but may lead to large numbers of events that are in conflict with themselves yet cannot be removed in general. As an example of a flow event structure, the next one corresponds to the LOTOS expression (∗) above:

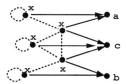

Bundle event structures

Bundle event structures [La91] have been defined in order to avoid the inevitable self-conflicting events in flow event structures. The causality relation is represented by so-called *bundles*. A bundle is a multi-edge between a set of conflicting events and another event. We graphically represent a bundle by a set of arrows connected by small line segments, e.g.

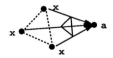

The interpretation is: if a happens, exactly one of the x events has to have happened already. A bundle is a straightforward generalization of the causal arrow. Therefore the enabling condition is simpler than in flow event structures which makes the analysis of event structures easier. The bundle event structure for LOTOS expression (∗) above is

Stable event structures
Stable event structures [Wi89] have also been proposed; they can be used in order to avoid the unique enabling property of prime event structures. There is no explicit causality relation; instead, enabling relations are recorded explicitly. Constructions are simpler than for prime event structures. Stable event structures are attractive from a theoretical point of view. However, because of their greater expressive power they are harder to analyse in general. Their graphical representation is in general less attractive than the representations of the other models.

A calculus to define correct transformations of LOTOS specifications

T. Massart

Laboratoire d'Informatique Théorique & Helios-B Group, Université Libre de Bruxelles, CP 212
Bld. du Triomphe, 1050 Brussels, Belgium
e-mail: MASSART@HELIOS.IIHE.RTT.BE

Abstract

We present a basic agent calculus which uses simple actions and contains 6 kinds of operators: the sequence, the choice, the parallel composition, the recursion, the hiding and the relabelling operator. This calculus is used to define correct transformations. As an example, we solve a problem of distribution of an agent into several locations (places): we provide an equality preserving transformation which transforms an agent P into subagents $<Q^1, Q^2, ..., Q^n>$ which synchronize by using a reliable medium M. We also show that, since LOTOS may be mapped on this calculus, it may be used as a theoretical basis for LOTOS developments.

1. Introduction

Process calculi and algebraic specification languages have been used in the recent years to examine the correct design of distributed systems [17, 9]. The basic idea is to start from a very abstract specification S (called agent in the following) which describes the functionality of the system and to refine (as often as needed) this specification into an agent S', adding implementation details of this system. This method called stepwise refinement needs to be correct with respect to some implementation relation R [8] which links S to S'; this relation R ensures that the desired properties described in S are preserved in S'.

The difficulty in such an approach arises from the fact that the person specifying a system prefers to use a full specification language, like LOTOS [5], which allows him to 'easily' specify systems. Unfortunately it is a very difficult task to directly define correct refinements for LOTOS specifications.

To simplify the search of correct refinements of LOTOS specifications, two solutions can be thought of:

1°) define these transformations on the underlying semantical model, i.e. on the Labelled Transition System model [6] (LTS for short).

2°) define these transformations on a basic calculus on which LOTOS can be mapped and which keeps the structure of the specifications.

Using the method 1°, the refinement would be specified by an LTS. This solution may be intractable since it does not use the structure of the initial specification and since the number of states of the LTS corresponding to an agent is generally huge if not infinite. The approach 2°

allows us to define compositional transformations based on the structure of the agents. This also allows us to 'map' these transformations to LOTOS. By this method we would get correct refinements transforming LOTOS specifications to refined ones. Since it is possible to define compositional transformations which encompass complete classes of cases, we would be able to build tools to automatically perform these transformations.

To illustrate such an approach we have taken the bisimilarity relation (or more precisely the bisimulation congruence also called equality relation [15]) as the implementation relation. This relation is sometimes too strong to get a meaningful implementation of an agent [8]. However, since equality relates agents with equivalent external behaviours, it is an obvious candidate for such an implementation relation.

We shall define classes of equality preserving transformations and apply them to the problem of distribution [2, 4, 7]: if P is an agent and we know the location where each action of P must occur (called *place* [2] in the following), we shall construct an equal agent composed by one subagent per place which synchronize by using a reliable medium. Note that in [2, 4] a solution of this problem is provided for a restricted algebraic calculus, but the formal relation between the initial and the final agent is not examined. In [7], the simplification of the problem and the use of the so called expansion theorem imply that the model corresponds to a finite LTS; therefore the subagents also correspond to finite LTS and have no algebraic structure.

In our approach we have as well a formal implementation relation (equality) which guaruantees correctness of the transformation as well as a subagent structure which resembles the structure of the inital agent.

2. The Basic Calculus

In this section we briefly define the syntax and the operational semantics of the calculus we shall use. The operational (interleaving) semantics is restricted to the set of agents, i.e. the set of expressions without free variables (see [10, 14] for a more detailed discussion on this subject).

Assume a finite or countably infinite unstructured set, $\mathcal{L}$, of labels or observable actions, and a separate element τ, the internal or unobservable action ($\tau \notin \mathcal{L}$). *The set of actions*, denoted $\mathcal{A}ct$, is defined as $\mathcal{A}ct =_{df} \mathcal{L} \cup \{\tau\}$. Let $a, b, \ldots$ range over $\mathcal{A}ct$ and S range over sets of visible actions. We define relabelling functions Φ from $\mathcal{L}$ to $\mathcal{L}$, and extend Φ to $\mathcal{A}ct$ by decreeing that $\Phi(\tau)=\tau$. Assume also a countably infinite set $\mathcal{X}$ of agent variables, also called variables, ranged over by X, Y, ...; the *set $\mathcal{E}$ of agent expressions*, also called expressions and ranged over by E, E_1, F,...is defined as the smallest set which contains the following expressions:

$\quad$ X (*variable*) | a.E (*prefix*) | $\sum$ **E** (*summation*) | $E_1 |_S E_2$ (*composition*) |
$\quad$ E\S (*hiding*) | E[Φ] (*relabelling*) | fix$_X$ X=E (*recursion*)

where **X** is a set of agent variables, and **E** = $<E_X>_{X \in \mathbf{X}}$ is an **X**-indexed family of agent expressions in $\mathcal{E}$. The operators are given in the order of decreasing priority. If **E** is empty, $\sum$**E** is denoted **0**. If **E** is finite and $|\mathbf{E}| \geq 2$, e.g. **E** = $\{E_i \mid 0 \leq i \leq n\}$, for convenience, instead of $\sum$**E** we may write $E_1 + E_2 + \ldots + E_n$, with the E_i's written in any order since no order is given for the elements of the family **E**.

We can also consider **X** as an I-indexed family of distinct variables and **E** as an I-indexed family of expressions, for some indexing set I, and denote $\text{fix}_i\ X = E$ instead of $\text{fix}_X\ X = E$. This alternate notation will generally be used in the following. Similarly the family **E** in $\sum E$ may be indexed by some indexing set I.

In $\text{fix}_X\ X=E$, the variables $Y \in X$ occurring in any $E \in E$ are bound by the fix operator. For an expression E, Vars(E) is the set of free (i.e. not bound) variables of E. An agent expression E is an *agent* if it contains no free variables, i.e. if Vars(E) = $\emptyset$; $\mathcal{P}$ is the set of all the agents, ranged over by P, P_1, P_2, Q, R, ...

The operational semantics of this calculus is defined from the *transition relations* $\xrightarrow{a}$, included in $\mathcal{P} \times \mathcal{P}$, defined for each $a \in \mathcal{A}ct$. This definition follows the structure of agents and is obtained with an inference system. The <u>complete</u> set of axioms and inference (or transition) rules (or more precisely inference schema) associated with the defined operators is given in table 2.1 where **fix X=E** abbreviates the **X**-indexed family $<\text{fix}_X\ X = E>_{X \in X}$; if **P** is a **Y**-indexed family of <u>agents</u> and **X** is a set of variables with $X \subseteq Y$, E{P/X} is obtained by the substitution in E of each free occurrence of the variable X by P_X, for all $X \in X$.

The semantics of an agent is given by the associated Labelled Transition System LTS = $<\mathcal{P}, \mathcal{A}ct, T, ->$ where the transition relations T are derived from Table 2.1.

Prefix	$a.P \xrightarrow{a} P$	(in particular: $\tau.P \xrightarrow{\tau} P$)
Summation	$\dfrac{P_j \xrightarrow{a} P'_j}{\sum P \xrightarrow{a} P'_j}$ $(P_j \in P)$	
Composition	$\dfrac{P_1 \xrightarrow{a} P'_1}{P_1 \mid_S P_2 \xrightarrow{a} P'_1 \mid_S P_2}$ (a∉ S)	$\dfrac{P_2 \xrightarrow{a} P'_2}{P_1 \mid_S P_2 \xrightarrow{a} P_1 \mid_S P'_2}$ (a∉ S)
	$\dfrac{P_1 \xrightarrow{a} P'_1 ,\ P_2 \xrightarrow{a} P'_2}{P_1 \mid_S P_2 \xrightarrow{a} P'_1 \mid_S P'_2}$ $(a \in S)$	
Hiding	$\dfrac{P \xrightarrow{a} P'}{P \setminus S \xrightarrow{a} P' \setminus S}$ (a ∉ S)	$\dfrac{P \xrightarrow{a} P'}{P \setminus S \xrightarrow{\tau} P' \setminus S}$ $(a \in S)$
Relabelling	$\dfrac{P \xrightarrow{a} P'}{P[\Phi] \xrightarrow{\Phi(a)} P'[\Phi]}$	
Recursion	$\dfrac{E_X\{\text{fix X=E / X}\} \xrightarrow{a} P'}{\text{fix}_X\ X=E \xrightarrow{a} P'}$	

Table 2.1: Axioms and inference rules

The equality relation links the agents which are weakly bisimilar in any context (see e.g. [15] for a summary of the results on strong bisimilarity [16] (denoted ~), weak bisimilarity (denoted ≈) and equality (also called bisimulation congruence and denoted ≈^{c})).

Because of the syntax and the semantics of the fix operator it may often be interesting to know which agent corresponds to some subexpression C of an agent P. For instance, if P ≡ fix X=E with E ≡ fix Y = (a.X + Y), the expression (a.X + Y) corresponds to the agent

(a.X+Y){(fix Y=(a.X+Y)){fix X=E/X}/Y}{fix X=E/X} ≡(a.fix X=E) + (fix Y=a.(fix X=E)+Y)
(I.e., in this context, X *"stands for"* the agent fix X=E and Y for (fix Y=a.(fix X=E)+Y)).
These substitutions become quite difficult to denote when the level of nesting is higher than 2! We thus define the following useful notation:

Notation 2.1: *(list of substitutions)*

If $n \in N$,

$\forall\ 1 \le i \le n$: I^i is an indexing set,

$<X^1, X^2, ..., X^n>$ is a list of n families of variables where each X^i is I^i-indexed,

$<E^1, E^2, ..., E^n>$ is a list of n families of agent expressions where each E^i is J^i-indexed with $I^i \subseteq J^i, C \in \mathcal{E}$,

with $\forall\ 0 \le i \le n$: $\text{Vars}(E^i) \subseteq \cup_{n \ge j > i} X^j$ (in particular E^n is a family of agents), then

$C\{E^1/X^1, E^2/X^2, ..., E^n/X^n\}$ denotes the following
- if $n = 0$, $C\{\} \equiv C$ where $\{\}$ stands for the empty list of substitution,
- if $n \ge 1$ $C\{E^1/X^1, E^2/X^2, ..., E^n/X^n\}$
  $\equiv (C\{E^1\{E^2/X^2, ..., E^n/X^n\}/X^1\})\ \{E^2/X^2, ..., E^n/X^n\}$ □

It can be seen, by induction on the length n of the list of substitutions, that this definition is sound, and defines a sequence of substitutions (replacing occurrences of free variables by <u>agents</u>).

Mapping of LOTOS in our Basic Calculus

In [13, 11] it is shown that the LOTOS enabling and disabling are derived operators of our basic calculus. We have also proved in [10] that it is possible to translate any agent which uses the instantiation mechanism into one which uses a recursion expressed by the fix operator (and vice versa).

Moreover, since $\mathcal{L}$ is countably infinite, summation and recursion allow a countably infinite family as a parameter and since the composition is similar to the one in LOTOS, we can see that the translation of any LOTOS specification into an agent of our calculus is quite natural (an example of such a translation between LOTOS and a basic calculus is given in [3]) and for instance the following LOTOS specification:

>   *specification* Q [g,a,b,c] : *noexit*
>   *library* BasicNaturalNumber *endlib*
>   *behaviour*   P[g,a,b,c]
>   *where*
>   *process* P[g,a,b,c]: *noexit* :=
>   g?n:Nat;
>   ([n gt 0] -> b!n; (c; *stop* |[c]| c; *stop*)
>   []
>   [n le 0] -> a!n; P[g,a,b,c])
>   *endproc*
>   *endspec*

may be translated in a simplified way by the following (where in this example $\cup$ means that the two Σ are in fact two parts of the same summation:

$$Q \equiv \text{fix}_1 \left(\begin{array}{ll} P_1 = & \Sigma_{n>0} \ <g_n.\ b_n.\ (c.\ \mathbf{0} \ |_{\{c\}}\ c.\ \mathbf{0})> \\ \cup & \Sigma_{n\leq 0} \ <g_n.\ a_n.\ P_1> \end{array} \right)$$

Figure 2.1

Note also that a set of actions Δ corresponds to the LOTOS *exit*. When mapping a LOTOS specification into our calculus, all the parallel composition operators are synchronized at least through Δ (if *exit* is used). For instance the LOTOS parallel composition (a.*exit* |[a]| a.*exit*) could be mapped on (a.δ.0 $|_{\Delta \cup \{a\}}$ a.δ.0) with $\delta \in \Delta$ corresponds to the exit without offer.

Notations 2.2:

- In the following, we shall suppose that we have an injective mapping G between the set of LOTOS action-denotations (without query in its offers) and $\mathcal{A}ct$ with $G(i) = \tau$.
  To simplify our notation, we shall e.g. denote a!3!4 when we talk about the corresponding action $G(a!3!4)$ (where a is a LOTOS gate and 3, 4 are offers). We shall also denote the operators $|_{\{g\}}$ \\$\{g\}$ with g a gate to mean resp. $|_S$ and \\$S$ with
  $S = \{a = G(g\ \text{list})$ with the gate g and $\forall\ \text{list} \in$ list of offers without query$\}$ i.e. the set of actions corresponding to the gate g.
- We shall also suppose that the considered agents do not use the actions (gates) 'send_synchro' and 'receive_synchro'; these gates will be used to transmit synchronizations through the medium.
- Since the identity of expressions is defined up to the indexing of the various families occurring in them, in the following, we shall consider two special indexings for $\mathcal{X}$: N and N^*; N is the set of natural numbers and $N^* = \cup_{i \in N} N^i$ where N^i is the set of i-tuple of natural numbers: $N^i = \{<n_1, n_2, ..., n_i> : n_1,... n_i \in N\}$. We call them strings of natural numbers of length i.
  The inclusion of two strings of N^* is defined by the prefix property: if $\sigma_1, \sigma_2 \in N^*$, $\sigma_1 \subseteq \sigma_2$ if $\exists\ \sigma_3 \in N^*$: $\sigma_2 = \sigma_1 \times \sigma_3$ (where $\times$ is the concatenation operator).
  We shall use these indexings for variables, fix expressions and summations of $\mathcal{E}$; to be clear we shall denote X^i, E^i and fix^i $X = E$ when $i \in I \subseteq N$ and X_i, E_i and fix$_i$ $X = E$ when $i \in I \subseteq N^*$.
- Finally we would sometimes index the operators of an agent by strings of natural numbers. Formally we define $\mathcal{E}^{N^*}$ similarly to $\mathcal{E}$ but with some index from N^* associated to each expression, i.e. $\mathcal{E}^{N^*}$ is the smallest set which contains $<X, \sigma> \in \mathcal{X} \times N^*$ and also $<a.E, \sigma>, <\Sigma E, \sigma>, <E_1 |_S E_2, \sigma> <E \backslash S, \sigma> <E [\Phi], \sigma>, <\text{fix}_i X = E, \sigma>$ where all the expressions E and $E_i \in \mathcal{E}^{N^*}$ and $E \subseteq \mathcal{E}^{N^*}$
  Notice that if $E \in \mathcal{E}^{N^*}$ each subexpression of E is also indexed.
  If $E \in \mathcal{E}^{N^*}$, $ind(E)$ denotes its corresponding index.

3 Transformations

In this section we define a sequence of transformations which solve the distribution problem presented above. To simplify the problem, we will suppose that any alternative in a summation is in prefix form. We also suppose that we know the place of any action: to each prefix a.E in our agent P, $p(a)$ denotes the place where a must occur; furthermore for any given visible action a, $p(a)$ is the same in all prefixes in P. We shall also suppose that the hidding and relabelling operators 'preserve' the place of each action (The place may be seen as an attribute of the prefix). We also impose that all the possible first actions in a summation have the same place. This implies that the choice can be taken locally (In [7] a polling mechanism is described which allows distributed choices. This mechanism preserves the bisimilarity but in general not the equality between the initial agent and the distributed agent).

The transformations we shall present now will illustrate the kind of interesting developments that can be done in the field of correctness-preserving stepwise refinements of distributed systems. As mentionned above, we have studied compositional transformations: if an agent S is composed by several parts $S_1, S_2, ..., S_n$, a compositional transformation T of S is recursively defined as a function f whose parameters are transformations of parts S_i of S, i.e.
$$T(S) \equiv f(T(S_1), T(S_2), ..., T(S_n))$$
This approach allows us, through the definition of a single function f, to encompass a complete class of transformation cases.

To explain the method, we must first notice that an agent P implies constraints on the possible ordering of actions (This is also true for other models like Petri nets or event structures). The sequencing of actions is given by the prefix operator: if $First(Q)$ denotes the enabled actions of an agent Q, $P \equiv a.Q$ specifies that the action a must happen before any action of $First(Q)$ and in particular if $P \equiv a.b.0$, b can happen only after a has occurred. Now let us distribute the agent P into several subagents, say P_1 and P_2 linked by some medium M (M accepts any send_synchro and transmits the corresponding receive_synchro. In the following we shall suppose M to be defined as follows: M $\equiv$ fix X = $\Sigma_{\text{liste list of offers}}$ send_synchro!list. (receive_synchro!list.0 $|_\emptyset$ X) where list is any list of offers and may be empty) and let a occur in P_1 and b in P_2. One solution which preserves this ordering consists of transmitting through the medium M some 'message' to inform P_2 that a occurred in P_1. At reception of this message in P_2, the action b can be enabled. This is illustrated in figure 3.1.

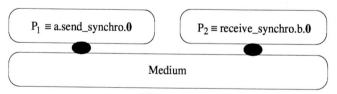

Figure 3.1

It can also be seen that if the transmissions through the Medium (send_synchro, receive_synchro) are hidden, the only possible behaviour of the new agent
$$P^d \setminus \{\text{send\_synchro}, \text{receive\_synchro}\} \equiv$$
$$((P_1 |_\emptyset P_2) |_{\{\text{send\_synchro}, \text{receive\_synchro}\}} M) \setminus \{\text{send\_synchro}, \text{receive\_synchro}\}$$

will be a.τ(send_synchro).τ(receive_synchro).b, where τ(a) denotes an action τ resulting from the hiding of an action a.
Therefore we have as required: $P^d \setminus \{send\_synchro, receive\_synchro\} \approx^c P$.

We have seen that with two places, an agent Q will distributes into Q_1 and Q_2. If we also have an agent R it will also be distributed into R_1 and R_2. Now, let us examine an agent P which is the composition of Q and R, i.e. $P \equiv Q \mid_S R$. Since we want compositional transformations, P should distribute into $P_1 \equiv (Q_1 \mid_S R_1)$ and $P_2 \equiv (Q_2 \mid_S R_2)$ (and the medium).

We can use the same idea for the other operators. It follows that if P is the agent to be distributed using M, the structure of the agent P_i (for each place i) which results from the distribution should be similar to the structure of P, except that P_i has only its local actions plus some actions send_synchro and receive_synchro for the synchronization with the agents P_j of the other places (In general P_i can still be simplified; our aim here is not to develop further on those simplifications which use simple laws as e.g. $P \mid_\emptyset \mathbf{0} \sim P$. A list of these laws is given in [10]).

However, care must be taken to properly identify the transmissions. For instance it may happen that several transmissions are ongoing at the same time. If for example the agent $P \equiv a.b.\mathbf{0} \mid_\emptyset c.d.\mathbf{0}$ has to be distributed and a, c have to happen at place 1 and b, d at place 2, we get, by applying the same principle:

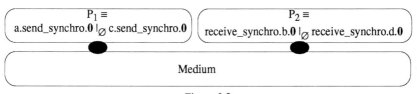

Figure 3.2

We can see that the transmissions are not properly identified, i.e. d may happen after a, or b may happen after c. To solve this problem we need separate identifications (id_1 and id_2 in this case) for the transmissions between the first subagents of the composition (Q_1 and Q_2) and between the second subagents of the composition (R_1 and R_2). This results in:

$P_1 \equiv a.send\_synchro!id_1.\mathbf{0} \mid_\emptyset c.send\_synchro!id_2.\mathbf{0}$

$P_2 \equiv receive\_synchro!id_1.b.\mathbf{0} \mid_\emptyset receive\_synchro!id_2.d.\mathbf{0}$

Another problem is that, due to recursion, some sequence of actions may be executed several times and in different 'contexts'. For instance for $P \equiv \text{fix } X = (a.b.\mathbf{0} \mid_\emptyset X)$ with a ocurring at place 1 and b at place 2, we have an unbounded number of prefixes a.b.0 in parallel. In this example we can see that $P \approx^c P^d \setminus \{send\_synchro, receive\_synchro\}$ since any b of P_2 may follow any a of P_1, where

$P^d \equiv (P_1 \mid_\emptyset P_2) \mid_{\{send\_synchro, receive\_synchro\}} M$

$P_1 \equiv \text{fix } X = (a.send\_synchro.\mathbf{0} \mid_\emptyset X)$

$P_2 \equiv \text{fix } X = (receive\_synchro.b.\mathbf{0} \mid_\emptyset X)$

But, as the following example shows, equality is not preserved in the general case:
Let $P \equiv \text{fix } X = (a.b.\mathbf{0} \mid_\emptyset (X \mid_{\{a,b\}} \mathbf{0}))$ with a at place 1 and b at place 2.

If we transform P into $P^d \equiv (P_1 \mid_\emptyset P_2) \mid_{\{send\_synchro, receive\_synchro\}} M$, with

$P_1 \equiv \text{fix } X = (a.send\_synchro.0 \mid_\emptyset (X \mid_{\{a,b\}} 0))$

$P_2 \equiv \text{fix } X = (receive\_synchro.b.0 \mid_\emptyset (X \mid_{\{a,b\}} 0))$,

we have that $P_1 \xrightarrow{a.send\_synchro} P'_1 \equiv 0 \mid_\emptyset (P_1 \mid_{\{a,b\}} 0)$ and

$P_2 \xrightarrow{receive\_synchro} P'_2 \equiv receive\_synchro.b.0 \mid_\emptyset (b.0 \mid_\emptyset (P_2 \mid_{\{a,b\}} 0) \mid_{\{a,b\}} 0)$.

Therefore $P^d \xrightarrow{a.send\_synchro.receive\_synchro} P^{d'} \equiv (P'_1 \mid_\emptyset P'_2) \mid_{\{send\_synchro, receive\_synchro\}} M'$ where $P^{d'} \not\xrightarrow{b}$, when obviously only $P \xrightarrow{a} P' \equiv (b.0 \mid_\emptyset (P \mid_{\{a,b\}} 0)$ is possible and $P' \xrightarrow{b}$, i.e. $P^d \setminus \{send\_synchro, receive\_synchro\}$ is even not trace equivalent to P!

A careful examination of the problem shows that it is again caused by a confusion at the reception of the transmitted synchronizations. In fact in this example the same piece of syntax is used several times in different contexts.

To solve this problem, one can transform the initial agent P so that it is always possible during the distribution transformation, to properly identify the various transmissions. If $P \equiv C[Q \mid_S R]$ (for some context $C[\ ]$), the distribution of Q and R may be defined such that the transmissions of synchronization messages between the subagents corresponding to Q ($Q_1,...Q_n$) are all different from the transmissions between the subagents corresponding to R ($R_1,...R_n$). Therefore the agent P^d, obtained after the distribution of P, will have two separate 'pools' (or partitions) of transmissions: one for the transimissions of $Q_1,...Q_n$ and one for the transmissions of $R_1,...R_n$. Therefore no confusion will be possible between the transmissions of $R_1,...R_n$ and those of $Q_1,...Q_n$.

A similar constraint is needed for the summation operator. Indeed if $P \equiv a.c.0 + b.d.0$ with a, b at place 1 and c, d at place 2, we distribute P into

$P^d \equiv (P_1 \mid_\emptyset P_2) \mid_{\{send\_synchro, receive\_synchro\}} M$ with

$P_1 \equiv a.send\_synchro!id_1.0 + b.send\_synchro!id_2.0$

$P_2 \equiv receive\_synchro!id_1.c.0 + receive\_synchro!id_2.d.0$

such that P_2 is able to determine with the identifier (id_1 or id_2) the alternative taken by P_1.

To allow the separation of the identifiers in partitions, we define a transformation called Indexing Unfolding which transform expressions E into expressions $E' \in \mathcal{E}^{N*}$ and will be used to slightly transform the initial agent P into an agent P' which may be distributed correctly.

Definition 3.1: *(Indexing Unfolding)*

The Indexing Unfolding $U : \mathcal{E} \times N^* \to \mathcal{E}^{N*}$ is defined recursively as follows:

- $U(X^i, \sigma) \equiv \langle X_{\sigma.i}, \sigma \rangle$,
- $U(a.E, \sigma) \equiv \langle a.U(E, \sigma), \sigma \rangle$,
- $U(\Sigma E, \sigma) \equiv \langle \Sigma \{U(E^i, \sigma.i)\}_{i \in I}, \sigma \rangle$ (ΣE is I-indexed) ,
- $U(E_1 \mid_S E_2, \sigma) \equiv \langle U(E_1, \sigma.1) \mid_S U(E_2, \sigma.2), \sigma \rangle$,
- $U(E_1 \setminus S, \sigma) \equiv \langle U(E_1, \sigma) \setminus S, \sigma \rangle$,
- $U(E_1 [\Phi], \sigma) \equiv \langle U(E_1, \sigma) [\Phi], \sigma \rangle$,
- $U(\text{fix}^i Y=F, \sigma) \equiv \langle \text{fix}_{\sigma.i} Y'=F', \sigma \rangle$ ($i \in I$) , with

$Y = \langle X^j \rangle_{j \in I}$, $\quad F = \langle F^j \rangle_{j \in I}$,

$Y' = \{X_{\sigma_1 x j} : \sigma_1 \in N^*, j \in I\}$,

$F' = \{U(F^j, \sigma_1) : \sigma_1 \in N^*, j \in I\}$ where $U(F^j, \sigma_1)$ has the index $\sigma_1 x j$. □

Note that we have used the notations 2.2 (e.g. X^i and X_σ to state that X is indexed by some $i \in N$ or $\sigma \in N^*$).

The indexing of expressions will be useful to determine the identifiers which should be associated with each transmission.

The Indexing Unfolding modifies the fix expressions and indexes all the operators with 'strings' of natural numbers.

However, we have the following propositions which show that, except for some slight modifications, the Indexing Unfolding completely 'preserves' the agents:

Proposition 3.2: [10]

$\forall \sigma \in N^*: P \sim U(P, \sigma)$ (where the indexing of $U(P, \sigma)$ is abstracted) □

Note: it is interesting to see [10] that if in this definition we modifiy the definition of the fix expressions in the following way: $F' \equiv \{U(F^j, \sigma_1 x j) : \sigma_1 \in N^*, j \in I\}$

we have that: $\forall P, \forall \sigma \in N^*, U(P, \sigma) \sim P$ and that the LTS of $U(P, \sigma)$ is acyclic!

The following proposition helps to understand the interest of the Indexing Unfolding.

Proposition 3.3: [12]

If $P \in \mathcal{P}$, $P' \equiv U(P, \sigma)$ with $\sigma \in N^*$ then

$\forall P'' \in Der(P')$ (where $Der(P')$ is the set of derivatives of P'), such that $P'' \xrightarrow{a} P^3$ using $b.Q \xrightarrow{b} Q$, and such that $P'' \xrightarrow{c} P^4$ using $d.Q' \xrightarrow{d} Q'$ we have that

$ind(b) = ind(d) \Leftrightarrow b = d, Q \equiv Q', P^3 \equiv P^4$ □

In other words, when two different actions are enabled simultaneously, they are properly identified by their indexes. These indexes will therefore be used as dentifiers of the synchronization transmissions.

We shall now define our distribution relation *Dist* which links unfolded agents to their distribution.

Definition 3.4: (—≼ , *Dist*)

If L is the set of actions corresponding to send_synchro, receive_synchro
(L = {a : a = G(send_synchro list) or a = G(receive_synchro list) $\forall$ list $\in$ list of offers without query}), and 1, 2, ... , n give the places,

—≼ is defined as the smallest relation between couples containing an expression of $\mathcal{E}^{N^*}$ and a list of substitutions and expressions of $\mathcal{E}$ satisfying the following axioms and inference rules, where

- *replist* is a list of substitution such that $\forall$ used expression E, E {*replist*} $\in \mathcal{P}$,

- I is an indexing set with $I \subseteq N^*$, J is an indexing set with $J \subseteq N$,
- $a \notin L$,   - $A \cap L = \emptyset$,
- Φ is a relabelling function with $\forall\ a \in L: \Phi(a) = a$ and $\Phi[L - L] \cap L = \emptyset$,
- $C^1, C^2, ..., C'^1, C'^2, ..., C^i{}_j, E^1{}_{ixj}, ... \in \mathcal{E}$
- $C, C_1, C_2, C_i, D_i, E_{ixj} \in \mathcal{E}^N$
- X is an I-indexed family of variables
- C and E are resp. I-indexed and IxJ-indexed families of expressions of $\mathcal{E}^N$,
- C^1, C^2 are I-indexed families of expressions of $\mathcal{E}$,
- E^1, E^2 are IxJ-indexed families of expressions of $\mathcal{E}$,
- *First*(P) gives the set of actions enabled in P

L1 $\quad\dfrac{}{<<X_{\sigma xi}, \sigma>, \{replist\}> \longrightarrow\!\!\!\!\!\prec\ <X_{\sigma xi}, X_{\sigma xi}, ..., X_{\sigma xi}>}$

L2 $\quad\dfrac{<C, \{replist\}> \longrightarrow\!\!\!\!\!\prec\ <C^1, C^2, ..., C^i, ..., C^n>,\ ind(C) = \sigma}{<<a.C, \sigma>, \{replist\}> \longrightarrow\!\!\!\!\!\prec\ <C'^1, C'^2, ..., C'^n>}$

where if $p(a)$ is the place of the action a and $d_1, d_2, ..., d_m$ are the list of places of the actions enabled in C and different from $p(a)$

$(d_1, d_2, ... d_m \in \{p(b): b \in First(C\{replist\})\} \setminus p(a))$, we have $\forall$ place i:

- if $i \notin p(a) \cup \{p(b): b \in First(C\{replist\})\}$: $C'^i \equiv C^i$
- if $i = p(a)$: $C'^i \equiv$ a.send_synchro!$p(a)$!d_1!σ.send_synchro!$p(a)$!d_2!σ....
  .send_synchro!$p(a)$!d_m!σ.C^i
- if $i = d_j$ $(i \in \{p(b): b \in First(C\{replist\})\} \setminus \{p(a)\})$:
  $C'^i \equiv$ receive_synchro!$p(a)$!d_j!σ.C^i

L3 $\quad\dfrac{\begin{array}{c}\forall\ i \in I: <C_i, \{replist\}> \longrightarrow\!\!\!\!\!\prec\ <C^1{}_i, C^2{}_i, ..., C^n{}_i>,\\ \text{and } \exists \text{ a place p with } C_i \equiv <a_i.D_i, \sigma x\sigma_i> (\sigma_i \in N^*) \text{ with}\\ p(a_i) = p \text{ and}\\ \forall\ i \neq j\ (i,j \in I): \sigma_i \not\subseteq \sigma_j \text{ and } \sigma_j \not\subseteq \sigma_i\end{array}}{<<\Sigma\ C, \sigma>, \{replist\}> \longrightarrow\!\!\!\!\!\prec\ <\Sigma C^1, \Sigma C^2, ..., \Sigma C^n>}$

L4 $\quad\dfrac{\begin{array}{c}<C_1, \{replist\}> \longrightarrow\!\!\!\!\!\prec\ <C^1{}_1, C^2{}_1, ..., C^n{}_1>,\\ <C_2, \{replist\}> \longrightarrow\!\!\!\!\!\prec\ <C^1{}_2, C^2{}_2, ..., C^n{}_2>,\\ ind(C_1) = \sigma x\sigma_1,\ ind(C_2) = \sigma x\sigma_2,\ \sigma_1 \not\subseteq \sigma_2,\ \sigma_2 \not\subseteq \sigma_1\end{array}}{\begin{array}{c}<<C_1 |_A C_2, \sigma>, \{replist\}>\\ \longrightarrow\!\!\!\!\!\prec\\ <(C^1{}_1 |_A C^1{}_2), (C^2{}_1 |_A C^2{}_2), ..., (C^n{}_1 |_A C^n{}_2)>\end{array}}$

L5 $\quad\dfrac{<C, \{replist\}> \longrightarrow\!\!\!\!\!\prec\ <C^1, C^2, ..., C^n>,\ ind(C) = \sigma}{<<C \setminus S, \sigma>, \{replist\}> \longrightarrow\!\!\!\!\!\prec\ <C^1 \setminus S, C^2 \setminus S, ..., C^n \setminus S>}$

L6 $\dfrac{<C,\{replist\}> \twoheadrightarrow C'_1,\ ind(C) = \sigma}{<<C\ [\Phi],\sigma>,\ \{replist\}> \twoheadrightarrow <C^1\ [\Phi], C^2\ [\Phi], \ldots, C^n\ [\Phi]>}$

$\forall\ i \in I, j \in J:$

L7 $\dfrac{<E_{ixj},\{\textbf{fix}\ X=E\backslash X,\ replist\}> \twoheadrightarrow <E^1_{ixj}, E^2_{ixj}, \ldots, E^n_{ixj}>\ \text{and}\ ind(E_{ixj}) = i}{<<\textbf{fix}_{ixj}\ X=E, i>,\{replist\}> \twoheadrightarrow <\textbf{fix}_{ixj}\ X=E^1, \textbf{fix}_{ixj}\ X=E^2, \ldots, \textbf{fix}_{ixj}\ X=E^n>}$

If $P, Q = <Q^1, Q^2, \ldots, Q^n>$ is resp. an indexed agent and a family of n subagents then $Q\ Dist\ P$ if $<<P,\sigma>, \{\}> \twoheadrightarrow Q$ for some $\sigma \in N^*$. □

Notes: The use of a list of substitutions {*replist*} is needed to calculate the set of actions enabled at some point; indeed we must determine $First(C\{replist\})$ where C is a subexpression of the agent P and $C\{replist\}$ is its corresponding agent.

In **L7**, the place of each action is considered to be part of this action.
In $C\{\textbf{fix}\ X=C\backslash X, replist\}$, the place of the corresponding actions in **fix** X=C must then be identical to the place of the corresponding actions in C.

First it may be seen that if $P' \equiv U(P, \sigma)$ and satisfies the restrictions explained in the beginning of §3, then it is always possible to have a family **Q** such that **Q** *Dist* P' (and indirectly P).

Now we have to prove that if **Q** *Dist* P we have $P \approx^c ((|_\varnothing\ Q)\ |_L\ M) \backslash L$ where $(|_\varnothing\ Q)$ stands for $(Q_1\ |_\varnothing\ (Q_2\ |_\varnothing\ \ldots\ (Q_{n-1}\ |_\varnothing\ Q_n)\ldots))$ and L is the set of actions corresponding to send_synchro, receive_synchro.

To achieve this proof, it may be interesting to develop some variation of the confluence notions described in [15].

Definition 3.5: *(Strong L-Confluence)*

If L is a set of actions, P is *Strongly L-Confluent* (SLC) if $\forall\ Q \in Der(P),\ \forall\ a \in \mathcal{A}ct, u \in L$, $Q \xrightarrow{a} Q_1$ and $Q \xrightarrow{u} Q_2$ for some Q_1, Q_2 imply

either: (case 1) $a = u$ and $Q_1 \sim Q_2$

or: (case 2)   for some Q_3, Q_4 with $Q_3 \sim Q_4$: $Q_1 \xrightarrow{u} Q_3$ and $Q_2 \xrightarrow{a} Q_4$

or: (case 3)   for some Q_3 with $Q_1 \sim Q_3$: $Q_2 \xrightarrow{a} Q_3$

graphically, if $Q \xrightarrow{a} Q_1$ and $Q \xrightarrow{u} Q_2$ then one of the following graph holds:

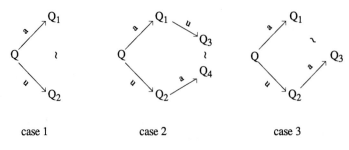

Figure 3.3

Notes:

- This definition defines a class of properties (one for each possible L); in particular τ can belong to L.
- We could have defined SLC without the third alternative; this notion would have been more restrictive and the obtained results would still be similar.
- Other confluence notions may be defined and are useful in calculi using interleaving semantics. For instance, we can see by the well known expansion theorem that P ≡ a.0 |∅ b.0 ~ Q ≡ a(0 |∅ b.0) + b.(a.0 |∅ 0). With this kind of semantics the summation operator does not 'really' express the choice between various alternatives but rather the possible interleaving of sequences. Therefore intuitively, this summation is confluent since the following diagram holds, where $Q_1 \equiv (0 \mid_\emptyset b.0)$, $Q_2 \equiv (a.0 \mid_\emptyset 0)$ and $Q_3 \equiv (0 \mid_\emptyset 0)$.

Figure 3.4

SLC has various nice properties; in particular we have the following

Proposition 3.6: [12]

If P is SLC and P $\overset{\sigma}{\to}$ P' for σ ∈ L* then P \L ≈ P' \L   □

Now to prove that if **Q** *Dist* P then P ≈^{c} ((|∅ Q) |$_L$ M) \L with

M ≡ fix X = $\Sigma_{p,q \in places,\ \sigma \in N^*}$ send_synchro!p!q!σ. (receive_synchro!p!q!σ.0 |∅ X)

several steps have still to be done.

At first it is easy to see that if M transmits a synchronization message, i.e.

$M \xrightarrow{\text{send\_synchro!p!q!}\sigma.\text{receive\_synchro!p!q!}\sigma} M'$ then $M' \sim M$.

Secondly, we have the following:

Proposition 3.7: [12]

If Q *Dist* P then $(|_\varnothing Q) |_L M$ is SLC.

Proof outline:

We construct a set which is closed under derivation and which contains all the agents $R \equiv (|_\varnothing R) |_L M$ which are a distribution of some agent.

If in addition for some agent R of this set we have $R \xrightarrow{a} R'$ and $R \xrightarrow{u} R''$ with $u \in L$ then one of the diagrams given in definition 3.5 must hold.

Intuitively this can be seen by two facts

1°) At any place, a subagent R_i can never receive a synchronization by two different ways (the synchronizations cannot be mixed). This is linked to proposition 3.3.

2°) Each send_synchro follows an action and each receive_synchro follows its corresponding send_synchro without possible alternative, this sequencing can never be cancelled.

□

This will allow us to forget the transmission of the synchronizations by firing them directly after the action which enables them.

Proposition 3.8: [12]

If Q *Dist* P then $P \approx^c ((|_\varnothing Q) |_L M) \setminus L$

Proof outline

If we prove that $S = \{ <P, ((|_\varnothing Q) |_L M) \setminus L> $ such that Q *Dist* $P\}$ is such that

$\forall <P, R> \in S, \forall a \in \mathcal{A}ct$:
   (i) $P \xrightarrow{a} P' \Rightarrow R \xRightarrow{a} R'$ with $P' S \approx R'$
   (ii) $R \xrightarrow{a} R' \Rightarrow P \xRightarrow{a} P'$ with $P' S \approx R'$

we can deduce ([15]) that S is a bisimulation up to $\approx$, hence $P \approx R$ ($\forall <P, R> \in S$). Moreover, this implies that $\forall <P, R> \in S$, $\approx$ is a rooted bisimulation w.r.t. $<P, R>$ and therefore [1] $P \approx^c R$.

The proof proceeds by transition induction, i.e. by induction on the length of the inference needed to infer the transition: the prefix case gives the initialisation case and the other form give the induction cases.

Let us e.g. prove that (i) is fulfilled in the prefix case. We suppose $P \equiv a.P' \xrightarrow{a} P'$ for some a and P'.

Then $R \equiv ((|_\emptyset\, Q) \,|_L\, M) \setminus L$ with $Q = <Q^1, Q^2, ..., Q^n>$ and by definition of *Dist*,
for $i = p(a)$, $Q^i \equiv a.\text{send\_synchro}!p(a)!j!\sigma....Q'^i$
for $j \in p(First(P'))$, $Q^j \equiv \text{receive\_synchro}!p(a)!j!\sigma.Q'^j$
for the other places k: $Q^k \equiv Q'^k$
such that P' *Dist* $\mathbf{Q'}$.
Then $R \xrightarrow{a} R' \xrightarrow{\tau(\text{send\_synchro}!p(a)!j!\sigma)} ... \xrightarrow{\tau(\text{receive\_synchro}!p(a)!j!\sigma)} R''$ with by 3.7 and 3.6,
$R' \approx R''$ and $R'' \sim R^3 \equiv ((|_\emptyset\, \mathbf{Q'}) \,|_L\, M) \setminus L$ with $\mathbf{Q'}$ *Dist* P'.

□

4 Example

Let us illustrate our transformation by distributing the example given in figure 2.1 where we suppose that actions g and c occur at place 1 and actions a and b at place 2.

To make it easier to understand let us only index the prefixes (actions) of the indexed agent given by the unfolding and denote the prefix $<a.E, \sigma>$ by $^\sigma a.E$.

We can see that $Q \sim Q' \equiv U(Q, \varepsilon) \equiv \text{fix}_1 <P_{\sigma x1} = E_{\sigma x1}>_{\sigma \in N^*}$ with

$E_{\sigma x1} \equiv \quad \sum_{n>0} <^{\sigma x n}g_n.\, ^{\sigma x n}b_n.\, (^{\sigma x n x 1}c.\, \mathbf{0} \,|_{\{c\}}\, ^{\sigma x n x 2}c.\, \mathbf{0})>$
$\qquad \cup \quad \sum_{n \leq 0} <^{\sigma x n}g_n.\, ^{\sigma x n}a_n.\, ^{\sigma x n}P_{\sigma x n x 1}>$

Then the corresponding distributed subagents are given by the following:

$Q_1 \equiv \text{fix}_1 <P_{\sigma x1} = E^1_{\sigma x1}>_{\sigma \in N^*}$, $\quad Q_2 \equiv \text{fix}_1 <P_{\sigma x1} = E^2_{\sigma x1}>_{\sigma \in N^*}$, with

$E^1_{\sigma x1} \equiv \quad \sum_{n>0} <g_n.\, \text{send\_synchro}!1!2!\sigma xn.\, \text{receive\_synchro}!2!1!\sigma xn.\, (c.\mathbf{0} \,|_{\{c\}}\, c.\mathbf{0})>$
$\qquad \cup \sum_{n \leq 0} <g_n.\, \text{send\_synchro}!1!2!\sigma xn.\, \text{receive\_synchro}!2!1!\sigma xn.\, P_{\sigma x n x 1}>$

$E^2_{\sigma x1} \equiv \quad \sum_{n>0} <\text{receive\_synchro}!1!2!\sigma xn.\, b_n.\, \text{send\_synchro}!2!1!\sigma xn.\, (\mathbf{0} \,|_{\{c\}}\, \mathbf{0})>$
$\qquad \cup \sum_{n \leq 0} <\text{receive\_synchro}!1!2!\sigma xn.\, a_n.\, \text{send\_synchro}!2!1!\sigma xn.\, P_{\sigma x n x 1}>$

where $Q \approx^c ((Q_1 \,|_\emptyset\, Q_2) \,|_{\{\text{send\_synchro,receive\_synchro}\}}\, M) \setminus \{\text{send\_synchro,receive\_synchro}\}$

It may be seen that Q_1 and Q_2 correspond e.g. resp. to the following simplified LOTOS processes (where a sort Natstring has been defined to represent strings of naturals):

Process P_1 [g,c,send_synchro,receive_synchro] (s:Natstring) *noexit* :=
   g?n:Nat;([n gt 0] -> send_synchro!1!2!s*x*n; receive_synchro!2!1!s*x*n; (c;*stop* |[c]| c;*stop*)
        [] [n le 0] -> send_synchro!1!2!s*x*n; receive_synchro!2!1!s*x*n;
                P_1[g,c,send_synchro,receive_synchro] (s*x*n))
endproc

Process P$_2$ [a,b,send_synchro,receive_synchro] (s:Natstring) *noexit* :=
   choice n:Nat[] ([n gt 0]-> receive_synchro!1!2!s$_x$n; b!n; send_synchro!2!1!s$_x$n; (*stop* |[c]| *stop*)
        [] [n le 0] -> receive_synchro!1!2!s$_x$n; a!n; send_synchro!2!1!s$_x$n;
                 P$_2$[a,b,send_synchro,receive_synchro] (s$_x$n))
endproc

Note: it is important to notice that during the "execution" of the system, the length of the identifier in the transmissions grows due to the choice and composition operators, but not due to the recursion.

5 Conclusion

We have presented a basic agent calculus which uses simple actions and a restricted number of operators. We have shown that a mapping between LOTOS and our calculus could be achieved; in particular, the LOTOS enabling and disabling operators are derived operators of this calculus [10, 11].

This calculus is used to model compositional transformations of agents and it provides a good basis for proving the correctness of such transformations. We have illustrated our approach by the resolution of the following distribution problem: given an agent P for which we know the *place* (localization) of each action, find a set of subagents (one for each place) such that the interleaved composition of the subagents synchronized using a reliable medium, gives a 'distributed' agent Q equal to the initial agent P. We have also shown that the definition of such compositional transformations is possible by the use of inference systems (as the one defined for *Dist*). These transformations preserve some of the structure of the initial agents.

We are conviced that it may be possible to 'map' such correct transformations to LOTOS to finally obtain correct refinements transforming LOTOS specifications to refined LOTOS specifications. It would also be possible to build tools to perform automatically these transformations.

Aknowledgments

The author would like to express its gratitude to Paul Van Binst the head of the Helios-B group, to Raymond Devillers the director of his thesis, to anonymous referees for their pertinent advises and to Michael Leuschel who has improved a preceding version of this paper.

References

1   J.C.M. Baeten, *Processalgebra*, (Kluwer, Deventer), 1986.
2   G.v. Bochmann, R. Gotzhein, *Deriving protocol specifications from service specifications*, in: Proceedings of the ACM SIGCOMM '86 Symposium, Vermont, USA, 1986.
3   E. Brinksma, *On the design of extended LOTOS (A Specification Language for Open Distributed Systems)*, Doctoral Dissertation, University of Twente, 1988.
4   R. Gotzhein, G.v. Bochmann, *Deriving protocol specifications from service specifications: an extended algorithm*, to be published in ACM TOPLAS, 1990.
5   ISO, *Information Processing Systems, Open Systems Interconnection, LOTOS, A Formal Description Technique Based on the Temporal Ordering Of Observation Behaviour*, IS 8807, 1988.
6   R. Keller, *Formal Verification of Parallel Programs*, CACM 19, pp371-384, 1976.

7   R. Langerak, *Decomposition of functionality: a correctness preserving LOTOS transformation*, in: L. Logrippo, R.L. Probert, H. Ural (eds.), Proceedings of the IFIP WG 6.1 Workshop 'Protocol Specification, Testing, and Verification, X', North-Holland, Amsterdam, 1990.
8   G. Leduc, *On the Role of Implementation relations in the design of Distributed Systems using LOTOS*, Doctoral dissertation of the Université de Liège, 1990.
9   T. Bolognesi, P. Boehm, A. Fantechi, E. Najm (eds.), *Correctness Preserving Transformation*, First deliverable of Task 1.2 of the Esprit Project 2304: LOTOSHERE, reference Lo/WP1/T1.2/n0020, April 1990.
10 T. Massart, *A Basic Agent Calculus and Bisimulation Laws for the Design of Systems*, Doctoral Dissertation, University of Brussels, 1990.
11 T.Massart, *A Basic Agent Calculus for the LOTOS Specification Language*, internal report ULB-LIT no 236 , 1991.
12 T.Massart, *An equality preserving distribution of agents*, internal report ULB-LIT no 240 , 1991.
13 T.Massart, *An agent calculus with simple actions where the enabling and disabling are derived operators*, to appear in Information Processing Letters.
14 T. Massart, R. Devillers, *Agents or Expressions: which Semantics for a Process Calculus*, Internal Report of The Laboratoire d'Informatique Théorique, no 230, University of Brussels, March 1991.
15 R. Milner, *Communication and Concurrency*, Prentice-Hall International, 1989.
16 D. Park, *Concurrency and Automata on Infinite Sequences*, Proc. 5th GI Conference, LNCS 104, Springer-Verlag, Berlin, 1981.
17 K.J. Turner, *A LOTOS-Based development Strategy*, in: S.T. Vuong (ed.), Proceedings of the 2nd International Conference 'FORTE'89 on Formal Description Techniques', North-Holland, Amsterdam, 1990.

Inverse Expansion [1]

S. Pavón[a]   M. Hultström[a]   J. Quemada[a]   D. de Frutos[b]   Y. Ortega[b]

[a] Departamento de Ingeniería de Sistemas Telemáticos, ETSI Telecomunicación, Universidad Politécnica de Madrid E-28040 MADRID SPAIN

[b] Departamento de Informática y Automática, Facultad de Ciencias Exactas, Universidad Complutense de Madrid, E-28040 MADRID SPAIN

Abstract

This article presents two algorithms for transforming a monolithic LOTOS behaviour into two processes composed by the parallel operator. These algorithms are particular cases of the overall concept *Inverse Expansion*, which is based on the inversion of the so-called *Expansion Theorem*. The transformations presented in this article maintain the observational equivalence. The main interest of these transformations is that they keep the parallelism of the original behaviour and make it explicit. The *Inverse Expansion* has several applications, like the decomposition of functionality, modularization, synthesizing of protocols, decomposition of tests, etc...

1 Introduction

In the design of complex systems it is highly desirable to use a top-down approach based on stepwise refinement, as it allows an incremental construction of the system. This design approach consists of a sequence of design steps, starting with the most abstract description of the system and ending with the actual system.

LOTOS [1] allows the formalization of the former design process [2], where the design step can be seen as a transformation of the specification produced in the previous step into a new, more refined, one. The designer must decide which transformation will be applied in each step, so that the requirements will be maintained during all the design process.

Correctness preserving transformations [3] can help the designer along the design trajectory. These transformations preserve the correctness of each new refinement, as they maintain some equivalence relation with the previous refinement. This article describes such a transformation with application in the design by stepwise refinement using LOTOS.

---

[1] This work was supported in part by the CEC within ESPRIT project 2304 LOTOSPHERE and by the Spanish National Research Programme on Information Technology & Communications within project MEDAS.

The general transformation is called *Inverse Expansion*, which is based on the inversion of the *Expansion Theorem* [1].

By *Inverse Expansion* we mean a set of correctness preserving transformations whose target is to decompose a LOTOS behaviour into a parallel composition of several sub-behaviours. The *Inverse Expansion* is related to other transformations described in the literature, such as the decomposition of functionality [4] [5] [6] or the protocol synthesis [7] [8] [9]. The main contribution of the *Inverse Expansion* with respect to the former algorithms, is that the potential parallelism executing in a specification is made explicit. The former algorithms achieve a very low degree of parallelism.

In this article two *Inverse Expansion* transformations are presented: the *Pure Interleaving Decomposition* and the *Visible Communication Decomposition*. They decompose a monolithic LOTOS behaviour into a parallel composition of two sub-behaviours. We also present the algorithms to implement these transformations. They have a reasonable complexity and will be performed by LOLA [10] in the future. The presented algorithms find solutions which are observational equivalent with the original behaviours. The solutions are also intuitively minimal in size. The transformations are restricted to the decomposition of one behaviour into two, but consecutive applications will allow to decompose it further.

The *Inverse Expansion* transformations presented cannot always be applied. For example, a behaviour may only be decomposed in pure interleaving if, in fact, the behaviour *results* from the composition in interleaving of two sub-behaviours. It must be analysed if the chosen decomposition can be applied to the overall behaviour before actually doing the decomposition. A general solution would imply the creation of hidden events which are strategically located in the specification to be decomposed, such that the resulting behaviours keeps its maximum potential parallelism.

The most relevant feature of these transformations is that they maintain all the parallelism existing in the original behaviours, and moreover make it explicit. They make a global analysis of the states and transitions of the behaviour to be decomposed. This analysis allows us to obtain a decomposition that keeps the existing parallelism.

The inverse expansion has many practical applications as for example, the decomposition of the specification in parts that adjust to the resources in the system, the derivation of the specification of a protocol from its service specification, modularization, the decomposition of a global tester in an *upper* and a *lower* test, etc.

The rest of the paper is organized as follows. Section 2 gives a general description of the transformations and further explains the concept *Inverse Expansion*. In section 3 we define the language (subset of LOTOS) used by the transformations. Section 4 presents the decomposition of a behaviour into two interleaving sub-behaviours. Section 5 describes the decomposition into two subbehaviours which evolve in interleaving and synchronize on their common actions. In section 6 a first approach to treat recursive behaviours is presented. Section 7 presents studies related with the concept *Inverse Expansion* and give conclusions and directions for further work. Finally in appendixes A and B the consistency and completeness of the algorithms presented in this paper are proved.

2 Description of the transformations

The transformations presented here impose some restrictions to the behaviours to be decomposed. They must be specified in a monolithic style [11], i.e. the behaviour will be expressed as alternatives of action prefixes and *stops*. These transformations are also limited to finitely branching, concrete, sequential behaviours [12]. This means that in each state the number of choices are finite, only one action is performed at the same time and the behaviours do not contain internal actions. Moreover in this version the behaviours must not be recursive. However, to deal with recursive behaviours does not seems difficult and a first approach can be found in section 6.

The behaviour to be decomposed can be described as follows:

$$B = \sum_{i \in I} a_i \, ; \, B_i$$

where each B_i is either the instantiation of a behaviour/process or alternatives of several action prefixes and *stops* (as B). By $\sum_{i=1}^{n} P_i$ we mean $P_1[\ ]P_2[\ ]...[\ ]P_n$.

The *Inverse Expansion* presented in this article can be formulated as:

$$B[A_0] = B_1[A_1] \, |[A]| \, B_2[A_2]$$

where $B[A_0]$ is the behaviour to be decomposed, $B_1[A_1]$ and $B_2[A_2]$ are the sub-behaviours we wish to generate and A is the set of actions on which B_1 and B_2 synchronize.

There are several degrees of freedom in the previous equation. The type of decomposition obtained depends on the sets A, A_1, and A_2. We impose the following restrictions on the gate sets: $A_0 = A_1 \cup A_2$ (all initial gates are present and no new gates are introduced) and $A = A_1 \cap A_2$ (all of the common gates are synchronization gates).

We will study two solutions to this decomposition problem:

Pure interleaving   Visible Communication

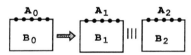 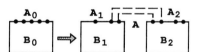

Given $B[A_0]$, A_1 and A_2 decompose such that $B[A_0] = B_1[A_1] \, ||| \, B_2[A_2]$, where $A_1 \cap A_2 = \emptyset$.

Given $B[A_0]$, A_1 and A_2 decompose such that $B[A_0] = B_1[A_1] \, |[A]| \, B_2[A_2]$, where $A = A_1 \cap A_2$.

The *pure interleaving* case is actually a particular case of the second case, however we think that this serves as a good introduction before dealing with the more complex transformation.

The inputs for the transformations are the behaviour $B[A_0]$ to be decomposed and the sets A_1 and A_2 assigned to each sub-behaviour.

3 The Language

This transformation has been developed for a subset of LOTOS, but would be applicable with slight changes, to any formal language based on labelled transition systems. In this version data types are not supported and the operators that are treated are *stop*, *action prefix*, *parallel* and *alternative*. The corresponding sublanguage of LOTOS can formally be defined in the following way:

constant operator	stop	$\rightarrow P$
action prefix operator	;	$L \times P \rightarrow P$
alternative operator	[ ]	$P \times P \rightarrow P$
parallel operator	|[ ]|	$P \times P(L) \times P \rightarrow P$

where P is the set of processes, L is the set of the visible actions, and $P(L)$ is the powerset of L. The parallel operator will be renamed to $|||$ for the case of pure interleaving. The axioms and the derivation rules are:

- **Action prefix:** $\qquad a; P - a \rightarrow P$

- **Alternative:** $\qquad \dfrac{P_1 - a \rightarrow P'_1}{P_1[\ ]P_2 - a \rightarrow P'_1} \qquad \dfrac{P_2 - a \rightarrow P'_2}{P_1[\ ]P_2 - a \rightarrow P'_2}$

- **Parallel:** $\qquad \dfrac{P_1 - a \rightarrow P'_1,\ P_2 - a \rightarrow P'_2,\ a \in A}{P_1|[A]|P_2 - a \rightarrow P'_1|[A]|P'_2}$

$$\dfrac{P_1 - a \rightarrow P'_1,\ a \notin A}{P_1|[A]|P_2 - a \rightarrow P'_1|[A]|P_2} \qquad \dfrac{P_2 - a \rightarrow P'_2,\ a \notin A}{P_1|[A]|P_2 - a \rightarrow P_1|[A]|P'_2}$$

4 Pure Interleaving Decomposition

In this section we will present a transformation to decompose a behaviour into two sub-behaviours composed in pure interleaving.

This decomposition can be described by: Given the behaviour $B[A_0]$ and the gate sets A_1 and A_2, decompose it into $B_1[A_1]$ and $B_2[A_2]$ such as $B_1[A_1] \ ||| \ B_2[A_2]$ will be observational equivalent with B, where $A_0 = A_1 \cup A_2$ and $A_1 \cap A_2 = \emptyset$. The restrictions on the behaviour to be decomposed are that no internal actions may be present and the behaviour must not be recursive.

Not every behaviour can be decomposed as previously described. Thus a boolean function *IsPar* is defined, which by studying the structure of the behaviour will decide if it is decomposable in this way or not.

The behaviour to be decomposed may offer in each state actions belonging to the first sub-behaviour and actions belonging to the second. However, the execution of these actions is not causally related, so the actions offered by one sub-behaviour will not affect the other sub-behaviour in any sense. Both sub-behaviours will evolve freely without any interactions between them. *IsPar* will analyse in each state and for all possible transitions that the evolution of each sub-behaviour does not affect the other. It checks that the set of actions offered by one of the sub-behaviours does not change if the other sub-behaviour produces an action.

The definition of *IsPar* is:

$$IsPar(A_1, A_2, B) =$$
$$\forall i \in I \qquad IsPar(A_1, A_2, B_i)$$
$$\text{and} \quad \forall i \in I \mid a_i \in A_1 \quad Rest(B, A_2) = Rest(B_i, A_2)$$
$$\text{and} \quad \forall i \in I \mid a_i \in A_2 \quad Rest(B, A_1) = Rest(B_i, A_1)$$
$$IsPar(A_1, A_2, stop) = true$$

where $B = \sum_{i \in I} a_i ; B_i$.

IsPar uses the restriction function *Rest*. For a given behaviour B, *Rest* extracts the traces beginning with actions of the sub-behaviour we want to generate. In these traces, the parts starting with an action of the other sub-behaviour are eliminated. Its definition is:

$$Rest(B, A_1) = \sum_{i \in I, a_i \in A_1} a_i; Rest(B_i, A_1)$$

where $B = \sum_{i \in I} a_i ; B_i$. A_1 is the gate set of the behaviour we wish to extract.

To conclude, the decomposition of a behaviour B into two interleaving sub-behaviours will only be possible if the function *IsPar* is satisfied, and the sub-behaviours will be $B_1[A_1] = Rest(B, A_1)$ and $B_2[A_2] = Rest(B, A_2)$.

Example: The decomposition of the behaviour B such as $A_1 = \{a, b\}$ and $A_2 = \{c, d\}$ is:

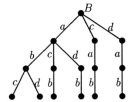

5 Visible Communication Decomposition

In this section we will present a transformation to decompose a monolithic behaviour into two sub-behaviours, which jointly evolve with visible communication.

The decomposition can be described by: Given the decomposable behaviour $B[A_0]$ and the sets of gates A_1 and A_2, decompose $B[A_0]$ into $B_1[A_1]$ and $B_2[A_2]$ such as $B[A_1] \ |[A]| \ B[A_2]$ is observational equivalent with $B[A_0]$, where $A_0 = A_1 \cup A_2$ and $A = A_1 \cap A_2$. The restrictions imposed are that B must not contain any internal events, nor any recursivity and it must be deterministic.

First we will develop a function to decompose the behaviour of $B[A_0]$ as described above. This function will only generate the right decomposition if it is possible to decompose the overall behaviour. In the subsection 5.2 we will develop a predicate which analyses if the behaviour $B[A_0]$ can indeed be transformed into $B_1[A_1] \ |[A]| \ B_2[A_2]$.

5.1 Decomposition

Two sub-behaviours composed in parallel may evolve in two ways:

1. In interleaving, when one of the sub-behaviours can produce an event in which the other does not need to synchronize.
2. With synchronization, when both sub-behaviours offer an event on which they synchronize and evolve at the same time.

These two types of evolutions are mixed in the overall behaviour $B[A_0]$. The function *Rest*, defined in the previous section, will not work for the visible communication decomposition. Synchronization events that only are present after interleaving actions will not be extracted by *Rest*.

For example, if we decompose the following behaviour B, using the function *Rest*, such that $A_1 = \{a, c_1, c_2\}$, $A_2 = \{c_1, c_2\}$ and $A = \{c_1, c_2\}$, we obtain:

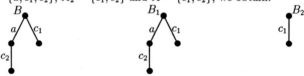

B_1 is a correct decomposition, due to that no new synchronization events are present after interleaving actions of B_2. However, B_2 is not a correct decomposition — we have lost the synchronization event c_2 which exists after the interleaving event of B_1. The correct decomposition for B_2 should include a choice of the event c_2. Thus, we define a new decomposition function, called *Decomp*, which takes the behaviour to be decomposed and the sets A_1 and A_2 as inputs, and depending on the order of the parameters yields B_1 or B_2. The definition of the decomposition function is:

$$Decomp(B, A_1, A_2) \;=\; DE(\; Rest'(B, A_1, A_2)\;)$$

The definition of DE is:
$$DE(B) = \sum_{j \in J} a'_j \;;\; B'_j$$

where:
$B = \sum_{i \in I} a_i \;;\; B_i$
$\forall i \in I, \exists j \in J \mid a_i = a'_j$
$\forall k, l \in J, k \neq l \Rightarrow a'_k \neq a'_l$
$\forall j \in J, B'_j = DE(\sum_{k \in K_j} B_k) \mid K_j = \{i \mid i \in I, a_i = a'_j\}$

and the definition of the function $Rest'$ is:

$$\begin{aligned}
Rest'(B, A_1, A_2) &= \sum_{i \in I, a_i \in A_1} a_i; Rest'(B_i, A_1, A_2) \\
&[\,] \sum_{i \in I, a_i \in A_2 - A_1} Sync(B_i, A_1, A_2) \\
Rest'(stop, A_1, A_2) &= stop \\
Sync(B, A_1, A_2) &= \sum_{i \in I, a_i \in A_1 \cap A_2} a_i; Rest'(B_i, A_1, A_2) \\
&[\,] \sum_{i \in I, a_i \in A_2 - A_1} Sync(B_i, A_1, A_2) \\
Sync(stop, A_1, A_2) &= stop
\end{aligned}$$

where: $B = \sum_{i \in I} a_i \;;\; B_i$.

The function $Rest'$ looks similar to the old decomposition function $Rest$. The only difference is that an auxiliary function, $Sync$, is needed for extracting the special synchronization events mentioned above, and that both gate sets are needed as input. The definition of the function $Rest'$ is divided in two parts:

- The first part corresponds to the old $Rest$ — i.e. it extracts the actions directly performed by the chosen sub-behaviour.

- The second part calls the function $Sync$ after the interleaving events performed by the other sub-behaviour.

The behaviour obtained from the function $Rest'$ may be non-deterministic. This arises from the function $Sync$, which extracts the synchronization events that may be performed after interleaving actions of the other sub-behaviour — these cannot be found anywhere else. However, $Sync$ has no possibility to differentiate between how many times the same synchronization event has been extracted. Thus, this event may be extracted more than once producing false non-determinism.

For example, if we only use $Rest'$ for the decomposition of the following behaviour B such that $A_1 = \{a,c\}$, $A_2 = \{c\}$ and $A = \{c\}$

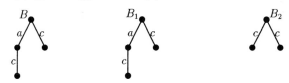

we obtain the above behaviours B_1 and B_2. The behaviour B_2 is non-deterministic, due to the fact that the c event is extracted by both the first and the second term of $Rest'$. The correct behaviour of B_2 is c ; $stop$, and the c action will synchronize with both c's of B_1.

The function DE will remove this false non-determinism obtained by $Rest'$. DE takes a behaviour B, and for each depth in the tree unifies the non-deterministic possibilities of one event to one transition. The behaviour obtained after applying DE will be trace equivalent with the original one.

Thus, if we know that the overall behaviour B is decomposable, then it can be decomposed into: $B_1[A_1] = Decomp(B, A_1, A_2)$ and $B_2[A_2] = Decomp(B, A_2, A_1)$.

Given a decomposable behaviour, $Decomp$ will find one B_1 and one B_2 of an infinite number of solutions (if $A \neq \emptyset$). For example, $Decomp$ decomposes the following behaviour as B_1 and B_2, where $A_1 = \{a, c_1, c_2\}$, $A_2 = \{b, c_1, c_2\}$, $A = \{c_1, c_2\}$: :

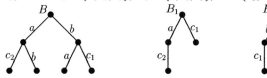

However, another decomposition could be:

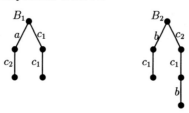

The other solutions are extensions of the decomposition produced by *Decomp*. They includes collections of branches beginning with synchronizations that are not feasible, i.e. B_1 and B_2 will never synchronize on these events.

Given a behaviour $B = B_1[A_1]|[A_1 \cap A_2]|B_2[A_2]$ and applying *Decomp* will give us a minimal solution. This minimal solution does not include unfeasible traces. Let $Min_{B_2}(B_1)$ denote the minimal behaviour of B_1 w.r.t. B_2, and similar for the minimal behaviour of B_2. We will define *Min* using trace semantics as our behaviours are deterministic.

Definition 1 (Synchronization actions of a trace) *Let A be the set of synchronization actions and let $\bar{A}$ be its complement (i.e. the set of interleaving actions). We define the synchronization actions of a trace $\sigma c \omega$, where $\sigma \in \bar{A}^*$, $c \in A^*$, $\omega \in (A \cup \bar{A})^*$, to be:*

$$S_A(\sigma c \omega) = \begin{cases} c\, S_A(\omega) & \text{if } c \neq \epsilon \\ \epsilon & \text{otherwise} \end{cases}$$

Definition 2 (Unfeasible traces) *Let A be the synchronization set of the behaviour B_1 and B_2 ($B_1|[A]|B_2$). Let $\alpha \in tr(B_1)$, then α is an unfeasible trace of B_1 w.r.t. B_2, iff $\neg \exists \beta \in tr(B_2)$ such as $S_A(\alpha) = S_A(\beta)$.*

Thus, $tr(Min_{B_2}(B_1)) = tr(B_1) - \mathcal{UT}_{B_2}(B_1)$, where $\mathcal{UT}_{B_2}(B_1)$ denotes the set of unfeasible traces of B_1 w.r.t. B_2, and vice versa for B_2.

5.2 Detection

As mentioned before, not every behaviour can be decomposed with only visible communication. We have developed a predicate *Decomposable* that will decide for a given behaviour B and the two subsets A_1 and A_2 if a visible communication decomposition is possible.

Let B_1 denote the result from $Decomp(B, A_1, A_2)$ and let B_2 denote the result from $Decomp(B, A_2, A_1)$. If the composition $B_1\ |[A]|\ B_2$ is not equal to original behaviour B, then the behaviour is *not* decomposable. This will hold if we are able to prove that given a decomposable behaviour our decomposition algorithm will yield a correct decomposition, this proof is included in the appendix B.

Decomposable is based on the definitions of the parallel composition and the fact that for deterministic behaviour observational equivalence is the same as trace equivalence. *Decomposable* takes as input the overall behaviour B and the sets A_1 and A_2.

Decomposable calculates the sub-behaviours obtained from the decomposition function and compares them with the original behaviour B. Comparison means checking that all the events offered in each state of B are also offered by the associated states of B_1 and B_2 and the other way round.

The definition of *Decomposable* is:

$$Decomposable(B, A_1, A_2) = Comp(B, Decomp(B, A_2, A_1), Decomp(B, A_1, A_2), A_1 \cap A_2)$$

where $B = \sum_{i \in I} a_i ; B_i$.

and the definition of *Comp* is:

$Comp(B, B_1, B_2, A) =$
$\quad \forall i \in I \mid a_i \in A, \exists j \in J, k \in K \qquad a_i = a_j = a_k \land Comp(B_i, B_{1j}, B_{2k}, A)$
$\quad$ and $\forall j \in J, k \in K \mid a_j = a_k, a_j, a_k \in A, \exists i \in I \quad a_i = a_j$
$\quad$ and $\forall i \in I \mid a_i \notin A, \exists j \in J \qquad\qquad\qquad a_i = a_j \quad \land Comp(B_i, B_{1j}, B_2, A)$
$\quad$ and $\forall j \in J \mid a_j \notin A, \exists i \in I \qquad\qquad\qquad a_i = a_j$
$\quad$ and $\forall i \in I \mid a_i \notin A, \exists k \in K \qquad\qquad\qquad a_i = a_k \quad \land Comp(B_i, B_1, B_{2k}, A)$
$\quad$ and $\forall k \in K \mid a_k \notin A, \exists i \in I \qquad\qquad\qquad a_i = a_k$
$Comp(stop, stop, stop, A) = true$

where $B_1 = \sum_{j \in J} a_j ; B_{1j}$ and $B_2 = \sum_{k \in K} a_k ; B_{2k}$.

The predicate $Decomposable(B, A_1, A_2)$ will be *true* if the overall behaviour is decomposable, if not it will be *false*.

6 Recursive Behaviours

As presented before, this version does not deal with recursive behaviours. However the transformations can easily be extended to manage recursive behaviours. We only have to consider where the recursive behaviours are situated. However, the solutions obtained may not be minimal in size. If this is to be accomplished, the original behaviour B ought to be minimized first. This type of algorithms can, for instance, be found in [13]. For example the decomposition of the next behaviour B such as $A_1 = \{a, b, d\}$ and $A_2 = \{b, c\}$ should generate the following B_1 and B_2:

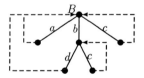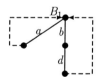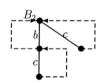

7 Conclusions and other works

In this paper we have presented two methods for decomposing a given behaviour into two sub-behaviours, one more general – for synchronization and interleaving – and one particular for the pure interleaving case. These transformations are specific cases of the general transformation technique which we call *Inverse Expansion*. We have proved the completeness and consistency of the two algorithms, and showed that observational equivalence is maintained between the original behaviour and the transformed behaviour. The main interest with the presented transformations is that they maintain the original parallelism and make it explicit.

This work can be extended in several directions. First of all, the limitations of the behaviours should be removed, for example we ought to be able to treat recursive and non-deterministic behaviours. The decomposition of recursive behaviours is easy to add, as can be seen in subsection 6. To treat non-deterministic behaviours is a more complex task which is under study. The algorithms should also be able to deal with full LOTOS, treatment of data types, etc... There is also a need for a more general algorithm that can decompose all kinds of behaviour and at the same time maintain the existing parallelism. This algorithm is a further elaboration of the transformations presented here, augmented with an algorithm that introduces internal synchronization events only in necessary places.

This work is a further elaboration of the similar algorithms presented in [4]. To our knowledge there do not exist any other work on *Inverse Expansion* with the point of view presented in this article. However, there are works on the *Inverse Expansion* with internal synchronization events added, but which do not maintain the existing parallelism. This type of algorithm can be found in [4], where a more general definition is presented, due to that a wider domain is treated: $B[A_0] = \textbf{hide} \ A_I \ \textbf{in} \ B_1[A_1] \ |[A_S]| \ B_2[A_2]$ where A_I are synchronization events introduced during the decomposition. And further in:

- [5] presents a method for deriving two distributed test sequences from a general test sequence specified in the monolithic style. It consists of decomposing a Local tester in a Lower and an Upper test by means of introducing synchronization events. The equivalence maintained between the general specification and the two parts in this paper is trace equivalence. The existing parallelism is not kept.

- [6] contains algorithms of different complexity for decomposing a LOTOS process into two subprocesses. The interaction between the two subprocesses is either synchronous or asynchronous communication. These algorithms maintain the observational equivalence, but do not keep the already present parallelism.

- In [7] it is presented an algorithm for obtaining an arbitrary number of protocol entities from a given service specification via introducing synchronization events. The overall behaviour is restricted to only include choices between events of the same protocol entity and the present parallelism is not kept.

Another type of transformations is based on protocol synthesizing. The idea here is to find one missing submodule specification, which together with the already specified submodules preserves some equivalence relation with the general specification. Some examples of this idea can be found in:

- In [8] this idea is developed based on finite-state machines. The algorithm presented in this paper finds the most general specification for the missing submodule . It is based on trace equivalence.

- In [9] this idea is based on CCS and on a procedure for solving equations on the form: $(A|X)L = B$, where X is the unknown submodule, A are the known submodules, L is the known channels over which the submodules communicates and B is the given specification. The obtained submodule is a result of automatic transformations and guidance of the user. Observational equivalence is maintained between the given specification and the composition of the submodules.

A Pure Interleaving Decomposition Proof

We will prove that the decomposition algorithm defined in section 4 is consistent (theorem 1) and complete (theorem 2). The relation maintained by this transformation is the observational equivalence.

Theorem 1 *If a behaviour* $B[A_0] = \sum_{i \in I} a_i$; B_i *satisfies* Ispar *then it can be decomposed as* $B_1[A_1] \;|||\; B_2[A_2]$ *where*

$$B_1 = Rest(B, A_1) = \sum_{i \in I, a_i \in A_1} a_i; Rest(B_i, A_1)$$
$$B_2 = Rest(B, A_2) = \sum_{i \in I, a_i \in A_2} a_i; Rest(B_i, A_2)$$
$$A_1 \cap A_2 = \emptyset$$
$$A_0 = A_1 \cup A_2$$

Proof: By induction on the depth of the behaviour B: The base of the induction corresponds to the case in which B is *stop*:

$$B[A_0] = stop \quad Rest(B, A_1) \;|||\; Rest(B, A_2) = stop \;|||\; stop = stop$$

As $B[A_0]$ satisfies *IsPar*, then the following properties are held:

$$\forall\, i \in I \mid a_i \in A_1 \quad Rest(B, A_2) = Rest(B_i, A_2) \qquad (1)$$
$$\forall\, i \in I \mid a_i \in A_2 \quad Rest(B, A_1) = Rest(B_i, A_1) \qquad (2)$$

So: $\quad B_1 \;|||\; B_2 = \quad Rest(B, A_1) \;|||\; Rest(B, A_2) \qquad$ (expansion)
$$= \sum_{i \in I, a_i \in A_1} a_i; (Rest(B_i, A_1) ||| Rest(B, A_2))$$
$$[\,] \sum_{i \in I, a_i \in A_2} a_i; (Rest(B, A_1) ||| Rest(B_i, A_2)) \quad \text{(equations 1 and 2)}$$
$$= \sum_{i \in I, a_i \in A_1} a_i; (Rest(B_i, A_1) ||| Rest(B_i, A_2))$$
$$[\,] \sum_{i \in I, a_i \in A_2} a_i; (Rest(B_i, A_1) ||| Rest(B_i, A_2)) \quad \text{(induction hypothesis)}$$
$$= \sum_{i \in I, a_i \in A_1} a_i; (B_i)$$
$$[\,] \sum_{i \in I, a_i \in A_2} a_i; (B_i)$$
$$= \sum_{i \in I} a_i\,;\, B_i \;=\; B$$

Lemma 1 *Let $B_1[A_1] = \sum_{i \in I_1} a_i; B_i$ and $B_2[A_2] = \sum_{j \in I_2} a_j; B_j$ be two behaviours such as $A_1 \cap A_2 = \emptyset$. Then*
$$Rest(B_1[A_1] \;|||\; B_2[A_2], A_2) = B_2[A_2]$$

Proof: By induction on the depth of B_2: The base of the induction corresponds to the case in which B_2 is *stop*:

$$Rest(B_1 \;|||\; stop, A_2) = Rest(\sum_{i \in I_1} a_i \;;\; B_i \;|||\; stop, A_2) = stop$$

$Rest(B_1 \;|||\; B_2, A_2) = Rest(\sum_{i \in I_1} a_i \;;(B_i \;|||\; B_2) \;[\;] \sum_{j \in I_2} a_j \;;(B_1 \;|||\; B_j), A_2)$
$= \sum_{j \in I_2} a_j \;;\; Rest(B_1 \;|||\; B_j, A_2)$
(application of the induction hypothesis)
$= \sum_{j \in I_2} a_j \;;\; B_j \;=\; B_2$

Theorem 2 *Every behaviour that could be decomposed into two sub-behaviours composed in pure interleaving, i.e. that could be expressed like $B_1[A_1] \;|||\; B_2[A_2]$, satisfy IsPar.*

Proof: By induction on the depth of B_1 and B_2. The base of the induction corresponds to the case in which B_1 and B_2 are *stop*. It is immediate to prove.
Let $B_1[A_1] = \sum_{i \in I_1} a_i \;;\; B_i$ and $B_2[A_2] = \sum_{j \in I_2} a_j \;;\; B_j$. Then

$IsPar(A_1, A_2, B_1|||B_2) = IsPar(A_1, A_2, \sum_{i \in I_1} a_i;(B_i|||B_2)[\;]\sum_{j \in I_2} a_j;(B_1|||B_j))$
$\qquad = \quad \forall\; i \in I_1 \quad IsPar(A_1, A_2, B_i|||B_2)$
$\qquad \text{and } \forall\; j \in I_2 \quad IsPar(A_1, A_2, B_1|||B_j)$
$\qquad \text{and } \forall\; i \in I_1 \quad Rest(B_1|||B_2, A_2) = Rest(B_i|||B_2, A_2)$
$\qquad \text{and } \forall\; j \in I_2 \quad Rest(B_1|||B_2, A_1) = Rest(B_1|||B_j, A_1)$

The two first conditions are satisfied by the induction hypothesis and the two last conditions are satisfied by the lemma 1.
□ Theorems 1 and 2 prove that the Pure Interleaving decomposition algorithm is consistent and complete.

B Visible Communication Decomposition Proof

We will prove that the decomposition algorithm defined in section 5 is consistent (i.e. when *Decomposable* is satisfied the behaviour is indeed decomposable and *Decomp* will find a correct decomposition) and complete (i.e. *Decomposable* is satisfied for all decomposable behaviours).

Theorem 3 proves the correctness of the decomposition — given the decomposable behaviour B, *Decomp* will find two behaviours which composed in visible communication are observational equivalent with B.

From now on we use the notation $Rest_1(B)$ for $Rest'(B, A_2, A_1)$, and $Rest_2(B)$ for $Rest'(B, A_1, A_2)$.

Lemma 2 *Let $B[A_0]$ be a deterministic behaviour that can be decomposed into $B_1[A_1]$ and $B_2[A_2]$ such as $B = B_1|[A]|B_2$, $A = A_1 \cap A_2$. Then for any trace $\beta \in (A_2 - A_1)^*$ such that $\beta \in tr(Rest_2(B))$, and $a \in A_1 - A_2$:*

$$tr(Rest_2(B^{a\beta})) \subseteq tr(Rest_2(B^\beta))$$

Proof: By induction on length of β. The next figure synthesizes the application of $Rest_2$ to $B^{a\beta}$ and B^β, where $b \in A_2 - A_1$, $c, c' \in A_1 \cap A_2$, $\alpha \in (A_1 - A_2)^* \cap tr(B^{a\beta})$ and $\alpha' \in (A_1 - A_2)^* \cap tr(B^\beta)$.

There are three cases to study:

- **b:** If $b \in tr(Rest_2(B^{a\beta}))$ then it cannot be causally related to the execution of action a, and thus $b \in tr(Rest_2(B^\beta))$. Now we must only prove that $tr(Rest_2(B^{a\beta b})) \subseteq tr(Rest_2(B^{\beta b}))$, but this is just the induction hypothesis. The base of the induction corresponds to the case in which there is no such an action b.

- **c:** For any $c \in tr(B^{a\beta})$ (or $c \in tr(Rest_2(B^{a\beta}))$) we have $c \in tr(Rest_2(B^\beta))$ (or $a; c \in tr(B^\beta)$, $\alpha' = a$) and $tr(Rest_2(B^{a\beta c})) \subseteq tr(Rest_2(B^{\beta ac}))$ ($\alpha' = a$). The first fact is a consequence of the independence of the execution of a and β in B. Thus $B^{a\beta c}$ is equal to $B^{\beta ac}$ and $tr(Rest_2(B^{a\beta c})) = tr(Rest_2(B^{\beta ac}))$ ($\alpha' = a$).

- **c':** As in the previous case, if $\alpha c' \in tr(B^{a\beta})$ then $a\alpha c' \in tr(B^\beta)$, and $tr(Rest_2(B^{a\beta \alpha c'})) = tr(Rest_2(B^{\beta a\alpha c'}))$ ($\alpha' = a; \alpha$).

Lemma 3 *Let $B_1[A_1]$ be a deterministic behaviour, let $C_2[A_2]$ be the behaviour $\sum_{\forall a \in A_2} a; C_2$ (i.e. $tr(C_2) = A_2^*$ or $C_2 \xrightarrow{a} C_2$, $\forall a \in A_2$) and $A = A_1 \cap A_2$. Then*

$$tr(Rest_1(B_1|[A]|C_2)) = tr(B_1)$$

Proof: By induction on length of traces of B_1. Let $B_1[A_1] = \sum_{i \in I} a_i; B_i$. Then

$$\begin{aligned}
tr(Rest_1(B_1|[A]|C_2)) &= tr(\ \sum_{i \in I, a_i \in A_1} a_i; Rest_1(B_i|[A]|C_2) \\
&\qquad [\,] \\
&\qquad \sum_{\forall a \in A_2 - A_1} Sync(B_1|[A]|C_2, A_2, A_1)\ ) \\
&= tr(\sum_{i \in I} a_i; Rest_1(B_i|[A]|C_2) \\
&\qquad [\,] \\
&\qquad Sync(B_1|[A]|C_2, A_2, A_1)\ ) \\
&= tr(\sum_{i \in I} a_i; Rest_1(B_i|[A]|C_2)) \quad \text{(induction hypothesis)} \\
&= tr(B_1)
\end{aligned}$$

Note that the traces of $Sync(B_1|[A]|C_2, A_2, A_1)$ are $tr(\sum_{i \in I, a_i \in A_1 \cap A_2} a_i; Rest_1(B_i|[A]|C_2))$ plus the traces produced by $Sync(B_1|[A]|C_2, A_2, A_1)$, which are the same.

The base of the induction corresponds to the case in which B_1 is *stop*.

Theorem 3 *Let $B[A_0]$ be a deterministic behaviour that can be decomposed into $B_1[A_1]$ and $B_2[A_2]$ such as $B = B_1|[A]|B_2$, $A = A_1 \cap A_2$. Then*

$$B = Decomp(B, A_2, A_1)|[A]|Decomp(B, A_1, A_2)$$

Proof: First of all note that as B is deterministic we can also take B_1 and B_2 deterministic. Besides $Decomp(B, A_2, A_1)$ and $Decomp(B, A_1, A_2)$ are also deterministic, and thus their parallel composition is too. So we have to prove observational equivalence of two deterministic behaviours, but for this kind of behaviours the observational equivalence is just trace equivalence. Then we have to prove that $tr(B) = tr(Rest_1(B)|[A]|Rest_2(B))$.

$\subseteq$ $tr(B) \subseteq tr(Rest_1(B)|[A]|Rest_2(B))$.

We will prove this by induction on the length of the traces of B ($t \in tr(B)$).

If B does not offer any trace ($t = \varepsilon$) then everything is trivial. Otherwise the traces of B will be $t = a; t'$, and we can distinguish three cases:

1. $a \in A_1 - A_2$

   Since $B = B_1|[A]|B_2$, we have $B_1 \xrightarrow{a} B_1^a$ and $B \xrightarrow{a} B^a$, where $B^a = B_1^a|[A]|B_2$. On the other hand $Rest_1(B)|[A]|Rest_2(B) \xrightarrow{a} Rest_1(B^a)|[A]|Rest_2(B)$. Now by the induction hypothesis we have $tr(B^a) = tr(Rest_1(B^a)|[A]|Rest_2(B^a))$. Thus to end this part of the proof it would be enough to prove that $tr(Rest_2(B^a)) \subseteq tr(Rest_2(B))$. This is proved in lemma 2 for a empty β.

2. $a \in A_2 - A_1$

   Analogous to previous case just interchanging A_1 and A_2 all along the proof.

3. $a \in A_1 \cap A_2$

   Since $a \in A$ we have $B \xrightarrow{a} B_1^a|[A]|B_2^a = B^a$. On the other hand $Rest_1(B)|[A]|Rest_2(B) \xrightarrow{a} Rest_1(B^a)|[A]|Rest_2(B^a)$ and to conclude we only have to apply the induction hypothesis.

$\supseteq$ $tr(B) \supseteq tr(Rest_1(B)|[A]|Rest_2(B))$.

$$tr(Rest_1(B)|[A]|Rest_2(B)) =$$
$$tr(Rest_1(B_1|[A]|B_2)|[A]|Rest_2(B_1|[A]|B_2)) \subseteq$$
$$tr(Rest_1(B_1|[A]|C_2)|[A]|Rest_2(C_1|[A]|B_2)) = \qquad \text{(lemma 3)}$$
$$(1) = tr(B_1|[A]|B_2) = tr(B)$$

where C_1 and C_2 fulfil that $tr(C_1) = A_1^*$ and $tr(C_2) = A_2^*$.

$\square$ $Decomp(B, A_2, A_1)|[A]|Decomp(B, A_1, A_2)$

Let B be a decomposable behaviour and B_1 and B_2 its decomposition using $Decomp$. Their behaviour can be expressed as:

$$B = \sum_{i \in I, a_i \in A_1 - A_2} a_i\ ;\ B_i\ []\ \sum_{i \in I, a_i \in A_2 - A_1} a_i\ ;\ B_i\ []\ \sum_{i \in I, a_i \in A_1 \cap A_2} a_i\ ;\ B_i$$

$$B_1 = \sum_{j \in J, a_j \in A_1 - A_2} a_j\ ;\ B_j\ []\ \sum_{j \in J, a_j \in A_1 \cap A_2} a_j\ ;\ B_j$$

$$B_2 = \sum_{k \in K, a_k \in A_2 - A_1} a_k\ ;\ B_k\ []\ \sum_{k \in K, a_k \in A_1 \cap A_2} a_k\ ;\ B_k$$

Then, due to the properties of the parallel composition and the correctness proof, the following equations hold:

$$\sum_{a_i \in A_1 - A_2} a_i\ ;\ B_i\ =\ \sum_{a_j \in A_1 - A_2} a_j\ ;\ (\ B_j\ |[A_1 \cap A_2]|\ B_2\ ) \tag{3}$$

$$\sum_{a_i \in A_2 - A_1} a_i\ ;\ B_i\ =\ \sum_{a_k \in A_2 - A_1} a_k\ ;\ (\ B_k\ |[A_1 \cap A_2]|\ B_1\ ) \tag{4}$$

$$\sum_{a_i \in A_1 \cap A_2} a_i\ ;\ B_i\ =\ \sum_{a_{jk} \in a_j \cap a_k} a_{jk}\ ;\ (\ B_j\ |[A_1 \cap A_2]|\ B_k) \tag{5}$$

The consistency follows from the correctness proof and from that $Decomposable$ will never hold for a behaviour not decomposable. The last fact is demonstrated easily. Let B be a behaviour *not* decomposable and let B_1 and B_2 be the result of applying $Decomp$ on B. Then, according to that B is not decomposable and the correctness, we know that $B[A] \not\approx B[A_1]\ |[A_1 \cap A_2]|\ B[A_2]$. This means that at least one of the equations 3, 4 and 5 will not hold. By structural induction it is proved that for each equation that do not hold, $Decomposable$ will neither hold.

The completeness of the algorithm means that we will find *all* decomposable behaviors and decompose them. If the behaviour is decomposable then equation 3, 4 and 5 hold. Structural induction is applied and it is proved that $Decomposable$ always yields $true$ when equations 3 to 5 hold, i.e when the behaviour is decomposable.

□ Our algorithm is consistent and complete.

C REFERENCES

[1] ISO. *LOTOS a Formal Description Technique based on the Temporal Ordering of Observational Behaviour.* IS 8807, TC97/SC21, 1988.

[2] LotosPhere Project. *Task 1.1 - task 3.3 2nd year deliverable. part i.* Technical Report Lo/WP1/T1.1/N0032/V02, ESPRIT Ref:2304, April 1991.

[3] LotosPhere Project. *Correctness preserving transformations.* Technical Report Lo/WP1/T1.2/N0020, ESPRIT Ref:2304, May 1990.

[4] Santiago Pavón Gómez. *Contribución al Análisis y Transformación de Especificaciones LOTOS.* PhD thesis, E.T.S.I. Telecomunicación, Madrid, Spain, 1990.

[5] C. Steenbergen. *Conformance Testing of OSI Systems.* MSc-Thesis., May 1986. University of Twente.

[6] R. Langerak. *Decomposition of Functionality: a Correctness Preserving LOTOS Transformation.* pages 203–218, Ontario, Canada, 1990. University of Ottawa, Dpt. of Computer Science, Tenth International IFIF WG 6.1 Symposium on Protocol Specification, Testing and Verification.

[7] F.Khendek, G.v.Bochmann, and C.Kant. *New results on deriving protocol specifications from service specifications.* SIGCOM '89 Symposium Communications Architectures & Protocols, Computer Communications Review, 19(4):136–145, September 1989.

[8] P. Merlin and G.V. Bochmann. *On the Construction of Submodule Specifications and Communication Protocols.* ACM, 5(1):1–25, January 1983. Transactions on Programming Languages and Systems.

[9] Joachim Parrow. *Submodule Construction as Equation Solving in CCS*.* Theoretical Computer Science, 68:175–202, 1989.

[10] J. Quemada, S. Pavon, and A. Fernandez. *State Exploration by Transformation with LOLA.* In Workshop on Automatic Verification Methods for Finite State Systems, Grenoble, June 1989.

[11] C.Vissers, G.Scollo, M.Sinderen and E. Brinksma. *On the use of Specification Styles in the Design of Distributed Systems.* Technical report, University of Twente, Fac. Informatics, Enschede, NL, 1989.

[12] R.J. van Glabbeek. *Comparative Concurrency Semantics and Refinement of Actions.* PhD thesis, Vrije University of Amsterdam, 1990.

[13] M. Llamas and J. Quemada. *Reducción de Expresiones de Comportamiento en LOTOS Finito.* In II Jornadas Sobre Concurrencia, Palma de Mallorca. Spain, September 1990.

A LOTOS Data Facility Compiler (DAFY)[1]

Eric Lallemand
Research Engineer

Guy Leduc
Research Associate F.N.R.S. [2]

Université de Liège, Institut d'Electricité Montefiore, B28, B-4000 Liège 1, Belgium
Tel: + 32 41 562691   Fax: + 32 41 562989
E-mail: u514401@bliulg11.bitnet   or   leduc@montefiore.ulg.ac.be

Abstract

If we take a look at existing LOTOS specifications, we notice that the description of the needed data types is very often huge. This causes the lack of concision of most descriptions of complex systems. We propose to tackle this problem in two steps. First, we define extensions to the LOTOS language allowing short definitions of most of the data types used in practical LOTOS specifications. Second, we propose a tool called "**DAFY**" (**D**ata **F**acilit**y** Compiler) which is able to translate these extensions into standard LOTOS.

1. Introduction

LOTOS (**L**anguage **O**f **T**emporal **O**rdering **S**pecification) was developed by FDT (Formal Description Technique) experts during the years 1981-1988. The basic idea behind LOTOS is that systems can be described by defining the temporal relation between events describing the externally observable behaviour of a system.

LOTOS has two relatively independent components:
- The first one deals with the description of the process behaviour of a system, and is based on a modification of CCS (Calculus of Communicating Systems - [Mil 80], [Mil 89]) and CSP (Communicating Sequential Processes - [Hoa 85]).
- The second one deals with the description of data structures and value expression and is based on the abstract data type language ACT ONE which was developed at the Technical University of Berlin ([EhM 85]).

Although it has been developed for OSI (Open Systems Interconnection), LOTOS is a Formal Description Technique which is generally applicable to distributed, concurrent information processing systems. LOTOS was developed with the purpose of allowing the production of system descriptions which are **unambiguous, complete, consistent, precise** and **concise**.

In fact, when we take a look at existing specifications, we notice that the description of the needed data types is often huge. This causes the lack of concision of most descriptions of complex systems. This problem has already been identified by G. Scollo in 1986. In order to solve it, he proposed to extend the language definition ([Sco 86]) with shorthand notations to be able to produce concise data type descriptions. However, most of the extensions proposed

---

[1] This work was partially supported by the Commission of the European Communities under the ESPRIT II programme in project OSI 95.
[2] Fond National de la Recherche Scientifique: National Fund for Scientific Research (Belgium)

by G. Scollo were not included in the standardized definition of the language. Thus, the problem remains unsolved as system descriptions using the extended language are neither internationally accepted by the scientific community nor tractable by LOTOS related tools.

2. The language extensions

The shorthand notations, proposed by G. Scollo in 1986 when LOTOS was not a standard yet, intended to ease the data definition work and to speed it up ([Sco 86]).

After a short description of the proposed facilities, we will evaluate their usefulness and we will look at the feasibility to define additional facilities.

2.1. The extensions proposed by G. Scollo

2.1.1. "Constant"

This language extension allows the easy definition of data types whose value domains (sorts) consist only of a finite number of constants whose names are the parameters of the extension invocation [1].

The operations defined within this type allow the comparison of the constants (equality, inequality). These operations are defined considering that constants of different names are different.

A more complete version of this extension also defines additional operations such that "less than", "less or equal", "greater than", "greater or equal". The results provided by these operations are based on an order relation which will somehow have to be defined by the user of this extension. This will be done in relation with the order of the names of the constants in the parameter field of the extension invocation.

2.1.2. "Map"

This facility allows the easy and explicit description of a function (possibly partial) between the two sorts which are the parameters of the extension invocation.

The operations defined by this type allow:
- the association of a (new) value to a term of the function domain;
- the generation of the value associated to a term of the function domain;
- the generation of the function domain;
- the comparison of two functions, ...

2.1.3. "OneOf"

LOTOS allows the use of the same name to refer to different operations (if it is possible to distinguish each occurrence of the same identifier because of either the nature of the operation arguments or the relative position of the operator with respect to its arguments). This feature is called "overloading" and it is not allowed to be used for sort identifiers. So it is not possible to use the same identifier to denote two different sorts.

This extension tries to remedy this situation by allowing the definition of a sort as the "union" of other value domains which are the parameters of the extension invocation.

---

[1] By "extension invocation", we mean the text to be typed by the specifier who uses the language extension.

The operations associated with this type allow the comparison of two terms of the "global" sort and to know to which "subsort" a term belongs.

2.1.4. "Set" and "String"

These facilities represent the well-known concepts used in mathematics or in computer science.

2.1.5. "Tuple"

This extension allows the definition of a sort as the cartesian product of a finite number of data domains which are the parameters of the extension invocation.

This type is similar to a "record" in PASCAL or to a "struct" in C.

The operations associated with this type allow the construction of a term (i.e. assign an initial value to all fields of the structure), the extraction of the value of a tuple component, the modification of one or several components of a tuple and at last the test of equality of two tuples.

Note that, as for the "Constant" extension, a more complete version of the "Tuple" extension is also available. This extended version defines and uses an order relation over the tuples.

2.2. Other extensions of the language ?

It may seem surprising that other abstract data types like those mentioned in [UhS 90] are neither included in the standard library nor proposed to be defined as language extensions. Are "Queues", "stacks", "trees", ... (which are very frequently used in ordinary programming language) useless in the LOTOS context ? It seems that the answer of this question is "yes". Indeed, the study of the protocol and service specifications of the transport and the session layers of the OSI model ([ISO 9571], [ISO 9572], [ISO 10022] and [ISO 10023]) illustrates that:
- Most data types used in the specifications could be specified by using the language extensions proposed by G. Scollo.
- Data types similar to "stacks" or "trees" are not used.
- Data types similar to "queues" are rather seldom. Moreover, each occurrence generally having specific characteristics, it would only be possible to specify a reduced version of this type which only takes account of the common characteristics of all the "queues" (which can be resumed in the "first in, first out" data access policy). Another reason that led us to reject this type as a possible extension is the impossibility to correctly and completely specify operations representing partial functions in ACT ONE. Indeed, a partial function is a function which is not defined on all the values of its domain. This is the case of the function which tries to extract the value of the first element of a queue as the result is undefined if the queue is empty.
- Other data types used in the specification are few, quite short and too particular to consider the creation of facilities enabling their substitution.

These results also take account of the fact that it is possible to specify some data types using processes ([Got 87], [Led 87], [Led 90]).

2.3. The treatment of the extensions

As the use of non-standard features is forbidden in LOTOS and as the extensions proposed by G. Scollo seem very useful, we decided to design a tool which translates an extended LOTOS specification (based on variants of these extensions) in a standard LOTOS specification. This tool will ease the specification task in two significant ways:
- it will permit the reduction of the length of the specifications written by specifiers;

- it will allow an easy definition of most of the needed data types.

Although the "Set" and "String" extensions proposed by Scollo were retained in the standard library, we have chosen to treat them because the extension invocations translated by DAFY will be much easier to use than the library types which have to be correctly actualized and renamed.

Although we only consider the extensions proposed by G. Scollo, the tool will be designed in a modular way in order to allow the incorporation of future extensions.

3. Definition of the extension invocation syntax and of the translations produced

3.1. The extension invocation syntax

When we defined the syntax to be used to invoke the extensions, we had to find a compromise between two opposite desires:
- On one hand, the desire to use a syntax as close as possible to the one used for abstract data types in LOTOS. The use of the extensions will then seem as natural as possible.
- On the other hand, the need for the translation tool to be able to distinguish the use of an extension from a standard data type definition (this is only possible if the syntax used for the extension invocations is different enough from the one used by standard LOTOS).

Taking the technical problem related to the design of a compiler into account, but considering that we wanted to produce a tool easy to use, we chose the following syntax for the extension invocations:

>   **type** *type_name* **isdafy** *extension_name*
>   *[**actualizedby** type_name_list **using**]*
>   *[**sortnames** sort_name]*
>   *[**opnnames** (operation_name **for** operation_name)+]*
>   **parnames** *identifier_list*
>   **endtype**

Parts between "[]" are optional and "(operation_name **for** operation_name)+" means the repetition of at least one "(operation_name **for** operation_name)" group.

Example of the use of this syntax:

>   **type** *Constant_3* **isdafy** *Constant*
>   **sortnames** *Const*
>   **parnames** *Const_1, Const_2, Const_3*
>   **endtype**

This example defines the "Constant_3" type and the "Const" sort whose only three terms are "Const_1", "Const_2" and "Const_3". In this invocation of the "Constant" extension, we chose to impose the produced sort name (which is by default chosen equal to the type name) but we did not ask the compiler to modify the operation names which are produced by default. This modification could have been done as in standard LOTOS using the "**opnnames**" keyword.

The only differences between an actualization in standard LOTOS and an extension invocation are:
- The use of the "**isdafy**" (**is da**ta **f**acilit**y**) keyword which effectively indicates that we will use a language extension rather than a previously defined data type;
- The non-use of the "**for** sort_name" after the "**sortnames**" keyword;

- The use of "**parnames**" followed by an identifier list. This word has been used in order to uniformly treat the parameters of all the extensions (the parameters of the "Constant" extension are operation names whereas the parameters of the other extensions are sort names).

Let us note that only the "**isdafy**" word is considered as a new keyword by the data facility compiler. The "parnames" word and the extension names ("Constant", "Map", "OneOf", ...) can be used as normal LOTOS identifiers (except "Constant+" and "Tuple+" which are used to design the extended version of the "Constant" and "Tuple" extensions; they are not standard LOTOS identifiers).

3.2 Translation of the extension invocations

3.2.1. The generic data type concept

The standard LOTOS allows the description of *parametrized data types* which can be considered as partial specifications where only some general features of the type are described and "holes" (formal sorts, operations and equations) are left to be filled later with further details. An example of such a parametrized data type is the well-known "Set" defined in the standard library annexed to the LOTOS language definition ([ISO IS 8807]). From this "Set" definition, it is possible to easily **generate** the definition of any set whose operations have the same properties as those specified in the initial type. For this reason, "Set" is considered as a **generic** data type definition.

By using the same LOTOS feature, it is possible to define generic data types by defining the operation properties of a "Map" (its domain and its range are the parameters), a "OneOf" for a given number of subsorts gathered (these sorts are the parameters), a "String" (the sort of the elements contained is the parameter), a "Tuple" of a given number of fields (the sorts of the fields are the parameters). An example of such a generic data type produced by DAFY and representing a "Tuple" of three fields is given between the 22nd and the 92nd line of the annex B.

There is no need to use parametrized data types to define sorts consisting only of a finite number of constants as only the constant names are unknown. Nevertheless, because of the *renaming feature* of the standard LOTOS, it is also possible to specify a **generic** type which defines a sort of a given number of constants whose names are adaptable at will. An example of a generic data type defining three constants is given between the 4th and the 20th line of the annex B.

Taking the preceding remark into account, we decided to produce the translations of the extension invocations in two stages:
- the production of a generic data type completely specifying the concepts used by the facility (possibly taking the number of parameters into account) and,
- the adaptation of the generic data type to the particularities of the facility invocation.

These translations will be produced at two different levels of specification by the data facility compiler:
- the generic data types needed by the complete set of extensions used in the source specification will be produced just before the "**behaviour**" symbol in order to give them global scope (cf. lines 4 to 92 of the annex B);
- the translations instantiating the generic data types will be produced where the extension invocations are detected (these translations are said "local"). (cf. lines 97 to 132 of the annex B).

Let us note that it is impossible to define a single generic data type to describe a "Tuple" of any number of fields because the properties of the operations depend upon this number. For the same reason, it is also impossible to define a single generic data type for a "Constant" or a

"OneOf" of any number of parameters. Thus, we will have to produce as many generic data types as the different numbers of parameters used in these three extensions.

3.2.2. Partial functions specification

We will not describe each line of the translations (local or generic) produced for each facility but we will rather describe the two major problems we had to face during the study of the translations and the way we solved them.

The semantics of the LOTOS language makes it impossible to describe partial operations completely and correctly ([EhM 85]). Two of the most common solutions used to overcome this problem are:
- "The *error value* solution": The use of an error value which will be returned if the function is undefined for the values of its arguments.
- "The *set* solution": The modification of the definition of the problematic operation such that it does not return a single value but a set of values. Thus, if the operation was originally defined for some arguments and returned "v", it will now return the singleton containing "v" and, if the operation was not defined, it will now return the empty set.

The use of the first solution very often leads to contradictions in the produced equations. The second solution is not free of problems either. Indeed, the insertion of the result of the operation in a set only delays the problem because it is not possible to specify a total function that could extract the solution possibly contained in the set.

Another solution would consist in simply not defining the behaviour of the operation if the represented function is not defined.

Considering that no solution is perfect, we decided initially to use the "set" solution to specify the properties of the partial operations of the "Map" and the "OneOf" facilities. Later, we extended DAFY very quickly (2 hours' work) in order to support the "undefined" solution.

3.2.3. Term rewriting systems

In order to simulate LOTOS specifications, and in particular to evaluate ACT ONE value expressions, the usual technique consists in translating the ACT ONE equations into a term rewriting systems. Classically, the equations of the data types definitions are interpreted as rewrite rules from left to right by the simulator[3]. This means that if the applying conditions of an equation are satisfied and if a portion of an expression matches the left hand part of the equation, then this portion of expression may be replaced by using the right hand part of this equation. The set of equations of the data type specification (also referred to as the equational theory associated with the specification) are then interpreted as what is commonly called a "term rewriting system".

However there are basic theoretical limitations to this translation process: some equational theories cannot be translated into terminating and confluent term rewriting systems. Consequently, some valid LOTOS specification (w.r.t. the syntax and static semantics defined in the standard [ISO IS 8807]) are not "simulable".

A term rewriting system is *terminating* ([Der 85]) iff no infinite derivations are possible (i.e. any sequence of successive applications of rewrite rules must terminate, that is derive a term which is irreducible).

---

[3] This is the case of the HIPPO V2.1 symbolic simulator of the ESPRIT/SEDOS LOTOS Toolset, but most of the other LOTOS tools apply similar translations.

A term rewriting system is *confluent* ([Der 85]) iff each correct value expression has at most one normal form (i.e. by any sequence of successive applications of rewrite rules, in any order, at most one irreducible term may be found).

In practice, when a specified equational theory makes it impossible to derive an ad-hoc terminating and confluent term rewriting system, it is necessary to modify in a significant way the equational theory itself. For example, the set equational theory can be translated if an order relation is correctly defined for the elements contained in the set. This is due to the fact that, to obtain a terminating and confluent rewrite system, one of the n! representations of a set containing n elements must be given a greater importance, and this can only be done if a correct order relation is defined over the elements of the set.

Taking the preceding remark into account, we decided to produce two translations for each data facility:
- The first one is said "theoretical" and is obtained without taking the limitations of simulator tools into account.
- The second one is said "simulable", and takes these limitations[4] into account and thus specifies variants of these types which generates terminating and confluent rewrite systems.

Being simpler, cleaner and more compact, the first one will be used as reference. Being "simulable" the second one will be used to validate the specification.

An example of a "simulable" translation produced by DAFY is given in the annex B. The only difference between this translation and the "theoretical" one corresponding to the same source specification is that lines 15, 17 and 18 are replaced, in the latter, by a single equation:
    "*c1 eq c2 = c2 eq c1;*"
In conjunction with the equations of the 13th, 14th and 16th lines, this equation expresses the same properties of the "eq" operation (constants of different names are different).

4. Design of the tool

The structure of the extension invocations makes it possible to use a compiler to translate them.

As the standard LOTOS and the proposed extension invocations satisfy the constraints related to the use of "lex" and "yacc" tools of the UNIX environment, we were able to use them to produce DAFY.

Proceeding this way, we certainly produced the tool faster than if we did it by hand, but above all it allows us to write a quite modular source code. Indeed, it is possible to easily modify the code either to extend the number of extensions treated by the compiler, or to modify the translations produced for an extension (in order to, for example, take account of the limitations specific to other simulators), or even to use another syntax for the extensions (provided that the new syntax satisfy the constraints imposed by "lex" and "yacc").

About 6 months work were needed to produce the code of DAFY which is divided into three major parts:
- the code needed to produce the lexical analyzer (about 2800 lines of "lex" code),
- the code needed to produce the syntactic analyzer (about 2500 lines of "yacc" code),

---

4 Being designed to be integrated with the SEDOS LOTOS Toolset, we will also have to take account of the fact that HIPPO does not support the standardized definition of the LOTOS language ([ISO IS 8807]). It only supports the draft international standard definition ([ISO DIS 8807]). This implies that some features allowed by the final definition of LOTOS are not supported (the renaming combined with the actualization is an example of such a feature).

- the code needed to produce the translations of all the data facilities (about 1400 lines of C).

This last part is contained in different files which contain all the procedures needed to produce the translation of one language extension.

Let us examine the main characteristics of the lexical analyzer and of the syntactic analyzer. They are the most important parts of the DAFY compiler (cf. Figure 1).

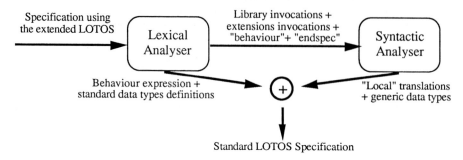

Figure 1: Structure of DAFY.

4.1. The lexical analyzer

The main characteristics of the lexical analyzer of the DAFY program are:
- It correctly identifies the lexical tokens defined in the clause 6.1 of the standard LOTOS definition [5] except the "*)" token which indicates the end of a comment and which must be preceded by a separator (sequence of spaces, of tabulations or carriage return) to be correctly recognized. The "behaviour" symbol is always correctly identified but for reasons of translation, it must be located on a new line (it can only be preceded by separators on its line).
- It correctly identifies the "isdafy" and "parnames" words which are used in the data facilities. These two words are not considered in the same way by the compiler. Indeed, "isdafy" is considered as a keyword (and can not be used as a normal LOTOS identifier) whereas "parnames" is not. This difference results from the fact that "isdafy" actually identifies an extension invocation in comparison to a normal data type definition.
- It recognizes a new type of identifier when it is used in extension invocations. These identifiers are built by using a LOTOS identifier concatenated to the string composed of the "*" character followed by a natural number (let "n" be this natural number). In fact, such an identifier represents a list of "n" LOTOS identifiers separated by a comma.
- It extracts the extension invocations, the library type invocations, the "behaviour" and the "endspec" symbols from the extended LOTOS specification. Only these parts are transmitted to the syntactic analyzer because they are the only parts needed to produce the translations.

---

[5] This clause defines the basic characters, the keywords, the special symbols and the format of the identifiers used in the standard LOTOS. It also defines the format of the comments which can be used in the specification.

4.2. The syntactic analyzer

The main function of the syntactic analyzer (as well as checking the syntax of the extension invocations and reporting the detected errors) is to "decode" the correct extension invocations. The decoding goes with a static semantic check of the following points:
- Is the number of parameters used in the invocation correct ? It must be equal to 1 for the "Set" and "String" extensions and equal to 2 for the "Map" facility;
- Are the renamed operations defined for the referenced facility ?
- Are all the parameters different if they must be so (for the "Constant" and "Map" facilities) ?
- Are all the library types used by the generic translations (which have global scope) invoked before the "behaviour" symbol ? If it is not so, warnings are reported in an error file.

Once the decoding and the semantic check of an extension invocation are finished, the local translation is produced if no error has been reported.

Then, the analyzer indicates in a variable the type of extension used and, if needed, the number of parameters used. This stage is needed in order to produce only the generic data types actually used by the local translations.

If the end of the source specification is reached without any error, the analyzer calls a procedure which inserts the generic data types used by all the local translations just before the "behaviour" symbol. If errors have been detected, they will be reported in an error file whose name must be given when starting DAFY.

Although the analyzer is not always able to correctly identify the nature of the errors encountered during the compilation, their location is correctly reported. This allows an easy debugging of specifications using the extended language. The DAFY compiler recovers rapidly and correctly after the detection of most of the errors.

4.3. The resulting translation tool

As the DAFY compiler supports the complete standard LOTOS, it can translate the extension invocations inside a specification using almost any standard LOTOS features. Indeed, in order to produce a specification which is tractable by DAFY, the specifier only needs to check that:
- the "*)" symbol indicating the end of a comment is preceded by at least a separator (space, tabulation or carriage return);
- the "behaviour" symbol is only preceded by separators on its line;
- the "isdafy" word is only used to indicate the use of a language extension (it may not be used as an identifier).

4.4. Integration of DAFY in ILOT

ILOT (Integrated LOTOS Toolset - [Sch 90]) is a program which was designed to integrate an editor (EMACS) and the tools of the SEDOS LOTOS Toolset (the "SCLOTOS" syntactic analyzer, the "LISA" semantic checker, the "HIPPO" symbolic simulator, ...) into a user-friendly environment. It was conceived on a SUN 3 workstation and uses many of the resources provided by SunView (Sun Visual Integrated Environment for Workstations) to ease the design and the treatment of a LOTOS specification.

In order to treat a specification using the extended language as easily as those using the standard language only, we have integrated DAFY in ILOT (cf. figure 2). With this new version of ILOT, it is almost possible to treat a specification without knowing that extensions of the language are used.

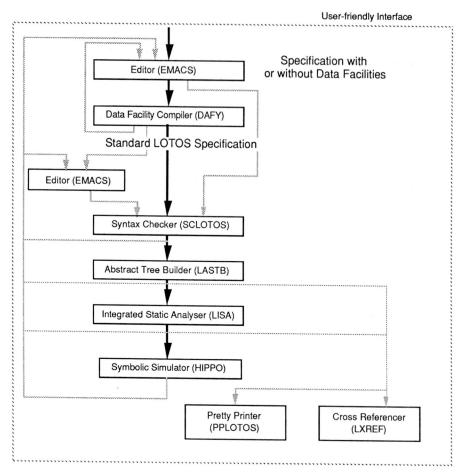

Fig. 2: Structure of ILOT.

5. Conclusion

We have developed a tool (called "**DAFY**" - **D**ata **F**acility Compiler) which translates language extensions into standard LOTOS. It allows the concise description of most of the data types frequently used in LOTOS specifications. We have integrated this tool into the user-friendly "ILOT" environment running on a SUN workstation.

The use of DAFY for the specification of the Transport Protocol showed us that this program allows the reduction of the size of the data type descriptions to about 60 % of the length of those using only standard language data types. The gain obtained by students with small examples has even been greater as they needed less than 30 lines of extension invocations to define all the necessary data types, while the translation of the invocations produced more than 300 lines. DAFY has been defined to produce a quite optimal code. Nevertheless, it is still possible to shorten the size of the produced code by suppressing the lines corresponding to operations which are automatically produced in the translation but not used in the remaining part of the specification.

When designing the tool, we wanted it to be:
- Easy to use. This led us to choose a syntax very close to the one used in standard LOTOS data type definitions.
- Modular in order to be able to extend it easily. Some examples of extensions that we could imagine are: the treatment of newly added language extensions (if the syntax used for the new extension is similar to the one used at the moment), to allow the production of other translations for the partial operations, to take the particularities and limitations of other LOTOS simulators into account, ...
- Portable : DAFY, initially developed on a "SUN 3" station, has been easily ported on a "SUN/SPARC" station and on a "DEC 3100" workstation.

6. Acknowledgments

We would like to thank professor A. Danthine of the "Systèmes et Automatique" department of the University of Liège who proposed the design of a data facility compiler. We would also like to thank F. Marso and Ch. Pecheur who helped us to realize DAFY. We are grateful to France Bierbaum, Professor Danthine's assistant, and to the students attending the course "Protocole de Réseaux d'ordinateurs". They have been the first users of this program and they provided valuable feedback to improve it.

7. Bibliography

[Der 85]   N. Dershowitz,
           Termination,
           in: J.-P. Jouannaud, ed., Rewriting Techniques and Applications, LNCS 202 (Springer-Verlag, Berlin Heidelberg New York Tokyo, 1985, ISBN 3-540-15976-2) 180-224.

[EhM 85]   H. Ehrig and B. Mahr,
           Fundamentals of Algebraic Specification 1, Equations and Initial Semantics,
           in: W. Brauer, B. Rozenberg, A. Salomaa, eds., EATCS , Monographs on Theoretical Computer Science (Springer Verlag, Berlin Heidelberg New York Tokyo, 1985, ISBN 3-540-13718-1).

[Got 87]   R. Gotzhein,
           Specifying abstract data types with LOTOS,
           in: G.v. Bochmann, B. Sarikaya, eds., Protocol Specification, Testing and Verification, VI (North-Holland, Amsterdam, 1987, ISBN 0-444-70126-5) 15-26.

[Hoa 85]   C.A.R. Hoare,
           Communicating Sequential Processes,
           (Prentice-Hall International, London, 1985, ISBN 0-13-153271-5).

[ISO DIS 8807] ISO/TC97/SC21/WG1/FDT/C,
           LOTOS - A Formal Description Technique based on the Temporal Ordering of Observational Behaviour,
           DIS 8807, July 1987.

[ISO IS 8807] ISO/IEC-JTC1/SC21/WG1/FDT/C,
           Information Processing Systems - Open Systems Interconnection - LOTOS, a Formal Description Technique Based on the Temporal Ordering of Observational Behaviour,
           IS 8807, February 1989.

[ISO 9571]   ISO/IEC-JTC1/SC21/WG6 Ad-hoc group,
              Information Technology - Open Systems Interconnection - LOTOS Description of the Session Service,
              TR 9571, Sept. 1989.
[ISO 9572]   ISO/IEC-JTC1/SC21/WG6 Ad-hoc group,
              Information Technology - Open Systems Interconnection - LOTOS Description of the Session Protocol,
              TR 9572, Sept. 1989.
[ISO 10023]   ISO/IEC-JTC1/SC6/WG4 Ad-hoc Group,
              Formal Description of ISO 8072 in LOTOS,
              DTR 10023, ISO/IEC-JTC1 N1519, Aug. 1991.
[ISO 10024]   ISO/IEC-JTC1/SC6/WG4 Ad-hoc Group,
              Formal Description of ISO 8073 in LOTOS,
              Revised text for DTR 10024, ISO/IEC-JTC1/SC6 N6978, Aug. 1991.
[Lal 90]   E. Lallemand
              Développement d'un outil d'aide à la définition des types de données en LOTOS,
              Graduate dissertation, University of Liège, June 1990.
[Led 87]   G. Leduc,
              The Intertwining of Data Types and Processes in LOTOS,
              in: H. Rudin, C.H. West, eds., Protocol Specification, Testing and Verification, VII, (North-Holland, Amsterdam, 1987, ISBN 0-444-70293-8) 123-136.
[Led 90]   G. Leduc,
              Process-oriented and data-oriented specifications in LOTOS
              Thesis annexed to the Agrégation dissertation, Université de Liège, Dept. Systèmes et Automatique, B28, B-4000 Liège, Belgium, 1990.
[Mil 80]   R. Milner,
              A calculus of communicating systems,
              LNCS 92 (Springer-Verlag, Berlin Heidelberg New York, 1980, ISBN 3-540-10235-3).
[Mil 89]   R. Milner,
              Communication and Concurrency,
              (Prentice-Hall International, London, 1989, ISBN 0-13-114984-9).
[Sch 90]   F. Schumacker,
              Interface conviviale à un ensemble d'outils LOTOS,
              Bulletin scientifique de l'Association des Ingénieurs Electriciens sortis de l'Institut d'Electricité Montefiore, 1/1990.
[Sco 86]   G. Scollo,
              Some facilities for concise data type definitions in LOTOS,
              Rept. ESPRIT/SEDOS/C1/WP/13/T, University of Twente, March 1986, also in: Potential Enhancements to LOTOS, ISO/TC97/SC21 N2015.
[UhS 90]   J. Uhl, H.A. Schmid,
              A Systematic Catalogue of Reusable Abstract Data Types,
              LNCS 460 (Springer-Verlag, New York Berlin Heidelberg, 1990, ISBN 0-387-53229-3).

Annex A : Specification using some extensions of the language

```
1     specification demo : noexit
2     library Boolean, Element, FBoolean, NaturalNumber, String,
      Octet endlib
3
4     behaviour
5     stop
6     where
7     type Address isdafy CONSTANT
8     sortnames Add
9     parnames Add1, Add2, Add3
10    endtype
11
12    type Data isdafy STRING actualizedby Octet using
13    parnames Octet
14    endtype
15
16    type Packet isdafy TUPLE actualizedby Address, Data using
17    opnnames DstAdd for comp1
18             SrcAdd for comp2
19             Data   for comp3
20    parnames Add*2, Data
21    endtype
22    endspec
```

Annex B : Translation produced by DAFY

```
1     specification demo : noexit
2     library Boolean, Element, FBoolean, NaturalNumber, String,
      Octet endlib
3
4     type dafy_constant3 is Boolean
5     sorts dafy_constant3
6     opns const1 : -> dafy_constant3
7          const2 : -> dafy_constant3
8          const3 : -> dafy_constant3
9          _eq_, _ne_ : dafy_constant3, dafy_constant3 -> bool
10    eqns forall c1, c2 : dafy_constant3
11         ofsort bool
12         c1 eq c1 = true;
13         const1 eq const2 = false;
14         const1 eq const3 = false;
15         const2 eq const1 = false;
16         const2 eq const3 = false;
17         const3 eq const1 = false;
18         const3 eq const2 = false;
19         c1 ne c2 = not (c1 eq c2);
20    endtype
21
22    type dafy_tuple_el1 is Element renamedby
23    sortnames dafy_tuple_el1 for Element
24    endtype
25
26    type dafy_tuple_el2 is Element renamedby
```

```
27        sortnames dafy_tuple_el2 for Element
28        endtype
29
30        type dafy_tuple_el3 is Element renamedby
31        sortnames dafy_tuple_el3 for Element
32        endtype
33
34        type dafy_tuple3_basic is
35            dafy_tuple_el1, dafy_tuple_el2, dafy_tuple_el3
36        sorts dafy_tuple3
37        opns cons : dafy_tuple_el1, dafy_tuple_el2, dafy_tuple_el3
                    -> dafy_tuple3
38             comp1 : dafy_tuple3 -> dafy_tuple_el1
39             comp2 : dafy_tuple3 -> dafy_tuple_el2
40             comp3 : dafy_tuple3 -> dafy_tuple_el3
41        eqns forall el1 : dafy_tuple_el1,
42                    el2 : dafy_tuple_el2,
43                    el3 : dafy_tuple_el3
44             ofsort dafy_tuple_el1
45                 comp1 (cons (el1,el2,el3)) = el1;
46             ofsort dafy_tuple_el2
47                 comp2 (cons (el1,el2,el3)) = el2;
48             ofsort dafy_tuple_el3
49                 comp3 (cons (el1,el2,el3)) = el3;
50        endtype
51
52        type dafy_tuple3_new is dafy_tuple3_basic
53        opns new_comp1 : dafy_tuple3, dafy_tuple_el1 -> dafy_tuple3
54             new_comp2 : dafy_tuple3, dafy_tuple_el2 -> dafy_tuple3
55             new_comp3 : dafy_tuple3, dafy_tuple_el3 -> dafy_tuple3
56        eqns forall t1 : dafy_tuple3,
57                    el1 : dafy_tuple_el1,
58                    el2 : dafy_tuple_el2,
59                    el3 : dafy_tuple_el3
60             ofsort dafy_tuple3
61                 new_comp1 (t1, el1) = cons (el1, comp2(t1), comp3(t1));
62                 new_comp2 (t1, el2) = cons (comp1(t1), el2, comp3(t1));
63                 new_comp3 (t1, el3) = cons (comp1(t1), comp2(t1), el3);
64        endtype
65
66        type dafy_tuple3_expanded is dafy_tuple3_new
67        opns
68         new_comp1_comp2 : dafy_tuple3, dafy_tuple_el1, dafy_tuple_el2
                           -> dafy_tuple3
69         new_comp1_comp3 : dafy_tuple3, dafy_tuple_el1, dafy_tuple_el3
                           -> dafy_tuple3
70         new_comp2_comp3 : dafy_tuple3, dafy_tuple_el2, dafy_tuple_el3
                           -> dafy_tuple3
71         new_comp1_comp2_comp3 : dafy_tuple3, dafy_tuple_el1,
                                  dafy_tuple_el2, dafy_tuple_el3
                                  -> dafy_tuple3
72        eqns forall t1 : dafy_tuple3,
73                    el1 : dafy_tuple_el1,
74                    el2 : dafy_tuple_el2,
75                    el3 : dafy_tuple_el3
76             ofsort dafy_tuple3
77          new_comp1_comp2 (t1, el1, el2) = cons (el1, el2, comp3(t1));
78          new_comp1_comp3 (t1, el1, el3) = cons (el1, comp2(t1), el3);
79          new_comp2_comp3 (t1, el2, el3) = cons (comp1(t1), el2, el3);
```

```
80          new_comp1_comp2_comp3 (t1, el1, el2, el3) = cons (el1, el2,
                                                                    el3);
81          endtype
82
83          type dafy_tuple3 is dafy_tuple3_expanded
84          opns _eq_, _ne_ : dafy_tuple3, dafy_tuple3 -> fbool
85          eqns forall t1, t2 : dafy_tuple3
86              ofsort fbool
87                  t1 eq t2 =
88                      (((comp1 (t1) eq comp1 (t2)) and
89                      (comp2 (t1) eq comp2 (t2))) and
90                      (comp3 (t1) eq comp3 (t2)));
91                  t1 ne t2 = not (t1 eq t2);
92          endtype
93
94          behaviour
95          stop
96          where
97          type Address is dafy_constant3 renamedby
98          sortnames Add for dafy_constant3
99          opnnames
100                 Add1 for const1
101                 Add2 for const2
102                 Add3 for const3
103         endtype
104
105
106         type Data_basic is String renamedby
107         sortnames Data for string
108         endtype
109
110         type Data is Data_basic actualizedby
111             Octet, Boolean, NaturalNumber using
112         sortnames Bool for FBool
113                 Nat for Fnat
114                 Octet for element
115         endtype
116
117
118         type Packet_basic is dafy_tuple3 renamedby
119         sortnames Packet for dafy_tuple3
120         opnnames
121                 DstAdd for comp1
122                 SrcAdd for comp2
123                 Data for comp3
124         endtype
125
126         type Packet is Packet_basic actualizedby
127             Address, Data, Boolean using
128         sortnames Bool for FBool
129                 Add for dafy_tuple_el1
130                 Add for dafy_tuple_el2
131                 Data for dafy_tuple_el3
132         endtype
133
134         endspec
```

The superimposition of Estelle programs:
A tool for the specification and implementation of observation and control algorithms [*]

Benoît Caillaud

I.R.I.S.A.

Campus Universitaire de Beaulieu

35042 RENNES cedex

FRANCE

E-mail : caillaud@irisa.fr

Keywords: Estelle, distributed program composition, superimposition, distributed algorithms, observers, normal form transformation.

Abstract

The *superimposition* is a composition of distributed programs. It is a convenient concept for the design and implementation of control and observation algorithms in distributed systems, such as snapshots, detection of termination, global time, property checking, mutual exclusion and garbage collection. The present paper deals with the implementation of the *superimposition* on the formal description language *Estelle*. It consists in a compiler which translates a static Estelle program with *superimposition* into a pure static Estelle program. Guidelines for programming observers and controllers of distributed systems specified in *Estelle* are given. The transformation techniques used for the compilation of *superimposed Estelle* programs into pure *Estelle* are also explained.

1 Introduction

Many distributed algorithms (communication protocols or any computation on a distributed abstract variable) split up into several simple and generic algorithms: in other words an algorithm is the composition of several paradigms [5, 4]. The *"relations"* (communications, synchronization, shared variables) between these blocks are quite often complex and very different from the mere parallel composition of two processes.

Unfortunately, when programming these algorithms, this compositionality disappears: the different blocks are mixed together because the programming language lacks of such

---

[*]This work has been done in the team "Algorithmes Distribués et Protocoles" of the IRISA and is partially supported by the PRC-GRECO C^3 of the CNRS.

powerful compositions. This is the cause of great difficulties in programming algorithms, and the source of many bugs in distributed systems.

This paper presents the implementation of a particular composition: the *superimposition* in the *Estelle* formal description language [2]. The *superimposition* has been first studied in [1]. It is a composition of distributed programs which enables a building blocks approach in many algorithms: the class of control and observation algorithms (termination detection, mutual exclusion, snapshots, etc) and some other algorithms such as garbage collection.

This paper is divided into three parts. First the *superimposition* is presented and defined (section 2). Then, in section 3 we introduce *Estelle* and show how the *superimposition* can be added to this language.We also deal with guidelines for programming observers and controllers using this composition. Lastly the implementation problem is raised (section 4): the principles of a transformation method of *superimposed Estelle* programs is given. The implementation of the method in the *Echidna* tool [9] is detailed. All along this paper the different concepts will be illustrated by a single concrete example: the particular snapshots algorithm [6].

2 What is the Superimposition ?

The presentation of this concept is divided into three parts: the first one describes the principles of the *superimposition*. The second one is an example of distributed algorithm using the *superimposition*. And the last part deals with the principles of the implementation of the *superimposition*.

2.1 The principles of the superimposition

2.1.1 An informal explanation of the Superimposition

The aim of this section is not to define the *superimposition* completely, in an axiomatic way, but is rather to give the reader some highlights on that concept. A complete description of the *superimposition* on CSP is given in [1] and section 2.1.2 defines the *superimposition* in the model of communicating finite state machines[1].

The *Superimposition* is an asymmetric composition of two distributed programs (P and Q) — it is denoted $\frac{P}{Q}_K$ where K is a set that describes some synchronizations, as it will be explained later. We call P the top program and Q the bottom one.

The main purpose of the *superimposition* is to give a convenient construction in order to program distributed observers or controllers. The top program is the observer, and the bottom one, the observed system.

In order to perform observation or control on the bottom distributed program Q, the top program P needs two mechanisms:

- A read-only asynchronous access to the variables of Q.

---

[1]The model on which Estelle is based is an extension of the communicating finite state machines model. It is easier to explain what the superimposition is, in a simple model, rather than going directly in the complex Estelle model.

- The possibility of detecting or forbidding some of the communications[2] of Q.

It is not easy to share variables between two distant processes, and distributed synchronization costs a lot in communications and time. That is why it has been chosen to associate to each process of Q, a process of P. There is a one to one mapping from the processes of P to the processes of Q. Therefore the processes are associated by pairs (P_i, Q_i). Two associated processes share the same memory. Only the process P_i can read asynchronously in an atomic action the local variables of Q_i. This mechanism is called "*peek*".

The control and detection of communications is performed by synchronizing the sendings and receivings of messages by a similar action. For instance, if Q_i sends a message towards Q_j, then this emission will be synchronized with a message sending from P_i to P_j. From this constraint it is easy to show that the communication graphs of the top program P and of the bottom one Q are isomorphic.

Every communication need not to be symchronized: there can be some free communications that are not synchronized with any communication of the other layer. The set K is the set of pairs of synchronized communications.

There cannot exist any communication between the observer and the observed program: they are confined into two distinct closed layers. Since the observer cannot modify the variables of the bottom program, any finite computation of Q superimposed in $\frac{P}{Q} K$ is a legal computation of the bottom program Q, taken aside. This is a very important property for observation: the *superimposition* preserves the partial correctness[3] of the bottom program. The total correctness of the bottom program is not necessarily preserved since the top program can deadlock the bottom one in a non terminating state.

Figure 1 illustrates the different principles of the *superimposition* which can be summed up in the five following rules:

1. The two programs are confined into two distinct closed layers. There cannot be any communication crossing the layers.
2. To each process of the bottom layer is associated a process of the top layer.
3. The processes of the top layer and of the bottom layer are concurrent.
4. A process of the top layer can read asynchronously the state of its associated process, in an atomic action (the "*peek*" mechanism).
5. Some pairs of communications respectively of the top program and of the bottom one are synchronized, with the constraint: the communications must be similar — i.e. on the same edge of the communication network, and both a sending or a receiving.

2.1.2 Some more details

Estelle is based on an extension of the model of the Communicating Finite State Machines (CFSM for short). We will formally define the *superimposition* in this model.

---

[2] And other events such as process creation and network reconfigurations. Generally speaking, any externally visible event can be detected and controlled — i.e. any event that can be seen from the outside of a process of Q, and no internal event of any process of Q.

[3] A program is said partially correct if, when it terminates properly, it performs the right computation.

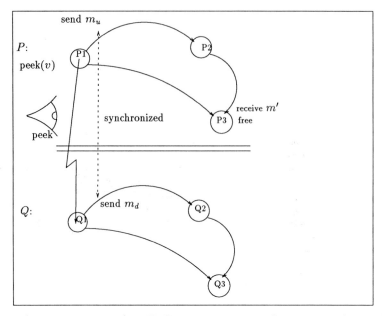

Figure 1: (send m_u, send m_d) $\in K$, the two messages sendings are synchronized. The event receive m' on process P_3 is not synchronized with any event of the process Q_2 since m' is free.

Let P and Q be two distributed programs over the same network $G = (V, E \subset V \times V)$. The program P is the parallel composition of the processes $(P_i)_{i \in V}$, and identically for Q:

$$\begin{cases} P = \|_{i \in V} P_i \\ Q = \|_{i \in V} Q_i \end{cases}$$

We define $S = \dfrac{P}{Q} K$ as the parallel composition of the blocks $S_i = \dfrac{P_i}{Q_i} K$.

$$S \equiv \frac{\|_{i \in V} P_i}{\|_{i \in V} Q_i} K \equiv \|_{i \in V} \frac{P_i}{Q_i} K$$

The set K is defined as follows:

- If Σ_P and Σ_Q are the finite sets of externally visible events of P and Q respectively then $K \subset \Sigma_P \times \Sigma_Q$.
- We say that K is *well defined* if and only if for all pair $(\alpha, \beta) \in K$, if α is a message sending (resp. receiving) from P_i to P_j, $(i,j) \in E$, then β is a message sending (resp. receiving) from Q_i to Q_j.

Let us denote:

$$\begin{cases} \mathcal{L} : (\alpha,\beta) \longmapsto \alpha \\ \mathcal{R} : (\alpha,\beta) \longmapsto \beta \end{cases}$$

An automaton A is represented by $(S_A, i_A \in S_A, T_A \subset S_A \times \Sigma_A \times S_A)$, where S_A is the finite set of states, i_A is the initial state, and T_A is the finite set of transitions — i.e. the set of the triplets (e, α, f) where e is the *"from"* state, f the *"to"* state and α the atomic action (internal or communication) of the transition.
The notation $P_i : e \xrightarrow{\alpha} f$ means that P_i is in the state e and fires the transition $(e, \alpha, f) \in T_{P_i}$. This notation can be generalized to a couple of processes: $\frac{P_i}{Q_i} K : (e, f) \xrightarrow{(\alpha,\beta)} (e', f')$ means that P_i and Q_i synchronously fire the respective transitions (e, α, e') and (f, β, f'). The synchronization can be defined by an operational semantics using the notation defined above:

$$\begin{cases} \dfrac{\left(P_i : e_1 \xrightarrow{\alpha} e_2\right) \wedge \left(Q_i : f_1 \xrightarrow{\beta} f_2\right) \wedge (\alpha,\beta) \in K}{\frac{P_i}{Q_i} K : (e_1, f_1) \xrightarrow{(\alpha,\beta)} (e_2, f_2)} \\[2em] \dfrac{\left(P_i : e_1 \xrightarrow{\alpha} e_2\right) \wedge f \in S_{Q_i} \wedge \alpha \notin \mathcal{L}(K)}{\frac{P_i}{Q_i} K : (e_1, f) \xrightarrow{\alpha} (e_2, f)} \\[2em] \dfrac{e \in S_{P_i} \wedge \left(Q_i : f_1 \xrightarrow{\beta} f_2\right) \wedge \beta \notin \mathcal{R}(K)}{\frac{P_i}{Q_i} K : (e, f_1) \xrightarrow{\beta} (e, f_2)} \end{cases}$$

The *"peek"* mechanism can't be detailed here since finite state automata do not have variables.

2.2 An example: the particular snapshots

All along the paper, the different concepts will be illustrated with a real example: the particular snapshots. This algorithm is described in [6].
A snapshot of a distributed system is the collection of the local states of each process and of the state of each communication channel, such that there is no encountered received message that hasn't been sent (figure 2).
Being able to compute global states of a distributed system is useful for debugging, or saving the state of a computation so that it can be restarted in case of a failure (hardware failure for instance).

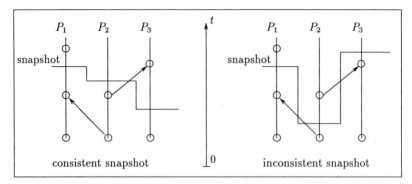

Figure 2: Two snapshots on the same computation: a consistent one and an inconsistent one. This diagram represents the message exchanges between the different processes. The events (circles) are sorted by increasing time. An arrow represents a message. The head of the arrow represents the receiving of the message and its emission is represented by the origin of the arrow.

The solution given in [6] computes a particular class of snapshots: snapshots with empty channels. Therefore a global state is completely defined by the set of local states of the processes.

2.2.1 The algorithmical foundations

The observer $P \equiv \|_{i=1...n} P_i$ computes particular snapshots of the observed program $Q \equiv \|_{i=1...n} Q_i$.
This algorithm contains two mechanisms:

- The first one computes the number of messages in transit in the channels of the observed program Q. This information is useful in order to know whether a snapshot is consistent and particular (no message in transit). However this information is global and can not be computed locally. For this purpose, we use a token going round the observers. It is a vector in Z^n, counting the number of messages sent towards the n processes of the observed program Q, and not yet received. Initially a null vector is sent by a special "*master*" process[4].
- The second mechanism consists in a synchronization between the observers and the observed processes: The observers can detect the communications of the observed program and insert marks into the channels in order to synchronize one another.

The observer P computes particular global states of the observed system Q. Each observer P_i holds a local vector of counters mt, and behaves as follows:

- When the site i sends a message to j, the observer performs: $mt_i[j] \leftarrow mt_i[j] + 1$
- When the site i receives a message from j: $mt_i[i] \leftarrow mt_i[i] - 1$
- When the observer P_i receives the token, with the vector $count$:

---
[4]The "*master*" process can be a distinct process or integrated in one of the observer processes.

- It waits until a *mark* is received on every input edge coming from an observer which has already been visited by the token[5].
- Then it records the local state of its bottom process.
- It computes $count \leftarrow mt + count$.
- It sends a *mark* on every output edge going to an unvisited observer.
- The token is sent to the next observer with the value mt.
- The process performs: $mt \leftarrow 0$.

- When the token comes back to the master, if $count = 0$ then the "*master*" broadcasts a message telling the observers to send him back the recorded local states.

The following theorems state that this algorithm eventually computes particular snapshots and can not deadlock:

Theorem 1 (Partial correctness) *If the channels are FIFO, reliable and if the "master" detects $count = 0$ at the end of the "tour" then the set of all the recorded local states is a particular snapshot.*

Theorem 2 (Total correctness) *If the underlying program accepts the inputs in any order and in a finite time then the token comes back in finite time*[6].

The proofs of these two theorems can be found in [6].

2.2.2 An application of the superimposition

This algorithm implicitly uses the superimposition: the observation of a communication is done by synchronizing the underlying communication with the send or the receive of an empty message of the observer. The markers are implemented by free messages of the upper program on the same channels. The ring is implemented by free channels — i.e. channels which are not composed with any channel of the underlying program. The copy of the local state is performed by the *peek* mechanism

2.3 The implementation: by compilation

The principles of the implementation of the *superimposition* will first be informally explained. Then it will be detailed in the case of the CFSM model.

2.3.1 The principles

The principle (see figure 3) is to replace each pair of superimposed processes by an equivalent single process. And to replace each pair of partially or totally composed channels by a single channel. Each pair of synchronized messages is implemented by a single message, carrying the two data fields.
The *peek* mechanism is simply achieved by sharing the same variable. The compiler should check whether the observer does not modify a peeked variable.

---

[5]This can be achieved with several implementations: the token may be passed from observer to observer in increasing process identity order; or the token may contain the set of visited process identities.

[6]We assume that every message is delivered in a finite time.

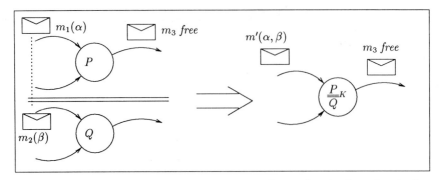

Figure 3: The principle of the implementation: compiling each pair of synchronized message in a single message

2.3.2 On finite state automata

In the model of the communicating finite state automata, the processes communicate through fifo channels. Each process is described by a finite state automaton. Each transition is labelled by an external action (send, receive) or an internal one.
If the two automata P and Q are defined as follows:

$$\begin{cases} P = (S_P, i_P \in S_P, T_P \subset S_P \times \Sigma_P \times S_P) \\ Q = (S_Q, i_Q \in S_Q, T_Q \subset S_Q \times \Sigma_Q \times S_Q) \end{cases}$$

The *superimposition* of two automata P and Q, relatively to K is implemented by the automaton $S \equiv \frac{P}{Q}K$ defined as follows:

$$\frac{P}{Q}K = (S_P \times S_Q, (i_P, i_Q), T_{\frac{P}{Q}K})$$

Where $T_{\frac{P}{Q}K}$ is defined by the three following rules:

$$\begin{cases} (a,\alpha,b) \in T_P \land (c,\beta,d) \in T_Q \land (\alpha,\beta) \in K \iff ((a,c), \phi(\alpha,\beta), (b,d)) \in T_{\frac{P}{Q}K} \\ (a,\alpha,b) \in T_P \land \alpha \notin \mathcal{L}(K) \land c \in S_Q \iff ((a,c), \alpha, (b,c)) \in T_{\frac{P}{Q}K} \\ a \in S_P \land (b,\beta,c) \in T_Q \land \beta \notin \mathcal{R}(K) \iff ((a,b), \beta, (a,c)) \in T_{\frac{P}{Q}K} \end{cases}$$

The function ϕ defines the composition of two similar actions into a single action: for instance, let us assume that α is an emission from P_i to P_j and β an emission from Q_i to Q_j. Then $\phi(\alpha,\beta)$ is the sending of a message from $\frac{P_i}{Q_i}K$ to $\frac{P_j}{Q_j}K$.

It should be noted that the rules defining the transitions set $T_{\frac{P}{Q}K}$ come directly from the three rules of the operationnal semantics defined section 2.1.2.

3 Estelle and the *Superimposition*

This section is a quick overview of the *static* restriction of the *Estelle* specification language. Then the extension of *Estelle* to the *superimposition* is detailed.

3.1 Restriction: static Estelle

We have implemented the *superimposition* in a restriction of *Estelle*: *Static Estelle*. In *Static Estelle* the network is static — i.e. once it has been defined at initialization time, it cannot be changed anymore.
Such a restriction is achieved by the following rule:

| In static Estelle, the parent process of any process is inactive. |

That means that the process embodying a process does not contain any transition. Therefore the network is defined at `initialize` time (with the `init`, `connect` and `attach` instructions). After the `initialize` phase, the graph cannot be modified. The other channel and process control instructions (`detach`, etc) are useless and are forbidden in *Static Estelle*.

It should be noted that this restriction has been taken for reasons of simplicity of the implementation and is not inherent to the *superimposition* concept. The case of a dynamic network with process creations and destructions is raised in the section 6.

3.2 Adding the superimposition

We have chosen to define the *superimposition* in its algebraic distributed form: $\|_{i \in V} \frac{P_i}{Q_i} K$ where each P_i and Q_i is a process. Therefore we must define a new process type corresponding to the superimposition of two processes: $\frac{P_i}{Q_i} K$.

Since in *Estelle* a process P_i is the association of a `module` P_i^m with a body P_i^b, we must define the module corresponding to the *superimposition* of the modules P_i^m and Q_i^m. The binding set K is defined there.

Identically, the behaviours of the *superimposed module* $\frac{P_i^m}{Q_i^m} K$ must be defined as the *superimposition* of a body P_i^b for the *module* P_i^m over a body Q_i^b for the *module* Q_i^m: $\frac{P_i^b}{Q_i^b} K$.

The *superimposed* modules or bodies can be manipulated and referenced as any other module or body. There is no difference between a simple and a composed module or body. The use of init, connect, attach, etc is exactly the same.

This section is divided into three parts: the first one defines the syntax of the *superimposition* of two **module** declarations. The second one defines the syntax of the declaration of a *superimposed* body. The third one describes the syntax of the *external choice* output construction.

3.2.1 On modules

The set K is defined in the following way:

- We need to declare the pairs of bound interaction points that hold synchronized events. They must be compatible (i.e. if one of them is an array of interaction points, then the other one must also be an array, with the *same* index type). Each pair of bound interaction points defines a new interaction point of the module $S_i^m \equiv \dfrac{P_i^m}{Q_i^m} K$.

- Some pairs of messages respectively from the channel of the upper interaction point, and from the channel of the lower interaction point are synchronized. The following consistency rule insures that K is well-defined: the roles of two synchronized messages must either be the respective roles of the interaction points or their conjugates.

Consequently, we can give a syntax for the extension of Estelle:

```
module module-name ( formal-parameter-list );
    superimpose  module-up ( p-list-up )
    over         module-down ( p-list-down );
                    | bind ip-up over ip-down   |
    { ip { port :  | up ip-up                   | ; }*}
                    | down ip-down              |
    { compose ip-up.message-up over ip-down.message-down ; }*
end;
```

Where *p-list-up* and *p-list-down* are two sublists of the formal parameter list of the superimposed module. These allow us to share the parameters passed at the init time between the two constitutive modules, *module-up* and *module-down*.

The free interaction points of the upper (resp. lower) module *module-up* (resp. *module-down*) are renamed with the **up** (resp. **down**) construction. All ports of *module-up* and *module-down* must appear exactly once.

The set of composed message pairs is specified by a last of compose statements.

3.2.2 On bodies

A body for a complex of superimposed pair of modules is the superimposition of two bodies, respectively for the upper and lower modules of the complex. The set of variables that are subject to "*peeks*" is declared there.

The syntax is:

```
body body-name for module-name ;
    superimpose body-up over body-down ;
    { peek { var-up := var-down ; }*}
end;
```

var-up must be a variable of the upper body, declared in the **var** field of the body. And *var-down* must also be a variable of the lower body, with the same scope. They must be assignment type compatible as the syntax prompts it.
Then any reference to *var-up* is actually a reference to *var-down*.
In order to follow the specifications of the superimposition it is forbidden to put *var-up* either on the left hand side of an assignment or as a variable parameter of a procedure or function call.

3.2.3 External choice output

The concept of *external / internal choice* is well known in process algebra (see [7]). But this concept is not very important in pure Estelle. However the following example shows that it is an important concept in superimposed Estelle. This example explains what *external / internal choice* is:
Let us assume a process **machine** simulating a coffee machine. It has two interaction points: one for input (**m1**) and one for output (**m2**). This process awaits for an input on **m1**: either **tea** or **coffee**. Then it outputs a **tea** or **coffee** message on **m2**.
We want to check that **machine** behaves correctly: if we send **tea** then we get **tea** and if we send **coffee**, we get **coffee** on **m2**. For this purpose we superimpose over **machine** a process that checks the communications of **machine**. The **body** of the observer and the synchronizations between the observer and the underlying process **machine** are given figure 4.
The first part of the observer is correct because the choice between the two transitions depends only on the message present on **o1**. The **when** construction has an *external choice* semantics.
But the second part is not correct since deadlocks are possible with a *pure* Estelle semantics for the **output** statement. There is a nondeterministic choice from the states **stea** and **scoffee**: this is *internal choice*.
However this example is correct if we add to Estelle an **output** construction with an *external choice* semantics — i.e. an **output** statement in the *clause* part of a **transition**. As a matter of fact, an **output** event cannot be delayed since the channels are unbounded. Therefore an *external choice* semantics for the **output** construction is useless in pure Estelle. But a message sending construction with an *external choice* semantics is required for the purpose of the observation of **output** events (see figure 4). In VEDA [8] the observation of an event is performed by a **when** transition which has an external choice semantics.
For reasons of simplicity of the implementation it has been chosen not to change the syntax of the transition, yet it would have been better to put the *external choice output* in the clause part of the transition:

```
body bobserver for mobserver;
  state ok, stea, scoffee, wrong;
  initialize to ok
    begin
    end;
  (* first part *)
  trans from ok to stea
    when o1.tea
      begin
      end;
  trans from ok to scoffee
    when o1.coffee
      begin
      end;
  (* second part *)
  trans from stea to ok
    begin
      output o2.tea
    end;
  trans from stea to wrong
    begin
      output o2.coffee
```
```
    end;
  trans from scoffee to ok
    begin
      output o2.coffee
    end;
  trans from scoffee to wrong
    begin
      output o2.tea
    end;
end;
module mcomplex;
  superimpose mobserver over mmachine;
  ip c1: bind o1 over m1;
     c2: bind o2 over m2;
  compose o1.tea     over m1.tea;
  compose o1.coffee  over m1.coffee;
  compose o2.tea     over m2.tea;
  compose o2.coffee  over m2.coffee;
end;
body bcomplex for mcomplex;
  superimpose bobserver over bmachine;
end;
```

Figure 4: The Estelle body for the observer process and the composition of the observer over the machine

> An output **statement at the beginning of a transition without** when **clause has an external choice semantics.**

This does not change the behaviour of a non superimposed process because a *free* message sending cannot be delayed. Likewise the partial correctness of the bottom program in a superimposed complex is not changed.

3.3 An example of superimposed Estelle program: the particular snapshots

A first example using superimposition in Estelle is given section 3.2.3. The present section gives a second example: the implementation of the particular snapshots algorithm presented in section 2.2.

Two difficult points must be solved for the implementation of this algorithm:

- How should we implement the snapshot of a local state? If we assume that the state of the underlying process is coded in a single variable (such as a record), then a single *peek* on that variable catches the local state.
- How should we implement the marks? The marks are simply free messages of the superimposed channel.

The channel type for the observers is:

```
channel ch_obs (in_o,out_o);
  by out_o : obs;
              mark;
channel ch_ring(in_a,out_a);
  by out_a: token(visit: vbool; cmt: vcount);
  by out_a: snap(stat_global: g_stat);
```

The module type of the observer processes is:

```
body pss for mpss;
  var mt: vcount;
      peek_local_state: the_state;
      local_state: the_state;
      wait: vbool;
      visit: vbool;
  state idle,wait_mark;
  initialize to idle
    begin
      all k:site do mt[k] := 0
    end;
  trans from idle,wait_mark
    any k:site do
    when in_obs[k].obs
    begin
      mt[me] := mt[me] - 1
    end;
  trans from idle,wait_mark
    any k:site do
    begin
      output out_obs[k].obs;
      mt[k] := mt[k] + 1
    end;
  trans from idle to wait_mark
    when in_ring.token(visited,cmt)
    begin
      all k:site do
        begin
          wait[k] := visited[k];
```

```
          visit[k] := visited[k];
          mt[k] := mt[k] + cmt[k]
        end;
      visit[me] := true
    end;
  trans from wait_mark
    any k:site do
    provided wait[k]
    when in_obs[k].mark
    begin
      wait[k] := false
    end;
  trans from wait_mark to idle
    provided not vector_or(wait)
    begin
      local_state := peek_local_state;
      all k:site do
        if not visit[k]
          then output out_obs[k].mark;
      output out_ring.token(visit,mt);
      all k:site do mt[k] := 0
    end;
  trans
    when in_ring.snap(global_state)
    begin
      global_state[me] := local_state;
      output out_ring.snap(global_state)
    end;
end;
```

Figure 5: The Estelle body for the observer processes.

```
module mcomplex(z:integer;me: site);
  superimpose mpss(me) over mcalculus(me);
  ip in_complex: bind in_obs over in_calculus;
     out_complex: bind out_obs over out_calculus;
     in_ring: up in_ring;
     out_ring: up out_ring;
  compose in_obs.obs over in_calculus.info;
  compose out_obs.obs over out_calculus.info;
end;
body complex for mcomplex;
  superimpose pss over calculus;
  peek peek_local_state := e;
end;
```

Figure 6: The Estelle module for the *superimposition* of the particular snapshots module over the observed module.

```
module mpss(me: site);
  ip in_obs: array[site] of ch_obs(in_o);
     out_obs: array[site] of ch_obs(out_o);
     in_ring: ch_ring(in_a);
     out_ring: ch_ring(out_a);
end;
```

The figure 5 gives the body of the observer. For reasons of simplicity of the code of the body pss, the network is assumed to be totally connected.

It must be pointed out that this body uses the external choice in order to observe the outputs of the underlying process.

And the superimposition of the observer over the underlying process is defined figure 6

In the observer the statement local_state := peek_local_state performs an atomic copy of the state of the underlying process.

The interaction points `in_ring` and `out_ring` are free interaction points of the module `mpss`. The message type `mark` is free, therefore not synchronized with any event of the underlying process. Since the channels are FIFO, a composed message[7] (`obs`, `info`) cannot overtake a mark.

3.4 Some Guidelines

The two examples presented section 3.2.3 and 3.3 show that the superimposition is proper to the purpose of distributed observers.

Furthermore, it offers the ability to associate to each message of the underlying system some information — this method is called "piggy backing". This is used by the logical clocks defined in [10]: This observation algorithm computes the causality partial order on the events of the underlying system. This is achieved by mapping to each event a vector of positive integers. The partial orders on events is defined by the canonical partial order on integer vectors. For this purpose each message is stamped by the vector of integers corresponding the message emission.

Such a logical clock is useful mainly for debugging distributed systems. But it is also used by many distributed algorithms as a building block.

It is possible to use the superimposition in a different manner: the top program performs a given distributed computation assumed that the underlying program carries out a particular control flow. An election algorithm relying on a graph traversal algorithm is given in [1].

4 An informal explanation of the transformation method

The transformation of an Estelle specification with *superimposition* into a pure Estelle specification consists in rewriting every superimposed `module` or `body` in an equivalent non superimposed one.

The composition of two modules consists in replacing every pair of partially or totally bound interaction points by a single interaction point with a new channel type. This channel type derives from the channel types of the two interaction points.

The composition of two bodies relies on the composition of two automata described in section 2.3.2. But a preliminar normal form transformation is necessary because the transitions in Estelle are not limited to a single atomic action as in the CFSM model.

This normal form transformation consists in replacing each flow control statement (in the sequential part of each transition) containing a synchronized event by an equivalent automaton containing only atomic transitions — i.e. transitions with at most one `when` statement or one synchronized `output` statement.

Both normal form transformation, modules and bodies composition algorithms are detailed in [3].

---

[7] We assume that `info` is the only message type of the underlying program. If there were several messages it would be sufficient to compose each of them with `obs`.

5 The implementation of the compiler

A compiler for the *superimposition* has been implemented. It generates pure *Estelle* code which can be compiled by the *Echidna* compiler [9], for several target machines: Sun Workstation and parallel machines such as intel iPSC/2, networks of Sun Workstations, and the Transputer-based Tnode.
Several *superimposed* distributed algorithms have been implemented in *Estelle* and tested on these parallel machines.
The *superimposition* compiler has been written in CAML[8] — except for the parser which is derived from the parser of the *Echidna* compiler and is written in pascal.

6 Conclusion

This implementation of the *superimposition* shows that, first of all, it is possible to write transformation systems for the Estelle language in a few months (it took actually about 2 months), although the syntax of Estelle is quite big. Secondly it allowed us to experiment the *superimposition* and some superimposed algorithms, therefore proving that it is a valuable program composition technique.
The normal form used in the transformation algorithm is not particular to the *superimposition*. It seems to be general to many transformation methods of Estelle programs. A stronger normal form is given in [11]: it consists in replacing every transition containing conditional, loop statements or procedure calls by an equivalent automaton without any flow control statement. In the normal form of the present paper this transformation is required only when the conditional or loop statement contains a bound interaction.
Lastly, the use of a strongly typed language has been of great help for the implementation of the superimposition compiler, since most bugs were detected at compilation time.
There are several interesting research directions for the superimposition:

- A global (not distributed) superimposition of two *specifications* seems possible — i.e. $\frac{\|_{i \in V} P_i}{\|_{i \in V} Q_i} K$ instead of $\|_{i \in V} \frac{P_i}{Q_i} K$. It would allow a complete observation of a specification without changing a single line in it. The distributed superimposition would be an intermediate form.
- Some restrictions in the current implementation can be easily removed: **goto** statements and **delay** clauses. However, the *Echidna* compiler (which was used to test the code generated by the superimposition compiler) has the same restrictions.
- Integrating the superimposition in dynamic Estelle seems possible. It is just required that the processes and edges creations/destructions are treated as externally visible events, so that the superimposed process could be synchronized on it and perform a similar action, in order to maintain the equality of the networks.
- Optimizing the generated code is an important problem since the normal form transformation widely increases the size of the generated code.

---
[8]CAML is a dialect of Milner's ML, developed by the INRIA [12]. It is a functional strongly typed polymorphic language.

- The correctness proof of the transformation method, although tedious, seems possible and is an important deal since the correctness of this compositional programming method is entirely grounded on this proof.

References

[1] L. Bougé and N. Francez. A compositional approach to superimpostion. In *Proc. of the 15th ACM SIGACT-SIGPLAN Symposium on Principle of Programming Languages*, pages 240–249, San Diego, California, January 1988.

[2] S. Budkowski and P. Dembinski. An introduction to Estelle: a specification language for distributed systems. *Computer Networks and ISDN Systems*, 14:3–23, 1987.

[3] B. Caillaud. *The superimposition of Estelle programs: A tool for the implementation of observation and control algorithms*. Rapport de Recherche 1102, INRIA, October 1989.

[4] K. M. Chandy and J. Misra. *Parallel program design : a foundation*. Addison-Wesley, 1988. 516 p.

[5] E. Gafni. Perspectives on distributed network protocols: a case for building blocks. In *Proceedings of the MILCOM'86, Monterey, California*, October 1986.

[6] J.M. Hélary, N. Plouzeau, and M. Raynal. A characterization of a particular class of distributed snapshots. In *Proc. International Conference on Computing and Information (ICCI'89), Toronto*, North–Holland, may 23–27 1989.

[7] M. Hennesy. *Algebraic Theory Of Processes*. MIT Press, Cambridge, 1988.

[8] C. Jard, R. Groz, and J.F. Monin. Development of VEDA: a prototyping tool for distributed algorithms. In *IEEE Trans. on Software Engin.*, March 1988.

[9] C. Jard and J.-M. Jézéquel. A multi-processor Estelle to C compiler to experiment distributed algorithms on parallel machines. In *Proc. of the 9th IFIP International Workshop on Protocol Specification, Testing and Verification, University of Twente, The Netherlands*, North Holland, 1989.

[10] F. Mattern. Virtual time and global states of distributed systems. In Cosnard, Quinton, Raynal, and Robert, editors, *Proc. Int. Workshop on Parallel and Distributed Algorithms Bonas, France, Oct. 1988*, North Holland, 1989.

[11] B. Sarikaya, G. V. Bochmann, and J-M. Serre. *A method of validating formal specifications*. Technical Report 86 – CC – 01, Concordia University, January 1986.

[12] P. Weis, M.V. Aponte, A. Laville, M. Mauny, and A. Suárez. *The CAML reference manual*. Rapport Technique 121, INRIA, septembre 1990.

FORMAL DESCRIPTION TECHNIQUES, IV
K.R. Parker and G.A. Rose
Elsevier Science Publishers B.V. (North-Holland)
© 1992 IFIP. All rights reserved.

Design and Implementation of an Application Interface for LOTOS Processors

Kazuhito Ohmaki[1], Hirosato Tsuji[2], Kenjiroh Yamanaka[3], Yoshikazu Sato[4], Yoshinori Itabashi[5], and Toshihiko Shimizu[6]

[1]Electrotechnical Lab., 1-1-4 Umezono, Tsukuba, Ibaraki 305, Japan
(E-mail: ohmaki@etl.go.jp)

[2]Mitsubishi Electric Corp., 5-1-1 Ofuna, Kamakura, Kanagawa 247, Japan
(E-mail: hirosato@isl.melco.co.jp)

[3]Nippon Telegraph and Telephone Corp., 3-9-11 Midori-Cho, Musashino, Tokyo 180, Japan
(E-mail: yamanaka@sdesun.ntt.jp)

[4]Oki Electric Industry Co., Ltd., 1-2-27 Shiromi, Chuo-ku, Osaka 540, Japan
(E-mail: sato@kansai.oki.co.jp)

[5]Matsushita Electric Industrial Co., Ltd., 3-10-1 Higashi Mita, Tama-Ku, Kawasaki, Kanagawa 214, Japan *(E-mail: itabashi@trl.mei.co.jp)*

[6]Nihon Unisys, Ltd., 2-17-51 Akasaka, Minato-Ku, Tokyo 107, Japan
(E-mail: shimizu@sted.unisys.co.jp)

Abstract

LOTOS has attracted a lot of attention as a suitable language for formal description techniques, and a number of LOTOS processors have been proposed and implemented, that include specification simulators, test case generators, property checkers, and structural editors. Those varieties of LOTOS processors should ideally be implemented based on a common *LOTOS kernel* interfaced with a set of well defined *interface library functions*, the combination of which provides sufficiently powerful functionality for LOTOS system in a very flexible development environment. This approach is particularly advantageous because it yields *portable* systems. The purpose of this paper is to report our project of designing such a kernel, *LIpS (LOTOS Interpretation Server)*, and the set of interface functions, which we call *service functions* of LIpS. We believe that our kernel together with these service functions can implement virtually all LOTOS processors, and therefore serves as a general purpose LOTOS processor development environment. Moreover, the grammar handled by our kernel contains extensions to standard LOTOS that allows separate compilation and treatment of non-determinism.

1 Introduction

We have designed and been implementing an application interface for LOTOS processors. There are various LOTOS processors such as simulators, test case generators, property checkers, structural editors, and so forth ([1, 2], etc.). To make these kinds of LOTOS processors flexible (i.e., portable, extensible, or modifyable), it is necessary to design a primitive LOTOS kernel and to provide an application interface library to use this kernel. All LOTOS processors should be implemented using the routines defined in this library. This is a quite common approach to keep the application portability, especially in the area of window management systems (e.g. [3]).

We have designed a LOTOS kernel named *LIpS (LOTOS Interpretation Server)* and defined a set of library functions to interface in between LIpS and application programs (i.e., LOTOS processors). We call these functions as the *service functions* of LIpS. Any application should be implemented using these service functions. To make a LOTOS system extensible, the service functions of LIpS should be as small but flexible as possible.

LIpS is a LOTOS interpretation server in the sense that it is designed to behave as a server and all applications are treated as clients of LIpS. LIpS supports the following functionalities:

- Any LOTOS specification can be separately input into LIpS. LIpS analyzes these partial specifications.

- LIpS transforms a (partial) LOTOS text into an internal language named *Arbalotos*. This internal language directly reflects a flattened canonical LOTOS specification defined by ISO 8807 [4], but is enhanced to treat partially developed LOTOS specifications.

- LIpS performs an automatic simulation for the non-determinism in a LOTOS specification. We extend the inference rules of the transitions for dynamic behaviour listed in ISO 8807 in order to handle both a "weighted" transition system and a value generation.

- we provide a set of service functions to probe the ADT specifications, for the ADT part.

In this paper, we show the design policy of LIpS, the list of the service functions, and their concepts.

2 Design policy

Figure 1 shows the relations between application programs and LIpS. Each LOTOS processor communicates the LIpS via its service functions of LIpS.

LIpS is designed so that application programs can satisfy the following conditions:

1. The applications should be able to handle the real-scale protocols and services specifications:
   The applications have to treat all of syntax and semantics defined in the LOTOS ISO standard [4]. Moreover, The applications have to process these specifications with a reasonable response time.

2. The applications should provide the good user interface according to the users' skill: For the beginners, the applications should provide easier user interfaces, but, for the experts, their user interfaces should be more effective and concise. For example, the experimental small specifications might be processed interactively, and the large specifications for the actual protocols should be autonomously processed using some automatic event selection mechanisms.

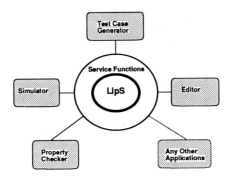

Figure 1: LIpS and application programs

3. The applications should run on distributed computer systems:
This is because the users wish to use the computer resources effectively. Moreover, the tools, which will be developed in future, can re-use a part of the same software as used in old ones.

One possible solution for LIpS to satisfy these conditions is to design LIpS as a server. The application programs of any LOTOS processor is running on a client computer using LIpS as a server.

Typical roles of the server and the client would be

- **Server Side** (i.e. LIpS):
    - Syntax analysis
    - Static semantic analysis
    - Dynamic semantic analysis
    - Deduction of inference rules for dynamic behaviours
- **Client Side**:
    - Logic Analyzer of LOTOS specifications
    - Simulator
    - Test Case Generator
    - Structured Editor

3 Service functions of LIpS

Table 1 shows almost all service functions of LIpS. In Table 1,

- **Server Open, Server Close, and other miscellaneous functions:**
  These are to enable or disable LIpS, and to get some general information on LIpS.

- **Specification Entry functions:**
  These are to input a part of specifications, called *module*, into LIpS. LIpS syntactically parses modules. Typical modules are process definitions or type definitions. We define the module in Section 4.

- **Specification Deletion functions:**
  These are to get rid of a module of from LIpS. Syntactical correctness of a specification is preserved even after the deletion.

- **Specification Information Listing functions:**
  These are to show the header text of a module, e.g. the header part of a process definition or a type definition.

- **Specification Text Getting functions:**
  These are to get the whole text of a module, e.g. the whole text of a process definition or a type definition.

- **Simulation functions:**
  These are to simulate a module. Even if a LOTOS specification is not completely correct from the viewpoint of the static semantics defined in ISO 8807 [4], LIpS can perform a simulation when data types or processes used by the simulated process are already entried into LIpS. This is one of significant points of LIpS.

- **ADT manipulation functions:**
  These are to evaluate a term defined by a type declaration or to set a strategy of term rewritings for the evaluation.

- **Internal language manipulation functions:**
  These are to save, load, or flatten the the internal language.

4 Modules and related service functions

We define the modules of a LOTOS specification. Then we explain the service functions related with the module handling.

LIpS treats the following parts of a specification as *modules*: **Spec**, **Proc**, and **Type**.

- Specification module   **Spec**
- Process module   **Proc**
- Data type module   **Type** $\begin{cases} \textbf{Global-Type} \\ \textbf{Local-Type} \end{cases}$

The data type module **Type** is either **Global-Type** or **Local-Type**, according to its textual position. **Global-Type** is a **Type** whose scope covers a whole specification. **Local-Type** is a **Type** whose scope is only local for a part of a specification. **Type** is a user-defined type or the standard library.

In Table 1, there are functions qualified as "..._spec()", "..._proc()", "..._global_type", or "..._type". These functions manipulate modules **Spec**, **Proc**, **Global-Type**, or **Local-Type**, respectively.

We examplify how the specification entry functions for **Spec** in Table 1. The module **Spec** is defined by the following BNF:

Functionalities	Service Functions
Server open, Server close, and miscellaneous	LIpS_open_server(), LIpS_close_server(), LIpS_help_server(), LIpS_version(), LIpS_error()
Specification entry	LIpS_entry_org_spec(), LIpS_entry_spec(), LIpS_entry_spec_id(), LIpS_entry_spec_init_be(), LIpS_entry_global_type(), LIpS_entry_global_lib(), LIpS_entry_proc(), LIpS_entry_type(), LIpS_entry_lib()
Specification deletion	LIpS_init_spec(), LIpS_delete_spec(), LIpS_delete_spec_id(), LIpS_delete_init_be(), LIpS_delete_global_type(), LIpS_delete_global_lib(), LIpS_delete_proc(), LIpS_delete_type(), LIpS_delete_lib()
Specification information Listing	LIpS_list_spec(), LIpS_list_global_type(), LIpS_list_proc(), LIpS_list_type()
Specification text getting	LIpS_get_org_spec(), LIpS_get_spec(), LIpS_get_global_type(), LIpS_get_global_lib(), LIpS_get_proc(), LIpS_get_type(), LIpS_get_lib(), LIpS_get_init_be(), LIpS_get_be(), LIpS_get_lib_type(), LIpS_get_indent_set()
Simulation	LIpS_simu_start(), LIpS_simu_menu(), LIpS_simu_next(), LIpS_simu_mark(), LIpS_simu_unmark(), LIpS_simu_go(), LIpS_simu_dump(), LIpS_simu_restore(), LIpS_simu_depth(), LIpS_simu_relabel(), LIpS_simu_expname(), LIpS_simu_end()
ADT manipu.	LIpS_adt_Eval(), LIpS_adt_EvalEnv(), LIpS_adt_EvalCont(), LIpS_adt_AS(), LIpS_adt_GlobalTypeEnvironment(), LIpS_adt_LocalTypeEnvironment(), LIpS_adt_DefaultOpnStrategy(), LIpS_adt_GlobalOpnStrategy(), LIpS_adt_LocalOpnStrategy()
Internal language manipu.	LIpS_save_il(), LIpS_load_il(), LIpS_flatten_spec()

Note: Each function is headed by "LIpS_" to distinguish from the other libraries.

Table 1: Service functions of LIpS

```
specification  =  " specification "
                  specification-identifier
                  formal-parameter-list
                  [ global-type-definitions ]
                  " behaviour "
                  behaviour-expression
                  [ local-definitions ]
                  " endspec "
```

Specification entry functions for **Spec** in Table 1 perform the following facilities:

- LIpS_entry_org_spec():
  This inputs a whole text represented by the non-terminal symbol specification (i.e., a text from **specification** to **endspec**) into LIpS.

- LIpS_entry_spec():
  This inputs a text of specification except for behaviour-expression and local-definition.

- LIpS_entry_spec_id():
  This inputs (renames) the text of specification-identifier.

- LIpS_entry_spec_init_be():
  This inputs the text of behaviour-expression.

Other functions for the module **Spec** are analogous to those of entry functions. The modules **Proc** and **Type** and their service functions are similarly defined as well.

"Specification entry" functions listed in Table 1 perform the syntax analysis of a LOTOS text. The static semantic analysis according to [4] has to be explicitly performed by a client using the function LIpS_flatten_spec() in Table 1. This function constructs an internal language representation which will be mentioned in Section 7. "Specification deletion" functions in Table 1 perform the deletion of a corresponding part of an internal language representation. To re-analyze the static semantics, the client should call LIpS_flatten_spec() again.

5 Simulation for non-determinism

LIpS supports the autonomous execution for non-determinism in a LOTOS specification. This is performed using weighted both inference rules and value generation.

The simulation functions of LIpS listed in Table 1 perform the inference rules for dynamic behaviours defined in ISO 8807.

In order to debug a specification, LIpS

- simulates a partially correct specification,

- shows a menu of next possible transitions and behaviour expressions,

- simulates by stepwise,

- saves and restores its status, and

- makes limitation on transitions to avoid infinite loops.

In case of encountering the non-determinism, LIpS continues to simulate a specification according to in-lined comments. These are designed to simulate large specifications. When encountering these comments, LIpS

- calculates the weights according to the Table 2 of Subsection 5.1, and
- calculates the next value candidates according to the comments for value generations of Subsection 5.2.

5.1 Weighted inference rules

An existing simulator (e.g. [1]) has a user interface to simulate specifications by one step at a time. This simulation is performed through a communication tree selected manually by means of a event menues offered at each step. This interface is flexible with respect to selection of events, because selections from menus are done by a user. However, it is too flexible and complicated to simulate a large specification, because all selections should be done by a user. An automatic traversal on a communication tree is useful for simulating a large specification.

Nevertheless, the automatic traversal has still another problem. If all selections in a simulation are managed by a system, the simulation will not always satisfy users' requirements. To simulate a large specification efficiently, we will need not only an automatic traversal mechanism, but also some control mechanism by which users' requirements reflects menu selections done by the system.

To realize this control mechanism, we have enhanced the inference rules listed in Section 7 of the ISO 8807 [4] so that the inference rules include a "weight" information. Using weights, the user can inform his/her requirements for simulation (e.g. probability or priority of events) to the system.

Those enhanced inference rules can be formalized as shown in Table 2. Weights are written in the comment texts as follows:

$$(* \ \%W \ = \ <floating \ num> \ *) \ \text{or} \ (* \ \%w \ = \ <floating \ num> \ *)$$

We can assign weights to operators as follows:

operators	possible positions
[], I[]I, [>	both sides
>>	only left hand side
process definitions	in front of :=

For example, we can write as follows in cases of [] -operator and a process definition:

```
A (* %w = 3.5 *) [] (* %w = 0.5 *) B

process Test[A,B](x,y) (* %w = 0.9 *) : exit :=
     <process body>
endproc
```

name	axioms and inference rules
inaction	no rules
termination	$exit \xrightarrow[1.0]{\delta} stop$
action-prefix	$\mu; B \xrightarrow[1.0]{\mu} B$
choice	$\dfrac{B_1 \xrightarrow[x]{\mu^+} B_1'}{B_1(* \ y_1 \ *)[](* \ y_2 \ *)B_2 \xrightarrow[x \cdot y_1]{\mu^+} B_1'}$ $\qquad$ $\dfrac{B_2 \xrightarrow[x]{\mu^+} B_2'}{B_1(* \ y_1 \ *)[](* \ y_2 \ *)B_2 \xrightarrow[x \cdot y_2]{\mu^+} B_2'}$
composition	$\dfrac{B_1 \xrightarrow[x]{\mu} B_1' \quad \mu \notin \{a_1,...,a_n\}}{B_1(* \ y_1 \ *)|[a_1,...,a_n]|(* \ y_2 \ *)B_2 \xrightarrow[x \cdot y_1]{\mu} B_1'(* \ y_1 \ *)|[a_1,...,a_n]|(* \ y_2 \ *)B_2}$ $\dfrac{B_2 \xrightarrow[x]{\mu} B_2' \quad \mu \notin \{a_1,...,a_n\}}{B_1(* \ y_1 \ *)|[a_1,...,a_n]|(* \ y_2 \ *)B_2 \xrightarrow[x \cdot y_2]{\mu} B_1(* \ y_1 \ *)|[a_1,...,a_n]|(* \ y_2 \ *)B_2'}$ $\dfrac{B_1 \xrightarrow[x_1]{g^+} B_1' \quad B_2 \xrightarrow[x_2]{g^+} B_2' \quad g \in \{a_1,...,a_n,\delta\}}{B_1(* \ y_1 \ *)|[a_1,...,a_n]|(* \ y_2 \ *)B_2 \xrightarrow[min(x_1 \cdot y_1, x_2 \cdot y_2)]{g^+} B_1'(* \ y_1 \ *)|[a_1,...,a_n]|(* \ y_2 \ *)B_2'}$
hiding	$\dfrac{B \xrightarrow[x]{\mu^+} B' \quad \mu \notin \{a_1,...,a_n\}}{B \backslash [a_1,...,a_n] \xrightarrow[x]{\mu^+} B' \backslash [a_1,...,a_n]}$ $\qquad$ $\dfrac{B \xrightarrow[x]{g} B' \quad g \in \{a_1,...,a_n\}}{B \backslash [a_1,...,a_n] \xrightarrow[x]{i} B' \backslash [a_1,...,a_n]}$
enabling	$\dfrac{B_1 \xrightarrow[x]{\mu} B_1'}{B_1(* \ y \ *) >> B_2 \xrightarrow[x \cdot y]{\mu} B_1'(* \ y \ *) >> B_2}$ $\qquad$ $\dfrac{B_1 \xrightarrow[x]{\delta} B_1'}{B_1(* \ y \ *) >> B_2 \xrightarrow[x \cdot y]{i} B_2}$
disabling	$\dfrac{B_1 \xrightarrow[x]{\mu} B_1'}{B_1(* \ y_1 \ *)[>(* \ y_2 \ *)B_2 \xrightarrow[x \cdot y_1]{\mu} B_1'(* \ y_1 \ *)[>(* \ y_2 \ *)B_2}$ $\qquad$ $\dfrac{B_1 \xrightarrow[x]{\delta} B_1'}{B_1(* \ y_1 \ *)[>(* \ y_2 \ *)B_2 \xrightarrow[x \cdot y_1]{\delta} B_1'}$ $\dfrac{B_2 \xrightarrow[x]{\mu^+} B_2'}{B_1(* \ y_1 \ *)[>(* \ y_2 \ *)B_2 \xrightarrow[x \cdot y_2]{\mu^+} B_2'}$
instantiation	$\dfrac{B_P(\phi,y) \xrightarrow[x]{\mu^+} B_P'(\phi,y) \quad \phi = [a_1/g_1,...,a_n/g_n] \quad \text{process } P[g_1,...,g_m](* \ y \ *) := B_P \ \text{endproc}}{P[a_1,...,a_m] \xrightarrow[x]{\mu^+} B_P'(\phi,y))}$
relabeling	$\dfrac{B \xrightarrow[x]{g} B' \quad \phi=[a_1/g_1,...,a_n/g_n] \quad a/g \in \phi}{B(\phi,y) \xrightarrow[x \cdot y]{a} B'(\phi,y)}$ $\qquad$ $\dfrac{B \xrightarrow[x]{g} B' \quad \phi=[a_1/g_1,...,a_n/g_n] \quad a/g \notin \phi}{B(\phi,y) \xrightarrow[x \cdot y]{g} B'(\phi,y)}$

[Symbols]

$g, g_1, \ldots, a, a_1, \ldots$: gates
μ : gates or an internal action(**i**)
g^+ : gates or the action δ with **exit**
μ^+ : gates, **i**, or δ
$B, B', B_1, \ldots, B_1', \ldots$: behaviour expressions
$x, y, x_1, \ldots, y_1, \ldots, z$: non-negative real numbers

Table 2: Weighted inference rules

5.1.1 Examples to use the weighted inference rules

In this subsection, we state several examples to use the weighted inference rules supported by LIpS.

> *The readers of this paper should note that LIpS only provides the transitions according to the rules listed in Table 2. The way to use these rules is heavily depending on each application program of LIpS.*

There are two cases to use weights as follows:.

1. Choice for the non-determinancy:
   For example,

   a;b;stop (* %w=0.5 *) [] (* %w=2.0 *) a;c;stop

   is interpreted such that, when a is offered, the weight for the left choice is 0.5 and one for the right is 2.0. That is, the possibility of the left choice is 0.2 and 0.8 for the right.

2. Choice from the alternatives according to the environment:
   For example,

   a;b;stop (* %w=0.5 *) [] (* %w=2.0 *) b;c;stop

   is interpreted that a and b are offered from the outer environment with the probability 0.2 and 0.8, respectively.

In case of the operator [], the word "probability" is appropriate to interpret the assigned-value. But in case of |[]|, we can not treat this value as probability. This is the reason why we use the word "weight" in stead of "probability".

5.1.2 Interpretations of weights

There are two possibilities of the interpretation of weights. One is to select the "heaviest" weighted path, and the other is to select the paths according to the probability. These two interpretations are different. Suppose that we have the following three different transitions from a behaviour expression A:

$A - a,0.5 \rightarrow A'$
$A - a,0.7 \rightarrow A''$
$A - b,0.8 \rightarrow A'''$

According to the first interpretation, we have to select the last transition. On the other hand, according to the other interpretation, the possibilities for the selections of these three transitions are 0.25, 0.35, and 0.4, respectively.

5.1.3 An example of the calculation of weights

Suppose that the following behaviour expression is given at the start of simulation.

$$\frac{a;b;exit-a,1.0 \to b;exit}{(a;b;exit \; [] \; (* \; \%w=0.4 \; *) \; c;d;exit)- a,1.0 \times 1.0 = 1.0 \to b;exit} \Leftarrow C$$

$$\frac{c;d;exit-c,1.0 \to d;exit}{(a;b;exit \; [] \; (* \; \%w=0.4 \; *) \; c;d;exit)-c, \; 1.0 \times 0.4 = 0.4 \to d;exit} \Leftarrow D$$

$$\frac{c;d;exit-c,1.0 \to d;exit}{(c;d;exit \; (* \; \%w=2 \; *) \; [] \; (* \; \%w=0.2 \; *) \; d;a;exit))-c,1.0 \times 2.0 = 2.0 \to d;exit} \Leftarrow E$$

$$\frac{d;a;exit-d,1.0 \to a;exit}{(c;d;exit \; (* \; \%w=2 \; *) \; [] \; (* \; \%w=0.2 \; *) \; d;a;exit))-d,1.0 \times 0.2 = 0.2 \to a;exit} \Leftarrow F$$

$$\frac{C}{A|[c]|B-a,1.0 \times 0.5 = 0.5 \to b;exit(* \; \%w=0.5 \; *)|[c]|(*\% \; w=1.5 \; *)B}$$

$$\frac{F}{A|[c]|B-d,0.2 \times 1.5 = 0.3 \to A(* \; \%w=0.5 \; *)|[c]|(* \; \%w=1.5 \; *)a;exit}$$

$$\frac{D,E}{A|[c]|B-c,min(0.4 \times 0.5, 2.0 \times 1.5) = 0.2 \to d;exit(* \; \%w=0.5 \; *)|[c]|(* \; \%w=1.5 \; *)d;exit}$$

Figure 2: An example of the calculation of weights

```
(a;b;exit [] (* %w=0.4 *) c;d;exit)
   (* %w=0.5 *) |[c]| (* %w=1.5 *)
(c;d;exit (* %w=2 *) [] (* %w=0.2 *) d;a;exit)
```

From this behaviour expression, LIpS calculates the weighted transitions to get the results of the service function LIpS_simu_menu() according to the inference steps shown in Figure 2. In this figure, we let the behaviour expressions (a; b; exit [] (* %w=0.4 *) c; d; exit) and (c;d;exit (* %w=2 *) [] (* %w=0.2 *) d;a;exit)) be A and B, respectively. This calculation obeys the rules in Table 2.

LIpS will list the following three candidates of transitions as a result of the function LIpS_simu_menu().

1: $A|[c]|B$ $-a,0.5\to$ $A|[c]|a;exit$
2: $A|[c]|B$ $-c,0.2\to$ $b;exit|[c]|B$
3: $A|[c]|B$ $-d,0.3\to$ $d;exit|[c]|d;exit$

If the application program select the first transition using the function LIpS_simu_next(), then the next behaviour expression will become $b;exit|[c]|B$ in LIpS.

5.1.4 Example to use weights

Simulation for special conditions

Let E1 and E2 be processes which communicate with each other through a noisy channel process CHAN of which error rate is 10%. To simulate this situation, we can describe weights as follows:

```
process A[G,H] : noexit :=
   hide M,N in E1[G,M]|[M]|CHAN[M,N]|[N]|E2[N,H]
   where
      process E1[G1,G2] : noexit :=
```

```
        ....
        endproc
        process E2[G1,G2] : noexit :=
        ....
        endproc
        process CHAN[G1,G2] : noexit :=
           G1?x:int;( i; G2!x; CHAN[G1,G2]
                       (* %w = 0.9 *) [] (* %w = 0.1 *)
                       i; CHAN[G1,G2] )
        endproc
endproc
```

If we change weights to 1 and 0 in stead of 0.9 and 0.1, respectively, we can simulate the case when the communication errors never occur. Using weights, we can simulate a specification according to particular conditions of communication.

Fair scheduling

Let B and C be processes which should perform the fairness of their execution. This situation is described as follows:

```
        process A[G] : noexit :=
           B[G]|||C[G]
           where
              process B[H] (* %w = 0.9 *) : noexit :=
              ....; B[H]
              endproc
              process C[H] (* %w = 0.9 *) : noexit :=
              ....; C[H]
              endproc
        endproc
```

A weight described in a process definition is increased by a process instantiation. If the number of selected events offered by B is greater than by C, weights of events offered by B is decreased by 10%. Therefore, the probability to select events from C is increased, and the fairness of the process scheduling is achieved in the simulation.

There are several approaches to introduce probability or priority into process algebras [6, 7, 8]. The application programs towards these approaches would be implemented using the simulation service functions of LIpS.

5.2 Value generation

During simulation, we have to assign some actual values for variables in case of the variable declarations in **choice** statements or action denotation.

We have been designing two different ways to describe for the implicit generation of values to be assinged. These are written as expressions in comment texts using %G or %g.

5.2.1 Enumeration

Using comments with %G-option, we write as (* %G x = *Generator* *) where x is a variable. The syntax of *Generator* is defined as:

- *Generator ::= Constant {"," Constant } ["," G-expression]*
- *G-expression ::= Term* which contains no variables other than x

For example, we can write

```
choice x,y : Int  (* %G x=0,2,4   y=1,3,5  *)
       w,z : Bool (* %G w=true  z=false    *)
         n : Nat  (* %G n=s(s(0)), s(s(n)) *) [] ...
```

The values are assigned to variables so that

- $< x, y > = < 0, 1 >, < 0, 3 >, < 0, 5 >, < 2, 1 >, < 2, 3 >, ...,$ and
- $n = s(s(0)), s(s(s(s(0)))), s(s(s(s(s(s(0)))))), ...$

in these orders.

5.2.2 "FOR" constructs

Expressions for the value generation are placed on either

- after the operator [] in case of choice statements, or
- just before selection predicates in case of action denotations

We write expressions for generators (* %G x = *Generator* *) as well. The syntax of *Generator* is defined as:
Generator ::= <variable> "=" <initial value list> ";"
                 <generator expression> ";" <number of applications>

<initial value list> and <generator expression> are evaluated according to the function *recon* defined in Section 7.3.3 of ISO 8807 [4]. <number of applications> is an integer to indicate the number of applications of <generator expression>. This is similar to the "FOR" constructs of C language.

For example, we can write

```
choice x : Nat []
  (* %g x = 0 ; s(x) ; 5 *)
  (* %g y = x ; s(y) ; 5 *) ...
  ...
```

In this example, values are assigned to variables so that
$$<x,y> = < 0, 0 >, <s(0),s(0)>, <s(s(0)),s(s(0))>,$$
$$..., <s(s(s(s(s(0))))),s(s(s(s(s(0))))) >$$

in these orders.

6 ADT manipulation

We realize the ADT part of LIpS using a conditional term rewriting system. In this section, we show the design decisions to make a feasible ADT interpreter.

6.1 Functionalities of the ADT simulation

The service functions for ADT manipulation listed in Table 1 are divided into two kinds of facilities. In order to debug the ADT parts in a specification, LIpS can

1. print rewrite rules,
2. trace reduction steps,
3. set trace depth levels,
4. set maximum number of reduction steps,
5. set maximum number of operations in a term,
6. set maximum number of reduction depth levels,
7. evaluate terms with a type environment,
8. set rewrite strategies, and
9. evaluate terms.

These are similar facilities implemented by [1]. We can set parameters using in-line comments in case of LIpS.

6.2 Semantics check

We have to translate a LOTOS text into a CLS (canonical LOTOS specification). LIpS does not generate a CLS but translates into an internal representation including the information of CLS using Arbalotos.

It is impossible to implement the LOTOS system according to the exact dynamic semantics for ADT defined in [4]. We restrict the equations in order to fix the values assinged to the variables in equations [10], so that

- $var(L) \supseteq var(R)$ and
- $var(L) \supseteq var(L_i)$ and $var(L) \supseteq var(R_i)(i = 1 \ldots n)$

for all conditional equations $L_1=R_1,\ldots,L_n=R_n$ => $L=R$. $var(t)$ is a set of all variables in a term t.

There are many ways to interpret conditional equations as a term rewriting system (TRS). We define a reduction relation $\rightarrow$ on TRS generated by conditional equations so that

$$t_1 \rightarrow t_2 \quad iff \quad \exists asg, c[\,], \exists L_1=R_1,\ldots,L_n=R_n => L=R \in Conditional\ Equations \bullet$$
$$t_1 = c[asg(L)] \wedge t_2 = c[asg(R)] \wedge \forall i \in \{1\ldots n\} \bullet asg(L_i) \downarrow = asg(R_i) \downarrow$$

where $c[\,]$ is a context decided by rewrite strategies, asg is an assignment, and $t \downarrow$ is a normal form of a term t.

The congruent relation $\equiv$ generated by TRS is define as follows:

$$t_1 \equiv t_2 \quad iff \quad t_1 \downarrow = t_2 \downarrow$$

6.3 Rewrite strategy

Each operation identifier has a rewrite strategy which decide an order of subterms to be rewritten. Following rewrite strategies are available.

- leftmost-innermost
- leftmost-outermost
- projection
- parallel-outermost
- if-then-else

We can specify rewrite strategies with two ways. The first one is to use service function in simulation time. The other way is to specify using comments such as

```
type T is TT
  sorts S
  opns    a(* %s=lmim *), _b_(* %s=lmom *), c  : S, S -> S
  eqns ...
entype
```

7 Internal representation language

The internal representation language is named Arbalotos. Any Arbalotos representation includes the information of both a syntax tree and a flattened structure. Figure 3 shows an overall structure of an Arbalotos representation.

The information stored in a representation is proportional to the size of the LOTOS text. Some redundant information such as parenthesis, space characters, of comments are eliminated. The representation contains enough information for the general purpose usage to many application programs.

The service functions of LIpS related with the internal language in Table 1 perform to save and restore internal representations and to re-flatten it. Figure 4 shows an example of flattening operation on an internal representation for the LOTOS text

```
sap1?x:int; sap2!x of int; stop
```

In this figure, the two boxes for the variable x are "unified" to point a sort int in ADT part, after flattened.

Since LIpS performs the entry or deletion of modules in a part of a specification, its internal structure has to keep both the flattened information (i.e. the canonical LOTOS specification) and a syntax structure of a LOTOS text as shown in Figure 4.

8 Concluding remarks

We have designed an application interface for LOTOS processors, in order to make a variety of LOTOS processors flexible, and implemented a prototype of LIpS. This prototype

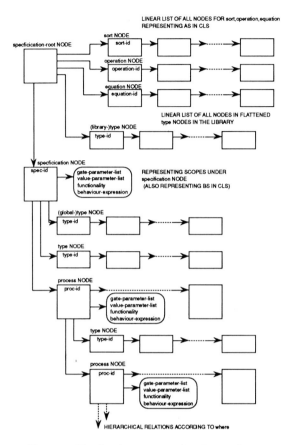

Figure 3: Top level structure of an internal representation

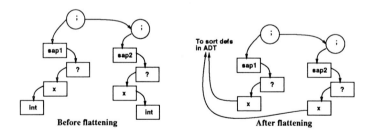

Figure 4: The internal structure before and after flattening

is not a server but realizing most fucntions listed in Table 1. We have demonstrated the prototype of LIpS at Interoperable Networking Event '91 (INE'91) held in this November in Tokyo, Japan. LIpS will become a server which can be used through a network within a year.

Our project started from April, 1990, after some amount of the feasibility study for a year. The authors are participating almost every two weeks as a working group on Formal Description Techniques held by INTAP (Interoperability Technology Association for Information Processing, Japan), and making detailed documents of LIpS.

There are fourteen researchers in this working group. Besides of designing and implementing LIpS, other researchers in the working group are specifying OSI application layers such as CCR, the implementation specification of TP, OSI management, and so forth, using LOTOS. The main purpose of the working group is to assess the usefulness of LOTOS.

Acknowledgements

A part of this work was performed at INTAP by the R & D Interoperable Database System supported by NEDO (New Energy and Industrial Technology Development Organization).

References

[1] Software Environment for Design of Open Distributed Systems, HIPPO-LOTOS Simulator, University of Twente, The Netherlands.

[2] T.de Miguel, T.Robles, J.Salvachua, "TOPO: A Full LOTOS to C Compiler", *Tool Demonstrations of FORTE'90*, Madrid 1990.

[3] J.Gettys, R.Newman, and R.W.Sheifler, "Xlib - C Language X Interface, Protocol Version 11," MIT and DEC, Sept. 1987.

[4] ISO 8807, "Information Processing Systems - Open System Interconnection - LOTOS - A formal description technique based on the temporal ordering of observational behaviour," 1989.

[5] P. van Eijk, C.A. Vissers, M. Diaz eds., "The Formal Description Technique LOTOS," *North-Holland*, 1989.

[6] A.Giacalone, C.C.Jou, and S.A.Smolka, "Algebraic Reasoning for Probabilistic Concurrent Systems," *Proc. of Working Conference on Programming Concepts and Methods*, IFIP TC 2, Sea of Gallilee, Israel, April 1990.

[7] R.v.Glabbeek, S.A.Smolka, B.Steffen, and C.Tofts, "Reactive, Generative, and Stratified Models of Probabilistic Processes," *CWI Report CS-R9020*.

[8] R.Cleaveland and M.Hennessy, "Priorities in Process Algebras," *Information and Computation 87*, pp.58-77, 1990.

[9] R.B.Alderden, "Functionality of an ADT Interpreter," The same book as [5].

[10] S.Kaplan, "Conditional Rewrite Rules," *Theor. Comput. Sci.*, Vol.33, No.2, pp.175-193, 1984.

Formal specification, validation and implementation of an Application protocol with Estelle

C.T. Nguyen, P. Hunel, M.-C. Vialatte

Université Blaise Pascal - Clermont II, Laboratoire d'Informatique,
F-63177 AUBIERE CEDEX, FRANCE
Tel.: (33) 73 40 76 29, Email : mcv@frsun12.bitnet

Abstract
We present in this paper our experience in using Estelle for the development of an application protocol and the methodology we have applied for the development process. During this process we used various tools for specification, verification and implementation phases : EWS, Xesar, ISODE; a quality analysis has also been done with LOGISCOPE. We discuss and assess on the experience and propose some general features for an Integrated Project Support Environment.

1. INTRODUCTION

In the past few years it has appeared necessary to adopt a precise methodology to develop complex distributed applications [1] [2]. The interest in the Formal Description Techniques (FDT) for designing communication protocols has already been proved. Some of the better known are Estelle [3] and LOTOS [4] standardized by ISO. Some tools have been designed and are now available. For example, there are the NIST Integrated Tool Set [5], the ESTIM tool [6], the Estelle WorkStation(EWS) [7], the BULL Estelle Debugger [8], and others. They provide an Estelle Compiler, sometimes a development environment, but rarely tools for protocol verification and testing.

We present in this paper our experience in applying Estelle for the development of an application protocol named ELDA [9]. This work is supported by GDF/DETN/SIMA company.

To support all the stages of the development, we have used two sets of tools, EWS for the simulation and the implementation, and Xesar [10] for the protocol verification. In order to check the quality of implementation we have also used LOGISCOPE [11] based on software engineering techniques.

The first section presents the ELDA protocol and how we have specified it in Estelle. The next sections deal with the simulation and verification of ELDA with EWS and Xesar. In the final section, we describe the implementation stage, and report the measurements on implementation results. We conclude on assessments about the ELDA project with FDT Estelle and its future.

2. ELDA SPECIFICATION

2.1. Presentation

The first stage of our experience consists in specifying ELDA in a formal manner with Estelle. We do not present here the Estelle language and many tutorials can be found in [12] [13]. Before describing the ELDA specification in Estelle, we introduce the main aspects of ELDA.

The protocol to be implemented is called ELDA; it has been designed by EDF/GDF [9] for their specific needs. According to OSI concepts, ELDA is a connectionless application layer protocol using the X400 Message Transfer Service (MTS) [14].

Its main objective is to provide transfer and handling services of data batches. A data batch contains user data and control information required for the management of the data batch by the users and by ELDA provider. The role of ELDA is to send data batches, to store them, to deliver them to the recipient user, to provide and to update control information. The data batches are stored in mailboxes called data batch box and ELDA provides local service for the mailbox management including creation, destruction and various accesses. The data batch handling is carried out by exchanging reports between ELDA entities. An optional alarm service may activate ELDA user entities when specific events happen. The ELDA provider is composed of as many entities as implied sites; these entities exchange protocol data units (PDU) by means of MTS. The structure of an ELDA entity is shown in figure 9.

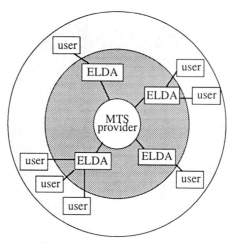

Figure 1. ELDA Application model

The service elements, shown in figure 8, offered by ELDA may be classified in two categories depending on the way they are processed : in the first category, we find the services which need only local actions; the services of the second category are combinations of local and remote actions.

The sequence of events in the services of the first category is the following : a user entity generates a request primitive, then the local ELDA entity processes it, and finally returns a confirmation primitive to the user entity. Such a service concerns neither other users, nor other ELDA entities, nor MTS provider.

However, the services of the second category imply at least one user entity, two ELDA entities and the MTS provider. In addition to the local action of each implied ELDA entity, these services generate at least one PDU exchange processed by the MTS provider.

2.2. Formal ELDA protocol specification requirements.

The formal specification of ELDA is actually done from a specification in natural langage described in [9]. At the beginning of our study, the specification does not contain any formalism nor semi-formalism as classified in [15]. The only exception is the specification of ELDA-PDU which was written in ASN1 [16]. Originally, the ELDA service is given by means of OSI abstract service primitives. The ELDA protocol is defined by ELDA-PDU, some procedural aspects, with the use of MTS service primitive.

The order in which different ELDA-primitives are executed by the protocol entities is described by means of time sequence diagrams. However these diagrams describe only certain examples of sequences and not all possible ones. This limited description of the protocol in natural language has led to the requirement of its formal specification.

We have chosen Estelle because at the time we have started the project, numerous tools supporting Estelle could be easily found.

The specification of the ELDA protocol defines the behaviour of an ELDA entity.

2.3. Estelle specification of an ELDA entity

The specification of an ELDA entity is achieved in two main steps : the first step consists in determining all events that an ELDA entity has to perform and how the entity may react to these events; the second step consists in the ELDA translation from these events and their corresponding behaviour into Estelle transitions. The specification is completely event-driven. Events that may happen consist mainly in the reception of user ELDA request primitives, MTS provider confirmation or indication primitives, and in internal time-out. The behaviour that an ELDA entity may have is clearly represented by a one state automaton.

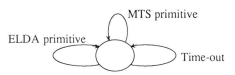

Figure 2. ELDA state automaton

We have to specify the actions to be done by the ELDA entity for each event. These actions are divided into two groups. The first deals with local actions. The second group concerns remote actions; in this case, the ELDA entity reacts by requesting MTS provider service.

Once these aspects have been determined, the translation into Estelle language can be done very easily :
 - primitives are translated, into Estelle interactions : primitive sending is specified by the Estelle OUTPUT statement and primitive reception is specified by the Estelle

WHEN clause.
- time out are dealt with by DELAY clause.
- local actions are specified by Pascal statements.

Thus the transitions of an ELDA entity look like :

```
TRANS
    When EA.ELDA_user_request (parameters)
    Begin
        Local-actions...
        OUTPUT EA.ELDA_user_confirmation (parameters);
        Local-actions...
    End;

TRANS
    When EA.ELDA_user_request (parameters)
    Begin
        Local-actions...
        OUTPUT ELDA_user.ELDA_conf (parameters);
        OUTPUT MTS_provider.MTS_request (parameters);
        ...
    End;

TRANS
    When MTS_provider.MTS_indication (parameters)
    Begin
        Local-actions...
        OUTPUT EA.ELDA_user_indication (parameters);
        ...
    End;

TRANS
    DELAY (time)
    Begin
        actions...
    End;
```

2.4. Results

Estelle is well suited for this type of protocol which is a asychronous one. We actually found very easy to describe such a protocol with available features. We have also appreciated the feature of describing, as Estelle primitives, all local actions like I/O primitives which may not directly be connected with the protocol. If one writes the specification with respect to the legibility, the specification becomes clearer and the quality of the basis document also increases.

We did not use all the Estelle features, nor the extensions proposed as Rendez-vous mechanism in [17].

We have written 650 lines in Estelle for a reduced ELDA entity, and 2500 lines in C for the external primitives.

3. VALIDATION

This specification of an ELDA entity is based on an ELDA description in natural language, all the classical problems of the interpretation of specification in natural language have to be solved. As the protocol specification is critical for the reliability of later implementations, it is necessary to ensure that this specification does not contain any errors. In order to overcome this problem, two complementary validation techniques are applied :

The first one, which is described in the next section, is to build a simulation and verify the correctness of the specification by executing some scenarios.

The second technique is to formally verify properties of the protocol.

To support validation stage, we use EWS for the first technique, and Xesar for the second one.

3.1. Simulation

3.1.1. Estelle Workstation

We present here a brief reminder of the components of the EWS environment. Estelle WorkStation (EWS) is the result of the European Esprit Project 1265 entitled Sedos Estelle Demonstrator. EWS is a software environment for designing distributed systems. It provides an open pre-industrial prototype which has been tested on selected application areas such as space protocols, solar power plant control, flexible assembly cell driving system. A detailed presentation and some examples can be found in [7].

EWS contains a syntax oriented editor, a translator, a code generator, a simulator generator, an implementor and two libraries of procedures. Figure 3 describes the general EWS architecture.

The translator performs source analysis of the Estelle specification, semantics check, and, if there is no error, produces an intermediate form of the specification. The purpose of the code generator is to produce source files in a common programming langage from the intermediate form. Presently, only C is available.

EWS combines generated C files with the simulation library and produces a debuging oriened simulator of the specified system. This simulator provides an interactive execution of the specified system. It proposestwo simulation modes : one controlled by the operator, and the other fully automatic. It also contains debugging capabilities such as enabling or disabling breakpoints or variable displaying and modification.

The EWS debugger/simulatoir allows designers to simulate Estelle specifications.

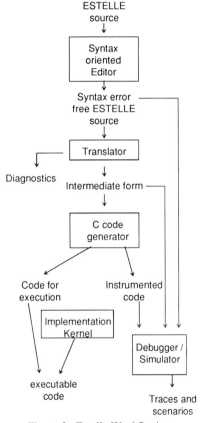

Figure 3. Estelle WorkStation

The dialogue with the user is performed by an interface which offers various functions. The user can select which transition to be fired next or he can choose an automatic simulation worked out by a random selection of the transitions to fire. With regard to our research, the user friendly interface that EWS contains is sufficient to make possible a quick learning phase.

The implementation library contains the procedures which realize all the Estelle specific features (modules, channels, interactions, and their handling). It must be linked with procedures required for the installation in a host.

3.1.2. System architecture

After specifying the behaviour of an ELDA entity in Estelle, our aim is to build a simulation system for the validation of the specification. To do this, we have to put the ELDA entity in a system that makes possible the testing and verification of our specification. ELDA is conceived in a layered architecture which includes user entities for the upper layer and Service provider for the lower layer. A simulation architecture for ELDA must contain the three levels.

The simulation system must contain users of ELDA service (EU) which may generate ELDA request primitives and receive ELDA confirmation primitives, and a MTS provider that implements MTS. As ELDA is a protocol which may imply the cooperation of several ELDA entities and provides a broadcast service, at least three ELDA entities are required in the system. This leads to the following architecture :

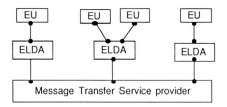

Figure 4. Simulation system architecture

With the objective of simulation and verification of the specification, we avoid making assumptions for the behaviour of ELDA user. So, the EU must be able to generate all kinds of possible ELDA primitive and in any order. Therefore, the behaviour of the EU in this architecture consists in generation of testing sequences that make all kinds of scenarios. Furthermore, we must assume that the MTS provider may act successfully or may fail during message transfer.

We must now describe this architecture in an Estelle system specification.

Estelle makes this task easy by its abstract features and high level concepts. Thus, it is possible to adopt a step by step refinement process to describe this without irrespective of the implementation characteristics.

First, we specify the architecture in Estelle concepts : all entities can be fairly specified by modules connected by channels.

This leads to the following description :

```
Channel ELDA_service (user, provider);
by user:
    ELDA_request (parameters : type);
by provider:
    ELDA_confirmation (parameters : type);
    ELDA_indication (parameters : type);

Channel MTS_service (user,provider);
by user:
    MTS_request (parameters : type);
by provider:
    MTS_confirmation (parameters : type);
    MTS_indication (parameters : type);

Module EU_header systemactivity;
    ELDA_sap: ELDA_service(user) Common queue;
end;

Module ELDA_header systemactivity;
    ELDA_sap:ELDA_service(provider) Common queue;
    MTS_sap: MTS_service(user) common queue;
end;

Module MTS_provider_header systemactivity;
    MTS_sap: MTS_service(provider) common queue;
end;

Body ELDA_body for ELDA_header external;
Body EA_body for EA_header external;
Body MTS_provider_body for MTS_provider_header;
```

All the required modules have been written in Estelle by hand. An interesting alternative can be used as in [18] to assist the designer to construct his whole system in a more systematic way.

3.1.3. Results

With the simulation stage, many aspects have become more precise and some problems and questions about ELDA protocol have been raised [19] especially after testing scenarios with the use of MTS primitive.

The simulation technique consists in building up scenarios executing specific services.

The simulation allows us to check specific behaviours of the modules in normal and abnormal situations: during the execution of each scenario, we check how modules react to events, how their state and data are modified, which interactions are exchanged and what are the value of their parameters. For example we have simulated the repetition of protocol elements in case of a transmission failure. The complex conflict problems have been solved by a step by step simulation.

EWS is quite good for this task, we have especially appreciated the possibility of saving and restoring scenarios and also dynamically handling states and variables. Contrary to the experience reported in [20] with another tool, we believe that the use of EWS in such tasks is quite convenient.

But this task is heavy and the explosive number of scenarios, due to the non-determinist behaviour of the user entities, makes the simulation unable to do a complete validation of the specification: The general properties cannot be verified in an exhaustive way; however if the running of some scenarios makes possible the detection of some deadlocks, but we cannot guarantee that all of them have been detected. Moreover, during the execution of the scenarios, the observation of queues and modules states shows possible unspecified interactions.

EWS provides no mechanism nor way to define the Service for the verification of the protocol, it is not possible to verify automatically the specific properties. One way to improve EWS may be to include the notion of observers as in VESAR [21] or in EDB [8]. With this plan we can perform the verification of specific properties as shown in [22].

To assess with the use of EWS, we outline the main advantages of EWS to be :
The user-friendly interface, making initial learning more simplified,
EWS can assist effectively in the protocol design and correction of errors,
EWS does not constrain strictly the used model (real size protocol like ELDA can be processed easily)
EWS is a very good support for teaching Estelle (we have also experimented it for teaching tasks at the university).

3.2. Verification

3.2.1. Xesar description

Xesar is a formal verification tool which implements model checking techniques We present here concisely the Xesar tool, although a more complete description can be found in [10] and in [23]

Xesar verifies properties of a protocol specified in Estelle/R (a dialect of ISO-Estelle). The formalism used to specify the properties is branching time logic CTL [24].

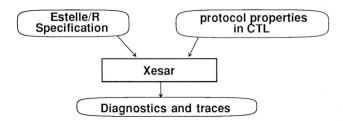

Figure 5. Xesar General Functionning

As users of Xesar, we have noted two characteristics. They come from the method itself and have some consequences upon the studied system.

The verification done by Xesar is based on the system state graph which must be built before any check. This graph contains all the possible states of the analized system. The consequence is that this method forbids dynamic creation of entities (INIT clause in Estelle). If the analyzed system contains such features, the use of Xesar leads us either to build a new static system or to decompose it into static sub-specification which can be validated. In either case, the validation does not apply to the initial model and some complementary analysis is needed.

The second characteristic is that Xesar implements the Rendez-vous mechanism for module communication. This mechanism models synchronous communication. But when the studied system contains asynchronous communications, this model by Rendez-vous is not adapted. The consequences are that the model introduces unexpected deadlocks.

3.2.2. Discussion

Three difficulties have restricted the results we may expect from the use of this tool.

First, we have had to divide our system into some smaller ones, each of them being small enough to be studied by XESAR. This restriction hangs some doubts over the obtained results.

Second, if some properties like deadlock freeness are obvious, it is quite difficult to decide how to express the protocol service or the correct behaviour of the entities.

Finally, except very simple properties like sequence of few events, the writing of temporal logic formulas requires a good knowledge.

In fact, the use of Xesar allows us to verify only simple properties.

All these difficulties lead us to look for other tools which implement techniques like observers [25] [21] or Petri Nets, directly [26][27], or after some translation from an Estelle specification [28].

4. AUTOMATIC IMPLEMENTATION

4.1. Integration in a host

4.1.1. Structure of an Estelle derived process

Estelle WorkStation allows us to compile an Estelle entity specification into a C program and then to build an executable program by linking it with the implementation library and some private procedures.

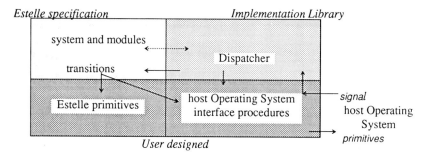

Figure 6. Structure of an Estelle derived process

The private procedures contain communication features in order to install the specification in a host and to allow it to communicate with other processes. This communication interface must be integrated in the specification; this modification of the specification is quite a minor one.

4.1.2. Inter-Process Communication

Any inter-process communication may be used; we have experimented two techniques on a SUN 3/80 workstation, running SUNOS 4.03 :
- UNIX message operations (msg) for communications inside the host :

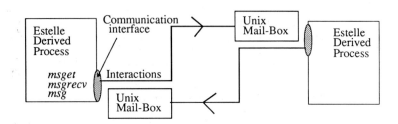

- BSD 4.3 Socket based TCP connections for communications between several networked hosts .

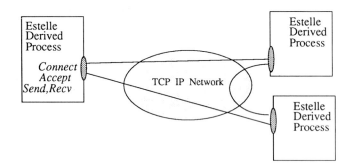

Moreover we have combined the two techniques which may easily interwork :

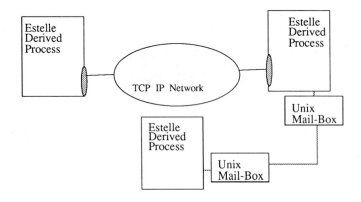

For doing these implementations we had to be very careful to adjust the communications interfaces, especially the TCP by selecting the most suitable features of sockets (we chose non blocking sockets) and to manage correctly the timer interruptions.

However once the interface is well defined, it becomes rather easy to install such processes in hosts systems.

4.1.3. Architecture of an application

We may also note that it's up to the designer to build the architecture and to distribute the suitable Estelle modules in the processes. For instance, we have put in a process one ELDA entity and two EU entities, and in another process, only one ELDA entity.

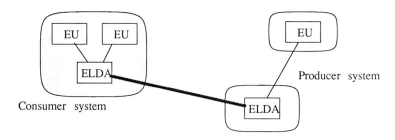

Figure 7. An example of Derived Processes

In this case, the numbers of lines of the different system sources are :

	Estelle source	generated C source	external C primitives
Producer	1600	3895	3100
Consumer	1860	4815	3100

4.2. Measurement

To see the advantages of a Formal Description Technique and its associated tools, such as EWS, we tried to compare the program produced by the Estelle Workstation with another one, which performs the same processing, but was obtained by direct C programming.

To compare these two programs, we have chosen to apply the same environmental, static and dynamic measures, listed in [29], to them.

Environmental analysis consists in evaluating the design and development process in order to check whether the product development process conforms to quality assurance rules. The non-existence of concrete environmental measures led us to make a qualitative comparison of the two design and development processes. This was done according to a scale model of the Mc Call [30] quality tree which proposes a factor and criterion decomposition of software quality. Regarding the factors of maintainability, testability and flexibility, the automatically generation is more efficient especially because of the good instrumentation of the EWS environment, the opportunity of using automatically validation and the verification methods offered by the formal specification stage, and the adaptability of Estelle language for protocol specification which makes easier the programmer's work. However, regarding the factors of reusability and portability, the direct implementation performs better because of the low software independance of EWS.

Static measures have been carried out by Logiscope [11] which performs Halstead [31] and Mc Cabe [32] complexity measures, and the results have been analized with a statistical software. This static analysis shows that the automatically generated C program has a less complex structure, as the EWS generator does not need to cut complex procedures into lower levels as programmer does, and because of the program organization. Nevertheless, we must point out that static measures were applied to generated C source program and not to the Estelle program. It is very possible that we would obtain differing results with another generator. However, when we compare the automatic implementation control graphs to the manual implementation control graphs, we observe that the most important manual implemented procedures take a more complex structure than the automatic implemented procedures. And when we analyse call graph of each implementation, we can observe recursive calls of procedures in the manual implementation graph that reduce the graph complexity but not the application lisibility.

Using the UNIX tools for dynamic measures, we have noted that the automatically generated process needed on average, three times more memory (150 Kbytes vs 50 Kbytes and two times more CPU time (0.4 to 0.6 s vs 0.2 to 0.3). But this evident inefficiency of the automatically generated process in dynamic analysis is a minor disadvantage if the protocol has to be implemented in a powerful computer.

Nevertheless, we must insist on the fact that the results had been achieved with EWS generator. This is an experimental result, and it would be necessary to compare this result with others obtained with another generatot.

So, in the sum, we can conclude that the automatic generation presents more advantages to the designers, but the generator must be improved in order to obtain a perfect interoperability between two processes, the one automatically generated and the other direct implemented, and to provide better performances.

4.3. FUTURE INTEGRATION

For all the implementations we carried out, the ELDA-PDUs are exchanged without using the Basic Encoding Rules of ASN1 [33]. Presently, we are trying to cope with this problem by using an ASN1 compiler. Many compilers already exist such as PLC409 [34] or CX409 [35]. We are studying the interfacing of the EWS implementation kernel with POSY/PEPY ASN1 compiler of ISODE environment [36]. The main task is to transfer all values to be encoded/decoded from the Estelle implementations towards ISODE interface structures. At this stage, we have not adjusted the interface. Nevertheless many experiments have already been done as in [37] or as in [38] with EDB and PLC409.

The second point we are studying is the integration of a real MTS package. Indeed, we have only implemented an Estelle test version. However, after the different tests we have carried out, it is our opinion that EWS is suitable to be interfaced with any package.

5. CONCLUSION

This approach by using FDT and various tools covers a wide part of communication software development cycle. The Estelle tools used in this project are suitable for the kind of application we have to deal with.

The results we have obtained encourage us to use the same methodology in the design and development of an infra-red LAN protocol [39]. However the situation is rather different since there is no specification yet, even in natural language.

During the development process of ELDA protocol, we used various tools (EWS, Xesar, ISODE, LOGISCOPE). However it was difficult to get these tools to directly communicate because each of them is specific, with its particular user interface, specific data representation or data transformation. So to make these tools cooperate, we have had to interface them by hand which increases the production process complexity. To solve this problem, it will be interesting to set up a development environment integrating tools of the software life cycle various phases. This environment would allow tools to share data stored in a common format. Morever, the integrated tools should show a uniform user interface in order to make designer task easier. Such an environment is usually known as an Integrated Project Support Environment (IPSE). It aims at reducing the software protocol development cost. It should also guarantee the quality of the development process and the quality of the final product.

6. ACKNOWLEDGEMENTS

This work is supported by GDF/DETN/SIMA company.
The authors wish to thank their colleagues from Equipe Réseaux & Protocoles for stimulating discussion, A. Ternot, J.M. Drain and A. Sudret from GDF/DETN/SIMA for their helpful support. Special thanks to B. Traverson from INRIA for all his help and to Bridget, Margaret and Maureen for reviewing this paper.

7. REFERENCES

1 M. Diaz, C.A.Vissers, J.P.Ansart, "Software Environment for the Design of Open distributed Systems" in FDT Estelle, results of the ESPRIT SEDOS Project, Edited by M.Diaz and al., North Holland 1989.

2 C. Rieu, J.J. Mercier, M.C. Vialatte, "A Tool for Specification and Semi-automatic Implementation of Transfer Protocols", Proceedings of the International Conference on Computer Communication ICCC'88, Tel Aviv, Israel, October 1988.

3 ISO IS 9074, "Estelle, a Formal Description Technique based on an extended state transition model", November 1988.

4 ISO IS 8807, "Lotos, a Formal Description Technique based on the Temporal ordering of Observational Behaviour", 1988.

5 R. Sijelmassi, B. Strausser, "NIST Integrated Tool Set for Estelle", Proceedings of the Third International Conference on Formal Description Techniques FORTE'90, Madrid, Spain, November 5-8, 1990.

6 P. de Saqui-Sannes, J.P. Courtiat, "ESTIM : The Estelle Simulator Prototype of The ESPRIT-SEDOS Project", Proceedings of the First International Conference on Formal Description Techniques (FORTE 88), September, 1988.

7 "SEDOS Estelle Demonstrator", Esprit Project 1265, Workshop at Brussels, May 1989.

8 S. Budkowski, "Chaîne d'outils Estelle, aide au développement de protocoles de communication", FIRTECH, France, January 29-30, 1990.
9 "Echange de Lots de données entre Applications. Proposition de norme (version 4)", FJIDSTT 1661-1, EDF/GDF, 1988.
10 J.L. Richier, C. Rodriguez, J. Sifakis, J. Voiron, "Xesar user's Guide", September 1987.
11 "Logiscope, notice technique", VERILOG, Toulouse, France, october 1988.
12 S. Budkowski, P. Dembinski, "An Introduction to Estelle; a Specification Language for Distributed Systems", Computer Networks and ISDN Systems, Vol. 14, pp 3-23, 1987
13 R.L. Tenney, "A Tutorial Introduction to Estelle", Invited paper at the First International Conference on Formal Description Techniques, Stirling, September 1988.
14 ISO DIS 10021-4 / CCITT X411, "Message Oriented Text Interchange System, Message Transfer System - Abstract Service definition and Procedures", September 1988.
15 G. von Bochmann, "Protocol Specification for OSI" in Computer Networks and ISDN systems 18, p.167-184, 1989/1990.
16 ISO IS 8824, "Information Processing Systems - Open Systems Interconnection - Specification of Abstract Syntax Notation One (ASN1)".
17 J.P. Courtiat, "Introducing a rendez-vous mechanism in Estelle: Estelle*", The FDT Estelle, Results of ESPRIT/SEDOS Project, edited by M. Diaz and al. , North Holland 1989.
18 E. Lallet, A. Lebrun, J.F. Martin, S. Budkowski, "Un outil de génération automatique de l'environnement d'exécution de spécifications Estelle" in proceedings of CFIP 91, Pau, France, September 17-19, 1991.
19 C.T. Nguyen, M.C. Vialatte, "Expérimentation de Estelle sur ELDA : commentaires sur le protocole ELDA", rapport technique GDF/SIMA, January 1991.
20 M. Guilmet, P. Thomas, B. Traverson, "Design, Implementation and Validation of a multi-peer protocol using Estelle" in proccedings of FORTE'90 Edited by J. Quemada, J. Manas, E. Vasquez, DIT-UPM.
21 B. Algayres, V. Coelho, and al., "VESAR: Un outil pour la spécification et la vérification formelle de protocoles", CFIP 91, Pau, France, September 17-19, 1991.
22 R. Groz, "Automated verification of logical properties of protocols on simulation, using an observer approach", Thèse de l'université de Rennes I, mention informatique.
23 E.M. Clarke, E.A. Emerson and A.P. Sistla, "Automatic verification of Finite-state concurrent system using Temporal Logic Specifications", ACM TOPLAS 8 (2), 1986.
24 J.L. Richier, C. Rodriguez, J. Sifakis, J. Voiron, "Verification in Xesar of the sliding window protocol", in proceedings of IFIP international meeting on Protocol Specification, testing and Verification, Zurich, May 5-8, 1987
25 C. Jard, R. Groz, J.F. Monin, "Development of VEDA : a Protyping Tool for Distributed Algorithms", IEEE Transactions on Software Engineering, 14 (3) March 1998.

26 P. Azema, G. Papanagiotakis, "Protocol analysis by using predicate nets", 5th Workshop on Protocol Specification, Testing and Verification, Toulouse, France, June 1985.
27 P. de Saqui-Sannes, J.P. Courtiat, "From the simulation to the verification of Estelle* specifications", Proceedings of the Second International Conference on Formal Description Techniques(FORTE 89),Vancouver, Canada, December 5-8, 1989.
28 B. Zouari, P. Estraillier, "Le projet PETRISTELLE. Validation Formelle de systèmes à partir de spécifications Estelle", FIRTECH, France, January 29-31, 1990.
29 P. Hunel, Rapport de DEA d'Informatique, Université Blaise Pascal-Clermont II, 1990
30 J.A. McCall, "Factors in software quality", General Electric nr. 77C1502, June 1977.
31 M.H. Halstead, "Element of Software Science", Elsevier, North-Holland, New-York, 1977
32 T.J. McCabe, "A complexity measure", IEEE Trans. on Soft. eng., December 1976.
33 ISO IS 8825, "Information Processing Systems - Open Systems Interconnection - Specification of Basic Encoding Rules for Abstract Syntax Notation One(ASN.1) 1987.
34 "PLC409, The Presentation Layer Compiler X409/ASN1, Product general Information", A/MKI/PLC409/PGI, Marben, Paris, France, 1988
35 "Présentation générale de CX409", Audilog SA, Montigny-le-Bretonneux, France, 1989
36 T.R Marshall, "The ISO Development Environment user's manual volume 4", 1989.
37 P. Dembinski, "Interfacing ASN1 and Estelle : A pratical approach" In Proceedings of the Third International Conference on Formal Description Techniques FORTE'90, Madrid, Spain, November 5-8, 1990, Edited by J. Quemada, J. Manas, E. Vasquez, DIT-UPM, 1990.
38 J. Toutain, S. Budkowski and al., "Développement de FTAM à partir de sa spécification en Estelle" in proceedings of DNAC 1989 p. 181-192, Eyrolles 1989.
39 M.C. Vialatte, Misson M., "La recherche en informatique à l'université de Clermont-Ferrand, Equipe Réseaux et Protocoles" in La lettre de l'ADMIRA, number 10, March 1989.

service	Description	Request	Ind.	Conf
MB-create	Creation of Mail-Box	×		×
MB-modify	Modification of Mail-Box	×		×
MB-consult	Consultation of Mail-Box	×		×
History-consult	Consultation of history	×		×
MB-delete	Deletion of Mail Box	×		×
Consume	Consumation of Data-Batch	×		×
Alarm	Alarm set	×		×
Product	Production of Data-Batch	×		×
Send	Sending of deferred Data-Batch	×		×
BATCH-delete	Deletion of DATA-Batch	×		×
BATCH-deliver	Delivery of DATA-Batch		×	
BATCH-notify	Notification of DATA-Batch		×	
Consummation-notify	Notification of DATA-Batch consummation		×	

Figure 8. Service primitives

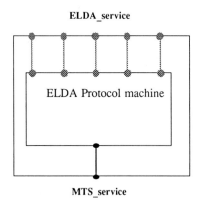

Figure 9. Structure of an ELDA entity

Specification and Validation of a Simple Overtaking Protocol using LOTOS

Patrik Ernberg
Lars-åke Fredlund
Bengt Jonsson*
Swedish Institute of Computer Science
Box 1263, S-164 28 Kista, Sweden

Abstract

We present a LOTOS specification of a simple protocol for overtaking between vehicles. The main purposes of this paper are to evaluate the applicability of LOTOS and related tools for the early design stages in the construction of a protocol, in particular in a new application domain where features such as positioning of cars must be modeled, and to illustrate the use of available validation tools.

1 Introduction

During the last decade, increasing attention has been given to the use of Formal Description Techniques (FDTs) for protocol specification and validation. In this paper, we present a case study where we (1) use FDTs to specify and validate a protocol in the early stages of the design process, (2) use FDTs in a new application domain where new system aspects (such as e.g. positioning of cars) must be modeled, and (3) use various automated validation tools to detect errors at an early stage of the design. The chosen protocol is intended to coordinate vehicles on a road, in order to reduce the risk of accidents when vehicles overtake each other.

The specification of the overtaking protocol has been a part of our effort in the PROMETHEUS project. One of the aims of this project is to use communication protocols between intelligent cars to improve traffic safety. Some desirable functions in PROMETHEUS are informally specified in [PRO89]. The overtaking protocol in this paper is our simplified design inspired by the specification of safe overtaking in [PRO89].

Variations of the overtaking protocol have been specified by us using communicating labelled transition systems (LTSs) [ELN+89, LNEF90, EFH+91]. An overtaking protocol based on the one in this paper has also been specified in PSF_d [Mul91]. For the

---

*Authors' email: pernberg@sics.se; bengt@sics.se; fred@sics.se

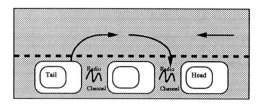

Figure 1: The Overtaking Scenario

present specification, we have chosen LOTOS [BB89]. LOTOS has been successfully used to specify and validate large protocols [EVD89] and is an accepted ISO standard [ISO87]. Tools for validating reasonable size LOTOS specifications are starting to emerge [Eij89, QPF90, Tre89], and the Caesar tool [GS90] can translate LOTOS specifications into LTSs. In addition, LOTOS provides certain constructs which are desirable when specifying medium to large sized software systems [Ern91]. These constructs are, for example, data types, process instantiation, and operators which improve the structure and legibility of a specification.

In Section 2 we present the overtaking protocol and specify it formally in LOTOS. We will assume that the reader has basic familiarity with LOTOS and refer to [BB89] for a concise introduction to the language. The validation of the protocol specification is presented in Section 3 and a discussion of our results and conclusions are presented in Sections 4 and 5.

2 Specification of the Overtaking Protocol

In this Section we will first describe the overtaking protocol informally and list some basic assumptions that we made regarding its functionality. We then formalize this informal description in LOTOS.

2.1 Informal Description of the Overtaking Protocol

The scenario in which the overtaking protocol operates assumes a queue of cars following each other. In the following, we will assume that the queue consists of three vehicles: a Head vehicle, a Middle vehicle, and a Tail vehicle (see Figure 1). Each vehicle in the queue can communicate with the immediately preceding and succeeding vehicles through unique radio channels.

A driver who intends to overtake the vehicle in front initiates a protocol entity in his own vehicle, which in its turn will initiate a negotiation with a protocol entity in the vehicle in front. Henceforth, the vehicle requesting permission to overtake will be referred to as a *client* vehicle whereas the requested vehicle will be referred to as a *server* vehicle. The *server* vehicle decides if overtaking is possible, in which case a positive response is sent to the *client* vehicle. If overtaking is not possible, the *server* waits for the next overtaking request from the client. Once a *client* vehicle has initiated an overtaking negotiation, it will keep on negotiating until it is given a positive acknowledgment from the *server* vehicle, i.e. it is not possible to abort an overtaking. A vehicle may only overtake its directly preceding vehicle. To pass two vehicles, at least two overtaking protocol negotiations must be performed.

To keep our specification of the overtaking protocol relatively simple, we have made certain assumptions regarding the environment as well as the involved vehicles and communication channels. We will mention a few general assumptions here and point out others as we explain the protocol specification:

- We only consider a fixed and finite number of vehicles in the queue, i.e. we do not allow vehicles to join or leave the queue. This also means that we do not allow the *head* vehicle to overtake or the *tail* vehicle to be overtaken.

- The channels used to negotiate the overtaking are simplex mediums which are presumed to be unreliable: they may nondeterministically lose messages but not alter the contents of messages.

- We assume that the environment will remain "friendly" once a vehicle has received a go ahead signal from the preceding vehicle, i.e. no unexpected events, such as the sudden appearance of a large moose on the road, will occur.

2.2 Formal Description of the Overtaking Protocol in LOTOS

Our formal specification consists of Vehicle processes which communicate with each other through the Medium process, and during an overtaking through the Overtake_Medium process. We call primitives that are exchanged between vehicle and medium processes *Protocol Data Units* (PDUs). These will all be prefixed with a "p_ot_". Primitives that are exchanged between the vehicle and the overtaking service user[1] are referred to as *Service Primitives* and are prefixed with "ot_". A rcv or a snd value is appended to all PDUs to distinguish the sending of a PDU from the reception of a PDU.

2.2.1 Formal Specification of the Vehicle Process

The Vehicle process has three gates for communication purposes. Below we give a brief description of each gate.

S   The interface between the overtaking service user and the vehicle.

M   The interface between the vehicle and the communication medium which is used to send messages to the succeeding and preceding vehicles in the queue.

---

[1] A user of the overtaking service in a given vehicle may either be the physical driver of the vehicle or another process in the vehicle

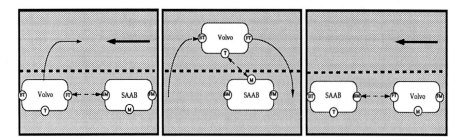

Figure 2: An overtaking situation

Ot The interface between the vehicle and the overtaking medium, used only at the moment of overtaking.

Each Vehicle has knowledge of the communication medium addresses of the succeeding and the preceding vehicles (B and F), and the overtaking medium address of the preceding vehicle (Op). Additionally, a Vehicle has information about its own name (car), and whether it is at the head, middle, or tail of the vehicle train (pos).

The address of the recipient of a PDU is added before the message is sent over the selected medium. For example, M!F!snd!pdu sends pdu to the preceding vehicle over the M gate (via the Medium process). During an overtaking, the protocol takes care to swap the information of addresses between the two involved vehicles (via the OT medium) to reflect the new ordering of vehicles in the queue.

The passing of addresses between the processes involved in an overtaking scenario is illustrated in Figure 2. The scenario consists of a road with two-way traffic, with two vehicles, Volvo and Saab, travelling from left to right. In the other lane, traffic normally flows from right to left. In each vehicle process, the name of the vehicle as well as the current values of the F, B, and Op addresses are illustrated. In the Volvo vehicle, for example, the F address has the value FT, the B address has the value BT, and the Op address has the value T. The figure starts in the left hand configuration, and tries to illustrate how the values of the F, B and Op addresses change during an overtaking. The connection between a pair of addresses, a communication channel, is implemented by the Medium and Overtake_Medium processes. In the figures such a connection is illustrated by an arrow between two vehicles. The initial situation of the figure is that the Volvo vehicle is negotiating an overtaking with the Saab vehicle. The overtaking then starts and the two vehicles communicate address values. Finally, when the overtaking has finished, the Volvo vehicle is at the head of the queue. Our specification of a Vehicle can be divided into three parts:

1. A description of how an overtaking entity can become either a server or a client in a given overtaking scenario, formalized in the LOTOS process Vehicle.

2. A client part, to enable the local service user to overtake safely, specified in the LOTOS process Client.

3. A server part, to serve the overtaking request initiated by another overtaking entity, formalized in the LOTOS process Server.

```
process Vehicle[S,M,OT](F:M_Port,B:M_Port,Op:Ot_Port,pos:Position,car:CarId):noexit :=
         S!ot_req!car!pos[pos <> Head]; Client[S,M,OT](F,B,Op,pos,car)
      [] M!B!rcv!p_ot_req[pos <> Tail]; Server[S,M,OT](F,B,Op,pos,car)
endproc
```

If the Vehicle process first accepts an overtaking request ot_req from the service user, which is not possible at the head of the queue (i.e. [pos <> head]), the vehicle becomes a client. If however a p_ot_req PDU is received from a succeeding vehicle the vehicle becomes a server.

The client process starts by sending a p_ot_req to the preceding vehicle announcing its intention to overtake, and awaits a response. A timer may then either time out (client_timer), in which case the Client process is restarted (which will resend p_ot_req), or a positive acknowledgment is received (p_ot_conf_ok) from the preceding car, thus initiating the actual overtaking procedure. If a positive acknowledgment arrives too late from the preceding car, i.e. the client_timer has already timed out and the client wants to send a new overtaking request p_ot_req, the system may deadlock since the medium only supports simplex communication (there is a conflict between the sending of p_ot_req and the reception of p_ot_conf_ok). This problem is resolved by accepting "old" acknowledgments in the Client, but ignoring them since they are out-of-date.

The client starts the actual overtaking procedure by informing the service user that overtaking is about to begin (ot_begin). The client then sends its own position, its own overtaking medium address, and the communication medium address of its successor to the server via the overtaking medium. When the client receives the servers's position and the addresses to the vehicle preceding the server, the client first informs the service user that the overtaking has been successfully completed (ot_end), and then restarts the Vehicle process with updated addresses and position.

```
process Client [S,M,OT](F:M_Port,B:M_Port,Op:Ot_Port,pos:Position,car:CarId):noexit :=
       hide client_timer in
       M!F!snd!p_ot_req;
            (    client_timer!car; Client[S,M,OT](F,B,Op,pos,car)
            []
                 M!F!rcv!p_ot_conf_ok;
                 S!ot_begin!car!pos;
                 OT!Op!B!Op!pos;
                 OT!Op?s_F:M_Port?s_Op:Ot_Port?s_pos:Position;
                 S!ot_end!car!pos;
                 Vehicle[S,M,OT](s_F,F,s_Op,s_pos,car))
       [] M!F!rcv!p_ot_conf_ok; Client[S,M,OT](F,B,Op,pos,car)
endproc
```

The server part is activated when a p_ot_req PDU is received from a succeeding vehicle. This will result in an ot_ind service primitive being sent to the overtaking service user.

We assume that the overtaking service user has the intelligence to decide if it is reasonable to overtake and appropriate responses are given to the server. The service user might for example decide that overtaking is safe if no approaching vehicle can be detected. If the response is negative, the server will await another p_ot_req from the succeeding vehicle. Otherwise, if the response is positive, this will be forwarded to the succeeding vehicle by means of a p_ot_conf_ok, and the server will be ready for the actual overtaking. In order to avoid deadlocks in the system, the Server_answer and Server_ok processes have been modified to handle the case when the client times out and resends the overtaking request p_ot_req (either due to slow processing in the server, or message loss in the communication medium).

```
process Server[S,M,OT](F:M_Port,B:M_Port,Op:Ot_Port,pos:Position,car:CarId):noexit :=
            S!ot_ind!car!pos;
                (    S!ot_resp_no!car!pos; M!B!rcv!p_ot_req; Server[S,M,OT](F,B,Op,pos,car)
                 []  S!ot_resp_ok!car!pos; Server_answer[S,M,OT](F,B,Op,pos,car))
endproc

process Server_answer[S,M,OT](F:M_Port,B:M_Port,Op:Ot_Port,pos:Position,car:CarId)
    :noexit :=
            M!B!snd!p_ot_conf_ok; Server_ok[S,M,OT](F,B,Op,pos,car)
         [] M!B!rcv!p_ot_req; Server[S,M,OT](F,B,Op,pos,car)
endproc

process Server_ok[S,M,OT](F:M_Port,B:M_Port,Op:Ot_Port,pos:Position,car:CarId)
    :noexit :=
            OT!Op?c_B:M_Port!F?c_Op:Ot_Port!Op?c_pos:Position!pos;
            Vehicle[S,M,OT](B,c_B,c_Op,c_pos,car)
         [] M!B!rcv!p_ot_req; Server[S,M,OT](F,B,Op,pos,car)
endproc
```

The server part of the overtaking synchronization is activated upon the reception of the client's position and the addresses to the client's succeeding vehicle. In the same communication, the server transmits its own position, and the addresses of its preceding vehicle. After this synchronization (over the overtaking medium), the Vehicle process is restarted with addresses and position parameters updated to reflect the result of the overtaking.

2.2.2 Formal Specification of the Communication medium

The communication medium used for negotiating overtakings is modelled as two static channels, each channel connecting two ports. Using actual LOTOS gates for this purpose is not possible because LOTOS gates cannot be communicated in a process synchronization. Instead we modelled these abstract ports using addresses (constant values of a LOTOS type), and a global gate M. Each channel thus connects a fixed address (which can be communicated in a process synchronization) to another fixed address. As previously mentioned, the communication channels are lossy and simplex.

```
process Medium[M]:noexit :=
        M_Channel[M](F_Tail,B_Middle) ||| M_Channel[M](F_Middle,B_Head)
endproc

process M_Channel[M](P1:M_Port,P2:M_Port):noexit :=
        hide medium_loss in
            M!P1!snd?pdu:PDUsort;
                (   M!P2!rcv!pdu;   M_Channel[M](P1,P2)
                [] medium_loss; M_Channel[M](P1,P2))
            [] M!P2!snd?pdu:PDUsort;
                (   M!P1!rcv!pdu;   M_Channel[M](P1,P2)
                [] medium_loss; M_Channel[M](P1,P2))
endproc
```

2.2.3 Formal Specification of the Overtaking medium

The overtaking medium is similar to the communication medium, except that the medium is perfect and one-way. Thus only one address per vehicle is needed: if the vehicle is a client in the current overtaking scenario, it communicates only with the preceding vehicle; if it is acting as a server, it communicates only with the succeeding one. The vehicles involved in the overtaking swap the following communication medium addresses: the overtaking vehicle receives the address of the vehicle in front of the overtaken vehicle, and the overtaken vehicle receives the address of the vehicle behind the overtaking vehicle. The vehicles also exchange their positions (e.g. tail and middle positions) and their overtaking medium addresses.

```
process Overtake_Medium[OT]:noexit :=
        Ot_Channel[OT](ot_Tail, ot_Middle) ||| Ot_Channel[OT](ot_Middle, ot_Head)
endproc

process Ot_Channel[OT](P1:Ot_Port,P2:Ot_Port):noexit :=
        OT!P1?c_B:M_Port?c_Op:Ot_Port?c_pos:Position;
        OT!P2!c_B?s_F:M_Port!c_Op?s_Op:Ot_Port!c_pos?s_pos:Position;
        OT!P1!s_F!s_Op!s_pos;
        Ot_Channel[OT](P1,P2)
endproc
```

3 Validation of the Overtaking Protocol

In this section, we present the different tools and methods used when validating the Overtaking protocol. It should be emphasized that the process of proving the protocol correct was closely intertwined with the specification work. In order to make the verification methods work well, care had to be taken to write the specification in a verifiable way.

In order to make verification possible, we restricted the queue to a length of three vehicles.

The vehicles are called Volvo, Saab, and BMW, and are initially in this order with BMW at the head of the queue. Below we present a skeleton specification of the Overtaking protocol for three vehicles:

```
hide M, OT in
       ( Vehicle[S,M,OT](F_Tail, B_Tail, ot_Tail, Tail, Volvo)
       ||| Vehicle[S,M,OT](F_Middle, B_Middle, ot_Middle, Middle, Saab)
       ||| Vehicle[S,M,OT](F_Head, B_Head, ot_Head, Head, BMW))
                            |[M,OT]|
         (Medium[M] ||| Overtake_Medium[OT])
```

Parameters prefixed with F_ and B_ are communication medium addresses to the preceding and succeeding vehicles, while those prefixed with ot_ are overtaking medium addresses to the preceding vehicle. Notice that each vehicle also has a name and a current position. Below, the different tools and methods will be described in the order in which they were applied.

3.1 Simulation

When our specification had become reasonably complete, we simulated it using the Hippo[Tre89] tool. The simulator essentially performs a step by step expansion of the protocol, allowing the user to specify which nondeterministic steps should be taken. We stepped through a number of key scenarios that were central to the workings of the protocol. We checked, for instance, that the tail vehicle could overtake the middle vehicle, and that the new tail vehicle could then overtake the new middle vehicle. Several errors in the protocol were discovered by testing such selected scenarios. The errors were fixed and the simulation repeated until no more errors were found.

3.2 Expansion and Minimization

Once we were fairly sure that the LOTOS specification was correct, we translated it into a labelled transition system using the Caesar[GS90] tool. This produced a transition graph with 89879 states and 286716 transitions. The transition system was then minimized with respect to observation equivalence, using the Aldébaran[Fer89] tool, to produce a graph with 156 states and 318 transitions.

3.3 Projection

To get a better understanding of the result of the minimization we used *projections*, i.e. looking at only a subset of all primitives which are visible to the environment. Technically, this can either be done by hiding additional ports explicitly in the LOTOS specification using the hide operator, or by renaming unwanted actions to the internal action (i) using a tool working on LTSs, and then minimizing the result using Aldébaran. The latter method is often preferred as it can be done on an already minimized automaton and specific actions at a certain port may also be hidden.

The projections were displayed graphically using the Auto and Autograph tools[SV89, RdS89], resulting in an increased understanding of how and why the protocol works. As an example of a picture created by Autograph, the projection of the actions of the Volvo vehicle for the three vehicle scenario can be found in Figure 3.

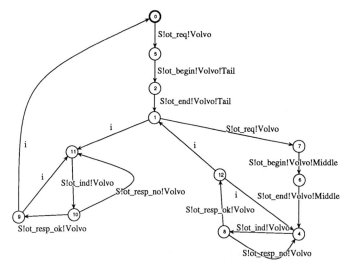

Figure 3: The graphical representation of the actions of the Volvo vehicle.

State 0 is the initial state, with the Volvo at the tail of the queue. State 1 represents the state when the Volvo has just overtaken to reach the middle position in the queue, and in state 4 the Volvo has reached the head of the queue.

3.4 Model Checking

In the previous section, a method of validation based on projections was presented. This essentially involved looking at a sufficiently small subset of visible primitives and judging if these behaved according to our intuition. An alternative method of validating the protocol is to use model checking. This amounts to proving that the specification satisfies a set of properties expressed in a modal logic. In the following, we will make use of the modal μ-calculus. We will briefly introduce the calculus here, and refer to [Sti87, Sti89] for more in depth descriptions of the logic as well as more general discussions about temporal logics for communicating systems.

3.4.1 The μ-calculus

The μ-calculus is a propositional modal logic with relativized modal operators. The set of formulas of the logic is defined as follows:

- tt is a formula
- if P and Q are formulas then so are $\neg P$, $P \vee Q$, and <e>P where e is an event.

The truth of a proposition in the μ-calculus is defined relative to a transition system. We use a satisfaction relation, denoted $\models$, to define when a proposition is true in a state. $S \models P$ should be read: "the proposition P is true in the state S". The semantics of the formulas is defined as follows:

- $S \models$ tt for all states S. The proposition tt is the most primitive proposition and is satisfied by all states.
- $S \models \neg P$ if and only if not $S \models P$.
- $S \models P \vee Q$ if and only if $S \models P$ or $S \models Q$.
- $S \models$<e>P if and only if there exits a transition labelled with event e from state S to state S' and $S' \models P$.

We also have the derived modal operators ff $\equiv \neg$tt, P $\wedge$ Q $\equiv \neg(\neg$P $\vee \neg$Q$)$, and $[e]P \equiv \neg$<e>$\neg P$. Furthermore, we shall use the two derived operators $[-]P$ and <->P, where "$-$" can be regarded as wild card events. Thus, a state satisfies $[-]P$ if all its derivatives satisfy P, and it satisfies <->P if it has a derivative that satisfies P.

In order to further increase the expressive power of the language we introduce maximal and minimal fixpoint operators. The maximal fixpoint operator, $\nu X.(P)$, can be interpreted as the infinite conjunction $P_0 \wedge P_1 \wedge, ...$, where $P_0 =$ tt and $P_{i+1} = P[P_i/X]$. This operator is useful for expressing invariance properties. The minimal fixed point operator $\mu X.(P)$ is the dual of the maximal one and can be interpreted as the infinite disjunction $P_0 \vee P_1 \vee, ...$, where $P_0 =$ ff and $P_{i+1} = P[P_i/X]$. This constructor is useful for expressing eventuality properties.

3.4.2 Validating the Overtaking protocol using the μ-calculus

The general method of validation involves taking the minimized LTS produced by Caesar and feeding it into the Concurrency Workbench. It is then possible to verify that the LTS satisfies a given μ-calculus formula using the model checking algorithm in the Concurrency Workbench (see [CPS89, Mol91] for a description of the model checking implementation in the Concurrency Workbench). Most interesting properties described in the μ-calculus make use of fixed point operators. Unfortunately, these are, at least to a novice, rather unintuitive. The best way of using them is therefore to define some well-understood properties and code these as macros. Below, we define some macros which have proved useful when specifying desirable behaviors:

$$\begin{aligned}
AG\ P &\equiv \nu X.(P \wedge [-]X) \\
EF\ P &\equiv \mu X.(P \vee <->X) \\
A(P\ U\ Q) &\equiv \mu X.(Q \vee (P \wedge [-]X \wedge <->\text{tt}))
\end{aligned}$$

$AG\ P$ holds in a state s if P holds in every state reachable from s. This macro is used to describe a property which invariantly holds for a labelled transition system. $EF\ P$ holds in a state s if P holds in some future state reachable from s. $EF\ P$ can be used to describe properties which will eventually hold in some future state. $A(P\ U\ Q)$ holds in a state s if Q is guaranteed to hold in some future state and P holds in every state until then. Using the macros defined above, we can go on and specify some interesting properties which the Overtaking protocol should satisfy:

Property 1 *The protocol does not contain any deadlocks.*

In order to specify that no deadlock occurs we merely have to make sure that the initial state can perform an event and that all states reachable from the initial state can perform an event:

$$NoDeadlock = AG\ \texttt{<->tt}$$

Property 2 *It is always possible for all vehicles to reach a state where they can initiate an overtaking operation.*

This property states that there exist no "sink" states in the protocol from which other states are unreachable. An alternative formulation of the above property could be that there exist no future states where the S!ot_req action remains invariantly deadlocked.

$$NoSink = \neg EF\ AG\ [S!ot\_req]\texttt{ff}$$

Property 3 *Once the tail vehicle has started overtaking, neither the tail vehicle nor the middle vehicle will attempt to start overtaking before the tail vehicle has finished overtaking.*

This property says that all overtaking operations performed by the tail vehicle are safe.

$$\begin{aligned}SafeOver\ =\ &AG\ [S!ot\_begin!Tail]\\&(A(([S!ot\_begin!Tail]\texttt{ff} \wedge [S!ot\_begin!Middle]\texttt{ff})\ U\ \texttt{<}S!ot\_end!Tail\texttt{>tt}))\end{aligned}$$

A similar formula could also be written for the case when the middle vehicle engages in an overtaking operation. For the sake of simplicity, both Properties 2 and 3 have been defined using service primitives which do not include any information about vehicle names. Of course, the μ-calculus formulas which are applied directly to a graph produced by Caesar from the specification in Section 2 would have to take vehicle names into account as well.

It should also be noted that the list of properties presented here is by no means exhaustive. We have only described a few interesting properties to give a flavor for what behaviors can concisely be described in the μ-calculus. Both the above properties could be described as safety properties which state that no undesirable events will ever happen. A further property which could be desirable in an overtaking protocol could be that the protocol is live in some sense:

Property 4 *A middle vehicle will always eventually be informed of a tail vehicle's request to overtake.*

The above property is not crucial for the protocol to be safe, but is desirable if we want the protocol to be fair and eventually handle a vehicle's request. Below we give the μ-calculus formalization of the property.

$$LiveOver = AG\ [S!ot\_req!Tail](A(\mathtt{tt}\ U\ <S!ot\_ind!Middle>\mathtt{tt}))$$

It turns out that this property is not satisfied by the overtaking protocol. The reason is that other overtaking requests from vehicles in the queue may always be handled before the first request i.e. the vehicle may be permanently starved. This property is similar to the mutual exclusion properties described in [Wal89, Sti91].

4 Discussion

In this section we discuss some issues regarding the specification of the Overtaking protocol in LOTOS. We divide our discussion into three parts. The first part discusses issues related to the LOTOS language. In the second part, we discuss the tool environment and the restrictions that it places on the specification and validation. Lastly, we consider our particular protocol and possible enhancements which can be made to the specification.

4.1 Comments about LOTOS

All communication events in our protocol have a direction in the sense that there is always a sender and a receiver. LOTOS communications do not distinguish between senders and receivers. We therefore had to append a value to each action indicating if it was intended as a send operation or a receive operation. For example, sending to the vehicle in front may be accomplished by the action $M!F!\mathtt{snd}!pdu$. The communication medium will pass this message along to the vehicle in front (if no message loss occurs) where it can be received using $M!B!\mathtt{rcv}?pduvar: PDUtype$.

A shortcoming of LOTOS is that it is not possible to pass gates between processes. Our specification circumvents this problem by coding the ports as abstract data types, and passing these as values between processes. This solution has the disadvantage that we have to introduce an explicit medium for communication between vehicles. A cleaner specification could probably have been achieved by using a specification formalism such as the π-calculus [MPW89a, MPW89b], where port names can be passed as parameters between processes. In [FO91] this problem is discussed in more detail.

4.2 Comments about the Tool Environment

While specifying and validating our specification we made extensive use of a collection of different tools. The fact that we could move between different tools and analyze our protocol using different methods made the work more efficient. To ease the process of working with different tools "common formats" for LTSs have been suggested [FMdS91]. Besides the problem of tool interaction, tools also place restrictions on what can be realistically verified. We were therefore forced to specify our Overtaking protocol in a verifiable way. The most serious restrictions were due to the Caesar verification tool:

- The specification had to be finite-state (we only consider a finite, fixed amount of vehicles), and furthermore, had to satisfy the more restrictive *static control constraints* (e.g. the parallel operator is not allowed in a recursive process, see [GS90]).

- Care had to be taken to cut down the size of the specification, otherwise the statespace would become too large for effective analysis.

As specifications become larger, verification becomes more difficult and simulation and testing are often the only possible methods of validation. In contrast to Caesar, Hippo can be conveniently used for large specifications. Simulation is an informative method of validation because of its interactive nature. In our example, simulating the protocol often gave us more understanding of how the protocol worked than using projection or model checking techniques.

4.3 Comments about the Overtaking Specification

We have deliberately made our specification simple to make it easy for the reader to follow the specification and to allow for verification using tools which can only cope with a very limited state space. Several improvements could be made to the existing protocol:

- A driver should be allowed to abort an overtake operation.

- No attempts have been made to model the rest of the environment in an explicit way. A good protocol should take into account vehicles in the opposite lane as well as unexpected events such as obstacles on the road.

- Assuming a fixed queue size is unrealistic. The protocol should cater for attachments to and detachments from the vehicle queue.

- The protocol should maybe make use of only one medium, i.e. the overtaking medium is not needed. We have in fact experimented with, and verified several scenarios where the overtaking medium is absent.

5 Conclusions

We have presented a simple specification of an Overtaking protocol in LOTOS and illustrated the application of different automatic validation techniques. Our goal was mainly to exercise LOTOS and its associated tools for early design and validation of a protocol.

Our experience suggests that LOTOS is an appropriate language to use for the early stages in the design of a protocol; the structural constructs available in LOTOS make it possible to produce concise specifications. The validation techniques, involving a number of different methods and tools also seem applicable in the early design process.

As the specification becomes more complex, verification using the Caesar tool becomes more difficult. Our present specification is close to the limit of what the current version of Caesar can efficiently handle. In fact, the limits of Caesar considerably influenced our design. On the other hand, our specification is quite loosely synchronized leading to a relatively large state space. Validation techniques based on simulation tools such as Hippo are useful even for specifications with large state-spaces.

The virtues of LOTOS should facilitate going from an early specification to a more enhanced design. It would be interesting to try to improve the specification in this paper with some of the suggestions presented in Section 4.3 in order to verify this conjecture.

6 Acknowledgments

This work has been partially funded by the ESPRIT/BRA project 3006 CONCUR, and the Swedish Telecommunication Administration (project PROCOM).

We would like to thank Joachim Parrow for valuable comments on earlier versions of the paper. We are particularly grateful to Kim Laraqui and Ala Nazari, Swedish Telecom Radio, for fruitful discussions which set the foundations for the work presented in this paper.

References

[BB89]   T. Bolognesi and E. Brinksma. Introduction to the ISO specification language LOTOS. In P. van Eijk, C. Vissers, and M. Diaz, editors, *The Formal Description Technique LOTOS*, pages 77–82. North-Holland, 1989.

[CPS89] R. Cleaveland, J. Parrow, and B. Steffen. A semantics-based verification tool for finite-state systems. In *Proc. Protocol Specification, Testing, and Verification IX*. North-Holland, 1989.

[EFH+91] P. Ernberg, L. Fredlund, H. Hansson, B. Jonsson, F. Orava, and B. Pehrson. Guidelines for specification and verification of communication protocols, 1991. SICS Perspective Report No. 1.

[Eij89] P. Eijk. Lotos tools based on the Cornell Synthesizer Generator. In E. Brinksma, G. Scollo, and C. Vissers, editors, *Proc. Protocol Specification, Testing, and Verification IX*. North-Holland, 1989.

[ELN+89] P. Ernberg, K. Laraqui, A. Nazari, C. Odmalm, B. Pehrson, and M. Svärdh. A PROMETHEUS - PROCOM framework, a specification model for PROMETHEUS functions and communication services. In *PROMETHEUS pro-*

ceedings of the 2nd Workshop, Stockholm. SICS and Swedish Telecom Radio, 1989.

[Ern91] P. Ernberg. CCS as a method of specification and verification: Analysis of a case study. Technical Report T91:05, SICS, 1991.

[EVD89] P. van Eijk, C. Vissers, and M. Diaz, editors. *The Formal Description Technique LOTOS.* North-Holland, 1989.

[Fer89] J-C. Fernandez. Aldébaran: A tool for verification of communicating processes. Technical Report RTC 14, IMAG, Grenoble, 1989.

[FMdS91] J-C. Fernandez, E. Madelaine, and R. de Simone. Fc: A common format representation for automata. Manuscript, 1991.

[FO91] L. Fredlund and F. Orava. Modelling dynamic communication structures in LOTOS. In *Proc. 4th International Conference on Formal Description Techniques*, 1991.

[GS90] H. Garavel and J. Sifakis. Compilation and verification of LOTOS specifications. In L. Logrippo, R. Probert, and H. Ural, editors, *Proc. Protocol Specification, Testing, and Verification X.* North-Holland, 1990.

[ISO87] ISO Information Processing Systems - Open Systems Interconnection. LOTOS - a formal description technique based on the temporal ordering of observational behaviour. DIS 8807, 1987.

[LNEF90] K. Laraqui, A. Nazari, P. Ernberg, and L. Fredlund. Communication systems architecture - a case study. In *PROMETHEUS Proceedings of the 3rd Workshop.* Swedish Telecom Radio and SICS, 1990.

[Mol91] F. Moller. The Edinburgh Concurrency Workbench (Version 6.0). Technical Report LFCS-TN-34, Deptartment of Computer Science, University of Edinburgh, 1991.

[MPW89a] R. Milner, J. Parrow, and D. Walker. A calculus of mobile processes, part I. Technical Report ECS-LFCS-89-85, Department of Computer Science, University of Edinburgh, 1989. Accepted for publication in *Information and Computation.*

[MPW89b] R. Milner, J. Parrow, and D. Walker. A calculus of mobile processes, part II. Technical Report ECS-LFCS-89-86, Department of Computer Science, University of Edinburgh, 1989. Accepted for publication in *Information and Computation.*

[Mul91] H. Mulder. Specification of a simple overtaking protocol using PSF_d. In R. Milner and F. Moller, editors, *ESPRIT Basic Research Action No 3006 CONCUR - Deliverable Task 1.4 Case Studies.* 1991.

[PRO89]   PROMETHEUS. Functions or how to achieve PROMETHEUS objectives, 1989. PROMETHEUS Office, Stuttgart.

[QPF90]   J. Quemada, S. Pavon, and A. Fernandez. State exploration by transformation with LOLA. In J. Sifakis, editor, *Automatic Verification Methods for Finite State Systems, LNCS 407*. Springer-Verlag, 1990.

[RdS89]   V. Roy and R. de Simone. An Autograph primer. Technical Report 112, INRIA, Sophia Antipolis, 1989.

[Sti87]   C. Stirling. Modal logics for communicating systems. *Theoretical Computer Science*, (49):311–347, 1987.

[Sti89]   C. Stirling. Temporal logics for CCS. In *LNCS 354*. Springer-Verlag, 1989.

[Sti91]   C. Stirling. An introduction to modal and temporal logics for CCS. In *Proceedings of the Joint UK/Japan Workshop on Concurrency, LNCS 491*. Springer-Verlag, 1991.

[SV89]   R. de Simone and D. Vergamini. Aboard Auto. Technical Report 111, INRIA, Sophia Antipolis, 1989.

[Tre89]   J. Tretmans. HIPPO: A LOTOS simulator. In P. Eijk, C. Vissers, and M. Diaz, editors, *The Formal Description Technique LOTOS*, pages 391–396. North-Holland, 1989.

[Wal89]   D.J. Walker. Automated analysis of mutual exclusion algorithms using CCS. *Formal Aspects of Computing*, 1:273–292, 1989.

Protocol Trace Analysis based on Formal Specifications *

M.C. Kim[†], Samuel T. Chanson and Son T. Vuong

Department of Computer Science
University of British Columbia
Vancouver, B.C., Canada V6T 1W5

Abstract

Test case generation and trace analysis are two important topics in protocol testing research. In this paper, we present a model based on the formal description technique *Estelle* that combines these two functions in a unified framework. Our model handles both control and data flows. Symbolic evaluation is used to detect and delete infeasible paths which may be the results of path selection. Practical considerations such as out of order message sequences that may occur in a real test environment are also addressed. The application of this method to the trace analysis of *X*.25 *LAPB* shows that it can manage frame collision, control and data flows of the protocol rigorously.

1 Introduction

Research activities in protocol testing can be roughly divided into test case generation and trace analysis [Bochm 89a]. However, as in the case for software testing, most of the work has been on test case generation rather than on trace analysis.

Just as there are formal description techniques for protocol specification, *CCITT* and *ISO* have jointly developed a notation to describe test suites for *OSI* conformance testing known as the Tree and Tabular Combined Notation (*TTCN*) [ISOb]. A test suite specified in *TTCN* consists of a collection of tables defining the different aspects of the test cases, such as service primitives, *PDU*'s and their parameters, constraints on parameter values and dynamic behaviors (interactions). The interaction order is defined in terms of a tree where each branch from the root to a leaf represents a possible execution sequence. A *TTCN* test case contains the trace analysis function by expressing verdicts explicitly. This approach gives rise to issues such as how to generate, validate, and manage test suits. Currently, most of the test cases in use have been created manually in an informal manner.

Recently there are works that aim at generating test suites systematically as a result of translation from formal protocol specifications (e.g., [Ural 87] [Sarik 87]), and to validate *TTCN* test cases with respect to a formal protocol specification as a result of inverse translation [Bochm 89b].

An approach is to make an oracle function which determines whether the message streams exchanged between two protocol entities conform to the formal protocol specification. Even

---

*This work was supported in part by the Canadian Institute for Telecommunications Research.

[†]Kim is also a member of technical staff of Korea Telecom.

though the approach is most suitable for trace analysis, it can be used for test case validation [Bochm 89b], test case generation [Ural 86, Gorli 90] and reducing test case complexity[Wvong 90]. We believe it is possible to combine the applications into one system using a common framework.

So far, few people have taken advantage of the close relationship between test case generation and trace analysis and applied the large body of research results in software test case generation (or, for that matter, in protocol test case generation) to protocol trace analysis. Also there has been no attempt to build one system to generate test cases and analyze traces with respect to formal protocol specifications using a unified framework. Even though the constraints on test case generation and trace analysis procedures are different, some of the techniques used in test case generation for software testing such as static data flow analysis and symbolic evaluation can be used to augment the generality, correctness, efficiency, and diagnostics of trace analysis.

In this paper, we describe the design of a trace analyzer that works with *Estelle* specifications. The trace analysis is performed using a two phase scheme: a path selection phase based on the control flow (with or without data flow) of the protocol specification followed by an infeasible path detection and deletion phase using symbolic evaluation. This scheme can be extended to include test case generation.

The design objectives are listed below:

- Generality: the analysis is based on the extended finite state machine ($EFSM$) model. Thus, the technique will work with any protocol specifications that can be mapped into an $EFSM$ (see for example [Karjo 90]).
- Extendability: the trace analyzer can be easily extended to perform test case generation function using common functionalities and the same system view.
- Correctness: infeasible paths are detected and eliminated using symbolic evaluation. In general, determining which paths are not executable is equivalent to the halting problem, but unexecutable paths may be eliminated by detecting inconsistencies in the path conditions using symbolic evaluation.
- Efficiency: the analyzer should be so efficient that it may perform the analysis on-line. The two-phase scheme greatly enhance the performance of the trace analyzer.
- Diagnostics: the analyzer should help to identify the cause of errors when they occur.
- Practicality: the system should be able to handle real life protocols and testing environments.

This paper is primarily on trace analysis and some related work is given in section 2. Section 3 outlines some basic theories in finite state machines relevant to trace analysis. In section 4, our model based on extended finite state machines is presented, and the relationship between extended finite state machines and finite state machines is given. The model is extended to different test architectures in section 5, and illustrated using $X.25$ $LAPB$ as a case study in section 6. We discuss the relationship between trace analysis and test case generation in section 7 and outline how the model can be used to generate test cases. Finally section 8 concludes the paper.

2 Related Works

[Ural 86] contains the concepts of protocol trace analysis. The work was to validate a protocol implementation - SFR_K (System Functionality Representative_K) in their terminology, according to the protocol specification *SFR_K - 1*. The *SFR_K - 1* is assumed to be acceptable as a reference for consistency checking. In *trace checking*, *SFR_K - 1* is employed as a test oracle which determines whether or not an observed trace of *SFR_K* is permissible. In *trajectory checking*, all allowed responses to a stimulus are included in a tree-structured trajectory. The paper proposes that a *Prolog* procedure implementing an abstract SFR_K based on *Estelle* can be used as a generator to produce interaction sequences and as a validator to check observed interaction sequences. This requires *Estelle* specifications to be translated into *SFRs* in *Prolog* and the *SFRs* to be capable of reverse execution. However, not all *Prolog* programs are reversible because of the arithmetic evaluation and depth first search rules of *Prolog*. In order to execute the *Prolog* programs reversibly, the *Prolog* programs have to be structured properly, for example, by checking loops whenever transitions are visited. Furthermore, the automatic translation of *Estelle* specifications into *Prolog* is quite complicated.

In [Bochm 89b] a test trace analyzer called *TETRA* was constructed by modifying a *LOTOS* interpreter. *TETRA* takes interaction parameters into account and uses backtracking to determine whether the tree of possible execution histories defined by the specification includes the observed trace of interactions. For nondeterministic choices which are not directly visible, backtracking is necessary until either a right path is located or there is no match. In order to avoid backtracking over all possible paths, the system instantiates interaction parameters as late as possible until their values can be determined from the constraints of the specification and/or subsequent observed input or output values. Nonetheless, certain features of *LOTOS* such as non well-guarded expressions and general *CHOICE* statements can easily explode the number of paths that have to be processed. Also, currently *TETRA* cannot be used for test case generation and there are limitations when the behavioral tree of the protocol is too complex.

Mockingbird [Gorli 90], on the other hand, can be used as both a generator - producing test cases whose properties conform to the specification, and an acceptor - validating test cases against the specification. The specification language is a combination of context-free grammars and constraint systems. The semantics of the specification are based on constraint logic programming (*CLP*). However, not all *CLPs* are reversible because of the possible infinite recursions generated by the unfair method of rule selection in *CLP*. The model is not suitable for real-life protocols.

In [Wvong 90] a trace analyzer is used to simplify test cases. Test cases only need to describe the expected behaviors of the protocol implementation. The unexpected behaviors are checked by the analyzer. The technique was applied to an implementation of *LAPB*.

There has been much work on static data flow analysis [Oster 81, Podgu 90] and symbolic evaluation [King 76, Clark 85] in software engineering. Static data flow techniques require the selection of subpaths based on particular sequences of definitions and references to the variables in the program without execution. It is used to detect suspicious or erroneous use of data, such as referencing undefined variables and defining variables without subsequent usage. Symbolic evaluation is a program technique that derives algebraic representations, over the input values, of the computations and their applicable domains. Thus symbolic evaluation describes the relationship between the input data and the resulting values, whereas normal execution computes numeric values but loses information about the way in which the numeric values are derived. Static data flow analysis methods can be used to detect paths containing suspect sequences of events but cannot determine if these paths are executable. Symbolic evaluation can be used to determine which paths are unexecutable by computing the consistency of path conditions and thus can greatly simplify the complexity of trace analysis.

3 Experiments on Finite State Machines

Our approach uses some principles of the finite state machine model. The reader is assumed to have a basic knowledge of finite state machines. In this section, only the principles and theories relevant to trace analysis are outlined.

A *finite state machine* is an abstract model consisting of a finite number of states, a finite number of input symbols, and a finite number of output symbols. Every possible combination among input symbol, output symbol, present state and next state of a finite state machine is described by either a *transition table* or a *transition diagram*. An *experiment* performed on a finite state machine consists of applying one or more input sequences, observing the corresponding output sequences, and drawing a conclusion about the internal behavior of the machine. A machine is assumed to be finite, deterministic, reduced, strongly connected, and completely specified, and is available to the experimenter as a *black box*, which means that he has access to its input and output terminals, but cannot inspect the internal structures.

The experimenter may have to consider a class of problems, known as *measurement and control problems*, to conduct experiments on a machine for which the transition table is supplied. The control problem is concerned with finding input sequences that take a given machine from a known initial state to a predesignated terminal state. The measurement problem is the identification of the unknown initial state of the machine. The general machine control problem that brings the machine to a specified final state from an unknown initial state can be viewed as being composed of two distinct subproblems: a measurement problem followed by a simple control problem.

The experiments are classified into *synchronizing experiments*, *homing experiments*, and *distinguishing experiments* according to the purpose of the experiments [Gill 62, Henni 68]. A synchronizing experiment consists of the application of a fixed input sequence that is guaranteed to leave the machine in a particular final state. A homing experiment consists of the application of either a preset or an adaptively chosen input sequence such that the resulting output sequence uniquely specifies the machine's final state. A distinguishing experiment is similar to a homing experiment except that it is used to determine a machine's initial state. The homing experiment is solvable but not all distinguishing experiments are solvable [Gill 62].

Typically, solutions to the measurement and control problem make use of the information contained in the machine's transition table in conjunction with the machine's response tree [Gill 62, Henni 68]. A *response tree* is generated from the transition table, and is basically a graphical presentation of the results obtained when different input sequences are applied to the machine. The different paths through this tree correspond to the possible input sequences that might be used in an experiment. The *nodes* of this tree correspond to the possible states that the machine can be in after the application of the input sequences that lead to those nodes. The *level* of a node corresponds to the *length* of the input sequence required to reach the node. A path through a response tree terminates whenever certain termination rules are satisfied. The response tree approach is, in effect, an exhaustive tree search process. Theorem 1 below gives an upper bound on the lengths of the simple preset homing experiments [Gill 62].

Theorem 1 *The homing problem for a v-state sequential machine M with m admissible state can always be solved by a simple preset experiment of length L_{hs} where $L_{hs} \leq (v-1)(m-1)$.*

The *admissible states* of machine M means the initial states of the machine. A *simple experiment* is one which is performed on a single copy of the machine, and an experiment is *preset* if the entire input sequences are predetermined independent of the outcome of the experiment.

4 Unified Model for Trace Analysis and Test Case Generation

Our model is based on *extended finite state machines*. The *extented finite state machine* is an abstract model using a *program segment* on each transition instead of an input/output message pair of the finite state machine. Thus, there can be predicates, variables, and a sequence of actions associated with each transition. A specification written in *Estelle* or *SDL* is an extended finite state machine, and trace analysis can be viewed as experiments on the extended finite state machine.

First, we note the differences between test case generation and trace analysis with respect to path analysis methods for control and data flows:

1. In test case generation, the initial and final states of each path are supposed to be known. This is not the case for trace analysis, so we need to determine the initial and final states from the observed input and output message sequences. Even for finite state machines which deal with control flow only, determining the initial state is not always possible (see section 3). This condition is even more complicated for extended finite state machines which deal with both control and data flows.

2. In test case generation, every possible path of a formal specification has to be considered. Trace analysis, on the other hand, needs only consider a finite number of paths that comply with the observed sequence of input and output messages. Actually, generating all test cases can be done efficiently. The problem is in the identification of the infeasible paths from among the paths produced. For example, data flow techniques that attempt to generate only feasible paths by excluding inconsistent branch predicates have been shown to be $NP - complete$ [Gabow 76]. However the techniques for the restricted class of program flow graphs which are trees are not NP-complete [Gabow 76]. This suggests, therefore, that trace analysis can be done faster than test case generation in general.

3. As a consequence of point 2 above, the paths which have to be considered in trace analysis are finite in number and are a subset of those for test case generation. The trace contains information to determine the actual number of loop iterations, specific values of parameters, and the outcome of conditional statements. The absence of this information is largely responsible for the inefficiency in test case generation.

We start with an *Estelle* specification which is supposed to be error-free and which conforms to the standards. Furthermore, the specification is assumed to be single module, without state lists, procedures and functions as a result of transformations. Unlike Normal Form Specification(NFS) [Sarik 87], however, we allow conditional statements which helps to avoid the transition explosion problem which can occur in NFS for complex protocols.

Definition 1 *A single-module Estelle specification E is defined as a 5-tuple $E=<S,P,\Delta,I_o,D>$ where*

- *S is a set of states on E,*
- *P is a set of program segments on each transition of E,*
- $\Delta \subseteq S \times P \times S$ *is a relation of the transitions,*
- I_o *is the initial state, and*
- *D is declaration and/or initialization of variables and interaction parameters.*

Definition 2 *A finite state machine F is defined as a 4-tuple $F=< S, L, \Sigma, I_o >$ where*

- *S is a set of states on F,*

- L is a set of labels on each transition of F and is represented in the format "input symbol/output symbol",
- $\Sigma \subseteq S \times L \times S$ is a relation of the transitions, and
- I_o is the initial state.

Procedure 1 *Mapping from Estelle specification E to finite state machine F.*

For program segment $P_i(labelL_i)$ between states A and B of $E(F)$ in Definition 1(2) respectively, a transition ξ in E is defined as $\xi_E = <A, P_i, B>$ and a transition ξ in F is defined as $\xi_F = <A, L_i, B>$.

P_i, contains interaction primitives $I(p_1, \cdots, p_n)/O(q_1, \cdots, q_n)$ where

- I and O are input and output interaction primitives respectively,
- $(p_1, \cdots, p_n)$ and $(q_1, \cdots, q_n)$ are sets of input and output interaction primitive parameters respectively.

The mapping from ξ_E to ξ_F is given by the following:

if the domain size of every interaction parameter is small, then

$\xi_F = <A, L_i, B>$ iff $L_i = I \times p_1 \times \cdots \times p_n \: / \: O \times q_1 \times \cdots \times q_n$ is valid with respect to P_i, else

$\xi_F = <A, L_i, B>$ iff $L_i = I/O$ is valid with respect to P_i

In other words, when the domain sizes of the parameter are small (i.e., the possible combinations of parameter values are manageable), the parameters are included. Otherwise, they are left out to avoid state explosion. In the latter case, symbolic evaluation is used to detect and discard infeasible paths that may be generated as a result (see Definition 3 below).

Definition 3 *AllPath(X,S_i,S_o,C) is the set of all executable paths from the initial state S_i to the final state S_o of an Estelle (or finite state machine) specification X with Constraints C.*

The constraints C bounds the set of feasible paths and include restrictions on the iteration number of **while** loops and transition loops, and conditions limiting the domain space of variables and interaction parameters for *Estelle*. Since finite state machines have no program segments and do not deal with data and predicates, the constraints C_f of a finite state machine derived from an *Estelle* specification E using Procedure 1 is a subset of the constraints C_e of E.

Theorem 2 *Given finite state machine F obtained from an Estelle specification E using Procedure 1, AllPath(F,S_i,S_o,C_f) $\supseteq$ AllPath(E,S_i,S_o,C_e)*

The proof is obvious when we note that $C_e \supseteq C_f$.

Definition 4 *The set of test cases T_c generated from specification X (E or F) with constraints C, initial state S_i, and final state S_o, is $T_c = \{t \mid t = T(AllPath(X, S_i, S_o, C))\}$ where T is a one-to-one function from a path to a test sequence t.*

Definition 5 *Conformance testing is defined as $M \: conf_c \: X$ if $EXT(M)|_{T_c} \subseteq EXT(X)$ where EXT is the external behavior function.*

This definition states that an implementation M of a specification X with constraints C passes a conformance test using test case T_c if the external behaviors of the test is a subset of the allowable behaviors specified by X.

Definition 6 *As a generalization of conformance testing in Definition 5, the following definition is useful for trace analysis:* $M \text{ conf } X \text{ if } \forall C \ \forall S_i \ \forall S_o, \ M \text{ conf}_c X$

If X in *Definition 6* is replaced by F of *Definition 2*, then $M \text{ conf} F$ turns out to be the *homing problem* discussed in section 3. *Theorem 1* gives the bound of message length to uniquely identify the machine's final state. Thus, after at most L_{hs} messages, the state of the implementation is known and subsequent traces can be determined if they are legal paths according to the specification. The actual length is usually much shorter than the bound given in Theorem 1.

We now outline our proposed procedure for trace analysis/conformance testing as follows: Given an *Estelle* specification and its implementation M,

1. Transform the *Estelle* specification into the form given in *Definition 1*,

2. Apply *Procedure 1* to map the *Estelle* specification E obtained in step 1 into its finite state machine representation F.

3. In accordance with *Definition 6* for trace analysis and *Definition 5* for conformance testing,

    (a) Select from F the set of paths satisfying the input and output messages in the case of trace analysis, and all the paths from the given initial state to the given final state with constraints for test case generation,

    (b) Detect and delete the infeasible paths using symbolic evaluation if necessary,

    (c) Assign verdict.

We may have information loss on transformation by *procedure 1*. The loss is the difference on *AllPath* between F and E in *Theorem 2* due to reduction of the constraints. For example, an empirical study on the number of feasible versus infeasible paths for several programs using control flow only[Wood 80] shows almost every program has a significant number of infeasible paths out of all the paths generated. The infeasible paths can be detected and deleted by symbolic evaluation [King 76, Clark 85]. Some of the infeasible paths may also be detected using static data flow analysis, but the result is not as satisfactory because the method gives only the necessary (not sufficient) condition for deleting infeasible paths [Podgu 90].

There are three basic methods for symbolic evaluation [Clark 85]: *path-dependent symbolic evaluation* describes data dependencies for a path specified by the user or the system; *dynamic symbolic evaluation* produces a trace of the data dependencies for particular input data sequence; *global symbolic evaluation* represents the data dependencies for all paths in a program. In our case, we use symbolic evaluation to select a set of paths which satisfy path condition consistency out of the set of paths matching the input and output message sequences. This can be considered as an extension of path-dependent symbolic evaluation. Even though we may not know the values of internal variables which have an effect on the execution of the specification, they can be inferred by using path condition consistency based on the following rules:

1. We can select a path (or a set of paths) from the specification which matches the observed trace with respect to the interaction primitives and their parameters.

2. Once the path(s) is determined, the values of some internal variables on the path can be obtained from the specification.

3. The values of the other internal variable can be inferred from the interaction primitive parameters.

Verdicts on external behaviors are dependent on the characteristics of the application: whether we know the initial state, the final state, and the constraints. If we have non-ambiguous T_c of *Definition 5*, then it is possible to determine if the implementation conforms to the specification. In trace analysis where the initial and final states as well as the constraints are not known as in *Definition 6*, what we can say about the correctness of the implementation depends on the length of the observed path length. For a given protocol, there is a threshold path length l_t less than or equal to that given by *Theorem 1* which will differentiate every possible ambiguity on the path (see section 6 for l_t for $LAPB$). For message sequences of length less than or equal to l_t, only if $EXT(M) \not\subseteq EXT(X)$ can one conclude the implementation contains error(s). However, $EXT(M) \subseteq EXT(X)$ does not necessarily imply conformance.

5 Trace Analysis in External Test Architectures

In the last section, we have outlined the basic technique for determining whether a trace of input and output messages is permissible with respect to a specification given as an extended finite state machine. However, the method assumes it is possible to observe the input and output messages correctly and in the order they are generated. If observation is to be done external to the implementation under test(IUT), it may not be possible to have access to the interaction points to both the upper and the lower interfaces of the IUT directly, and the assumptions may no longer hold.

It is known that local observers are unable to detect all errors [Bochm 89a]. We will assume that a system clock will timestamp all events occurring at the IUT, and that a test architecture such as the Ferry [Chans 89] or Astride [Rafiq 90] is used to transfer all local observations to the global analyzer with timing information. The problem remains as to how to organize the local traces into one global trace with the input and output messages ordered properly. This is difficult since messages may be generated spontaneously by the IUT (i.e., without external stimuli) and message delays may occur inside the IUT.

We will use the following notations to describe the order of message sequences.

Notation 1 *Suppose an input message p_i results in a response message q_i. This input and output sequence is represented as $p_i < q_i$.*

Notation 2 *Suppose the two message sequences $p_i < q_i$ and $p_{i+1} < q_{i+1}$ have no order relationship between them. This is expressed as $\{p_i < q_i \ ; \ p_{i+1} < q_{i+1}\}$.*

Notation 3 *If the message pair $p_i < q_i$ is completed before the sequence $p_{i+1} < q_{i+1}$ starts, the composite message sequence is represented as $p_i < q_i << p_{i+1} < q_{i+1}$.*

The order relationship on messages p_i and q_i can be determined if the timestamps of input message $t(p_i)$ and output message $t(q_i)$ as well as the round trip delay δ between the IUT and the observer is available [Wvong 90]:

1. If $t(q_i) < t(p_i)$, then $q_i < p_i$,
2. If $t(q_i) > t(p_i) + \delta$, then $p_i < q_i$,
3. If $t(p_i) < t(q_i) < t(p_i) + \delta$, then $q_i \not< p_i$ and $p_i \not< q_i$.

In case 3 where there is uncertainty on the order of messages, we may consider every possible set of sequences that satisfies the constraints of the program paths of the formal specification.

For example, Table 1 gives all the possible composite sequences of the two message sequences where $t(p_1) < t(p_2)$ and $t(q_1) < t(q_2)$.

			Time $\rightarrow$			Resulting Seqs
Case 1	q_1q_2	p_1		p_2		$q_1q_2p_1p_2$
2		p_1	q_1q_2	p_2		$p_1q_1q_2p_2$
3		p_1		p_2	q_1q_2	$p_1p_2q_1q_2$
4	q_1	p_1	q_2	p_2		$q_1p_1q_2p_2$
5	q_1	p_1		p_2	q_2	$q_1p_1p_2q_2$
6		p_1	q_1	p_2	q_2	$p_1q_1p_2q_2$

Table 1.

In the above example, each message might be spontaneous without external stimulus. This example is one of the more complex situations that can arise in practice. If there is an order relationship between messages p_i and q_i, the number of possible cases will be reduced.

6 Case Study

We now demonstrate the feasibility of the proposed methodology by applying it to a specific protocol, the $X.25$ $LAPB$ protocol as specified by ISO 7776 [ISOa].

The given Estelle specification of $LAPB$ [1] was translated into the finite state machine diagram of Appendix A using *procedure 1* described in section 4.

The translation was done under the following conditions:
- we had a single module Estelle specification,
- we had access to the the interaction points at the upper and the lower interfaces,
- we integrated the parameters of those interaction primitives with very small domain space for each of their parameters into their message types (see below for details),
- timer operations were not considered even though including them will not be difficult.

From Appendix A we note that there are identical input and output messages such as the sequences g/j and h/k (marked with an * in the appendix). Not only are the message types and parameter values identical, they also end in the same states. Thus, if these sequences are observed without leading message sequences before them, it is not possible to determine the states from which the message sequences start. Note also that transition loops such as $w/\_$ and $v/\_$ (marked ** in Appendix A) may make the threshold value of the homing sequence path length l_t large. However in this example the transition loops $w/\_$ and $v/\_$ are used for exception handling so the iteration number is likely to be small. The threshold value of path length l_t (measured in terms of number of messages) for $X.25$ $LAPB$ is, from Appendix A, given by

$l_t = 2 + 2\times$ (the iteration number of loop transitions).

$LAPB$ has interaction parameters such as Address, P/F, $N(S)$ and $N(R)$. The address, whose value is either A or B, identifies the intended receiver of a command frame and the transmitter of a response frame. Frames containing commands transferred from the DCE to the DTE contain the address A and frames containing responses transferred from the DCE to the DTE contain the address B. In the case of DTE, the address is the reverse of the above. In order to differentiate polling and response to polling, $LAPB$ uses the P/F bit which has the value 0 or 1.

---
[1] The *Estelle* specification can be obtained from the authors on request.

Each I frame contains a send sequence number $N(S)$. Also all I frames and supervisory frames contain $N(R)$, the expected send sequence number of the next received I frame. For sequence numbers based on *modulo 8* or higher, the possible combinations of $N(S)$ and $N(R)$ are large and will cause a large amount of transitions if integrated into the control flow. Therefore we have included only the data variables Address and P/F into the control flow (for $LAPB$, this includes all transitions except for those associated with the self loop at state ABM). This means the transitions from ABM to ABM must be handled differently from the rest. The transitions from ABM to ABM will produce infeasible paths which must be detected and deleted. No infeasible paths will be produced for the other transitions, since the data values are integrated into the interaction primitives.

We demonstrate our approach using two examples from [Wvong 90]. The first example deals with a trace which has no data transfer but involves frame collision. In trace (a) of Figure 1, the DCE and the DTE send $DISC$ commands at the same time ($DISC$ collision). The DCE then tries

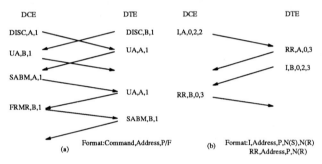

Figure 1: Sequence of Events in Traces

to initiate link set up. Finally the DCE requests link reset by sending a $FRMR$ response, and the DTE resets the link. *Note that in our example, the trace analyzer is located near the DCE side and is observing the behavior of the DTE at the lower interface.* Based on the timestamps on each message (given in [Wvong 90] but not shown in Figure 1) and information on request and response of the messages, we obtain the message sequences $\{DISC, A, 1 < UA, A, 1; \_ < DISC, B, 1 << UA, B, 1 < \_\} << SABM, A, 1 < UA, A, 1 << FRMR, B, 1 < SABM, B, 1$ for the interaction point at the lower interface. Here "$\_$" means the message is either null or not observable from the trace. However, it can be deduced from the specification that the first "$\_$" is $DISCREQ$ from the upper interaction point. There are three transitions, namely $ABM \rightarrow SEND\_DM, SEND\_DISC \rightarrow SEND\_DISC$, and $WAIT\_SABM \rightarrow SEND\_DM$ which can produce the message pair $DISC < UA$. From the figure in Appendix A, only one of them satisfies the constraints of the observed trace:

Transitions : $ABM \xrightarrow{A} SEND\_DISC \xrightarrow{B} SEND\_DISC \xrightarrow{C} SEND\_DM$

Messages seqs: $\overbrace{DISCREQ < DISC, B, 1}^{A} << \overbrace{DISC, A, 1 < UA, A, 1}^{B} << \overbrace{UA, B, 1 < \_}^{C}$

Therefore the trace (a) is valid according to the formal specification.

The second example contains data transfer: the DCE and DTE exchange I frames as shown in

Figure 1(b). Based on the timestamp on each message and information on request and response messages, we obtain the message trace

$\overbrace{I, A, 0, 2, 2/RR, A, 0, 3}^{A} << \_/I, B, 0, 2, 3 << \overbrace{RR, B, 0, 3/\_}^{B}$ for a transition from ABM to ABM. The first "$\_$" can be inferred to be $DATAREQ$ from the upper interaction point.

To analyze the input/output sequences A and B, an examination of transitions $t11$ and $t13$ (see Appendix B) shows there are 96 and 192 paths respectively even before the **while** statements are considered. This means that if we adopt the Normal Form Specification [Sarik 87] instead of *Definition 1*, the number of Normal Form Transitions (one per path) will be enormous.

The *Estelle* source must not contain procedures and functions in our method; the procedures and functions must be expanded. Also system functions such as allocation and deallocation of space should be deleted as they do not affect the outcome of trace analysis but unnecessarily complicate the processing.

To improve efficiency in the analysis, we use a technique similar to program slicing [Weise 81]. Paths which do not modify program variables are bypassed unless subsequent trace shows the assumption to be incorrect. For example, *IsCorrectAck* of transition $t11$ generates some paths which contain conditional statements only but do not update any program variables. These paths are bypassed by assuming the path in bold arrow. If the assumption is invalid, inconsistencies will show up in subsequent external behaviors of the IUT such as **output** statements. In our example, **output** statements of transitions $t11$ and $t12$ show the assumption to be correct using symbolic evaluation.

Of the four paths between points B and C of the flow chart in Appendix B, three of them containing *output P.AckIndication* are candidate paths by rule 1 of path condition consistency listed in section 4. With this information, we can deduce the predicate $frame \wedge .NR <> LastRxNR$ by rule 2, but we do not know whether $TimerRecovery = false$. Just after point C in the flow chart, the 2 paths containing $WriteSFrame(RR,1,A)$ are candidate paths by rule 1, and this allows us to decide that $LocalRNR = false$ by rule 2. These paths can be differentiated by whether they include *S.DataIndication* from the upper interaction point. The path containing *S.DataIndication* (in bold line) is selected. Transition $t22$ containing *WriteIFrame* from D to E in the flow chart gives us the values of a bunch of variables such as $RemoteRNR=false$, $TimerRecovery=false$, $frame \wedge .NS=VS$ and $frame \wedge .NR=VR$ by rule 2. These in turn allow us to select paths which are dependent on internal variables. For example the information on $TimerRecovery=false$ which was unknown between points B and C, provides enough information to select one path (in bold line) out of the three candidate paths. Also the second I frame in the trace contains $frame \wedge .NR$ gives the value 3 for the internal variable VR because of the assignment statement $frame \wedge .NR := VR$ just after point D in the flow chart. Now, since the I frame's $frame \wedge .NS$ has value 2, the predicate $frame \wedge .NS <> VR$ which appears between points C and D, is inferred to be false by rule 3. Thus, the correct path between points C and D is the one marked in bold line and it matches the observed trace. Furthermore, *clearrecovery* in *ReadSFrame* just after point E evaluated to false using the values of variables already known to us. The values of interaction parameters of RR, the interaction primitive type RR itself, the value of *clearrecovery*, and the predicate $RemoteRNR = false$ eliminate all but one path in transition $t13$ between points E and F that satisfies all the constraints. As a result we have one path satisfying the observed input and output message trace. Therefore the trace (b) is valid according to the formal specification.

7 Test Case Generation

Early work on automating the selection of test cases are based on the finite state machine model. The model is used to describe the control flow of a protocol and has been widely used in test case generation. More recently, the data flow of a protocol is taken into consideration as well by using the extended finite state machine model.

As mentioned earlier, test case generation and trace analysis share some common functions which can be depicted using Figure 2. The *Path Selection* phase generates a set of paths with respect

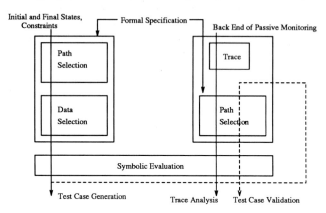

Figure 2: Test Case Generation and Trace Analysis

to the initial and final states of F in the case of test case generation, and with respect to the observed input and output sequences (trace) in the case of trace analysis as described in section 4. In order to make the number of paths manageable, we make use of *structural constraints* which place limitations on transition loops, **while** statements, and intermodule communications. We have described *AllPath*, the most powerful criterion in data flow analysis. The *Data Selection* phase generates a set of test data for each path selected in the Path Selection phase for test case generation. However, in trace analysis, a trace can be viewed as a test case with the verdicts removed and muddled with the environmental effects such as uncertainty of the message order and/or loss of the test data. In the Data Selection phase, in order to make the number of test cases finite, we make use of *data constraints* which place limitations on the variables and input interaction parameters. If the domain of variables and input parameters of the protocol is finite, the problem is NP-complete but may be solved in reasonable time [Chun 90].

Recently, test case generation approaches with respect to *Estelle* have been proposed using data flow analysis for test path selection [Ural 87], a hybrid method combining the control and data flows [Sarik 87], and Constraint Logic Programming for generating only feasible test cases with constraints on the parameters of input interactions [Chun 90]. [Podgu 90] compares a number of data flow path selection criteria. One of the major weaknesses of all data flow criteria is that they are solely based on syntactic information and do not consider semantic issues such as infeasible paths. The presence of a data flow anomaly does not imply that execution of the program will definitely produce incorrect results; it only implies that it may produce incorrect results.

Our model, which handles both control flow and data flow, can be used not only for trace analysis but also for test case generation. For example, if we transform the Estelle specification of $LAPB$ into F by *procedure 1*, we can generate all possible execution paths $AllPath(F, S_i, S_o, C)$. By selecting specific initial and final states with constraints for test case generation, the paths can be structured as a tree. Since all paths except those transitions from the state ABM to ABM of $LAPB$ cover every possible combination of data flow, we do not need to use the Data Selection phase on them. However, paths containing the transition from ABM to ABM have a large number of value combinations on variables and input interaction parameters even though their domains are finite. For these paths, data selection can be done by random, static data flow analysis [Ural 87], constraints [Chun 90], or simply by exhaustive enumeration.

8 Summary

We have presented the basic techniques to perform trace analysis using *Estelle* specifications. Indeed, since the model is based on extended finite state machines, it will work with any specifications that can be translated into extended finite state machine representations. In order to avoid transition explosion as a result of normalization of *Estelle* specifications, we include the conditional statements and introduce symbolic evaluation to detect and discard infeasible paths. Some practical issues such as trace analysis using an external test architecture were also discussed. The technique was illustrated using $LAPB$ to show that it can handle some of the hard problems such as frame collisions and data flow rigorously. We also show the relation between trace analysis and test case generation and briefly discuss how our framework can be extended to include test case generation.

References

[Bochm 89a] Gregor v. Bochmann, Rachida Dssouli, and et al, *Trace Analysis for Conformance and Arbitration Testing*, IEEE Tr. on Software Engineering, pp. 1347 - 1356, November 1989.

[Bochm 89b] Gregor v. Bochmann, D. Desbiens, and et al, *Test Result Analysis and Validation of Test Verdicts*, 3rd Int'l Workshop on Protocol Test Systems, October 1990.

[Chans 89] S. T. Chanson, B. P. Lee, and et al, *Design and Implementation of a Ferry Clip Test System*, Ninth Int'l Symposium on Protocol Specification, Testing, and Verification, June 1989.

[Clark 85] L. A. Clarke, D. J. Richardson, *Application of Symbolic Evaluation Methods*, The Journal of Systems and Software 5, pp. 15 - 35, 1985.

[Chun 90] Woojik Chun, Paul D. Amer, *Test Case Generation for Protocols Specified in Estelle*, Proceedings of The Third Int'l Conference on Formal Description Techniques, pp. 197 - 209, 1990.

[Gabow 76] Harold N. Gabow, Shachindra N. Matheshwari, and et al, *On Two Problems in the Generation of Program Test Paths*, IEEE Tr. On Software Engineering, Vol. SE-2, No. 3. pp. 227 - 231, Sept. 1976.

[Gill 62]   A. Gill, *Introduction to the Theory of Finite-State Machines*, McGraw-Hill, New York, 1962.

[Gorli 90]   Michael M. Gorlick, Carl F. Kesselman, and et al, *Mockingbird: A Logical Methodology for Testing*, The Journal of Logic Programming, pp. 95 - 119, January/March 1990.

[Henni 68]   Frederick C. Hennie, *Finite-State Models for Logical Machines*, John Wiley & Sons, Inc., 1968.

[ISOa]   ISO 7776, *Information processing systems - Open Systems Interconnection - Description of the X.25 LAPB-compatible DTE data link procedures.*

[ISOb]   ISO DS 9646-3, *OSI Conformance Testing Methodology and Framework Part3: The Tree and Tabular Combined Notation(TTCN)*, 1990.

[Karjo 90]   G. Karjoth, *A Compilation of Algebraic Process Based on Extended-Action Derivation*, Third Int'l Conference on Formal Description Techniques, 1990.

[King 76]   James C. King, *Symbolic Execution and Program Testing*, CACM, Vol 19, No 7, pp. 385 - 394, July 1976.

[Oster 81]   L. J. Osterweil, L. D. Forsdick, and et al, *Error and Anomaly Diagnosis through Data Flow Analysis*, Computer Program Testing, edited by B. Chandrasekaran and S. Radicchi, North-Holland Publishing Co., pp. 35 - 64, 1981.

[Podgu 90]   Andy Podgurski and Lori A. Clarke, *A Formal Model of Program Dependences and Its Implications for Software Testing, Debugging, and Maintenance*, IEEE Tr. on Software Engineering, Vol. 16, No. 9, pp. 965 - 979, Sept. 1990.

[Rafiq 90]   O. Rafiq and R. Castanet, *Experience with the Astride Testing Approach*, Proceedings of the IFIP TC6 Int'l Conference on Computer Networking COMNET'90, 1990.

[Sarik 87]   Behcet Sarikaya, Gregor V. Bochmann, and et al, *A Test Design Methodology for Protocol Testing*, IEEE Tr. on Software Engineering, pp. 518 - 531, May 1987.

[Ural 87]   Hasan Ural, *Test Sequence Selection Based on Static Data Flow Analysis*, Computer Communications, Vol 10, No 5, pp. 234 - 242, Oct. 1987.

[Ural 86]   Hasan Ural and Robert L. Probert, *Step-Wise Validation of Communication Protocols and Services* , Computer Networks and ISDN Systems 11, pp. 183 - 202, 1986.

[Weise 81]   M. Weiser, *Program Slicing*, IEEE 5th Int'l Conference on Software Engineering, pp. 439 - 449, 1981.

[Wood 80]   Marin W. Woodward, David Hedley, and et al, *Experience with Path Analysis and Testing of Programs*, IEEE Tr. on Software Engineering, pp. 278 - 286, May 1980.

[Wvong 90]   R. Wvong, *A New Methodology for OSI Conformance Testing Based on Trace Analysis*, Master Thesis, UBC, Oct. 1990. See also *LAPB Conformance Testing using Trace Analysis*, 11th int'l Symposium on Protocol Specification, Testing, and Verification, pp. 248 - 261, June 1991.

Appendix A. Result of Applying Procedure 1 to X.25 LAPB

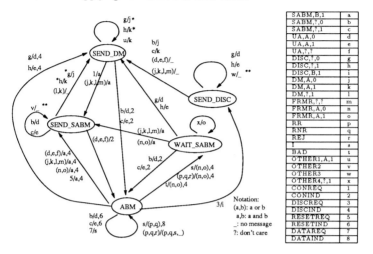

Appendix B. Flowchart for Example 2 in Section 6

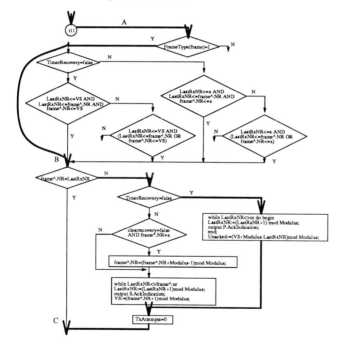

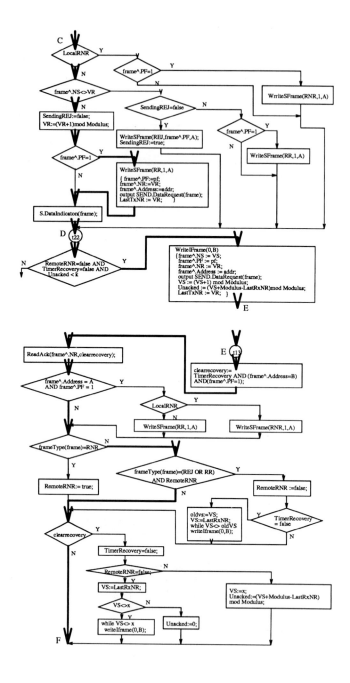

Inheritance in LOTOS

Steve Rudkin

BT Group Technology and Development, St Vincent House, 1 Cutler Street, Ipswich, IP1 1UX, United Kingdom

Abstract
Inheritance is a powerful technique, supporting reusability of specifications and/or implementations. However the formal description technique LOTOS was designed before object oriented techniques became widely accepted, and so does not provide explicit support for the concept. This paper examines the extent to which the existing facilities of LOTOS can be used to achieve the desired effect.

1 Introduction

Many benefits have been cited for object oriented design e.g. [1,2]. One of the notable characteristics is the support for re-use provided through the property of encapsulation and the mechanism of inheritance. This has led to suggestions [3] that, in future, software ICs will be commonplace. Meyer [4] has pointed out that if software libraries are to succeed, the code must be accompanied with precise specifications of their functionality. These specifications should be defined using formal specification techniques.

[5,6,7] suggest LOTOS [8] as a suitable candidate. LOTOS is an internationally standardized formal description technique, designed for the specification of OSI protocols and services. However, its foundation on the notions of concurrency and communication has enabled it to be usefully applied to the more general problem area of distributed systems design. Tutorials on LOTOS are available in, for example, [9,10]. Development of LOTOS began before object oriented techniques became widely accepted, so whilst concepts such as encapsulation are a fundamental part of its design, there is no analogue of inheritance in LOTOS.

This is unfortunate as inheritance is a powerful technique, supporting reusability of specifications and/or implementations [11]. Different languages place varying emphasis on the semantic relationship between objects related by inheritance. By interpreting inheritance in a formal language we can give it a precise definition. Also the formal specifier is offered an alternative to composition for the support of re-use.

Despite differences of opinion concerning the best implementation of inheritance, a number of features are common to all interpretations of inheritance. Firstly, inheritance is a technique for incrementally modifying existing class definitions, and secondly recursion in the parent class definition must be re-directed to the child when used as part of the child definition [12]. It is this latter point which has proved to be the biggest issue in developing a suitable interpretation of inheritance in LOTOS. [13] proposes a simple solution but only for terminating LOTOS processes.

This paper presents two incremental modification techniques for LOTOS. The first is only for terminating templates. It differs from the proposal of [13], in that this one guarantees subtyping. This ensures that instances of a derived class can be used, wherever instances of the parent class are expected. This result should be of interest to anyone concerned with conformance in LOTOS, irrespective of their interest in object oriented techniques. The second technique is effective for both terminating and recursive class definitions. This is achieved by introducing a third primitive process. LOTOS already has **stop** and **exit**. Now **self** is introduced. This technique is also shown to guarantee subtyping.

The remainder of the paper is structured as follows. Section 2 introduces the basic terminology of the object oriented paradigm; our interpretation of inheritance is presented in section 3. Section 4 summarizes the issues addressed by this paper, i.e. subtyping and redirection of self-references. Sections 5 and 6 propose the different modification techniques. Section 5 largely addresses the subtyping problem; redirection is only partially treated. Section 6, on the other hand, focuses on the redirection problem, but then applies some of the subtyping results of section 5. Conclusions are drawn in section 7.

2 Basic Object Oriented definitions

Wegner [14] categorizes object oriented languages according to their support for the concepts of *object*, *class* and *inheritance*. *Object-based* languages support objects. *Class-based* languages support objects and classes. *Object oriented* languages support objects, classes and inheritance.

An object combines state and behaviour in a single encapsulated entity. The property of encapsulation means that an object's state may change only as a result of internal events or as a result of explicitly defined interaction with the environment. Classes provide a basis for structuring large or small collections of objects. Finally, inheritance allows existing definitions to be manipulated and reused in definitions of newer objects. The object oriented paradigm also demands a model of communication between objects.

LOTOS is constructed on the concepts of observable and hidden behaviour together with the notion of synchronization. These provide a solid basis for a formal interpretation of the object oriented paradigm. Observability and hiding support encapsulation: internal interaction is hidden from the environment; observable behaviour defines a prescribed interface to the object. Synchronization is used to model communication. Support for the notions of class and inheritance is less obvious. However [5] provides an interpretation of classes in LOTOS and establishes the main requirements for a definition of inheritance. This paper attempts to provide an appropriate LOTOS interpretation of inheritance.

In the remainder of this section relevant object oriented concepts (template, class, instance, type, and encapsulation) are introduced and interpreted in LOTOS. Their definitions are taken from Open Distributed Processing (ODP) [15].

- **Template** The specification of the common features of a collection of objects.

  A template is an abstraction of a collection of objects. As identified in [5,6], a LOTOS process definition[1] corresponds to the class template.

- **Class (of objects)**[2] The set of all objects possessing the common features specified by a given template (the class template).

  A set of LOTOS process instantiations[1] related to a given process definition by a chosen membership relation is said to be a class.

- **Instance (of class)** An object is said to be an instance of a class when it is related to the class template by the chosen membership relation.

  The membership relation is discussed in detail later. For now it is sufficient to know that it encompasses process parameter-instantiation; An instantiation of a LOTOS process definition is an instance of the class whose template is the process definition.

- **type**[2] A predicate determining the instances of a class. An object is (an expression) of the type if and only if the object is an instance of the class.

  An object template together with the chosen membership relation is a type.

- **Encapsulation** The property resulting from modelling a system object as an object interacting with other objects only at defined interfaces. Encapsulation is central to the object oriented philosophy. It is however not the concern of this paper.

As a short illustration of these concepts, consider the following Buffer example. (It is assumed that a datatype describing sort *queue* and operations *hd, tl* and *appends* has already been defined.)

```
process BUFFER [in,out] (q:queue): noexit:=
    in?x:element; BUFFER[in,out](x appends q)
[]
    [q ne empty] -> out!hd(q); BUFFER[in,out](tl(q))
endproc
```

This LOTOS process definition is a template, which can be instantiated to produce objects such as BUFFER[in,out](empty) and BUFFER[in,out](x appends empty). Each of these objects is an instance of the BUFFER class. The value-parameter list should also contain a formal parameter denoting the instance name; a particular name would be given to this parameter during instantiation. However to keep the examples here as simple as possible, this parameter has been omitted in this paper.

BUFFER objects are encapsulated in that the state is observable only in a strictly controlled way. The scope of q:queue is limited to the BUFFER process. The only way in which *q* can be accessed is through *in* and *out*. So, for example, the whole of *q* cannot be read at once. BUFFER objects can be composed with other objects through synchronization on *in* and *out*.

---
[1] The terms *process definition* and *process instantiation* are chosen in accordance with their usage in the formal definition of the LOTOS syntax [8].

[2] The concepts of *class* and *type* here are actually called *template class* and *template type* in [15].

3 Inheritance

In this section we clarify informally what is intended, in this paper, by the term *inheritance*. The informal interpretation, given here, is used to explain the issues, which had to be addressed in order to formulate a formal definition of inheritance in LOTOS.

According to ODP [15], inheritance is an incremental modification technique that allows one template to be defined as a modification of another existing template. With the chosen membership relation fixed, the derived template defines the *derived class*, and the older template defines the *parent class*. The set of templates which are linked in this way by incremental modification defines an **inheritance hierarchy**.

In contrast, a **type hierarchy** links templates whose types are related by logical implication, i.e. whose classes are related by set inclusion. The subtype implies the supertype, and the class of the subtype is a subset of the class of the supertype. Note we cannot necessarily use the words *derived class* and *parent class* here, because the templates may not be related by incremental modification.

In this paper, we wish to define a particular inheritance mechanism. It must conform to the ODP definition and redirect self-references appropriately. But additionally we require the inheritance hierarchy to be a sub-graph of the type hierarchy. Now, [5] characterizes inheritance as a binary operation: $s = t \oplus m$, where s and t are templates and m is a behaviour expression, (which may also be a template). Pursuing this characterization, we require an incremental modification mechanism ($\oplus$), which

1. implies subtyping i.e $s = t \oplus m \Rightarrow type(s)$ *is-a-subtype-of* $type(t)$

2. redirects self-reference in accordance with Cook's proposal [12].

4 Inheritance in LOTOS: problems

In LOTOS the choice operator most simply captures the notion of incremental modification. However as it stands, it is not suitable for modelling the above definition of inheritance; both enumerated requirements are violated.

4.1 The subtyping problem

Informally, T_s *is-a-subtype-of* T_t means 's satisfactorily substitutes for t in an environment expecting t'. Even from this informal definition, it should be clear that $t[]m$ cannot generally be a subtype of t; non-determinism is introduced when m is unstable, or when the initials of m and the initials of t have a non-empty intersection.

Furthermore non-determinism can also be introduced through the combination of redirection and choice. For example consider

P = a ; (P [] b ; P)) and
Q = (a; (Q [] b ; Q)) [] b ; c ; Q.
Here $Q = a, b \Rightarrow c; Q =a\not\Rightarrow$ but $\not\exists P' \cdot P = a, b \Rightarrow P' =a\not\Rightarrow$

i.e. Q can fail when P cannot, so Q is not a subtype of P. So for a variety of reasons the LOTOS choice operator does not guarantee subtyping.

4.2 The redirection problem

Consider the following behaviour.

```
process BUFFER2 [in,out,flush,delete] (q:queue): exit(nat):=
    in?x:element; BUFFER2[in,out,flush,delete](x appends q)
[]
    [q ne empty] -> out!hd(q); BUFFER2[in,out,flush,delete](tl(q))
[]
    flush; BUFFER2[in,out,flush,delete](empty)
[]
    delete; exit(length(q))
endproc
```

BUFFER2 is very similar to BUFFER: it differs only in the addition of two extra branches of behaviour. BUFFER2 is a prime example of a template, that should be amenable to definition through inheritance. We wish to identify ⊕ such that BUFFER3 is bisimulation congruent to BUFFER2, where BUFFER3 takes the form:

```
process BUFFER3 [in,out,flush,delete] (q:queue): exit(nat):=
    BUFFER[in,out](q)
⊕
    (flush; BUFFER3[in,out,flush,delete](empty)
    []
    delete; exit(length(q)))
endproc
```

However if choice is substituted for ⊕, then the result is not bisimulation congruent to BUFFER2. The reason (as identified by Cook [12]), is that, any reference in the derived template definition (BUFFER3) to the parent template (BUFFER), should be redirected to the derived template. And of course the choice operator does not do this.

The remainder of this paper analyses in detail how these two problems can be overcome.

5 Solving the subtyping problem

To address the subtyping problem (characterised in clause 4.1) we must first introduce an interpretation of class membership in LOTOS.

5.1 Class membership in LOTOS

As in [5], the conformance relation of [16] (denoted $conf$) is used here to model the membership relation, i.e. it is used to relate objects to templates.

Conformance measures the functionality of a (possibly abstract) implementation against its specification. Let Q and P be processes. Then the statement that Q conforms to P (written $Q\ conf\ P$) signifies that Q is a valid implementation of P [3].

Now [5] considered only basic LOTOS. Here we wish to model inheritance in standard LOTOS, and therefore we must also consider parameterised processes. Clearly in the creation of an instance from a template we must allow the formal parameters of the process denoting the template to be instantiated. So our membership relation is defined by parameter-instantiation.conf [4], where '.' denotes composition of relations[5].

We can now say three important things. Firstly, an object a instantiates template t iff $a\ parameter\text{-}instantiation.conf\ t$. Secondly, the pair $(t,\ parameter\text{-}instantiation.conf)$ defines a type and thirdly, $\{a|a\ parameter\text{-}instantiation.conf\ t\}$ defines a class. Notice that through the membership relation, types and classes embody a notion of behavioural compatibility.

5.2 Inducing subtyping

In this paper we wish to define the incremental modification mechanism (denoted $\oplus$) such that the subtyping hierarchy always includes the class hierarchy. This means that when the incremental modification mechanism is used to add new functionality, we can be sure that an instance of the derived class will be acceptable where an instance of the parent class was expected. Again following [5] we can guarantee subtyping through a special case of conformance, namely extension.

$$Q\ extends\ P \Rightarrow T_Q\ is\ a\ subtype\ of\ T_P \quad (1)$$

An implementation which offers *at least* the **good** behaviour of the specification is said to *extend* the specification:

$Q\ extends\ P$ if
(i) $\text{Traces}(Q) \supseteq \text{Traces}(P)$ and
(ii) $Q\ conf\ P$

To ensure that incremental modification implies subtyping, it is sufficient, from rule 1, to impose condition 2.

$$s = t \oplus m \Rightarrow s\ extends\ t \quad (2)$$

where s and t are LOTOS process definitions (*class templates*), $\oplus$ represents the required incremental modification mechanism and m is a behaviour expression.[6] So whenever C_s

---

[3] A formal definition of $conf$ is included at the start of appendix A.
[4] For the sake of brevity, we have ignored relabelling in this presentation.
[5] So $a\ R.S\ c \Leftrightarrow \exists b \cdot a\ R\ b \wedge b\ S\ c$.
[6] In this paper we constrain the effect of incremental modification to behaviours only - the ACT-ONE types of t can be used in m but not modified.

is a derived class of class C_t then T_s is a subtype of T_t (where C_s and T_s respectively denote the class and type defined by s).

5.3 LOTOS incremental modification definition

It is likely that a number of incremental modification mechanisms could be defined in LOTOS. Here we wish to define just one, based on the LOTOS choice operator. In this section, we restrict our consideration to terminating templates only. Self-referencing templates are allowed; they can be defined either from scratch or in terms of a terminating template, but either way they cannot be incrementally modified directly.

$$s_{term} = t_{term}[]m \text{ is an incremental modification with the required properties if}: \quad (3)$$

a) t_{term} is a non-recursive template;
b) m is a modifier behaviour containing no type definitions;
c) m is stable;
d) The initial events of m are distinct from the initials of t_{term};
e) No initial events of s_{term} or t_{term} occur in either the body of s_{term} or in the body of t_{term}.

When these conditions are satisfied we can write $s_{term} = t_{term} \oplus m$. These conditions are sufficient to ensure [7]:

$$s_{term} = t_{term} \oplus m \Rightarrow s_{term} \text{ extends } t_{term} \quad (4)$$

Furthermore the conditions required for definition 3 also ensure [8]:

$$s_{term} = t_{term} \oplus m \Rightarrow s_{self-ref} \text{ extends } t_{self-ref} \quad (5)$$

where a self-referencing template can be defined from a terminating template as follows:

$$s_{self-ref} = s_{term} \gg accept \ldots in \; s_{self-ref}. \quad (6)$$

Thus an inheritance hierarchy derived from terminating templates induces one type hierarchy for the terminating templates and another (similar) type hierarchy for the associated self-referencing templates.

Consequently, $t_{self-ref}$ can be incrementally constructed by first modifying s_{term} according to definition (3) and then applying equation (6). [13] takes a similar approach to the incremental modification of self-referencing templates, but does not attempt to guarantee subtyping.

The main problem with this approach is that it can treat self referencing templates only if they contain no exits; equation (6) necessarily redirects all exits as self-references. The next section lays a foundation to overcome this, and in such a way that the subtyping guarantee still holds.

---

[7] The formal definition of the conditions and the proof are given under proof 1 of appendix A.
[8] See proof 2 in appendix A.

6 Solving the redirection problem

In this section we show how the LOTOS choice operator can be used (even with self-referencing processes) as the basis of incremental modification. As characterised in section 4.2, the main issue is to ensure that self references are redirected correctly. The annex of [13] discusses two approaches. The first proposed solution removes the possibility of templates having both terminating and self-referencing branches of behaviour. The second proposal overcomes this by introducing a new operator into LOTOS, to redirect process self-references. The new operator simultaneously marks the source and destination of the redirection. Unfortunately the operator is not formally defined.

In this paper we propose the alternative approach of marking the redirection source and destination separately. This has a number of advantages. Firstly the changes to the language are small and secondly the LOTOS object templates would closely resemble OO programming languages in the way that recursion is represented. The required effect can be achieved through two simple steps.

6.1 Introduce Primitive Process: self

Firstly, a third primitive process is introduced. LOTOS already has *stop* and *exit*. To these *self* is added. Additionally a third kind of functionality is added. The *self* process denotes a source of redirection. The functionality list now takes the form:

functionality-list = colon-symbol exit-self-list | colon-symbol noexit-symbol
exit-self-list   = exit-list | self-list | self-list exit-list
exit-list   = exit-symbol[open-parenthesis-symbol sort-list close-parenthesis-symbol]
self-list   = self-symbol[open-parenthesis-symbol sort-list close-parenthesis-symbol]
exit-symbol   = exit
self-symbol   = self
noexit-symbol   = noexit

If any *exits* appear in the body of the process, then the functionality-list displays an exit-list. If any *selfs* appear in the body of the process then the functionality list displays a self-list. If neither of these conditions are satisfied, then the functionality-list displays the *noexit* symbol.

With the new process *self* we have to introduce its associated special event σ and enabling operator $\gg_\sigma$. The primitives $self, \sigma, \gg_\sigma$ behave in exactly the same way as $exit, \delta$ and standard LOTOS enabling (which will be denoted $\gg_\delta$ in future). Appendix B details the new inference rules. Now instead of writing BUFFER we would write BUFFER4:

```
process BUFFER4 [in,out] (q:queue): self(queue):=
    in?x:element; self(x appends q)
[]
    [q ne empty] -> out!hd(q); self(tl(q))
endproc
```

Note that the use of *self* reflects the style of object oriented programming languages such as Smalltalk [17].

6.2 Introduce Redirection Operator: *

Secondly, we must introduce an operation * which marks the destination of any redirection initiated by *self*:

$*P[g1...gn](x1,...,xn) =$
$P[g1...gn](x1,...,xn) \gg_\sigma accept\ y1 : t1,...,yn : tn\ in\ * P[g1...gn](y1,...,yn)$

where $t1...tn$ are the types of the actual parameters $y1...yn$ (as in the self-list of P).

Therefore by proof 3 in appendix A, *BUFFER4 [in,out] (q:queue) is bisimulation congruent to BUFFER. As a result, the LOTOS choice operator can now be used to define a process (*BUFFER5), which is an incremental modification of BUFFER4, and is bisimulation congruent to BUFFER2:

```
process BUFFER5 [in,out,flush,delete] (q:queue): self(queue) exit(nat):=
    BUFFER4[in,out](q)
[]
    flush ; self(empty)
    []
    delete ; exit(length(q))
endproc
```

Notice that (just as with *exit*) all instantiations of *self* must bear values whose sorts match those in the functionality list. Strictly speaking, the need to specify a self-list is redundant, as it is identical to the list of sorts in the value-parameter list.

The choice of when to apply * depends on the intended effect [18]. If the normal effect of the LOTOS operator is intended i.e. if we do not wish self-references to be re-directed, then we must write the choice of behaviour between two processes as $*P[] * Q$. This describes the situation where the environment has to choose between P and Q behaviour once and forever.

When we do wish self-references to be re-directed, * is applied to the whole choice expression: $*(P[]m)$. This represents the object which inherits from P, is modified by m, and which (assuming P and m include *self*) can offer both P and Q behaviour after behaving like P or like Q.

For example, BUFFER5 inherits from BUFFER4, so that after the occurrence of any branch of behaviour (except delete which leads to *exit*), all branches are again available. Conversely, a simple choice between BUFFER4 and the modifier would allow the environment to choose BUFFER4 and then would never offer the modifier behaviour again.

6.3 Discussion

Generally, self references are re-directed to the closest containing process, which is operated on by *. Consider the following example.

```
process BUFFERCHOICE[in1,out1,in2,out2,delete2,flush2](q1,q2:queue):exit(nat):=
    *BUFFER4[in1,out1](q1) [] *BUFFER5[in2,out2,delete2,flush2](q2)
endproc
```

Here we have a process which offers a choice of two kinds of buffer - the first event chooses which of the two kinds of behaviour will be subsequently offered. Clearly, the self-references in each BUFFER should be redirected: to *BUFFER4 in the case of *in1* or *out1*; and to *BUFFER5 otherwise. Self-references should not be redirected to BUFFERCHOICE, as that would allow one kind of buffer to be chosen at the start and then later, the other kind to be chosen.

When using the * operator the following principles should be applied. These could be checked statically.

- Ensure that all *selfs* are redirected using *. As a side effect of this we must extend our definition of instantiation to include the operator *_ :

  instantiation = *.parameter-instantiation.conformance.

  This ensures that any *selfs*, introduced through freedom permitted by conformance, are resolved. Note that for all processes S, **S = *S; the first application of * removes every σ, $\gg_\sigma$ and *self* from S, and inference rule 7.5.3.3e of appendix B then applies.

- Disallow the direct use of $\gg_\sigma$. This operator should only be available to the specifier indirectly, through use of the * operator.

6.4 Subtyping guaranteed

In section 5, an inheritance operator $\oplus$, defined as a constrained version of the LOTOS choice operator, was introduced. Using this operator, it was shown that, derived terminating templates were necessarily subtypes of their parents (predicate 4). Furthermore it was shown that self-referencing templates generated from a derived terminating template (by rule 6), must be a subtype of the self-referencing template which was generated from the parent terminating template (predicate 5).

This last result is applicable whether the terminating template uses *exit* or *self* (with the self-referencing template being generated using $\gg_\delta$ and $\gg_\sigma$ respectively). We can therefore apply this result to the modification operator in section 6, concluding that

$$*(P \oplus m) \text{ is-a-subtype-of } * P$$

where $\oplus$ and * are defined in sections 5 and 6 respectively. Notice that condition a) of the definition of $\oplus$ (which demands that P is a terminating template) means that P cannot reference itself. But *self* is permitted.

7 Conclusions

Two incremental modification techniques have been defined.

The first inheritance technique (introduced in section 5) is applicable only for terminating templates. Self-referencing templates can be treated only if they contain no *exits*. In such cases they can be described in terms of a terminating component template and the enable operator. The modification technique can then be applied to the terminating component. But templates which contain a mixture of terminating and self-referential behaviour cannot be modified, significantly damaging the power of this technique. Nevertheless the technique is shown to guarantee subtyping between the derived and the parent terminating templates and between the associated self-referencing templates.

The second mechanism (defined in section 6) is a more powerful interpretation of inheritance. It can deal with all kinds of template (but at the price of a change to LOTOS). This technique is also shown (using the results of section 5) to guarantee subtyping.

Applying Wegner's categorization of languages, summarized in section 2, it is clear that LOTOS is inherently object-based. Following [5], LOTOS can additionally be considered to be class-based. However, LOTOS provides limited scope for modelling inheritance, making it only partially object-oriented; LOTOS would have to be enhanced, for example as proposed in section 6, to make it fully object oriented.

Whether the benefits of the proposed extension outweigh the cost is not clear. Is inheritance important enough to require changes to the LOTOS standard, and to justify the increase in complexity of the language?

Acknowledgements

Many thanks are due to Jeremy Jacob (PRG, Oxford University) for the inspiration which led to the second modification mechanism, and to Tim Regan (University of Sussex) and Chris Smith (BT) for checking the proofs. Any remaining errors are, of course, the responsibility of the author.

References

[1] G Booch. Object Oriented Development. IEEE Transactions on Software Engineering, Vol SE12 No 2, February 1986.

[2] B Meyer. Object-oriented Software Construction. Prentice Hall 1988.

[3] B J Cox. An Evolutionary Approach. Addison Wesley 1987.

[4] B Meyer. The New Culture of Software Development. Journal of Object Oriented Programming Nov/Dec 90.

[5] E Cusack S Rudkin and C Smith. An Object-oriented interpretation of LOTOS. The 2nd International Conference on Formal Description Techniques (FORTE89), December 1989.

[6] S Black. Objects and LOTOS. 2nd International Conference on Formal Description Techniques for Distributed Systems and Communications Protocols (FORTE89).

[7] T Mayr, Specification of object-oriented systems in LOTOS, Formal Description Techniques - Proceedings of the first international conference on formal description techniques

(Stirling, September 1988), North Holland 1989.
[8] ISO IS 8807, LOTOS - a formal description technique based on the temporal ordering of observed behaviour, 1988.
[9] K J Turner. The formal specification language LOTOS - a course for users. Technical report, Department of Computer Science, Stirling University, 1987.
[10] T Bolognesi, E Brinksma. Introduction to the ISO Specification Language LOTOS, Computer Networks and ISDN Systems 14 (1987) 25-59, North-Holland.
[11] S B Zdonik P Wegner. Type similarity, inheritance and evolution, or what "like" is and isn't like. Technical report, Brown University, 1987.
[12] W Cook and J Palsberg. A Denotational Semantics of Inheritance and its Correctness. In OOPSLA '89, 1989.
[13] ISO/IEC. Information Retrieval, Transfer and Management for OSI - Working Document - Architectural Semantics, Formalisms and Specification Techniques. ISO/IEC JTC1/SC21 N6082, June 1991.
[14] P Wegner, Dimensions of object-based language design, Object Oriented Programming, Systems, Languages and Applications 87, Orlando, Florida, September 1987.
[15] ISO/IEC. Information Retrieval, Transfer and Management for OSI - Committee Draft - Basic Reference Model of Open Distributed Processing - Part 2: Descriptive Model. ISO/IEC JTC1/SC21 N6079, June 1991.
[16] E Brinksma, G Scollo Formal notions of implementation and conformance in LOTOS, Technical Memorandum (INF-86-13), University of Twente, December 1986.
[17] A Goldberg, D Robson; Smalltalk-80 The Language and its implementation, Addison-Wesley, 1983.
[18] E Cusack. Refinement, Conformance and Inheritance, presented at Workshop on the Theory and Practice of Refinement, Open University, January 1989.

A Proofs

Throughout this section the following conventions hold.

a, b, c denote events.
r, s, t denote strings of events and ϵ denotes the empty string.
s_{term}, t_{term}, P, Q and m denote behaviour expressions.
A, B denote sets of events.
The meanings of $P = a \Rightarrow$, $Q = s \Rightarrow$, $Q = s \Rightarrow Q_1 = a \not\Rightarrow$ etc. are defined in [16]. A formal definition of conformance is included here.

Definition (conformance)
Let Q and P be processes.
   Q conf P iff
   $\forall s \epsilon Traces(P). \forall A \subseteq L(P)$
      if $\exists Q'. \forall a \epsilon A. Q = s \Rightarrow Q' = a \not\Rightarrow$
      then $\exists P'. \forall a \epsilon A. P = s \Rightarrow P' = a \not\Rightarrow$

Proof 1: $s_{term} = t_{term} \oplus m \Rightarrow s_{term}$ extends t_{term},
where $s_{term} = t_{term} \oplus m \Rightarrow$
$s_{term} = t_{term}[]m$
and

a) t_{term} is a non-recursive template;
b) m is a modifier behaviour containing no type definitions;
c) m is stable;
d) $\forall s^1_{term}, s^2_{term} | s^1_{term} \neq_{tc} s^2_{term} \cdot s_{term} =b\Rightarrow s^1_{term} \land s_{term} =b\Rightarrow s^2_{term}$ implies
$t_{term} =b\Rightarrow s^1_{term} \land t_{term} =b\Rightarrow s^2_{term}$, where $=_{tc}$ denotes testing congruence defined in [8].
(The initial events of m are distinct from the initials of t_{term}.)
e) $\forall b. s_{term} =b\Rightarrow \lor t_{term} =b\Rightarrow$ implies $b \notin B$, where $B = \{L(R)|s_{term} =c\Rightarrow R \lor t_{term} =c\Rightarrow R\}$.
(No initial events of s_{term} or t_{term} occur in the body of s_{term} or in the body of t_{term}.)

$$s_{term} =a\not\Rightarrow \forall a \in A \text{ implies} \quad (defn\ of\ []\ and\ condition\ c) \tag{1}$$
$$t_{term} =a\not\Rightarrow \forall a \in A$$
$$s_{term} =s \Rightarrow s'_{term} =a\not\Rightarrow \forall a \in A \text{ implies} \quad (defn\ of\ []\ and\ condition\ d) \tag{2}$$
$$t_{term} =s \Rightarrow t'_{term} =a\not\Rightarrow \forall a \in A \lor$$
$$m =s \Rightarrow m' =a\not\Rightarrow \forall a \in A \land t_{term} =hd(s)\not\Rightarrow$$

Thus s_{term} conf t_{term}. Moreover $tr(s_{term}) \supseteq tr(t_{term})$, so s_{term} extends t_{term}.

Proof 2: $s_{term} = t_{term} \oplus m \Rightarrow s_{self-ref}$ extends $t_{self-ref}$,
where $s_{self-ref}$ and $t_{self-ref}$ are non-divergent.

In the following proof we denote s_{term} and t_{term} by Q and P respectively. First we record condition (e) as an assumption.

$$\forall b \cdot Q =b\Rightarrow \lor P =b\Rightarrow \text{implies } b \notin B, \text{where } B = \{L(R)|Q =c\Rightarrow R \lor P =c\Rightarrow R\} \tag{1}$$

Now we proceed by proving $Q = P \oplus m \Rightarrow \forall n. Q^n \text{ conf } P^n$, using the principle of induction. (Q^{n+1} denotes $Q^n \gg Q$, where $Q^1 = Q$.) The base case holds from proof 1.

$$Q \text{ conf } P \tag{2}$$

We assume the induction hypothesis.

$$Q^n \text{ conf } P^n \tag{3}$$

Next we must prove $Q^{n+1} \text{ conf } P^{n+1}$. This is of the form $X \Rightarrow Y$, so we assume X and prove Y.

$$For\ any\ A \cdot Q^{n+1} =s\Rightarrow Q^{n+1}_1 =a\not\Rightarrow \forall a \in A \land P^{n+1} =s\Rightarrow \quad Assumption \tag{4}$$

Considering the first conjunct of predicate 4, we can say either s is a non-terminated trace of Q^n (by non-terminated we mean $last(s) \neq \delta$), or it is a trace which enters the n+1th iteration of Q.

$$(Q^n =s\Rightarrow Q^n_1 =a\not\Rightarrow \forall a \in A \land last(s) \neq \delta) \lor (\exists r_1, t_1 \cdot s = r_1\frown t_1 \land \tag{5}$$
$$Q^n =r_1\Rightarrow exit \land Q =t_1\Rightarrow Q_1 =a\not\Rightarrow \forall a \in A)$$

Similarly, considering the second conjunct of predicate 4, we can say either s is a non-terminated trace of P^n or it is a trace which performs at least one observable event in the n+1th transition of P, i.e. that $t_2 \neq \epsilon$. We are able to insist here that t_2 is non-empty because conjunct 2 is concerned only with observable traces. We cannot insist on this with conjunct 1 of predicate 4, because it is considering refusals.

$$(P^n =s\Rightarrow \wedge last(s) \neq \delta) \vee (\exists r_2, t_2 \cdot t_2 \neq \epsilon \wedge s = r_2\frown t_2 \wedge P^n =r_2\Rightarrow exit \wedge P =t_2\Rightarrow) \quad (6)$$

Thus from predicates 4, 5 and 6 we produce four separate cases:

Case 1:
$$(Q^n =s\Rightarrow Q_1^n =a\not\Rightarrow \forall a \in A) \wedge (P^n =s\Rightarrow) \wedge last(s) \neq \delta$$

Applying predicate 3 gives
$$P^n =s\Rightarrow P_1^n =a\not\Rightarrow \forall a \in A$$

and since the last event of s is not δ, this gives
$$P^{n+1} =s\Rightarrow P_1^{n+1} =a\not\Rightarrow \forall a \in A$$

Case 2:
$(\exists r_1, t_1 \cdot s = r_1\frown t_1 \wedge Q^n =r_1\Rightarrow exit \wedge Q =t_1\Rightarrow Q_1 =a\not\Rightarrow \forall a \in A) \wedge$
$(\exists r_2, t_2 \cdot t_2 \neq \epsilon \wedge s = r_2\frown t_2 \wedge P^n =r_2\Rightarrow exit \wedge P =t_2\Rightarrow)$

Applying predicate 1, and considering initials of Q we deduce $hd(t_1) \notin tl(t_2)$. Similarly considering initials of P we get $hd(t_2) \notin tl(t_1)$. And since in case 2 we have $s = r_1\frown t_1 = r_2\frown t_2$ then $r_1 = r_2 \wedge t_1 = t_2$. So equating r_1 with r_2 and t_1 with t_2 in case 2 gives

$$(\exists r,t \cdot s = r\frown t \wedge Q^n =r\Rightarrow exit \wedge Q =t\Rightarrow Q_1 =a\not\Rightarrow \forall a \in A \wedge P^n =r\Rightarrow exit \wedge P =t\Rightarrow)$$

Weakening this by dropping uninteresting terms and applying predicate 2 gives

$$\exists r,t \cdot s = r\frown t \wedge P^n =r\Rightarrow exit \wedge P =t\Rightarrow P_1 =a\not\Rightarrow \forall a \in A$$

from which we can deduce
$$P^{n+1} =s\Rightarrow P_1^{n+1} =a\not\Rightarrow \forall a \in A$$

Case 3:

$(Q^n=s\Rightarrow Q_1^n=a\not\Rightarrow \forall a \in A \wedge last(s) \neq \delta) \wedge (\exists r_2, t_2 \cdot t_2 \neq \epsilon \wedge s = r_2\frown t_2 \wedge P^n=r_2\Rightarrow exit \wedge P=t_2\Rightarrow)$

By predicate 1, s may contain at most n initials of P or Q. Since $t_{self-ref}$ cannot be divergent P cannot contain empty traces leading to termination or deadlock. Thus r_2 must contain exactly n initial events of P or Q. So since $s = r_2\frown t_2$, it must be true that $t_2 = \epsilon$.

But this contradicts the predicate that $t_2 \neq \epsilon$. Therefore this case is empty.

Case 4:

$(P^n =s\Rightarrow \wedge last(s) \neq \delta) \wedge (\exists r_1, t_1 \cdot s = r_1\frown t_1 \wedge Q^n =r_1\Rightarrow exit \wedge Q =t_1\Rightarrow Q_1 =a\not\Rightarrow \forall a \in A)$

By predicate 1, s may contain at most n initials of P or Q. Since $s_{self-ref}$ cannot be divergent Q cannot contain empty traces leading to termination or deadlock. Thus r_1 must contain exactly n initial events of P or Q. So since $s = r_1\frown t_1$, it must be true that $t_1 = \epsilon$. So
$$Q =\epsilon\Rightarrow Q_1 =a\not\Rightarrow \forall a \in A$$
But $P =\epsilon\Rightarrow$ (any process can), so by predicate 2
$$P =\epsilon\Rightarrow P_1 =a\not\Rightarrow \forall a \in A \tag{7}$$
Moreover $Q^n =r_1\Rightarrow exit$. And since both $P^n =s\Rightarrow$ and predicate 3 must hold true,
$$P^n =r_1\Rightarrow P_1 =a\not\Rightarrow \forall a \in L \setminus \{\delta\} \tag{8}$$
Assume $P^n =s\Rightarrow P_1 =\delta\Rightarrow$ then by predicate 7 we have
$$P^{n+1} = r_1\Rightarrow P_1 =a\not\Rightarrow \forall a \in A \tag{9}$$
If $P^n =s\Rightarrow=\delta\not\Rightarrow$ then directly from predicate 8 we have
$$P^n =s\Rightarrow P_1 =a\not\Rightarrow \forall a \in A$$
which in turn gives predicate 9.

So each case is either empty or results in predicate 9. Thus by discharging assumption 4 we can conclude that $Q^{n+1}\ conf\ P^{n+1}$. Discharging assumption 3 gives
$$Q^n\ conf\ P^n\ implies\ Q^{n+1}\ conf\ P^{n+1}$$
So finally applying the principle of induction we have
$$\forall n \cdot Q^n\ conf\ P^n$$
From the definition of the LOTOS choice operator $tr(Q) \supseteq tr(P)$. So, as required:
$$\forall n \cdot Q^n\ extends\, P^n$$

Proof 3: $A = []\{a_j; exit(E_1 \ldots E_n) | j \in I\} \gg accept(x_1 : t_1, \ldots x_n : t_n)\ in\ A$
$\Leftrightarrow$
$A = []\{a_j; A(E_1 \ldots E_n) | j \in I\}$

Generally a_j are parameterized events dependent on $x_1 \ldots x_n$, and which may be used to define $E_1 \ldots E_n$. These definitions and the results of appendix B of [8]) give:

$$\begin{aligned}
A &= []\{a_j; exit(E_1 \ldots E_n) | j \in I\} \gg accept(x_1 : t_1, \ldots x_n : t_n)\ in\ A \\
&= []\{a_j; exit(E_1 \ldots E_n) \gg accept(x_1 : t_1, \ldots x_n : t_n)\ in\ A | j \in I\} \quad (defn\ of\ []) \\
&= []\{a_j; i; [E_1/x_1 \ldots E_n/xn]A | j \in I\} \quad (by\ d2b) \\
&= []\{a_j; i; A(E_1 \ldots E_n) | j \in I\} \quad (by\ h) \\
&= []\{a_j; A(E_1 \ldots E_n) | j \in I\} \quad (by\ m1)
\end{aligned}$$

The h step is allowed provided A is a process which takes x1..xn as formal parameters.

B Inference rules for self

ISO8807 Clause 7.5.3.2c.
Add the following axioms to the existing axioms for exit.
$self - \sigma \longrightarrow stop$ is an axiom.
$self(E_1, \ldots, E_n) - \sigma v_1 \ldots v_n \longrightarrow stop$ is an axiom iff
$v_i = [E_i]$ if E_i is a ground term $(1 \leq i \leq n)$
$v_j \in Q(s_i)$ if $E_i = any\ s_i$ $(1 \leq i \leq n)$, where
$Q(s) = \{[t] \mid t \text{ is a ground term of sort } s\}$ and $[t] = \{t' \mid t \equiv_{pres} t'\}$.

ISO8807 Clause 7.5.3.3e.
Add the following rules to the existing rules for $\gg_\delta$.
$x_1 \ldots x_n$ are variable instances and
$t_1 \ldots t_n$ are ground terms with $[t_1] = v_1, \ldots, [t_n] = v_n$

If $B = B_1 \gg_\sigma accept\ x_1, \ldots, x_n\ in\ B_2$, then

$$\frac{B_1-a\longrightarrow B_1'}{B-a\longrightarrow B_1' \gg_\sigma accept\ x_1 \ldots x_n\ in\ B_2} \quad name(a) \neq \sigma.$$

$$\frac{B_1-\sigma v_1 \ldots v_n \longrightarrow B_1'}{B-i\longrightarrow [t_1/x_1,\ldots,t_n/x_n]B_2}$$

ISO8807 Clause 7.5.3.3f.
Replace the existing rules with the following rules.
If $B = B_1[> B_2$

$$\frac{B_1-a\longrightarrow B_1'}{B-a\longrightarrow B_1'[> B_2} \quad name(a) \notin \{\delta, \sigma\}.$$

$$\frac{B_1-\delta v_1 \ldots v_n \longrightarrow B_1'}{B-\delta v_1 \ldots v_n \longrightarrow B_1'}$$

$$\frac{B_1-\sigma v_1 \ldots v_n \longrightarrow B_1'}{B-\sigma v_1 \ldots v_n \longrightarrow B_1'}$$

$$\frac{B_2-a\longrightarrow B_2'}{B-a\longrightarrow B_2'}$$

ISO8807 Clause 7.5.3.3g.
Change the conditions on each inference rule so that the specified set of gates contains σ. i.e. $name(a) \notin \{g_1, \ldots, g_n, \delta, \sigma\}$ for the first two rules, and $name(a) \in \{g_1, \ldots, g_n, \delta, \sigma\}$ for the third inference rule.

Mixing LOTOS and SDL Specifications*

Heinz Saria[a], Heinrich Nirschl[a], and Carl Binding[b]

[a]Alcatel Austria - ELIN Research Centre, Ruthnergasse 1-7, A-1210 Wien, Austria

[b]IBM Research Division, Zurich Research Laboratory, 8803 Rüschlikon, Switzerland

Abstract

This paper describes an approach to intermix specifications written in the CCITT specification language SDL with specifications expressed in the ISO specification language LOTOS. First, we introduce a model of the inter-communication. This model is based on asynchronous communication between the LOTOS and SDL specifications. After that we present a formal language that allows us to express the transformation of SDL signals to LOTOS events and vice versa. The transformation rules are flexible enough to handle SDL concepts like process IDs and channels for which no direct counterpart in LOTOS exists. This mixing scheme is currently implemented in conjunction with a common run-time environment for SDL and LOTOS.

1 Introduction

The goal of the RACE project *Specification and Programming Environments for Communication Software* (SPECS) [5, 14] is to create a software engineering environment for the construction of large bodies of software, in particular of communication systems in the context of the European Integrated Broadband Communication (IBC) effort. The project has been concerned with establishing a methodological framework and a supporting toolset to assist the process of software development. Starting with informal requirements, a rigorization phase leads to formally specified software components. To these, various analysis and verification tools can be applied. Ultimately, code generation tools can derive executable code from the formal specifications.

To date, SPECS has essentially supported two so-called formal *tower-languages* in which specifiers can express the system behaviors. These are the CCITT specification language SDL [4] and the ISO specification language LOTOS [8]. Both languages are mapped onto a common semantical model based on the common representation language, CRL [13]. Various tools operate on this intermediate representation: logical model checkers, as well as an animator tool are part of the SPECS toolset. Code generation is also based on the intermediate representation from which C code is derived.

---

*The research by the authors was supported by RACE project no. 1046, Specification and Programming Environment for Communication Software (SPECS). This paper expresses the opinion of the authors and does not necessarily reflect the views of the SPECS consortium.

This code is linked with a special purpose run-time environment and can be executed in various target environments.

One of the important goals of the SPECS project has been to address the intermixing of specifications expressed in the different tower languages. The motivation for such mixing has several rationales:

1. It allows the reuse of existing specifications even if they are written in a language different from the one used for the new specification.

2. Specifications written by a set of people with different backgrounds can be combined.

3. Depending on the problem at hand, some of its sub-problems might be better expressed in one or the other specification language. These "modules" can then be combined into one single system.

Such language mixing can be done at the semantic level via a mapping of the various tower languages into the CRL for analysis and verification purposes. Mixing can also be achieved at the operational level by using an execution model which associates the different inter-process communication paradigms of the specification languages, i.e. where we relate LOTOS *events* with SDL *signals* and vice versa. Our work is based on the latter alternative.

We have designed a special-purpose language to express the intermixing of SDL and LOTOS specifications. The syntax of this *interconnection language* (ICL) is relatively simple, but appears appropriate to solve the problem at hand. A dedicated ICL compiler interacts with the SDL and LOTOS compilers to establish the linkage between the various C modules generated by the SDL and LOTOS compilers. To that effect, the ICL compiler generates code that invokes features of the common run-time environment to support the transformation of LOTOS events onto SDL signals and vice versa. The run-time environment also provides operations for inter-process communication between components originally specified in both tower languages.

To our knowledge, no previous work related to such intermixing of the standard specification languages SDL and LOTOS exists. Traditional compiler and operating system technologies ensure inter-language communication at the level of a *procedure call* by using a common procedure calling convention. In contrast, our work achieves interoperation at a level of *inter-process communication*. This approach is partly based on the special role that inter-process synchronization and communication play in SDL and LOTOS. Unlike conventional sequential programming languages, inter-process communication is built into SDL and LOTOS and thus it was essential to find a means of relating SDL's asynchronous, message based inter-process communication style with LOTOS' synchronous multi-way rendezvous style of inter-process communication.

The remainder of this paper describes our approach in more detail. A brief description of the tower specification languages SDL and LOTOS is given in Section 2. Section 3 presents an overview of our intercommunication model and the language in which this model can be expressed. In Section 4 the semantics of the mixing scheme is informally described by means of an example. Section 5 contains a presentation of the common run-time environment and its support for our mixing scheme. The paper concludes with a discussion of the results and the current status of the work.

2 SDL and LOTOS

The ISO specification language LOTOS [8, 3] can be divided into a *data part* and a *control part* (also called *process part*). The data part relies on the theory of *abstract data types* defined by a set of equations using the concrete syntax of ACT-ONE [6]. Implementation techniques for the LOTOS data part can be based on *rewrite-systems* [10, 7, 9]. In practice, however, the symbolic manipulations performed in these systems are too inefficient and implementations of the abstract data types are built using a conventional programming language such as LISP, Pascal, or C.

The process part, in turn, is based on the notion of *process algebra* [1] in which a calculus of synchronizing and communicating processes is formulated. The operands of this calculus are process expressions and the operators combine these expressions into further, composite process expressions. Amongst the operators, we find *parallel operators* to specify interleaved and synchronized execution of the operand processes. A *disable* operator can be used to describe forced termination by one process of another process. The *choice* operator is available to express non-deterministic execution of either operand process.

Inter-process synchronization and communication in LOTOS is based on the concept of multi-way rendezvous with associated value passing, value matching, or value generation. Conceptually such synchronization takes place over so-called *gates* at which processes submit event offers. Event offers may contain data arguments with which a process can request "input" (the ? operator) or offer "output" (the ! operator). When the appropriate number of processes have submitted matching event offers at a given gate, the synchronization at that gate takes place and the individual processes proceed with their execution. (In LOTOS terminology, this is also called the occurrence of an *event* or an *action*.) The determination of which processes must propose event offers and the actual event matching depends on the relation between the processes (i.e. interleaved or synchronized), the data arguments involved, as well as optional *selection-predicates*. For a detailed description of LOTOS event unification, see [11, 2].

Similar to LOTOS, the CCITT specification language SDL [4, 12] can also be divided into a *data* and a *process part*. The data part is similar to the LOTOS data part and shall not be further discussed here. The SDL process part, however, is fundamentally different in that it uses a model of pair-wise, unidirectional, and asynchronous communication based on message sending. SDL messages or *signals* consist of a name, a list of data values, the identification of the sender process, and the identification of the receiver process and can be sent directly between processes or routed via so-called *channels* that connect SDL *blocks*[1]. SDL, in contrast to LOTOS, thus supports both, explicit and implicit addressing of the receiving process.

---
[1] A *block* is a grouping and encapsulation abstraction provided by the language.

3 Overview of the Mixing Model

When mixing LOTOS and SDL specifications, one specification is considered a component of the other specification's external environment. Since each language expects the communication behavior between the specification and its environment to obey its own communication model, some transformation is needed to map the different communication models onto each other.

In essence, to mix SDL and LOTOS specifications two problems must be solved:

- LOTOS events and SDL signals differ in their information content: For instance, the information contained in a LOTOS event alone is not sufficient to create an SDL signal. In particular, the SDL related routing information is missing from a LOTOS event. In the case of SDL $\rightarrow$ LOTOS communication, creation of a LOTOS event offer from an SDL signal may sometimes require inclusion of an SDL PId value as an event parameter.

- The nature of inter-process communication is different in SDL and LOTOS: LOTOS uses a multi-way rendezvous mechanism for inter-process communication, whereas SDL uses an asynchronous, pair-wise message exchange inter-process communication model.

Our mixing model does not specifically address the data part. Indeed, both languages use an equivalent data model based on initial algebras defined by a set of abstract data type specifications. Hence, once an implementation technique has been chosen, both the SDL and LOTOS systems can use the same common data type library and the mixing is no problem. In our work, we map abstract data types of either tower language into concrete C data type implementations. For example, the LOTOS sort *Nat* and the SDL data type *integer*, are both mapped onto C's *int* type. A similar scheme works for more abstract data types such as queues, lists, or stacks: we simply need to associate the same concrete C data type with the appropriate specification language data types. This can be done in a simple way by using naming equivalence.

Other differences in the execution model of the tower languages do not play a role in our mixing scheme. This is due to the fact that we only transform *externally* visible events or signals onto input signals or event offers. Hence, LOTOS' non-determinism in event execution versus SDL's deterministic sequencing of input and output actions is no issue: the mixing component only becomes aware of a LOTOS event *after* it has happened, the determination of the occurrence is irrelevant. In other words, the mixing component always *accepts* any event offer from the LOTOS subsystem and thus does *not* influence the determination of event occurrence. Similarly, the presence of timers in an SDL system play no role: only SDL signals that leave the SDL system become visible to the mixing model, the point in time when they are sent is of no concern.

3.1 Transformations between LOTOS events and SDL signals

The first item addressed by our mixing scheme is the generation of compatible inter-process communication items, i.e. signals and event offers, from inter-process communication items of the other language. Some special rules are introduced in Tables 1 and 2 to define generic transformations for the generation of *signal* ↔ *event* conversions. Amongst other problems, the rules address the fact that LOTOS events are more abstract than SDL signals since they do not explicitly contain sender and receiver information. In fact, LOTOS events do not need the concept of "direction" at all, since LOTOS uses a multi-way communication paradigm. As a consequence of this paradigm, LOTOS also has no notion of a *channel* to route information. In our model, such routing information is associated with a LOTOS event via appropriate ICL statements. For instance, one can specify to which SDL signal a LOTOS event is transformed and the signal is then routed to one particular SDL process. The actual routing is performed by some SDL compiler generated code which, upon invocation, returns one possible routing for a given signal type. It is, of course, also possible to pass explicit routing information from the SDL system to the LOTOS system which can later be used as an argument in a LOTOS event to determine the routing of an SDL signal.

On the other hand, since SDL signals contain more information, it is sometimes necessary to encode that additional information into the value-list of the corresponding LOTOS event. For instance, the identity of the sending SDL process can become an explicit LOTOS event parameter.

Before considering the transformation from LOTOS events to SDL signals and vice versa, we introduce the following notation: We denote SDL signals with name s and with value-list vl that are routed via channel ch, from sender process $send$ to receiver process rec, as $\langle s, vl, ch, send, rec \rangle$. LOTOS event offers at gate g with a value-list vl are denoted as $\langle g, vl \rangle$. Quoted strings in teletype font (such as `"subgate"`) denote constants, unquoted variable names (such as vl) are used to indicate that a value is 'copied' from the signal to the event or vice versa. A star ("$\star$") is a special value indicating that no specific value is given. We shall also use the operator "$\frown$" to denote the concatenation of values and value-lists.

SDL → LOTOS: We need to express transformations of the form $\langle s, vl, ch, send, rec \rangle \rightarrow \langle g, vl \rangle$. In order to compensate for the difference in information content, we considered the following:

- When analyzing LOTOS specifications, it can be observed that LOTOS gates sometimes directly express 'signals' and sometimes are used like 'channels' on which several signals are multiplexed. In the second case, a further qualification by means of data values is needed to identify the signal (rules 1.2, 1.4, 1.6, 1.8 below). (In LOTOS, this technique is also called *subgating*.)

- In SDL, process instances are identified by so-called PId (*process instance identifier*) values which are automatically available. In practice, PIds are often used to establish explicit communication between specific process instances. Hence, the ICL allows for the inclusion of an SDL PId into a LOTOS event offer as an additional, explicit parameter for possible later use (rules 1.3, 1.4, 1.7, 1.8 below).

The rules of Table 1 handle a large number of signal to event transformations. In fact, each rule adds several elements into the relation SIGtoEV $\subseteq$ Signal $\times$ Event, where Event is the set of all LOTOS events and Signal is the set of all SDL signals.

(1.1)	$\langle$"s"$, vl, \star, \star,$"LPid"$\rangle$	$\rightarrow$	$\langle$"g"$, vl\rangle$
(1.2)	$\langle$"s"$, vl, \star, \star,$"LPid"$\rangle$	$\rightarrow$	$\langle$"g"$,$"subgate"$^\frown vl\rangle$
(1.3)	$\langle$"s"$, vl, \star, pid_S,$"LPid"$\rangle$	$\rightarrow$	$\langle$"g"$, vl^\frown pid_L\rangle$
(1.4)	$\langle$"s"$, vl, \star, pid_S,$"LPid"$\rangle$	$\rightarrow$	$\langle$"g"$,$"subgate"$^\frown vl^\frown pid_L\rangle$
(1.5)	$\langle$"s"$, vl,$"c"$, \star,$"LPid"$\rangle$	$\rightarrow$	$\langle$"g"$, vl\rangle$
(1.6)	$\langle$"s"$, vl,$"c"$, \star,$"LPid"$\rangle$	$\rightarrow$	$\langle$"g"$,$"subgate"$^\frown vl\rangle$
(1.7)	$\langle$"s"$, vl,$"c"$, pid_S,$"LPid"$\rangle$	$\rightarrow$	$\langle$"g"$, vl^\frown pid_L\rangle$
(1.8)	$\langle$"s"$, vl,$"c"$, pid_S,$"LPid"$\rangle$	$\rightarrow$	$\langle$"g"$,$"subgate"$^\frown vl^\frown pid_L\rangle$

Table 1: Generic transformation rules from signals to events

Since SDL signals are strongly typed, vl refers only to value lists that are consistent with the definition of "s". If we assume that the value list of "s" consists of one boolean value the rule 1.2 adds $\langle$"s"$, \langle$true$\rangle, \star, \star,$"LPid"$\rangle \rightarrow \langle$"g"$,$"subgate"$^\frown \langle$true$\rangle\rangle$, $\langle$"s"$, \langle$false$\rangle, \star, \star,$"LPid"$\rangle \rightarrow \langle$"g"$,$"subgate"$^\frown \langle$false$\rangle\rangle$ to SIGtoEV.

The rules have been designed to enable a distinguished treatment of cases that take into account semantic differences in the use of SDL signals and their information contents. The following interpretation is associated with the individual rules:

Rule 1.1: If a signal with name "s" is sent by some SDL process to the LOTOS subsystem (denoted by the fake process identifier "LPid"), it may be transformed to a LOTOS event over gate "g" with value-list vl. As an example, the SDL signal s(varValue,91) can be transformed to the LOTOS event g!varValue!91. Note that simple copying of value-lists is possible because we assume that LOTOS and SDL values have been mapped to the same concrete implementation.

Rule 1.2: In this case signal "s" is transformed to an event over "g" where the value list starts with the specific value "subgate".

Rule 1.3: The sender PId pid is appended to the value-list of the generated LOTOS event. pid_S refers to the SDL representation of the PId value and pid_L refers to the equivalent LOTOS representation. There must be a suitable correspondence between values of the two different representations: Since SDL PIds are isomorphic to the natural numbers, it is rather natural to use the LOTOS sort *nat* for SDL PId values.

Rule 1.4: Combination of 1.2 and 1.3.

Rule 1.5–8: Like 1.1–4 with the with the exception that only signals "s" arriving on channel "c" are transformed.

A more sophisticated scheme of placing "subgate" and pid_L on arbitrary positions within the generated LOTOS value list can be envisioned. However, for clarity's sake, we shall stick to this simple scheme. If several rules apply to the same signal, one of them is chosen non-deterministically.

LOTOS → SDL: The generic transformations for this direction are given in Table 2.

(2.1)	$\langle \texttt{"g"}, vl \rangle$	→	$\langle \texttt{"s"}, vl, \star, \texttt{"LPid"}, \star \rangle$
(2.2)	$\langle \texttt{"g"}, \texttt{"subgate"}^\frown vl \rangle$	→	$\langle \texttt{"s"}, vl, \star, \texttt{"LPid"}, \star \rangle$
(2.3)	$\langle \texttt{"g"}, vl^\frown pid_L \rangle$	→	$\langle \texttt{"s"}, vl, \star, \texttt{"LPid"}, pid_S \rangle$
(2.4)	$\langle \texttt{"g"}, \texttt{"subgate"}^\frown vl^\frown pid_L \rangle$	→	$\langle \texttt{"s"}, vl, \star, \texttt{"LPid"}, pid_S \rangle$
(2.5)	$\langle \texttt{"g"}, vl \rangle$	→	$\langle \texttt{"s"}, vl, \texttt{"c"}, \texttt{"LPid"}, \star \rangle$
(2.6)	$\langle \texttt{"g"}, \texttt{"subgate"}^\frown vl \rangle$	→	$\langle \texttt{"s"}, vl, \texttt{"c"}, \texttt{"LPid"}, \star \rangle$
(2.7)	$\langle \texttt{"g"}, vl^\frown pid_L \rangle$	→	$\langle \texttt{"s"}, vl, \texttt{"c"}, \texttt{"LPid"}, pid_S \rangle$
(2.8)	$\langle \texttt{"g"}, \texttt{"subgate"}^\frown vl^\frown pid_L \rangle$	→	$\langle \texttt{"s"}, vl, \texttt{"c"}, \texttt{"LPid"}, pid_S \rangle$

Table 2: Generic transformation rules from events to signals

The individual rules of Table 2 have a similar interpretation to the ones of Table 1. Analogously to the relation SIGtoEV there is a relation EVtoSIG which contains all the transformations generated by the rules of Table 2.

Table 3 now gives a concrete syntax for the generic transformations described in Table 1 and Table 2. Brackets ("[|]") denote optional constructs "{}" denotes repetition, terminal symbols (keywords) are quoted. Note that we do not need the "?" operator in action transformations: value acceptance is expressed with "!*". This has the advantage of not only supporting the acceptance of any value of a given sort, but also to express the acceptance of any value list of some given sorts. Note also how the concrete syntax of Table 3 handles PId values: explicit inclusion of the SDL PId value into the data exchanged between SDL and LOTOS is expressed through value matching for a PId value in the concrete syntax of the non-terminal ⟨action⟩. (The sender PId value is implicitly always present in SDL signals). Table 4 gives some examples for the rather obvious correspondence between ICL constructs and transformation rules.

⟨ICL⟩	:=	{ ⟨ICLstatement⟩ }
⟨ICLstatement⟩	:=	⟨signal⟩ '->' ⟨action⟩
	|	⟨action⟩ '->' ⟨signal⟩
⟨signal⟩	:=	'SIGNAL' ⟨signalname⟩'(*)' ['VIA' ⟨channelname⟩]
⟨action⟩	:=	'ACTION' ⟨gatename⟩['!'⟨value⟩]'!*'['!PID']
⟨signalname⟩	:=	*SDL syntax of a signal name*
⟨gatename⟩	:=	*LOTOS syntax of a gate name*
⟨channelname⟩	:=	*SDL syntax of a channel name*
⟨value⟩	:=	*LOTOS syntax of a value*

Table 3: Concrete Syntax of the SDL/LOTOS Interconnection Language (ICL)

ICL statement	Rule
SIGNAL s(*) -> ACTION g!*	1.1
SIGNAL s(*) VIA c -> ACTION g!*	1.5
SIGNAL s(*) VIA c -> ACTION g!subgate!*	1.6
ACTION g!subgate!* -> SIGNAL s(*)	2.2
ACTION g!*!PID -> SIGNAL s(*)	2.3

Table 4: Correspondence between concrete syntax and transformation rules

3.2 Synchronous versus Asynchronous Communication

The second problem to be addressed in our intermixing scheme is to resolve the differences in inter-process communication paradigms between SDL and LOTOS. The inter-process communication style also appears in the communication between a system specified in LOTOS or SDL and its *environment*[2]. LOTOS uses synchronous, multi-way communication gates and SDL relies on asynchronous communication ports. This means that if a LOTOS event occurs on an externally visible gate, then both the specification and the environment have not only exchanged data, but they also have synchronized their execution states. In the case of SDL, the situation is quite different: There is no direct means for the environment to detect whether a signal has been *accepted* by an SDL process or not. The notion of "accepted" is not even clearly defined for SDL. It could mean that the signal has been enqueued in the receiver's input queue, that it has been removed from the receiver's input queue, or that the processing triggered by the signal is in a certain state. The same holds for signals from SDL to its environment.

The only possibility to enforce synchronization between an SDL specification and its environment is to use an explicit synchronization protocol between the communicating processes. This would, of course, require drastic changes in specification style and extensive modifications of existing SDL specifications. Furthermore, no easy cookbook approach for such synchronization appears possible. Therefore, we decided to allow a certain degree of asynchronous behavior at the border of a LOTOS specification. We will discuss our solution for the two directions separately.

LOTOS → SDL: LOTOS events can be transformed to SDL signals as discussed in Section 3.1 and sent to external SDL "in-channels". Since SDL channels have a buffer-like behavior, no additional constructions are needed.

SDL → LOTOS: Since LOTOS does not provide means for buffering events, we had to introduce a buffering entity into the SDL → LOTOS communication scheme. We have chosen to use a single first-in, first-out, buffering queue for the SDL → LOTOS communication. SDL signals are stored in that queue, eventually taken out, trans-

---
[2] The term *environment* refers to the components of the overall system that were *not* specified in either tower language, but which can nevertheless communicate with the specified system.

formed into LOTOS event offers, and offered to the LOTOS specification. Other solutions are possible, in particular a scheme where several buffering queues are used: for example, one queue for each SDL "out"-channel. Although the latter scheme changes the mixing semantics, it is of no consequence to our general considerations. Especially, it has no impact on the ICL. We selected the one-queue solution because of the implicit preservation of the order of signal delivery: Signals are submitted to the LOTOS sub-system in the same order as they passed the border of the SDL system.

When the combined system can execute either inter-language communication, i.e. either an SDL signal can be generated from a LOTOS event or a LOTOS event offer can be created from an SDL signal and submitted to LOTOS, one of the possible actions is chosen non-deterministically by the system. As an example, consider the statements SIGNAL s(*) -> ACTION g!* and ACTION g!* -> SIGNAL s(*). We assume that "s" with value list vl has been sent and therefore "g" with the same value list is the first element in the queue between SDL and LOTOS. Now an event $\langle$"g", $vl\rangle$ offered by LOTOS can either synchronize with the queue (i.e. receive "s" from SDL) or it can trigger the sending of a new "s" from LOTOS to SDL and the system arbitrarily chooses one option.

4 Semantics of Mixed Specifications

For every signal s that is received from the SDL side SIGtoEV determines what to do. If no entry $s' \to ev$ exists in SIGtoEV that matches s then nothing happens, if one such entry exists it is transformed into ev and queued. $s' = \langle$"s", $vl, \star,$ "LPId", $\star\rangle$ matches all signals s with name "s" and receiver address "LPId", $\langle$"s", "c", $\star,$ "LPId", $\star\rangle$ matches all signals s with name "s" and receiver address "LPId" that have been received on channel "c", etc. If several entries exist one is chosen indeterministically. The first element in the queue between SDL and LOTOS ($Q_{SDL \to LOTOS}$) is offered to the LOTOS side.

The occurrence of an event ev offered from the LOTOS side is determined by the relation EVtoSIG (cf. Section 3.1) and the first element in $Q_{SDL \to LOTOS}$. If no matching $ev \to s$ pair is in EVtoSIG and ev is the first element of $Q_{SDL \to LOTOS}$ then ev occurs and is removed from the queue. If no queue synchronization is possible and matching $ev \to s$ pairs exist in EVtoSIG then one of them is chosen and s is sent. If both $Q_{SDL \to LOTOS}$ and EVtoSIG allow ev events one is chosen randomly. If none of them is willing to accept ev then it cannot happen until it is offered by the queue (EVtoSIG is statically determined).

If the channel of the generated signal s is $\star$ then the signal is sent without giving a channel; if the receiver PId is $\star$, then the signal is sent without giving an explicit receiver address. Expressed in SDL terms, $\langle$"s", $vl, \star,$ "LPid", $\star\rangle$ is equivalent to OUTPUT s(vl) (the sender address is an implicit part of the signal), $\langle$"s", $vl, \star,$ "LPid", $pid_S\rangle$ is equivalent to OUTPUT s(vl) TO pid_S, $\langle$"s", $vl,$ "c", "LPid", $\star\rangle$ is equivalent to OUTPUT s(vl) VIA c, etc.

Below an example is given (Figure 1). In this simple example, we have a LOTOS subsystem that can always accept an event of the form g!0, g!1, g!3, ... (in our notation $\langle$"g", "0"$\rangle$, ...) or generate an event h!91. (The LOTOS operator "[]" denotes a choice,

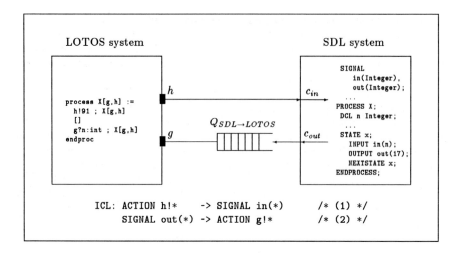

Figure 1: Interconnection Example

the ";" denotes sequence, and "g?n:nat" expresses the ability to accept any "g"-action with a natural number value[3].) The SDL subsystem is a one-state process that waits for the reception of a signal "in" which carries a data value of type natural number (in our notation $\langle$"in"$, n, \star, \star, \star\rangle$) and which sends a signal "out" with value "17" to LOTOS.

The ICL statements that have been used to express the intermixing of the two systems are also given in Figure 1: statement (1) corresponds to rule 2.1 and statement (2) to rule 1.1. Again, note here the use of "!*" to express acceptance by the LOTOS subsystem of an event offer containing any value of any sort.

When the system starts, the queue between SDL and LOTOS ($Q_{SDL \to LOTOS}$) and the channels of the SDL system (c_{in}, c_{out}) are empty. While the SDL subsystem is waiting for the reception of in(n), it is blocked. The LOTOS subsystem however can execute event h!91 which is then transformed to signal in(91) and sent to SDL. After reception of this signal, out(17) will be sent from the SDL subsystem, transformed to g!17, and put into $Q_{SDL \to LOTOS}$. The event offer is then dequeued and offered to the LOTOS subsystem which can execute the LOTOS action "g?n:nat". Of course, LOTOS has also the possibility to perform another h event to be transformed to signal in at any time between.

---

[3] Formally, $g?n : nat; \ldots \equiv choice\ n : nat [] g!n; \ldots$.

5 Run-time Support for Mixing

In this section we first describe the overall run-time environment features that relate to each specification language, i.e. SDL and LOTOS. We then present the features that can be used by the ICL compiler to implement our mixing scheme.

5.1 The Run-time Environment

The run-time environment supporting both SDL and LOTOS provides two essential aspects for the implementation of the tower languages. These are

- *Concurrency*: The run-time environment supports so-called *lightweight* threading within one UNIX address space. These threads are used to implement LOTOS and SDL processes where the exact mapping of LOTOS or SDL processes to run-time provided threads is a function of the compilers. (Currently, this mapping is one-to-one in the case of SDL, the LOTOS compiler will merge several LOTOS processes into one run-time thread in some situations.)

- *Communication and synchronization*: Both tower languages have a concept of inter-process communication. LOTOS also integrates inter-process synchronization into its communication model. The message based, asynchronous SDL communication is supported by the run-time environment's *send* and *receive* calls. LOTOS multi-way synchronization with associated data exchange is supported by the *synch* operation where synchronization occurs if all involved processes have submitted matching event offers.

The above abstractions are implemented in a library that is linked with the C code generated by the SDL and LOTOS compilers. The library contains functions for process creation and destruction. Processes, once created, can be suspended, resumed, and disabled. Inter-process communication gates can be created dynamically and existing processes can be bound to these gates. The LOTOS semantics of parallel process execution, i.e. interleaving and synchronization, can be specified in the association of processes and gates. Processes then synchronize by submitting event offers at a given gate: A unification phase determines whether the event offers match according to the LOTOS synchronization semantics. SDL message passing is provided through calls for sending and receiving signals; the latter of these calls also allows the specification of enabling-conditions and continuous signals. Timer support for SDL is provided by features to start a new timer, to reset an active timer, and to test for a timer's state. Time-out messages are sent as prioritized messages. (A detailed description of that run-time environment can be found in [2].)

The above functionality implements the process or control part of the tower languages. Data support can be provided in several ways: either via hand-coded C routines which implement the operations of the abstract data types contained in the specification or via invocation of a rewrite-system that evaluates data expressions. Seen from the run-time environment, data items are merely represented as 32 bit entities which can be either a data value or a pointer to the value. All data operations are invoked via

C function calls. The compilers generate these calls based on the original specification and a naming scheme that associates SDL or LOTOS operator names with C function names.

5.2 Support for Mixing

Based on the model described in Section 3, the run-time environment has to support the following:

- Creation of SDL signals upon occurrence of LOTOS events.
- Generation and queuing of LOTOS event offers from SDL signals.

We first discuss the LOTOS→SDL communication scheme. It is implemented as follows:

1. An association between a run-time provided gate abstraction and two C functions is created. One of the C functions, *Ev2Sig*, will translate a LOTOS event into an SDL signal when invoked by the run-time environment. This function implements the transformations of Table 2. It is generated by the ICL compiler, based on the ICL specification. Please note, that sig and chan are out-parameter. For transformations with PId handling the receiver PId is written into the Message structure. For the example given in Figure 1, the following pseudo-C code is required:

```
Signal Ev2Sig(ev, sig, chan)
Event    ev;    /* Event to be transformed. */
Message *sig;   /* Signal to be sent. */
Channel *chan;  /* Channel on which sig has to be sent */
{
  < create SDL signal "in" >;
  < copy data from LOTOS event "h" into SDL signal "in" >;
  *sig = < signal "in" >;
  *chan = NULL;
}
```

The other C function, *Recvr* determines which SDL process, i.e. which run-time environment thread, is to receive the signal. Of course, this function is trivial for rules that contain the receiver identification explicitly (transformations 2.3, 2.4, 2.7, 2.8). The *Recvr* function is:

```
Thread Recvr(sigid, chan)
int sigid;    /* Signal identification. */
Channel chan; /* Channel on which signal will be sent. */
{
  < invoke SDL compiler generated code that maps signal identifiers
    onto SDL PIds >;
  < return thread-id of receiving SDL process >;
}
```

The above function interacts with the SDL compiler in that it is the SDL compiler that has to generate some bookkeeping code which associates an SDL signal with an SDL process for the cases in which the destination PId is not contained in the LOTOS event.

2. When an event occurs at a gate for which one of the above associations exists, the run-time environment first up-calls the *Ev2Sig* function. That function disassembles the LOTOS event descriptor and packs the values into an SDL signal structure. *Ev2Sig* handles all events over a given gate. In general it is a case statement over all possible transformations where the entries are applied randomly.

3. A second up-call from the run-time environment to the *Recvr* determines which thread is to receive the SDL signal.

4. If both up-calls succeed, the run-time environment sends the signal to the receiving thread. This thread then uses the standard *receive* call to effectively receive an SDL signal which was sent after a LOTOS event occurred at a given gate.

In the above scheme, several failures can occur. For instance, no SDL thread might currently be enabled to receive the specific signal type when the associated LOTOS event occurs[4]. In these cases, the run-time environment emits a warning and aborts the operating system process running the specifications.

The LOTOS → SDL inter-communication required a few minor modifications and extensions to the SPECS run-time environment.

- A new function to create LOTOS→SDL associations had to be provided. Its arguments consist of a reference to a LOTOS gate and two function handles embodying the *Ev2Sig* and the *Recvr* up-calls. The call returns a handle to an *association*. This *associate* call also has its inverse, called *dissociate* which can be used to break a previously created association.

- The internals of the run-time environment had to be modified to perform the generation and sending of an SDL signal whenever a LOTOS action on a gate, for which a LOTOS→SDL association exists, occurs.

The case of the SDL to LOTOS communication was solved without modifications to the run-time environment. A dedicated thread is created for each SDL channel by the code generated by the ICL compiler. It receives all SDL signals that are to be transformed to LOTOS events if received on that channel, creates LOTOS event offers, and submits these to the LOTOS sub-system via a thread implementing $Q_{SDL \to LOTOS}$. $Q_{SDL \to LOTOS}$ always offers the first event in the queue to the LOTOS system, using the run-time environment's *synch* call. In our example the intermediate thread's code is:

```
void SDL2LOTOS_C_OUT()
{
    <enable reception of SDL signal "out">;
```

---

[4] Recall that SDL processes are dynamic, i.e. a given SDL process that can receive some specific signal type need not exist at all times.

```
  for (;;) {
    <receive signal "out" from SDL sub-system>;
    <analyze signal and translate it into LOTOS event offer "h">;
    <enqueue generated event in Q(SDL->LOTOS)>;
  }
}
```

6 Conclusion

We have shown that it is possible to combine of LOTOS and SDL specifications without modifying the languages. This is achieved by viewing the specification in one language as part of the other language's environment. The connection is described by a simple, special-purpose language. The implementation on a common SDL and LOTOS run-time environment required only small extensions to the support needed by either LOTOS or SDL alone. The feasibility of such intermixing increases the possibility of reuse of specifications as sub-systems in a larger context and allows for the use of the most appropriate specification language for a given task.

We now are extending the mixing scheme in two directions:

- Support the combination of several LOTOS and/or SDL specifications.

- Allow nested combination (i.e. combination of mixed systems).

This will support the assembly of large systems from smaller parts which are complete, self-contained specifications and can therefore be understood and analyzed separately.

7 Acknowledgements

Georg Karner contributed substantially to the definition of the Interconnection Language (ICL). Ed Mumprecht, Günter Karjoth, and Liba Svobodova improved the overall readability of this paper through their insightful comments. This work was partly supported by the Austrian "Innovations und Technologiefonds".

References

[1] J. Bergstra and J.W. Klop. Process Algebra for Synchronous Communication. *Information and Control*, 60:109–137, 1984.

[2] C. Binding. Executing LOTOS Behavior Expressions IBM Research Report RZ 2118 (#73402), IBM Research Division, Zürich Research Laboratory, 8803 Rüschlikon, Switzerland, May 1991.

[3] T. Bolognesi and E. Brinksma. Introduction to the ISO Specification Language LOTOS. *Computer Networks and ISDN Systems*, 14(1):25–29, January 1989.

[4] CCITT. *Functional Specification and Description Language (SDL)*. CCITT, Geneva, Switzerland, 1989. CCITT Blue Book, Volume X.

[5] The SPECS Consortium and J. Bruijning. Evaluation and Integration of Specification Languages. *Computer Networks and ISDN Systems*, 13(2):75–89, 1987.

[6] H. Ehrig and H. Mahr. *Fundamentals of Algebraic Specification*, volume 6 of *EATCS Monographs on Theoretical Computer Science*. Springer-Verlag, New York, 1985.

[7] H. Garavel. Compilation of LOTOS Abstract Data Types. In *Second International Conference on Formal Description Techniques, FORTE 89*, pages 195–214. IEEE Computer Society, ACM SIGCOMM, December 1989. Vancouver, B.C., Canada.

[8] ISO. *LOTOS-A Formal Description Technique Based on the Temporal Ordering of Observational Behavior*. International Organization for Standardization – Information Processing Systems – Open Systems Interconnections, 1987. Draft International Standard 8807.

[9] L. Jadoul, L. Duponcheel, and W. van Puymbroeck. An Algebraic Data Type Specification Language and its Rapid Prototyping Environment. In *11th International Conference on Software Engineering*, pages 74–84. ACM SIGSOFT, May 1989.

[10] D.E. Knuth and P.B. Bendix. Simple Word Problems in Universal Algebras. In J. Leech, editor, *Computational Problems in Abstract Algebra*. Pergamon Press, Oxford, 1970. QA 266 C59 1970.

[11] S. Nomura, T. Hasegawa, and T. Takizuka. A LOTOS Compiler and Process Synchronization Manager. In *Tenth International IFIP Symposium on Protocol Specification, Testing, and Verification*, pages 165–184. IFIP WG 6.1, June 1990.

[12] R. Saracco and P.A.J. Tilanus. CCITT SDL: Overview of the Language and its Applications. *Computer Networks and ISDN Systems*, 13:65–74, 1987.

[13] SPECS Consortium. *Definition of MR and CRL, Version 2.0*. Deliverable 46/SPE/WP5/DS/A/004/b1, Version 3, RACE Project 1046 (SPECS), December 1989.

[14] SPECS Consortium. *The project SPECS*. Deliverable 46/SPE/WP1/DS/A/004/b1, Version 6, RACE Project 1046 (SPECS), September 1991.

$\Lambda\beta$: a Virtual LOTOS Machine[1]

José A. Mañas and Joaquín Salvachúa

Dpt. Ingeniería Telemática, Technical University of Madrid, E-28040 Madrid, Spain

Abstract

LOTOS behaviour semantics are usually presented in a declarative style that permits to evaluate which events are possible at each stage, and which is the behaviour after an event occurs. In order to generate code that implements these operational semantics, an imperative model is very convenient for efficiency. A virtual machine ($\Lambda\beta$-machine for LOTOS Behaviour Machine) is presented in this paper that provides such an imperative point of view, but still keeps independent of implementation details, effectively providing an intermediate representation for either interpretation or generation of code for any systems programming language. An abstract model of execution is presented, and then the virtual machine is presented by describing its instructions, the relationship to LOTOS constructs, and its dynamic semantics. C code generation is briefly commented too.

1 INTRODUCTION

LOTOS [1] is a very complicated language both syntactically and semantically. Generation of executable code out of a LOTOS specification is a task that must be tackled in several stages to keep complexity under control.

LOTOS is composed of two clearly distinguishable parts: data and behaviour. The data part is pretty complex due to the overloading and structuring facilities, and scope (or visibility) laws. In this paper it is assumed that some kind of *library* exists that provides the functions to perform operations on data types, to evaluate values and predicates, and most notably there is a function available to check for equality of value expressions according to initial semantics.

For the behaviour part, a clear operational semantics is provided in [1]. It may be directly implemented by means of a set of rewrite rules working on some abstract syntax representation. This approach is followed, for instance, in simulators [2, 3], but its efficiency is not satisfactory for a compiler. LOTOS is able to specify highly concurrent systems, where very many activities may be involved at any moment: the exact control threads that exist at each stage of execution, as well at their interrelationship, are only known at run-time.

---

[1]This work has been partly funded by the European Space Agency under contract number 103290, and by the Spanish National Research Programme on Information Technology & Communications within project MEDAS.

In this framework, code generation is an enormous task, and plenty of implementation decisions have to be taken to move from very high level LOTOS to very low level machine code. Furthermore, as experience is gained on the understanding of the language, and implementation issues, these decisions may be subject to severe changes. In order to keep complexity under control, and permit easy maintenance, it is of paramount importance to identify intermediate stages, and keep them clearly isolated. If this isolation is achieved, each one of the stages may be easily replaced without disturbing the others.

In TOPO [4] (a LOTOS compiler) two such intermediate stages are identified and used. First stage is the $\Lambda\beta$-machine presented below, where the syntactic and semantic complexity of LOTOS has been resolved by the semantics analyzer, and an abstract model to implement LOTOS has been chosen. Still it is open to several concrete implementations. $\Lambda\beta$-machine stands for LOTOS Behaviour Machine. The second stage is a systems programming language. Currently, TOPO is able to produce either the widely available C language, or the promising Ada. Some hints about the final implementation decisions taken in TOPO with respect to deriving C code are shown below.

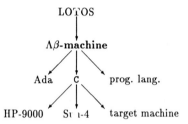

Some naive points of view are frequently found when speaking about LOTOS implementations. It is far too easy to identify LOTOS processes and Operating System processes, and make a one to one mapping. That would be nice, but may be completely unrealistic, and it must be clear that the $\Lambda\beta$-machine presented in this paper leaves that path open to future considerations. There are two basic considerations to take into account:

- Tail recursive process instantiation just models conventional loops (*for, while, until,* ...). They might be implemented as real processes, but the overhead is too high to be worth. Actual experience shows that process instantiation most often falls into this category.

- There is "real" parallelism in LOTOS expressions built out of the *parallel* operators. These parallel threads of control do not necessarily get a name in the user's specification, that is, there is not necessarily a **process** for each branch. A single name, a LOTOS **process**, may well be behaving as a couple of unnamed actual processes at run-time, after "splitting" around some parallel operator.

$\Lambda\beta$-machine carefully avoids taking any compromising decision on this critical issue of mapping to real machine processes. Concurrent threads of control exist, but its mapping is delayed to the code derivation stages. Notice, that this decision is sometimes not possible at all. For instance, if the target machine is to run under a mono-process O.S. (e.g. under MS–DOS), there are few opportunities to pass concurrency control to the O.S.

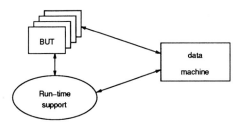

Figure 1: $\Lambda\beta$-machine Run Time Model

2 THE ABSTRACT MODEL

This section presents an abstract model for the run-time components of a system derived from a LOTOS specification. There are three basic building blocks (see figure 1): a collection of BUTs, a data machine, and a run-time support. Their functionality and interrelationship is described below.

The BUTs (for Behaviour UniTs), are derived from LOTOS behaviour specification. There is initially a single BUT that behaves as the main behaviour in the specification. As concurrent control threads are spawn, further BUTs appear. The data machine provides an implementation of the data specification. The run-time support (sometimes called Kernel) provides centralized control on active BUTs, keeps information about BUTs relation patterns, selects partners for a rendezvous [5], and schedules the allocation of time slots for BUTs activities.

BUTs call the data machine for data evaluation, and guards resolution. The run-time support calls the data machine for predicate resolution, and for deciding equality of terms according to initial semantics. BUTs are activated under control of the kernel. It holds a table of active BUTs that encompasses both the code to execute and their private data. It exactly reflects the role of an O.S. kernel that keeps a table of active processes: code and data segments. BUTs have independent activity, and inform the kernel of relevant events that require coordination with other BUTs. The kernel provides system calls to inform of synchronization patterns and to spawn new BUTs. The kernel recovers control when the BUT makes an offer to participate in an event. The behaviour of BUTs closely resembles that of processes in conventional O.S. User processes get time slots from the kernel. The processes rely on the kernel to coordinate with other processes, and use system calls to access kernel data structures.

The rest of the paper is devoted to describe BUTs in terms of a virtual behaviour machine.

2.1 Related Work

Although the authors are not aware of any other virtual machine for LOTOS, several papers have been published that propose their own run-time organization. For may of them, blocks with a similar functionality to our BUTs may be identified. Then, the virtual machine described below may be used in several other environments.

It seems that many of the proposed implementation models for LOTOS [6, 7, 8, 9, 10] rely on some activity units modeling the behaviour of independent parts of the specification, and that these units rely on external communication to resolve rendezvous. The kernel may be centralized as in [8], or more or less distributed as in [6, 7, 9, 10]. As far as this minimal model is followed, $\Lambda\beta$ may be used as an intermediate stage for code generation; isolating front-end analysis, and back-end code generation.

3 THE LANGUAGE

The $\Lambda\beta$-machine is defined by its (programming) language. It is a stack machine driven via a number of instructions that may be classified into three major groups:

stack: The stack will be basically used to perform data evaluation, and as intermediate stage to store data for other instructions. It is a polymorphic stack, that may hold: booleans, integers, data, gates, and experiments.

automata: The activity of the BUT is described by means of a state machine that moves between states upon successful synchronization.

kernel: Eventually, the BUT will block waiting for some synchronization to take place. The BUT will make a *kernel call* to offer a rendez–vous.

One of the most simple instructions removes one item from the stack: POP.

3.1 Data Evaluation in the Stack

For data there is a clear distinction between a *variable* and a *value*. A variable is a buck ready to contain a *value*. Variables are local to BUTs, but values may be exchanged. Within a BUT a variable is uniquely identified (or denoted) by its **index**. Values may exist either on the stack or loaded into some variable.

`P_VAR variable_index`	push the index of a variable
`P_VAL variable_index`	push a data value
`L_VAR variable_index`	load a variable taking a value from the stack.
`I_VAR total_number_of_variables variable_parameters`	

I_VAR is intended for BUT instantiation. At that moment, room is made for all the variables in the BUT. Those coming as actual parameters are directly loaded. The others, internal variables, will be loaded as their values become known. Data values are passed through the stack between the caller and the callee.

Usually, data are evaluated on the stack, and eventually loaded into some indexed position by means of L_VAR, or directly used from the stack.

EVAL operation number_of_arguments
It takes N operands from stack, and calls the **operation** with so many arguments, pushing the result back to the stack. Arguments to **EVAL** are removed from the stack.

EQUAL sort
Takes 2 arguments from the stack, checks them for equality, according to the initial algebra semantics for their **sort**, and pushes the result (a **boolean**) back to the stack.

3.2 Gate Manipulation

For gates, there exists no concept of contents and container. There is no similar concept to pass data values. Gates are statically identified by means of an index, and dynamically handled by means of relabeling. Gate identification is a very specific problem derived from the very peculiar mechanisms of LOTOS, most notably the relabeling concept. Gate values are not truly shared between BUTs. Gates are not passed during process instantiation, as data values are. Gates have a rather isolated existence inside their definition scope, and only when offers exported from the scope are considered outside, is the involved gate changed from referring to the local name, to refer to the external name. This mechanism of changing names *on leave* is known as "dynamic relabeling", and only requires to know gate indexes in their scope, and indexes correspondences at scope boundaries.

$\Lambda\beta$ assumes the following handling of gate indexes. During semantics analysis, a unique index is given to each gate declared in the scope of a process definition. This is a direct mapping for gates declared as formal gates. Other gates, as those declared by means of **hide** operators, get an scope extended to the innermost enclosing process definition. This scope extension should not make any harm at run time, since semantics analysis did its job previously.

These gate indexes are directly used as gate identification at run-time. Special care must be paid to relabeling, that may only occur during process instantiation, and sum- and par-expressions. In these places, a translation between the index above, and the index below is needed.

Since relabeling implies to inform the kernel, there is a single local instruction on gates,

    P_GTE gate_index   push the index onto the stack.

3.3 BUT Description Instructions

This set of instructions is organized as pairs of instructions:

```
B_xxx  < argument > ...
  < body >
E_xxx
```

denoting the Beginning and End of some description. This model has been chosen to easily match syntax parentheses in most programming languages. Easy code generation out of this is a must.

These instruction pairs do not make any sense by themselves, but strictly organized in a certain context. Therefore, we shall use a bit of BNF (Backus–Naur Form) to denote their relationship, but still more information will be provided later on, when dealing with the mapping from LOTOS to $\Lambda\beta$.

The outmost instruction pair in a $\Lambda\beta$ description:

```
lbc ::  B_LBC  specification_name
          [ BUT_definition ]+
          [ predicate ]*
        E_LBC
```

The code for $\Lambda\beta$ will describe 1 or more BUTs. There is always at least one, corresponding to the *main* behaviour in a LOTOS specification. This main BUT is always labeled as 0. There are as many more as **process** definitions in the source specification. Therefore there is a one to one mapping of processes to BUTs.

LOTOS **predicates** on **action prefix expressions** are translated into boolean valued functions. There may be no predicate at all in a LOTOS specification.

```
BUT_definition ::  B_CRT  BUT_#  process_name
                     initial_state
                     [ state ]*
                   E_CRT
```

Each LOTOS **process** is mapped to a $\Lambda\beta$ behaviour unit. It is modeled as a state machine. There is at least one initial state, and there may be more.

```
initial_state ::  B_ENT  0
                    [ I_VAR  number_of_variables  parameter_variables ]
                    state_description
                  E_ENT
```

```
state ::  B_ENT  state_#
            state_description
          E_ENT
```

BUTs must be initialized upon instantiation. Actual arguments are provided in the stack, and must be loaded onto the formal variables.

Some activities may be carried on per state. Local variables may be introduced via **let expressions** in LOTOS. These variables do exist from the initialization stage of the BUT instantiation, when all the variables in the BUT were created (where creation just means making room for them). But the value for a variable is not known at the initialization time, and it must be evaluated in a concrete state.

Furthermore, guards may show up in certain states. They must be evaluated, and react to their result.

Once all the local variables are evaluated, and guards are evaluated and found to be passed, the BUT may proceed to instruct the Kernel of the next synchronization requirements.

```
state_description :: [ local_definition  |  guard ]*
                     kernel_call

local_definition :: B_LET
                       [ value_expression
                           [ L_VAR var_index ]+
                         POP                     ]+
                     E_LET
```

LET constructs load a data value in one or more BUT variable(s). `value_expression` will evaluate a data expression onto the stack. This value is loaded into as many variables as required, and removed.

Guards may be stated by giving to expressions that are to check for equality, or by giving a single `bool` expression to be compared against `true`. During semantics analysis, the second case is expanded with the second expression, and there is no longer but a single situation.

```
guard :: B_GRD
            value_expression
            value_expression
         EQUAL sort
         E_GRD
```

A boolean value is pushed on top of the stack. If it is `false`, the BUT stops. Otherwise, it may continue.

LOTOS specification predicates, are transformed into boolean valued functions. LOTOS accepts two formats for predicates, either two terms, or only one. This second case is transformed into the first one during the analysis phase, by expanding a "true" value. The stack is used for guard evaluation:

```
predicate :: B_PRD  predicate_#
                value_expression
                value_expression
            EQUAL sort
            E_PRD
```

3.4 Kernel Call Instructions

State transition is performed upon successful synchronization. Since more partners may be involved in synchronization, each BUT will just inform the kernel of its synchronization requirements, both architecture and offers, and wait for the kernel to inform of the success.

```
kernel_call :: synchronization_pattern | synchronization_offer

synchronization_pattern :: hiding_expression
   | enable_expression    | disable_expression | BUT_instantiation
```

```
                    | parallel_expression | choice_expression | relabelling

synchronization_offer :: stop_expression | internal_action
                        | external_offer  | exit_expression
```

For most of these kernel calls, with the exceptions of stop and BUT instantiation, the following state(s) is(are) indicated to the kernel, for it to return control back to the adequate continuation state.

```
hiding_expression :: [ P_GTE gate_index ]+
                     MK_HD  next_state  number_of_gates
```

This instruction informs the kernel of the creation of new gate on which synchronization may take place. The stack is used as intermediate storage for the values of the new gate(s).

```
enable_expression :: [ P_VAR variable_index ]*
                     MK_EN  enabling_state  enabled_state  number_of_variables
```

Two BUTs are spawned under a LOTOS enable operator. A similar spawn occurs below for the operators disable and parallel. A few variables may be used to capture exit values. The stack is used as intermediate storage for the indexes of the variables to be used in capturing exit values.

```
disable_expression :: MK_DIS normal_state disabling_state

parallel_expression :: parallel_explicit
     | parallel_interleaving | parallel_synchronization

parallel_explicit :: [ P_GTE gate_index ]*
                     MK_PE  state  state  number_ gates

parallel_interleaving :: MK_PI state state

parallel_synchronization :: MK_PS state state
```

Two BUTs are spawned under a LOTOS parallel operator. There are three possibilities, corresponding to full synchronization, interleaving, and synchronization limited to some explicit gates The stack is used as intermediate storage for the values of the gate(s) on which synchronization is required.

```
choice_expression :: MK_CH state state
```

The BUT may offer a number of exclusive choices. These are grouped in pairs to simplify the code. Some states will just split into two choices. By composition of states of this kind, as many choices as needed may be "simultaneously" offered for synchronization.

BUT_instantiation :: [value_expression]*
                    [P_GTE gate_index]*
                    MK_PR BUT_# number_gates number_values

A BUT may eventually call another one. In fact, the old one does not exist any longer, but is replaced by the new one. The stack is used as an intermediate stage for actual gates and values.

There is an implicit relabeling in BUT_instantiation. There may also be explicit relabeling as a consequence of the compile time expansion of sum- and par-expressions
$$\text{choice } g \text{ in } [a, b, c] \: [] \: B \rightarrow (B)[a/g] \: [] \: (B)[b/g] \: [] \: (B)[c/g]$$

RLBL outer_gate_index inner_gate_index
instructs the kernel about the correspondence between gate indexes.

3.5 Offers for Rendezvous

The simplest of the offers are the no-offers: stop and internal event. There is just nothing after stop, and there is a next_state after en internal event.

stop_expression :: MK_ST

internal_action :: MK_I next_state

In action denotations, a number of experiments are offered on a gate for consideration by the environment. If the pattern is accepted, the BUT will move to the next state. The complexity arises from the large (and variable) number of items to consider in making such an offer; the stack is used to organize the recollection:

external_offer :: [experiment]*
                  MK_AD next_state gate number_exps predicate

experiment :: single_offer | multiple_offer

single_offer :: value_expression
                MK_EXP "!" sort

multiple_offer :: P_VAR variable_index
                  MK_EXP "?" sort

For a multiple offer, a variable must be identified that holds the data value that will be eventually used in the rendez-vous. A partner is expected to provide a single value for synchronization to succeed. This value is stored in the variable whose index is provided.

Lastly, it is quite similar to offer an exit since there may be concrete values offered as exit status, or multiple values. Single offers are handled as gate !value, while multiple offers are handled as gate ?fv: sort, where fv is just a funny variable that is never used.

exit_expression :: [experiment]*
                   MK_EX number_of_offers

4 SEMANTICS

The Λβ-machine consists of four principal registers:

S **The Stack:** used to hold intermediate results.

F **The Frame:** (or environment) used to bind values to variables.

C **The Code:** used to hold the Λβ-machine code being executed.

K **The Kernel Tree:** (a pointer to) used as a directed graph to preserve synchronization structure between concurrent behaviour units, as well as to remember next state after synchronization for offers.

The entire state of a BUT can be denoted by giving the content of its four registers. Thus, each instruction in the machine can be described by giving the state of the machine before and after its execution. We call this a *machine transition*. We will write it in the form
$$(S, F, C, K) \rightarrow (S', F', C', K')$$
where the tuple on the left of the arrow gives the state before, and the tuple on the right, the state after. When we wish to indicate that part of a tuple in the state before is repeated in the state after, we shall split apart relevant information on the left hand side, by expanding the structure of the corresponding register, and repeat the same pieces on the right hand side, as appropriate.

BUTs may be in a stable or in an unstable state. Unstable BUTs shall be denoted as $(S, F, C, K)^*$, the superscript is removed for stable states. Unstable BUTs will perform spontaneous transitions until a stable state is reached. Then, control is given to the kernel. Eventually the kernel will return the control by marking the BUT as unstable.

The complete system is described by a collection of BUTs, each one with its own state, plus a shared Kernel Tree. It holds dynamic information related to the BUT synchronization environment. A BUT is allowed to extend the Kt along its branch, but has no other opportunity to make use of it, nor to access the dynamic environment via it.

The Kt holds the following types of information

- hide {set of gate indexes}
- >> [list of variable indexes]
- I[]I {set of gate indexes}
- other operators: [>, |||, ||, []
- relabel {pairs of gate indexes}

Lastly, BUT may provide offers for synchronization to the kernel, being each of these offers composed of
<gate, list of experiments, predicate>

The code is organized in such a way that given a BUT identification, b, and a BUT entry point, e, the next instruction may be found as C_e^b. When only one BUT is involved in a transition, we shall write the shorter form C_e to identify entry e of current BUT. When strict sequencing of instructions is the rule, we shall use structural decomposition on the left hand side, $c : C$, to denote that current instruction c is followed by the code C.

The initial state of the system is denoted by an empty Kt, and a single unstable BUT that holds the main behaviour of the specification: an empty stack, and a fresh (empty) frame.

$$(\text{nil}, \text{NewFrame}, C_0^0, \text{nil})^*$$

By convention, the main BUT is number 0, and the first entry of every BUT is number 0. In the remainder of this section, we provide the transitions for each $\Lambda\beta$-machine instruction.

4.1 Stack Manipulation Instructions

$(s : S, F, \text{POP} : C, K)^* \to (S, F, C, K)^*$

where the top element on the stack S is removed. The code steps to the next instruction.

$(S, F, \text{P\_VAR } i : C, K)^* \to (i : S, F, C, K)^*$

$(S, F, \text{P\_VAL } i : C, K)^* \to (F(i) : S, F, C, K)^*$

$(v : S, F, \text{L\_VAR } i : C, K)^* \to (v : S, F[F(i) \mathrel{\cdot\!-} v], C, K)^*$

$(S, F, \text{I\_VAR } t\ i : C, K)^* \to (\text{pop}^i(S), F', C, K)^*$
where $F' \leftarrow F[F \leftarrow \text{allocate}(t), \forall j \in [0..i-1] F(j) \leftarrow \text{top}^j(S)]$

$(S, F, \text{EVAL } o\ n : C, K)^* \to (v : \text{pop}^n(S), F, C, K)^*$
where $v \leftarrow o(\text{top}^0(S), \ldots \text{top}^{n-1}(S))$

$(s_0 : s_1 : S, F, \text{EQUAL } s : C, K)^* \to ((s_0 =_s s_1) : S, F, C, K)^*$

$(S, F, \text{P\_GTE } i : C, K)^* \to (i : S, F, C, K)^*$

The following instructions have no semantics meaning (they are just for syntax bracketing): B_LBC and E_LBC, B_CRT and E_CRT, B_ENT and E_ENT, B_LET and E_LET, and B_GRD. However, B_CRT associates a BUT identification to the following code, and this information will be saved somewhere for later use when evaluating C_e^b. B_ENT associates an entry number to the following code, and this information will be saved somewhere for later use when evaluating C_e^b.

$(\text{true} : S, F, \text{E\_GRD} : C, K)^* \to (S, F, C, K)^*$
$(\text{false} : S, F, \text{E\_GRD} : C, K)^* \to (\text{nil}, \text{nil}, \text{nil}, K)$

where the value on top of the stack is used to either step to the next instruction, that is another unstable state (and the machine goes on); or to a stable state, namely the stop state.

$(S, F, \text{MK\_HD } c\ n, K)^* \to (\text{pop}^n(S), F, C_c, K')^*$

where $K' \leftarrow \text{hide}\{\text{top}^i(S), i = 0..n-1\} : K$

The Kt is extended with a hiding node that holds the indexes of the gates that only exist under this node.

$(S, F, \text{MK\_EN } c_1\ c_2\ n, K)^* \rightarrow \{(S', F, C_{c_1}, K')^*, (S', F, C_{c_2}, K')\}$
where $S' \leftarrow \text{pop}^n(S)$
and $K' \leftarrow\ >> [\text{top}^i(S), i = 0..n-1] : K$

The BUT splits into two concurrent machines. One of them, the enabling branch, is still unstable and needs further unfolding. The other one, the enable side, is just recorded onto the Kernel Tree.

$(S, F, \text{MK\_DIS } c_1\ c_2, K)^* \rightarrow \{(S, F, C_{c_1}, K')^*, (S, F, C_{c_2}, K')^*\}$
where $K' \leftarrow [>: K$

The machine splits in two unstable pieces, both of them working under a Kt enriched with a disabling node.

$(S, F, \text{MK\_PE } c_1\ c_2\ n, K)^* \rightarrow \{(S', F, C_{c_1}, K')^*, (S', F, C_{c_2}, K')^*\}$
where $S' \leftarrow \text{pop}^n(S)$
and $K' \leftarrow |[]|\{\text{top}^i(S), i = 0..n-1\} : K$

The machine splits into two unstable machines, that need further unfolding. The parameters are recorded into the Kt.

$(S, F, \text{MK\_PI } c_1\ c_2, K)^* \rightarrow \{(S, F, C_{c_1}, K')^*, (S, F, C_{c_2}, K')^*\}$
where $K' \leftarrow ||| : K$

$(S, F, \text{MK\_PS } c_1\ c_2, K)^* \rightarrow \{(S, F, C_{c_1}, K')^*, (S, F, C_{c_2}, K')^*\}$
where $K' \leftarrow || : K$

$(S, F, \text{MK\_CH } c_1\ c_2, K)^* \rightarrow \{(S, F, C_{c_1}, K')^*, (S, F, C_{c_2}, K')^*\}$
where $K' \leftarrow [] : K$

$(S, F, \text{MK\_PR } B\ g\ v, K)^* \rightarrow (\text{pop}^g(S), \text{NewFrame}, C_0^B, \texttt{relabel}\{\text{top}^i(S) \leftrightarrow i, i = 0..g-1\} : K)^*$

where internal index i is associated to external index $\text{top}^i(S)$.

$(S, F, \text{RLBL } e\ i : C, K)^* \rightarrow (S, F, C, \texttt{relabel}\{e \leftrightarrow i\} : K)^*$

$(S, F, \text{MK\_ST}, K)^* \rightarrow (\text{nil}, \text{nil}, \text{nil}, K)$

$(S, F, \text{MK\_I } c, K)^* \rightarrow (S, F, C_c, K)$

An offer $< i, nil, nil >$ is handed to the kernel, and the BUT stabilizes. Upon occurrence, the state becomes unstable, and the BUT resumes at C_c.

$(S, F, \text{MK\_AD } c\ g\ e\ p, K)^* \rightarrow (\text{pop}^e(S), F, C_c, K)$

An offer $< g, [\text{top}^i(S), i = 0..e - 1], p >$ is handed to the kernel,

$(v : S, F, \text{MK\_EXP } "!" \ s : C, K)^* \rightarrow (\text{experiment}("!", v, s) : S, F, C, K)^*$

$(i : S, F, \text{MK\_EXP } "?" \ s : C, K)^* \rightarrow (\text{experiment}("?", i, s) : S, F, C, K)^*$

$(S, F, \text{MK\_EX } e, K)^* \rightarrow (\text{nil}, \text{nil}, \text{nil}, K)$

An offer $< \text{exit}, [\text{top}^i(S), i = 0..e - 1], nil >$ is handed to the kernel.
The complete LOTOS machine follows the following instruction cycle:

start $(\text{nil}, \text{NewFrame}, C_0^0, \text{nil})^*$
LOOP FOREACH unstable BUT
            WHILE unstable
                perform $\Lambda\beta$-machine instruction
        select a collection of offers for rendezvous
        IF (collection found) THEN
                perform rendezvous AND mark the selected collection as unstable
        ELSE exit loop
ENDLOOP

The selection of partners for rendezvous is a complicated algorithm that is performed by the run time support. Details may be found in [5]. Upon finding enough and convenient partners for participating in a rendezvous, the kernel tree may need to be pruned. This situation happens for mutually exclusive offers, namely:

- []: when a branch of a choice operator is selected, the other ones must be removed;
- [>: when the disabling branch is selected, the normal behaviour must be removed.

Lastly, when an **exit** event occur, if there is a branch waiting at an enabling operator, the enabled branch becomes unstable.
This completes the dynamic semantics of the $\Lambda\beta$-machine.

5 IMPLEMENTATION

There are very many ways to get an implementation of the $\Lambda\beta$-machine as described above. The language is intended not to take any further implication on the implementation than those stated above in section 2. Here we shall briefly provide some hints about the current implementation in TOPO, most concretely the C implementation.

C is basically a single-task language. Although there are means to create and manage several tasks, it greatly relays on the O.S. facilities to create, communicate, and manage these tasks. For these reasons, the current implementation is a single UNIX process. This has permitted easy port to systems that don't support real multiprocessing, for instance to MS–DOS.

Generated code is parameterized with respect to an instantiation frame that holds state information, both BUT entry and variable values. This permits to use the C code as reentrant functions. The kernel keeps as many frames as active BUTs, and takes care of their allocation on BUT creation, and removal upon termination.

Functionally, the code is a collection of coroutines emulated in C. Pieces of code for the Kernel and the BUTs give control to each other alternating their roles. The status of each BUT instantiation is held in its internal variables. No assembler code is used anywhere, nor any knowledge is assumed about target machine stack. Coroutines are strictly implemented in conventional C code to guarantee portability.

Being the Kt a centralized and shared facility, its access must be severely restricted. The visibility of the Kt from the BUTs is only via register K. And K only points to a leave of the Kernel Tree. BUTs do not look deeper into K, but are only allowed to "dress it" with further structuring information. In practice, K is a "read only" register that BUTs use to call run time support libraries that do effective changes on the Kt. Thus, only kernel code has write rights on the Kernel Tree.

TOPO extends the language with annotations [4]. These permit to perform external actions upon event occurrences, as well as allow the environment to influence behaviour. $\Lambda\beta$-machine has a few more instructions to bridge these annotations from LOTOS onto the target language. These extra instructions pass information unprocessed, so that it is interpreted in the target language. For instance, it does not make any difference to write annotations in C or in Ada, but the output of code generation is supposed to feed the appropriate compiler. These extra instructions have been not presented in this paper, since they have no semantics relevance, but interested readers may find the details in [11].

6 CONCLUSIONS

$\Lambda\beta$-machine, an abstract machine for LOTOS, has been presented. It is designed as an intermediate stage after the semantics analysis of users' specification, but before actual code derivation for some systems programming language. All the syntactic and semantics richness of LOTOS has been removed. Therefore, $\Lambda\beta$-machine is not intended for humans. Code generation for a programming language must be an straightforward activity from the $\Lambda\beta$-machine code. Still, a number of implementation decisions are open. For instance, run–time data structures, and mapping to O.S. processes are open options. Very many implementations may be derived. Currently there exist two such code derivators, for C and Ada. The C implementation has been briefly sketched to demonstrate some of the open opportunities.

Many models presented in the literature seem to fit into the abstract model assumed by $\Lambda\beta$-machine, and might benefit from the intermediate stage provided by $\Lambda\beta$ before actual code generation. Symbolic interpreters might as well benefit from $\Lambda\beta$-machine, provided it is enriched with handles back into the source text to allow for nice listings. These extra instructions would be semantically null.

$\Lambda\beta$-machine has been used in TOPO for over three years. During this period, it has suffered several changes. In fact, it is still subject to changes looking for a clear distinction of roles between generating $\Lambda\beta$-machine code, and deriving actual code from it. Although designed to be independent of the target language, experience in deriving code for a second language (i.e. Ada) helped to make it truly independent from final code.

References

[1] ISO. *Information Processing Systems – Open Systems Interconnection – LOTOS - A Formal Description Technique Based on the Temporal Ordering of Observational Behaviour*. IS-8807. International Standards Organization, 1989.

[2] L. Logrippo et al. An Interpreter for LOTOS A Specification Language for Distributed Systems. *Software Practice and Experience*, 18(4):365–385, April 1988.

[3] P. van Eijk. The Design of a Simulator Tool. In P. van Eijk et al., editors, *The Formal Description Technique LOTOS*, pp. 351–390. North-Holland, 1989.

[4] J. A. Mañas et al. From LOTOS to C. In K. J. Turner, editor, *Formal Description Techniques, I*, pp. 79–84, Stirling, Scotland, UK, 1989. IFIP, North-Holland. Proceedings FORTE'88, 6–9 September, 1988.

[5] J. A. Mañas et al. The TOPO Implementation of the LOTOS Multiway Rendezvous. Tech. rep., Dpt. Telematics, Techical Univ. Madrid, Spain, Jan. 1991.

[6] E. Dubuis. An Algorithm for Translating LOTOS Behaviour Experssions into Automata and Ports. In Vuong [12], pp. 163–177.

[7] Q. Gao et al. Distributed Implementation of LOTOS Multi-Rendezvous. In Brinksma et al. [13].

[8] S. Nomura et al. A LOTOS Compiler and process Synchronization Manager. In L. Logrippo et al., editors, *Protocol Specification, Testing, and Verification X*, pp. 165–184, Ottawa, Ontario (CA), June 1990. IFIP, Elsevier Science B.V. (North-Holland).

[9] P. Sjödin. A Distributed Algorithm for Synchronous Process Communication at Ports. In Brinksma et al. [13].

[10] G. v. Bochmann et al. On the Distributed Implementation of LOTOS. In Vuong [12], pp. 133–146.

[11] J. A. Mañas et al. The $\Lambda\beta$-machine in TOPO. Technical report, Dpt. Telematics Engineering Techinal Univ. Madrid, Spain, June 1990.

[12] S. T. Vuong, editor. *Formal Description Techniques, II*, Vancouver (CA), 1990. IFIP, Elsevier Science B.V. (North-Holland). Proceedings FORTE'89, 5–8 Dec., 1989.

[13] E. Brinksma et al., editors. *Protocol Specification, Testing, and Verification IX*, Enschede (NL), June 1989. IFIP, Elsevier Science B.V. (North-Holland).

A Complete Example

```
specification sample : noexit
                B_LBC sample
                B_CRT 0 sample
                B_ENT 0
                    I_VAR 0 0
  type Natural_numbers is
    sorts nat
    opns 0: -> nat
         s: nat -> nat
  endtype
behaviour
  hide send, receive in
                        P_GTE 0
                        P_GTE 1
                        MK_HD   1 2
                        E_ENT
  ( producer [send] (0)
                        B_ENT 3
                            EVAL 0 0
                            P_GTE 0
                            MK_PR 3 1 1
                            E_ENT
    |||
                        B_ENT 2
                            MK_PI 3 4
                            E_ENT
    consumer [receive]
                        B_ENT 4
                            P_GTE 1
                            MK_PR 2 1 0
                            E_ENT
  )
  |[ send, receive ]|
                        B_ENT 1
                            P_GTE 0
                            P_GTE 1
                            MK_PE 2 5 2
                            E_ENT
  buffer [send, receive]
                        B_ENT 5
                            P_GTE 0
                            P_GTE 1
                            MK_PR 1 2 0
                            E_ENT
                        E_CRT
where
  process producer [g] (n: nat) : noexit :=
                B_CRT 3 producer
                B_ENT 0
                    I_VAR 1 1
    g !n ;
                                    P_VAL 0
                                    MK_EXP ! 7
                                    MK_AD 1 0 1 -1
                                    E_ENT
    producer [g] (s(n))
                                B_ENT 1
                                    P_VAL 0
                                    EVAL s 1
                                    P_GTE 0
                                    MK_PR 3 1 1
                                    E_ENT
  endproc                       E_CRT

  process consumer [g] : noexit :=
                B_CRT 2 consumer
                B_ENT 0
                    I_VAR 1 0
    g ?x: nat ;
                                    P_VAR 0
                                    MK_EXP ? 7
                                    MK_AD 1 0 1 -1
                                    E_ENT
    consumer [g]
                                B_ENT 1
                                    P_GTE 0
                                    MK_PR 2 1 0
                                    E_ENT
  endproc                       E_CRT

  process buffer [a, b] : noexit :=
                B_CRT 1 buffer
                B_ENT 0
                    I_VAR 1 0
    a ?d: nat ;
                                    P_VAR 0
                                    MK_EXP ? 7
                                    MK_AD 2 0 1 -1
                                    E_ENT
    b !d ;
                                B_ENT 2
                                    P_VAL 0
                                    MK_EXP ! 7
                                    MK_AD 3 1 1 -1
                                    E_ENT
    buffer [a, b]
                                B_ENT 3
                                    P_GTE 0
                                    P_GTE 1
                                    MK_PR 1 2 0
                                    E_ENT
  endproc                       E_CRT
endspec                         E_LBC
```

Tool Demonstration: FORSEE

Jonathan Billington, Geoff Wheeler, Brian Keck and Ken Parker
Telecom Australia Research Laboratories, Clayton, Victoria. 3168
j.billington@trl.oz.au, g.wheeler@trl.oz.au, b.keck@trl.oz.au, k.parker@trl.oz.au

Abstract
We briefly describe the FORSEE environment being developed by the Telecom Research Laboratories. FORSEE currently has 3 components: Design/CPN, a graphical editor and simulator; TORAS, a reachability analysis tool; and PROMPT, an automatic implementation tool.

1 Introduction

The development of quality software will play a key role in the provision of advanced services to customers of telecommunications and information providers. Furthermore, ultra-reliable systems will be required to manage the networks providing these services. It will be important to be able to provide new services quickly in response to customer demand, and to reliably and quickly extend software systems to provide enhanced services. Therefore better ways of developing and maintaining telecommunications software are the subject of active research.

One approach to satisfying these requirements uses mathematically based techniques (*formal methods*) for specifying systems. Formal specifications are mathematical models of the systems we wish to create. It is standard practice in engineering disciplines to build models of systems before we go to the expense of constructing the actual system. This is so that we can gain confidence in the final product by experimenting with a physical model (wind tunnel testing of aeroplanes is an example), or by analysing mathematical models (the frequency response of electrical filters is usually determined this way). We can do the same with software, as long as we are prepared to master the necessary mathematical techniques.

Telecommunications networks and the services they provide are distributed and concurrent. The trend to multiparty connections, multiple calls per connection and the simultaneous use of different features will see an increase in the amount of concurrency inherent in telecommunication services. It is therefore necessary for the mathematical techniques we use to be able to specify and analyse concurrent systems.

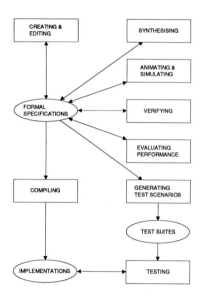

Figure 1: FORmal Systems Engineering Environment (FORSEE)

2 FORSEE

To make the use of formal methods practical, an environment needs to be developed in which designers can create and manipulate formal specifications. In a project being undertaken by the Telecom Research Laboratories aimed at improving the quality of telecommunications specifications and software, the environment has been called FORSEE: a FORmal Systems Engineering Environment. Some of the activities and relationships we envisage for FORSEE are illustrated in figure 1. The figure shows facilities for creating and maintaining specifications, formally refining service specifications (synthesising protocols), animating/simulating, verifying and evaluating performance. There is also a set of compilers which produce implementations (for different target machines), and a test scenario generator for generating test cases for a tester.

Within the FORSEE project, the mathematical technique currently being used for the specification of telecommunication systems is based on Petri nets. This is because Petri nets have been formulated with concurrency in mind; are executable; and have a sound mathematical basis with a number of techniques for their analysis. They also have a graphical form which facilitates specification animation. (A disadvantage is that they have no constructs to help with structuring specifications, although hierarchical Coloured Petri nets have addressed this to some extent [3]).

We have concentrated on the development of a verification tool, TORAS (TOol for the

Reachability Analysis of Specifications), and an automatic implementation tool, PROMPT, which translates a formal specification into 'C' code. We have purchased a Coloured Petri Net graphical editing and simulation system, Design/CPN, which will form the basis of a front end for FORSEE. Our current efforts are to integrate Design/CPN with TORAS and then with PROMPT.

2.1 TORAS

TORAS allows Petri net specifications to be analysed by reachability analysis — the generation of all the states and state sequences of the system reachable from a given initial state. The state explosion problem inherent in reachability analysis has been tackled by the use of some advanced algorithms which greatly reduce the state space of concurrent systems [5], while retaining properties of the system such as deadlock and livelock. An overview of TORAS and some of its initial applications and future plans have already been reported [6]. For example, for a simple resource sharing scheme with 100 processes, the full state space is about 10^{47} and it contains a deadlock. The reduced state space is about 30,000 states, and it preserves the deadlock. This can be generated on a Sparcstation 1 in about 4 minutes. Since then, TORAS has been applied to the verification of the IEEE 802.6 Configuration Control protocol and this has revealed a deadlock on start-up.

2.2 PROMPT

PROMPT [1, 4] provides a development environment for communications software. It comprises four elements: a compiler; a debugger; a control interface; and a log file analyser. The compiler takes as input an eXtended Net Language (XNL) (a language based on Petri nets and structured data) and transforms it into C language code. The debugger operates at the XNL level and provides facilities for stepping through the specification. The control interface allows several XNL specifications to be run simultaneously and user control of events to be logged for later interpretation by the log file analyser.

PROMPT was developed by Unico Computer Systems, Melbourne, with support from Telecom Australia's product development fund. The system is written in 'C' and designed to be portable across platforms that support the standard C run-time environment. The same is true for the output code.

Recent enhancements to PROMPT to greatly improve its usability and usefulness have occurred following a major application of PROMPT to the development of level 3 of the Message Transfer Part of CCITT's Common Channel Signalling System No. 7 [4]. These enhancements include X-windows interfaces, the ability to execute user-written C language modules from XNL, a comprehensive script-driven testing facility, the encoding and decoding of all ASN.1 data types, the extension and complete revision of the documentation as well as other changes to improve the performance of PROMPT and make it easier to use.

2.3 Design/CPN

Design/CPN is a package developed by Meta Software Corporation (USA) for the graphical editing and simulation of Coloured Petri Nets (CPNs). CPNs are high-level Petri nets in the sense that they contain symbolic information and allow much more compact representations of systems. They have a well defined semantics, a number of analysis techniques, and can be considered as a combination of Abstract Data Types and Petri nets within the same algebraic foundation. CPNs have matured over the last decade, and later this year the first text book on CPNs will be published.

Details of Design/CPN can be found in a recently published Petri net tool list [2]. It is written in C and Standard ML and runs on Apple Macintoshes, IBM PCs and Sun Workstations.

3 Acknowledgements

The work on FORSEE has involved a number of people other than the authors including: our colleague at the Telecom Research Laboratories, Greg Findlow; and Geoff Illing, Lee Lester and Richard Sievers from Unico Computer Systems. We would also like to mention the contribution of David Kinny in developing the PROMPT compiler and Dr Antti Valmari of the Technical Research Centre of Finland, who implemented the state space generator of TORAS.

The permission of the Executive General Manager Research, Telecom Australia, to present this paper is hereby acknowledged.

References

[1] J. Billington and D. Kinny. Computer aided protocol engineering. In *Proceedings of the Conference on New Business Applications of Information Technology*, pages 69–73, Melbourne, 26-27 April 1989.

[2] F. Feldbrugge. Petri Net Tool Overview 1989. In G. Rozenberg, editor, *Advances in Petri Nets 1989*, pages 151 – 178. Springer-Verlag, Berlin, January 1990. Lecture Notes in Computer Science, Vol. 424.

[3] P. Huber, K. Jensen, and R.M. Shapiro. Hierarchies in Coloured Petri Nets. In *Proceedings of the 10th International Conference on Application and Theory of Petri Nets*, pages 192 – 209, Bonn, West Germany, June 1989.

[4] K.R. Parker. The PROMPT Automatic Implementation Tool - Initial Impressions. In Juan Quemada, Jose Manas, and Enrique Vazquez, editors, *Conference Record of FORTE90*, pages 701 – 707, Madrid, November 1990. included in List of Tool Demos.

[5] A. Valmari. Stubborn sets for reduced state space generation. In *Proceedings of the Tenth International Conference on the Application and Theory of Petri Nets*, Bonn, West Germany, 28-30 June 1989. First paper of Supplement to the Proceedings.

[6] G. Wheeler, A. Valmari, and J. Billington. Baby TORAS eats Philosophers but thinks about Solitaire. In *Proceedings of the Fifth Australian Software Engineering Conference ASWEC'90*, pages 283 – 288, Sydney, Australia, 23-25 May 1990.

Tool Demonstration: Tools for Process Algebras

Eric Madelaine ** and Didier Vergamini * [1]

**INRIA
Route des Lucioles, Sophia Antipolis
06565 Valbonne Cedex (France)
email: madelain@sophia.inria.fr

*CERICS
Avenue Albert Einstein, Sophia Antipolis
06565 Valbonne Cedex (France)
email: dvergami@sophia.inria.fr

1 Introduction

The notion of *process algebra* was first introduced by Milner, and is now widely used as a framework for modeling parallelism and concurrency, and as a foundation for verification tools in this area. We present a set of tools including: ECRINS, for the definition of process algebra using structural operational semantics, the computation of the behaviours of open terms, and the proof of algebraic laws, making a link between operational and algebraic semantics; AUTO, for automata construction from finite terms of the MEIJE algebra, and for analysis of automata by reduction and abstraction; MAUTO that generalises AUTO for various process algebras, for example leading to an integration in the LOTOSPHERE tool environment; and finally AUTOGRAPH, a graphical editor for hierarchical networks of automata, for creating AUTO inputs, and for displaying resulting automata.

2 ECRINS

ECRINS gives a syntax for defining process algebra by giving together the syntactic and operational semantics definition of its operators. Figure 1 shows a part of the ECRINS definition of CCS.

The main functionalities of ECRINS are the evaluation of behaviours of open terms and the proof of strong bisimulation laws. The behaviours of a term can be computed in an automatic way, but the termination of a such computation is not decidable; the set of immediate behaviours may even be infinite. In such cases, the evaluator can be used in a user-driven way, using either interactive guidance or tactic programs. In the evaluation of an open term, the system is able to make formal assumptions on the behaviour of free process variables; the result of the evaluation is a set of conditional rules similar to the operational rules defining an operator.

---

[1] The development of these tools is partially supported by ESPRIT BASIC RESEARCH ACTION 3006: CONCUR

Whenever two (open) terms have a finite set of rules, they can be compared with respect to an extended version of strong bisimulation [4]. This gives us the ability to prove algebraic laws of any operator expressible in our semantics definition format. Such bisimulation proofs can be mixed with algebraic reasoning based on rewriting. [5] gives an example of the use of ECRINS for proving equivalence between MEIJE and BASIC LOTOS terms.

```
operator parallel:: Processus   Processus --> Processus
syntax   // left 2
semantics
   left-parallel           p -- a -->p'
                       ------------------------------
                       p // q -- a --> p' // q
   all-parallel  p -- a --> p' & q -- b -->q' & (b inverse a)
                       ------------------------------------------------
                       p // q -- tau --> p' // q'
   right-parallel          q -- b -->q'
                       ------------------------------
                       p // q -- b --> p // q'
```

Figure 1: A part of the ECRINS definition of CCS

3   AUTO

The system AUTO is dedicated to the analysis of finite closed terms of a fixed process algebra called MEIJE[1]. The finiteness property is imposed by restriction of the syntax of terms. The main goal of this system is to provide functionalities for computing automata that are reductions of abstractions of terms. Abstractions are parameterised by user-defined abstract actions, while reduction is defined using the classical notion of bisimulation. AUTO uses weak and strong bisimulation congruence properties to reduce structurally the components of a system before combining them rather than building first a huge global automaton and reducing it afterwards. This allows to deal with potentially enormous systems. AUTO now uses improved algorithms to compute strong, weak and branching bisimulation grace to a new tool called FCTOOL: the interface between the two systems is a so-called *common format* for transition systems. This format is used by several other verification systems such as the CWB [3], and ALDEBARAN[6]; giving access to other (complementary) analysis techniques, including various equivalences and preorders, and model checking. AUTO also provides *debugging* functionalities: a sequence of actions computed on an abstract automaton can be projected on the initial term, enabling the user to see what concrete sequences of actions and synchronisations lead to a given abstract behaviour. Figure 2 shows a screen dump of a session of AUTO.

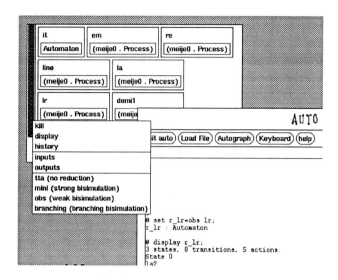

Figure 2: An AUTO session

4 MAUTO

MAUTO is a generalisation of AUTO to a large family of process algebra. The syntactic restrictions that guarantee the finiteness of the semantics, and the algorithm of automata generation from terms are compiled from the ECRINS definition of the process algebra [7]. Our main application is an instantiation of MAUTO for BASIC LOTOS inside the *lite* environment developed by the LOTOSPHERE ESPRIT project; an example of specification and proof using this environment is described in [8].

5 AUTOGRAPH

AUTOGRAPH is a graphical editor for hierarchical networks of automata. It is able to produce input terms for AUTO, and to display automata produced by AUTO (and MAUTO). The placement of the vertices of an automaton can be provided automatically, and modified by the user. Figure 3 shows a screen dump of session of AUTOGRAPH. The usage of AUTO and AUTOGRAPH is described through an example in [2].

References

[1] G. Boudol. Notes on algebraic calculi of processes. In K. Apt, editor, *Logics and Models of Concurrent Systems, NATO-ISA series F13*, 1985.

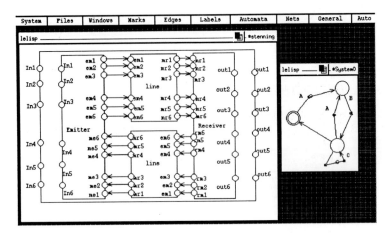

Figure 3: An AUTOGRAPH session

[2] G. Boudol, R. de Simone, and D. Vergamini. Experiment with AUTO and AUTO-GRAPH on a simple case sliding window protocol. Rapport de Recherche RR870, INRIA, July 1988.

[3] R. Cleaveland, J. Parrow, and B. Steffen. The concurrency workbench. In *Proc. of the Workshop on Automated Verification Methods for Finite State Systems*, number 407 in LNCS. Springer-Verlag, 1989.

[4] R. de Simone. High level devices in Meije-Sccs. *Theoretical Computer Science*, 40, 1985.

[5] G. Doumenc, E. Madelaine, and R. de Simone. Proving process calculi translations in ECRINS: The PureLotos --> Meije example. Rapport de recherche RR1192, INRIA, Mars 1990.

[6] Jean-Claude Fernandez. Aldebaran: A tool for verification of communicating processes. Rapport technique SPECTRE C14, Laboratoire de Génie Informatique — Institut IMAG, Grenoble, September 1989.

[7] E. Madelaine and D. Vergamini. Finiteness conditions and structural construction of automata for all process algebras. In R. Kurshan, editor, *proceedings of Workshop on Computer Aided Verification*, New-Brunswick, June 1990. AMS-DIMACS.

[8] E. Madelaine and D. Vergamini. Specification and verification of a sliding window protocol in LOTOS. In *FORTE'91 conference*. IFIP, Sydney, 1991.

Tool Demonstration:
A Cross Compiling Experiment:
a PC Implementation of a LOTOS Spec.[1]

José A. Mañas and Joaquín Salvachúa and Tomás de Miguel

Dpt. Ingeniería Telemática, Technical University of Madrid, E-28040 Madrid, Spain

Abstract

An abracadabra protocol entity is implemented in a PC running MS-DOS. The protocol was initially specified using LOTOS. After annotating it to add implementation details, a LOTOS to C compiler, TOPO, is used to generate code. This code is ported to a PC. The result is an autonomous system that will be used to demonstrate conformance testing scenarios involving the use of formal description techniques.

1 INTRODUCTION

LOTOS [1] is a specification language superbly adequate to describe complex behaviour of systems. It was explicitly designed for protocol specification, and it may be reasonable expected that these specifications will be used to assist in the derivation of test suites to assess systems derived from them.

LOTOS specifications are usually regarded as highly abstract, what implies that a significant amount of effort is needed to derive a working system from them. Implementation details on resources and interfaces to the real world have to be added. These additions introduce the risk for extra errors, and the conformance of the final system has to be assessed by testing.

The experiment reported below provides a testbed that permits to run demonstrations on the functionality of the implementation of the abracadabra protocol, as well as to plug it into testing environments, either conventional ones, or new ones based on FDTs.

The abracadabra protocol is a realistic example of communications protocols. It is connection oriented, providing bidirectional data exchange, and using an alternating bit protocol to deal with line errors and duplicates. Up to N retries are attempted, under control of a timer that expires after P seconds, where both N and P are open parameters. Both user and medium initiated disconnections are considered.

There are several objectives intended by the experiment reported below. (1) To put to work on an autonomous piece of hardware a non-trivial communications protocol originally

---

[1]This work has been partly funded by Telefónica I+D under contract C68/91, and by the National Research Programme on Information Technology & Communications within project MEDAS

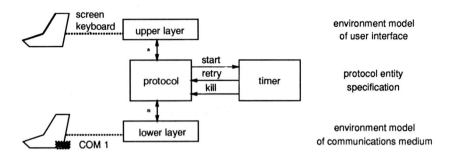

Figure 1: Annotated Specification Architecture

specified in LOTOS. (2) To measure the performance that may be expected from porting LOTOS specs into the PC world. (3) To run conformance testing experiments both against conventional testers, and against test systems based on FDTs.

2 PROCEDURE: METHOD AND TOOLS

The abracadabra protocol is becoming a classic example of protocol specification experiments. A first specification using LOTOS was produced by one of the authors, and published in [2]. The revised version (updated to [1]) is used in this experience; this is the version to appear in [3].

The specification was enriched by means of annotations [4] in order to take into consideration implementation details, and real world entities. Most of the annotations were provided by means of specifying an environment that is fold into the specification [5]. The resulting LOTOS text is self-contained, and output actions are performed as side-effects of event occurrences. The overall architecture is shown in figure 1.

The Upper_Layer maps events on gate a onto screen and keyboard, while events on gate m are mapped onto COM1 by Lower_Layer.

The protocol entity specification, **Abracadabra_Protocol**, had to be modified slightly in order to introduce real time for the timeout clock. This is needed since the timer is specified as an internal resource, whose interface is hidden, and not accessible from the environment. Therefore, we had to go to the lines describing the timer resource, and add a delay annotation.

Both the upper and the lower layer are specified as two interleaved interfaces for incoming and outgoing events:

```
Upper_Layer [a] ::=
  hide keyboard in
    Incoming_Events [a, keyboard]  |||  Outgoing_Events [a]

Incoming_Events [a, kb] ::=
  (*| wait user_input_available () |*)
  kb ?sp (*| default user_input () |*) : SP ;
```

```
    a !sap1 !sp ;
    Incoming_Events [a, kb]

Outgoing_Events [a] ::=
    a !sap1 ?sp: SP
    [isConInd (sp) or isConConf (sp) or isDatInd (sp) or isDisInd (sp) ]
    (*| C send_asp (success[1]); |*) ;
    Outgoing_Events [a]
```

The availability of user input triggers the offer of a service primitive to the protocol entity. For service primitives input into the protocol entity, busy wait is used (i.e. active polling) both for key board input, and for COM1 receptions. This is a simple mechanism that is acceptable in this case since the target system is autonomous and fully (and uniquely) devoted to run the abracadabra protocol. More sophisticated means may be used if active wait were not acceptable (see [5]). For outgoing events, it is much simpler: the environment just get the service primitive, and sends it.

The ADT compiler in TOPO is used to derive implementations directly from the formal specification. This applies even for data types from the standard library as booleans and natural numbers. The operations provided by the compiler are used to build service primitives. There is a special case regarding user data, that in the formal specification is just a sort, but which contents are not specified. In our implementation, user data are strings of characters of variable length, ended by CR (end of line). These strings are handled by means of annotations, and only a pointer goes into the LOTOS world in order to refer to it. External C code takes care of line encoding/decoding.

Notice that on the receiver part, a local queue of received messages is maintained by the entity. The operations on this queue are specified in LOTOS, and ultimately refer to values of sort user–data. These references are implemented as pointers to character strings that are allocated outside from LOTOS.

TOPO 1R7 was used to generate code on a Sun system. Then, the generated code, as well as the run time libraries for behaviour and data, were copied into a PC. The MicroSoft C Compiler (v6.00) was used to compile the pieces and to bring them together. No optimization flag was used. Behaviour run time library had to be slightly adapted to take into account MS-DOS system calls to get time information. This is due to the fact that TOPO assumes a UNIX run-time environment, that is quite similar, but small details need to be adjusted.

Direct coding in C was needed to provide non–blocking interfaces to the keyboard, and to the communication line, COM1. This specific code is in a separate file, and provides a set of functions that are instantiated from the annotations in the specification.

The original LOTOS specification comprised 503 lines, after removing comments. 88 lines were added as annotaed environment. 32 annotations were needed: 22 to link external data types, 2 delays, 2 waits, 2 defaults, 3 pieces of C code, and 1 include.

TOPO generated 3000 lines of C code for data, and 2000 for behaviour. To these figures we must add the run time libraries for data and behaviour (200 and 4000 resp.).

The executable image requires 100 Kbytes. The target PC is a Tandom 386SX with 1Mb of main memory, at 20MHz, running MS-DOS 3.33. With the communication port set to 9600 bps, a direct connection of the COM1 ports of two PCs running the abracadabra implementation, yields a performance bounded by the speed of the serial port.

3 FUTURE WORK

We plan to use the the experience reported to run some performance experiments in order to measure the degradation caused from using a high level description technique and automatic compilation.

The system will be exercised against a conventional tester developed at Telefónica I+D (a branch of the Spanish PTT). The same protocol was specified using EDIPPO [6], a tool of their own that accepts extended automata specifications, and generates a test suite for conformance testing. The system runs on a VAX/VMS machine. Line coding of PDUs was agreed on the beginning, to permit communication with their lower tester. The testing will be a conventional black-box test, using the serial line, the keyboard and the screen of the PC as points of control and observation (PCOs). This experiment will permit to validate by testing the implementation of the protocol entity.

We plan as well to derive test sequences from the formal specification in LOTOS, and follow a similar path to get another PC implementation that is a tester of the one reported above. The test scenario will be composed by two PCs exchanging PDUs on the serial port, plus an operator performing the upper tester procedures. This experience will permit to validate the implementation of the tester, that may be used to test other implementations of the protocol.

References

[1] ISO. *Information Processing Systems – Open Systems Interconnection – LOTOS – A Formal Description Technique Based on the Temporal Ordering of Observational Behaviour.* IS-8807. International Standards Organization, 1989.

[2] ISO. *Working Draft for the Guidelines for Application of Estelle, LOTOS and SDL.* ISO/IEC JTC 1/SC 21/N2549. International Standards Organization, March 1988.

[3] J. A. Mañas et al. Abracadabra Protocol: Formal Description in LOTOS. In K. Turner, editor, *Using Formal Description Techniques.* John Wiley & Sons, (to appear).

[4] J. A. Mañas et al. From LOTOS to C. In K. Turner, editor, *Formal Description Techniques, I*, pages 79–84, Stirling, Scotland, UK, 1989. IFIP, North-Holland.

[5] J. A. Mañas et al. Tool Support to Implement LOTOS Formal Specifications. *Computer Networks and ISDN Systems*, 1992. Submitted for Publication.

[6] D. R. López et al. On the Use of the EDIPPO Facilities for CATG. In J. Kroon, editor, *WPTS IV*, The Hague (NL), October 1991. IFIP. Submitted.

Tool Demonstration:
The Lotosphere Integrated Tool Environment *Lite*

The Lotosphere Consortium
edited by Peter van Eijk
pve@cs.utwente.nl
University of Twente, Fac. Informatics
P.O. Box 217
7500 AE Enschede, NL

Abstract

This document describes some of the LOTOS tools that were produced in the Lotosphere project, and that are demoed during the FORTE 91 conference.

1 Introduction

Lotosphere is an ESPRIT II project (number 2304), of which the goal is to expand the formal description technique LOTOS (ISO 8807) into a viable, industrial, system design and development method. One of the work packages is devoted to the development of an industrially applicable integrated set of tools. Collectively, this set of tools is called *Lite*.

Lite is ongoing work. Parts of it are already applicable for realisticly sized developments, whereas other parts still need more development.

In this paper we briefly review the structure and components of *Lite*, and present some of the organisational background.

2 The Structure of *Lite*

The access to the various tools is organised through a calling program. In the architecture of *Lite* there are three important types of objects. Of course there is the LOTOS text, on which the editors work. Then there is a common representation encoding semantically correct specifications, on which most tools work. Finally, there is a common format for reports, which can be merged by a tool into the textual presentation.

Lite offers its functions through an X11 based window interface.

3 The Components of *Lite*

Editing. *Lite* offers, apart from access to conventional text editors, a structure editor and an editor for graphical LOTOS.

The *structure editor*, also called a template or syntax directed editor, is based on the Grammatech Synthesizer Generator. It supports structural and textual editing with incremental static semantics checking. The structure editor guides the user in the correct use of LOTOS and also provides different views or projections from a specification; for example process headers.

The *graphical* editor is based on the current ISO draft international standard for G-LOTOS.

Static Semantics Checking. Apart from the structure editor, there is a batch semantics checker, generating a common representation file. This one too checks conformance against International Standard IS 8807.

Report generation. *Lite* contains several tools that generate reports from correct LOTOS specifications. Reports convey information on the specification from a specific point of view, and can be used as an aid in the (manual) validation of a specification.

Cross-reference reports are useful to resolve overloading: for an operator the correct definition and the relevant equations are indicated, even if there are several operators with the same name.

The *dependency report* provides the user with a report on the logical dependency order among process definitions and among type definitions. In a sense the dependency report is a complexity measure, and based on this report one might decide to change the structure of a specification in order to lower the complexity and improve understandability.

A *gate-sort report* flags "suspicious mismatches" of sort lists on communicating events.

In the works, but probably ready for the demo, is a tool to report on the executability of the equational data type specification.

Simulation. The simulator allows the user to explore, manually or automatically, the tree of possible behaviour of the specification. This tool is fully symbolic, which makes it possible to study a trace of events without the need to instantiate the variables. On top of this, it uses an advanced technique called 'abstract data type narrowing' to resolve conflicting predicates symbolically. This reduces the size of simulation trees dramatically in comparison with earlier LOTOS simulators, in particular on so-called constraint oriented specifications.

Compilation. The compiler tool compiles almost all of LOTOS processes and abstract data types into executable C code. Certain design decisions that cannot be represented in LOTOS can be added in the specification as special comments called annotations. The annotations address topics like association of abstract data types with machine data types, in particular for integers, booleans, characters, etc., resolving value generation and association of a delay to an internal event that represents a timer.

Transformation. A number of correctness preserving transformations helping in the design process are incorporated in *Lite*. Some are interactive, available through the structure editor, others are run as separate tools.

Regrouping of parallel processes (RPP). RPP is a transformation that takes an expression consisting of a number of processes composed with parallel operators and transforms these into an expression, with strong bisimulation equivalent behaviour, in which the processes are grouped differently. The original configuration of processes might be a good presentation of the logical structure (architecture) of the system, and the regrouping might reflect the intended partitioning of processes over processors.

Bipartition of functionality (BP). BP is a transformation that splits a single process into two processes communicating in a prescribed configuration. The original and the pair of communicating processes are weak bisimulation equivalent.

There are also tool functions to produce a basic LOTOS model of a specification. Such transformations are approximations, forgetting part of the information carried by data; they preserve most liveness properties.

Verification. Currently verification of equivalence is possible on basic LOTOS specification. Behaviour equivalence verification includes strong or observational equivalence between two specifications (typical a service and the corresponding protocol, or two successive versions of a specification in a refinement-based methodology), and the minimization and graphical visualization of abstract views of a specification.

Work is under way concerning the integration of a model checking tool, based on a temporal logic language. After construction of a finite automaton using the preceding method, or directly (e.g. with the simulator), it will be possible to check whether temporal logic formulas are satisfied by the model.

Testing. Test generation and analysis can be done in *Lite* through the use of the simulator and compiler. The output of the simulator contains a set of acceptable tests. According to the semantics of LOTOS, these can then be executed, using either the simulator or compiler, by putting them in parallel with a specification.

Additionally there is a tool to derive canonical testers of LOTOS specifications. The currently available tool is based on the CO-OP method and works for basic LOTOS. This tool is currently being extended to full LOTOS.

4 More Information

The Lotosphere Partners

The Lotosphere consortium consists of the following organisations (those listed with a dagger (†) participate in the tools work package). Alcatel Standard Electrica, Ascom Tech†, British Telecommunications†, C.N.R.–CNUCE†, Gesellschaft für Mathematik und Datenverarbeitung†, C.N.R.–Instituto Elaborazione Informazione†, Institut National de Recherche en Informatique et en Automatique†, Laboratoire d'Automatique et d'Analyse des Systèmes du CNRS, Océ Nederland, PTT–Research Neher Laboratories†, SYSECA Logiciel, Technische Universität Berlin†, Universidad Politécnica de Madrid†, University of Stirling, University of Twente†.

Acknowledgements

The development of *Lite* is the joint responsibility of a number of organisations. The emphasis of each organisation is as follows. Ascom Tech works on one of the compiler approaches, and does integration work. BT contributes to the work on testing. CNR–CNUCE works on the graphical editor and on correctness preserving transformations. GMD works on ADT completion and persistency tools. INRIA works on verification tools and prerequisite transformations. RNL is working on report generator and lister functions. TUB works on narrowing and term rewriting machines, and ADT executability tests. UPM works on compilation and the user interface. UT works on the structure editor, testing tools, and the advanced simulator.

This paper was assembled from contributions by a number of persons working in the project.

Further Information

For further information concerning *Lite* or the LotosPhere project, consult Jeroen van de Lagemaat, Lotosphere project coordinator, INF-TIOS, University of Twente, P.O. Box 217, 7500 AE Enschede, Netherlands, Tel +31 53893792, e-mail lagemaat@cs.utwente.nl.

Superposition Refinement of Parallel Algorithms

R.J.R. Back
Åbo Akademi University, Department of Computer Science

K. Sere *
Utrecht University, Department of Computer Science

Abstract

Superposition refinement enhances an algorithm by superposing one computation mechanism onto another mechanism, in a way that preserves the behavior of the original mechanism. Superposition seems to be particularly well suited to the development of parallel and distributed programs. An originally simple sequential algorithm can be extended with mechanisms that distribute control and state information to many processes, thus permitting efficient parallel execution of the algorithm. We will in this paper show how superposition of parallel algorithms is expressed in the refinement calculus. We illustrate the power of this method by a case study, showing how a distributed broadcasting algorithm is derived through a sequence of superposition refinements.

1 Introduction

A common way of constructing programs is to start from an existing program that achieves part of what is needed, and add code to this program so that additional requirements are satisfied. Often this will require that some changes are done to the original program, so that the extensions fit into it. When the changes in the original program are small, in the sense that the underlying computation is essentially unchanged, we refer to this construction method as *superpositioning*.

Superposition seems to be useful in most fields of programming, because it permits us to construct a complicated program by a sequence of successive enhancements, each of which is reasonably small and usually encodes a single design decision. In other words, it permits us to tackle one issue at the time, rather than having to make a joint design decision and settle a number of interrelated design questions all at the same time.

Superposition as a method for program refinement has come up in a number of different contexts, e.g. in the works of Dijkstra et al. [11], Back and Kurki–Suonio et al. [4,14], Chandy and Misra [9], Francez et al. [8,12], Katz [13] and others.

---

*On leave from Åbo Akademi University, Department of Computer Science, SF–20520 Turku, Finland

In this paper we will study superposition of parallel programs, within the *action system* framework for parallel and distributed computations. This was introduced by Back and Kurki–Suonio in [4], together with one form of superpositioning. Action systems have similarities with other event–based formalisms like UNITY of Chandy and Misra [9], interacting processes of Francez [12] and shared actions of Ramesh and Mehndiratta [17] among others. The system behavior is in these formalisms described in terms of the events or actions which processes in the system carry out in co–operating with each other.

Action systems support the construction of parallel and distributed systems in a stepwise manner [4,18]. Stepwise refinement of action systems starts with a specification of the intended behavior of the system, given as a sequential statement. The goal is to construct an action system that satisfies certain criteria and fits into some predefined syntactic category [4,5] for which an efficient implementation on the assumed distributed architecture can be given.

Superposition refinements of action systems are done in order to increase the degree of parallelism of the program, as well as distribute control in the program. For instance, modifications can be made in order to distribute some shared variables among the processes in a distributed system, to add some information gathering mechanism to the system which replaces direct access to a shared variable, to detect some stable property (such as termination) of an action system or in order to impose some communication protocol upon the processes executing an action system. These changes are done in such a way that the original computation is not disturbed while new functionality is added to the code.

Superposing one mechanism onto another often constitutes a rather large refinement step, the correctness of which can be quite difficult to establish using only informal reasoning. Therefore, a formal treatment of the method is needed. The *refinement calculus* provides a general formal framework for carrying out program refinements and proving the correctness of each refinement step. We will here show how to describe superposition of action systems within this calculus.

Refinement calculus is a formalization of the stepwise refinement method based on the weakest precondition calculus of Dijkstra [10]. It was proposed by Back [1,2] and has later been further elaborated by several researchers [7,15,16].

The refinement calculus is based on the assumption that the notion of correctness we want to preserve is *total correctness*. Total correctness is an appropriate correctness notion for *parallel algorithms*, programs that differ from sequential algorithms only in that they are executed in parallel, by co–operation of many processes. They are intended to terminate, and only the final results are of interest. The refinement calculus and the action system formalism together provide an uniform foundation for the derivation of parallel algorithms by stepwise refinement [6,18].

The refinement calculus can also be extended to stepwise refinement of reactive programs, as shown in [3]. The methods for handling superposition described here carry over to this more general framework without much changes. For brevity, we will restrict ourselves here to the original version of the refinement calculus, where total correctness is required to be preserved.

We proceed as follows. In section 2, we give a very brief overview of the basic notions of the refinement calculus, to the extent needed in this paper. In section 3, the action systems formalism is presented. In Section 4 the superposition method is first described informally, and then formally within the refinement calculus. Its application to an example superposition step is described in detail in Section 5. We use the derivation of a distributed broadcasting algorithm as a general case study for illustrating the method. Section 6 gives an overview of the whole derivation of the distributed broadcasting algorithm. We end with some concluding remarks in section 7.

Besides showing how to carry out superpositions in the refinement calculus, we will also give special attention to the way program derivations using superposition are presented. Traditionally, program derivations following the refinement paradigm show all the intermediate versions in the derivation in full. We will try to compress this information and remove redundancy, hopefully without sacrificing understandability of the derivation. We use a tabular description of a superposition derivation, showing the initial specification of the program and the successive changes carried out on the program components.

2 Refinement calculus

We consider the language of guarded commands of Dijkstra [10], with some extensions. We have two syntactic categories, statements and actions. *Statements* S are defined by

$$
\begin{aligned}
S ::= \quad & x := e & & (assignment\ statement) \\
| \quad & \{Q\} & & (assert\ statement) \\
| \quad & S_1; \ldots; S_n & & (sequential\ composition) \\
| \quad & \text{if } A_1 \;[\!]\; \ldots \;[\!]\; A_m \text{ fi} & & (conditional\ composition) \\
| \quad & \text{do } A_1 \;[\!]\; \ldots \;[\!]\; A_m \text{ od} & & (iterative\ composition) \\
| \quad & \text{begin var } x;\ S \text{ end} & & (block\ with\ local\ variables)
\end{aligned}
$$

Here $A_1, \ldots, A_m$ are actions, x is a list of variables, e is a list of expressions and Q is a predicate.

An *action* (or *guarded command*) A is of the form

$$A ::= g \to S$$

where g is a boolean expression (the *guard* of A, denoted gA) and S is a statement (the *body* of A, denoted sA). We will say that an action is *enabled* in a certain state, if its guard is true in that state.

The *assert statement* $\{Q\}$ acts as *skip* if the condition Q holds in the initial state. If the condition Q does not hold in the initial state, the effect is the same as *abort*. Thus, $skip = \{true\}$ and $abort = \{false\}$. The other statements have their usual meanings.

The *weakest preconditions* of the assignment statement, sequential, conditional and iterative composition are defined as in [10]. The weakest precondition of the assert statement

is $\text{wp}(\{Q\}, R) = Q \wedge R$. The weakest precondition for the block statement is
$$\text{wp}(\textbf{begin var } x; S \textbf{ end}, R) = (\forall x : \text{wp}(S, R)).$$
A statement S is said to be *(correctly) refined* by statement S', denoted $S \leq S'$, if
$$(\forall\, Q : \text{wp}(S, Q) \Rightarrow \text{wp}(S', Q)).$$
This is equivalent to the condition
$$(\forall\, P, Q : P[S]Q \Rightarrow P[S']Q).$$
Here $P[S]Q$ stands for the total correctness of S w.r.t. precondition P and postcondition Q. In other words, refinement means that whatever total correctness criteria S satisfies, S' will also satisfy this criteria (S' can satisfy other total correctness criteria also, which S does not satisfy).

Intuitively, a statement S is refined by a statement S', if (i) whenever S is guaranteed to terminate, S' is also guaranteed to terminate, and (ii) any possible outcome of S' for some initial state is also a possible outcome of S for this same initial state. This means that a refinement may either extend the domain of termination of a statement or decrease the nondeterminism of the statement, or both.

Two statements S and S' are *refinement equivalent*, denoted $S \equiv S'$, if they refine each other. This means that they are guaranteed to terminate on the same set of initial states, and will produce the same set of possible outcomes on these initial states.

The refinement relation is reflexive and transitive. Hence, if we can prove that $S_0 \leq S_1 \leq \ldots \leq S_{n-1} \leq S_n$, then $S_0 \leq S_n$. This models the successive refinement steps in a program development: S_0 is the initial high level specification statement and S_n is the final executable and efficient program that we have derived through the intermediate program versions $S_1, \ldots, S_{n-1}$. Each refinement step preserves the correctness of the previous step, so the final program must preserve the correctness of the original specification statement.

The refinement relation is monotonic w.r.t. the statement constructors. For any statement $S(T)$ that contains T as a substatement, we have that
$$T \leq T' \Rightarrow S(T) \leq S(T').$$

Notation for replication In our examples we will need to use a lot of replicated structures, so we will adopt a convenient notation for these. A **for** -clause will state that the previous declaration or statement is replicated, once for each value of the index variable. If the operator between the statements is not sequential composition, then it has to be indicated explicitly. Thus, we have that

$$
\begin{array}{rcl}
x_i : \tau_i \textbf{ for } i \in < 1, 2, \ldots, m > & = & x_1 : \tau_1;\ x_2 : \tau_2;\ \ldots;\ x_m : \tau_m \\
S_i \textbf{ for } i \in < 1, 2, \ldots, m > & = & S_1;\ S_2;\ \ldots;\ S_m \\
[\!]\ S_i \textbf{ for } i \in < 1, 2, \ldots, m > & = & S_1 [\!]\ S_2 [\!]\ \ldots [\!]\ S_m.
\end{array}
$$

In stead of lists, the index may range over sets when the ordering of the elements does not matter. Also, we may write just a comma for **for** , when space is scarce.

$$S: v_1,\ldots,v_m := v_0,\ldots,v_0 \equiv$$
```
                          begin S'
                          var rec.i ∈ bool for i ∈ V;
                          rec.0 := true
                          rec.i := false for i ∈ V − {0};
                          do
                          ▯ ¬rec.i → v.i := v.0; rec.i := true
                          for i ∈ V − {0}
                          od
                          end
```

Figure 1: Two refinement equivalent programs, S and S'.

Example Let $V = \{0, 1, 2, \ldots, m\}$ be a set of indices, and let $v.0, v.1, v.2, \ldots, v.m$ be a set of variables indexed by V. Then the two programs in Figure 1 are refinement equivalent. Both will always terminate, and will establish the same final state for a given initial state: each variable $v.i$ will have the value $v.0$. The proof that program S' has this effect is based on loop invariant

$$(\forall i : 1 \leq i \leq m : rec.i \Rightarrow v.i = v.0).$$

The local variable $rec.0$ is not really needed, but turns out to be useful in the derivations to follow.

Refinement of actions We also define weakest preconditions for actions, by

$$\text{wp}(g \to S, R) \quad = \quad g \Rightarrow \text{wp}(S, R).$$

Refinement between statements can then be extended to a notion of refinement between actions. Let A and A' be two actions. Action A is *refined* by action A', $A \leq A'$, if

$$(\forall Q : \text{wp}(A, Q) \Rightarrow \text{wp}(A', Q)).$$

LEMMA 1 *Let A and A' be two actions. Then $A \leq A'$ if and only if*

(i) $\{gA'\}; sA \leq sA'$ and

(ii) $gA' \Rightarrow gA$.

In other words, action A is refined by action A' if and only if (i) whenever A' is enabled, the body of A is refined by the body of A' and (ii) A is enabled whenever A' is enabled.

3 Action systems formalism

An *action system* $\mathcal{A}$ is a statement of the form

$$\mathcal{A} = \textbf{begin var } x; S_0; \textbf{do } A_1 \,\|\, \ldots \,\|\, A_m \textbf{ od end} : v$$

on *state variables* $y = x \cup v$. The *global* variables v are indicated explicitly for notational convenience. Each variable is associated with some domain of values. The set of possible assignments of values to the state variables constitutes the *state space*. The initialization statement S_0 assigns initial values to the state variables.

The behavior of an action system is that of Dijkstra's guarded iteration statement [10] on the state variables: the initialization statement is executed first, thereafter, as long as there are enabled actions, one action at a time is nondeterministically chosen and executed.

Let $\mathcal{P} = \{p_1, \ldots, p_k\}$ be a partitioning of the state variables y in action system $\mathcal{A}$. The tuple $(\mathcal{A}, \mathcal{P})$ is called a *partitioned action system*. We identify each partition p_i in a partitioned action system with a *process*. The variables in p_i are then the variables belonging to this process. We say that action A *involves* process p_i, if it refers to a variable in p_i.

Let pA be the set of processes involved in action A in a partitioned action system $(\mathcal{A}, \mathcal{P})$, i.e., $pA = \{p \in \mathcal{P} \mid A \text{ involves } p\}$. Two actions A and B are *independent* if $pA \cap pB = \emptyset$. An implementation may permit actions that are independent in some partitioning to be executed in parallel. As two independent actions do not have any variables in common, their parallel execution is equivalent to executing the actions one after the other, in either order.

A hierarchy of partitioned action systems was defined in [5]. For every class of action systems in this hierarchy, there is an efficient implementation of action systems onto some (centralized or distributed) machine architecture. These classes are, however, rather restricted, so the task of constructing an action system that fits some specific class can be quite hard.

A stepwise method for constructing an action system that fits some specific implementation class was put forward in [6,18]. The idea is that a more or less sequential system is transformed into an action system with the required characteristics. The action systems in the first steps do not, e.g., have to respect the process boundaries, and the network topology can be allowed to be arbitrary. In later versions, these restrictions will then be enforced, by making suitable modifications of the action system.

The derivation is done within the refinement calculus. A set of transformation rules and methods was developed to assist in the derivation procedure. In this paper we will develop yet another transformation rule, superposition refinement, which was not considered explicitly in [6,18].

3.1 Example: A broadcasting algorithm

Let (V, E) be a connected graph with V a finite set of nodes and E a finite set of edges on V. Let the nodes denote processes and the edges denote communication channels between the processes. Each process is assumed to know the identities of its direct neighbors. Node 0 knows additionally the identities of all the nodes in the network. Communication can only take place between nodes directly connected by an edge, but may be bidirectional.

begin C	**begin** C'	**begin** C''
$v.i := v.0,\ i \in V - \{0\};$	**begin** S'	**var** $rec.i \in bool,\ i \in V;$
$R;$	**var** $rec.i \in bool,\ i \in V;$	$rec.0 := true;$
end	$rec.0 := true;$	$rec.i := false,\ i \in V - \{0\};$
	$rec.i := false,\ i \in V - \{0\};$	**do**
	do	$\quad \llbracket\ \neg rec.i \rightarrow$
	$\quad \llbracket\ \neg rec.i \rightarrow$	$\qquad v.i := v.0;$
	$\qquad v.i := v.0;$	$\qquad rec.i := true$
	$\qquad rec.i := true$	$\quad$ **for** $i \in V - \{0\}$
	$\quad$ **for** $i \in V - \{0\}$	**od**;
	od	R
	end;	**end**
	R	
	end	

Figure 2: Initial specification C, first refinement C' and second refinement C''.

Each node $i \in V$ has a variable $v.i$. We are requested to design an action system that assigns (broadcasts) the value $v.0$ to each variable $v.i,\ i \in V - \{0\}$. The termination of the broadcast must be detected by node 0, after which this node initiates some other computation R. The algorithm should work for any connected graph V, E, and should behave as a wave algorithm.

Program C in Figure 2 is an initial specification of the required effect. Program C' in Figure 2 shows a first refinement of this specification. We have simply taken the refinement of Figure 1 and, using monotonicity, replaced the assignment statement in C by its refinement S'. A second refinement C'' moves the statement R inside the block. This refinement is correct under the assumption that the variables $rec.i$ do not appear in R, an assumption that we will make here.

Neither C nor its two refinements C' and C'' are, however, in the form of action systems, because of the trailing continuation R. An action system refinement of C'' is C_1, shown in Figure 3. Here we have made R into a single action. The auxiliary variable $rest$ has been introduced in order to guarantee that R is executed only when all the assignments have been carried out, and that it is then executed only once. We have given names to the individual actions in this system, for ease of reference.

Using the methods described in [6,18] the correctness of $C \leq C' \leq C'' \leq C_1$ is easily established (in fact, these are all equivalences). Hence, by transitivity, C_1 is a correct refinement of our initial specification C.

We want to place the auxiliary variables $rec.i$ in the same process as the variables $v.i$, $i \in V$. The auxiliary variable $rest$ will be placed in the same process as the root $v.0$. This would give us the partitioning $\mathcal{P} = \{p_i | i \in V\}$ of the action system C_1, where

$$p_0 = \{v.0, rec.0, rest\},$$
$$p_i = \{v.i, rec.i\},\quad i \in V - \{0\}.$$

```
begin C₁
  var rec.i ∈ bool for i ∈ V;
    rest ∈ bool;
  rec.0 := true;
  rec.i := false for i ∈ V − {0};
  rest := true;
  do
    [A.i] ¬rec.i →
      v.i := v.0; rec.i := true
    for i ∈ V − {0}
    [B] (∀i ∈ V.rec.i) ∧ rest →
      rest := false; R
  od
end : v.i ∈ val for i ∈ V
```

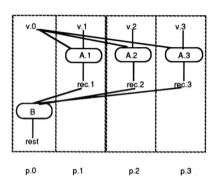

Figure 3: An action system refinement C_1 of specification C, and a partitioning of this action system

Figure 3 shows this partitioning graphically. It shows that node 0 has to communicate directly with every other node in the graph, first to communicate the value $v.0$ and then later to detect termination. This violates the requirement that communication only takes place along the edges in the graph. Thus, this action system is not an acceptable solution to the problem we posed above. In Section 5 we will show how superposition is used to construct a refinement of action system C_1 that does satisfy our communication constraints.

4 Superposition refinement of action systems

Let

$$\mathcal{A} = \text{begin var } x; S_0; \text{do } A_1 \,[\!]\, \ldots \,[\!]\, A_m \text{ od end} : v \text{ and}$$
$$\mathcal{A}' = \text{begin var } x, z; S_0'; \text{do } A_1' \,[\!]\, \ldots \,[\!]\, A_m' \,[\!]\, B_1 \,[\!]\, \ldots \,[\!]\, B_n \text{ od end} : v$$

be two action systems with the same global variables v. The action system $\mathcal{A}'$ has some new local variables z, in addition to the local variables x that $\mathcal{A}$ also has. For each *old action* A_i in $\mathcal{A}$ there is a corresponding *new action* A_i' in $\mathcal{A}'$. The *auxiliary actions* B_j in $\mathcal{A}'$ do not correspond to any actions in $\mathcal{A}$.

The action system $\mathcal{A}$ is correctly refined by $\mathcal{A}'$, $\mathcal{A} \leq \mathcal{A}'$, if the following conditions are satisfied, for some assertion $I(v, x, z)$ on the state variables:

(1) *Initialization:*

  (a) The new initialization S_0' has the same effect on the old variables v, x as S_0, and

(b) it will establish $I(v,x,z)$.

(2) *Old actions:*

   (a) The body of each new action A'_i has the same effect on the old variables v, x as the corresponding old action A_i when $I(v,x,z)$ holds,

   (b) each new action A'_i will preserve $I(v,x,z)$, and

   (c) the guard of each new action A'_i implies the guard of the corresponding old action A_i, when $I(v,x,z)$ holds.

(3) *Auxiliary actions:*

   (a) None of the auxiliary actions B_j has any effect on the old variables v, x when $I(v,x,z)$ holds, and

   (b) each auxiliary action B_j will preserve $I(v,x,z)$.

(4) *Termination of auxiliary actions:* Executing only auxiliary actions in an initial state where $I(v,x,z)$ holds will necessarily terminate.

(5) *Exit condition:* The exit condition of the new action system implies the exit condition of the old action system when $I(v,x,z)$ holds.

Often a new action A'_i that is to replace an old action is constructed by simply strengthening the guard and adding some assignments to the new variables z, i.e., $A'_i = gA_i \wedge gC_i \rightarrow sA_i; sC_i$. In this case, we only need to check case (b) in condition (2), because the other conditions will be trivially satisfied. Similarly for the initialization statement: if $S'_0 = S_0; T_0$, where T_0 only assigns values to the new variables z, then we only need to check case (b) of condition (1). The other conditions, (3) – (5), have to be checked as before. This special case corresponds to the usual notion of *syntactic superposition*, which thus simplifies the proof obligations.

4.1 Formalization of the rule

The superposition method is more formally expressed by the following theorem.

THEOREM 1 *(Superposition for action systems) Let*

$$\mathcal{A} = \textbf{begin var } x; S_0; \textbf{do } A_1 \, [\!] \, \ldots \, [\!] \, A_m \textbf{ od end} : v \text{ and}$$
$$\mathcal{A}' = \textbf{begin var } x, z; S'_0; \textbf{do } A'_1 \, [\!] \, \ldots \, [\!] \, A'_m \, [\!] \, B_1 \, [\!] \, \ldots \, [\!] \, B_n \textbf{ od end} : v.$$

Let $g\mathcal{A}$ be the disjunction of the guards of the A_i actions, $g\mathcal{A}'$ the disjunctions of the guards of the A'_i actions and $g\mathcal{B}$ the disjunction of the guards of the B_j actions. Then $\mathcal{A} \leq \mathcal{A}'$ if the following conditions hold, for some invariant $I(v,x,z)$:

   (1) $S_0 \leq \textbf{begin var } z; S'_0; \{I\} \textbf{ end}$.

(2) $A_i \leq \text{begin var } z; I \to A'_i; \{I\} \text{ end, for } i = 1, \ldots, m$.

(3) $true \to skip \leq \text{begin var } z; I \to B_j; \{I\} \text{ end, for } j = 1, \ldots, n$.

(4) $I \text{ [do } B_1 \text{ [} \ldots \text{ [} B_n \text{ od]} true$.

(5) $I \wedge g\mathcal{A} \Rightarrow (g\mathcal{A}' \vee g\mathcal{B})$.

The action $I \to A'_i; \{I\}$ in condition (2) can equivalently be written as a single action $I \wedge gA'_i \to sA'_i; \{I\}$. A similar rewriting can be done for condition (3).

We will not use the superposition proof method on this level of formality in the sequel, but will be content with using the informal description of the method first given in the case study below. Most of the actual refinements we will consider are actually rather simple, with all statements being deterministic and always terminating.

4.2 Describing superpositions

We will describe a superposition as shown in Figure 4. The symbol • is either + or empty. If an action on the right hand is preceded by a +, then only the additions to the corresponding left hand action is shown. We define

$$\begin{aligned}
\text{var } x + \text{var } z &= \text{var } x; z \\
S + S' &= S; S' \\
A + A' &= gA \wedge gA' \to sA; sA' \\
\{I\} + \{I'\} &= \{I \wedge I'\}.
\end{aligned}$$

We leave the right hand side position empty if the action is unchanged in the refinement. If there is no left hand action, then the right hand action is a new auxiliary action. In all other cases, the right hand side action is to replace the corresponding left hand side action in the action system. The invariant used in the superposition rule is shown after the loop.

We only permit additions to the list of local variables in superposition. We may also chain a number of successive superpositions, each new superposition providing a new column in the tabular representation of a program derivation.

5 A first superposition refinement: $\mathcal{C}_2$

We will exemplify superposition refinement by showing how to change the way in which the value $v.0$ is passed among the nodes in program $\mathcal{C}_1$. In $\mathcal{C}_1$ process 0 is assumed to communicate with every other process in the network. It was, however, required that only the edges of the graph should be used for communication. We therefore add a mechanism that only uses the permitted connections to broadcast the value $v.0$. Each process, upon receiving the value $v.0$, forwards it to all other processes that it is directly connected to.

$$
\begin{array}{lcl}
\textbf{begin } N & & \textbf{begin } N' \\
\textbf{var } x; & + & \textbf{var } z \\
S_0 & \bullet & S_0' \\
\textbf{do} & & \textbf{do} \\
\quad [\!]\ gA_1 \to sA_1 & \bullet & \quad [\!]\ gA_1' \to sA <_1 \\
\quad \vdots & & \quad \vdots \\
\quad [\!]\ gA_m \to sA_m & \bullet & \quad [\!]\ gA_m' \to sA_m' \\
& & \quad [\!]\ gB_1 \to sB_1 \\
& & \quad \vdots \\
& & \quad [\!]\ gB_n \to sB_n \\
\textbf{od} & & \textbf{od} \\
\{I\} & \bullet & \{I'\} \\
\textbf{end} : v \in val & & \textbf{end}
\end{array}
$$

Figure 4: Describing a superposition

The mechanism is implemented by adding a queue $q.i$ for each $i \in V$. This queue will hold the values node i has received from other nodes to which it is directly connected in the graph. The queue $q.i$ will thus contain one or more copies of the value $v.0$. When node i finds its queue non–empty, it extracts the first value from it, assigns this value to its own variable $v.i$ and then forwards it to all nodes directly connected to itself. The rest of queue $q.i$ is ignored. The set $H.i$ will hold the indices of those nodes that are directly connected to node i and that have not yet been sent the value $v.0$ from node i.

It is easy to check that the following is an invariant of action system $\mathcal{C}_1$:

$$
\begin{aligned}
Inv.1: \quad & (rest \Rightarrow Inv.11 : (\forall i \in V : rec.i \Rightarrow v.i = v.0)) \\
& \wedge \\
& (\neg rest \Rightarrow (\forall i \in V : rec.i)).
\end{aligned}
$$

The following additions to the loop invariant $Inv.1$ describe the way in which the new variables are to be used in the resulting action system $\mathcal{C}_2$:

$$
\begin{aligned}
Inv.2: \quad rest \Rightarrow \quad & Inv.21 : (\forall i \in V : (\forall j,k : q.i.j = k \Rightarrow k = v.0)) \\
\wedge \quad & Inv.22 : (\forall i \in V.H.i \subseteq E(i)) \\
\wedge \quad & Inv.23 : (\forall (k,i) \in E : i \notin H.k \Rightarrow q.i \neq <> \vee rec.i)
\end{aligned}
$$

We will use the multiple assignment statement as a convenient notation for working with lists (as queues will be represented). If x is a variable of type $value$ and q is a variable of type $value\ list$, then $x, q := q$ will assign the first element of q to x and remove it from q. Similarly, $q := q, x$ will add x as last element to q.

This superposition turns the action system into a wave algorithm. The refinement is shown in Figure 5.

$$\begin{array}{ll}
\textbf{begin } \mathcal{C}_1 & + \quad \textbf{begin } \mathcal{C}_2 \\
\textbf{var } rec.i \in bool \textbf{ for } i \in V; & \quad\quad \textbf{var } q.i \in value\ list \textbf{ for } i \in V; \\
\quad rest \in bool; & \quad\quad\quad\ H.i \in index\ set \textbf{ for } i \in V;
\end{array}$$

$$\begin{array}{ll}
rec.0 := true; & + \quad q.i :=<> \textbf{ for } i \in V; \\
rec.i := false \textbf{ for } i \in V - \{0\}; & \quad\ H.i := E(i) \textbf{ for } i \in V; \\
rest := true; &
\end{array}$$

$$\begin{array}{ll}
\textbf{do} & \textbf{do} \\
{[A.i]}\ \neg rec.i \to & [A.i]\ \neg rec.i \wedge q.i \neq <> \to \\
\quad v.i := v.0;\ rec.i := true & \quad v.i, q.i := q.i;\ rec.i := true \\
\textbf{for } i \in V - \{0\} & \textbf{for } i \in V - \{0\} \\[1em]
{[B]}\ (\forall i \in V.rec.i) \wedge rest \to & [B] \\
\quad rest := false;\ R & \\[1em]
 & [C.k.i]\ rec.k \wedge i \in H.k \to \\
 & \quad q.i := q.i, v.k; \\
 & \quad H.k := H.k - \{i\} \\
 & \textbf{for } (k,i) \in E \\
\textbf{od} & \textbf{od} \\
\{Inv.1\} & + \quad \{Inv.2\} \\
\textbf{end} : v \in val & \textbf{end}
\end{array}$$

Figure 5: Superposition of forwarding mechanism

5.1 Proof of correctness of superposition

Let us now show that $\mathcal{C}_1 \leq \mathcal{C}_2$ holds, using the superposition rule. The invariant of the rule will be $Inv.1 \wedge Inv.2$.

(1) *Initialization:*

  (a) The new initialization has the same effect on the old variables as the old initialization, because only assignments to the new variables $q.i$ and $H.i$ were added.

  (b) The new initialization will establish $Inv.1 \wedge Inv.2$. The fact that $Inv.1$ is established follows already from the fact that $Inv.1$ is an invariant of the old action system and from (a). The fact that also $Inv.2$ is established is easily seen: $Inv.21$ holds because all queues $q.i$ are initialized to empty, $Inv.22$ holds because each $H.i$ is initialized to $E(i)$ and $Inv.23$ holds initially, because $i \notin H.k$ holds for no $(i,k) \in E$.

(2) *Old actions $A.i$ and B:*

  (a) The body of each new action $A.i$ has the same effect on the old variables as the corresponding old action $A.i$ when $Inv.1 \wedge Inv.2$ holds. This follows from

$Inv.21$, by which the assignment $v.i := v.0$ is equivalent to assigning to $v.i$ the first element of queue $q.i$. For the B action, the condition holds trivially, because the new B action is the same as the old B action.

(b) Each new action A'_i will preserve $Inv.1 \wedge Inv.2$. The fact that $Inv.1$ is preserved again follows from (a) above. That $Inv.2$ is also preserved is easily seen: $Inv.21$ is clearly preserved, as values are only removed from $q.i$, $Inv.22$ is preserved because $H.i$ is unchanged and $Inv.23$ is preserved, because at the same time as $q.i$ may become empty, $rec.i$ is set to true. The B action does not change any variables that are constrained by the new invariant, so the condition holds trivially in this case.

(c) The guard of each new action A'_i implies the guard of the corresponding old action A_i, when $Inv.1 \wedge Inv.2$ holds, because the new guard has an added conjunct. For the B action, the condition holds trivially.

(3) *Auxiliary actions $C.k.i$:*

(a) None of the auxiliary actions $C.k.i$ has any effect on the old variables when $Inv.1 \wedge Inv.2$ holds, because these actions do not assign to any of the old variables.

(b) Each auxiliary action $C.k.i$ will preserve $Inv.1 \wedge Inv.2$. The fact that $Inv.1$ is preserved follows again from (a). $Inv.21$ is preserved, because by $Inv.11$, $v.k = v.0$, so the new value added to $q.i$ is $v.0$. $Inv.22$ is preserved, because we are only removing elements from $H.k$ in this action. Finally, $Inv.23$ is preserved, because $q.i$ is made non-empty by the action.

(4) *Termination of auxiliary actions $C.k.i$:* Executing only auxiliary actions in an initial state where $Inv.1 \wedge Inv.2$ holds will necessarily terminate. This follows from the fact that there can be only finitely many elements in all sets $H.k$ altogether, and each auxiliary action will remove one element from one of these sets.

(5) *Exit condition:* The exit condition of the new action system implies the exit condition of the old action system, whenever $Inv.1 \wedge Inv.2$ holds. This is really the only nontrivial proof obligation in this superposition. We will prove the counterpositive of the statement, which means that we have to show that

$$(\exists i \in V : \neg rec.i) \vee ((\forall i \in V : rec.i) \wedge rest)$$
$$\Rightarrow$$
$$(\exists i \in V : \neg rec.i \wedge q.i \neq <>) \vee ((\forall i \in V : rec.i) \wedge rest) \vee$$
$$(\exists (k,i) \in E : rec.k \wedge i \in H.k).$$

If $(\forall i \in V : rec.i) \wedge rest$ holds, then this implication hold trivially. Assume therefore that it does not hold, i.e. that $\neg rec.i$ holds for some $i \in V$. Assume that $rec.i \vee q.i = <>$ holds for every $i \in V$. As the graph is connected, there must exist a path from 0 to i. We have that $rec.0$ is true and $rec.i$ is false. Hence, on this path there must exist a node k such that $rec.k$ is true, but for successor j of node k on this path, $rec.j$ is false. By assumption, this means that $q.j =<>$. By invariant $Inv.23$, this again means that j must be in $E(k)$. Hence, there does exist a pair $(k,j) \in E$ such that $rec.k$ and $j \in H.k$.

6 Additional superposition steps

We continue here the derivation of our broadcasting algorithm. Figure 6 shows the whole derivation in tabular form, as a sequence of successive superpositions. The initial version $\mathcal{C}_1$ has already been derived above, as well as the first superposition $\mathcal{C}_2$. Here we will describe two more successive superpositions of this action system, $\mathcal{C}_3$ and $\mathcal{C}_4$.

A requirement we had was that the termination of the broadcast should be detected by node 0. Hence, we must make all the nodes report to node 0 when they have received their value. This will be done in two superposition steps, first adding a mechanism that constructs a dynamic spanning tree rooted at node 0 at the same time as the values are being forwarded, giving $\mathcal{C}_3$. Then, we add a mechanism that sends acknowledgments back to the root whenever a value has been received by a node, resulting in $\mathcal{C}_4$. We do not show the correctness proofs of these steps here, for brevity.

6.1 Adding a dynamic spanning tree construction: $\mathcal{C}_3$

We construct a spanning tree among the nodes in the graph in the following way. Each node i considers as its father the node from where it received the value $v.0$. Variable $f.i$ holds the index of the father for node i. The queue $fq.i$ holds for each node i the indices of the nodes that have sent values to node i through queue $q.i$. In addition to the previous invariants, we also maintain the invariance of

$$Inv.3: \quad rest \Rightarrow \quad Inv.31: (\forall i \in V - \{0\}.rec.i \Rightarrow (f.i, i) \in E)$$
$$\wedge \quad Inv.32: (\forall k \in V.\forall i \in V - \{0\}.\forall j.fq.i.j = k \Rightarrow rec.k \wedge (k, i) \in E)$$
$$\wedge \quad Inv.33: (\forall k \in V - \{0\}.rec.k \Rightarrow fpath(0, k))$$

where $fpath$ is the least relation that satisfies the condition $fpath(i, j) = f.j = i \vee fpath(i, f.j)$ for any two nodes i, j in V.

Checking the correctness of the superposition is in this case quite simple, as no new auxiliary actions are introduced, and the guards of the old actions are unchanged. The fact that the new conjuncts of the invariant are preserved is relatively straightforward to check.

6.2 Adding backward acknowledgements: $\mathcal{C}_4$

Having added a spanning tree construction, we may use the spanning tree to forward acknowledgements towards node 0.

begin C_1	begin C_2	begin C_3	begin C_4
var $rec.i \in bool, i \in V$; $rest \in bool$;	+ **var** $q.i \in value\ list, i \in V$; $H.i \in index\ set, i \in V$;	+ **var** $f.i \in index, i \in V'$; $fq.i \in index\ list, \in V'$;	+ **var** $ack.i \in index\ list, i \in V$; $VS \in index\ set$;
$rec.0 := true$; $rec.i := false\ i \in V - \{0\}$; $rest := true$;	+ $q.i := <>$ **for** $i \in V$; $H.i := E(i)$ **for** $\in V$;	+	+ $ack.i := <>$ **for** $i \in V$; $VS := V - \{0\}$;
do	**do**	**do**	**do**
$[A.i] \neg rec.i \rightarrow$ $v.i := v.0$; $rec.i := true$ **for** $i \in V - \{0\}$	+ $[A.i] \neg rec.i \land q.i \neq <> \rightarrow$ $v.i, q.i := q.i$; $rec.i := true$ **for** $i \in V - \{0\}$	+ $[A.i]\ true \rightarrow$ $f.i, fq.i := fq.i$ **for** $i \in V - \{0\}$	+ $[A.i]\ true \rightarrow$ $ack.(f.i) := ack.(f.i), i$ **for** $i \in V - \{0\}$
$[B]\ (\forall i \in V.rec.i) \land rest \rightarrow$ $rest := false; R$	$[B]$	$[B]$	$[B]\ VS = \emptyset \land rest \rightarrow$ $rest := false; R$
	$[C.i] \neg rec.k \land i \in H.k \rightarrow$ $q.i := q.i, v.k$; $H.k := H.k - \{i\}$ **for** $(k, i) \in E$	$[C.k.i]\ true \rightarrow$ $fq.i := fq.i, k$ **for** $(k, i) \in E$	$[C.k.i]$
			$[D.k]\ ack.k \neq <> \rightarrow$ **begin var** $a \in index$; $a, ack.k := ack.k$; $ack.(f.k) := ack.(f.k), a$ **end** **for** $k \in V - \{0\}$
			$[E]\ ack.0 \neq <> \rightarrow$ **begin var** $a \in index$; $a, ack.0 := ack.0$; $VS := VS - \{a\}$ **end**
od	**od**	**od**	**od**
$\{Inv.1\}$	+ $\{Inv.2\}$	+ $\{Inv.3\}$	+ $\{Inv.4\}$
end : $v \in val$	**end**	**end**	**end**

Figure 6: Tabular representation of entire derivation

Each node i holds a queue $ack.i$ of received acknowledgements. When node i receives value $v.0$ it acknowledges this by placing an acknowledgement message into $ack.(f.i)$, i.e., into the acknowledgement queue of its father. Whenever its ack–queue is non–empty, node i forwards the acknowledgements to its father. Node 0 keeps track of the nodes whose acknowledgements it has not yet received, in the set VS.

The superposition will preserve the invariance of

$Inv.4$:
$\quad rest \Rightarrow Inv.41 : (\forall i \in V. \forall j \in V - \{0\}. \forall k : ack.i.k = j \Rightarrow rec.j \wedge j \in V - \{0\})$
$\quad \wedge \quad Inv.42 : VS = \{j \mid \neg rec.j\} \cup \{j \mid (\exists i, k : ack.i.k = j)\}$.

The correctness of this superposition refinement can again be checked by our rule. This superposition is less trivial than the preceding one. The main difficulty this time is to show that the auxiliary actions necessarily terminate, if executed alone. This will follow from the fact that the father links established in the previous step form a tree that is rooted at 0.

6.3 Final program

Let us finally put all the superposition steps together. In Figure 7 we show the complete action system $\mathcal{C}_4$ that results from the refinement steps we have described. It is a wave algorithm, as required. The final process network is generated with the variable partitioning $\mathcal{P} = \{p_i \mid i \in V\}$, where

$$p_0 = \{v.0, rec.0, rest, q.0, H.0, f.0, fq.0, ack.0, VS\},$$
$$p_i = \{v.i, rec.i, q.i, H.i, f.i, fq.i, ack.i\}, \quad i \in V - \{0\}.$$

In this partitioning, all the communication takes place between nodes directly connected to each other. None of the actions involve more than two adjacent processes. Furthermore, termination is detected by node 0 as was originally requested.

By transitivity of refinement, the final action system $\mathcal{C}_4$ will be a correct refinement of the initial specification $\mathcal{C}$.

7 Conclusions

We have shown how the superposition refinement rule for action systems can be formalized within the refinement calculus. Due to this formalization, superposition can be applied as a program transformation rule when doing program derivation in the refinement calculus framework. A methodology based on the use of program transformation rules was put forward in [6,18]. The superposition rule complements the collection of rules presented in these works.

The main emphasis of this paper was to show the practical usefulness of the rule. We claim that our broadcasting example, which is far from trivial, shows that the method is of practical value. Another larger example on application of the superposition rule is given in [5] where a compiler from action systems to occam is derived.

The method to structure superposition derivations should also be of interest. Using a tabular representation, only the new information needs to be shown at each step.

Acknowledgements

The work reported here was supported by the FINSOFT III programme sponsored by the Technology Development Centre of Finland. The stay of Kaisa Sere at the Utrecht University was supported by the Dutch organisation for scientific research under project nr. NF 62-518 (Specification and Transformation Of Programs, STOP). We are grateful to Jan van de Snepscheut for a critical review of the derivation.

References

[1] R. J. R. Back. *Correctness Preserving Program Refinements: Proof Theory and Applications*, volume 131 of *Mathematical Center Tracts*. Mathematical Centre, Amsterdam, 1980.

[2] R. J. R. Back. A calculus of refinements for program derivations. *Acta Informatica*, 25:593–624, 1988.

[3] R. J. R. Back. Refinement calculus, part II: Parallel and reactive programs. In J. W. de Bakker, W.-P. de Roever, and G. Rozenberg, editors, *Stepwise Refinement of Distributed Systems: Models, Formalisms, Correctness. Proceedings. 1989*, volume 430 of *Lecture Notes in Computer Science*, pages 67–93. Springer-Verlag, 1990.

[4] R. J. R. Back and R. Kurki-Suonio. Decentralization of process nets with centralized control. In *Proc. of the 2nd ACM SIGACT–SIGOPS Symp. on Principles of Distributed Computing*, pages 131–142, 1983.

[5] R. J. R. Back and K. Sere. Deriving an occam implementation of action systems. In *Proc. of the 3rd Refinement Workshop BCS FACS/IBM UK Laboratories/Oxford University*, Hursley Park, England, January 1990. (to appear).

[6] R. J. R. Back and K. Sere. Stepwise refinement of parallel algorithms. *Science of Computer Programming*, 1(1):133–180, January 1990.

[7] R. J. R. Back and J. von Wright. Refinement calculus, part I: Sequential nondeterministic programs. In J. W. de Bakker, W.-P. de Roever, and G. Rozenberg, editors, *Stepwise Refinement of Distributed Systems: Models, Formalisms, Correctness. Proceedings. 1989*, volume 430 of *Lecture Notes in Computer Science*, pages 42–66. Springer-Verlag, 1990.

[8] L. Bougé and N. Francez. A compositional approach to superposition. In *Proc. of the 14th ACM Conference on Principles of Programming Languages*, pages 240–249, San Diego, California, USA, January 13–15 1988.

[9] K. Chandy and J. Misra. *Parallel Program Design: A Foundation*. Addison–Wesley, 1988.

[10] E. W. Dijkstra. *A Discipline of Programming*. Prentice–Hall International, 1976.

[11] E. W. Dijkstra, L. Lamport, A. J. Martin, C. S. Scholten, and E. F. M. Steffen. On-the-fly garbage collection: An exercise in cooperation. *Communications of the ACM*, 21:966 – 975, 1978.

[12] N. Francez and I. R. Forman. Superimposition for interacting processes. In J. C. M. Baeten and J. W. Klop, editors, *CONCUR '90 Theories of Concurrency: Unification and Extension. Proceedings*, volume 458 of *Lecture Notes in Computer Science*, pages 230–245, Amsterdam, the Netherlands, August 1990. Springer–Verlag.

[13] S. M. Katz. A superimposition control construct for distributed systems. Technical Report STP–286–87, MCC, August 1987.

[14] R. Kurki-Suonio and H.-M. Järvinen. Action system approach to the specification and design of distributed systems. In *Proc. of the 5th International Workshop on Software Specification and Design*, pages 34–40. ACM Software Engineering Notes 14(3), May 1989.

[15] C. C. Morgan. The specification statement. *ACM Transactions on Programming Languages and Systems*, 10(3):403–419, July 1988.

[16] J. M. Morris. A theoretical basis for stepwise refinement and the programming calculus. *Science of Computer Programming*, 9:287–306, 1987.

[17] S. Ramesh and S. L. Mehndiratta. A methodology for developing distributed programs. *IEEE Transactions on Software Engineering*, SE–13(8):967–976, 1987.

[18] K. Sere. *Stepwise Derivation of Parallel Algorithms*. PhD thesis, Department of Computer Science, Åbo Akademi University, Turku, Finland, 1990.

begin $\mathcal{C}_4$
var $rec.i \in bool$ **for** $i \in V$; $rest \in bool$;
  $q.i \in value\ list$ **for** $i \in V$;
  $H.i \in index\ set$ **for** $i \in V$;
  $f.i \in index$ **for** $i \in V - \{0\}$;
  $fq.i \in index\ list$ **for** $i \in V - \{0\}$;
  $ack.i \in index\ list$ **for** $i \in V$; $VS \in index\ set$;

$rec.0 := true;\ rec.i := false$ **for** $i \in V - \{0\}$; $rest := true$;
$q.i :=<>$ **for** $i \in V$;
$H.i := E(i)$ **for** $i \in V$;
$fq.i :=<>$ **for** $i \in V - \{0\}$;
$ack.i :=<>$ **for** $i \in V$; $VS := V - \{0\}$;

do
$[A.i]\ \neg rec.i \wedge q.i \neq <> \rightarrow$
    $v.i, q.i := q.i;\ rec.i := true;$
    $f.i, fq.i := fq.i;\ ack.(f.i) := ack.(f.i), i$
for $i \in V - \{0\}$

$[B]\ VS = \emptyset \wedge rest \rightarrow rest := false;\ R$

$[C.k.i]\ rec.k \wedge i \in H.k \rightarrow$
    $q.i := q.i, v.k;\ H.k := H.k - \{i\};\ fq.i := fq.i, k;$
for $(k, i) \in E$

$[D.k]\ ack.k \neq <> \rightarrow$
    begin var $a \in index$;
    $a, ack.k := ack.k;\ ack.(f.k) := ack.(f.k), a$
    end
for $k \in V - \{0\}$

$[E]\ ack.0 \neq <> \rightarrow$
    begin var $a \in index$;
    $a, ack.0 := ack.0;\ VS := VS - \{a\}$
    end
od
$\{Inv.1 \wedge Inv.2 \wedge Inv.3 \wedge Inv.4\}$
end : $v.i \in value$ **for** $i \in V$

Figure 7: Resulting action system.

Specification and Verification of a Sliding Window Protocol in LOTOS

Eric Madelaine [**] and Didier Vergamini [*]

[**]INRIA
Route des Lucioles, Sophia Antipolis
06565 Valbonne Cedex (France)
email: madelain@mirsa.inria.fr

[*]CERICS
Avenue Albert Einstein, Sophia Antipolis
06565 Valbonne Cedex (France)
email: dvergami@mirsa.inria.fr

Abstract

We give an example of protocol verification in Lotos, using automata-based verification tools available inside the Lotosphere Integrated Tool Environment (Lite). The current state of tools imposes a dedicated, *behaviour oriented*, specification style. The example we consider is a Sliding Window protocol. We present the specification of the various components of the protocol, and analyse its behaviour for various quality of the underlying communication media: we prove that the protocol is able to recover from the loss, the duplication, and the shuffling of messages. We give time and space measurements of the verification activities, highlighting the methods for *state explosion* control.

Keywords: verification, process calculus, parallelism, concurrency, lotos, protocol, transition system, behavioural semantics, automata

1 Introduction

Lotos is a formal description technique for protocols and distributed systems. It is a specification language rather than a programming language, and as such encourages the writing of system behaviours at a very abstract level. Having a clear mathematical semantics, such a specification technique gives a sound background to the first steps of the development of a system, eliminating the ambiguities usually present in "natural language" specifications. It is also the basis for the definition of so-called "correctness preserving transformations", to be used for transforming a specification into a more refined one, or closer to implementation. Finally, it is used for further verification activities, such as proving that a specification matches some requirements. These requirements may be stated in some logical language, or even in Lotos itself, the correctness being expressed then as a mathematical relation between the specification and the requirement. A classical example in the framework of layered protocols is the requirement of equivalence between the service of a given layer and the system composed of protocol entities of that layer and the service of the underlying layer.

Those verification activities require large amounts of mathematical reasoning, and cannot be conducted on anything but toy examples without the help of software tools. Such tools are nowadays in the process of emerging from pure research laboratories. There exists a large variety of tools that may be applied to the verification of behaviours, ranging from logical and algebraic reasoning support, usually very interactive, to model-checkers and tools based on extensive analysis of automata. In the first family one can mention the general theorem-prover HOL [11], that supports logical deduction in any high-order logic specified by the user, or the process-algebra specialist PAM [13], that supports term rewriting and inductive reasoning in equationally specified process algebras; the PSF proof assistant [16] has similar functionalities. These tools are essentially interactive, and the work of building proofs for reasonable-size examples is tedious. The model-checking family is better developed in the framework of hardware design. It supports automated reachability analysis without explicit computation of the underlying automaton, allowing for verification of logical formulas on very large systems (see e.g. [8]). There exists currently no such technique supporting proofs in the framework of Lotos behavioural equivalence: the explicit computation of automata is required.

A number of verification tools based on automata analysis have been elaborated during the last decade [2,7,4,12], offering various verification approaches for various process algebras. Our tool AUTO was first developed for a clone of Milner's SCCS calculus [17] called MEIJE [3]. It has been generalised recently [15] to a large class of operationally specified algebras, generating the functions building automata from terms directly from the operational semantics rules of the operators; this has been the basis of a BasicLotos version of Auto, that has been connected to the Lotosphere Tool Environment.

Few tools have been developed that deal specificly with verification of (full) Lotos specifications. Exceptions are Lola [19], that applies expansion theorems as a mean for correctness-preserving transformations; and Caesar [10], that uses user-described finite approximations of data-types for implementation and verification of Lotos specifications.

The protocol

The Sliding Window Protocol we consider was first introduced by N.V. Stenning ([22]). It is a protocol ensuring a correct data-transfer over very poor quality communication lines: the underlying lines may duplicate, loose, or change the order of messages. Messages are stamped by numbers bounded by an integer characterising the protocol that we name its size. Each protocol entity maintains a bounded window permitting the reordering of messages before delivering them. Acknowledging is done modulo the size of the protocol, allowing for acknowledgement of packs of data-messages by a single message. The size of windows, the buffering capacity of the lines, and the protocol size must fulfill a given arithmetic relation for the protocol to behave correctly.

Being an intermediate scale example, the sliding window protocol has inspired several studies since the original paper by Stenning. Those in the framework of process algebras are of interest for us:

In [5], the protocol is described in MEIJE, using the lowest meaningful sizes (lines and windows of capacity 2, protocol size 6), and its behaviour is analysed using AUTO.

In [20], the protocol is written in Estelle/R, and some temporal logic properties are verified using the XESAR tool.

In [6], three versions of the protocol are expressed both in the process algebra ACP and in the PSF language. They differ slightly from our version, for their messages carry both data and acknowledging information. Only the most complex of the three versions has a receiving window of size greater than 1, enabling message reordering. No verification whatsoever is performed on those specifications.

In [1], several versions of the protocol are specified in Lotos, illustrating various Lotos specification styles, concentrating on the adaptation of various style to the different steps of the development methodology.

Section 2 presents the tools we used for developing and analysing the protocol. Section 3 discusses the *behaviour oriented* specification style, and details the design of the protocol and its components. Section 4 explains how one obtains a (reduced) global automaton for the whole specification, and gives some comments on performances. Section 5 illustrates the verification of some partial behavioural properties of the system.

2 The Lotosphere Tool Environment

One of the main goal of this paper is the illustration of tool usage for both specification and verification activities. We have written our Sliding Window protocol in Lotos, with a strong help from tools. We have used tools for editing, checking the syntax and the static semantics, simulating parts of the protocol, and finally for building and analysing the global automaton of the system, and comparing various versions of the protocol.

The Lotosphere Integrated Tool Environment (*Lite*), provided by the Lotosphere consortium [1], is a programming environment for Lotos programs, containing a window interface managing several functionalities, summarised in figure 1.

The Lite interface manages a number of menus activating the various tools, and takes care of the correct sequencing of tools: when activating a tool, all required intermediate files are produced automatically. The main internal representation of a Lotos specification is the so-called *Common Representation* (CR), that serves as input for many tools in the environment. A file in CR form contains a representation of the abstract syntax tree of a specification guaranteed to conform to the syntax and the static semantics of Lotos.

The creation of a Lotos specification may be done with one's preferred editor. Additionally, *lite* provides a structure editor in which one can create or edit specifications in a syntax directed manner, with on-the-fly and incremental semantic checking. There is also a graphical editor based on the ISO GLOTOS graphical language, allowing for edition of mixed graphics and text. Each of these methods produces Lotos text files to be used by the environment.

---

[1]Lotosphere is the ESPRIT2 project n° 2304

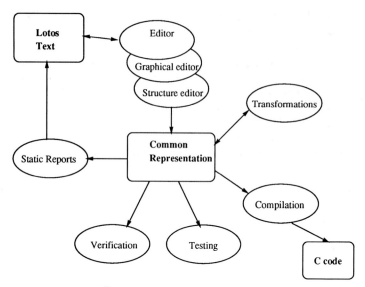

Figure 1: Lite main functions

A CR file is produced from a text file by a batch tool that checks its syntax and its static semantics. Usually this tool is called automatically when needed, though there is a menu button for calling it explicitly. The structure editor can also produce directly CR files.

Various report generators tools can be run on a specification, dealing e.g. with cross-references, with static dependences amongst processes and types, and with the type structure of gates.

Early debugging of (part or whole of) a specification can be done with the simulator. It builds interactively a simulation tree, proposing menus of events at each step. Events contain predicates that are dealt with in a purely symbolic way: in classical simulators, you need give values to variables before being able to compute predicates; here the simulator uses the equations from the data-types and a narrowing algorithm to solve the predicates at the symbolic level. Events with a predicate that has no solutions are automatically pruned out of the event menu. For those that remain, the system can propose interactively solutions to the user.

Additionally, the simulator is able to find out whether a newly created state in the simulation tree has already been encountered, pruning further the search space. Whenever this process terminates with a finite set of states, the tool can output an Extended Finite State Machine in Lotos syntax (or in CR) that is equivalent to the original specification, but is purely state oriented.

Some transformations are available within the system. Some of them are correctness preserving: they transform a specification into a new one which behaviour is equivalent to the former behaviour. Such transformations may be used during refinement steps, for example when one aims at a more resource-oriented version of a specification. Examples are the rearrangement of interaction points (splitting or regrouping of gates) and the regrouping of parallel processes (changing the geometry of a system).

The compiler is able to translate a Lotos specification into C-code. It takes as input a Lotos specification with some restrictions (e.g. no external gates), and with some annotations (linking e.g. Lotos events to system calls). The produced code contains an extended finite machine that implements the behaviour part of the specification, and rewrite systems that implement the data part. There is a run-time environment with the compiler that enables to run test sequences in an efficient way.

The test generation tool and the behaviour verification tool are currently restricted to BasicLotos (i.e. without data) specifications. There are transformations in *lite* for extracting a BasicLotos program from a Lotos specification. Those are necessarily approximations, because they loose information on data. Yet, they preserve some liveness properties, and they are used for behaviour analysis with the verification tools.

The behaviour verification tool is named AUTO [14,5,9]. A naive usage of the tool inside *lite* is possible, for simple activities such as the construction and graphical drawing of an automaton, or the comparison of two specifications by strong or weak equivalences. A more serious knowledge of the verification methods and of the tool is useful for further analysis, or when something goes wrong.

Verification in AUTO is based on the construction of finite transition systems. There are several instances of AUTO, depending on the input formalism. The version available within *lite* is tailored for BasicLotos. Not all BasicLotos programs have a finite transition systems, and an important step before any verification activity is a syntactic check for finiteness [15]. Afterwards, the usual verification activities are: the construction of automata from programs, the minimisation and the comparison of automata along various behavioural equivalences, the construction of *abstract* automata using abstract actions (each representing a set of sequences of concrete actions), the computation of specific paths (e.g. leading to deadlocks) and of their representatives in the corresponding concrete automaton. A companion system, AUTOGRAPH [5,21], also accessible inside *lite*, allows for a graphical display of the automata computed by AUTO, whenever they are small enough. The geometrical placement of states and edges in AUTOGRAPH can be done through an automatic layout algorithm, or in a user-driven way.

In order to compute bisimulation equivalences, AUTO manipulates the explicit representation of automata. The main problem with such techniques is of course the size of the manipulated structures. From small programs containing many synchronised or interleaved components, one can obtain very big automata. The "state explosion" can be reduced within AUTO by several methods. Essentially "global" automata should not be constructed by brute force, but reductions by congruences should be used whenever possible, while building automata of components. AUTO provides functions that apply reductions modulo strong, weak, or branching bisimulation on each component automatically, in a bottom-up way. Using such techniques may require a good knowledge of the structure of the specification under study, for it is often critical to assemble (and reduce) strongly connected components as soon as possible, in order to built small intermediate structures.

Throughout the remaining sections of the paper, we shall concentrate on the use of the verification tools. The structure editor, the batch CR-building tool, and the simulator have also been used extensively during the development of the example.

3 Specification of the Protocol

3.1 Lotos versus BasicLotos

The computation of a finite model for a Lotos specification encounters two basic difficulties: the use of data types with infinite carriers, and the unbounded creation of processes.

We already have mentioned that infinite data-types should be approximated in some way; a very rough approximation is the brute projection into BasicLotos that forgot all kind of data (e.g. in events, predicates, and process parameters). The Lotos to BasicLotos transformations currently available in *lite* are no much more than that. The CAESAR tool implements a finer approximation that uses a (user-specified) finite expansion of data-types. However, the expansion is performed directly during the transition system computation, preventing for any reduction of the state space by structural (congruent) methods. This limits the applicability of the method to small sized cases.

Unbounded process creation could be solved in a similar manner, approximating the original specification through finite expansion. Such a method is not yet available in the tools, only potentially infinite creation is detected using sufficient syntactic conditions.

When designing a specification with the idea of verifying its behaviours with the automated tools, one could from the beginning restricted itself to BasicLotos, getting rid of these approximation problems. Rather, we would use a new *style* of specification, with restrictions ensuring an easier mapping to finite operational models.

We call *"behaviour oriented specification"* a Lotos specification with no mixing of data and control, or more syntactically, with no predicates (in offers, nor in guards). E. Najm used a similar approach in [18], calling it "verification oriented style". Behaviour oriented specifications are more easily mapped to BasicLotos terms: no logical analysis of data-type predicates is required. Still we have to deal with the matching of value offers; a solution is to create new gate names for each possible value involved in such a matching, and to map each matching event to a *pure* event at one of the new gate names. If the types involved in matching offers have finite carriers, the expansion will preserve any behavioural property. In other cases, one would rely either on a finite approximation (à la Caesar), or on more symbolic methods, that are out of the scope of this paper.

In practice, writing pure (expanded) BasicLotos might prove lengthy, and very cumbersome. We have chosen here a mixed approach: we have a full Lotos version of our protocol, that uses generic processes with events bearing data when possible, but no predicates, and an expanded version of the protocol in which those generic processes have been expanded. The expansion has been done by hand, because the corresponding tools do not exist yet in *lite*, though in our case, it would be an easy task. The expanded version is pure

BasicLotos, so the *lite* tools can be applied directly with no further manual encoding. The two complete specifications (non-expanded and expanded) are in the full version of the paper.

3.2 Overall Structure

Our protocol consists in an emitter and a receiver communicating through two communication media. All messages are tagged by an integer bounded by the characteristic size of the protocol. In the original paper from Stenning [22], the minimal size of the tag range is given as the sum of the life duration of a message in the medium and the sizes of the windows in the receiver and in the emitter. In the sequel, we are using the smallest significant sizes for each of these parameters to build our specification: the life duration of a message will be 2, as the size of the windows. Thus, each message will be tagged with an integer modulo 6.

We have pictured in figure 2 the network of processes involved in our specification. The emitter takes messages from the outside, sends them via a first medium and waits for acknowledgements from a second medium. The receiver takes messages from the first medium, delivers them to the outside and sends acknowledgements via the second medium.

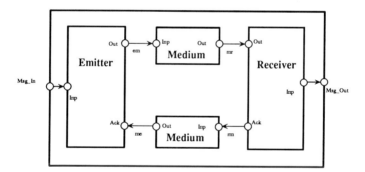

Figure 2: The global net

Here follows a Lotos specification of the network. The corresponding BasicLotos specification distinguishes events on a given gate that carry different values, by using as many different gate names as possible values; here messages are indexed modulo 6, so there are 6 different gates for each gate of the system and of its components (e.g. In1, ..., In6 for the external gate Msg_In, and Out1, ..., Out6 for the Out gate of each component, etc).

---------- The protocol network ----------
```
process Stenning[Msg_In, Msg_Out] : noexit
:= hide em, rm in
    (hide me in Emitter [Msg_In, em, me] |[me]| Medium [rm, me])
    |[em, rm]|
    (hide mr in Receiver [Msg_Out, mr, rm] |[mr]| Medium [em, mr])
endproc
```

3.3 The Communication Media

The specification of the communication medium must *implement* the notion of life duration. For this, we use as many atomic cells as the life duration, composed in a linear network. The messages are pushed from one cell to the following. A medium cannot hold a given message while delivering an unbounded number of different other messages: a line in which several consecutive messages can overtake a given message is not allowed. Each cell is a one-place buffer with a special gate on which a message may be duplicated. We give here the Lotos specification of a cell and a drawing of its behaviour in figure 3.

---------- A line cell ----------
```
process LineCell [Inp, Out, Dup] : noexit
:=
  Inp?n:Index ; (Loop[Dup](n) [> Out!n ;  LineCell [Inp, Out, Dup])
where
  process Loop[g](n) : noexit := g!n ; Loop[g](n) endproc
endproc
```

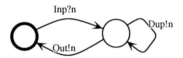

Figure 3: The line cell : a duplicating one-place buffer

After expansion over the finite sort **Index**, we get the BasicLotos program:

---------- A line cell (expanded) ----------
```
process LineCell [In1,In2,...,Out1,Out2,...,Dup1,Dup2,...] : noexit
:=
    In1 ; (Loop[Dup1] [> Out1 ; LineCell [In1,In2,...])
 [] In2 ; (Loop[Dup2] [> Out2 ; LineCell [In1,In2,...])
 [] In3 ; ...
where
  process Loop[g] : noexit := g ; Loop[g] endproc
endproc
```

We obtain several kinds of line using two such cells with various synchronisation schemes. For instance, a perfect medium is obtained by hiding all duplication messages and by connecting the output of the first cell with the input of the second one (cf figure 4, left side). The right half of figure 4 shows a disordering, duplicating and loosing medium, obtained by connecting the duplicating gates of the cells on the output of the network, the output gate of the first cell on the input gate of the second cell, and hiding the output gate of the second cell.

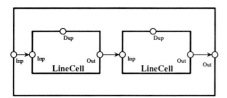 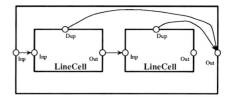

Figure 4: A perfect medium; and a disordering, loosing, and duplicating medium

───────────────────────────────── A perfect Medium ──

```
process Medium [Inp,Out] : noexit
:= hide Push, Dummy in
        LineCell[Inp, Push, Dummy ]
        |[Push]|
        LineCell[Push, Out, Dummy]
endproc
```

The interested reader may specify additional media, taking care of respecting the *bounded life duration* condition; our experiments include a duplicating medium, and a loosing and duplicating medium.

3.4 The emitter

We have made here, as in [5], the choice of specifying the emitter in a (resource-oriented) distributed way, as a network of 6 identical cells, each cell dealing with a different message tag (see the network in figure 7).

In the generic specification of a cell, two gates are used to indicate that a cell is entering and leaving the window (Win, Leave_Win). At every moment, two cells are inside the window; each can be active or not. An active cell can get its input message (on gate Inp); synchronously, the next cell becomes active (gate Prev_Inp). A cell, after receiving its message, delivers it repetitively (gate Out) until it receives the corresponding acknowledgement (gate Ack), or the following cell receives its own acknowledgement, and tells it to leave the window (gate Free). Figure 5 sketches one possible behaviour of the emitter (in each successive state of the emitter, the current window is outlined at its external border, and active cells have their numbers circled).

We give first the specification of a cell, described by three mutually recursive processes, each corresponding to one possible state of a cell (out of the window, in the window, or

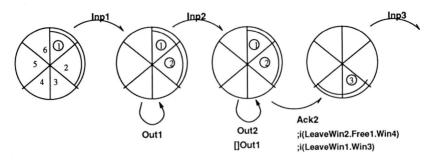

Figure 5: The emitter and its sliding window

active): figure 6 shows the behaviour of such a cell, as computed by AUTO and displayed with AUTOGRAPH.

―――――――――――――――――――――――――――――― A cell of the emitter ――
```
process BasicEmitCell [Inp, Prev_Inp, Out, Ack, Win, Leave_Win, Free] : NOEXIT
 :=
  Ack;BasicEmitCell [Inp, Prev_Inp, Out, Ack, Win, Leave_Win, Free]
  [] Free;BasicEmitCell [Inp, Prev_Inp, Out, Ack, Win, Leave_Win, Free]
  [] Win;InWindow [Inp, Prev_Inp, Out, Ack, Win, Leave_Win, Free]
  [] Prev_Inp;
      (Loop1[Ack]
       [> Win; ActiveCell [Inp, Prev_Inp, Out, Ack, Win, Leave_Win, Free])
endproc (* BasicEmitCell *)
```

―― (continued) ――
```
process InWindowCell
       [Inp, Prev_Inp, Out, Ack, Win, Leave_Win, Free] : NOEXIT
 :=
  Prev_Inp; ActiveCell [Inp, Prev_Inp, Out, Ack, Win, Leave_Win, Free]
endproc (*  InWindowCell  *)
```

―― (continued) ――
```
process ActiveCell [Inp, Prev_Inp, Out, Ack, Win, Leave_Win, Free] :NOEXIT
 :=
  Inp;
    (Loop1[Out]
     [>
      ((Ack; Leave_Win;
            BasicEmitCell[Inp, Prev_Inp, Out, Ack, Win, Leave_Win, Free])
       []
       Free; Leave_Win;
            BasicEmitCell[Inp, Prev_Inp, Out, Ack, Win, Leave_Win, Free]))
endproc (* ActiveCell *)
```

The emitter is obtained by putting all the cells into a network as pictured in figure 7. The Win, Leave_Win, and Free gates are connected through local (hidden) wires: when cell$_i$

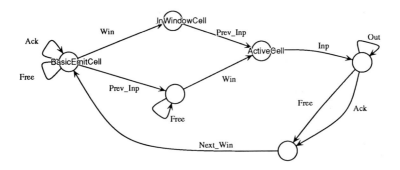

Figure 6: The automaton of one emitter cell

leaves the window, $cell_{i+2}$ enters the window, and $cell_{i-1}$ is freed. Each Inp!i external gate is connected both to gate Inp of $cell_i$, and to gate Prev_Inp of $cell_{i+1}$, so that an event on Inp!i activates $cell_{i+1}$. The corresponding Lotos specification is available in the full version of the paper.

3.5 The receiver

The receiver is very similar to the emitter. Differences come from the fact that acknowledgements are sent only when needed, i.e. when the cell is the last one in the window, allowing the receiver to bufferise messages arriving in disorder. The corresponding specification is also available in the full version of the paper.

4 Computing the global behaviour

We have computed and reduced along weak congruence the global automaton of the system for each possible lines. All the results are isomorphic. Figure 8 shows this automaton, as drawn through AUTOGRAPH. Its visible behaviour is that of a 4-places buffer that transmits messages in the correct order, with no loss nor duplication. This is of course to be understood under the usual fairness assumptions: if a medium is completely blocked, the protocol will wait forever.

This shows clearly that our protocol matches its (informal) requirement: it recovers from faults in the media.

The following table shows the performances of the verification tool for the various versions of the media. Time measurements have been done on a Sparc station (Sun4/40 with 24Mbytes of memory).

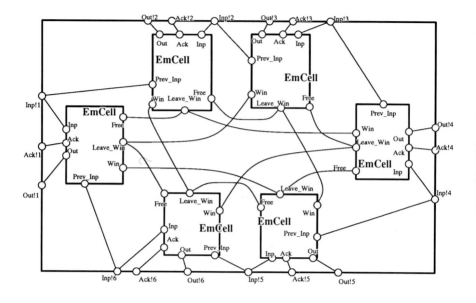

Figure 7: The emitter

Line		EM+BackL		REC+ForwL		Global
	reduced		reduced		reduced	unreduced
Perfect	43/84	2064/6924	624/2382	1032/3564	162/762	744/2544
		27 sec		17 sec		12 sec
Loosing &	37/114	1776/7962	240/1146	888/4068	174/906	432/1692
Duplicating		30 sec		16 sec		8 sec
Duplicating	49/138	2352/9522	684/2772	1176/5076	180/828	984/3762
		32 sec		20 sec		17 sec
Worst	37/144	1776/8496	432/2034	888/4476	294/1458	432/1728
		33 sec		20 sec		8 sec

For each half of the system, and for each possible line, we have computed an automaton, and reduced it along weak congruence. In each case, we have reported the size (number of states/number of transitions) of the automata before and after reduction, and the time for building the component starting from its (already reduced) subparts, including both construction and reduction times.

The overall automaton, after reduction, has 30 states and 48 transitions in all cases. Building the overall automaton using no component-wise reduction might be beyond the capacity of the system; one may evaluate its size to more than 10.000 states and 100.000 transitions.

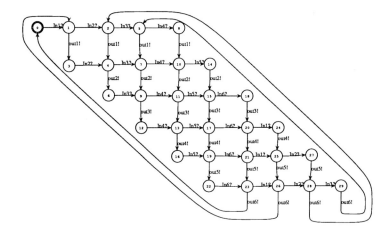

Figure 8: The global behaviour

We have reported here only the figures obtained with the optimal combinations of components. Application of component-wise reductions is most efficient when assembling strongly connected parts as soon as possible. However, it is often difficult to predict which combinations amongst the four parts of the protocol will lead to the most reduced sub-parts. Here the experience has proved that building the system in other combinations is much more expensive (up to 30 times longer).

5 Partial Properties

The global behaviour as pictured in figure 8 is small enough to be fully understood by a human reader. This is a very peculiar case where reduction techniques are giving by themselves a satisfactory result. Indeed, one could have started with this 4-place faithful buffer as a *specification* of the desired behaviour, and proved that the protocol has an external behaviour equivalent to its specification. This is not the general case, naturally, and analysis of results is often much more difficult, especially when the global automaton is much bigger, and when one does not have a predefined specification to be proven equivalent to.

In such case, we rely on *abstraction* techniques, aiming at the proof that some *partial ordering properties* do hold. AUTO offers functions for reducing a system after hiding all but a given set of actions, and more advanced methods using a notion of abstract actions (sets of sequences of concrete actions); the derived abstract transition system is usually smaller than the original system, and reflects the behaviour of the specification along a partial point of view.

We use here only the simplest, *reduction with hiding* function. Once we have computed the global system, we want to prove that it verifies some properties such as:

- the inputs (respectively the outputs) are correctly sequenced,
- an input is always followed by the corresponding output.

We used AUTO reduction mechanisms, keeping visible respectively the sets of all inputs actions, of all output actions, and of one input and its corresponding output action. The results are pictured in figure 9, and are those which were expected.

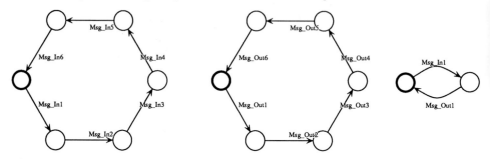

Figure 9: The results of reduction with hiding along various action sets

6 Conclusion

We have presented a Lotos specification of a Sliding Window Protocol, and shown that it behaves as we intended, recovering from various sorts of faulty communication media. The protocol has been written in a *behaviour oriented* way, suitable for exhaustive analysis, with no interaction of the data part over the behaviour control. Converting a Full-Lotos specification into behaviour oriented style is a highly semantical work, rarely decidable. Expanding behaviour oriented specification into a finite model is much easier. Starting from a generic (but behaviour oriented) specification of the protocol, it would be interesting, once we have tools supporting the transformation, to create and compare instances of the protocol with various values of its sizes.

The development and verification of the specification has been done entirely inside the *lite* environment, shortening the overall effort to less than 15 man*days. Obtaining a first Lotos specification correct with respect to syntax and static semantics was rather fast, with the help of the tool environment. The simulator has been used also at that step to get confidence in the behaviour of components, and to compute the first steps of behaviour of the whole system.

Then the verification tools have been used throughout several cycles of debugging, starting with the smallest components, and assembling them progressively. Finally the resulting protocol entities have been checked against the various media, computing its global behaviour, and proving some partial ordering properties. As we started with a behaviour oriented specification containing only finite data types, the BasicLotos approximation involved is bisimulation-preserving, and the properties we proved on the BasicLotos term are indeed properties of the original Lotos specification.

This illustrates one possible application of the verification method, as a debugging aid beyond mere simulation. One could also imagine having from the start stated that the requirement to be reached was the behaviour of some sort of faithful buffer, and proved brutally that the system is equivalent to its requirement, expressed itself in Lotos. This situation is rather frequent in the framework of protocols, where one specifies both a service and a protocol at each layer, and wants to prove that the protocol ensures the corresponding service. In such cases a simple application of the *observational equivalence* function of the verification tool will do the work.

Acknowledgements The authors would like to especially thank Robert De Simone for his helpful contribution in this paper.

References

[1] Guidelines for the application of ESTELLE, LOTOS, and SDL. ISO TR 10167.

[2] T. Bolognesi and M. Caneve. Squiggles: A tool for the analysis of LOTOS specifications. In *Formal Description Techniques*. North-Holland, 1989.

[3] G. Boudol. Notes on algebraic calculi of processes. In K. Apt, editor, *Logics and Models for Concurrent Systems*. Springer-Verlag, 1985.

[4] G. Boudol, V. Roy, R. de Simone, and D.Vergamini. Process calculi from theory to practice: Verification tools. In *Proc. of the Workshop on Automated Verification Methods for Finite State Systems*, number 407 in LNCS. Springer-Verlag, 1989.

[5] G. Boudol, R. De Simone, and D. Vergamini. Experiment with AUTO and AUTOGRAPH on a single case of sliding window protocol. Technical Report RR870, INRIA, 1988.

[6] J.J. Brunekreef. A formal specification of three sliding window protocols. Technical Report P9102, CWI, January 1991.

[7] R. Cleaveland, J. Parrow, and B. Steffen. The concurrency workbench. In *Proc. of the Workshop on Automated Verification Methods for Finite State Systems*, number 407 in LNCS. Springer-Verlag, 1989.

[8] O. Coudert, C. Berthet, and J.C. Madre. Verification of synchronous sequential machines based on symbolic execution. In *Proc. of the Workshop on Automated Verification Methods for Finite State Systems*, number 407 in LNCS. Springer-Verlag, 1989.

[9] R. de Simone and D. Vergamini. Aboard AUTO. Technical Report RT111, INRIA, October 1989.

[10] H. Garavel and J. Sifakis. Compilation and verification of lotos specifications. In *proceedings of the 10th International symposium on Protocol Specification, Testing and Verification*, Ottawa, 1990. IFIP, North-Holland.

[11] M.J. Gordon. HOL, a proof generating system for higher order logic. In Birstwisle G. and Subrahmanyam P.A., editors, *VLSI specification, verification, and synthesis*, pages 73–128, Calgary, Canada, January 1987. Kluwer academic press, Boston.

[12] H. Korver. The current state of bisimulation tools. Technical Report P9101, CWI, January 1991.

[13] H. Lin. Pam: A process algebra manipulator. Technical Report 2/91, University of Sussex, February 1991.

[14] E. Madelaine and D. Vergamini. AUTO: a verification tool for distributed systems using reduction of finite automata networks. In S.T. Vuong, editor, *Formal Description Techniques, II*. NORTH-HOLLAND, Vancouver, December 1989.

[15] E. Madelaine and D. Vergamini. Finiteness conditions and structural construction of automata for all process algebras. In R. Kurshan, editor, *Proceedings of Workshop on Computer Aided Verification*, New-Brunswick, June 1990.

[16] S. Mauw and G.J. Veltink. An introduction to PSF_d. In J. Diaz and F. Orejas, editors, *Proc. of Int. Joint Conf. on Theory and Practice of Software Development*, number 352 in LNCS, pages 272–285. Springer-Verlag, 1989.

[17] R. Milner. Calculi for synchrony and asynchrony. *Theoretical Computer Science*, 25:267–310, 1983.

[18] E. Najm. A verification oriented specification in LOTOS of the transport protocol. In *The Formal Description Technique LOTOS*. North-Holland, 1989.

[19] J. Quemada and S. Pavón. Transformating LOTOS specifications with LOLA. In *Formal Description Techniques*, Stirling, 1989. North-Holland.

[20] J. Richier, C. Rodriguez, J. Sifakis, and J. Voiron. Verification in XESAR of the sliding window protocol. In *Proceedings of the Seventh IFIP Symposium on Protocol Specification, Testing, and Verification*, 1987.

[21] V. Roy and R. de Simone. An AUTOGRAPH primer. Technical Report RT112, INRIA, October 1989.

[22] N. V. Stenning. A data transfer protocol. *Computer Networks*, 1:99–110, 1976.

//
Protocol Verification System for SDL Specifications Based on Acyclic Expansion Algorithm and Temporal Logic

Hironori Saito[a], Toru Hasegawa[a] and Yoshiaki Kakuda[b]

[a]R&D Laboratories, Kokusai Denshin Denwa Co., Ltd.(KDD)
1-15 Ohara 2-chome, Kamifukuoka-shi, Saitama 356, Japan

[b]Dept. of Information and Computer Sciences, Osaka University
1-1 Machikaneyama-cho, Toyonaka-shi, Osaka 560, Japan

Abstract

This paper describes a system which verifies that the behaviors of a protocol specified in SDL meet requirements. Requirements are expressed using a branching-time temporal logic for a concise and unambiguous description. The verification system first generates a set of state transition graphs consisting of executable transitions, and then evaluates the branching-time temporal logic formula on the graphs. Using an extended acyclic expansion algorithm, the state transition graph is obtained for each process, while the existing verification methods use a global state transition graph that represents the behaviors of the whole protocol system consisting of all processes. Since only the graphs of the processes relevant to the requirements are examined, the verification can be executed more efficiently. The verification is illustrated in the paper by the verification of a broadcasting protocol for requirements such as fair termination among processes.

1. Introduction

Along with the progress of the information society, more and more complex protocols have been designed and implemented for communication systems. As protocols become more complex, it becomes more difficult to manually design error-free protocol specifications. Since errors in the specification causes unnecessary incorrect implementation, the techniques in protocol engineering[6] to detect errors are now essential in designing protocol specifications.

In general, protocol errors can be classified into two categories. Errors general to all protocol specifications are called logic errors. Undefined message reception, deadlock, and channel overflow fall into this category. On the other hand, a logically correct protocol specification may include errors in the sense that its behavior is different from what the protocol designers expect. These types of errors are called semantic errors. A protocol verification system in this paper is a system which automatically checks whether a protocol specification meets the protocol designers' requirements.

For the verification system, a protocol specification is described in Specification and Description Language, SDL[8], recommended by CCITT, and requirements are expressed using a branching-time temporal logic. The logic enables concise and unambiguous description of requirements on a temporal ordering of events or state reachability.

In the previous verification methods using the temporal logic[1],[2], verification is executed on a global state transition graph which represents the behavior of the whole protocol system consisting of all processes. This is considered a drawback of these methods in terms of efficiency, since requirements for practical protocols are occasionally related to a transition sequence of one process or transition sequences of some processes. In contrast, the verification system executes verification efficiently. Since the acyclic expansion algorithm generates a state transition graph for each process, not a large global state transition graph, only the graphs of the processes relevant to the requirements are examined.

This paper is organized as follows. First, Section 2 outlines the verification system. The protocol model and the description method of requirements for protocol specifications are given in Section 3 and Section 4, respectively. Section 5 explains the verification method, based on which the verification system has been developed. In Section 6, the verification is illustrated by the example of a broadcasting protocol. Finally, some concluding remarks are provided in Section 7.

2. Outline of the System

For practical and efficient protocol verification, the verification system has been developed to have the following features. First, the requirements are expressed unambiguously and concisely using a branching-time temporal logic (BTL). Second, all possible behaviors of the protocol are examined. This is because all executable state transitions are obtained by the acyclic expansion algorithm which is extended such that it can compute values for variables at each state and evaluate an enabling condition for each transition. The resulting state transition graphs are related to one another by information on sequences that interact among processes. This information on interacting sequences facilitates verification for requirements regarding precedence of reached states, e.g., fair termination among processes. Finally, the most distinctive feature is that the verification is performed efficiently using only the executable state transition graphs of the processes relevant to the requirements.

The verification system is realized as software implemented on a SPARCstation. Since all the programs are written in C language and all the inputs and outputs use ASCII characters, it can be run on any UNIX workstation.

The configuration of the verification system with the data flow is shown in Fig. 1. The

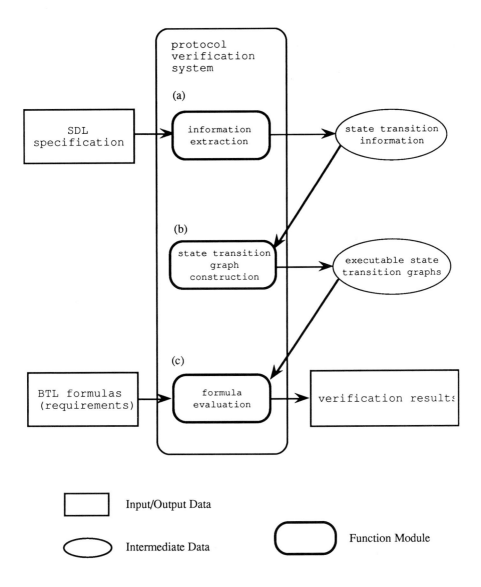

Fig. 1 Configuration of the protocol verification system.

system is composed of three main parts: (a) information extraction, (b) state transition graph construction, and (c) formula evaluation parts. Given an SDL specification, which is syntactically correct[10], and BTL formulas representing requirements, the verification is executed according to the following procedures, where the procedures (1), (2), (3) are executed by the parts (a), (b), (c), respectively.

(1) Information of state transitions, including variables and enabling conditions for transitions, is extracted out of the input SDL specification. Variables defined in each process are set to the initial values.

(2) State transition graphs consisting of executable transitions are constructed from the extracted information using the extended acyclic expansion algorithm. At the same time, the values of variables are computed for each state.

(3) The BTL formulas representing requirements are evaluated on the executable state transition graphs relevant to the formulas. The final results are obtained through this evaluation.

3. Protocol Model

In the verification system, a protocol is treated as extended FSMs that exchange messages through channels between them. The protocol model has the following assumptions.

(1) State transitions are deterministic, and time for a transition is zero.

(2) Every channel is an FIFO queue. That is, messages are received in the same order as transmitted.

The assumption (2) implies that no message is lost or corrupted in channels.

A protocol is characterized by a set of states, a set of messages, a set of variables, and so on. The definition of protocol is given as follows.

Definition 1: Let N be the number of processes. Protocol P is an 8-tuple P=(Q, o, M, V, E_o, B, D, succ), where Q=(Q_1, $\cdots$, Q_N), o=(o_1, $\cdots$, o_N), M=(M_{12}, $\cdots$, $M_{N\,N-1}$), V=(V_1, $\cdots$, V_N), E_o=(E_{o1}, $\cdots$, E_{oN}), B=(B_1, $\cdots$, B_N), D=(D_1, $\cdots$, D_N), D_i=$D^1_i \cup D^2_i$ ($1 \leq i \leq N$), succ=($succ_1$, $\cdots$, $succ_N$), and $succ_i$ is a partial function mapping, $Q_i \times B_i \times D^1_i \times (M_{ij} \cup M_{ji}) \times D^2_i \rightarrow Q_i$, for all j.

Here, Q_i is the set of states of process i and o_i is the initial state of process i. M_{ij} represents the set of messages to be transmitted from process i to process j. V_i represents the set of variables in process i, and E_{oi} represents the set of initial values for all variables in V_i. B_i represents the set of enabling conditions in process i, and, D^1_i and D^2_i represent the set of pre-computations and post-computations, respectively. Variables in V_i can be used in those conditions and computations. The function $succ_i(s_i, b_i, d^1_i, x, d^2_i)$ gives the state which process i enters from state s_i after executing d^1_i, transmission of $x \in M_{ij}$ or reception of $x \in M_{ji}$, and d^2_i if b_i is true. A state transition (or transition, for short) is defined including these operations. It is assumed that D^1_i and D^2_i don't have any computation which is iterated infinitely.

Definition 2: $(s_i, b_i, d^1_i, x, d^2_i)$ is a state transition iff $s_i \in Q_i$, $b_i \in B_i$, $d^1_i \in D^1_i$, $d^2_i \in D^2_i$ and a message $x \in M_{ij} \cup M_{ki}$ for some i, j, k ($1 \leq i \leq N$, $1 \leq j \leq N$, $1 \leq k \leq N$). A transition $(s_i, b_i, d^1_i, x, d^2_i)$ is said to be a send-transition if $x \in M_{ij}$ and a receive-transition if $x \in M_{ki}$ for some i, j, k.

A transition in the protocol model is depicted in Fig.2(a). Note that b_i may be True (always true) and d^1_i and d^2_i may be no operations.

In an SDL specification, an INPUT (reception) and more than one OUTPUT (transmission) may appear in one transition. So, the verification system divides the transition into plural transitions, each of which has either a reception or a transmission. An intermediate state is generated between each pair of the transitions. For example, transitions in SDL in Fig.2(b) are divided into three transitions as shown in Fig.2(c), where i_state is an intermediate state.

Definition 3: A global state is a pair G=(S,C) such that $S=(s_1,\cdots,s_N)$, $C=(c_{12},\cdots,c_{ij},\cdots,c_{NN-1})$, where $1 \leq i \leq N$, $1 \leq j \leq N$, $i \neq j$. The initial global state is a pair $G_0=(S_0, C_0)$ such that $S_0=(o_1, \cdots, o_N)$ and $C_0=(\varepsilon,\cdots,\varepsilon)$, where ε denotes an empty message sequence.

A send-transition $(s_i, b_i, d^1_i, x, d^2_i)$ is said to be executable, iff b_i is true at state s_i and there exists a global state $G=((s_1,\cdots,s_i,\cdots,s_N),C)$ which can be reached by executable transitions from G_0. A receive-transition $(s_i, b_i, d^1_i, x, d^2_i)$ is said to be executable, iff b_i is true at state s_i and there exists a global state $G=((s_1,\cdots,s_i,\cdots,s_N), (c_{12},\cdots,c_{ji},\cdots,c_{NN-1}))$ which can be reached by executable transitions from G_0, where the head of the message sequence in c_{ji} is x.

Even if a transition is defined in a specification, it is not necessarily executable. Executable transition sequences can be efficiently obtained by the acyclic expansion algorithm, which generates an executable state transition graph for each process. In the following, the definitions of least state, least sequence, least global state, and interacting sequences are given. These are deeply related to construction of executable state transition graphs by the algorithm.

Definition 4: The least state $L_j(s_i, Y)$ is the last state that process j must have reached when process i reaches a state s_i by transmitting and receiving all messages in Y. The least sequence $R_j(s_i, Y)$ is a sequence of messages to be transmitted and received by process j from o_j to $L_j(s_i, Y)$. Here, Y denotes a sequence of messages from o_i to s_i.

For convenience, "transmit and receive all messages in a message sequence Y" is expressed as "execute Y," hereinafter.

Definition 5: The least global state for a state s_i reached by executing Y is a global state $G=((s_1, \cdots, s_j, \cdots, s_N),(c_{1\,2}, \cdots, c_{pq}, \cdots, c_{N\,N-1}))$, where s_j is $L_j(s_i, Y)$ for all j and $c_{p\,q}$ ($p \neq q$) is a messages sequence in the channel from process p to q after every process j has executed $R_j(s_i, Y)$.

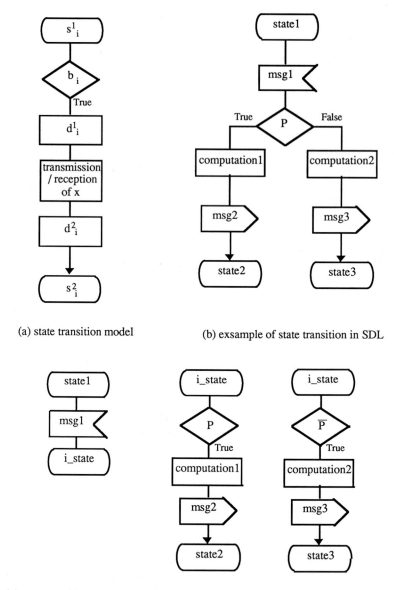

Fig. 2 state transition in the protocol model

It is easily understood that, for all i, the least global state for the initial state o_i is the initial global state $G_0=(S_0, C_0)$.

For an executable state transition from s_i to s_i', we can consider a least global state transition from G to G', where G is the least global state for s_i and G' is that for s_i'. During the least global state transition from G to G', a sequence of transitions that must have occurred before the transition from s_i to s_i' is executed in every process.

Definition 6: N sequences $(Y_1, \cdots, Y_j, \cdots, Y_N)$ are said to be a set of interacting sequences for a state s_i iff Y_j is $R_j(s_i, Y_i)$ for each process j $(1 \leq j \leq N)$, where Y_i is a sequence of transitions from state o_i to state s_i in process i.

In the acyclic expansion algorithm, least global states are used to obtain executable transitions, and every time an executable transition is obtained and attached to a transition graph, the least global state for the state reached by the executable transition is also obtained. As a result, each state in the obtained transition graphs has information of the least global state for the state. Since the least global state for a state s_i is reached by least global state transitions from the initial global state, a set of interacting sequences for s_i can be easily obtained using the least global state information.

4. Requirements

Requirements for protocols are unambiguously described using the branching-time temporal logic[1],[2],[5] (BTL). The advantage of BTL is that it can deal with all sequences at once. This enables description and reasoning of requirements such as "for every sequence from a state s_i, $\cdots$" or "there exists a sequence from s_i such that $\cdots$." As a result, concise description of requirements is possible.

For the verification system, a requirement is given as a BTL formula defined at a state of a process. We call this state "current state." The formal syntax of BTL is given as follows. AP is the underlying set of atomic propositions.
(1) Every atomic proposition $p \in AP$ is a formula.
(2) If f_1 and f_2 are formulas, then $\neg f_1$, $f_1 \wedge f_2$, $f_1 \Rightarrow f_2$, $\forall X f_1$, $\exists X f_1$, $\forall [f_1 U f_2]$ and $\exists [f_1 U f_2]$ are also formulas.

Here, the symbols $\neg$, $\wedge$, $\Rightarrow$ denotes negation, logical product, implication, respectively. X is the nexttime operator; the formula $\forall X f_1$ means that f_1 holds in every successor of the current state, and $\exists X f_1$ means that f_1 holds in some successors of the current state. U is the until operator; the formulas $\forall [f_1 U f_2]$ means that for every sequence there exists an initial prefix of the sequence such that f_2 holds at the last state and f_1 holds at all other states along the prefixes, and $\exists [f_1 U f_2]$ means that there exists such an initial prefix of the sequence for some sequence.

Using these operators, it is possible to speak about various kinds of requirements. For example, "For every sequence, f_0 eventually holds" is expressed as a formula, $\forall[\text{True} U f_0]$.

The semantics of BTL formulas is defined with respect to an executable state transition graph $W_i = (H_i, T_i, P_i)$, where
(1) H_i is a finite set of reachable states of process i.
(2) T_i is a finite set of executable transitions of process i.
(3) $P_i : H_i \rightarrow 2^{AP}$ assigns to each state the set of atomic propositions true in that state.

Although BTL formulas are defined on the graph W_i, BTL formulas can contain propositions speaking about the behaviors of processes other than process i. Such a formula can be evaluated using the least global state information for each state in W_i and interacting sequences obtained from least global states.

5. Protocol Verification Method

As mentioned in Section 2, the verification system is composed of three main parts, (a), (b), and (c) in Fig.1. The part (a) extracts information of state transitions in each process out of an SDL specification. The part (b) constructs a state transition graph for each process using the information of state transitions. And the part (c) evaluates a BTL formula on the obtained executable state transition graphs.

The procedures for construction of executable state transition graphs by the part (b) are further detailed in the following. The number of processes is denoted by N.

Let Z_i be a temporary set of least global states for states of process i ($1 \leq i \leq N$). Let W_i be a temporary executable state transition graph for process i. Initially, $Z_i = \phi$.
(1) For each i ($1 \leq i \leq N$), add to Z_i the initial least global state G_0. Let W_i be a node representing the initial state o_i with the information of the least global state for o_i (e.i., G_0) and the initial values of variables.
(2) If $Z_i = \phi$ for all i ($1 \leq i \leq N$), then go to (3). While there exists i such that $Z_i \neq \phi$, pick up a least global state G for a state s_i from Z_i, remove it from Z_i, and execute (2.1) and (2.2) for every executable send-transition from s_i. If s_i has no executable transition, then start this step from the beginning.
   (2.1) Let $(s_i, b_i, d^1_i, x, d^2_i)$ be the executable send-transition from s_i and let $s'_i = \text{succ}_i(s_i, b_i, d^1_i, x, d^2_i)$, where $x \in W_{ij}$. Obtain the least global state G' for s'_i from G, and add G' to Z_i. Derive values for variables at s'_i from those at s_i. Expand the graph W_i by attaching an edge and a node representing a transition from s_i to s'_i and a state s'_i, respectively. The information of G' and the variable values at s'_i are assigned to the node.
   (2.2) Find an executable receive-transition $(s_j, b_j, d^1_j, x, d^2_j)$ in process j, where x is the same message as in (2.1). Obtain the least global state G'' for the next state $s'_j = \text{succ}_j(s_j, b_j, d^1_j, x, d^2_j)$ from the least global state for s_j, and add G'' to Z_j. Derive variable values at

s'_j from those at s_j. Expand the graph W_j by attaching an edge and a node representing a transition from s_j to s'_j and a state s'_j, respectively. The information of G" and the variable values at s'_j are assigned to the node. Repeat this step (2.2), until all executable receive-transition for x have been processed.

(3) Output the obtained executable state transition graphs $W_1, \cdots, W_N$. Stop.

When the above procedures are finished, a set of executable state transition graphs, in which every node representing a state has the information of the least global state and the values for variables, is obtained. In part (c), a BTL formula representing a requirement is evaluated on the obtained graphs. If the formula is defined at a state s_i, evaluation is executed on the graph W_i.

For example, suppose that "$\forall [\text{TrueU} f_0]$ at o_i" is given as a requirement, where f_0 is a proposition. Then, every node of the graph W_i is searched starting the node for o_i up to the final node of every path, checking whether f_0 holds at each node. If f_0 is a proposition on variable values, the information of variable values are used. If f_0 is related to interacting sequences, the information on least global states attached to each node is used, since an interacting sequence is identical with a set of least global state transitions. If a node where f_0 holds is found in every path of W_i, then "$\forall [\text{TrueU} f_0]$ at o_i" is evaluated as true, otherwise false.

6. Protocol Verification Example

In this section, a verification example is presented using a protocol called broadcasting protocol[9]. This is a typical example of multi-process distributed protocols, among which are connectivity test protocols, minimum-hop-path protocols and path-updating protocols for routing[7],[9]. Automatic verification of such protocols has not been made by the previous techniques[1],[2],[3].

The broadcasting protocol consists of N (≥ 2) processes, representing communication nodes, and L ($\leq N \times N$) channels, representing communication links. Each process is connected by channels to some other processes called neighbors, and each process except one process has a pointer indicating one of its neighbors called preferred neighbor. The pointers form a directed tree routed at the process which does not have a pointer. This process is called SINK. (An example is shown in Fig. 3.) Intuitively, a message containing the information to be broadcast, MSG, is sent uptree from SINK to the leaves of the tree, and its acknowledgement, MSGACK, is sent downtree to SINK. Each process i has a set of variables, $\{Ni(k) \mid 0 \leq k \leq N-1, k \neq i\}$. Each value of $Ni(k)$ has the following meaning.

"NIL"   process i has not received yet any message from the neighbor k.
"RCVD"   process i has received MSG or MSGACK from the neighbor k.
"FINAL" process i has received MSG or MSGACK from all neighbors.

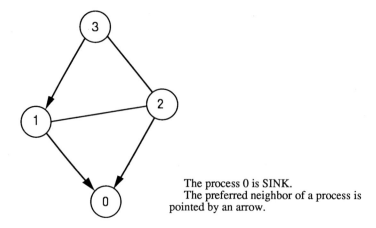

Fig. 3 Topology of the broadcasting protocol.

Fig. 4(a) and (b) show the action of SINK and that of an arbitrary process i except SINK, respectively, which are described in SDL. For convenience, OUTPUTs of the same message to all neighbors are specified as a single OUTPUT to "all neighbors."

Typical requirements for the protocol are: (1) MSG from SINK will be broadcast to all processes within finite time, and (2) MSGACK from all processes will be eventually delivered to SINK and all processes will terminate.

These requirements are formally described using the BTL as follows.
(1) $\forall\ j(1 \leq j \leq N\text{-}1)\ [\forall\ [\text{TrueUf}_1]$ at the initial state S1 of process j], where f_1 is a proposition that process j reaches state S2.
(2) $\forall\ [\text{TrueUf}_2]$ at the initial state S1 of SINK $\wedge\ \forall j(0 \leq j \leq N\text{-}1)\ [L_j(\text{the last state S3 in SINK}, Y) = $ the last state S3 in process j], where f_2 is a proposition that SINK reaches state S3, and Y is a sequence of messages from the initial state S1 to the last state S3 in SINK.

The first requirement represents reachability of state S2 in each process. The second requirement represents a fair termination for all sets of interacting sequences for SINK. The requirements on such kind of reachability and fairness are efficiently verified using interacting sequences by the verification system .

Given the SDL specification of the broadcasting protocol with the topology shown in Fig. 3, the verification for the requirements expressed as the above BTL formulas has been performed by the verification system. As the actual input to the system, the specification in the textual Phrase Representation (SDL/PR) was used, while the specification is expressed using

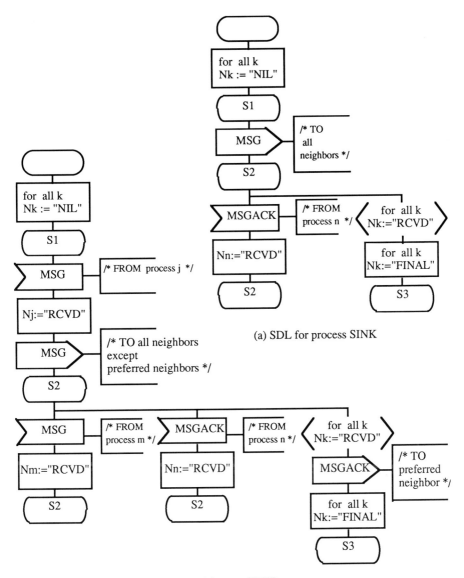

(a) SDL for process SINK

(b) SDL for an arbitrary process i (except SINK)

Fig. 4 SDL/PR for Processeses in the broadcasting protocol

the Graphic Representation (SDL/GR) in Fig.4. In Fig. 3, a process and a channel between processes are denoted by a circle and a line which connects two of the circles, respectively. The preferred neighbor of a process is indicated by an arrow on the line. Note that collection of the preferred neighbors forms a directed tree routed at SINK.

The executable state transition graphs obtained are shown in Fig. 5. (Intermediate states are omitted for convenience.) In Fig. 5, ovals denote states, arrows denote executable transitions, labels attached to a state s_i denote the least global state for s_i and a set of values of the variables Ni(k), and labels attached to an arrow denote messages transmitted or received during the transitions. In Fig. 5, states connected by dotted lines are equivalent states. If two states representing the same state in the specification have the same least global state and same values for every variable, then they are regarded as the same state. In the figure, bold lines represent a set of interacting sequences for S3 of SINK. A sequence chart representing these interacting sequences is shown in Fig. 6. Each set of interacting sequences thus corresponds to a sequence chart.

The formula (1) is evaluated on a graph M_j, and the formula (2) is evaluated on M_0 using the least global state information. As seen in Fig. 5, the formula (1) becomes true because state S2 is included in every sequence of executable transitions to reach the final states S3 in all processes. The formula (2) also becomes true for the following reason. The process SINK reaches state S3 through any sequences of executable transitions. All the values of $L_j(s_i, Y)$ at state S3 in SINK are S3 as denoted by (3, 3, 3, 3) in the figure. The given two requirements are thus proven to be satisfied.

7. Conclusion

This paper has presented a protocol verification system for SDL specifications based on the acyclic expansion algorithm and a temporal logic.

The distinctive features of the system is as follows.

(1) A requirement is expressed unambiguously and concisely as a branching-time temporal logic formula.
(2) All possible behaviors of the protocol, e.i., all executable state transitions of each process are obtained by the acyclic expansion algorithm extended such that it can compute values for variables at each state and evaluate an enabling condition for each transition.
(3) Among the state transition graphs consisting of executable transitions of each process, only the graphs of the processes relevant to the requirement are examined to evaluate the formula representing the requirement.

Considering that many practical communication systems consist of a number of processes and that usually only some of the processes are involved in a requirement, the presented verification system provides efficient verification for practical protocols. The verification has

523

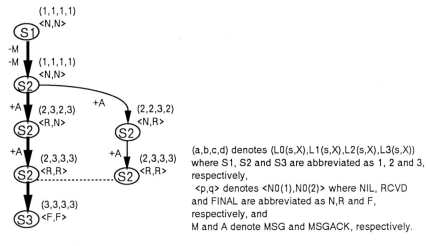

(a) Executable state transition graph of process 0 (SINK)

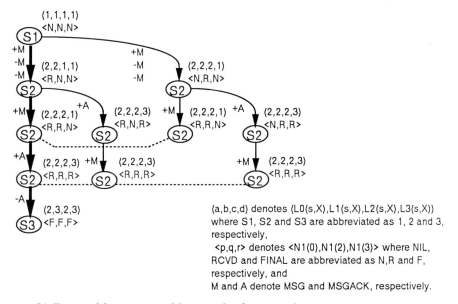

(b) Executable state transition graph of process 1

Fig. 5 Executable state transition graphs for the broadcasting protocol

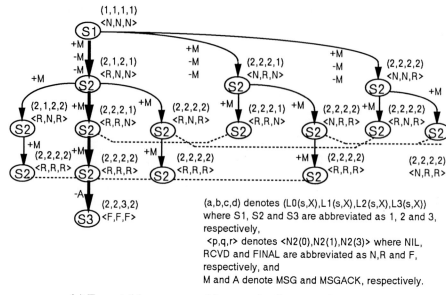

(c) Executable state transition graph of process 2

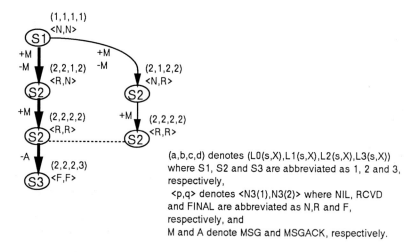

(d) Executable state transition graph of process 3

Fig. 5 Executable state transition graphs for the broadcasting protocol (continued).

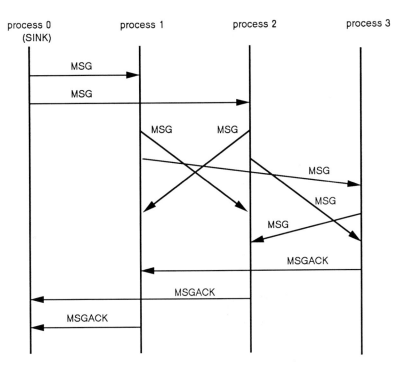

Fig. 6 Sequence chart for interacting sequences.

been illustrated by application to the broadcasting protocol. It is expected that the protocol verification system will be of wide applicability in practical protocol specification design.

Acknowledgements

The authors would like to express their sincere thanks to Dr. K. Ono, Dr. M. Yamada, Dr. Y. Urano, Mr. S. Ando and Mr. K. Konishi of R&D Laboratories of Kokusai Denshin Denwa Co., Ltd.(KDD) for their general guidance and encouragements. They greatly appreciate Mr. Y. Wakahara of KDD R&D Laboratories for his useful suggestions on this study. Thanks are also due to the members of Mitsubishi Research Institute, Inc., especially Mr. N. Yanagawa, for their support to development of the protocol verification system.

References

[1] A. R. Cavali and F. Horn : "Proof of specification properties by using finite state machines and temporal logic," Protocol Specification, Testing and Verification VII, pp.221-233, North Holland (1987).

[2] E. M. Clark, E. A. Emerson and A. P. Sistla: "Automatic verification of finite-state concurrent systems using temporal logic specifications," ACM Trans. on Programming Languages and Systems, 8, 2, pp.244-263 (April 1986).

[3] T. A. Joseph, T. Raeuchle and S. Toueg : "State machines and assertions (An integrated approach to modelling and verification of distributed systems)," Tech. Rep. TR84-652, Dept. of Computer Science, Cornell University (Nov. 1984).

[4] Y. Kakuda, Y. Wakahara and M. Norigoe: "An acyclic expansion algorithm for fast protocol validation," IEEE Trans. Soft. Eng., SE-14, 8, pp.1059-1070 (Aug. 1988).

[5] Y. Kakuda and Y. Wakahara : "Automatic protocol verification using temporal logic with predicate," IEICE Japan, Tech. Group Paper FTS89-14 (June 1989) in Japanese.

[6] M. T. Liu : "Protocol engineering," Advances in Computers, 29, pp.79-195 (1989).

[7] P. M. Merlin : "Specification and validation of protocols," IEEE Trans. Commun., COM-27, 11, pp.1671-1680 (Nov. 1979).

[8] CCITT Recommendation Z.100, Melbourne (Nov. 1988).

[9] A. Segall : "Distributed network protocols," IEEE Trans. on Information Theory, IT-29, 1, pp.23-35 (Jan. 1983).

[10] Y. Wakahara, Y. Kakuda, A.Ito and E. Utsunomiya : "Escort: an environment for specifying communication requirements," IEEE Software, pp.38-43 (March 1989).

Process Algebra Traces Augmented with Causal Relationships

C.J. Fidge

Key Centre for Software Technology, Department of Computer Science, The University of Queensland, Queensland 4072, Australia

Abstract

Process algebraic specification languages, i.e., CSP, CCS, LOTOS, etc., are semantically founded in the notion of interleaved traces of events. Unfortunately such traces are inadequate when the dimension of "real" time is considered since a totally ordered trace cannot model two or more time-consuming events overlapping in time. As a first step towards solving this problem, it is explained how, through a simple notational device, conventional traces can be augmented to retain causal event relationships. As a concrete illustration, a constructive definition of Basic LOTOS is given in terms of partially ordered traces. The resultant properties are discussed and their applicability outlined. An implementation of these concepts, as a trace generator, is described.

1 Introduction

The "process algebra" specification languages, i.e., CSP (Hoare, 1985), CCS (Milner, 1989), and their numerous derivatives, are defined using interleaving operational semantics. Typically the behaviour of a CSP operator is defined as a set of sequential traces, whereas CCS-like languages use a tree of possible transitions. However the net effect is equivalent; in both cases a total ordering is imposed on all events, with those that may occur "concurrently" being arbitrarily interleaved. This approach has two serious drawbacks.

Firstly, parallelism operators are not primitive: any process definition containing a parallelism operator can be replaced by an equivalent expression that does not use parallelism (Degano et al., 1988). For example, the following LOTOS (ISO, 1987) behaviour expression,

$$(\text{a; stop}) \; ||| \; (\text{b; stop}) \qquad (1)$$

i.e., actions a and b performed in parallel, may generate the following traces

$$\{\langle\rangle, \langle a\rangle, \langle a, b\rangle, \langle b\rangle, \langle b, a\rangle\}$$

exactly the same set of traces defined by

$$(\text{a; b; stop}) \; [] \; (\text{b; a; stop}) \qquad (2)$$

i.e., a choice between action a followed by b, or *vice versa*.

Secondly, the interleaving model hinders attempts to introduce the dimension of "real" time into the languages (e.g., Janicki and Koutny, 1990). Although interleaving is adequate for describing logical behaviour, temporal modelling requires the ability to represent two or more events occurring at exactly the same instant. Attempts to overcome this in the past have involved extending traces to either sequences of bags of simultaneous events (e.g., Liu and Shyamasundar, 1990; Gerber et al., 1988), or sequences of time/event pairs (e.g., Reed and Roscoe, 1987). Unfortunately the events must be instantaneous; time-consuming actions, with distinct start and end points, cannot be modelled in this way[1].

Herein we take a first step toward overcoming these problems by introducing a simple notational device for augmenting traditional totally ordered traces with sufficient information to recover the causal relationships between events, i.e., we define "partially ordered traces". A constructive definition and its practical implementation are then described for Basic LOTOS.

A number of papers on partially ordered semantics for CCS have appeared recently, but these have been mathematically oriented and somewhat intimidating. Our aim here is to show that the benefits of partial orders can be introduced into LOTOS clearly and unobtrusively.

2 Notation

The behaviour of process algebraic operators can be defined using the set of all possible totally ordered *traces* they allow, where a trace is a sequence of *events* (i.e., dynamic instances of static *actions*) up to some point in time (Hoare, 1985). (Strictly speaking fine points such as nondeterminism must be captured separately via the "refusals" of a process, but this is not central to our current concerns.) For instance, the possible traces of the following LOTOS behaviour expression

$$(\text{a; b; stop}) \; [] \; (\text{c; exit}) \qquad (3)$$

are

$$\{\langle\rangle, \langle a\rangle, \langle a, b\rangle, \langle c\rangle, \langle c, \delta\rangle\}$$

where δ is the special event representing successful termination. Our aim is to preserve this model, merely augmenting it in an unobtrusive way to allow the partial ordering to be recovered.

We define a *partially ordered trace* to be sequence of events, each of which is subscripted with a set of transitive *successor pointers*. These pointers are indexes to the positions

---

[1] Attempting to model time-consuming actions with separate "start" and "finish" events introduces the further complication of requiring indivisible event sequences (c.f., Gorrieri et al., 1990).

of those following events in the trace, if any, that the current event can directly causally affect.

For example, behaviour expression

```
(a; (b; exit ||| c ; exit)) >> (d; stop)
```

may generate the following partially ordered trace

$$\langle a_{\{2,3\}}, b_{\{4\}}, c_{\{4\}}, d_{\{\}} \rangle \tag{4}$$

This trace tells us that event a preceded both b and c and that these two events preceded d in the partial ordering. However neither b or c are successor to one another—they can thus be seen to have occurred in parallel, a fact not derivable from the totally ordered trace $\langle a, b, c, d \rangle$.

Referring back to the motivational examples in the introduction, expression 1 defines the following partially ordered traces

$$\{\langle\rangle, \langle a_{\{\}}\rangle, \langle a_{\{\}}, b_{\{\}}\rangle, \langle b_{\{\}}\rangle, \langle b_{\{\}}, a_{\{\}}\rangle\}$$

whereas example 2 has traces

$$\{\langle\rangle, \langle a_{\{\}}\rangle, \langle a_{\{2\}}, b_{\{\}}\rangle, \langle b_{\{\}}\rangle, \langle b_{\{2\}}, a_{\{\}}\rangle\}$$

Although their conventional traces are indistinguishable, the above partially ordered traces clearly model the difference between the two examples. With this new notation the parallelism operator is now fundamental—there is no way to generate a trace such as $\langle a_{\{\}}, b_{\{\}} \rangle$ without it.

When considered as digraphs there are clearly many equivalent partially ordered traces. For instance trace 4 above is isomorphic to

$$\langle a_{\{2,3\}}, c_{\{4\}}, b_{\{4\}}, d_{\{\}} \rangle \tag{5}$$

although their totally ordered interpretations differ.

Representations in which a successor of an event appears earlier in the trace, e.g.,

$$\langle a_{\{3,4\}}, d_{\{\}}, b_{\{2\}}, c_{\{2\}} \rangle$$

need not be considered since the corresponding totally ordered traces are not valid traces of the original behaviour expression.

3 Formal Treatment

Our goal is to define a function *potraces* which, given a LOTOS behaviour expression, will return the set of all possible partially ordered traces that the expression may perform. To facilitate the definition of this function it is helpful to know which events an expression may perform at the next step. We will therefore freely borrow formal notation for "traces" from Hoare (1985) and "labelled transition rules" from Bolognesi and Brinksma (1987).

The central issue is the need to identify which future events each event must point to. For instance expression

$$(a;\ b;\ \text{stop})\ |||\ (c;\ d;\ \text{stop}) \qquad (6)$$

may generate the following totally ordered trace

$$\langle c, a, d, b \rangle$$

Although event c is followed in the sequence by events a, d and b, it can only causally affect, and hence point to, event d. That is,

$$\langle c_{\{3\}}, a_{\{4\}}, d_{\{\}}, b_{\{\}} \rangle$$

To achieve this we need additional information. Therefore, for the purposes of the formal definition only, we use an internal representation in which all behaviour expressions B are superscripted with a unique "process identifier" p, one for each dynamic parallel process created. These identifiers must be allocated in such a way that it is possible to tell whether one process is a descendant of another process or not. Also each event e in a trace is superscripted with a set of process identifiers Q denoting all processes that participated in its performance. To avoid needlessly cluttering the following rules, we allow the superscripts to be omitted where they are not relevant.

3.1 Trace Operators

To simplify the definition of the trace derivation rules we first introduce some operators on traces (c.f., Hoare, 1985). Let the *head* events of a trace be all those events with no predecessors in the partial ordering and the *tail* events be all those without successors. For example, trace

$$\langle a_{\{3\}}, b_{\{3,4\}}, c_{\{5,6\}}, d_{\{6\}}, e_{\{\}}, f_{\{\}} \rangle$$

has head events a and b and tail events e and f.

Concatenation. The concatenation operator, "$\wedge$", joins two traces by making all tail events in the first trace point to all head events in the second. For example,

$$\langle a_{\{2,3\}}, b_{\{\}}, c_{\{\}} \rangle ^\wedge \langle d_{\{2,4\}}, e_{\{\}}, f_{\{4\}}, g_{\{\}} \rangle = \langle a_{\{2,3\}}, b_{\{4,6\}}, c_{\{4,6\}}, d_{\{5,7\}}, e_{\{\}}, f_{\{7\}}, g_{\{\}} \rangle$$

Notice that the pointers in the second trace must all be incremented by the length of the first trace.

Termination. This is a predicate which is true iff the given trace has successfully terminated, i.e., it has one tail event and that event is δ. For example,

$$term(\langle a_{\{\}}, b_{\{\}} \rangle) = \text{False}$$

$$term(\langle a_{\{3\}}, b_{\{3\}}, \delta_{\{\}} \rangle) = \text{True}$$

Composition. The trace "composition" operator (c.f., Hoare, 1985), ";", is similar to concatenation but has a special meaning with respect to successfully terminated traces. If the first argument has successfully terminated then it removes the last event (i.e., δ

and all pointers to it), and concatenates the traces. If the first trace has not successfully terminated then it simply returns the first argument. For example,

$$\langle a_{\{\}}, b_{\{\}}\rangle; \langle c_{\{3\}}, d_{\{3\}}, e_{\{\}}\rangle = \langle a_{\{\}}, b_{\{\}}\rangle$$

since the first trace has not terminated, but

$$\langle a_{\{3\}}, b_{\{3\}}, \delta_{\{\}}\rangle; \langle c_{\{3\}}, d_{\{3\}}, e_{\{\}}\rangle = \langle a_{\{3,4\}}, b_{\{3,4\}}, c_{\{5\}}, d_{\{5\}}, e_{\{\}}\rangle$$

Prepend. The prepending operator, "$\stackrel{P}{\frown}$", adds a new event to the start of a trace t, so that it points to every event e^Q in t where there exists a process identifier in set Q that is equal to, or a descendant of, any process identifier in set P, and no predecessors of e^Q in the partial ordering defined by t exhibit this property. This operator is central to the definition of partially ordered traces. It allows a new event to selectively point to only those events that it may causally affect since they were performed by the same parallel process, or offspring of the current parallel process. For example, assume that we are going to insert a new event c, performed by process set $\{2\}$, at the start of the following trace $\langle a_{\{3\}}^{\{1\}}, d_{\{\}}^{\{2\}}, b_{\{\}}^{\{1\}}\rangle$. (This situation arises when constructing the traces of example 6.) The new event will point to event d since that event was also performed by the same process, but it will not point to event a nor b since these events were not performed by process 2, or a "child" of process 2. That is,

$$c \stackrel{\{2\}}{\frown} \langle a_{\{3\}}^{\{1\}}, d_{\{\}}^{\{2\}}, b_{\{\}}^{\{1\}}\rangle = \langle c_{\{3\}}^{\{2\}}, a_{\{4\}}^{\{1\}}, d_{\{\}}^{\{2\}}, b_{\{\}}^{\{1\}}\rangle$$

As with the concatenation operator the pointers in the second argument must be adjusted to account for the new trace length.

3.2 Trace Derivation Rules

In this section we give rules for deriving the set of partially ordered traces associated with all Basic LOTOS operators.

Inaction. The stop operator is the unit of the LOTOS algebra. It does nothing and can therefore only generate the empty trace:

$$potraces(\texttt{stop}^p) = \{\langle\rangle\}$$

Action prefix. When some action a is performed, followed by some behaviour expression B, then that action is simply prepended to the traces of B:

$$potraces((a;B)^p) = \{\langle\rangle\} \cup \{a \stackrel{\{p\}}{\frown} t \mid t \in potraces(B^p)\}$$

For the internal action i we will assume that the special event τ is left in the trace to mark the occurrence of the "unobservable" event:

$$potraces((\texttt{i};B)^p) = \{\langle\rangle\} \cup \{\tau \stackrel{\{p\}}{\frown} t \mid t \in potraces(B^p)\}$$

Choice. A choice between two behaviour expressions B and C simply generates all possible traces for both:

$$potraces((B[]C)^p) = potraces(B^p) \cup potraces(C^p)$$

Successful termination. The exit operator can only perform the special action δ indicating normal termination:

$$potraces(\texttt{exit}^p) = \{\langle\rangle, \langle\delta_{\{\}}^{\{p\}}\rangle\}$$

Enabling. The sequential composition operator, >>, allows the second argument to proceed when the first has successfully terminated:

$$potraces((B\texttt{>>}C)^p) = \{s; t \mid s \in potraces(B^p) \wedge t \in potraces(C^p)\}$$

Disabling. The disabling operator, [>, allows the first behaviour expression to be interrupted at any time before it successfully terminates by the second:

$$\begin{aligned}potraces((B\texttt{[>}C)^p) = {} & \{s \mid s \in potraces(B^p) \wedge term(s)\} \cup \\ & \{s{\frown}t \mid s \in potraces(B^p) \wedge t \in potraces(C^p) \wedge \neg term(s)\}\end{aligned}$$

The first of these sets covers the maximal, successfully terminating, traces of behaviour expression B. The second set describes those traces where B has not yet terminated or the execution of B is interrupted by that of C.

The above definitions have all been straightforward; they differ little from their counterparts in Hoare (1985). The same process identifier p has been used throughout since all events have been performed within one particular process. The remaining operators are more complex since they must cater for multiple parallel processes and the possibility that a particular event involves the participation of two or more processes.

Hiding. The hide operator allows the actions named in the set A to be performed by process B as if they are internal actions. The definition is therefore in two parts, firstly for the unaffected actions, and secondly for the "hidden" ones.

$$\frac{B^p - a^Q \to B1^p \wedge a \notin A}{\{a \stackrel{Q}{\frown} t \mid t \in potraces((\texttt{hide }A\texttt{ in }B1)^p)\} \subseteq potraces((\texttt{hide }A\texttt{ in }B)^p)}$$

This is read as "if behaviour expression B (in process p) is capable of performing action a (involving subprocesses Q of p) and then transforming into expression $B1$, and a is not in the set of hidden events A, then the set of traces defined by prepending a to the traces of $B1$ is a subset of the partially ordered traces of B with actions A hidden" (c.f., Bolognesi and Brinksma, 1987). The set of process identifiers Q is used to allow for the possibility that B consists of several parallel processes, one or more of which perform action a.

Where the event to be performed is in the set of hidden events the rule is almost identical except that the action name is replaced by τ:

$$\frac{B^p - a^Q \to B1^p \wedge a \in A}{\{\tau \stackrel{Q}{\frown} t \mid t \in potraces((\texttt{hide }A\texttt{ in }B1)^p)\} \subseteq potraces((\texttt{hide }A\texttt{ in }B)^p)}$$

Finally, the above rules do not explicitly state that the null trace is possible, i.e.,

$$\{\langle\rangle\} \subseteq potraces((\texttt{hide }A\texttt{ in }B)^p)$$

Together the three rules above fully define the possible traces of **hide**; no other traces are possible.

General Parallelism. In the general parallelism operator two behaviour expressions B and C are performed independently except that they share a user-defined set of actions S, and the special termination action δ, which they must perform simultaneously. Firstly consider the case where process B can perform an event in isolation:

$$\frac{B^{p'} - a^Q \rightarrow B1^{p'} \wedge a \notin S \cup \{\delta\}}{\{a \stackrel{Q}{\frown} t \mid t \in potraces((B1 \mid S \mid C)^p)\} \subseteq potraces((B \mid S \mid C)^p)}$$

Process identifiers p', and p'' below, are distinct "children" of identifier p. The above rule prepends any event that may be performed by process B to the traces of events performed by the entire parallel construct. The $\stackrel{Q}{\frown}$ operator ensures that event a will only point to those events performed by $B1$ or its offspring.

A complementary rule defines the traces created by the second process performing an event in isolation:

$$\frac{C^{p''} - a^R \rightarrow C1^{p''} \wedge a \notin S \cup \{\delta\}}{\{a \stackrel{R}{\frown} t \mid t \in potraces((B \mid S \mid C1)^p)\} \subseteq potraces((B \mid S \mid C)^p)}$$

When an action is shared by both processes they must simultaneously perform it:

$$\frac{B^{p'} - a^Q \rightarrow B1^{p'} \wedge C^{p''} - a^R \rightarrow C1^{p''} \wedge a \in S \cup \{\delta\}}{\{a \stackrel{Q \cup R}{\frown} t \mid t \in potraces((B1 \mid S \mid C1)^p)\} \subseteq potraces((B \mid S \mid C)^p)}$$

Since the shared event involved the participation of all processes named in sets Q and R, their union is used by the $\frown$ operator.

Once again, for completeness, the null trace must be considered:

$$\{\langle\rangle\} \subseteq potraces((B \mid S \mid C)^p)$$

The remaining parallelism operators are merely special cases of the general parallelism operator above.

Full Synchronisation. With the $||$ operator all events are shared except for the special internal event τ. Either the first,

$$\frac{B^{p'} - \tau^Q \rightarrow B1^{p'}}{\{\tau \stackrel{Q}{\frown} t \mid t \in potraces((B1 \mid\mid C)^p)\} \subseteq potraces((B \mid\mid C)^p)}$$

or second,

$$\frac{C^{p''} - \tau^R \rightarrow C1^{p''}}{\{\tau \stackrel{R}{\frown} t \mid t \in potraces((B \mid\mid C1)^p)\} \subseteq potraces((B \mid\mid C)^p)}$$

process can perform an internal event alone, but any other event must be shared:

$$\frac{B^{p'} - a^Q \rightarrow B1^{p'} \wedge C^{p''} - a^R \rightarrow C1^{p''} \wedge a \neq \tau}{\{a \stackrel{Q \cup R}{\frown} t \mid t \in potraces((B1 \mid\mid C1)^p)\} \subseteq potraces((B \mid\mid C)^p)}$$

As usual the only other trace allowed is null:

$$\{\langle\rangle\} \subseteq potraces((B \mid\mid C)^p)$$

Pure Interleaving. With the ||| operator there are no shared events except the special termination event δ. (Partially ordered traces make "pure interleaving" a misnomer for the ||| operator because it is now used in those cases where all actions from different operands are unordered, rather than interleaved.) Either the first,

$$\frac{B^{p'} - a^Q \to B1^{p'} \land a \neq \delta}{\{a \stackrel{Q}{\frown} t \mid t \in potraces((B1 \mid\mid\mid C)^p)\} \subseteq potraces((B \mid\mid\mid C)^p)}$$

or second,

$$\frac{C^{p''} - a^R \to C1^{p''} \land a \neq \delta}{\{a \stackrel{R}{\frown} t \mid t \in potraces((B \mid\mid\mid C1)^p)\} \subseteq potraces((B \mid\mid\mid C)^p)}$$

process may independently perform any event, except for δ:

$$\frac{B^{p'} - \delta^Q \to B1^{p'} \land C^{p''} - \delta^R \to C1^{p''}}{\{\langle \delta_{\{\}}^{Q \cup R}\rangle\} \subseteq potraces((B \mid\mid\mid C)^p)}$$

Again, only the null trace is otherwise possible:

$$\{\langle\rangle\} \subseteq potraces((B \mid\mid\mid C)^p)$$

Finally, parameterised process definitions may be used to associate a name with a behaviour expression. The introduction of partially ordered traces has no significant effect on the way process definitions are described. See Bolognesi and Brinksma (1987) for their formal treatment.

4 Properties

Each partially ordered trace can be represented as a digraph. Whenever two or more traces are interpreted as partially ordered and define the same digraph, e.g., as do traces 4 and 5 in section 2, they are considered to be identical. Given this assumption most of the LOTOS laws for observation congruence (ISO, 1987), denoted $\approx^c$, are valid for partially ordered traces. The principal distinction is the expansion theorem for parallelism.

(**Internal action and hide.** To simplify the rules in section 3.2 it was assumed that τ explicitly appears in traces. Unfortunately this assumption invalidates desirable laws such as

$$a;\mathtt{i};B \approx^c a;B$$

This problem can be corrected by defining more complex rules for action prefix and hiding, or via a postprocessing function to remove τ from traces. However, since this is irrelevant to our central theme, i.e., improved definition of parallelism, we ignore this distraction from now on.)

Expansion theorem. Assume $\sum\{B_1,\ldots,B_n\}$ denotes $B_1[]\cdots[]B_n$. Let $B = \sum\{b_i;B_i \mid i \in I\}$ and $C = \sum\{c_j;C_j \mid j \in J\}$. Now that parallel composition is primitive, and cannot be simulated via action prefix and choice, the expansion theorem for general parallelism no longer holds, i.e.,

$$B \mid [A] \mid C \not\approx^c \quad \sum\{b_i;(B_i \mid [A] \mid C) \mid b_i \notin A \wedge i \in I\}$$
$$[] \quad \sum\{c_j;(B \mid [A] \mid C_j) \mid c_j \notin A \wedge j \in J\}$$
$$[] \quad \sum\{a;(B_i \mid [A] \mid C_j) \mid a \in A \wedge a = b_i = c_j \wedge i \in I \wedge j \in J\}$$

For instance,

$$(b;\ \text{stop} \mid [] \mid c;\ \text{stop})$$

has partially ordered traces

$$\{\langle\rangle, \langle b_{\{\}}\rangle, \langle b_{\{\}}, c_{\{\}}\rangle, \langle c_{\{\}}\rangle, \langle c_{\{\}}, b_{\{\}}\rangle\}$$

whereas

$$(b;\ (\text{stop} \mid [] \mid c;\ \text{stop}))\ []\ (c;\ (b;\ \text{stop} \mid [] \mid \text{stop}))$$

has a different set of traces

$$\{\langle\rangle, \langle b_{\{\}}\rangle, \langle b_{\{2\}}, c_{\{\}}\rangle, \langle c_{\{\}}\rangle, \langle c_{\{2\}}, b_{\{\}}\rangle\}$$

Parallel. The remaining laws involving parallelism, e.g., for associativity, etc., are still valid. Most notably,

$$B \mid [] \mid C \approx^c B \mid\mid\mid C$$
$$B \mid [A] \mid C \approx^c B \mid\mid C, \quad (L(B) \cup L(C)) \subseteq A$$

where $L(X)$ is the observable "alphabet" of behaviour expression X.

To compensate for the loss of the expansion theorem we add the following two laws,

$$(a;B \mid\mid a;C) \approx^c a;(B \mid\mid C)$$
$$(a;B \mid [A] \mid a;C) \approx^c a;(B \mid [A] \mid C), \quad a \in A$$

In other words, when all parallel behaviour expressions synchronise on the same action we can substitute prefix. Such synchronisation is never possible for $\mid\mid\mid$ (excluding δ).

5 Application

To demonstrate the practical value of partially ordered traces we return to the motivation mentioned in section 1, real-time analysis of specifications. Consider the following specification of a distributed system,

$$(a;\ b;\ d;\ e;\ \text{stop} \mid [d] \mid c;\ d;\ f;\ \text{stop})$$

Assume that we are told that each parallel process will reside on its own dedicated processor and that, either through experimental measurement or formal analysis, the following absolute-time durations have been established for each of the actions:

action	duration
a	1
b	2
c	4
d	2
e	5
f	1

Our task now is to determine whether or not this specification will satisfy two real-time requirements: (i) the end of action a and the start of action d must always be separated by at least 3 time units, and (ii) action f must always be completed within 9 time units of the start of the computation.

The set of "maximal" totally ordered traces (i.e., those that have terminated, either successfully or due to deadlock) for this computation is

$$\{\langle a,b,c,d,e,f\rangle, \langle a,c,b,d,e,f\rangle, \langle c,a,b,d,e,f\rangle,$$
$$\langle a,b,c,d,f,e\rangle, \langle a,c,b,d,f,e\rangle, \langle c,a,b,d,f,e\rangle\}$$

The third and sixth of these traces show actions a and d separated only by action b. Since b has duration 2 this suggests that requirement (i) has not been met.

The first three traces show action f taking place after all others. Adding the durations for actions a to e thus gives a starting time for f of 14 time units from the beginning of the computation. Requirement (ii) also appears to be violated.

These naïve conclusions can be shown to be erroneous, however, when we use partially ordered traces. Consider the following maximal trace:

$$\langle a_{\{2\}}, b_{\{4\}}, c_{\{4\}}, d_{\{5,6\}}, e_{\{\}}, f_{\{\}}\rangle$$

(All six traces above are isomorphic to this single trace when partial orders are considered.) Graphically we can represent this as

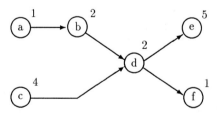

where we have annotated each node with the duration of the action.

Observe that in such a representation the time at which each action begins is the length of the *longest* path back to the origin of the graph. For instance, although action d follows a and b (3 time units in total), it must also wait for action c to complete, and hence cannot begin until 4 time units after the beginning of the computation. A simple (and automatable) graph traversal procedure allows us to arrive at the following time values for each action:

action	start time	stop time
a	0	1
b	1	3
c	0	4
d	4	6
e	6	11
f	6	7

It is clear from this table that both requirements (i) and (ii) *are* in fact satisfied by the specification (given the assumption about dedicated processors). Actions a and d are separated by exactly 3 time units and action f ends at time 7. The additional information concerning concurrency made available by the subscripts has given us an insight into the real-time behaviour of this specification not possible from the set of totally ordered traces alone.

Partially ordered semantics are valuable in other contexts too. It has been argued that they offer multiple observers an accurate distinction between parallelism and nondeterminism, allow for modelling of continuous time, make reasoning about liveness properties easier, and offer support for variable granularity, i.e., where a previously "atomic" action is refined into subactions (Pratt, 1986).

6 Implementation

To validate the rules in section 3 we have implemented a partially ordered trace generator for Basic LOTOS in the functional language Miranda[2] (Turner, 1986). All of the above rules, plus parameterised process definitions, were implemented.

Inevitably trace generators suffer severely from a "state explosion" and ours is no exception. In an attempt to optimise the generator, and avoid overwhelming the user with output, there are two ways in which the number and size of traces produced are restricted.

Firstly, only maximal traces are returned. For instance example 3 returns the following traces only

$$\{\langle a_{\{2\}}, b_{\{\}}\rangle, \langle c_{\{2\}}, \delta_{\{\}}\rangle\}$$

(although the full set of traces is easily derived by taking all prefixes of the maximal traces).

Secondly, the maximum length of each trace generated can be limited (default 20). Users must beware of this feature since it can lead to misleading traces. Consider the following example

(a; (b; exit ||| c; exit))

with a maximum trace length set to only two. The traces generated under these circumstances are:

$$\{\langle a_{\{2\}}, b_{\{\}}\rangle, \langle a_{\{2\}}, c_{\{\}}\rangle\}$$

---

[2]Miranda is a trademark of Research Software Ltd.

The fact that event a precedes both b and c at the same time is not obvious due to the premature truncation of the traces. Of course a maximum trace length of four or more in this case will result in the full set of traces being generated:

$$\{\langle a_{\{2,3\}}, b_{\{4\}}, c_{\{4\}}, \delta_{\{\}}\rangle, \langle a_{\{2,3\}}, c_{\{4\}}, b_{\{4\}}, \delta_{\{\}}\rangle\}$$

(In its present form the tool does not recognise that the two traces above are equivalent when interpreted as partially ordered.)

Despite these optimisations the trace generator still rapidly exhausts heap space when used with non-trivial examples. Nevertheless, it has sufficed to confirm the validity of the derivation rules above.

7 Related Work

Attempting to define non-linear semantics for process algebraic languages is by no means a new goal. This section contrasts our achievements herein with some of the prominent work in this area.

Nielsen et al. (1990) offer a taxonomy for representations of the behaviour of concurrent, nondeterministic systems. Their classifications are, from least to most powerful,

Firing sequences: the system generates strings of events. A given string contains no information concerning choice or concurrency.

Traces: each computation is represented by a set of equivalent firing sequences. Information regarding concurrency is retained (due to the equivalence of differently interleaved sequences) but choice is lost.

Non-sequential processes: each computation is represented as a labelled partially-ordered set of events. Again information about concurrency is retained, but not choice.

Labelled event structures: all possible computations are represented by a single partially ordered set of event occurrences. Information regarding both concurrency and choice is retained.

They then formally prove that traces, non-sequential processes and finite configurations extracted from labelled event structures are equivalent.

In terms of this classification we can see that our original starting point in section 1, i.e., a totally ordered trace, is equivalent to only the first level, "firing sequences". Our solution remains compatible with this traditional notion while simultaneously providing the benefits of partial ordering. Each trace generated by *potraces* can also be interpreted as partially ordered, by considering the subscripts, in which case they are equivalent to the third classification, "non-sequential processes".

Motivated by a desire to make parallelism a first-class operator, Degano et al. (1990) recently defined the operational semantics of CCS via a "partial ordering derivation relation". Each CCS term is decomposed into sets of *sequential* processes. Where there is parallelism a derivation rule may change only part of the global state, leaving the remainder unaltered. Each rule therefore has the form

$$I - [\mu, R] \to I'$$

where I is a set of sequential terms, μ is the action performed, I' is the set of terms resulting from an element of I performing μ and R is a causal ordering relation between sequential terms. R is used to hold those terms from I which are concurrent with the performance of μ, i.e., the terms in R are "caused" by set I but do not follow μ in the partial ordering.

Strong parallels can be drawn between the key features of these derivation rules and the work described herein. Where Degano et al. (1990) decompose CCS agents into their sequential components we have used so-called "process identifiers" to make the same distinction. Where they use relation R to maintain knowledge of causal relationships, we explicitly construct these via the "prepending" operator. Indeed, like our work, the derivations of Degano et al. (1990) may be "observed" as either interleavings or partial orders of events, thus also yielding a power equivalent to either "firing sequences" or "non-sequential processes". (Whenever a derivation rule resolves a nondeterministic choice the information about that choice is discarded, i.e., "branching-time" structure is not preserved.)

An approach equivalent to the fourth category is that of Reisig (1984). He (non-constructively) defines partially ordered operational semantics for CSP aided by an exceptionally clear graphical representation. The semantics of a process are represented by a relation between configurations (local states) and actions; each configuration leads to the next via an action and *vice versa*. All possible behaviours for a CSP program are represented in a single (typically infinite) tree, and particular computations are subsets of this tree. An interesting feature of this tree-like representation is the precise distinction it displays between nondeterminism and concurrency. Concurrent behaviour appears as actions with two or more outgoing arcs, and nondeterministic choice between possible futures appears as a state with two or more outgoing arcs.

In an earlier work Degano et al. (1987) described a tree-based representation of computations that respects branching-time and is thus also equivalent to a "labelled event structure". The nodes of this tree are computations, constructed using the trace derivation rules mentioned above, ordered by a prefix relation. This higher-level structure thus maintains knowledge of nondeterministic alternatives, information not found in individual partially ordered traces.

That we do not match the sophistication of Reisig (1984) or Degano et al. (1987) is a measure of our desire to keep the model as simple as possible, and anchored to the traditional low-level notion of totally ordered traces. It should be stressed that the set of partially ordered traces defined by *potraces* contains *all* possible behaviours. Such a set does not satisfy the criteria for categorisation as a "labelled event structure" merely because those points at which nondeterministic choices affected future behaviour are not readily identifiable. (Differing traces with identical prefixes *can* be used to identify branching-time decisions, but a genuine labelled event structure makes these points explicit.)

There have been a number of earlier designs for partially ordered trace semantics, particularly for CCS—see Degano et al. (1990) for an extensive list of references. Also note that partial orders have received considerable attention outside the domain of process algebraic languages (e.g., Pratt, 1986; Janicki and Koutny, 1990).

8 Conclusion

This brief paper has introduced a notation for defining partially ordered traces for the process algebraic specification languages. A formal definition for Basic LOTOS, and a corresponding "trace generator" implementation, have been discussed. We have aimed to retain the pleasing simplicity and elegance that has made the totally ordered trace model so popular during the last decade. By avoiding too onerous a presentation we hope to have convinced the reader that the concepts underlying partially ordered semantics are not as formidable as the more mathematically oriented work in this field may seem to suggest.

Acknowledgements. I wish to thank all those who reviewed earlier drafts of this paper for their helpful suggestions, and the FORTE referees for their insightful comments. This work was supported by an Australian Postdoctoral Research Fellowship and an Australian Telecommunications and Electronics Research Board Project Grant.

References

BOLOGNESI, T. and BRINKSMA, E. (1987): Introduction to the ISO Specification Language LOTOS, *Computer Networks and ISDN Systems*, 14(1), pp. 25–59.

DEGANO, P., DE NICOLA, R., and MONTANARI, U. (1988): A Distributed Operational Semantics for CCS Based on Condition/Event Systems, *Acta Informatica*, 26, pp. 59–91.

DEGANO, P., NICOLA, R. D., and MONTANARI, U. (1987): Observational Equivalences for Concurrency Models, In Wirsing, M., editor, *Formal Description of Programming Concepts III*, pp. 105–132. North-Holland.

DEGANO, P., NICOLA, R. D., and MONTANARI, U. (1990): A Partial Ordering Semantics for CCS, *Theoretical Computer Science*, (75), pp. 223–262.

GERBER, R., LEE, I., and ZWARICO, A. (1988): *A Complete Axiomatization of Real-Time Processes*, Technical Report MS-CIS-88-88, University of Pennsylvania.

GORRIERI, R., MARCHETTI, S., and MONTANARI, U. (1990): A2CCS: Atomic Actions for CCS, *Theoretical Computer Science*, (72), pp. 203–223.

HOARE, C. (1985): *Communicating Sequential Processes*, Prentice-Hall.

ISO (1987): *Information Processing Systems - Open Systems Interconnection - LOTOS - A Formal Description Technique Based on the Temporal Ordering of Observational Behaviour*, International Organisation for Standardisation, ISO/TC 97/SC21.

JANICKI, R. and KOUTNY, M. (1990): Observing Concurrent Histories, In Zedan, H., editor, *Real-Time Systems, Theory and Applications*, pp. 133–142. Elsevier.

LIU, L. and SHYAMASUNDAR, R. (1990): Static Analysis of Real-Time Distributed Systems, *IEEE Transactions on Software Engineering*, 16(4), pp. 373–388.

MILNER, R. (1989): *Communication and Concurrency*, Prentice-Hall.

NIELSEN, M., ROZENBERG, G., and THIAGARAJAN, P. (1990): Behavioural Notions for Elementary Net Systems, *Distributed Computing*, 4(1), pp. 45-57.

PRATT, V. (1986): Modeling Concurrency with Partial Orders, *International Journal of Parallel Programming*, 15(1), pp. 33-71.

REED, G. and ROSCOE, A. (1987): Metric Spaces as Models for Real-Time Concurrency, In Main, M. et al., editors, *Mathematical Foundations of Programming Language Semantics*, pp. 331-343. Springer-Verlag, LNCS 298.

REISIG, W. (1984): Partial Order Semantics versus Interleaving Semantics for CSP-like Languages and its Impact on Fairness, In Paredaens, J., editor, *Automata, Languages and Programming, 11th Colloquium*, v. 172 Lecture Notes in Computer Science, pp. 403-413.

TURNER, D. (1986): An Overview of Miranda, *ACM SIGPLAN Notices*, 21(12), pp. 158-166.

Fairness in LOTOS

Cheng Wu and Gregor v. Bochmann

Département d'informatique et de recherche opérationnelle, Université de Montréal, C.P. 6128, Succ "A", Montréal, P.Q., Canada, H3C 3J7

Abstract
Fairness is an important concept related to specification languages that are based on concurrent and non-deterministic computation models; it is related to liveness. In this paper we formally introduce fairness into the LOTOS specification language by employing the standard LOTOS semantics together with a formalism which states restrictions on fair infinite execution sequences. We extend three fairness concepts of CSP, namely process, guard and channel fairness, to LOTOS. Certain features of LOTOS, such as the dynamic creation of processes, the dynamic relation between gates and processes, and related membership in multi-way rendezvous, not present in CSP, make the definition of fairness difficult. We introduce the concept of "transition groups", which leads to a general notion of fairness, and use LOTOS action indexes to define the concepts of process, alternative and channel for LOTOS. We explain how a fair execution model for LOTOS can be obtained, and demonstrate the use of these concepts by showing how fairness assumptions can be used to prove liveness properties for a given LOTOS specification.

1. INTRODUCTION

Specification languages such as LOTOS[1], CSP[2], etc. are used to describe distributed systems which are based on concurrent and non-deterministic computation models. Fairness is an important property related to such models, which is related to liveness [3]. Liveness properties are usually described as "good things will eventually happen" and fairness properties are usually described as "if something is always or infinitely often ready then it will eventually happen". So, if one can show that a "good thing" meets some conditions such as being always or infinitely often ready, then fairness assumptions will lead to the related liveness properties, that is, "it will eventually happen". For example, a fairness property of an unsafe channel could be "if a sender insists on (always) putting messages into the channel, the receiver will receive infinitely many messages". It is obvious that the liveness property of "message A will eventually reach its receiver through the unsafe channel" holds if the sender repeatedly puts message A into the channel.

Besides obtaining proof systems, another motivation for studying fairness properties is to design execution models or algorithms which provide fair execution. This makes sure that properties proved to hold at the specification level based on fairness assumptions will also hold for the implementation.

A variety of fairness properties have been proposed in the context of different specification languages. For example, three kinds of fairness, namely process fairness, guard fairness and channel fairness, are defined for CSP [4]; process fairness has also been defined in CCS [5,6]. So far, little work has been done about fairness in LOTOS.

LOTOS [1,7] is an FDT (Formal Description Technique) which has been standardized within ISO (International Standard Organization). It was developed for formally specifying communication protocols and services in the context of OSI (Open System Interconnection) standards. However, it is suitable for many other applications in distributed systems. A LOTOS specification usually describes two aspects. The aspect of interaction parameters and associated data structures and operations is described using an abstract data type formalism. The aspect of the temporal ordering of the interactions is described using a formalism close to CCS [8]. In this paper, we are principally concerned with the latter aspect.

LOTOS prescribes infinite execution sequences without regard to fairness. For example, for the specification of an unsafe channel

```
process unsafe_channel[send, receive]:noexit:=
    send; (i; unsafe_channel[send,receive]
    []
    receive; unsafe_channel [send,receive])
endproc
```

the execution sequence **send, i, send, i, ...** is allowed by LOTOS semantics, which means the channel may lose all input messages.

Certain features of LOTOS make the definition of fairness difficult. Recursion in LOTOS can be used to define a loop (e.g. **P[g]:= g;P[g]**), as well as the dynamic creation of processes (e.g. **P[g]:= g; (g; stop) ||| P[g]**). Gates in LOTOS do not uniquely determine the process performing the action (e.g. **P[g]:= (g; stop) ||| (g;stop)**). In addition, multi-way rendezvous is allowed in LOTOS and the number of processes involved in a rendezvous may change dynamically from one occurrence of a rendezvous to another. Because of all of these aspects, it is not very clear what fairness means in the context of LOTOS specifications.

In this paper, we introduce fairness into Basic LOTOS. We do not mean by this to change the current standard definition of LOTOS, but rather to introduce fairness restrictions. We follow the approach of the so-called 'two level semantics', that is, we first introduce an unfair model, and then define certain restrictions which must be satisfied for fair execution sequences. We employ the standard LOTOS semantics [1] at the first level. We define process, alternative (guard) and channel fairness in LOTOS by defining suitable restrictions. They are extensions of the corresponding fairness concepts in CSP [4]. We also show the application of the fairness definitions, namely the proof of liveness properties and the construction of fair execution models.

The paper is organized as follows. Section 2 is a short introduction to linear temporal logic and labelled transition systems, two formal systems which are used in this paper. In Section 3, we introduce the concept of "grouping transitions", which provides a framework for defining fairness. We describe the intuitive meanings of our fairness definitions for LOTOS in Section 4, and define these concepts formally in Section 5. Section 6 discusses the proof of liveness properties based on fairness assumptions. Section 7 discusses the construction of fair execution models. Finally, Section 8 contains some conclusions.

2. THEORETICAL FRAMEWORK

2.1. Linear Temporal Logic

Fairness properties are related to infinite execution histories. Usually so-called "weak fairness" and "strong fairness" properties are described informally as "if permanently (always) A then eventually B" and "if infinitely often A then eventually B" respectively. Temporal Logic can be used to describe temporal concepts such as *permanently(always), infinitely often* and *eventually* [3,4,9].

Besides ordinary logical operators **or, and, not**, and $\Rightarrow$ (implies), Linear Temporal Logic [10,11] uses two temporal operators $\Diamond$ and $\Box$. The expression $\Box P$ (read "henceforth P") means that P is true now and will always be true in the future, and $\Diamond P$ (read "eventually P") means that P is true now or will be true sometimes in the future. These operators are usually interpreted based on a computation model of state sequences. The two temporal operators can also be combined. For example, $\Diamond\Box$ P means from a certain time onwards permanently P and $\Box\Diamond$ P means infinitely often P.

Now we are able to define the concepts of "weak fairness" and "strong fairness", mentioned above, in terms of temporal logic. A property of the forms $\Diamond\Box$ A $\Rightarrow \Diamond$B is a weak fairness assertion, and a property of the form $\Box \Diamond$A $\Rightarrow \Diamond$B is a strong fairness assertion.

2.2. Labeled transition systems

In this section, we consider Labeled Transition Systems, the model in which the LOTOS semantics is defined [1]. We will show how the concepts of temporal logic can be used in this context to define fairness properties.

Definition 2.1. A *labeled transition system* is a triple $\text{LTS}=(S,T,\{\text{-t->}\}_{t \in T})$ where,
- S is a countable set of states
- $T = \{t_1, t_2, ...\}$ is a set of labeled transitions
- $\{\text{-t->}\}_{t \in T}$ is a set of binary relations on S ($S \times S \supseteq$ -t->) in bijection with the labeled transitions.

A sequence of transitions, starting from some initial state of the transition system, defines at the same time a sequence of states which are reached after each of the transitions. This sequence of states may be used to defined temporal properties, using the formalism of temporal logic. One particular state predicate we are interested in indicates whether a transition of a given label is enabled in a given state, as given in Definition 2.3. However, we are also interested in the question whether a given type of transition has been executed, as defined in Definition 2.4; however, this information is not directly visible from a given state. Therefore we introduce the concept of "transition state" which corresponds to the pair of a transition label and a state, where the label corresponds to the last executed transition which led to the state in question.

Definition 2.2. An *execution history* **h** is a sequence of transition states $s_0(\varepsilon), s_1(t_1), s_2(t_2), ...$, where $s_i \in S$, $t_i \in T$ and $<s_{i-1},s_i> \in$ -t_i->, and $s_0(\varepsilon)$ is an initial transition state.

Definition 2.3. For a given state $s \in S$, a transition labelled **t** is said to be *enabled* iff $\exists s'$ (s -t -> s'). For a given transition state s(t'), a transition labelled **t** is said to be *enabled*, written as ENABLED(t), iff **t** is enabled at s.

Definition 2.4. For a given transition state s(t') in an execution history **h**, a transition labelled **t** is said to be *executed*, which is denoted as EXECUTED(t), iff **t** = t'.

We can combine the two assertions ENABLED and EXECUTED with the two temporal operators $\Box$ and $\Diamond$, which are defined in Section 2.1. For instance, $\Diamond\Box$ ENABLED(t) means transition **t** is (from a certain time onwards) **always** enabled; $\Box\Diamond$ ENABLED(t) means transition **t** is **infinitely often** enabled; $\Box\Diamond$ EXECUTED(t) means transition **t** is **infinitely often** executed. For the example of Figure 1, for the execution history $\mathbf{h} = s_1(\varepsilon), s_2(t_3), s_1(t_3), s_2(t_3),...$ (that is alternatively $s_1(t_3)$ and $s_2(t_3)$), $\Diamond\Box$ ENABLED(t_1)= **false**, $\Box\Diamond$ENABLED(t_1)=**true**, and $\Box\Diamond$ EXECUTED(t_3)=**true**.

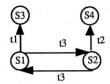

Figure 1: A labeled transition system

Therefore the following definitions are reasonable:

Definition 2.5. (Weak fairness for a labeled transition *t*) An infinite execution history **h** respects *weak fairness* for a labeled transition **t** if it satisfies

◊☐ ENABLED(t) ⇒ ☐◊ EXECUTED(t)

Definition 2.6. (Strong fairness for a labeled transition *t*) An infinite execution history **h** respects *strong fairness* for a labeled transition **t** if it satisfies

☐◊ ENABLED(t) ⇒ ☐◊ EXECUTED(t)

2.3. Serialized models vs. overlapping models

In some literature, two types of models, namely *a serialized model* and *an overlapping model*, are considered to specify distributed systems (see [3]). The overlapping model is closer to the nature of distributed systems, while the serialized model is easier to reason about. The two models are different as far as fairness is concerned. Caused by a so-called *conspiracy* phenomenon in the overlapping model, a fair execution history for the overlapping model may not be fair for the serialized model (see also [3]). In the rest of this paper, we consider only the serialized model, because the LOTOS semantics are defined on an interleaving (serialized) model [1].

3. GROUPING LABELED TRANSITIONS

In certain papers (e.g.[12]), fairness properties are related to the idea of "grouping interesting events". That is, properties are described in the following form: "if a group of events which are of interest become possible infinitely often, then events of this group will happen infinitely often". In this section, we introduce several concepts which are related to grouping labeled transitions. They will provide the later basis for defining fairness for LOTOS specifications.

3.1. Grouping labeled transitions

The following definitions, theorems and corollaries are always with respect to a labeled transition system **LTS=(S,T,{-t->}** $_{t \in T}$**)**, as defined in the previous section.

Definition 3.1. We call a *transition group* **g** any non-empty sub-set of **T**. We call a *grouping* **G={g1, g2,...}** any set of groups such that **T** = $\cup_{g \in G}$ **g**. (Note: groups need not be disjoin).

Definition 3.2. A transition group **g** of **T** is said to be enabled at state s∈ S, denoted as ENABLED(g), if ∃t∈ g such that ENABLED(t).

Definition 3.3. Let **h** be an execution history, a labeled transition group **g** of **T** is said to be executed in **h**, denoted as EXECUTED(g), if $\exists t \in g$ such that EXECUTED(t).

Definition 3.4. (g-fairness) The followings are fairness properties with respect to a transition group **g**

(*weak g-fairness*) $\Diamond\Box$ ENABLED(g) $\Rightarrow \Box\Diamond$ EXECUTED(g)
(*strong g-fairness*) $\Box\Diamond$ ENABLED(g) $\Rightarrow \Box\Diamond$ EXECUTED(g)

Definition 3.5. (G-fairness) The followings are fairness properties with respect to a grouping **G** of transitions

(*weak G-fairness*) $\forall g \in G\ (\Diamond\Box$ ENABLED(g) $\Rightarrow \Box\Diamond$ EXECUTED(g))
(*strong G-fairness*) $\forall g \in G\ (\Box\Diamond$ ENABLED(g) $\Rightarrow \Box\Diamond$ EXECUTED(g))

Theorem 3.1.
strong g-fairness $\Rightarrow$ weak g-fairness
strong G-fairness $\Rightarrow$ weak G-fairness

Proof (omitted).

Theorem 3.2. Given a finite number of transition groups g_i (i = 1,...,n) and $g = \bigcup_{i=1}^{n} g_i$. Any execution history **h** which is strongly g_i-fair for all i=1,...,n is also strongly g-fair.

Proof See the proof in [13].

Note the theorem above is not true for weak fairness, which is shown by the example in Figure 1. Let $g=\{t1,t2\}$, $g_1=\{t1\}$ and $g_2=\{t2\}$, the execution history $h = s_1(\epsilon), s_2(t_3), s_1(t_3), s_2(t_3),...$ (that is alternatively $s_1(t_3)$ and $s_2(t_3)$), respects weak g_1-fairness as well as weak g_2-fairness, but not weak g-fairness.

Definition 3.6. (Minimal Liveness) Weak T-fairness is called *Minimal Liveness*.

Minimal Liveness ensures that as long as there are transitions possible, the system will make a move, that is, execute a transition. In other words, Minimal Liveness ensures that the system stops only if it enters a terminal or blocked state.

Corollary 3.1. (of Theorem 3.1 and Theorem 3.2) Let **T** be finite and **G** be any grouping, then

strong G-fairness $\Rightarrow$ Minimal Liveness.

Proof See the proof in [13].

Corollary 3.2. (of Theorem 3.2) Let **T** be finite and let **G'** and **G"** be two groupings such that for all $g" \in G"$, there exists $G' \supseteq G$ such that $g" = \bigcup_{g \in G} g$, then

strong **G'**-fairness $\Rightarrow$ strong **G"**-fairness

3.2. Process fairness

In this section, we define process fairness for a distributed system based on the concepts of Section 3.1. Distributed systems usually involve a collection of processes. Process fairness is informally described as "if a process is always (or infinitely often) enabled, then it is infinitely often executed".

We use a Labeled Transition System to describe a distributed system. A transition is *local* if it is contributed by one process, that is, it specifies a local action of that process; a transition is *joint* if it is contributed by more than one process, that is, it corresponds to communication among several processes (rendezvous). Then we have the following definitions:

Definition 3.7. (Process) Given a process **P**, we call $p = \{t \mid f_P(t)\}$ the *transition group of process P*, where $f_P: T \rightarrow \{true, false\}$ is the *process assignment function* for process **P** which is defined as

$f_P(t) = $ **true**   if **t** denotes either a local action of process **P** or a communication in which process **P** is involved, or

            false   otherwise.

Definition 3.8. (Fairness for process P)
1) *Weak fairness for process P* is weak fairness in respect to the transition group of **P**;
2) *Strong fairness for process P* is strong fairness in respect to the transition group of **P**.

4. PROCESS, ALTERNATIVE AND CHANNEL FAIRNESS IN LOTOS

It is known that different fairness properties can be defined for a given computation model or specification language. For LOTOS, for instance, "gate fairness" can be defined as follows: if a gate is always (infinitely) enabled, it will be eventually executed. But gates in LOTOS do not uniquely determine the process or the alternative performing the action. For example, the "gate fairness" above does not ensure that the LOTOS program P[a]:= a; P[a] [] a; stop will eventually terminate when gate **a** is always enabled. So, the question turns out to be : What kind of fairness concepts are suitable for LOTOS?

"Process", "guard" and "channel" are three important concepts in CSP[2]. Related fairness definitions are given in [4]. We believe that such concepts are also important for LOTOS. In this paper we show how these concepts can be defined using the concept of transition groups, and how their definition can be extended to the more general context of LOTOS specifications.

4.1. Process, guard and channel fairness in CSP

Process, guard and channel are three important concepts which are related to the syntax of CSP. The syntax of a subset of CSP used in [4] is the follows, where neither the parallel operator ([...||...]) nor the choice operator (*[...]) is allowed to be used in a nested fashion.

Statements: S::= skip | x:=t | *[b1,c1 -> S1 [] ... [] bm,cm -> Sm] | S1;S2
(where t is an integer expression, b is a boolean expression and c is either
Pi!x or Pj?y, i,j $\in \{1, ...n\}$)

Programs: [P1::S1 || ... || Pn::Sn]
(where Pi, i$\in \{1...n\}$, is called a process. Processes have no shared variables)

The parallel operator [...||...] defines parallelism, that is, in the expression [**P1::S1** || ... || **Pn::Sn**], Pi (i = 1, ..., n) are called *processes* and can be executed in parallel with any **Pj** (j = 1, ..., n and j ≠ i), that is, the actions of **Pi** and **Pj** can be executed in any sequence (interleavings). The choice operator *[...] defines *alternatives*, that is, for the expression *[**b1,c1 -> S1 [] ... [] bm,cm -> Sm**], bi and ci (i = 1, ..., m) are called *guards* and if bi and ci are true Si is said be enabled and may be executed, and if there are more than one Si that are enabled then there is non-determinism. A pair of guards <g', g"> is called a *channel* if g' and g" are syntactically matching communication commands (e.g., Pi!x in Pj and Pj?y in Pi).

Informally, the related fairness concepts defined in [4] for CSP can be described as follows:

Weak (Strong) Process Fairness: Any process, that becomes permanently (infinitely often) enabled, must execute (infinitely often).

Weak (Strong) Guard Fairness: Any alternative, the guards of which become permanently (infinitely often) true, must be chosen (infinitely often).

Weak (Strong) Channel Fairness: Any channel, that becomes permanently (infinitely often) enabled, must be chosen (infinitely often).

If a labeled transition system is given for a CSP program, then the concepts process, guard and channel of CSP defined in [4] can be viewed as three ways of grouping transitions from the "grouping transition" point of view. More specifically, if we consider the transition system where each transition is labeled by either an action (denoting a local action of a process) or a pair of actions (denoting a rendezvous) (see the example of Figure 2), then we call a "process" the group of transitions containing an action which belongs to a syntactic CSP process; a "guard" the group of transitions containing an action which is in a specific position (of one syntactic CSP process) in the text of the CSP program; and a "channel" the group of transitions whose pair of actions (two syntactically matching actions) are in two specific positions (of two syntactic CSP processes) in the text of the CSP program. Then process, guard and channel *fairness* can be defined based on the framework of Section 3.

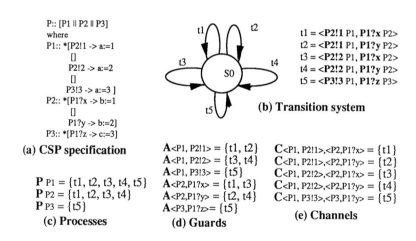

Figure 2: A CSP specification and its transition system

For example, the CSP program in Figure 2 defines three processes, six guards and channels. The execution history $h1 = s_0(\varepsilon), s_0(t_5), s_0(t_5), s_0(t_5), ...$ (that is, $h1$ consists of an infinite sequence of t_5 transitions) does not respect process fairness, because $P2$ is infinitely often enabled, but is not executed. The execution history $h2 = s_0(\varepsilon), s_0(t_5), s_0(t_1), s_0(t_5),$

$s_0(t_1),...$ (that is alternatively t_5 and t_1) does respect process fairness, but does not respect guard fairness, because $A_{P2!2} = \{t3, t4\}$ is infinitely often enabled and is not executed. The execution history $h3 = s_0(\varepsilon), s_0(t_1), s_0(t_3), s_0(t_5), s_0(t_1), s_0(t_3), s_0(t_5),...$ (that is, repeated sequence of t_1, t_3, and t_5) does respect guard fairness, but does not respect channel fairness, because $C_{<P2!1,P1?y>} = \{t2\}$ is infinitely often enabled and is not executed.

4.2. Process, alternative and channel fairness in LOTOS

In the context of CSP, as discussed above, the syntactic structure of the program reflects the structure of processes, alternatives and gates, directly. The process structure is static. This is not the case in LOTOS, where process instances may be created dynamically, possibly leading to complex communication relations between these processes, as defined by dynamically identified gates and multi-party rendezvous. In this dynamic setting, it is not so clear what the natural grouping of transitions is, related to the dynamically changing structure of processes.

In the following we propose groupings that correspond to the CSP groupings described above for the case of static process structure, and which seem also natural in the case of dynamic processes, as discussed below. For process fairness, we introduce a process hierarchy, where each process instance is the "father" of the process instances it creates. The transitions of the "child" processes are considered part of the "father's" transitions, as far as fairness for the "father" process is concerned. Concerning alternative fairness, we distinguish not only the syntactic alternatives shown in the program text, but also distinguish between a given alternative being executed by one or the other process instance. This allows a finer kind of alternative fairness, related to a particular process instance. Similar considerations apply for channel fairness. Note that such distinctions are not necessary in the static context of CSP where each alternative belongs to only one process instance.

In LOTOS, the keyword **process** is used to introduce a so-called process definition, that is, a process identifier and a behavior which it represents. In order to create a process instance, the process identifier must be invoked in a behavior expression. An initial process is defined which executes the behavior of the specification. We consider the following example:

    specification two_processes[a]:noexit:=
       behavior P[a](1) || P[a](2)
       where
       process P[a](x:int) :noexit:=
       a!x; P[a](x) [] a?y:int; P[a](x)
       endproc
    endspec

It contains one processes definition and two process instances executing in parallel, namely P[a](1) and P[a](2). The process definition contains two alternatives (a!1) and (a?y:int); we distinguish whether these alternatives are executed by the process instances P[a](1) or P[a](2). The specification contains three channels <a!1, a?y:int>, <a?y:int, a!2>, and <a?y:int, a?y:int> between P[a](1) and P[a](2); the fourth (syntactic) channel <a!1, a!2> does not allow any rendezvous, since the parameter values do not match.

In general, however, these concepts are not very clear because, in contrast to CSP, process instances can be created dynamically in LOTOS, possibly an unlimited number in the case of recursion (for example P:= a; ((b;stop) |||P)). Two process instances, possibly created by different father processes, may refer to the same process definition. For example, in the example above, P[a](1) and P[a](2) are two process instances of P[a](x:int); in the example of Figure 3, Q[a,b] creates P1[a,b], P2[a], and P3[b]. Note that process creations are introduced by the parallel operator || and |||. In the following, one process instance is called a *super-process* of the other if the former creates directly or indirectly the latter. Analogously, we have the concept of *sub-process*. As mentioned above, we consider that a super-process contains the transitions of its sub-processes. In the following, we introduce the concepts of "process", "alternative" and "channel" at the (dynamic) instance level, instead of at the (static) syntactic level (as done above for CSP). We will use again the idea of "grouping labeled transitions" to define these concepts and the corresponding fairness concepts.

For a given LOTOS specification, we assume that a labeled transition system is given according to the semantic definition of LOTOS, and that each of its transitions is labeled by a list of actions (LOTOS gates) $<a_{p1}, a_{p2}, ..., a_{pn}>$ ($n>0$). Transition $<a_{pi}>$ denotes a local action of process instance p_i, and $<a_{p1}, a_{p2}, ..., a_{pn}>$ ($n>1$) denotes a rendezvous which involves the process instances p_i ($i=1..n$) which do the action a_{pi}. For example, Figure 3(b) shows the transition system of the specification of Figure 3(a), which defines the same behavior as the CSP program shown in Figure 2.

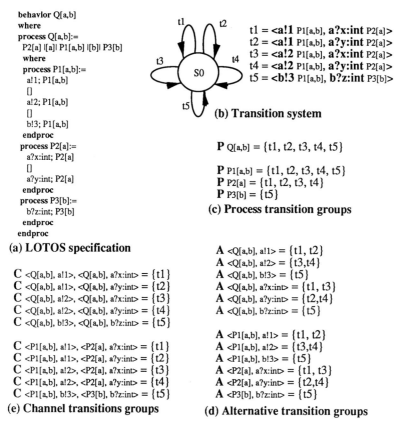

Figure 3: A LOTOS specification and its transition system

We define a *process transition group* P_p to be the group of transitions containing an action which belongs to a specific process instance **p** or its sub-process instances. We define an *alternative transition group* $A_{<p,l>}$ to be the group of transitions containing an action which is defined at a specific position l in the text of the LOTOS program and belongs to a specific process instance **p** or its sub-process instances. Finally, we define a *channel transition group* $C_{<p1,l1>,<p2,l2>,...,<pn,ln>}$ ($n \geq 1$) to be the group of transitions containing an action which is defined at a specific position l_i in the text of the LOTOS program and belong to a specific process instance p_i or its sub-process instances for each i (i=1..n). For example, the specification of Figure 3 defines four process transition groups, twelve alternative transition groups and ten channel transition groups (see Figure 3(c)). In this example, we use the interaction parameters (1 and z:int, etc.) to distinguish the different positions in the text of the specification. As the behavior of this specification is the same as for the CSP specification of Figure 2, it is not surprising that the process, alternative and channel transition groups of Figure 3 include those of Figure 2. However, Figure 3 also contains the groups belonging to the super-process **Q,** corresponding to the initial behavior of the specification.

Now we can define fairness properties as follows: for a given LOTOS specification, an execution history **h** is said to respect process (alternative, channel) fairness if it respects process (alternative, channel) transition group fairness for each process (alternative, channel) transition group defined for the LOTOS specification.

It is clear that alternative fairness, as defined here, ensures that the LOTOS program P[a]:= a; P[a] [] a; stop will eventually terminate when gate **a** is always enabled, which can not be guaranteed by "gate fairness" as mentioned at the beginning of this section.

It is obvious that the above concepts are extensions of the ones for CSP. The sub-set of CSP of Section 4.1 only allows two-way rendezvous and does not allow for process creation.

5. FORMALIZATION OF LOTOS FAIRNESS CONCEPTS

In this section, we will formalize the fairness concepts for LOTOS. For a given LOTOS specification, we first define a (syntactic) index for each action (gate) in the specification. Then, we build a labeled transition system with each of its transitions being labeled by a list of indexed actions. Finally, we characterize the groups of transition which we are interested in, based on action indexes, and define related fairness concepts based on the framework of Section 3.

5.1. LOTOS action indexes

In this section we define an index for each action in the LOTOS specification. For this purpose, we first consider the abstract syntax of the specification which is a set of trees. Each tree represents a process definition in the specification. We call each tree a *reference tree* and the set of trees the *reference forest*. In a given tree, internal nodes are LOTOS operators and leaf nodes are either actions (LOTOS gates) or **process** names which denote **process** instantiations (the word **process** here is a LOTOS term) (see Figure 4 (a) and (b)). Then we define *reference indexes* for each node of the reference forest. Reference indexes are assigned in such a way that no reference index occurs more than once at different nodes. Actually reference indexes define positions in the text of the LOTOS specification. For example, Figure 4(a) and (b) show reference forests with reference indexes. Let **RI** be the set of reference indexes for a given LOTOS specification. It is obvious that **RI** is finite.

Secondly we define a *reduction tree* for the given LOTOS specification. A reduction tree is obtained by replacing the process names (leaf nodes) of the reference tree with their (tree form) definitions (see Figure 5(a) and (b)). It is obvious that the reduction tree may be infinite due to recursion. Then we define indexes for the nodes of the reduction tree based on the reference indexes of the related reference forest. The following Table 5.1. shows the rules of building a reduction tree as well as the rules of indexing nodes of the tree, where l_B denotes the reference index of the related definition of **B** in the reference forest, $l_1 \cdot l_2$ is the concatenation of l_1 and l_2, and ε denotes the empty string. For example, Figure 5(a) and (b) show reduction trees with indexes. The leaf nodes of the reduction tree represent actions and their indexes are so-called action indexes which will be used in the rest of this paper. An index of an action is a tuple

<p,l>, where **p** and **l** are strings in **RI*** . We call **p** a *process index* (p-index), which is a process instance identification to which the action belongs, process instance **p1** is a super-process of process instance **p2**, written **p2≥p1**, if **p1** is prefix of **p2**. We call **l** a *location index* (l-index), which records the position of the action in the text of the LOTOS specification (l has a similar meaning as the control point of CSP in [4]).

Table 5.1.:

0) **behavior** → B (initial behavior)	B is indexed as <ε,ε>;
1) B → a; B1 (sequential execution)	if B has index <p,l> then **a** is indexed as <p, l·l$_a$>, B1 is indexed as <p, l$_{B1}$>;
2) B → B1 >> B2 (sequential execution)	if B has index <p,l> then B1 is indexed as <p, l·l$_{B1}$>, B2 is indexed as <p, l$_{B2}$>;
3) B → B1 [] B2 (alternatives) B → B1 [> B2 (B1 possibly disrupted by B2)	if B has index <p,l> then B1 is indexed as <p, l·l$_{B1}$>, B2 is indexed as <p, l·l$_{B2}$>;
4) B → B1 ‖ B2 (coupled parallelism) B → B1 ‖[S]‖ B2 (coupled parallelism) B → B1 ‖‖ B2 (independent parallelism)	if B has index <p,l> then B1 is indexed as <p·l$_{B1}$, l>, B2 is indexed as <p·l$_{B2}$, l>;
5) P → Bp (process invocation)	if P has index <p,l>, then Bp is indexed as <p, l>

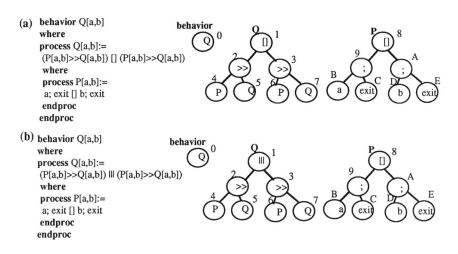

Figure 4: Reference forests and indexes

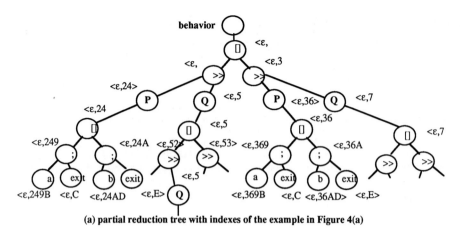

Figure 5: Two examples of reduction trees

The rationale for the above rules are as follows. For the rules concerning sequential execution and alternatives (in a broad sense, namely for the LOTOS operators ;, >>, [], and [>) the process index does not change, but the location index records the position corresponding to the LOTOS text. For the operators || and |||, two subprocesses are created, identified by a process index which has the index of the father process as prefix. In the case of a process invocation, neither the process index nor the location index are changed, since this construct corresponds to tail recursion and is normally used to define same form of looping behavior (conceptually no new "process").

In the example of Figure 5(b), for instance, the action **a** with index <2,49B> means that **a** belongs to the process instance **2**, as well as to process ε which is the super-process of the former. In the example of Figure 5(a), the index <ε,249B> of action **a** means that it belongs to the alternative **24** in the definition of Q as well as to the alternative **9B** in the definition of P (see Figure 4(a)). The **Q** node indexed by $<\varepsilon,5>$ appearing more than once in Figure 5(a) shows a loop in process ε.

5.2. Process, alternative, and channel transition groups, and the formalization of LOTOS fairness concepts

We can easily have a labeled transition system for a given LOTOS specification by directly applying the standard inference rules[1]. But here we are interested in having a labeled transition systems where each of its transitions is labeled by a list of indexed actions, instead of being labeled by a single LOTOS gate. This can be done by changing the standard inference rules as shown in the following two examples. In the following, we use notations such as **B**, **B1**, **B1'**,..., etc. to denote ordinary behaviors (behaviors without indexes) and **g**, **g1**,..., etc. to denote ordinary gates (gates without indexes). We use notations such as $\mathbf{B_I}$, $(\mathbf{B})_I$, $\mathbf{B1_{I1}}$,..., etc. to denote behaviors with indexes and $\mathbf{g_s}$, $\mathbf{g_r}$, $\mathbf{g_{s1}}$,..., etc. to denote gates with index. We use $=>_I$ to denote the application of the indexing rules defined in Table 5.1.

The standard LOTOS rules:

(1) g; B - g -> B

(2) $\dfrac{\text{B1 - g -> B1' and B2 - g -> B2' and g} \in \text{S}}{\text{B1 |S| B2 - g -> B1' |S| B2'}}$

are rewritten as:

(1)
$\dfrac{(g; B)_I =>_i g_s; B_{I'}}{(g; B)_I - <g_s> -> B_{I'}}$

(2)
$\dfrac{(B1|S|B2)_I =>_i B1_{I1}|S|B2_{I2} \text{ and } B1_{I1} - <g_{s1},...,g_{sn}> -> B1'_{I1'} \text{ and } B2_{I2} - <g_{r1},...,g_{rm}> -> B2'_{I2'} \text{ and } g \in S}{(B1 |S| B2)_I - <g_{s1},...,g_{sn},g_{r1},...,g_{rm}> -> B1'_{I1'} |S| B2'_{I2'}}$

Now we group transitions by using the action indexes and give related fairness definitions. The following definitions are in respect to a labeled transition system with a set of transitions **T** whose elements are lists of indexed actions. In the following definitions, **t** denotes an element of **T**.

Definition 5.1 (Process) Given a process **P**, we call the group $\{t \mid f_P(t)\}$ the *process transition group* of process **P** where $f_P: T \to \{\text{true, false}\}$ is the *process assignment function* for process **P** which is defined as

$f_P(<a_{<p1,\ l1>}\ ...,a_{<pn,\ ln>}>) =$
    true   if there is an $a_{<pi,li>}$ such that $p_i \geq p$, or
    false   otherwise

Definition 5.2 (Alternative) Given an alternative <p,l> (the alternative l in process p), we call the group $\{t \mid f_{<p,l>}(t)\}$ the *alternative transition group* of alternative <p,l> where $f_{<p,l>}$: T -> {true, false} is the *alternative assignment function* for alternative <p,l> which is defined as

$f_{<p,l>}(<a_{<p1, \; l1>} \ldots, a_{<pn, \; ln>}>) =$
    true   if there is an $a_{<pi,li>}$ such that $p_i \geq p$ and $l_i = l$, or
    false   otherwise

Definition 5.3. (Channel) Given a channel <p1,l1>,...,<pm,lm>, we call the group $\{t \mid f_{<p1,l1>,\ldots,<pm,lm>}(t)\}$ the *channel transition group* of channel <p1,l1>,...,<pm,lm> where $f_{<p1,l1>,\ldots,<pm,lm>}$: T -> {true, false} is the *channel assignment function* for channel <p1,l1>,...,<pm,lm> which is defined as

$f_{<p1,l1>,\ldots,<pm,lm>}(<a_{<p'1, \; l'1>} \ldots, a_{<p'n, \; l'n>}>) =$
    true   if n≥m and for all <p_i,l_i> there is an $a_{<p'j,l'j>}$ such that $p'_j \geq p_i$ and $l'_j = l_i$, or
    false   otherwise

Definition 5.4. (Process, Alternative, Channel fairness) *Weak (strong) process (alternative, channel) fairness* is weak (strong) fairness with respect to the transition groups of all processes (alternatives, channels) defined by the LOTOS specification.

Corollary From Theorem 3.1, we have the following: strong process (alternative, channel) fairness implies weak process (alternative, channel) fairness.

From the above definitions, it is obvious that for each process transition group **pg** there exists a set of alternative transition groups **AG'** such that $pg = \cup_{ag \in AG'} ag$ and for each alternative transition group **ag** there exist a set of channel transition groups **CG'** such that $ag = \cup_{cg \in CG'} cg$. Therefore, if T is finite, from Corollary 3.2, we have the following: strong channel fairness implies strong alternative fairness, and the latter implies strong process fairness.

6. PROVING LIVENESS

As discussed in Section 1, for concurrent and non-deterministic computation models such as in LOTOS, fairness properties (sometimes called fairness assumptions) are important for proving liveness properties. To build a proving system, one first needs to formalize the underlying computation model and its related fairness assumptions in a common formalism. Then the interesting liveness properties can be described in the same formalism. Finally, one uses the axioms and inference rules of the formalism to prove, manually or mechanically, the liveness properties of the specified system.

Temporal logic provides various axioms and inference rules [10,14]. Together with certain fairness assumptions, which are defined in terms of temporal logic, this formalism can be used to prove liveness properties for concurrent and non-deterministic computation models [4,3,14]. LOTOS semantics can be defined in terms of labeled transition systems [1] as well as temporal logic [15,16]. We believe that the fairness formalisms given in Sections 3 and 5 can be used as a basis for building a proof system for LOTOS specifications.

[13] shows several examples (including an example of dynamic creation of processes) of proving liveness for LOTOS specifications based on the fairness assumptions defined in this paper. it is also shown that the fairness assumptions are useful for proving liveness properties for more complex LOTOS specifications, such as the OSI Transport Service specification [17].

7. ON THE FAIR EXECUTION OF LOTOS SPECIFICATIONS

In this section, we discuss the construction of a 'fair execution model'. A fair execution model is one which will only produce finite or infinite execution sequences that are allowed by the specification and satisfy certain fairness assumptions (see Sections 3 and 5). Such a fair execution model is therefore a means for executing LOTOS specifications that satisfy those liveness properties that can be proved based on the underlying fairness assumptions, as discussed in the section above.

It is known that there are several ways of constructing fair execution model. One of them is based on **random choice**: whenever the system has several choices, it randomly selects one of them. [13] uses counters to count the execution time related to process, alternative and channel transition groups. The more a transition group is executed, the bigger its related counter is. The system always executes the transition group whose counter has the smallest value to ensure strong fairness respecting related transition groups. The results presented in [13] are based on the execution model of [18] in a centralized environment.

8. CONCLUSIONS

Fairness has been being studied in relation to various specification languages. In this paper, we defined process fairness, alternative fairness and channel fairness for LOTOS. these concept are extensions of those defined for CSP [4].

Certain features of LOTOS, such as the dynamic creation of processes, the dynamic relation between gates and processes, and related membership in multi-way rendezvous, not present in CSP, make the definition of fairness difficult. However, by introducing the concept of "transitions groups", we generalized the problem of defining fairness. The introduction of the concept of "action indexes" allows us to define the concepts of processes, alternatives and channels for LOTOS. We use temporal logic not only for clearly defining fairness properties, but also for proving liveness properties of LOTOS specifications, based on underlying fairness assumptions.

We have also considered the construction of fair execution models for LOTOS specifications. The approach of Section 7 works in a centralized environment. However, it turns out to be much more difficult to ensure fairness in a distributed execution environment [19,20]. This area needs further study.

ACKNOWLEDGEMENTS

This work was performed within the IDACOM-NSERC-CWARC Industrial Research Chair on Communication Protocols and was also supported by the Natural Sciences and Engineering Research Council of Canada under a strategic research grant, and the Ministry of Education of Quebec.

REFERENCES

1 "LOTOS - A formal description technique based on the temporal ordering of observational behavior", ISO, DIS 8807, 1987.
2 C. A. R. Hoare, "Communication Sequential Processes", Comm ACM 21(8), pp. 666 - 677, 1978.
3 Nissim Francez, "Fairness", Springer-Verlag New York, 1986.

4 Kuiper R, de Roever WP, "Fairness assumptions for CSP in a temporal logic framework", In Bjorner D (ed) Proceeding of TC.2 Working Conference on the Formal Description of Programming Concepts, Garmisch Partenkirchen, North Holland, 1983.
5 Costa, G., Stirling, C., "A fair calculus of communicating systems", Acta Informatica 21, pp. 417 - 441, Springer - Verlag, 1984.
6 Costa, G., Stirling, C., "Weak and strong fairness in CCS", Procs. of Symposium on Mathematical Foundations of Computer Science, Prague, LNCS 176, pp. 245 - 254, 1984.
7 T. Bolognesi and E. Brinksma, "Introduction to the ISO Specification Language LOTOS", Computer Network and ISDN Systems, vol. 14, no. 1, pp. 3- , 1987.
8 R. Milner, "A Calculus of Communicating Systems", Lecture Notes in CS, No. 92, Springer Verlag, 1980.
9 J. Parrow, "Fairness properties in process algebra", Ph.D. thesis, Dept. of Computer Systems, Uppsala University, Uppsala, Sweden, 1985.
10 Pnueli, A. "The temporal logic of programs", in Proceedings of the 18th Symposium on the Foundations of Computer Science, IEEE, Providence, Nov. 1977, pp. 46-57.
11 Pnueli, A. "The temporal semantics of concurrent programs", in Lecture Notes in Computer Science, vol. 70: Semantics of Concurrent Computation. Springer-Verlag, New York, 1979, pp. 1-20.
12 J.P. Queille and J. Sifakis, "Fairness and related properties in Transition Systems - a temporal logic to deal with fairness", Acta Informatica 19, pp. 195 - 220, Springer - Verlag, 1983.
13 Cheng Wu and Gregor v. Bochmann, "Fairness in LOTOS", Publication #769,Dept. I.R.O. Universite de Montreal, April 1991.
14 Owicki, S., "Proving Liveness Properties of Concurrent Programs", ACM Transactions on Programming Languages and Systems, vl. 4, no.3, July 1982, pp. 455-495.
15 A. Fantechi, S.Gnesi, C. Laneve, "An expressive temporal logic for basic LOTOS", FORTE'89, Vancouver, Canada, 1989.
16 A. Fantechi, S. Gnesi, G. Ristori, "Compositional logic semantics and LOTOS", Tenth International IFIP WG 6.1 Symposium on Protocol Specification, Testing and Verificaton, Ottawa, Canada, June, 1990.
17 ISO TC97/6/WG4/N317, "Formal Description of ISO8072 in LOTOS", 1987.
18 Cheng Wu and Gregor v. Bochmann, "An execution model for LOTOS specifications", GLOBCOMM'90, San Diego, Dec., 1990.
19 Cheng Wu, Gregor v. Bochmann and Mingyu Yao, "Fairness of N-party synchronization and its implementation in a distributed environment", in preparation, 1991.
20 Paul C. Attie, Ira R. Forman, Eliezer Levy, "On Fairness as an abstraction for the design of distributed systems", 1990.

A LOTOS Based Calculus with True Concurrency Semantics

Jean-Pierre Courtiat & Rosvelter João Coelho da Costa[*]

LAAS/CNRS
7, Avenue du Colonel Roche – 31077 Toulouse Cedex – France
Tel: 61336200 - Fax: 61336411
E-mail: courtiat@laas.laas.fr, rosvelte@laas.laas.fr

Partially ordered (multi)sets, have been introduced as a general model aiming at capturing "true concurrency" semantics in concurrent systems. The work presented in this paper starts with the definition of a new notation for representing partially ordered multisets. This notation is then extended by introducing LOTOS based operators, leading to the definition of a new calculus, POtLOTOS (Partial Order tiny LOTOS). A partial order operational semantics of POtLOTOS is finally provided as well as the characterization of a (partial order) strong bisimulation equivalence.

Introduction

In the past few years many algebraic calculi have been proposed for describing concurrent systems (for instance [22, 8, 2, 3]). These approaches are strongly related to the arbitrary interleaving semantics which leads to defining a total ordering of events. Nevertheless, although many (or even all) interesting properties of a distributed system may be analyzed following the arbitrary interleaving semantics [18, 23, 14, 20, 17], it has recently been pointed out that this approach is not always convenient (see [30, 33, 6] for an introductory discussion).

An alternative approach is to consider that events are concurrent if they are not causally related, which leads to considering a partial order semantics for expressing concurrency. Although many believe that partial order semantics (some times called "true concurrency" semantics) is the "right way" for expressing concurrency, this approach has often been rejected, essentially because it appears to be much more difficult to formalize within an algebraic framework. In the past few years, however, several attempts have been made to define partial order semantics for CCS / CSP and related languages (see [29, 36, 6, 21, 16] for a representative sample and further references).

The need to express true concurrency semantics in LOTOS [5, 19] has recently been pointed out by C. Vissers [35] who states that "real parallelism has nothing to do with the question whether or not one can observe that events take place at the very same moment, but with the question whether events are taking place independently".

---

[*] On leave from the Dept. of Computer Science and Statistics of the Universidade Federal de Santa Catarina (Florianópolis-Brazil). Supported by a research assistantship of Brazilian government (MEC/CAPES) Proc. 100/88-11.

The purpose of this paper is to illustrate a way to extend LOTOS with a true concurrency semantics preserving the basic features of LOTOS. Our approach, based on a new notation for representing pomsets (partially ordered multisets) [29], relies on the following basic intuition: one may informally consider that elementary processes in LOTOS are expressed by means of strings (totally ordered multisets) of actions, on the top of which operators have been provided for composing and synchronizing these elementary processes, whereas, in the proposed approach, elementary processes are expressed by pomsets of actions. Previous work following the same approach but considering a set of composition operators close to the ones of CCS has been presented in [11]. In this paper the same basic ideas are developed taking into account the composition operators of LOTOS.

The paper is organized as follows: section 1, which contains the basic intuitions behind our proposal, deals with the definition of a new notation for representing pomsets leading to the characterization of a Simple Partial Order Calculus, SPOC; in section 2, SPOC is extended by introducing LOTOS-based operators, leading to the definition of a new calculus, POtLOTOS (Partial Order tiny LOTOS), preserving both partial ordering among events and the branching-time structure for non-determinism; an operational semantics of POtLOTOS is provided as well as the characterization of strong bisimulation equivalence.

1 A Notation for Representing Pomsets

Partially ordered sets are a very basic concept in Mathematics and Computer Science. In particular, partially ordered sets (and related concepts such that labeled partially ordered sets and pomsets) are currently being used as a basic model for describing the behavior of concurrent systems [29, 21, 4]. In this section, we will introduce a new notation for representing pomsets. An early version of this notation has been presented in [10], and the current version of the notation has been extensively described in [12], where the proofs omitted in this section can be found.

A set X and a transitive, reflexive and antisymmetric relation $\preceq: X \times X$, define a *partially ordered set* (*poset* in short). A *labeled poset* (*lpo* in short) $(X, \preceq, A, l)$ extends a poset $(X, \preceq)$ by introducing a *set of actions* A and a *labeling function* $l : X \to A$. Lpo's express the fact that events correspond to occurrences of actions.

For instance, figure 1 shows the usual graphical representation of the lpo defined by $X = \{1,2,3,4,5\}$, $\preceq = \{(1,2),(1,3),(2,3),(1,4),(1,5),(4,5)\} \cup Id_X$, $A = \{a,b,c\}$, and $l = \{(1,a),(2,b),(3,c),(4,a),(5,b)\}$. In general, concurrent systems are not characterized by an unique lpo, but rather by a class of *isomorphic labeled posets*. The term *pomset* [29] has been used in the current literature to refer to an isomorphism class of an lpo.

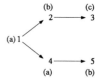

Figure 1 Labeled poset

1.1 Syntax

Now, we introduce a notation for denoting (finite) pomsets. We start by defining the syntax of the notation and then introduce basic conversion rules leading to the definition of canonical syntactical forms for terms expressed in the notation.

Let $\mathcal{X} = \{1, 2, \ldots\}$ be an infinite set of *names*. We will use w, x, y, z to stand for arbitrary names, with distinct letters denoting distinct names, unless otherwise stated. We will use C, D to denote finite subsets of $\mathcal{X}$. Let furthermore $\mathcal{A} = \{\mathsf{a}, \mathsf{b}, \mathsf{c}, \ldots\}$ be a set of actions, and $\alpha, \beta, \ldots$ stand for arbitrary actions.

Definition 1. *(Atom)* An *atom* with respect to $\mathcal{A}$ is defined as any triple (D, α, x), shortly noted by $_D\alpha_x$ ([1]). The following functions are also defined: $\delta(_D\alpha_x) = D$, $|_D\alpha_x| = \alpha$ and $\xi(_D\alpha_x) = x$. We will use $\mathcal{E}$ to denote the set of all atoms with respect to $\mathcal{A}$, and we will use (lightly italic) lowercase letters of the begin of the alphabet $a, b, c, \ldots$ to range over $\mathcal{E}$. □

Terms in the notation are simply strings (sequences) over $\mathcal{E}$, and we will use $\mathcal{T}$ to denote the set of all such terms, with *Nil* denoting the empty string. The triple $(\mathcal{T}, \cdot, \textit{Nil})$, where $\cdot : \mathcal{T} \times \mathcal{T} \to \mathcal{T}$ is the standard concatenation operator, defines the usual monoid over strings. In this section, $P, Q, \ldots$ are assumed to range over $\mathcal{T}$. Furthermore, as usual we will omit "$\cdot$" and "*Nil*" whenever there is no danger of confusion.

Intuitively, atom a represents the occurrence of action $|a|$. Thus, a term defines a set of $\mathcal{A}$-labeled events. Any atom b, present on the left of a, is a cause of a iff $\xi(b) \in \delta(a)$.

Example 1. $P = \mathsf{a}_1 \, _1\mathsf{b}_2 \, _2\mathsf{c}_7 \, _1\mathsf{a}_4 \, _1\mathsf{b}_5$ represents the lpo of figure 1. □

Definition 2. In the sequel, '$\equiv$' will be used to denote syntactic identity. Without any risk of ambiguity, '$\equiv$' will also be used to denote the (strongest) identity relation over terms defined as follows:

(i) $\textit{Nil} \equiv \textit{Nil}$ (ii) If $P \equiv Q$ and $C = D$, then $_C\alpha_x P \equiv \, _D\alpha_x Q$ □

Obviously, P defined above is not the unique term characterizing the lpo of figure 1. For instance, let $Q = \mathsf{a}_1 \, _1\mathsf{b}_2 \, _{1,2}\mathsf{c}_7 \, _1\mathsf{a}_4 \, _{1,4}\mathsf{b}_5$; although $Q \not\equiv P$, it should be clear that P and Q still represent the same lpo. Therefore, as the same lpo may be represented by several syntactic distinct terms, canonical representations are to be defined. For this purpose, the contraction and expansion conversion rules, which deal with the transitivity of the partial order relation, are introduced.

Definition 3. *(Contraction operation)* The contraction operation, $(C \triangleright x)P$, is defined by induction on P, as follows:

(i) $(C \triangleright x)\textit{Nil} \equiv \textit{Nil}$

(ii) $(\emptyset \triangleright x)P \equiv P$

(iii) $(C \triangleright x)_D\alpha_y P \equiv \begin{cases} _{D'}\alpha_y((C - \{y\}) \triangleright x)P & \text{if } x \not\equiv y \\ _{D'}\alpha_y P & \text{if } x \equiv y \end{cases}$ where $D' = \begin{cases} D - C & \text{if } x \in D \\ D & \text{otherwise} \end{cases}$ □

---

[1] If $D = \emptyset$, $_D\alpha_x$ is simply noted α_x.

Then, the following conversion rule may be defined:

THE CONTRACTION RULE:
$$_D\alpha_x P \xrightarrow{\triangleright} {_D\alpha_x}(D' \triangleright x)P \quad \text{for any } D' \subseteq D - \{x\}.$$

Conversely, we can formalize the dual of the contraction operation, namely the expansion operation.

Definition 4. *(Expansion operation)* The expansion operation, $(C \triangleleft x)P$, is defined by induction on P, as follows:

(i) $(C \triangleleft x)Nil \equiv Nil$
(ii) $(\emptyset \triangleleft x)P \equiv P$
(iii) $(C \triangleleft x)_D\alpha_y P \equiv \begin{cases} {_{D'}\alpha_y}((C - \{y\}) \triangleleft x)P & \text{if } x \not\equiv y \\ {_{D'}\alpha_y}P & \text{if } x \equiv y \end{cases}$ where $D' = \begin{cases} D \cup C & \text{if } x \in D \\ D & \text{otherwise.} \end{cases}$ □

In the same way, the following conversion rule may be defined:

THE EXPANSION RULE:
$$_D\alpha_x P \xrightarrow{\triangleleft} {_D\alpha_x}(D' \triangleleft x)P \quad \text{for any } D' \subseteq D - \{x\}.$$

In the sequel, we note respectively by '$\triangleright$' and '$\triangleleft$' the reflexive transitive closure of the relations induced by the contraction and expansion rules, and by '$\triangleleft\triangleright$' the transitive closure of their union.

Note that '$\triangleleft\triangleright$' is not symmetric; for instance, $_{1,2}a_3\,_{1,3}b_4\,_{2,3}c_5 \triangleleft\triangleright \,_{1,2}a_3\,_3b_4\,_3c_5$, but one may note that $_{1,2}a_3\,_3b_4\,_3c_5 \,\not\triangleleft\triangleright\, _{1,2}a_3\,_{1,3}b_4\,_{2,3}c_5$.

Definition 5. *(Min-/Max-forms)* A term P is said to be in *min-form* (*max-form*) iff $\not\exists P' \not\equiv P$ such that $P \triangleright P'$ ($\not\exists P' \not\equiv P$ such that $P \triangleleft P'$). □

Example 2. $P = a_1\,_1b_2\,_2c_3\,_1a_4\,_1b_5$ is in min-form and $Q = a_1\,_1b_2\,_{1,2}c_3\,_1a_4\,_{1,4}b_5$ is in max-form. □

Definition 6. *($\triangleleft\triangleright$-congruence)* P and Q are said to be $\triangleleft\triangleright$-*congruent*, in symbols $P \underset{\triangleleft\triangleright}{\equiv} Q$, iff either $P \triangleleft\triangleright Q$, or $Q \triangleleft\triangleright P$, or there exists a term R such that $P \underset{\triangleleft\triangleright}{\equiv} R$ and $R \underset{\triangleleft\triangleright}{\equiv} Q$. □

It is obvious that the $\triangleleft\triangleright$-congruence is also an equivalence relation, the $\triangleleft\triangleright$-*equivalence*.

The purpose of both min- and max- forms is essentially to define canonical syntactic forms with respect to the $\triangleleft\triangleright$-equivalence. For the sake of simplicity and without any loss of generality, only terms in their min-form will be considered in the sequel[1].

1.2 SPOC – a Simple Partial Order Calculus

Starting from the syntactic definition of the notation introduced previously, two basic conversion rules (namely the α-rule dealing with name substitution within a term, and the π-rule dealing with atom permutation within a term) will be defined, leading to a basic equivalence relation among terms and characterizing a Simple Partial Order Calculus.

---

[1] In fact, all results and definitions presented in the paper still hold (or are straightforward adapted) for any representation (from min- to max-forms). However, with this simplification hypothesis, many references to $\triangleleft\triangleright$-equivalence are avoided.

Note that (i) also holds for the conventional interleaving strong bisimulation equivalence defined for LOTOS. In fact, for the common subset of behavior expressions, our strong bisimulation equivalence is finer than the interleaving strong bisimulation equivalence defined for LOTOS. Moreover, all "non-interleaving laws" of LOTOS, such that the monoid laws for '[]' and '||' (the "absorption laws" where (i) and (ii) are only particular cases), etc., hold for both calculi.

Example 6. Figure 2 shows the Petri net representing the behavior of a very simple system composed of two processes: a producer and a consumer. The producer produces some resource, and then sends it to the consumer. The consumer receives the resource from the producer, and then consumes it. The unique constraint restricting the behavior of the two processes is that sending and receiving a resource should be atomic, i.e. the producer can only send a resource when the consumer is ready to receive it.

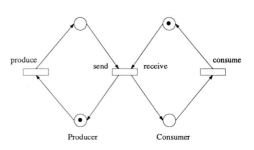

Figure 2 Producer/consumer

The behavior expressions for both producer (P) and consumer (C) are given by

$$P = (\mu X^1 \cdot {}_1 \mathbf{p}_{2\ 2} \mathbf{m}_3 X^3)^1 \qquad C = (\mu X^1 \cdot {}_1 \mathbf{m}_{2\ 2} \mathbf{c}_3 X^3)^1$$

with p, c and m having their obvious meaning. The specification of this producer/consumer system, S, is given by

$$S = P|[\mathrm{m}]|C = (\mu X^1 \cdot {}_1 \mathbf{p}_{2\ 2} \mathbf{m}_3 X^3)^1 |[\mathrm{m}]| (\mu X^1 \cdot {}_1 \mathbf{m}_{2\ 2} \mathbf{c}_3 X^3)^1$$

This specification is similar to the one which could be written using tLOTOS constructs, assuming a fixed-point notation for expressing recursive behaviors:

$$S_{\mathrm{tLOTOS}} = P|[\mathrm{m}]|C = (\mu X.\mathrm{p};\mathrm{m};X)|[\mathrm{m}]|(\mu X.\mathrm{m};\mathrm{c};X)$$

In fact, S can be considered as a "translation" of S_{tLOTOS} in POtLOTOS. The free name of S can be seen as the "binding point" to the context in which S will be placed, for instance $S^* = \mathrm{s}_l S$, where s_l is any atom characterizing a starting event for the producer/consumer system. Note that this notion of "binding point" is implicit in tLOTOS, for instance $S^*_{\mathrm{tLOTOS}} = \mathrm{s}; S_{\mathrm{tLOTOS}}$. In this case, all events in S_{tLOTOS} are in causal dependency with s. The notion of context in POtLOTOS is not so trivial as it is in tLOTOS. Indeed, we have a powerful mechanism in the calculus which is somewhat similar to the notion of "marking" of Petri nets. Current work dealing with the relationships between our approach and other true concurrency models such as Petri nets, event structures, etc., has demonstrated that many useful notions of such models are similar in our calculus [13].

Now, let $S' = {}_1 \mathbf{p}_{2\ 2} \mathbf{m}_3 (\mu X^3 \cdot {}_3 \mathbf{p}_{4\ 3} \mathbf{c}_5 \cdot {}_{4,5} \mathbf{m}_6 X^6)^3$. It should be clear that $S \sim S'$, and also that S' describes precisely true concurrency for the producer/consumer system specified by S.

Now, let $Q = a_6\ _6b_7\ _7c_8\ _6a_9\ _9b_{10}$, although $Q \neq P$ (defined in example 1), Q is expected to *"be equivalent to"* P as both terms represent the same pomset. Before defining formally this equivalence, some preliminary definitions are provided.

Name x is said to occur in atom a iff $x \in (\delta(a) \cup \{\xi(a)\})$. We note by $\sigma(a)$ the set of all names occurring in atom a, i.e. $\sigma(a) = \delta(a) \cup \{\xi(a)\}$. Furthermore, an occurrence of name x in P is said to be *bound* iff it is on the right of α within some sub-term $_D\alpha_x Q$ in P. Otherwise, it is said to be *free* in P. For example, in term $_{x,y}\alpha_x\ _y\beta_y\ _{y,x}\gamma_y$, the first occurrence of x is free and the others are bound; in the same way, the first two occurrences of y are free and the next three are bound.

Definition 7. The set of all free names of term P, noted as $\phi(P)$, is defined inductively as follows:

(i) $\phi(Nil) = \emptyset$ (ii) $\phi(aP) = \delta(a) \cup (\phi(P) - \{\xi(a)\})$

Term P is said to be *closed* iff $\phi(P) = \emptyset$. □

Definition 8. *(Substitution of names)* The substitution of z for all free occurrences of name x in P, in symbols $\{z/x\}P$, is defined by induction on the structure of P as follows:

(i) $\{z/x\}Nil \equiv Nil$

(ii) $\{z/x\}_D\alpha_y P \equiv \begin{cases} _{D'}\alpha_y P, & \text{if } y \equiv x \\ _{D'}\alpha_y \{z/x\}P, & \text{if } y \not\equiv x \land (y \not\equiv z \lor x \notin \phi(P)) \\ _{D'}\alpha_w \{z/x\}\{w/y\}P & \text{if } y \not\equiv x \land y \equiv z \land x \in \phi(P) \end{cases}$

where • $D' = \begin{cases} (D - \{x\}) \cup \{z\} & \text{if } x \in D \\ D & \text{otherwise} \end{cases}$ and • $w \notin \phi(P) \cup \{z\}$ □

Note that the third alternative of (ii) is intended to avoid name clashes.

Let us now define a conversion rule for substituting bound occurrences of names within a term:

THE α-RULE: $_D\alpha_x P \xrightarrow{\alpha} {_D\alpha_z}\{z/x\}P$ for any $z \notin \phi(P)$.

Definition 9. *(α-congruence)* Two terms P and Q are said to be α-*congruent*, in symbols $P \equiv_\alpha Q$, iff Q can be derived from P by applying the α-rule a finite number (possibly 0) of times. □

Proposition 1. The α-congruence is an equivalence relation (the α-*equivalence*).

Example 3. *(α-equivalent terms)* $P = a_1\ _1b_2\ _2c_3\ _1a_4\ _4b_5$ and $Q = a_6\ _6b_7\ _7c_8\ _6a_9\ _9b_{10}$ are α-equivalent, as $P \equiv_\alpha a_6\{6/1\}\ _1b_7\{7/2\}\ _2c_8\{8/3\}\ _1a_9\{9/4\}\ _4b_{10}\{10/5\} \equiv Q$. □

Let now P and Q be defined as: $P = a_1\ _1b_2\ _2c_3\ _1a_4\ _4b_5$ and $Q = a_1\ _1a_4\ _1b_2\ _2c_3\ _4b_5$. Although $P \not\equiv_\alpha Q$, it is clear that P and Q still represent the same pomset. Then, another rule is required for expressing the fact that the order of atoms within a term may be not relevant. This conversion rule is formally defined as follows:

THE π-RULE: $\qquad abS \xrightarrow{\pi} b'aS'$ if $\xi(a) \notin \delta(b)$

where $b' = {}_c\beta_z$, $S' = \{z/y\}S$ for $b = {}_c\beta_y$ and for some z satisfying:
$z \notin (\phi(S) - \{y\}) \;\wedge\; ((z \notin \delta(a) \wedge y \notin \phi(S)) \;\vee\; z \notin \sigma(a))$.

The two conversion rules defined so far, lead to establishing the following congruence relation:

Definition 10. *($\alpha\pi$-congruence)* Two terms P and Q are said to be *$\alpha\pi$-congruent*, in symbols $P \equiv_{\alpha\pi} Q$, iff Q can be derived from P by applying the α-rule or the π-rule a finite number (possibly 0) of times. □

Proposition 2. $abS \equiv_{\alpha\pi} baS$ if $\xi(a) \notin \delta(b) \wedge (\xi(b) \notin (\delta(a) \cup \phi(S)) \vee \xi(b) \notin \sigma(a))$. □

Proposition 3. The $\alpha\pi$-congruence is an equivalence relation (the $\alpha\pi$-equivalence). □

In [12], we give a more detailed presentation of SPOC. In particular, a formal characterization of SPOC in terms of lpo's is provided. In the next section, we will extend SPOC by introducing LOTOS-like operators leading to the definition of new concurrent calculus preserving both partial ordering among events and branching-time structure for non-determinism.

2 POtLOTOS - Partial Order tiny LOTOS

In order to illustrate our approach for providing a true concurrency semantics for LOTOS we consider, as a starting point, a subset of Basic LOTOS [5], called tiny LOTOS (tLOTOS in short). The major difference between tLOTOS and Basic LOTOS is that processes in tLOTOS, as in CCS, do not exit. As a consequence, operators '>>' (sequential composition) and '[>' (disrupt) are not supported. In addition to this major semantic difference, there are three main syntactic variations between tLOTOS and Basic LOTOS:

- Operator hide L in E is noted $E\backslash L$
- Internal action i of Basic Lotos is noted τ as in CCS
- Recursive processes are expressed by means of the classical fixed-point notation as in CCS.

Operators $STOP, ;, |[L]|, |||, ||, []$ have their same usual meaning as in Basic LOTOS. Based on the results presented in the previous section and using our notation for expressing pomsets, the basic intuition for providing a true concurrency semantics for tLOTOS, leading to the definition of POtLOTOS (Partial Order tiny LOTOS), is as follows:

- Actions of tLOTOS are replaced by atoms of the notation;
- Prefixing operator ";" of tLOTOS is replaced by a *partial prefixing operator* playing the same role as the concatenation operator of SPOC.

Thus, the additional structure induced by the atoms, together with the partial prefixing operator, permits to express a partial order among POtLOTOS events.

After this brief introduction emphasizing our intuition for providing a true concurrency semantics for LOTOS, the section is organized as follows: subsection 2.1 details formally the syntax of POtLOTOS and shows how the different conversion rules defined for SPOC may be extended to POtLOTOS; subsection 2.2 provides an operational semantics for POtLOTOS as well as a characterization of strong bisimulation equivalence among POtLOTOS behavior expressions; subsection 2.3 presents finally simple examples for illustrating some basic ideas and results discussed in this section.

2.1 Syntax

Let $\mathcal{G} = \{a, b, c, \ldots\}$ be a finite set of *gates* where L stands for an arbitrary subset of $\mathcal{G}$. Then, $\mathcal{A} = \mathcal{G} \cup \{\tau\}$, ranged over by $\alpha, \beta, \gamma, \ldots$, is the usual set of actions, where $\tau \notin \mathcal{G}$. Definition 1 is still valid. Remember that $a, b, c, \ldots$ range over atoms. Finally, we assume an infinite set $\mathcal{V}$ (disjoint of $\mathcal{X}$) of variables, ranged over by $\ldots, X, Y, Z$.

Definition 11. *(Behavior expressions)* Let $\rho : \mathcal{V} \to \mathbb{N}$ be an N-assignment, associating with every symbol X in $\mathcal{V}$ a natural number $\rho(X)$. We denote by $(X, n)\rho$ a new N-assignment defined by $\{(X, n)\} \cup \{(Y, \rho(Y)) | Y \neq X\}$. Then, set $\mathcal{T}_\rho$ of *behavior expressions*, with respect to some N-assignment ρ, is defined recursively as follows:

a. Bases:

   (i) $STOP \in \mathcal{T}_\rho$
   (ii) If $z_1, \ldots, z_n$ is a sequence of $n \geq 0$ names and $\rho(X) = n$, then $X^{z_1, \ldots, z_n} \in \mathcal{T}_\rho$

b. Recursive steps:

   (iii) If $a \in \mathcal{E}$ and $E \in \mathcal{T}_\rho$, then $aE \in \mathcal{T}_\rho$
   (iv) If $E, E' \in \mathcal{T}_\rho$, then $E[]E' \in \mathcal{T}_\rho$
   (v) If $E, E' \in \mathcal{T}_\rho$ and L is a subset of $\mathcal{G}$, then $E|[L]|E' \in \mathcal{T}_\rho$
   (vi) If L is a subset of $\mathcal{G}$ and $E \in \mathcal{T}_\rho$, then $E \backslash L \in \mathcal{T}_\rho$
   (vii) If $(x_1, \ldots, x_n)$ $z_1, \ldots, z_n$ is a sequence of (pairwise distinct) $n \geq 0$ names and $E \in \mathcal{T}_{(X,n)\rho}$, then $(\mu X^{x_1, \ldots, x_n}.E)^{z_1, \ldots, z_n} \in \mathcal{T}_\rho$

c. Closure: $E \in \mathcal{T}_\rho$ only if it can be obtained from bases (i) or (ii) by applying the operators defined in (iii) to (vii) a finite number of times.

In the sequel, we will use $\mathcal{T}$, ranged over by $E, F, \ldots$, to denote the union of all $\mathcal{T}_\rho$. □

Conventions: In order to avoid excessive use of parentheses, the usual priority order for the above operators is assumed. Furthermore, we will omit '*STOP*' when writing behavior expressions, whenever there is no danger of confusion. We will also use symbols |||, || to denote particular cases of the parallel composition operator $\_|[L]|\_$, respectively when $L = \emptyset$ and $L = \mathcal{G}$.

Operators $STOP, \_|[L]|\_, [], \_\backslash L$ have their usual meaning [5, 19]. The prefixing operation (aP), called *partial prefixing operation*, is equivalent to the concatenation operation presented in the previous section.

Construct $(\mu X^{x_1, \ldots, x_n}.E)^{z_1, \ldots, z_n}$ defines and immediately calls a parameterized recursive function with arity n. The meaning of this construct is similar to the one of the (conventional) parameterless case ($n = 0$), and will be detailed below after giving some preliminary definitions.

As in SPOC, '$\equiv$', which denotes syntactic identity, is also used for denoting the strongest identity relation over behavior expressions; we therefore assume a definition analogous to definition 2 for behavior expressions. Moreover, the same considerations related to canonical min-forms for SPOC (end of subsection 1.1) are also assumed for POtLOTOS, where, for convenience, we assume that they are sufficiently clear within the context of POtLOTOS.

An occurrence of variable X is said to be *bound* in E iff it is in a term $\mu X^{x_1,...,x_n}.E'$ in E, otherwise it is said to be *free*. In a similar way, an occurrence of name x is said to be *bound* in E iff either it is in a term $\mu X^{x_1,...,x,...,x_n}.E'$ in E, or it is on the right of α in a term $_D\alpha_x E'$ in E; otherwise, it is said to be *free*. For example, in $_z\alpha_x(\mu X^z._{x,z}\beta_x(_y\alpha_z Y^{y,z}\|[\gamma]\|_z\alpha_y {}_{y,x}\gamma_x X^z))^x$, there is not any free occurrence of x; there are only two free occurrences of z and y; the two occurrences of X are bound, and the unique occurrence of Y is free.

Definition 12. The set of all free names, noted as $\phi(E)$, and the set of all free variables, noted as $\varphi(E)$, of behavior expression E, is defined by induction on E as follows:

(i) $\phi(N\mathbf{i}) = \emptyset$ $\qquad\qquad\qquad\qquad\qquad\qquad\varphi(N\mathbf{i}) = \emptyset$
(ii) $\phi(X^{z_1,...,z_n}) = \{z_1,...,z_n\}$ $\qquad\qquad\varphi(X^{z_1,...,z_n}) = \{X\}$
(iii) $\phi(aE) = \delta(a) \cup (\phi(E) - \{\xi(a)\})$ $\qquad\varphi(aE) = \varphi(E)$
(iv) $\phi(E[]F) = \phi(E|[L]|F) = \phi(E) \cup \phi(F)$ $\qquad\varphi(E[]F) = \varphi(E|[L]|F) = \varphi(E) \cup \varphi(F)$
(v) $\phi(E\backslash L) = \phi(E)$ $\qquad\qquad\qquad\qquad\varphi(E\backslash L) = \varphi(E)$
(vi) $\phi((\mu X^{x_1,...,x_n}.E)^{z_1,...,z_n}) = \{z_1,...,z_n\} \cup (\phi(E) - \{x_1,...,x_n\})$ $\qquad\varphi((\mu X^{x_1,...,x_n}.E)^{z_1,...,z_n}) = (\varphi(E) - \{X\})$

Expression E is said to be x-/v-closed iff $\phi(E) = \emptyset / \varphi(E) = \emptyset$. $\square$

We use $\mathcal{P}$, ranged over by $P, Q, \ldots$, to denote the set of all v-closed behavior expressions.

Definition 13. (*Substitution of names within a behavior expression*) The substitution of z for all free occurrences of name x in behavior expression E, in symbols $\{z/x\}E$, is defined by induction on E as follows:

(i) $\{z/x\}STOP \equiv STOP$
(ii) $\{z/x\}X^{y_1,...,y_n} \equiv X^{z_1,...,z_n}$ where $z_i \equiv \begin{cases} z & \text{if } y_i \equiv x \\ y_i & \text{otherwise} \end{cases}$

(iii) $\{z/x\}_D\alpha_y E \equiv \begin{cases} _{D'}\alpha_y E & \text{if } y \equiv x \\ _{D'}\alpha_y\{z/x\}E & \text{if } y \not\equiv x \land (y \not\equiv z \lor x \notin \phi(E)) \\ _{D'}\alpha_w\{z/x\}\{w/y\}E & \text{if } z \equiv y \not\equiv x \land x \in \phi(E) \end{cases}$

where • $D' = \begin{cases} (D - \{x\}) \cup \{z\} & \text{if } x \in D \\ D & \text{otherwise} \end{cases}$ and • $w \notin \phi(E) \cup \{z\}$

(iv) $\{z/x\}(E|[L]|F) \equiv \{z/x\}E|[L]|\{z/x\}F$
$\{z/x\}(E[]F) \equiv \{z/x\}E[]\{z/x\}F$
(v) $\{z/x\}(E\backslash L) \equiv (\{z/x\}E)\backslash L$

(vi) $\{z/x\}(\mu X^{x_1,...,x_n}.E)^{y_1,...,y_n}$

$\equiv \begin{cases} (\mu X^{x_1,...,x_n}.E)^{z_1,...,z_j,...,z_n} & \text{if } x \in \{x_1,...,x_n\} \\ (\mu X^{x_1,...,x_n}.\{z/x\}E)^{z_1,...,z_j,...,z_n} & \text{if } x \notin \{x_1,...,x_n\} \land (z \notin \{x_1,...,x_n\} \lor x \notin \phi(E)) \\ (\mu X^{x_1,...,x_{i-1},w,x_{i+1},...,x_n}.\{z/x\}\{w/x_i\}E)^{z_1,...,z_j,...,z_n} & \text{if } x \notin \{x_1,...,x_n\} \land z \equiv x_i \land x \in \phi(E) \end{cases}$

where
- $z_j \equiv \begin{cases} z & \text{if } y_j \equiv x \\ y_j & \text{otherwise} \end{cases}$ and
- $w \notin \phi(E) \cup \{z, x_1, ..., x_{i-1}, x_{i+1}, ..., x_n\}$ □

Definition 14. *(Multiple substitution of names)* The substitution of $z_1, ..., z_n$ for all free occurrences of pairwise distinct names $x_1, ..., x_n$ in behavior expression E, in symbols $\{z_1, ..., z_n / x_1, ..., x_n\}E$, is defined recursively as follows:

$$\{z_1, ..., z_n / x_1, ..., x_n\}E \equiv \begin{cases} \{z_2, ..., z_n / x_2, ..., x_n\}\{z_1/x_1\}E & \text{if } z_1 \notin \{x_2, ..., x_n\} \vee x_1 \notin \phi(E) \\ \{z_2, ..., z_n / x_2, ..., x_{i-1}, w, x_{i+1}, ..., x_n\}\{z_1/x_1\}\{w/x_i\}E & \text{if } z_1 \equiv x_i \wedge x_1 \in \phi(E) \end{cases}$$

where $w \notin \phi(E) \cup \{z_1, x_2, ..., x_{i-1}, x_{i+1}, ..., x_n\}$. □

Definition 15. *(Variable substitution)* Let $E \in T_\rho$ and let $\mathcal{E}$ denote either a variable Z satisfying $X \in \varphi(E) \Rightarrow \rho Z = \rho X$, or a term $\mu V^{v_1,...,v_n}.F$ such that $F \in T_{(V,n)\rho}$ and $X \in \varphi(E) \Rightarrow \rho X = n$. Then, the substitution of $\mathcal{E}$ for all free occurrences of X in E, in symbols $[\mathcal{E}/X]E$, is defined by induction on the structure of E as follows ([1]):

(i) $[\mathcal{E}/X]STOP \equiv STOP$

(ii) $[\mathcal{E}/X]Y^{z_1,...,z_n} \equiv \begin{cases} \mathcal{E}^{z_1,...,z_n} & \text{if } X \equiv Y \\ Y^{z_1,...,z_n} & \text{otherwise} \end{cases}$

(iii) $[\mathcal{E}/X](_D\alpha_y E) \equiv \begin{cases} _D\alpha_y[\mathcal{E}/X]E & \text{if } y \notin \phi(\mathcal{E}) \vee X \notin \varphi(E) \\ _D\alpha_w[\mathcal{E}/X]\{w/y\}E & \text{otherwise} \end{cases}$
where $w \notin \phi(E) \cup \phi(\mathcal{E})$

(iv) $[\mathcal{E}/X](E|[L]|E') \equiv [\mathcal{E}/X]E|[L]|[\mathcal{E}/X]E'$
$[\mathcal{E}/X](E[]E') \equiv [\mathcal{E}/X]E[][\mathcal{E}/X]E'$

(v) $[\mathcal{E}/X](E\backslash L) \equiv ([\mathcal{E}/X]E)\backslash L$

(vi) $[\mathcal{E}/X](\mu Y^{y_1,...,y_n}.E)^{z_1,...,z_n}$

$\equiv \begin{cases} (\mu Y^{y_1,...,y_n}.E)^{z_1,...,z_n} & \text{if } Y \equiv X \\ (\mu Y^{y_1'',...,y_n''}.[\mathcal{E}/X]\{w_1, ..., w_m/y_1', ..., y_m'\}E)^{z_1,...,z_n} & \text{if } X \not\equiv Y \wedge (Y \notin \varphi(\mathcal{E}) \vee X \notin \varphi(E)) \\ (\mu W^{y_1'',...,y_n''}.[\mathcal{E}/X][W/Y]\{w_1, ..., w_m/y_1', ..., y_m'\}E)^{z_1,...,z_n} & \text{if } X \not\equiv Y \in \varphi(\mathcal{E}) \wedge X \in \varphi(E) \end{cases}$

where, for $1 \leq i \leq n$, $1 \leq j \leq m$
- $\{y_1', ..., y_m'\} = \{y_1, ..., y_n\} \cap \phi(\mathcal{E})$
- $y_i'' = \begin{cases} w_j & \text{if } y_i \equiv y_j' \\ y_i & \text{otherwise} \end{cases}$
- $w_1, ..., w_m$ are pairwise distinct names satisfying $w_j \notin \phi(\mathcal{E}) \cup \phi(E) \cup \{y_1, ..., y_n\}$
- $W \notin \varphi(E) \cup \varphi(\mathcal{E})$ □

The α-rule defined for SPOC may then be generalized for POtLOTOS by a set of three different conversion rules.

THE α-RULES:

- $_D\alpha_x E \xrightarrow{\alpha_1} {_D\alpha_z}\{z/x\}E$ for any $z \notin \phi(E)$
- $\mu X^{x_1,...,x_n}.E \xrightarrow{\alpha_2} \mu X^{x_1,...,x_{i-1},z,x_{i+1},...,x_n}.\{z/x_i\}E$ for any $z \notin \phi(E) \cup \{x_1, ..., x_{i-1}, x_{i+1}, ..., x_n\}$
- $\mu X^{x_1,...,x_n}.E \xrightarrow{\alpha_3} \mu Z^{x_1,...,x_n}.[Z/X]E$ for any $Z \notin \varphi(E)$

---

[1] $\phi(\mathcal{E}), \varphi(\mathcal{E}) = \begin{cases} \emptyset, Z & \text{if } \mathcal{E} = Z \\ \phi(F) - \{v_1, ..., v_n\}, \varphi(F) - \{V\} & \text{if } \mathcal{E} = \mu V^{v_1,...,v_n}.F \end{cases}$

Definition 16. (*α-congruence for behavior expressions*) Two behavior expressions E, F are said to be *α-congruent*, in symbols $E \equiv_\alpha F$, iff F can be derived from E by applying the α-rules a finite number (possibly 0) of times. □

Proposition 4. The α-congruence is an equivalence relation (the *α-equivalence*). □

Although the above definitions appear to be technically cumbersome, one may point out that their intuitive meaning is rather simple. Furthermore, one should note that they are, from a technical point of view, very close to Lambda-calculus.

Now, it is possible to define formally the meaning of the recursion definition introduced previously. The recursion definition $(\mu X^{x_1,\ldots,x_n}.E)^{z_1,\ldots,z_n}$ is characterized by the following conversion rule.

THE μ-RULE:
$$(\mu X^{x_1,\ldots,x_n}.E)^{z_1,\ldots,z_n} \xrightarrow{\mu} \{z_1,\ldots,z_n/x_1,\ldots,x_n\}[\mu X^{x_1,\ldots,x_n}.E/X]E$$

which corresponds to a slight modification of the usual μ-rule defined in the parameterless case. Intuitively, this rule indicates that the converted expression is obtained from E, first by substituting $\mu X^{x_1,\ldots,x_n}.E$ for all free occurrences of variable X in E and then by substituting $z_1,\ldots,z_n$ (actual parameters) for all free occurrences of names $x_1,\ldots,x_n$ (formal parameters).

As usual, the meaning of recursive behaviors is given by assuming that there exists a distinguished behavior expression Ω (the least defined behavior). For instance, divergent terms such that $\mu X.X$ are interpreted as Ω. The usual treatment given for the parameterless case (for instance, see [17]) can be straightforwardly adapted to the parameterized case.

Following the basic definitions introduced in this subsection, we are now ready to formalize an operational semantics for POtLOTOS.

2.2 Operational Semantics

The following set of axioms and inference rules, given in the Plotkins's SOS style [28], defines a partial order operational semantics for POtLOTOS. This operational semantics may be seen within a transitional framework [1], where "transitions" are labeled with "atoms" (instead of "actions"). In this way, the underlying Labeled Transition System (LTS) has an extra structure provided by the partial order relation induced by the atoms. The idea of extending LTS with a partial order relation among the transitions leading to defining a *Distributed Labeled Transition Systems* (DLTS) is not new. Several similar approaches have been proposed in the literature (see for instance [31, 15, 7]). Nevertheless, in the sequel we will not explicitly assume a DLTS as the underlying model of our operational semantics. Axioms and inference rules will instead be "interpreted" as proof constructions. So, proposition $E \xrightarrow{a} E'$ is valid if it can be derived (proven) by using the axioms and inference rules below. Roughly speaking, $E \xrightarrow{a} E'$ means that atom a may be derived from E.

Definition 17.

(i) $\dfrac{}{aE \xrightarrow{a} E}$

(ii) $\dfrac{E \stackrel{D\ \beta y}{\to} E'}{aE \stackrel{D\ \beta z}{\to} a\{z/y\}E'}$ if $\xi(a) \notin D$

for some z satisfying $z \notin (\phi(E') - \{y\}) \wedge ((z \notin \delta(a) \wedge y \notin \phi(E')) \vee z \notin \sigma(a))$

(iii) $\dfrac{E \stackrel{a}{\to} E'}{E[]F \stackrel{a}{\to} E' \quad F[]E \stackrel{a}{\to} E'}$

(iv) $\dfrac{E \stackrel{D\ \alpha x}{\to} E'}{E|[L]|F \stackrel{D\ \alpha z}{\to} (\{z/x\}E')|[L]|F \quad F|[L]|E \stackrel{D\ \alpha z}{\to} F|[L]|(\{z/x\}E')}$ if $\alpha \notin L$

for some z satisfying $z \notin \phi(F) \cup (\phi(E') - \{x\})$

(v) $\dfrac{E \stackrel{C\ \lambda x}{\to} E' \quad F \stackrel{D\ \lambda y}{\to} F'}{E|[L]|F \stackrel{C \cup D\ \lambda z}{\to} \{z/x\}E'|[L]|\{z/y\}F'}$ if $\lambda \in L$

for some z satisfying $z \notin ((\phi(E') - \{x\}) \cup \phi(F')) \vee z \notin ((\phi(F') - \{y\}) \cup \phi(E'))$

(vi) $\dfrac{E \stackrel{D\ \alpha x}{\to} E'}{(E\backslash L) \stackrel{D\ \tau x}{\to} (E'\backslash L) \text{ if } \alpha \in L \quad (E\backslash L) \stackrel{D\ \alpha x}{\to} (E'\backslash L) \text{ if } \alpha \notin L}$

(vii) $\dfrac{\{z_1,\ldots,z_n/x_1,\ldots,x_n\}[\mu X^{x_1,\ldots,x_n}.E/X]E \stackrel{a}{\to} E'}{(\mu X^{x_1,\ldots,x_n}.E)^{z_1,\ldots,z_n} \stackrel{a}{\to} E'}$ □

Axiom (i) is (intuitively) standard. Inference rules (iii)–(vii) have their same usual meaning as in LOTOS, and they have only been adapted for POtLOTOS. Inference rule (ii) requires a more detailed explanation. For this purpose, let us remember briefly the synchronization mechanism of LOTOS. Intuitively, an α-synchronization in LOTOS is obtained by considering "atomic execution" of two or more concurrent actions α, which is shown by the following LOTOS inference rules:

$$\dfrac{E \stackrel{a}{\to} E' \quad F \stackrel{a}{\to} F' \quad \alpha \in L}{E|[L]|F \stackrel{a}{\to} E'|[L]|F'} \qquad \dfrac{E \stackrel{a}{\to} E' \quad \alpha \notin L}{E|[L]|F \stackrel{a}{\to} E'|[L]|F \quad F|[L]|E \stackrel{a}{\to} F|[L]|E'}$$

The first rule characterizes occurrence of an α-synchronization. The interleaving induced by the second rule aims at two different goals: first it gives an "interpretation" of concurrency in terms of arbitrary interleaving of events, and second it permits concurrent actions to be offered within the context where $E|[L]|F$ will be placed (in order to possibly take part in others "α-synchronizations"). In POtLOTOS, the same intuitive reasoning is applied, i.e. actions are offered for synchronization by "constructing" arbitrary interleaving of atoms. Nevertheless, and contrary to LOTOS, this interleaving preserves the partial order among events. These two LOTOS inference rules are adapted for POtLOTOS by rules (iv) and (v), respectively. Furthermore, as there is another way for composing concurrent actions in POtLOTOS, i.e. by means of the partial prefixing operation, an additional inference rule, providing atom interleaving, has been defined in (ii). One may note that this rule is intuitively similar to the π-rule of SPOC.

Now let us give the POtLOTOS version of strong bisimulation equivalence.

Definition 18. *(Strong bisimulation) [27, 23]*

Let $R \subseteq P \times P$ be a binary relation between V-closed behavior expressions. Then we define a function $\mathcal{F}: 2^{P \times P} \to 2^{P \times P}$ as follows: $(P_1, Q_1) \in \mathcal{F}(R)$ iff for all $a \in \mathcal{E}$,

(i) whenever $P_1 \xrightarrow{a} P_2$ there exist $Q'_1 \equiv Q_1$ and Q_2 such that $Q'_1 \xrightarrow{a} Q_2$ and $(\exists (P'_2, Q'_2) \in R)$ such that $P_2 \equiv_\alpha P'_2$ and $Q_2 \equiv_\alpha Q'_2$.

(ii) whenever $Q_1 \xrightarrow{a} Q_2$ there exist $P'_1 \equiv P_1$ and P_2 such that $P'_1 \xrightarrow{a} P_2$ and $(\exists (P'_2, Q'_2) \in R)$ such that $P_2 \equiv_\alpha P'_2$ and $Q_2 \equiv_\alpha Q'_2$.

R is called a *strong bisimulation* iff $R \subseteq \mathcal{F}(R)$ (i.e. R is a pre-fixed-point of $\mathcal{F}$). If $(P, Q) \in R$ for some bisimulation R, P and Q are said to be *strongly bisimilar*, in symbols $P \sim Q$. □

Proposition 5.

(i) $R_1 \subseteq R_2 \Rightarrow \mathcal{F}(R_1) \subseteq \mathcal{F}(R_2)$ (i.e. $\mathcal{F}$ is monotonic).
(ii) $\sim$ is the largest pre-fixed-point of $\mathcal{F}$, i.e. $\sim = \bigcup \{R | R \subseteq \mathcal{F}(R)\}$. Moreover R is also the largest fixed-point (i.e. $R = \mathcal{F}(R)$) of $\mathcal{F}$.
(iii) $\sim$ is an equivalence relation, the *strong bisimulation equivalence*.

Proof It follows directly from definition 18 and from basic results in fixed-point theory (using the same proof scheme as in [23]). □

Proposition 6. The strong bisimulation equivalence $\sim$ is a congruence relation.

Proof Follows the same proof scheme given in [23] for the analogous proposition. □

2.3 Examples

Let us now give some simple examples for illustrating POtLOTOS. For making the use of the notation easier, we consider that, if the name of an atom in a term is missing, then it will assume any name not free within the scope of this atom. For example, $a_I (_I b_{?,I} d[]c_{I,?} a)$ can be assumed as $a_I (_I b_? {}_{?,I} d_?[]c_? {}_{I,?} a_I)$.

Example 4. (i) $ab \sim a\|\|b \not\sim a_I {}_I b[]b_I {}_I a$ (ii) $a_I(b[]_I c) \sim a_I {}_I c[[c]|(c[]b)$

(i) illustrates one of the basic ideas of our proposal; true concurrency between atoms a and b may be either expressed by ab (using partial prefixing operation) or by $a\|\|b$ (using parallel composition without any synchronization). Both behavior expressions are different from the third one which characterizes instead interleaving semantics.

(ii) illustrates the power of POtLOTOS, as the first behavior expression is much more simple and intuitive than the second one.

Example 5.

(i) $a(b[]c)[]ab[]b(a[]c) \sim (a(b[]c))[](b(a[]c))$
(ii) $a_I(b[]_I c)[]ab[]b_I(a[]_I c) \sim a_I(b[]_I c)[]b_I(a[]_I c)$

Note that for $\underset{I}{\sim}$ denoting the usual interleaving strong bisimulation equivalence, we have $S_{tLOTOS} \underset{I}{\sim} \mathtt{p;m;} \mu X.(\mathtt{p;c;m;} X[]\mathtt{c;p;m;} X)$ where clearly p and c are not concurrent activities.

Conclusion

One of the main results presented in this paper has dealt with the definition of a new approach for denoting pomsets. Furthermore two basic conversion rules have been established leading to the characterization of a Simple Partial Order Calculus (SPOC). Starting from the basic ideas developed for SPOC, a LOTOS based calculus called POtLOTOS with true concurrency semantics has been proposed. A partial order strong bisimulation equivalence very similar to the usual interleaving strong bisimulation equivalence has also been defined. In [11], the authors have developed a similar approach taking into account full basic CCS.

There have been earlier attempts aiming at providing partial order semantics for CCS/CSP based calculi, for example [7, 34, 15, 26, 24, 32, 25, 9]. Most of these attempts define a denotational and/or an operational semantics of these calculi based on an underlying partial order model (like Petri Nets, Event structures, ...). The calculus given in this paper seems to be much simpler than the previous ones and also provides a powerful abstract tool for dealing with the notion of distributed labeled transition systems. Furthermore, as POtLOTOS appears to be a natural extension of tLOTOS, in the sense that the basic and intuitive structure of LOTOS is preserved, it seems possible to generalize, within a partial-order framework, many results obtained using interleaving semantics. In particular, current work deals with an algebraic characterization of the partial order strong bisimulation equivalence introduced in the paper which relies on the introduction of a new operator ($a:E$) intended to capture local observations of a concurrent behavior. This operator seems to be "equivalent" to the asymmetric parallel operator of Castellani and Hennessy [9], and for the common subset of behaviors (as restriction, synchronization and recursion are not considered in [9]) our strong bisimulation equivalence coincides with theirs. Another solution for providing true concurrency semantics for CCS is proposed in [7], where a distributed labeled transition system model is defined with transitions being decorated by their proofs; the partial order relation among transitions is then induced from a partial order relation between the proofs. Although these approaches are somewhat intuitively similar to ours, they do not provide an abstract notion of a distributed labeled transition system being sufficiently expressive with respect to true concurrency models such that Petri nets and event structures.

Other directions of work deal currently with the generalization of weak bisimulation equivalence within our partial order framework, as well as with the study of formal relationships between our approach and other models expressing "true concurrency", in particular Petri nets.

Bibliography

[1] Arnold, A. Systèmes de transitions finis et sémantique des processus communicants. *Technique et Science Informatiques 9*, 3 (1990), 193–216.

[2] Austry, L., and Boudol, G. Algèbre de processus et synchronisation. *Theoretical Computer Science 30* (1984), 91–131.

[3] Bergstra, J. A., and Klop, J. W. Algebra for communicating processes with abstraction. *J. of Theoretical Computer Science 37* (1985), 77–121.

[4] Best, E., and Fernandez, C. *Non Sequential Processes: a Petri Net View*, vol. 13 of *EATCS Monographs on Theoretical Computer Science*. Springer-Verlag, 1988.

[5] Bolognesi, T., and Brinksma, E. Introduction to the ISO specification language LOTOS. *Computer Networks and ISDN Systems*, 14 (1987), 25–59.

[6] Boudol, G., and Castellani, I. Concurrency and atomicity. *TCS 59* (1988), 1–60.

[7] Boudol, G., and Castellani, I. Permutation of transitions: An event structure semantics for CCS and SCCS. In *Linear Time, Branching Time and Partial Order in Logics and Models for Concurrency*, J. de Bakker, W.-P. de Roever, and G. Rozenberg, Eds., vol. 354 of *LNCS*. Springer-Verlag, 1989, pp. 411–427.

[8] Brookes, S., Hoare, C., and Roscoe, A. A theory of communicating sequential processes. *J. of ACM 31* (1984), 560–599.

[9] Castellani, I., and Hennessy, M. Distributed bisimulation. *J. ACM 36* (1989), 887–911.

[10] Coelho da Costa, R. J., and Courtiat, J.-P. Definition of a new notation for representing pomsets (preliminary report). Rapport de Recherche 91121, LAAS, Mar. 1991.

[11] Coelho da Costa, R. J., and Courtiat, J.-P. POC: A partial order calculus for modeling concurrent systems. Rapport de recherche 91179, LAAS, May 1991.

[12] Coelho da Costa, R. J., and Courtiat, J.-P. SPOC – A simple partial order calculus for representing pomsets. In *Proceedings of the XVIII Integrated Seminar on Software and Hardware* (Santos/São Paulo - Brazil, Aug. 1991).

[13] Coelho da Costa, R. J., and Courtiat, J.-P. Using Petri nets as a model for Petri nets. In *Proceedings of Third IEEE Workshop on Future Trends of Distributed Computing Systems in the 1990's* (Taipei, Apr. 1992), IEEE Computer Society Press.

[14] De Nicola, R., and Hennessy, M. Testing equivalences for processes. *Theor. Comp. Sci. 34* (1984), 83–133.

[15] Degano, P., De Nicola, R., and Montanari, U. A partial ordering semantics for CCS. *Theor. Comp. Sci. 75* (1990), 223–262.

[16] Degano, P., and Montanari, U. Concurrent histories: a basis for observing distributed systems. *J. of Comput. System Sci. 34* (1987), 422–461.

[17] Hennessy, M. *An Algebraic Theory of Processes*. MIT Press, Cambridge, MA, 1988.

[18] Hoare, C. *Communicating Sequential Processes*. Prentice-hall, 1985.

[19] ISO. *8807: LOTOS - A formal Description Technique Based on the Temporal Ordering of Observational Behavior*, Aug. 1988.

[20] Lamport, L. What good is temporal logic. In *Proc. IFIP Congress '83* (Amsterdam, 1983), R. Mason, Ed., North-Holland, pp. 657–668.

[21] Mazurkiewicz, A. Trace theory. In *Advanced Course in Petri Nets*, W. Brauer, W. Reisig, and G. Rozenberg, Eds., vol. 255 of *LNCS*. Springer-Verlag, 1987, pp. 279–329.

[22] Milner, R. Calculi for synchrony and asynchrony. *Th. Comp. Sci. 25* (1983), 267–310.

[23] Milner, R. *Communication and Concurrency*. C.A.R. Hoare Series Editor. Prentice Hall, 1989.

[24] Nielsen, M. CCS- and its relationship to net theory. In *Advanced Course in Petri Nets*, W. Brauer, W. Reisig, and G. Rozenberg, Eds., vol. 255 of *LNCS*. Springer-Verlag, Bad Honeff 1986, 1987, pp. 393–415.

[25] Nielsen, M., Rosenberg, G., and Thiagarajan, P. S. Behavioural notions for elementary net systems. *Distributed Computing 4*, 1 (1990), 45–57.

[26] Olderog, E.-R. Operational Petri net semantics for CSP. In *Advances in Petri Nets 1987*, G. Rozenberg, Ed., vol. 266 of *LNCS*. Springer-Verlag, 1987, pp. 196–223.

[27] Park, D. Concurrency and automata in infinite sequences. vol. 104 of *LNCS*. Springer-Verlag, 1981, pp. 167–183.

[28] Plotkin, G. A structural approach to operational semantics. Report Daimi FN-19, Aarhus University (Denmark), 1981.

[29] Pratt, V. R. Modelling concurrency with partial orders. *Intern. J. of parallel Programming 15* (1986), 33–71.

[30] Reisig, W. Concurrency is more fundamental than interleaving. In *Bulletin EATCS*, vol. 35. June 1988.

[31] Stark, E. Concurrent transition system. *Th. Comp. Sci. 64* (May 1989), 221–269.

[32] Taubner, D. The representation of CCS programs by finite predicate/transition nets. In X^{th} *International Conference on Application and Theory of Petri Nets* (Bonn-Germany, 1989), pp. 348–370.

[33] van Glabbeek, R., and Goltz, U. Equivalence notions for concurrent systems and refinement of actions. Arbeitspapier 366, GMD, Feb. 1989.

[34] van Glabbeek, R., and Vaandrager, F. Petri net models for algebraic theories of concurrency. In *Proc. PARLE Conf.* (1987), A. N. J. W. de Bakker and P. Treleaven, Eds., vol. 259 of *LNCS*, Springer-Verlag.

[35] Vissers, C. FDTs for open distributed systems, a retrospective and a prospective view. In *IFIP Int. Symp. in Protocol Specification, Testing and Verification* (Ottawa-Canada, June 1990).

[36] Winskel, G. Event structures. In *Advanced Course on Petri Nets*, vol. 255 of *LNCS*. Springer-Verlag, 1987, pp. 325–392.

IFIP

The INTERNATIONAL FEDERATION FOR INFORMATION PROCESSING is a multinational federation of professional and technical organisations (or national groupings of such organisations) concerned with information processing. From any one country, only one such organisation – which must be representative of the national activities in the field of information processing – can be admitted as a Full Member. In addition a regional group of developing countries can be admitted as a Full Member. On 1 October 1991, 46 organisations were Full Members of the Federation, representing 70 countries.

The aims of IFIP are to promote information science and technology by:

– fostering international co-operation in the field of information processing;
– stimulating research, development and the application of information processing in science and human activity;
– furthering the dissemination and exchange of information about the subject;
– encouraging education in information processing.

IFIP is dedicated to improving worldwide communication and increased understanding among practitioners of all nations about the role information processing can play in all walks of life.

Information technology is a potent instrument in today's world, affecting people in everything from their education and work to their leisure and in their homes. It is a powerful tool in science and engineering, in commerce and industry, in education and adminstration. It is truly international in its scope and offers a significant opportunity for developing countries. IFIP helps to bring together workers at the leading edge of the technology to share their knowledge and experience, and acts as a catalyst to advance the state of the art.

IFIP came into official existence in January, 1960. It was established to meet a need identified at the first International Conference on Information Processing which was held in Paris in June, 1959, under the sponsorship of UNESCO.

Organisational Structure
The Federation is governed by a GENERAL ASSEMBLY, which meets once every year and consists of one representative from each Member organisation. The General Assembly decides on all important matters, such as general policy, the programme of activities, admissions, elections and budget.

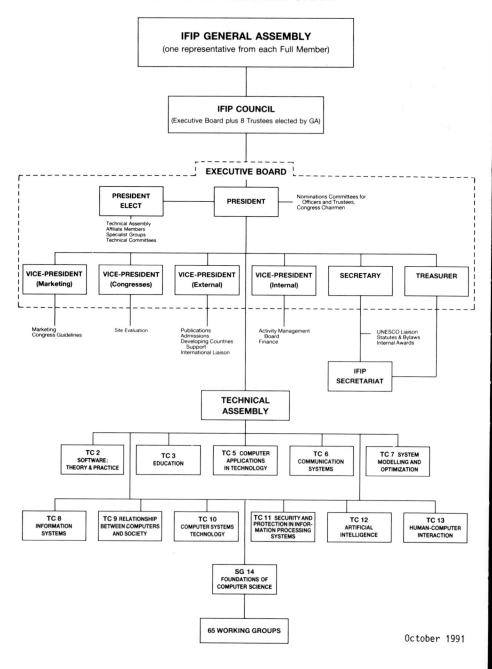

The day-to-day work of IFIP is directed by its Officers: the President, Vice-Presidents, Secretary and Treasurer, who are elected by the General Assembly and together constitute the EXECUTIVE BOARD.

The COUNCIL, consisting of the Officers and up to eight Trustees elected from the General Assembly, meets twice a year and takes decisions which become necessary between General Assembly meetings.

The headquarters of the Federation are in Geneva, Switzerland where the IFIP Secretariat administers its affairs.

For further information please contact:

IFIP Secretariat
attn. Mme. GWYNETH ROBERTS
16 Place Longemalle
CH-1204 Geneva, Switzerland
telephone: 41 (22) 28 26 49
facsimile: 41 (22) 781 23 22
Bitnet: ifip@cgeuge51

IFIP's MISSION STATEMENT

IFIP's mission is to be the leading, truly international, apolitical organisation which encourages and assists in the development, exploitation and application of Information Technology for the benefit of all people.

Principal Elements
1. To stimulate, encourage and participate in research, development and application of Information Technology (IT) and to foster international co-operation in these activities.
2. To provide a meeting place where national IT Societies can discuss and plan courses of action on issues in our field which are of international significance and thereby to forge increasingly strong links between them and with IFIP.
3. To promote internation co-operation directly and through national IT Societies in a free environment between individuals, national and international governmental bodies and kindred scientific and professional organisations.
4. To pay special attention to the needs of developing countries and to assist them in appropriate ways to secure the optimum benefit from the application of IT.
5. To promote professionalism, incorporating high standards of ethics and conduct, among all IT practitioners.
6. To provide a forum for assessing the social consequences of IT applications; to campaign for the safe and beneficial development and use of IT and the protection of people from abuse through its improper application.

7. To foster and facilitate co-operation between academics, the IT industry and governmental bodies and to seek to represent the interest of users.
8. To provide a vehicle for work on the international aspects of IT development and application including the necessary preparatory work for the generation of international standards.
9. To contribute to the formulation of the education and training needed by IT practitioners, users and the public at large.

Note to Conference Organizers

Organizers of upcoming IFIP Working Conferences are urged to contact the Publisher. Please send full details of the Conference to:

Mrs. STEPHANIE SMIT
Administrative Editor – IFIP Publications
ELSEVIER SCIENCE PUBLISHERS
P.O. Box 103, 1000 AC Amsterdam
The Netherlands
telephone: 31 (20) 5862481
facsimile: 31 (20) 5862616
email: s.smit@elsevier.nl

IFIP TRANSACTIONS

IFIP TRANSACTIONS is a serial consisting of 15,000 pages of valuable scientific information from leading researchers, published in 35 volumes per year. The serial includes contributed volumes, proceedings of the IFIP World Conferences, and conferences at Technical Committee and Working Group level. Mainstream areas in the IFIP TRANSACTIONS can be found in Computer Science and Technology, Computer Applications in Technology, and Communication Systems.

Please find below a detailed list of topics covered.

IFIP TRANSACTIONS A:
Computer Science and Technology
1992: 19 Volumes, US $ 1181.00/Dfl. 2185.00
ISSN 0926-5473

IFIP Technical Committees
Software: Theory and Practice (TC2)
Education (TC3)
System Modelling and Optimization (TC7)
Information Systems (TC8)
Relationship Between Computers and Society (TC9)

Computer Systems Technology (TC10)
Security and Protection in Information Processing Systems (TC11)
Artificial Intelligence (TC12)
Human-Computer Interaction (TC13)
Foundations of Computer Science (SG14)

IFIP TRANSACTIONS B:
Applications in Technology
1992: 8 Volumes. US $ 497.00/Dfl. 920.00
ISSN 0926-5481

IFIP Technical Committee
Computer Applications in Technology (TC5)

IFIP TRANSACTIONS C:
Communication Systems
1992: 8 Volumes. US 497.00/Dfl. 920.00
ISSN 0926-549X

IFIP Technical Committee
Communication Systems (TC6)

IFIP TRANSACTIONS FULL SET: A, B & C
1992: 35 Volumes. US $ 1892.00/Dfl. 3500.00

The Dutch Guilder prices (Dfl.) are definitive. The US $ prices mentioned above are for your guidance only and are subject to exchange rate fluctuations. Prices include postage and handling charges.

The volumes are also available separately in book form.

Please address all orders and correspondence to:

ELSEVIER SCIENCE PUBLISHERS
attn. PETRA VAN DER MEER
P.O. Box 103, 1000 AC Amsterdam
The Netherlands
telephone: 31 (20) 5862602
facsimile: 31 (20) 5862616
email: m.haccou@elsevier.nl